**Laurence Gardner**, Prior of the Celtic Church's Sacred Kindred of St Columba, is an internationally known sovereign and chivalric genealogist. Distinguished as the Chevalier Labhràn de Saint Germain, he is Presidential Attaché to the European Council of Princes – a constitutional advisory body established in 1946. He is formally attached to the Noble Household Guard of the Royal House of Stewart, founded at St Germain-en-Laye in 1692, and is the Jacobite Historiographer Royal.

# BLOODLINE OF THE HOLY GRAIL

## THE HIDDEN LINEAGE OF JESUS REVEALED

## Laurence Gardner

*Le Chevalier Labhràn de Saint Germain*

## ELEMENT
Shaftesbury, Dorset ● Rockport, Massachusetts
Melbourne, Victoria

**Dedicated to the Memory
of
Dr Whitman Pearson
a questing pilgrim of the eternal Grail**

© Element Books Limited 1996

Text © Chevalier Labhràn 1996

First published in Great Britain in 1996 by
Element Books Limited
This edition published in Great Britain
in 1997 by Element Books Limited Shaftesbury,
Dorset SP7 8BP

Published in the USA in 1996 by
Element Books, Inc.
PO Box 830, Rockport, MA 01966

Published in Australia in 1996 by
Element Books
and distributed by Penguin Australia Limited
487 Maroondah Highway, Ringwood, Victoria 3134

Cover design by Bridgewater Books
Design by Roger Lightfoot
Typeset by WestKey Ltd, Falmouth, Cornwall
Printed and bound in USA by Edwards Brothers Inc. Michigan

British Library Cataloguing in Publication
data available

Library of Congress Cataloging in Publication
data available

ISBN 1-86204-152-0

# CONTENTS

# LIST OF PLATES

# LIST OF MAPS

# LIST OF CHARTS

## Appendix V – Additional Genealogical Tables and Charts

# LIST OF DIAGRAMS
## AND ILLUSTRATIONS

# PICTURE CREDITS

Thanks must go to the sources below for permission to reproduce the following illustrations:

1, reproduction from Neumann, Eric, *The Great Mother*, Copyright © 1955 renewed © 1983, Princeton University Press, reproduced by permission of Princeton University Press; 2, reproduced courtesy of the Musée du Louvre, Paris, and the Bibliothèque Nationale de France; 3, acknowledgement to William Mackenzie, Glasgow; 4, acknowledgement to the Galleria Uffizi/Scala, Florence; 5, reproduced courtesy of The Visitors of the Ashmolean Museum, Oxford; 6, acknowledgement to the Bibliothèque Nationale de France, date c. AD 1300; 7, Notre Dame de Corbeil agency photographs acknowledgement to Giraudon, Paris; 8 and 9, reproduction courtesy of The Bridgeman Art Library, London, acknowledgement to the Galleria degli Uffizi, Florence; 10, acknowledgement to the Ministero per i Beni Culturali e Ambientali and the Galleria Nazionale di Capodimonte, Naples; 11, acknowledgement to the Church of St Mary Magdalene, and the Convent of Saint Mary Magdalene, Jerusalem; 12, reproduction from Taylor, John, *The Coming of the Saints*, courtesy of publisher: Artisan Sales, PO Box 1529, Muskogee, OK. 74402, USA, acknowledgement to Popperfoto; 13, acknowledgement to the Katholisches

Pfarramt St Maria Magdalena, Tiefenbronn; 14, from the *Sforza Book of Hours*, c. 1490 Italy; 15 & 16, permission Copyright © Peter Robson, courtesy of Entropic Fine Art Inc. Box 3, Newmarket, Ontario L3Y 4W3, Canada; 17, reproduction permission © *Crown Copyright*, RCHME, Royal Commission on the Historical Monuments of England; 18, photographic reproduction courtesy of © English Heritage; 19, illumination from the 16th century *Book of Wonders* by David Jovis; 20, acknowledgement to Notre Dame de Recollets, Verviers, Liège; 21 & 22, reproduction courtesy of Mike Green, photographer for the Friends of Rosslyn; 23, Private Collection; 24, courtesy of © Pitkin Guides; 25, Sir Thomas Malory, *The Birth Life and Acts of King Arthur*, acknowledgement to Thames & Hudson.

While every effort has been made to secure permissions, if there are any errors or oversights regarding copyright material, we apologise and will make suitable acknowledgement in any future edition.

# ACKNOWLEDGEMENTS

For their valued assistance in the preparation of this work, I am indebted to the good offices of the Celtic Church of the Sacred Kindred of Saint Columba, the Royal House of Stewart, the Keeper and Trustees of the Jacobite Records of Saint Germain, Le Président of the Counseil Européen des Princes, and the Ordo Supremus Militaris Templi Hierosolymitani. I would similarly like to thank all the archivists and librarians who have aided my quest, especially those at The British Library, Bibliothèque Nationale de France, Bibliothèque de Bordeaux, Somerset County Library, Birmingham Central Library, Glasgow Mitchell Library, and the National Library of Scotland.

Since this book is very much a synthesis of interrelated subject matter, I am greatly beholden to those specialist authors whose individual mastery in their respective fields has facilitated the coverage of specific aspects. Their personal research, expertise and preeminent published works have been invaluable. Apart from a comprehensive Bibliography, I have included selected reading material within the Notes and References, and have drawn particular attention to certain noteworthy writers in the general text.

My utmost gratitude is due to HRH Prince Michael of Albany for affording me privileged access to Household and Chivalric papers. I am also thankful to my wife, Angela and son, James, for their forbearance during my somewhat reclusive activity.

To my many good friends who have smoothed the path of this venture in one way or another I offer my appreciation. In particular, I am grateful to Chevalier David Roy Stewart, John Deering and Cliff Wadey. Also, for their professional knowledge of art and photography respectively, I am obliged to Peter Robson and Michael Deering.

Finally, to those without whom this edition would not exist despite all that went before, I owe inestimable thanks to Michael Mann, Chairman of Element Books, and to the inimitable John Baldock, whose fraternal guiding light shone the last miles home.

*Laurence Gardner*

# FOREWORD

*Bloodline of the Holy Grail* is a remarkable achievement in the field of genealogical research. Rare is the historian acquainted with such compelling facts as are gathered in this work. The revelations are entirely fascinating, and will surely be appreciated by many as real treasures of enlightenment. Herein, is the vital story of those fundamental issues which helped to shape the Christian Church in Europe and in the Crusader States.

To some, perhaps, aspects of this book will appear heretical in nature. It is the right of any individual to take this view since the inherent disclosures are somewhat removed from the orthodox tradition. However, the fact remains that Chevalier Labhràn has penetrated the very depths of available manuscripts and archival data concerning the subject, moving far beyond the bounds of any conventional domain. The resultant unveiled knowledge is presented in a very articulate, interesting and tantalising manner.

This work offers an incredible insight into centuries of strategic governmental alignments, together with their associated deceits and intrigues. For around two thousand years, the destinies of millions of people have been manipulated by unique, though often whimsical, personalities, who have perverted the spiritual aspirations of our civilization. With marvellous detail, the author has removed the constraints of vested interest to relate numerous suppressed accounts of our heritage. In so doing, he resurrects the politically silenced history of a resolute royal dynasty which the Church has long sought to vanquish in order to further its own ends. Now, in this new age of understanding, may the truth prevail, and may the Phoenix rise once again.

*HRH Prince Michael of Albany*
Head of the Royal House of Stewart

*Here is the Book of thy descent*
*Here begins the Book of the Sangréal.'*

*The   Perlesvaus*

# ONE

# ORIGINS OF THE BLOODLINE

## WHOM DOES THE GRAIL SERVE?

Following the Jewish Revolt in Jerusalem during the 1st century AD, the Roman overlords were reputed to have destroyed all records concerning the Davidic legacy of Jesus the Messiah's family. The destruction was far from complete, however, and relevant documents were retained by Jesus's heirs, who brought the Messianic heritage from the Near East to the West. As confirmed by the *Ecclesiastical History* of Eusebius, the 4th-century Bishop of Caesarea,[1] these heirs were called the *Desposyni* (ancient Greek for '*of the Master*'),[2] a hallowed style reserved exclusively for those in the same family descent as Jesus.[3] Theirs was the sacred legacy of the Royal House of Judah – a dynastic bloodline that lives on today.

During the course of this book, we shall study the compelling story of this sovereign lineage by unfolding a detailed genealogical account of the Messianic Blood Royal (the *Sangréal*) in direct descent from Jesus and his brother James. However, in order to cover this ground, it will firstly be necessary to consider the Old and New Testament Bible stories from a different perspective to that normally conveyed. This will not be a rewriting of history, but a reshaping of familiar accounts – bringing history back to its original base, rather than perpetuating the myths of strategic restyling by those with otherwise vested interests.

In this latter respect, there will undoubtedly be some who will contest what follows. Others will endeavour to uphold customary ideals by levelling destructive criticism against these pages. This being the case, one can but trust that such critics will have their contentions fully weighed, for as the Revd Lewis of Glastonbury identified in 1922, destructive criticism is often its own destroyer, while its intended prey remains better off for being attacked.

Meanwhile, this is a book genuinely written for the reader with an open mind and a questing spirit. Its authority rests with revelationary interpretations of ancient documents from the Holy Land, such as the Dead Sea Scrolls, and with the many Gospels and early texts that were conveniently obscured from the public domain. Recorded facts have also been culled from Celtic annals, and from chronicles of the Dark Ages, along with much information from the sovereign, saintly and chivalric archives of Europe.

Throughout the centuries, an ongoing Church and governmental conspiracy has prevailed against the Messianic inheritance. This heightened when Imperial Rome diverted the course of Christianity to suit an alternative ideal, and has continued to the present day.

Many apparently unconnected events of history have in fact been chapters of that same continuing suppression of the line. From the Jewish Wars of the 1st century through to the 18th century American Revolution and beyond, the machinations have been perpetuated by English and European governments in collaboration with the Anglican and Roman Catholic Churches. In their attempts to constrain the royal birthright of Judah, the High Christian movements have installed various figurehead regimes, including Britain's own House of Hanover – Saxe-Coburg–Gotha. Such administrations have been compelled to uphold specific religious doctrines, while others have been deposed for preaching religious forbearance.

Now, with the turn of the new Millennium at hand, this is a time for reflection and reform in the civilized world – and to accomplish such reform it is appropriate to consider the errors and successes of the past. For this purpose there is no better record than that which exists within the chronicles of the *Sangréal*.

The definition, *Holy Grail*, first appeared in the Middle Ages as a literary concept, based (as will be later discussed) on a series of scribal misinterpretations. It derived immediately as a translation from *Saint Grail*, and thence from the earlier forms *San Graal* and *Sangréal*. The Ancient Order of the Sangréal, a dynastic Order of the Scots Royal House of Stewart, was directly allied to the continental European Order of the Realm of Sion.[4] The knights of both Orders were adherents of the *Sangréal*, which (as given above) defines the true Blood Royal (the *Sang Réal*) of Judah: the *Bloodline of the Holy Grail*.

Quite apart from its dynastic physical aspect, the Holy Grail also has a spiritual dimension. It has been symbolized by many things, but as a material item it is most commonly perceived as a chalice, especially a chalice that contains, or once contained, the life-blood of Jesus. The Grail has additionally been portrayed as a vine, weaving its way through the annals of time. The fruit of the vine is the grape, and from the grape comes wine. In this respect, the symbolic elements of the chalice and the vine coincide, for wine has long been equated with the blood of Jesus. Indeed, this tradition sits at the very heart of the Eucharist (Holy Communion) sacrament, and the perpetual blood of the Grail chalice represents no less than the enduring Messianic bloodline.

In esoteric (hidden meaning) Grail lore, the chalice and vine support the ideal of *service*, whereas the blood and wine correspond to the eternal spirit of *fulfilment*. The spiritual Quest of the Grail is, therefore, a desire for fulfilment through giving and receiving service. That which is called the *Grail Code* is itself a parable for the human condition, in that it is the quest of us all to serve and, by serving, to achieve. The problem is that the precept of the Code has been overwhelmed by an avaricious society complex, based on the notion of the 'survival of the fittest'. Today, it is plain that wealth, rather than health, is a major stepping-stone towards being socially fit. Another criterion is obedience to the law.

But above all such considerations there is a further requirement: the requirement to toe the party line while paying homage to the demigods of power. This prerequisite has nothing to do with obeying the law or with behaving properly – it relies totally on not rocking the boat, and on withholding opinions that do not conform. Those who break ranks are declared heretics, meddlers and troublemakers, and as such are deemed socially unfit by their governing establishment. Perceived social fitness is consequently attained by submitting to indoctrination, and forsaking personal individuality in order to preserve the administrative status quo. By any standard of reckoning this can hardly be described as a democratic way of life.

The democratic ideal has been expressed as 'government *by* the people *for* the people'. To facilitate the process, democracies are organized on an electoral basis whereby the few represent the many. The representatives are chosen *by* the people to govern *for* the people – but the paradoxical result is generally government *of* the people. This is contrary to all the principles of democratic community and has nothing whatever to do with *service*. It is, therefore, in direct opposition to the Grail Code.

At a national and local level, elected representatives have long managed to reverse the harmonious ideal by setting themselves upon pedestals above their electorate. By virtue of this, individual rights, liberties and welfare are controlled by political dictate, and such dictates determine who is socially fit and who is socially unfit at any given time. In many cases this even corresponds to decisions on who shall survive and who shall not. To this end, there are many who seek positions of influence for the sheer sake of gaining power over others. Serving their own interests, they become manipulators of society, causing the disempowerment of the majority. The result is that instead of being rightly served, that same majority is reduced to a state of servitude.

It is not by any chance that from the Middle Ages the motto of Britain's Princes of Wales has been *Ich dien* (*I serve*). The motto was born directly from the Grail Code during the Age of Chivalry. Coming to power through hereditary lineage rather than being elected, it was important for those next in line to promote the ideal of *service*. But have the monarchs actually served? More to the point, whom have they served? In general – and certainly throughout the feudal and imperial eras – they have *ruled*, in collusion with their ministers and with the Church. *Rule* is not service, and it has no part in the justice, equality and tolerance of the democratic ideal. It is therefore quite inconsistent with the maxim of the Holy Grail.

Accordingly, this book, *Bloodline of the Holy Grail*, is not restricted in content to genealogies and tales of political intrigue, but its pages hold the key to the essential Grail Code – the key not only to a historical mystery but to a way of life. It is a book about good government and bad government. It tells how the patriarchal kingship of people was supplanted by dogmatic tyranny and the dictatorial overlordship of territory. It is a journey of discovery through past ages, with its eye set firmly on the future.

In this present age of computer technology, satellite telecommunications and an international space industry, scientific advancement takes place at an alarming rate. With each stage of development arriving ever more quickly, the functionally competent will emerge as the *survivors*, while the rest will be considered *unfit* by an impetuous establishment that serves its own ambitions but not its subjects.

So what has all this to do with the Grail? Everything. The Grail has many guises and many attributes – as will be revealed. Yet in whatever form it is portrayed, the Grail quest is governed by an overriding desire for honest achievement. It is the route by which all can *survive* among the *fit*, for it is the key to harmony and unity at every social and natural station. The Grail Code recognizes advancement by merit, and acknowledges community structure – but above all things it is entirely democratic. Whether apprehended in its physical or its spiritual dimension, the Grail belongs to leaders and followers alike. It belongs also to the land and the environment, enjoining that all should be as one in a common, unified *service*.

In order to be numbered among the *fit*, it is necessary to be fully informed. Only through awareness can preparation be made for the future. Dictatorial rule is not a route to information; it is a positive constraint designed to prevent free access to the truth.

Whom does the Grail serve? It serves those who quest despite the odds – for they are the champions of enlightenment.

## THE PAGAN IDOLS OF CHRISTENDOM

In the course of our journey we shall confront a number of assertions that may at first seem startling – but this is often the case when setting historical matters to rights, for most of us have been conditioned to accept certain interpretations of history as matters of fact. To a large extent we have all learned history by way of strategic propaganda, whether Church or politically motivated. It is all part of the control process; it separates the masters from the servants, and the fit from the unfit. Political history has, of course, long been written by its masters – the few who decide the fate and fortunes of the many. Religious history is no different, for it is designed to implement control through fear of the unknown. In this way the religious masters have retained their supremacy at the expense of devotees who genuinely seek enlightenment and salvation.

In relation to political or religious history it is a truism that establishment teachings often themselves border on the fantastic – but they are nonetheless rarely questioned. When less than fantastic, they are often instead so vague that they actually make little sense when examined with any depth of scrutiny.

In Biblical terms our Grail quest begins with the Creation, as defined in the book of Genesis. A little more than two centuries ago, in 1779, a consortium of London booksellers issued the mammoth 42-volume *Universal History*, a work that came to be much revered, and which stated with considered assurance that God's work of Creation began on 21 August 4004 BC.[5] A debate ensued over the precise month, for some theologians reckoned that 21 March was the more likely date. All agreed nevertheless that the year was accurate, and everyone accepted that there were only six days between cosmic nothingness and the emergence of Adam.

At the time of publication, Britain was in the grip of the Industrial Revolution. It was an unsettled period of extraordinary change and development but, as with today's rapid rate of advancement, there were social prices to pay. The prized skills and crafts of yesteryear became obsolete in the face of mass production, and society was regrouped to accommodate an economically-based community structure. A new breed of 'winners' emerged, while the majority floundered in an unfamiliar environment that bore no relation to the customs and standards of their upbringing. Rightly or wrongly, this phenomenon is called progress – and the relentless criterion of progress is that very precept propounded by the English naturalist Charles Darwin: the *survival of the fittest*.[6] The problem is that people's chances of survival are often diminished because they are ignored or exploited by their masters – those same pioneers who forge the route to progress, aiding (if not guaranteeing) their own survival.

It is easy now to appreciate that the 1779 *Universal History* was wrong. We know that the world was not created in 4004 BC. We also know that Adam was not the first man on Earth.[7] Such archaic notions have been outgrown – but to the people of the late 18th century this impressive *History* was the product of men more learned than most, and it was naturally presumed correct. It is therefore worth posing ourselves a question at this stage: How many of today's accepted facts of science and history will also be outgrown in the light of future discoveries?

Dogma is not necessarily truth: it is simply a fervently promoted interpretation of truth based on available facts. When new influential facts are presented, scientific dogma changes as a matter of course – but this is rarely the case with religious dogma. In this book we are particularly concerned with the attitudes and teachings of a Christian Church which pays no heed to discoveries and revelations, and which still upholds much of the incongruous dogma that dates from medieval times. As H G Wells so astutely observed during the early 1900s, the religious life of Western nations is 'going on in a house of history built upon sand'.

Charles Darwin's theory of evolution in *The Descent of Man* in 1871[8] caused no personal harm to Adam, but any thought of his being the first living human was naturally discredited. Like all the organic life-forms on the planet, humans had evolved by genetic mutation and natural selection through hundreds of thousands of years. The announcement of this fact struck religious-minded society with horror. Some simply refused to accept the new doctrine, but many fell into despair. If Adam and Eve were not the primal parents, there was no *Original Sin* – and the very reason for atonement was therefore without foundation!

The majority completely misunderstood the concept of 'natural selection'. They deduced that, if survival was restricted to the fittest, then success must be dependent on outdoing one's neighbour! Thus, a new sceptical and ruthless generation was born. Egotistical nationalism flourished as never before, and domestic deities were venerated as were the pagan gods of old. Symbols of national identity – such as Britannia and Hibernia – became the new idols of Christendom.

From this unhealthy base was generated an imperialist disease, and the stronger, advanced countries claimed the right to exploit less developed nations. The new age of empire-building began with an undignified scramble for territorial domain. The German *Reich* was founded in 1871 through the amalgamation of hitherto separate states. Other states combined to form the Austro-Hungarian Empire. The Russian Empire expanded considerably, and by the 1890s the British Empire occupied no less than one-fifth of the entire global landmass. This was the impassioned era of resolute Christian missionaries, many of them dispatched from Queen Victoria's Britain. With the religious fabric sorely rent at home, the Church sought a revised justification abroad. The missionaries were especially busy in such places as India and Africa, where the people already had their own beliefs and had never heard of Adam. More importantly, they had never heard of Charles Darwin!

In Britain a new intermediate stratum in society had emerged from the employers of the Industrial Revolution. This burgeoning middle-class set the true aristocracy and the governing establishment far beyond the reach of people at large, effectively creating a positive class structure – a system of divisions – in which everyone had a designated place. The 'chieftains' wallowed in Arcadian pursuits, while the middle-class opportunists competed for station through conspicuous consumption. The working man accepted his serfdom with songs of allegiance, a dream of *Hope and Glory*, and a portrait of the tribal priestess Britannia above his mantelshelf.

Students of history knew it would not be long before empires set their sights against each other, and they forecast a day when competing powers would meet in mighty opposition. The conflict began when France endeavoured to recover Alsace-Lorraine from German occupation, while the pair battled over the territory's iron and coal reserves. Russia and Austria-Hungary locked horns in a struggle for dominion of the Balkans, and there were disputes resulting from colonial ambitions in Africa and elsewhere. The fuse was lit in June 1914 when a Serbian nationalist murdered the heir to the Austrian throne, Archduke Francis Ferdinand. At this, Europe exploded into a great war, largely instigated by Germany. Hostilities were commenced against Serbia, Russia, France and Belgium, and the counter-offensive was led by Britain. The struggle lasted for more than four years, coming to an end when a revolt erupted in Germany, and Emperor (Kaiser) William II fled the country.

Following all the technological advancements of a manufacturing age, history had made little progress in social terms. Engineering achievements had led to unprecedented martial ability, while Christianity had become so fragmented as to be barely recognizable. Britain's pride emerged intact – but the German Reich was not of a mind to take its losses lightly. With the old regime overthrown, a fervent new party rose to dominance. Its despotic *Fuehrer* (leader), Adolf Hitler, annexed Austria in 1937 and swept into Poland two years later. The second great war – truly a World War – had begun: the fiercest territorial struggle to date. It was waged through six years, and was centred upon the very core beliefs of religion itself: the rights of everyone in a civilized environment.

Quite suddenly, the Church and the people realized that religion was not, and never had been, about dates and miracles. It was about belief in a neighbourly way of life, an application of moral standards and ethical values, of faith and charity and the constant quest for freedom and deliverance. At last any continuing general dispute about the evolutionary nature of human descent was put aside – that was the province of scientists, and the majority relaxed in acceptance of the fact.

The Church emerged as a far less fearful opponent of scholars, and the new environment was more agreeable to all concerned. For many, the text of the Bible had no longer to be regarded as inviolable dogma and venerated for its own sake. Religion was embodied in its precepts and principles, not in the paper on which it was printed. Indeed, the Bible was a book of history and record, a collection of ancient texts worthy of inquiry and study like any other.

This new perspective gave rise to endless speculative possibilities. If Eve had truly been the only woman in existence and her only offspring were three sons, then with whom did her son Seth unite to father the tribes of Israel? If Adam was not the first man on Earth, what actually was his significance? Who or what were the angels? The New Testament also had its share of mysteries. Who were the apostles? Did the miracles really happen? And most importantly, did the Virgin Birth and the Resurrection genuinely take place as described?

We shall consider all of these questions before we embark on the trail of the Grail Bloodline itself. In fact, it is imperative to understand Jesus's historical and environmental background, in order to comprehend the facts of his marriage and parental fatherhood. As we progress, many readers will find themselves treading wholly new ground – but it is simply the ground that existed before it was carpeted and concealed by those whose motives were to suppress the truth for the sake of retaining control. Only by rolling back the carpet and revealing this long-hidden ground can we succeed in our Quest for the Holy Grail.

## THE BLOODLINE BEGINS

It is now generally acknowledged that the opening chapters of the Old Testament do not accurately represent the early history of the world, as they appear to suggest.[9] More precisely, they tell the story of a family – a family that in time became a race comprising various tribes; a race that in turn became the Hebrew nation. If Adam can ever be said to have been the first of a type (notwithstanding the whole of human evolution behind

*Map 1* Qumran – Land of the Scrolls

him), then he was certainly a progenitor of the Hebrews and the tribes of Israel.[10]

Two of the most intriguing characters of the Old Testament are Joseph and Moses. Each played an important role in the formation of the Hebrew nation, and both have historical identities that can be examined quite independently of the Bible. Genesis 41:39–43 tells how Joseph was made Governor of Egypt:

> And Pharaoh said unto Joseph . . . Thou shalt be over my house, and according unto thy word shall all my people be ruled: only in the throne will I be greater than thou . . . and he made him ruler over all the land of Egypt.

Referring to Moses, Exodus 11:3 informs us similarly that:

> Moses was very great in the land of Egypt, in the sight of Pharaoh's servants, and in the sight of the people.

Yet for all of this status and prominence neither Joseph nor Moses appear in any Egyptian record under either of those names.

The annals of Rameses II (1304–1237 BC) specify that Semitic people were settled in the land of Goshen. It is further explained that they went there from Canaan for want of food. But why should Rameses' scribes mention this settlement at Goshen? According to standard Bible chronology the Hebrews went to Egypt some three centuries before the time of Rameses, and made their Exodus in about 1491 BC, long before he came to the throne. So, by virtue of this first-hand scribal record, the standard Bible chronology as generally promoted is seen to be incorrect.

It is traditionally presumed that Joseph was sold into slavery in Egypt in the 1720s BC, and was made Governor by the Pharaoh a decade or so later. Afterwards, his father Jacob (Israel)[11] and 70 family members followed him into Goshen to escape the famine in Canaan. Not-withstanding this, Genesis 47:11, Exodus 1:11 and Numbers 33:3 all refer to 'the land of Rameses' (in Egyptian, 'the house of Rameses').[12] This was a complex of grain storehouses built by the Israelites for Rameses II in Goshen some 300 years after they were supposedly there!

It transpires, therefore, that the alternative 'Jewish Reckoning' is more accurate than the 'Standard Chronology': Joseph went to Egypt not in the early 18th century BC but in the early 15th century BC. There he was appointed Chief Minister to Tuthmosis IV (ruled c. 1413–1405 BC). To the Egyptians, however, Joseph the Vizir was known as Yuya, and his story is particularly revealing not just in relation to the Biblical account of Joseph but also in respect of Moses. The Cairo-born historian and linguist Ahmed Osman has made an in-depth study of these personalities in their contemporary Egyptian environment, and his findings are of great significance.[13]

When Pharaoh Tuthmosis died, his son married his sibling sister Sitamun (as was the Pharaonic tradition) so that he could inherit the throne as Pharaoh Amenhotep III. Shortly afterwards he also married Tiye, daughter of the Chief Minister (Joseph/Yuya). It was decreed, however, that no son born to Tiye could inherit the throne. Because of the overall length of her father Joseph's governorship there was a general fear that the Israelites were gaining too much power in Egypt. So when Tiye became pregnant, the edict was given that her child should be killed at birth if a son. Tiye's Jewish relatives lived at Goshen, and she herself owned a summer palace a little upstream at Zarw, where she went to have her baby. She did indeed bear a son – but the royal midwives conspired with Tiye to float the child downstream in a reed basket to the house of her father's half-brother Levi.

The boy, Aminadab (born around 1394 BC), was duly educated in the eastern delta country by the Egyptian priests of Ra. In his teenage years he went to live at Thebes. By that time, his mother had acquired more influence than the senior queen, Sitamun, who had never borne a son and heir to the Pharaoh, only a daughter who was called Nefertiti. In Thebes, Aminadab could not accept the Egyptian deities and their myriad idols, and so he introduced the notion of Aten, an omnipotent God who had no image. Aten was thus an equivalent of the Hebrew 'Adonai' (a title borrowed from the Phoenician and meaning 'Lord') in line with Israelite teachings. At that time Aminadab (Hebrew equivalent of Amenhotep – 'Amun is pleased') changed his name to Akhenaten (servant of Aten).

Pharaoh Amenhotep then suffered a period of ill health. Because there was no direct male heir to the royal house, Akhenaten married his half-sister Nefertiti in order to rule as co-regent during this difficult time. When in due course Amenhotep III died, Akhenaten was able to succeed as Pharaoh – officially called Amenhotep IV.

Akhenaten and Nefertiti had six daughters and a son, Tutankhaten. Pharaoh Akhenaten closed all the temples of the Egyptian gods and built new temples to Aten. He also ran a household that was distinctly domestic – quite different from the kingly norm in ancient Egypt. On many fronts he became unpopular – particularly with the priests of the former national deity Amun (or Amen) and of the sun god Ra (or Re). Plots against his life proliferated. Loud were the threats of armed insurrection if he did not allow the traditional gods to be worshipped alongside the faceless Aten. But Akhenaten refused, and was eventually forced to abdicate in short-term favour of his cousin Smenkhkare, who was succeeded by Akhenaten's son Tutankhaten. On taking the throne at the age of about 11, Tutankhaten was obliged to change his name to Tutankhamun. He, in turn, was only to live and rule for a further nine or ten years, meeting his death while still comparatively young.

Akhenaten, meanwhile, was banished from Egypt. He fled with some retainers to the remote safety of Sinai, taking with him his royal sceptre topped with a brass serpent. To his supporters he remained very much the rightful monarch, the heir to the throne from which he had been ousted, and he was still regarded by them as the *Mose*, *Meses* or *Mosis* (heir/born of) – as in Tuth-mosis (*born of Tuth*) and Rameses (*fashioned of Ra*).

Evidence from Egypt indicates that Moses (Akhen-aten) led his people from Pi-Rameses (near modern Kantra) southward, through Sinai, towards Lake Timash.[14] This was extremely marshy territory and, although manageable on foot with some difficulty, any pursuing horses and chariots would have foundered disastrously.

Among the retainers who fled with Moses were the sons and families of Jacob (Israel). Then, at the instiga-tion of their leader, they constructed the Tabernacle[15] at the foot of Mount Sinai. Once Moses had died, they began their invasion of the country left by their forefa-thers so long before. But Canaan (Palestine) had changed considerably in the meantime, having been infiltrated by waves of Philistines and Phoenicians. The records tell of great sea battles, and of massive armies marching to war. At length, the Hebrews (under their new leader, Joshua) were successful and, once across the Jordan, they took Jericho from the Canaanites, gain-ing a real foothold in their traditional Promised Land.

Following Joshua's death, the ensuing period of rule by appointed 'judges' was a catalogue of Jewish disas-ter until the disparate Hebrew tribes united under their first king, Saul, in about 1055 BC. With the conquest of Palestine (Canaan) as complete as possible, David of Bethlehem – a descendant of Abraham – married Saul's daughter to become King of Judah (corresponding to half the Palestinian territory). By 1048 BC, he had also acquired Israel (the balance of the territory), becoming overall King of the Jews. The Bloodline of the Holy Grail had begun.

# TWO

# IN THE BEGINNING

## JEHOVAH AND THE GODDESS

Together with the military exploits of the Hebrews/
Israelites, the Old Testament describes the evolution of
the Jewish faith from the time of Abraham. The story is
not that of a unified nation devoted to the God Jehovah,
but tells of a tenacious sect who fought against all odds
to contrive the dominant religion of Israel. In their
opinion, Jehovah was male – but this was a sectarian
concept that gave rise to severe and manifold problems.

On the wider contemporary stage it was generally
understood that the creation of life must emanate from
both male and female sources. Other religions –
whether in Egypt, Mesopotamia, or elsewhere – accordingly had deities of both sexes. The primary male god
was generally associated with the sun or the sky, while
the primary goddess had her roots in the earth, the
sea, and fertility. The sun gave its force to the earth
and waters, from which sprang life: a very natural and
logical interpretation.

In relation to such theistic ideas, one of the more
flexible characters mentioned in Biblical texts is King
David's son, Solomon, celebrated not just for the mag-
nificence and splendour of his reign, but for the wisdom
of the man himself. Much later, Solomon's legacy was

**PATRIARCHS AND TRIBES OF ISRAEL**

crucial to emergent Grail lore because he was the true advocate of religious toleration. Solomon was king centuries before the period of the Israelites' captivity in Babylon, and he was very much a part of the old environment. During Solomon's era Jehovah was afforded considerable importance – but other gods were acknowledged as well. It was a spiritually uncertain age in which it was not uncommon for individuals to hedge their bets in respect of alternative deities. After all, with such a plethora of different gods and goddesses receiving homage in the region, it might have been shortsighted to decry all but one. Who was to say that the devout Hebrews had got it right!

In this regard then, Solomon's renowned wisdom was based on considered judgement. Even though he himself worshipped Jehovah, the God of a minority sect, he had no reason to deny his subjects their own gods (1 Kings 11:4–10). He even retained his own beliefs in the divine forces of nature, no matter who or what was at the head of them.

Veneration of the primary female deity was of long standing in Canaan, where she took the form of the goddess Ashtoreth. She was equivalent to Ishtar, the major goddess of the Mesopotamians, whose Sumerian temple was at Uruk (the Biblical Erech, modern Warka). In nearby Syria and Phoenicia the same goddess was reported by the ancient Greeks to have been called Astarte.

The Holy of Holies, or inner sanctuary, in Solomon's Temple was deemed to represent the womb of Ashtoreth (alternatively called Asherah, as mentioned several times in the Old Testament). Ashtoreth was openly worshipped by the Israelites until the 6th century BC. As the Lady Asherah, she was the supernal wife of El, the supreme male deity, and they were together the 'Divine Couple'. Their daughter was

Anath, Queen of the Heavens, and their son, the King of the Heavens, was called He. As time progressed, the separate characters of El and He were merged to become Jehovah. Asherah and Anath were then similarly conjoined to become Jehovah's female consort, known as the Shekinah or Matronit.

The name *Jehovah* is a late and somewhat Anglicized transliteration of *Yahweh*, which is itself a form of the four-consonantal Hebrew stem YHWH into which two vowels have been rightly or wrongly interpolated.[1] Originally, these four consonants (which only later became a sort of acronym for the One God) represented the four members of the Heavenly Family: Y represented El the *Father*; H was Asherah the *Mother*; W corresponded to He the *Son*; and H was the *Daughter* Anath. In accordance with the royal traditions of the time and region, God's mysterious bride, the Matronit, was also reckoned to be his sister. In the Jewish cult of the Cabbala (an esoteric discipline that reached its height in medieval times) God's dual male-female image was perpetuated. Meanwhile other sects perceived the Shekinah or Matronit as the female presence of God on Earth. The divine marital chamber was the sanctuary of the Jerusalem Temple, but from the moment the Temple was destroyed, the Matronit was destined to roam the Earth while the male aspect of Jehovah was left to rule the heavens alone.

In practical terms, the cementing of the Hebrew ideal of the One (male) God did not actually occur until after their 70 years of captivity in Babylon (around 536 BC). When the Israelites were first deported there by Nebuchadnezzar, they were effectively disparate tribes belonging to at least two major ethnic streams (Israel and Judah) – but they returned to the Holy Land with a common national purpose as Jehovah's 'Chosen People'.

Most of what we now know as the Old Testament (the Hebrew Bible) was first written down in Babylon.[2] It is hardly surprising, therefore, that Sumerian and Mesopotamian stories were grafted onto the early Jewish cultural tradition – including accounts of the Garden of Eden (the Paradise of Eridu[3]), the Flood[4], and the Tower of Babel.[5] The patriarch Abraham had himself migrated to Canaan from Ur of the Chaldees (in Mesopotamia), so the cultural grafting was doubtless justifiable, but the fact remains that stories such as that of Adam and Eve were by no means restricted to Hebrew tradition.

Alternatives to the *Adam and Eve* story in Genesis may be found in the writings of Greeks, Syrians, Egyptians, Sumerians and Abyssinians (ancient Ethiopians). In one version, Cain and Abel each had twin sisters, Luluwa and Aklemia. Elsewhere Seth had a sister called Noraia.

Yet other accounts tell of Adam's first consort, Lilith, before he was enchanted by Eve. Lilith was handmaiden to the Matronit, and she left Adam because he tried to dominate her. Escaping to the Red Sea, she cried 'Why should I lie beneath you? I am your equal!' A Sumerian terracotta relief depicting Lilith (dating from around 2000 BC) shows her naked and winged, standing on the backs of two lions. Although not a goddess in the traditional sense, her incarnate spirit was said to flourish in Solomon's most renowned lover, the Queen of Sheba. Lilith is described in the book of the esoteric Mandaeans of Iraq as the 'Daughter of the Underworld'.[6] Throughout history to the present day she has represented the fundamental ethic of female opportunity.

When the Israelites returned from Babylon to Jerusalem, the first five Books of Moses[7] were collated into the Jewish Torah (the Law). The rest of the Old Testament was, however, kept separate. For a number of

centuries it was regarded with varying degrees of veneration and suspicion, but in time the Books of the
Prophets[8] became especially significant in stabilizing
the Jewish heritage.[9] The main reason for hesitation was
that although the Jews were understood to be God's
Chosen People, Jehovah had not actually treated them
very kindly. He was their all-powerful tribal Lord and
had promised the patriarch Abraham to exalt their race
above all others. And yet, for all that, they had faced
only wars, famines, deportation and captivity! To
counter the nation's growing disenchantment, the
Books of the Prophets reinforced Jehovah's promise by
announcing the Coming of a Messiah, an anointed King
or Priest who would serve the people by leading them
to salvation.[10]

This prophecy was sufficient to ensure the rebuilding of Solomon's Temple and the Wall of Jerusalem . . .
but no Messianic saviour appeared. The Old Testament
ends at this point in the 4th century BC. Meanwhile the
bloodline of David continued, although not actively
reigning.

More than 300 years later a whole new chapter of
sovereign history began when the revolutionary heir of
Judah stepped boldly into the public domain. He was
Jesus the Nazarene, the King *de jure* of Jerusalem.

## HERITAGE OF THE MESSIAH

The New Testament picks up the story again in the final
years BC. But the untold intervening period was im-
mensely significant, for it set the political scene into
which the awaited Messiah was to make his entrance.

The era began with the rise to power of Alexander
the Great, King of Macedonia, who defeated the Persian
Emperor Darius in 333 BC. Destroying the city of Tyre
in Phoenicia, he then moved into Egypt and built Alex-

THE HOUSE OF HEROD
37 BC – AD 99

**ANTIPATER THE IDUMAEAN**
d. 48 BC
= *Cypros (Arabian)*

**HEROD THE GREAT**
King of Judaea from 37 BC
d. 4 BC
< – = *Ten wives including* = – >

| 1. | 2. | 3. | 4. | 5. | 6. | 7. |
|---|---|---|---|---|---|---|
| = *Doris (Idumaean)* | = *Mariamne I daughter of Alexander the Hasmonean (Jewess)* | = *Pallas* | = *Phaedra* | = *Mariamne II daughter of Simon Boethus High Priest (Jewess)* | = *Malthace of Samaria d. 4 BC (Samaritan)* | = *Cleopatra of Jerusalem (Jewess)* |

ANTIPATER
d. 4 BC

ARISTOBULOUS
d. 7 BC
= *Bernice niece of Herod the Great*

ALEXANDER
d. 7 BC
= *Glaphyra*

PHILIP
(Thomas)
= *Herodias* ▌

ARCHELAUS
Ethnarch
of Judaea
dep. AD 6
**EXILE IN GAUL**

HEROD-ANTIPAS
Tetrarch of
Galilee
dep. AD 39
**EXILE IN GAUL**
= 2. *Herodias* ▌

HEROD-PHILIP
Tetrarch of
Trachonitis
d. AD 34
= *Salome* ▲
*d.s.p.*

HEROD △
of Chalcis
d. AD 48
Regent of Agrippa II
= 1. *Mariamne g.dau of Joseph, bro. of Herod the Great*

ARISTOBULOUS
= *Jotape*

AGRIPPA I
b. 11 BC
King of Judaea
d. AD 44
= *Cypros (cousin)*

*Herodias* ▌
= 1. PHILIP (Thomas)
= 2. HEROD-ANTIPAS

*Salome* ▲
= 1. HEROD-PHILIP
= 2. ARISTOBULOUS

ARISTOBULOUS
= *Salome* ▲

HEROD-TIMOTHY

DRUSUS

AGRIPPA II
b. AD 27
King of Judaea
d. AD 99

*Berenice*
= 2nd wife of
HEROD of Chalcis △

*Mariamne*

*Drusilla*
= 2. Gov. Felix

andria in its stead. With full control of the enormous Persian Empire, Alexander then pressed on through Babylonia, moving ever eastwards, until he finally conquered the Punjab. At his early death in 323 BC his generals took control. Ptolemy Soter became Governor of Egypt, Seleucus ruled Babylonia, and Antigonus governed Macedonia and Greece. By the turn of the century, Palestine was also enveloped within the Alexandrian Empire.

At that stage a new force gathered momentum in Europe: the Republic of Rome. In 264 BC the Romans ousted the Carthaginian rulers of Sicily. They also captured Corsica and Sardinia. The great Carthaginian general Hannibal then retaliated by seizing Saguntum (in modern Spain) and advanced with his troops across the Alps, but he was checked by the Romans at Zama. Meanwhile Antiochus III – a descendant of the Macedonian general Seleucus – became King of Syria. By 198 BC he had rid himself of Egyptian influences to become master of Palestine. His son, Antiochus IV Epiphanes, occupied Jerusalem, an action that promptly gave rise to a Jewish revolt under the Hasmonaean[11] Judas Maccabaeus. He was killed in battle, but the Maccabees achieved Jewish independence in 142 BC.

In a continuing struggle, the Roman armies destroyed Carthage and formed the new province of Roman North Africa. Further campaigns brought Macedon, Greece and Asia Minor under Roman control. But disputes raged in Rome because the Carthaginian (or Punic) wars had ruined the Italian farmers while simultaneously enriching the aristocracy, who built large estates utilizing slave labour. The Democrat leader Tiberius Graccus put forward proposals for agrarian reform in 133 BC but was murdered by the Senatorial Party. His brother took up the farmers' cause, but he too was murdered, and the Democrat leadership passed to the military commander Gaius Marius.

By 107 BC Gaius Marius was Consul of Rome. The Senate found its own champion in Lucius Cornelius Sulla, who eventually deposed Marius and became Dictator in 82 BC. A horrifying reign of terror ensued until the Democrat statesman and general Gaius Julius Caesar gained popularity, and was duly elected to primary office in 63 BC.

In that same year, Roman legions marched into the Holy Land, which was already in a state of sectarian turmoil. The Pharisees, who observed the rather strict ancient Jewish laws, had risen in protest against the more liberal Greek culture. In so doing, they also opposed the priestly caste of Sadducees. The unsettled environment rendered the region ripe for invasion. Seeing their opportunity, the Romans, under Gnaeus Pompeius Magnus (Pompey the Great), subjugated Judaea and seized Jerusalem, having annexed Syria and the rest of Palestine.

Meanwhile the Roman hierarchy was undergoing its own upheavals. Julius Caesar, Pompey and Crassus formed the first ruling Triumvirate in Rome, but their joint administration floundered when Caesar was sent to Gaul, and Crassus went to supervise matters in Jerusalem. In their absence, Pompey changed political camps, deserting the Democrats for the Republican aristocrats – whereupon Caesar returned, and civil war ensued. Caesar was victorious at Pharsalus, in Greece, and gained full control of the Imperial provinces when Pompey fled to Egypt.

Until that time, Queen Cleopatra VII had been ruling Egypt jointly with her brother, Ptolemy XIII. But then Caesar visited Alexandria and liaised with Cleopatra, who had her brother assassinated and began to rule in her own right. Caesar went on to campaign in Asia

Minor and North Africa, but on his return to Rome in 44 BC he was murdered by Republicans on the Ides of March. His nephew Gaius Octavius (Octavian) formed a second Triumvirate with General Mark Antony and the statesman Marcus Lepidus. Octavian and Mark Antony defeated the foremost of Caesar's assassins, Brutus and Cassius, at Philippi in Macedonia, but Antony then deserted his wife Octavia (Octavian's sister) to join Cleopatra. At this, Octavian declared war on Egypt, and was victorious at the Battle of Actium, following which Antony and Cleopatra committed suicide.

Palestine at this juncture comprised three distinct provinces: Galilee in the north, Judaea in the south, and Samaria in between. Julius Caesar had installed the Idumaean Antipater as Procurator of Judaea, with his son Herod as the Governor of Galilee. Antipater was killed shortly afterwards, so Herod was summoned to Rome and there appointed King of Judaea.

To the majority of his subjects, Herod was an Arab usurper. He had converted to a form of Judaism, but he was not of the Davidic succession. In practice, Herod's authority was confined to Galilee; Judaea was actually governed by the Roman Procurator at Caesarea. Between the two of them, the regime was harsh in the extreme, and more than 3,000 summary crucifixions were carried out to coerce the population into submission.[12] Prohibitive taxes were levied, torture was commonplace, and the Jewish suicide rate leapt alarmingly.

This was the brutal environment into which Jesus was born: a climate of oppression controlled by a puppet monarchy backed by a highly organized military occupational force. The Jews were desperate for their long-awaited Messiah ('Anointed One', from the Hebrew *maisach* 'to anoint') – but there was no thought of this Messiah being divine. What the people wanted was a forceful liberator to secure their freedom from the

Roman overlords. Among the famous Dead Sea Scrolls, the text known as the *War Rule* sets out a strategy for the 'ultimate battle', naming the Messiah as the supreme military commander of Israel.[13]

## SCROLLS AND TRACTATES

The Dead Sea Scrolls are now the most useful aids to understanding the Judaean culture of the pre-Gospel era.[14] But they were discovered by pure chance as recently as 1947. A Bedouin shepherd boy, Mohammed ed-Di'b, was searching for a lost goat in the cliff-hill caves of Qumran, near Jericho, when he found a number of tall earthenware jars. Professional archaeologists were called in, and excavations were subsequently undertaken – not only at Qumran but at nearby Murabba'at and Mird in the Wilderness of Judaea.[15] Many more jars were discovered in 11 different caves. Altogether the jars contained some 500 Hebrew and Aramaic manuscripts, among them Old Testament writings and numerous documents of community record, some of their traditions dating back to about 250 BC. The Scrolls had been hidden during the Jewish Revolt against the Romans between AD 66 and 70, and were never retrieved. The Old Testament book of Jeremiah (32:14) states prophetically, 'Thus saith the Lord of Hosts . . . Take these evidences . . . and put them in an earthen vessel, that they may continue many days.'[16]

Among the more important manuscript texts, the *Copper Scroll* lists an inventory and gives the locations for the treasures of Jerusalem and the Kedron Valley cemetery. The *War Scroll* contains a full account of military tactics and strategy. The *Manual of Discipline* details law and legal practice along with customary ritual, and describes the importance of a designated Council of Twelve to preserve the faith of the land. The fascinating *Habakkuk Pesher* gives a commentary on the contemporary personalities and important developments of the era. Also in the collection is a complete draft of Isaiah which, at more than 30 feet (around 9 metres) in length, is the longest Scroll and is centuries older than any other known copy of that Old Testament Book.

To complement these discoveries, another significant find relating to the post-Gospel era had been made in Egypt two years earlier. In December 1945 two peasant brothers, Mohammed and Khalifah Ali, were digging for fertilizer in a cemetery near the town of Nag Hammadi when they came upon a large sealed jar containing 13 leather-bound books. The books' papyrus leaves contained an assortment of scriptures written in the tradition that was later to be called Gnostic (esoteric insight). Inherently Christian works but with Jewish overtones, they were soon known as the Nag Hammadi Library.[17]

The books were written in the ancient Coptic language of Egypt during early Christian times. The Coptic Museum in Cairo ascertained that they were in fact copies of much older works originally composed in Greek. Indeed, some of the texts were discovered to have very early origins, incorporating traditions from before AD 50. Included in the 52 separate tractates are various religious texts and certain hitherto unknown Gospels. They tend to portray an environment very different from that described in the Bible. The cities of Sodom and Gomorrah, for example, are not presented as centres of wickedness and debauchery but as cities of great wisdom and learning. More to our purpose, they describe a world in which Jesus gives his own account of the Crucifixion, and in which his relationship with Mary Magdalene reaches enlightening new proportions.

## SECRET CODES OF THE NEW TESTAMENT

The excavations at Qumran have produced relics dating from about 3500 BC, at which time, during the Bronze Age, the settlement was a Bedouin[18] camp. The period of formal occupation seems to have commenced in about 130 BC. Jewish historians describe a violent earthquake in Judaea in 31 BC,[19] confirmed at Qumran by a break between two distinct times of habitation.[20] According to the *Copper Scroll*, old Qumran was called Sekhakha. The second residential period began during the reign of Herod the Great (ruled 37–4 BC). Apart from the evidence of the Scrolls, a collection of coins has also been amassed from the ruins,[21] and they relate to a time-span from the Hasmonaean ruler John Hyrcanus (135-104 BC) to the Jewish Revolt of AD 66–70.

As we have already seen, the uprising in 168 BC – in which the Maccabees came to prominence – was prompted largely by the action of King Antiochus IV Epiphanes of Syria, who foisted a system of Greek worship upon the Jewish community. The Maccabees later reconsecrated the Temple but, successful as the Jews were against Antiochus, internal social damage had been done because the campaign had necessitated fighting on the Sabbath. A core of ultra-strict Jewish devotees known as the *Hasidim* (Pious Ones) strongly objected to this, and when the triumphant House of Maccabaeus took control and set up their own King and High Priest in Jerusalem, the Hasidim not only voiced their opposition but marched *en masse* out of the city, in order to establish their own 'pure' community in the nearby Wilderness of Qumran. Building work started in around 130 BC.

Many relics of the time have since been discovered, and during the 1950s more than a thousand graves were unearthed at Qumran. A vast monastery complex from the second habitation was also revealed, with meeting rooms, plaster benches, a huge water cistern, and a maze of water conduits. In the Scribes' room were ink-wells and the remains of the tables on which the Scrolls had been laid out – some more than 17 feet (c. 5 metres) in length.[22] It was confirmed that the original settlement had been damaged in the earthquake, and rebuilt by the incoming Essenes in the later Herodian era. The Essenes were one of three main philosophical Jewish sects (the other two being the Pharisees and the Sadducees).

Many Biblical manuscripts have been found at Qumran, relating to such books as Genesis, Exodus, Deuteronomy, Isaiah, Job, and others. There are in addition commentaries on selected texts, and various documents of law and record. Among these ancient books are some of the oldest writings ever found – pre-dating anything from which the traditional Bible was translated. Of particular interest are certain Biblical commentaries compiled by the Scribes in such a way as to relate the Old Testament texts to the historical events of their own time.[23] Such a correlation is especially manifest in the Scribes' commentary on the Psalms and on such prophetical books as Nahum, Habakkuk and Hosea. The technique applied to link Old Testament writings like these with the New Testament era was based on the use of 'eschatological knowledge',[24] a form of coded representation that used traditional words and passages to which were attributed special meanings relevant to contemporary understanding. These meanings were understood only by those who knew the code.

The Essenes were trained in the use of this allegorical code, which occurs in the Gospel texts in particular relation to those parables heralded by the words 'for those with ears to hear'. When the Scribes referred to the Romans, for example, they wrote of the *Kittim* –

*Map 2*  Old Testament Bible Lands

ostensibly a name for Mediterranean coastal people, which was also used to denote the Chaldeans, whom the Old Testament describes as ' ... that bitter and hasty nation which shall march through the breadth of the land to possess dwelling places that are not theirs' (Habakkuk 1:6). The Essenes resurrected the old word for use in their own time, and enlightened readers knew that *Kittim* always stood for 'Romans'.[25]

In order that the Gospels should be beyond Roman understanding, they were largely constructed with dual layers of meaning: evangelical scripture on the surface and political information beneath. The carefully directed messages were generally based on the substitution codes laid down by the Scribes.

Accordingly, references to 'Babylon' were actually references to Rome. But a working knowledge of the code was not available until some of the Dead Sea Scrolls were published. Only since then has an appreciation of the cryptic technique facilitated a much greater awareness of the political intelligence that was veiled beneath the Gospel texts. The most extensive work in this field has been conducted by the noted theologian Barbara Thiering, a lecturer at Sydney University from 1967.

Dr Thiering explains the code in very straightforward terms. Jesus, for example, was referred to as 'the word of God'. Thus a superficially routine passage – such as that in 2 Timothy 2:9, 'The word of God is not bound' – would be apprehended at once to concern Jesus, in this case meaning that Jesus was not confined. Similarly, the Roman Emperor was called 'the lion'. Being 'rescued from the lion's mouth' meant escaping the clutches of the Emperor or his officers.

Study of the Scrolls – particularly the *Pesharim*,[26] the *Manual of Discipline*, the *Community Rule* and the *Angelic Liturgy* – reveals a number of such coded definitions and pseudonyms [27] that were previously misunderstood or considered of no particular importance.

For instance, the 'poor' were not poverty-stricken under-privileged citizens; they were those who had been initiated into the higher echelons of the Community, and who on that account had been obliged to give up their property and worldly possessions. The 'many' was a title used for the head of the celibate Community, whereas the 'crowd' was a designation of the regional Tetrarch (Governor), and a 'multitude' was a governing council. Novices within the religious establishment were called 'children'; the doctrinal theme of the Community was the 'Way'; and those who followed the principles of the Way were known as the 'Children of Light'.

The term 'lepers' was often used to denote those who had not been initiated into the higher community, or who had been denounced by it. The 'blind' were those who were not party to the Way, and could therefore not see the Light. In these respects, texts mentioning 'healing the blind' or 'healing a leper' refer more specifically to the process of conversion to the Way. Release from excommunication was described as being *raised from the dead* (a term that is of particular importance and will be returned to later). The definition 'unclean' related mostly to uncircumcised Gentiles, and the description 'sick' denoted those in public or clerical disgrace.

Such information hidden in the New Testament was of considerable relevance when written, and it remains very important today. Methods of disguising the true meanings included allegory, symbolism, metaphor, simile, sectarian definition, and pseudonyms. The meanings were fully apparent, nonetheless, to *'those with ears to hear'*.

There are very similar forms of jargon in modern

English. Those of other countries would have difficulty understanding such common English expressions as 'the Speaker addressed the Cabinet', 'the Silk prepared his brief', or 'the Chair opposed the board'. So too was there an esoteric language of New Testament times – a language that included clouds, sheep, fishes, loaves, ravens, doves and camels. All of these classifications were pertinent, for they were all people – just as are today's screws, fences, sharks, angels, bulls, bears and stars.

Additionally, some of the esoteric terms in the New Testament were not merely descriptive of people's social status, but were titles – titles that also had special relevance to Old Testament tradition. The doctrine which the Community regarded as its guiding message was the 'Light', and that Light was represented by a high ranking triarchy (corresponding respectively to Priest, King and Prophet) who held the symbolic titles Power, Kingdom and Glory. In the clerical patriarchy, the *Father* was supreme and his two immediate deputies were designated his *Son* and his *Spirit*.[28] (Once again, this is crucial to our story, and we shall return to it.)

## ARMAGEDDON

Some of the most important non-Biblical records of the New Testament era have been preserved in the writings of Flavius Josephus, whose *Antiquities of the Jews* and *Wars of the Jews* were written from a personal standpoint, for he was the military commander in the defence of Galilee during the Jewish Revolt in the 1st century AD.

Josephus explains that the Essenes were very practised in the art of healing, and received their therapeutic knowledge of roots and stones from the ancients.[29] Indeed, the term 'Essene' may well refer to this expertise, in that the Aramaic word *asayya* meant physician, and corresponded to the Greek, *essenoi*.

A fundamental belief of the Essenes was that the universe contained the two cardinal spirits of Light and Darkness. 'Light' represented truth and righteousness, whereas 'Darkness' depicted perversion and evil. The balance of one against the other in the cosmos was settled by celestial movement, and people were individually apportioned with degrees of each spirit as defined by their planetary circumstances of birth. The cosmic battle between Light and Darkness was thus perpetuated within humankind, and between one person and another: some contained proportionately more light, others proportionately more dark.

God was held to be the supreme ruler over the two cardinal spirits, but for a person to find the Way to the Light required following a long and arduous path of conflict. Such a path culminated in a final weighing of one force against the other at a Time of Justification, later called the Day of Judgement. It was thought that as the time drew near, the forces of Darkness would gather in strength during a Period of Temptation. People would naturally be subject to this testing process. Those who followed the Way of Light thus sought to avoid the impending evaluation with the plea, 'Lead us not into Temptation, but deliver us from evil'.

By tradition, the Spirit of Darkness was identified with Belial (Worthless), whose children (Deuteronomy 13:13) worshipped gods other than Jehovah. The Spirit of Light was upheld by the hierarchy, and symbolized by a seven-branched candlestick, the *Menorah*. In the time of the Davidic kings, the Zadokite priest was considered the foremost proponent of the Light.

But just as the Spirit of Light had its representative on Earth, so too did the Spirit of Darkness. It was an appointment held by the Chief of the Scribes, and its purpose was to provide a formal 'opposition' within the hierarchical structure.[30] A primary responsibility of the designated 'Prince of Darkness' was to test female initiates within the celibacy, in which capacity he held the Hebrew title of *Satan* (Accuser). The equivalent title in Greek was *Diabolos* (Aggressor), being the origin of the English word *devil*. (Compare the idea of the Devil's Advocate who probes the background of potential candidates for canonization in the Roman Catholic Church.)

In the book of Revelation (16:16), the great final war between Light and Darkness, between good and evil, is forecast to take place at Armageddon (Har Megiddo, 'the heights of Megiddo'), a historically important Palestinian battlefield where a military fortress guarded the plains of Jezreel, south of the Galilean hills. The *War Scroll* describes in detail the forthcoming struggle between the Children of Light and the Sons of Darkness.[31] The tribes of Israel were to be on one side, with the Kittim (Romans) and various heathen factions on the other. In the context of this climactic war, however, there was no mention of an omnipotent Satan – such mythical imagery played no part in the Community's perception of the Final Judgement. The conflict was to be a purely mortal affair between the Light that was Israel and the Darkness of Imperial Rome.

Much later, the fundamental notion behind this ancient concept was adopted and adapted by the emergent Church of Rome. The symbolic battle of Har Megiddo was removed from its specific location and reapplied on a world scale, with Rome (the hitherto 'Darkness') usurping the 'Light' in its own favour. In order that the rule of the Catholic bishops should prevail, it was strategically decreed that the Day of Judgement had not yet come. Those who thereafter obeyed the revised principles of the Roman Catholic Church were promised the right of entry to the Kingdom of Heaven, as sanctified by the bishops. The one-time hill-fort of Har Megiddo was thereby invested with supernatural overtones, so that the very word *Armageddon* took on the hideous ring of apocalyptic terror: it implied the fearsome ending of all things, from which the only sure route to salvation was absolute compliance with the rule of Rome. In this regard, it has proved to be one of the most ingenious political manoeuvres of all time.

# THREE

## JESUS, SON OF MAN

### THE VIRGIN BIRTH

The Gospels of the New Testament are written in a manner not common to other forms of literature. Their method of construction was no accident, however, for they had a common specific purpose and were not intended to relate history. The aim of the Gospels was to convey an evangelical message (Greek *eu-aggelos* 'bringing good news') – the English word *Gospel* is an Anglo-Saxon translation from the Greek, meaning precisely the same thing. In large measure they can be regarded as enthusiastic propaganda and, on that basis, we should be wary of accepting their contents at face value.

The original unedited Gospel of Mark (inspired by Peter) was written in Rome in around AD 66. Clement of Alexandria, the 2nd-century Churchman, confirmed that it was issued at a time when the Jews of Judaea were in revolt against the Roman occupiers, and were being crucified in their thousands. The Gospel writer therefore had his own safety to consider, and could hardly present a document that was overtly anti-Roman. His mission was to spread the Good News, not to give cause for its condemnation. Mark's Gospel was a message of brotherly support, a promise of independent salvation for the needy people subject to the overwhelming domination of Rome. Such a forecast of deliverance eased the people's minds and took some of the pressure off the governors whose subjugation was felt throughout the growing Empire. The Gospel of Mark subsequently became a reference source for both Matthew and Luke whose authors severally expanded upon the theme.

The Gospel of Luke appears to have emerged from Antioch in about AD 80, and could indeed have been written by Luke 'the beloved physician' (Colossians 4:14). The account credited to Matthew (sponsored by the priest Matthew Annas) appeared first in Corinth about five years later. Both Matthew and Luke used the Mark version as a partial source. For this reason, the three are known together as the Synoptic Gospels (Greek, *syn-optikos* – '[seeing] with the same eye'), even though they do not concur in many respects.

The Gospel of John differs from them in content, style and overall concept, and is much more difficult to date. Published in Samaria, John's Gospel was compiled under the joint authorship of John Mark (Acts 12:12) and Philip the evangelist. It was influenced by the traditions of a particular community sect, and is far from naive in its account of Jesus's story. The Gospel consequently has its own following of believers who preserve its distinction from the other Gospels. It also includes countless small details which do not appear elsewhere – a factor that has led many scholars to conclude that it is a more accurate testimony in terms of both history and chronology. Although the Gospel of John did not see the light of day until after the other Gospels, it is likely that its unpublished content was compiled as early as AD 37.

The first published Gospel, that of Mark, makes no mention of the Virgin Birth. The Gospels of Matthew and Luke bring it into play with varying degrees of detail and emphasis, but it is totally ignored by John. In the past, as now, clerics, scholars and teachers have thus been faced with the difficulty of analysing the variant material, and they have made choices of belief from a set of documents that are very sketchy in places. As a result, bits and pieces have been extracted from each Gospel (whether or not the same information is contained in the others) to the extent that a whole new, unwritten Gospel has been concocted. Students are simply told that 'the Bible says' this, or 'the Bible says' that. When being taught about the Virgin Birth they are directed to Matthew and Luke. When being taught about other aspects they are directed to the Gospel or Gospels concerned – as if they were all intended to be constituent chapters of the same overall work – which of course they were not.

Through the passing years, various speculations about Biblical content have become interpretations, and these interpretations have been established by the Church as dogma. The emergent doctrines have been integrated into society as if they were positive facts. Pupils in schools and churches are rarely told that Matthew says Mary was a virgin but that Mark does not; or that Luke mentions the manger in which Jesus was placed whereas the other Gospels do not; or that not one Gospel makes even the vaguest reference to the stable which has become such an integral part of popular tradition. Selective teaching of this kind applies not only to the Nativity at Bethlehem but to any number of incidents in Jesus's recorded life. Instead, Christian children are taught a tale that has been altogether smoothed over; a tale that extracts the most entertaining features from each Gospel and merges them into a single embellished story that was never written by anyone.

The concept of the Virgin Birth of Jesus sits at the very heart of the orthodox Christian tradition. Even so, it is mentioned in only two of the four Gospels, and nowhere else in the New Testament. Matthew 1:18–25 reads:

> Now the birth of Jesus Christ was on this wise: When as his mother Mary was espoused to Joseph, before they came together, she was found with child of the Holy Ghost.
>
> Then Joseph her husband, being a just man, and not willing to make her a public example, was minded to put her away privily.
>
> But while he thought on these things, behold, the angel of the Lord appeared unto him in a dream, saying, Joseph, thou son of David, fear not to take unto thee Mary thy wife: for that which is conceived in her is of the Holy Ghost.
>
> And she shall bring forth a son, and thou shalt call his name Jesus: for he shall save his people from their sins.
>
> Now all this was done, that it might be fulfilled which was spoken of the Lord by the prophet, saying,
>
> Behold, a virgin shall be with child, and shall bring forth a son, and they shall call his name Emmanuel, which being interpreted is, God with us.

The 'prophet' referred to is Isaiah who, in 735 BC, when Jerusalem was under threat from Syria, proclaimed to the troubled King Ahaz, 'Hear ye now, O house of David . . . Behold, a virgin shall conceive, and bear a son, and shall call his name Immanuel' (Isaiah 7:13–14).[1] But there is nothing in this to suggest that Isaiah was predicting the birth of Jesus more than 700 years later. Such an anachronistic revelation would have been of little use to Ahaz in his hour of need! Like so many instances in the New Testament, this illustrates how events of the Gospels were often interpreted to conform to ambiguous prophecies.

Moreover, Mary and Joseph did not actually call their son Emmanuel (Hebrew, *Immanu-El* 'With us [is]

God');[2] they called him Jesus (Hebrew, *Yehoshua* 'Jehovah saves').

That apart, popular understanding of the Gospel text is based on numerous other misconceptions. The Semitic word translated as 'virgin' is *almah* – which actually means no more than 'a young woman'.[3] The Hebrew word denoting a physical 'virgin' (that is, *virgo intacta*) is *bethulah*. In Latin, the word *virgo* means no more than 'unmarried'; to imply the modern English connotations of 'virgin', the Latin word had to be qualified by a further adjective (*intacta*) denoting sexual inexperience.[4]

The physical virginity attributed to Mary becomes even less credible in relation to the dogmatic Catholic assertion that she was a virgin forever.[5] It is no secret that Mary had other offspring, as confirmed in each of the Gospels: 'Is this not the carpenter's son? Is not his mother called Mary? And his brethren, James, and Joses, and Simon, and Judas?' (Matthew 13:55). In both Luke (2:7) and Matthew (1:25), Jesus is cited as Mary's 'firstborn son'. The quotation from Matthew above furthermore describes Jesus as 'the carpenter's son' (that is, the son of Joseph), and Luke 2:27 clearly refers to Joseph and Mary as Jesus's 'parents'. Matthew 13:56 and Mark 6:3 both indicate that Jesus also had sisters.

The portrayal of Jesus as the son of a 'carpenter' is yet another example of how later language misinterpreted an original meaning. It is not necessarily a deliberate mistranslation, but it does show how some old Hebrew and Aramaic words have no direct counterparts in other tongues. The word translated into English as 'carpenter' represents the much wider sense of the ancient Greek *ho tekton*, which is in turn a rendition of the Semitic word *naggar*.[6] As pointed out by the Semitic scholar Dr Geza Vermes, this descriptive word could perhaps be applied to a trade craftsman, but could equally well define a scholar or teacher. It certainly did not identify Jesus and Joseph as woodworkers. More precisely it defined them as men with skills, learned men, who were masters of what they did. Indeed, one translation of the Greek, *ho tekton*, relates to 'a master of the craft', as may be applied to modern Freemasonry.

In much the same way, the mention in Luke of the baby Jesus's being placed in a manger has given rise to the whole concept of the Nativity being set in a stable, complete with its familiar cast of attentive animals. But, there is no basis whatever for this image; no stable is mentioned in any Gospel. In fact, Matthew 2:11 states quite clearly that the baby Jesus lay within a house: 'And when they were come into the house, they saw the young child with Mary his mother, and fell down, and worshipped him'.[7]

It is also worth noting that the precise words used in Luke 2:7 are to the effect that Jesus was laid in a manger because there was no room for the family '*in* the inn', not '*at* the inn',[8] as is so frequently misquoted. The journalist and biographer A N Wilson specifies that the original Greek (from which the New Testament was translated into English) actually states that there was 'no *topos* in the *kataluma*' – denoting that there was 'no *place* in the *room*'.[9] In reality, it was not at all uncommon for mangers (animal feeding boxes) to be used as substitute cradles.

## DYNASTIC WEDLOCK

According to Hebrews 7:14, Jesus was of the tribe of Judah. It is evident, therefore, that he was of the same family line as King David. The scriptures also say that Jesus was a 'Nazarene' – but this does not mean that he came from the town of Nazareth. Although Luke 2:39

implies that Joseph's family came from Nazareth, the term *Nazarene* (or *Nazarite*) was strictly sectarian, and had nothing whatever to do with the town.

In Acts 24:5, Paul is brought on a charge of religious sedition before the Governor of Caesarea: 'For we have found this man a pestilent fellow, and a mover of sedition among all the Jews throughout the world, and a ringleader of the sect of the Nazarenes'. The modern Arabic for 'Christians' is *Nasrani*, and the Islamic Koran refers to Christians as *Nasara* or *Nazara*. These variants ultimately derive from the Hebrew *Nozrim*, a plural noun stemming from the term *Nazrie ha-Brit* 'Keepers of the Covenant', a designation of the Essene Community at Qumran on the Dead Sea.[10]

It is actually a point of contention whether the town of Nazareth existed at all during Jesus's lifetime, for it does not appear on contemporary maps, nor in any books, documents, chronicles or military records of the period, neither of Roman nor of local compilation.[11] Even St Paul, who relates many of Jesus's activities in his letters, makes no allusion to Nazareth. This being the case, every reference to 'Nazareth' in English translations of the Gospels must be regarded as incorrect – stemming from a misunderstanding of the word *Nazarene*. As far as has been ascertained, the settlement of Nazareth (which does not feature in the Hebrew Talmud) was of no significance before the Roman destruction of Jerusalem in AD 70.

John the Baptist and Jesus's brother James were both Nazarites, but the sectarian term can be traced back to the Old Testament figures of Samson and Samuel. Nazarites were ascetic individuals bound by strict vows through predetermined periods, as related to Moses (Numbers 6:2–21). In the Gospel era, Nazarites were associated with the Essene Community of Qumran – the environment of Joseph and Mary.

The Community observed some highly regulated disciplines in relation to dynastic betrothal and matrimony – so we should refer the question of Mary's said virginity to this very specific context.

Both Matthew 1:18 and Luke 2:5 state that Mary was 'espoused' to Joseph, and she is thereafter referred to as his 'wife'. As determined in this regard, the word *espoused* does not mean betrothed or engaged – it refers to 'contractual wedlock'. But in what circumstance would a married woman also be 'virginal'? To answer this question we must refer to the original Hebrew word *almah*, the word that has generally, but incorrectly, been translated as 'virgin' (*virgo*), and incorrectly thought to mean *virgo intacta*.

As we have seen, the real meaning of *almah* was 'young woman' (and it had no sexual connotation). It was quite feasible, therefore, for Mary to be both an *almah* and Joseph's wife. Let us look again at how Matthew describes what followed. When Joseph learned of Mary's pregnancy, he had to decide whether or not to hide her away. It is of course perfectly normal for a wife to become pregnant, but this was not the case for Mary.

As the wife of a 'dynastic' husband, Mary would have been governed by the regulations applicable to Messianic (anointed) lines such as those of King David and Zadok the Priest. In fact, Mary was serving a statutory probationary period as a married woman of the dynastic hierarchy – a period of espousal during which sexual relations were forbidden – and Joseph would have had just cause for personal embarrassment when Mary was discovered to have conceived. The situation was resolved only when the high-ranking Abiathar priest (the designated Gabriel)[12] granted approval for the confinement.

From the time of King David, the dynasty of Abiathar (2 Samuel 20:25) was established in the hierarchy of senior priests. The line of Zadok was the primary priestly heritage, and the line of Abiathar was second in seniority. In addition to the traditional priestly styles, the Essenes also preserved the names of the Old Testament archangels within their governing structure.[13] Hence, the Zadok priest was also the archangel Michael, and the Abiathar priest (whatever his personal name) was also the angel Gabriel.[14] Being subordinate to the archangel Michael (the *Lord* – 'like unto God'), the Abiathar/Gabriel was the designated *Angel of the Lord* (the ambassador of the Michael-Zadok). This angelic system is detailed in the Book of 1 Enoch (4:9), and the *War Scroll* (9:15 – 17) also indicates the angels' order of ranking during the Gospel era.

In the Luke account, it was through the mediation of the angel Gabriel that Mary's pregnancy was granted approval, being of holy consequence. This is known as 'the Annunciation', but it was not so much a matter of announcing, as one of sanctioning.

Prior to Jesus's birth, the High Zadok (archangel Michael) was Zacharias.[15] His wife was Mary's cousin Elizabeth,[16] and his deputy, the Abiathar (angel Gabriel), was Simeon the Essene.[17] It was he who gave the formal consent for Mary's confinement, even though she and Joseph had disobeyed the rules of dynastic wedlock.

It is evident, then, that these dynastic rules were no ordinary matter, and were quite unlike the Jewish marital norm.[18] Parameters of operation were explicitly defined – dictating a celibate lifestyle except for the procreation of children, and then only at set intervals. Three months after a betrothal ceremony, a 'First Marriage', with anointing, was formalized to begin the *espousal* in the month of September. Physical relations were allowed after that, but only in the first half of December. This was to ensure that any resultant

Messianic birth occurred in the *Atonement* month of September. If the bride did not conceive, intimate relations were suspended until the next December, and so on.[19]

Once the probationary wife had conceived, a 'Second Marriage', with anointing, was performed to legalize the wedlock. However, the bride was still regarded as an *almah* (young woman) until completion of the Second Marriage, which was never celebrated until she was three months pregnant.[20] The purpose of this delay was to allow for the possibility of a miscarriage. Second Marriages thus took place in the month of March. The reason that full wedlock was not achieved until pregnancy had been firmly established was to accommodate the dynastic husband's legal change of wife if the first should prove barren.

In the case of Joseph and Mary, it is apparent that the rules of dynastic wedlock were infringed, since Mary gave birth to Jesus at the wrong time of year (Sunday 1 March, 7 BC).[21] Sexual union must therefore have taken place six months before the designated December, in June 8 BC[22] – at about the time of their initial betrothal – some three months before their First Marriage in the September. And so it was that *Mary not only conceived as an almah, but also gave birth as an almah* before her Second Marriage.

Once Mary's unauthorized pregnancy had been confirmed, Joseph would have been granted the choice of not going through with the Second Marriage ceremony. To save embarrassment he could have placed Mary in monastic custody ('put her away privily', as in Matthew 1:19), where the eventual child would be raised by the priests.

But if the child was a boy, he would be Joseph's firstborn descendant in the Davidic succession. It would have made little sense to bring him up as an unidentified orphan, leaving a possible younger brother to become his substitute in the kingly line. Joseph and Mary's unborn child was plainly a significant prospect and demanded special treatment as an exception to the general rule. The angel Gabriel would therefore have advised that, since a sacred legacy was at stake, Joseph should go ahead with the Second Marriage ceremony . . . 'for that which is conceived in her is of the Holy Ghost' (Matthew 1:20).

Following this dispensation, the normal rules would have been applied once more – the first being that no physical contact was allowed between man and wife until some while after the child had been born. 'Then Joseph being raised from his sleep did as the angel of the Lord had bidden him, and took unto him his wife: And knew her not till she had brought forth her firstborn son: and he called his name Jesus' (Matthew 1:24–25). All that remained was for the Gospel writers to wrap the whole sequence in a blanket of enigma, and this was made possible by the Old Testament prophecy of Isaiah.

In the early days of Christian belief, there were numerous Gospels of Jesus. It was not until AD 367, however, that the New Testament really began to take shape as we know it. At that time a collection of selected writings was put together by Bishop Athanasius of Alexandria. These texts were ratified and authorized by the Council of Hippo (AD 393) and the Council of Carthage (AD 397). In later years, the choice was strategically limited once again, and many important texts were excluded. Indeed, only four were finally approved by the Council of Trent in 1546: the Gospels of Matthew, Mark, Luke and John.[23]

Recently, the Nag Hammadi Codices have brought some additional Gospels to the fore. They include the Gospels of Philip, Thomas and Mary (Magdalene). In some cases the contents of individual tracts concur with passages from the New Testament, but in a number of instances they differ, sometimes markedly. It is a matter of some particular interest, for example, that the Gospel of Philip states 'Some say Mary conceived by the Holy Spirit. They are wrong. They do not know what they are saying.'

Another work, the book of James (*The Protevangelium*), was believed by Origen – the Christian Platonist of Alexandria (*c*. AD 185–254) – to have been written by James the brother of Jesus. This very early Christian book describes how Mary was one of the seven Temple nuns of Jerusalem – a sacred *almah*. For all practical purposes, in the light of this, it is correct (although ambiguous in the modern English sense) to say that a virgin conceived and bore a son.

## DESCENT FROM KING DAVID

Strange as it may seem, the Gospel of Mark – from which both Matthew and Luke took their leads – makes no mention of the Nativity. John 7:42 does allude to the birth at Bethlehem, but not as a mysterious event. Nor does John suggest that Mary's conception was virginal. In fact, he refers only to Jesus's Davidic descent: 'Hath not the scripture said, That Christ cometh of the seed of David, and out of the town of Bethlehem, where David was?' Even the Gospel of Matthew, which certainly implies the notion of Virgin Birth, opens with the statement, 'The book of the generation of Jesus Christ, the son of David, the son of Abraham.'

Paul's Epistle to the Romans 1:3 – 4 refers to 'Jesus Christ our Lord, which was made of the seed of David according to the flesh; And declared to be the Son of God'. Again, in Mark 10:47 and Matthew 22:42 Jesus is called the 'Son of David'. In Acts 2:30, Peter, referring to King David, calls Jesus the 'fruit of his loins, according to the flesh'.

At the beginning of the 2nd century, Bishop Ignatius of Antioch (a disciple of St John) wrote: 'Jesus Christ was conceived by Mary in God's plan, being sprung both from the seed of David and from the Holy Spirit'. Likewise, Acts 13:22–23 reads: 'I have found David the son of Jesse, … Of this man's seed hath God according to his promise raised unto Israel a Saviour, Jesus.'

All things considered, the divinity of Jesus is figuratively portrayed, whereas his human descent from David ('in accordance with the flesh') is consistently stated as a matter of fact.[24] Jesus was of the Davidic line, as confirmed on numerous occasions in the New Testament, through his father Joseph – an acknowledged descendant of the great King. This is the case even in Luke 1:32, despite the prior suggestion that Mary was a physical virgin and that divine agents had been at work, for the Gospel actually states that 'the Lord God shall give unto him the throne of his father David'.

References by Jesus to his 'heavenly Father' have led many to believe that he was the individual Son of God in a supernatural sense. The Christian Lord's Prayer, (in Matthew), however, specifically addresses 'Our Father', and there are many allusions in the New Testament to the notion that *all* believers are God's children (or God's sons). In this regard, John 1:12 states: 'But as many as received him, to them gave he power to become the sons of God'. Similarly, in Romans 8:14: 'For as many as are led by the Spirit of God, they are the sons of God.' And in 2 Corinthians 6:17–18: 'I will receive you, And will be a father unto you, and ye shall be my sons and daughters'. Also in 1 John 3:1: 'Behold, what manner of love the Father hath bestowed upon us, that we should be called the sons of God'.

Jesus generally referred to himself as the 'Son of Man' (as for instance in Matthew 16:13). When asked by the High Priest whether he was in truth the son of God, Jesus replied, 'Thou hast said'; implying that the priest had said it, not he (Matthew 26:63–64). Jesus answered in virtually identical terms as narrated in Luke (22:70): 'Then said they all, Art thou then the son of God? And he said unto them, Ye say that I am.'

Outside the Gospel texts, the ascription 'Son of Man' is also used in Acts 7:56 in respect of Jesus. The appellation had a special significance for it was directly related to the angelic structure. As the chief representative of the people, the Davidic dynast was not attached to the priesthood. Jesus's kingly line descended ultimately from the tribe of Judah, and held no hereditary priestly office at all: such rights were restricted to the Order of Aaron and the tribe of Levi. Instead the Davidic heir – at this time, Jesus – had a lay attachment to the angelic hierarchy as a spiritual *son* of the angel Gabriel. The name Gabriel meant 'Man of God' (Hebrew *Gebri-El*), and in the Old Testament imagery of the *Living Creatures* (Ezekiel 1:10) Gabriel represented the category of Man. Thus, Jesus was the Son of Man (of God).[25]

In his *de jure* capacity as the people's representative, Jesus personified the true sovereign practice of championing his subjects, even against the governing establishment. This was the form of Messianic obligation that was inherited by later *de facto* dynasts of his line, and which formed the basis of the Grail Code. As we shall see in due course, it meant that kings were the 'common fathers' of nations rather than the supreme governors of lands. It corresponds to the form of resolute guardianship symbolically upheld in literary romance. Never did a gallant bishop or valiant mayor race to the aid of an oppressed subject, or rescue a damsel in distress – for this was the domain and duty of princes and their appointed knights.

## THE MESSIANIC DISPUTE

One of Jesus's major problems was that he had been born into an environment of controversy over whether or not he was legitimate. It was for that very reason that Mary and Joseph took him to Simeon the Gabriel for legitimizing under the Law (Luke 2:25–35). Despite this endeavour by his parents, Jesus evoked a mixed response, and the Jews were polarized in two opposing camps on the subject of his lawful status in the kingly line. He had been conceived at the wrong time of year, and had been born before Joseph and Mary's wedlock was formalized in their Second Marriage. Six years later his brother James had been born within all the rules of dynastic wedlock, and there was no disputing his legitimacy. The opposing factions thus each had a prospective Messiah to support.

The Hellenists (westernized Jews) claimed that Jesus was the rightful Christ (Greek, *Christos* 'King') whereas the orthodox Hebrews contended that the entitlement lay with James. The argument persisted for many years, but in AD 23 Joseph – the father of both candidates – died, and it became imperative to resolve the dispute one way or the other.[26]

Through long prevailing custom, the Davidic kings were allied to the dynastic Zadokite priests, and the prevailing Zadok was Jesus's own kinsman, John the Baptist.[27] He had risen to prominence in AD 26 on the arrival of the Roman governor, Pontius Pilate. John the Baptist was very much of the Hebrew persuasion, but Jesus was a Hellenist. John therefore supported James, even though he acknowledged Jesus as legitimate and baptized him in the Jordan. It was because of

John's attitude that Jesus realized he must make a stand, for if the prospect of a revived Jewish kingdom were to gain momentum, he would undoubtedly lose out to his brother James. In view of this, he decided to create his own organized party of supporters: a party that would not follow any conventional social policy. His vision was straightforward, based on the logic that a split Jewish nation could never defeat the might of Rome. But he perceived too that the Jews as a whole could not accomplish their mission if they continued to hold themselves separate from the Gentiles (native non-Jews). His ambition for the Kingdom of Israel was one of harmonious, integrated society – and he was more than frustrated by the unbending Jews of rigid Hebrew principle.

Jesus knew full well that tradition had prophesied a Messiah who would lead the people to salvation, and he knew how desperately that Messiah was craved. John the Baptist was too much of a recluse to fulfil that role. James, meanwhile, was doing little to aid his own prospects, apart from relaxing in the comfort of High Priest Caiaphas and the Baptist's support.

And so, from a once reserved position, Jesus stepped into the public domain, resolving to give the people their long-awaited Messiah. After all, he was the first-born son of his father no matter what the wrangling priests and politicians had to say on the subject. More-over, he was the accepted Davidic dynast – the spiritual son of the angel Gabriel – in the eyes of the Hellenists, with support too from the Gentiles and Proselytes (baptized converts to Judaism). In a short while he gathered his disciples, appointed his twelve key apostles (delegates), and began his ministry.

In so doing, Jesus became a threat not only to Herod and his faction (the Herodians), and to the Romans in general, but also to the sectarian nationalists (the

*Map 3*  Gospel Locations

Pharisees and the Sadducees) who sought Jewish supremacy over the Gentiles. Disregarding his structured
background, Jesus ignored the rules of the Community
and challenged the establishment head-on. He sought
acceptance both as King and Priest in a world where he
perceived no selection by class, conviction, or fortune –
promoting an ideal of princely *service* that was to carve
its mark in time.

# FOUR

# THE EARLY MISSION

## WHO WERE THE APOSTLES?

For all his apparent humility, there is very little to portray anything faint-hearted or pacifist about Jesus. He knew full well that his task would make him unpopular in establishment quarters. Not only would the Roman regime be at his heels, but so too would the Jews' own governing body of legal elders, the powerful Sanhedrin. Nonetheless, Jesus made his entry in due accord, stating at the outset, 'Think not that I am come to send peace on earth: I came not to send peace, but a sword' (Matthew 10:34).

Under those circumstances, it seems rather odd that a group of everyday working men would give up their livelihoods for a leader who announced: 'Ye shall be hated of all men for my name's sake' (Matthew 10:22). There was no formal Christianity to preach in those early times, and Jesus promised neither earnings nor public status. The Gospels nevertheless appear to indicate that his envoys forsook their various employments and followed blindly into the unknown to become 'fishers of men'.

Who were these mysterious Apostles? Can anything of the Qumran Scribal Codes be applied to the texts, to make their identities and purpose more understandable?

Luke 6:13 and 10:1 tell that Jesus appointed 82 followers in all; 70 he sent out to preach, and 12 were designated his immediate circle. It is no secret to Bible readers that the Apostles were armed – even though Sunday-school tradition would have it otherwise. Indeed, Jesus made sure of their martial ability at the very start of his campaign, saying 'He that hath no sword, let him sell his garment, and buy one' (Luke 22:36).

All four Gospels agree that Simon was the first recruit; three Gospels also mention Andrew, his brother, at the same point. But there is some disagreement between John and the Synoptic Gospels about exactly where this recruitment took place. It was either at the Sea of Galilee (the Lake of Gennesaret) where the pair were mending their nets, or at Bethabara, beyond Jordan, at a baptism ritual. Moreover, the accounts differ again as to who was present at the time. John 1:28–43 states that John the Baptist was there, whereas Mark 1:14–18 claims that it all happened while the Baptist was in prison.

The account in John's Gospel is undoubtedly the more correct, for the first disciples were recruited in March AD 29. In *The Antiquities of the Jews*, Flavius Josephus of Galilee (born AD 37) indicates that Jesus began his ministry in the 15th year of the rule of Tiberius Caesar – that is AD 29. John the Baptist was not discredited until a year later, in March AD 30 (as confirmed in John 3:24). He was executed by Herod-Antipas of Galilee in September AD 31.

Luke 5:11 relates the story of Simon's enlistment as told in the Mark account, but makes no mention of Andrew. Next on the scene are James and John, the sons of Zebedee. Mark and Luke then declare that Jesus enrolled Levi. In Matthew, however, the next disciple is called not Levi but Matthew. In John, an early recruit is Philip, who is said to come from Bethsaida, the home-town of Simon and Andrew. Philip, in turn, brought Nathanael of Cana into the fold. From that point, no more is told of individual appointments.

Instead, it is next explained that Jesus gathered all his disciples together and from them chose his twelve personal delegates. Certain anomalies then become apparent. Levi disappears, as does Nathanael, but Matthew now appears in all listings. The Gospels of Matthew and Mark both name Lebbaeus Thaddaeus as one of the twelve, whereas the other Gospels do not – but Luke and Acts list Judas the brother of James in the twelve, whereas he does not appear in this context elsewhere. In Matthew and Mark we are also introduced to Simon the Canaanite, described in Luke and Acts as Simon Zelotes.

Mark narrates how Jesus gave Andrew's brother Simon the name of 'Peter' sometime after their meeting, but Matthew and Luke indicate that he had this other name already. From John we learn that Simon and Andrew were the sons of Jona, and that Jesus referred to James and John (the sons of Zebedee) as *Boanerges* or 'Sons of Thunder'. In Mark and Luke, the publican Levi is described as a son of Alphaeus; while listed among the final recruits is James, another son of Alphaeus. Thomas, a constant Apostle throughout the Gospels, is referred to in John and Acts as Didymus (the Twin).

This leaves only Philip, Bartholomew and Judas Iscariot, each of whom is listed by all the Gospel writers.

It is plain that the Apostles were not a group of sheep-like altruists, who abandoned all to join a charismatic faith-healer (even if he was of kingly descent). Jesus's prospects were unknown and, at that stage, he had not gained any divine reputation. It is therefore evident that something vital is missing from the Gospels. However, since they were compiled so as not to arouse the suspicions of the Roman overlords, much of their content was phrased in esoteric language for an audience who would understand what was written between the lines.

On many occasions our attention is drawn to specific textual passages by the words, 'He that hath ears to hear, let him hear' (as for instance Mark 4:9). In this regard, we now enter the enlightening world of the New Testament scribal codes – and there is no greater exponent of the ancient translatory art than Dr Barbara Thiering. For some 25 years Dr Thiering has been concerned with research into the Dead Sea Scrolls, and has opened doors to a wealth of new Gospel awareness. We shall now enter the door to the Apostles, and in so doing gain insight into the politically formidable role of Jesus as the Messianic descendant of King David.

## James and John

Jesus referred to James and John (the sons of Zebedee) by the descriptive Greek name of *Boanerges*: the 'Sons of Thunder' (Mark 3:17). This is a positive example of cryptic information aimed at initiates. 'Thunder' and 'Lightning' were the titles of two high-ranking ministers of the Sanctuary. The symbolic titles derived from references to the phenomena at Mount Sinai,[1] described in Exodus 19:16 – when thunder and lightning enveloped the mountain, and Moses went up from the camp to meet with God. The Sanctuary was emblematic of the Tabernacle (Exodus 25:8), and the Essene Sanctuary was at the Monastery of Mird, 9 miles south-east of Jerusalem – once the site of a Hasmonaean fortress.

The man known to Jesus as 'Thunder' was Jonathan Annas, the son of Ananus, the Sadducee High Priest from AD 6 to 15. Jonathan (which means '*Jehovah gave*') was alternatively called Nathanael (*'Gift of God'*), being essentially the same name. His counterpart and political rival, known as 'Lightning', was Simon Magus (also called Zebedee/Zebediah – *Jehovah hath given*), influential head of the Samaritan Magi. He is better known in the Gospels as Simon the Canaanite or Simon Zelotes (under which name he is discussed in the next subsection).

So, were James and John the 'sons of Thunder' (Jonathan Annas) or 'the sons of Lightning/Zebedee' (Simon Magus)? The answer is that they were both – not by birth, but by distinction. As *Boanerges*, James and John were spiritual sons (deputies) of the Ananus priests; they were also under instruction from Simon, who in due course was to hold the highest patriarchal office – that of the 'Father'.

At once we are presented with a very different picture of the Apostles' social prestige. Even James and John, who are identified as 'fishers', turn out to be prominent in Hellenist society. But why were they depicted (along with Peter and Andrew) in an environment of fishing boats? This is where the alternative account of John comes into its own, for symbolic fishing was a traditional part of the ritual of baptism.[2]

Gentiles who sought affiliation with the Jewish tribes could take part in the baptism but could not be baptized in the water. Although they joined the Jewish baptismal candidates in the sea, they were permitted only to receive priestly blessings after they had been hauled aboard ships in large nets. The priests who performed the baptism were called 'Fishers'. James and John were both ordained Fishers, but Simon and Andrew were among the lay net-haulers (fishermen). It was in an allusion to his own more liberal ministry that Jesus promised them canonical promotion, saying, 'I will make you to become fishers of men' (Mark 1:17).

The Apostles were clearly no ragtag band of righteous devotees but an influential Council of Twelve under their supreme leader Jesus the Christ (King). Only much later did his name become contracted to 'Jesus Christ', as if this were a proper name in its own right.[3] It is worth reminding ourselves here that the Qumran *Manual of Discipline* details the importance of a Council of Twelve to preserve the faith of the land.[4]

## Simon Zelotes

Simon Magus (or Zebedee) was head of the West Manasseh Magi,[5] a priestly caste of Samaritan philosophers who supported the legitimacy of Jesus. It was their ambassadors (the Magi, or wise men) who honoured the baby Jesus at Bethlehem. Simon was a master showman, and the manuscripts of his life deal with matters of cosmology, natural magnetism, levitation and psychokinesis.[6] He was a confirmed advocate of war with Rome, and was accordingly known as Simon *Kananites* (Greek, *the fanatic*). This was later mistranslated as Simon the Canaanite.

As an Apostle of Jesus, Simon was undoubtedly the most prominent in terms of social status, but he was also a keen Zealot commander, and was often called Simon *Zelotes* (the Zealot). The Zealots were militant freedom fighters set on vengeance against the Romans who had usurped their heritage and their territory. To the Roman authorities, however, the Zealots were simply *lestai* (bandits).

Already, the Apostles have assumed a more daunting identity than their familiar image, but their purpose remains the same: to support and defend the oppressed of their homeland, being themselves of the elite class.

Most were trained priests, therapeutics and teachers; they would have displayed merciful skills in healing, and been able to expound as orators of great wisdom and goodwill.

## Judas Iscariot

Another well-born nationalist leader of renown was Judas, who was Chief of the Scribes.[7] The Dead Sea Scrolls were produced under his tutelage and that of his predecessor, the fierce Judas of Galilee, founder of the Zealots.[8] Apart from his academic scholarship, Judas was the head of East Manasseh, and a warlord of Qumran. The Romans had a nickname for him: to them he was Judas *Sicarius* – the Assassin, the Hit-man (a *sica* was a deadly, curved dagger). The Greek form of the nickname was *Sikariotes* … and its corruption to *Sicariote* was in due course further corrupted to 'Iscariot'.[9]

Although always placed at the end of the Apostolic lists, Judas Sicariote would have been second in seniority only to Simon Zelotes.

## Thaddaeus, James and Matthew

Lebbaeus Thaddaeus is described as a son of Alphaeus, and is also called Judas (Theudas) in two of the Gospels. He was an influential leader of the Community, and yet another Zealot commander. For more than 50 years, from 9 BC, Thaddaeus was head of the Therapeutate, an ascetic order that evolved during the Egyptian occupation of Qumran. Thaddaeus was a confederate of Jesus's father Joseph, and took part in the rising against Pontius Pilate in AD 32.

James, said to be another son of Alphaeus, was actually Jonathan Annas, leader of the 'Thunder' party. The name *James* is an English variant of the name *Jacob*,[10] and the nominal style of 'Jacob' (James) was Jonathan's patriarchal entitlement. Just as the names of the angels and archangels were preserved within the higher priesthood, so too were the Jewish patriarchal names preserved by the Community elders. They were led by a triumvirate of appointed officials to whom were applied the titular names Abraham, Isaac and Jacob.[11] In this regard, Jonathan Annas was the Jacob patriarch for a time (the English equivalent being 'James').

As for Matthew (also called Levi), he too is described as a son of Alphaeus. He was in fact Matthew Annas (the brother of Jonathan) – later to succeed as High Priest from AD 42 until deposed by Herod-Agrippa I. Matthew was intimately concerned with the promotion of Jesus's work, and actively sponsored the Gospel issued under his name. As Jonathan's successor, he was the chief Levite priest, and held the nominal title of Levi. He was also an appointed publican (a Jerusalem tax official), responsible for the collection of public revenues from the Jews who had settled outside their homeland but were still liable to taxation.[12] Income from Asia Minor was collected by the Levites and deposited at the Treasury in Jerusalem: 'And as Jesus passed forth from thence, he saw a man, named Matthew, sitting at the receipt of custom' (Matthew 9:9). Similarly, in reference to the same event, 'He went forth, and saw a publican, named Levi, sitting at the receipt of custom' (Luke 5:27).

Thaddaeus, James and Matthew (Levi) are all described as 'sons of Alphaeus', but they were not *all* brothers. As elsewhere, the word *son* is here used to denote a *deputy* position. The style 'of Alphaeus' did not imply relation to a person or a place, for *Alphaeus* meant simply 'the Succession'.

## Philip, Bartholomew and Thomas

As John 1:45–49 indicates, Philip was an associate of
Jonathan Annas (alternatively known as Nathanael).
An uncircumcised Gentile Proselyte,[13] Philip was
head of the Order of Shem.[14] The Coptic Gospel of
Philip was written in his name.

Bartholomew (also known as John Mark) was Philip's
evangelical and political companion. He was chief of
the Proselytes, and an official of the influential Egyptian
Therapeutate at Qumran.[15]

The Gospels say little about Thomas, but he was
among the most influential of Christian evangelists,
known to have preached in Syria, Persia and India. He
was eventually lanced to death at Mylapore, near Ma-
dras. Thomas – originally Crown Prince Philip – was
born into the Herod family,[16] but lost his inheritance
when his mother, Mariamne II, was divorced by King
Herod after she tried to assassinate him. Philip's half-
brother, Herod-Antipas, later became Tetrarch of Galilee. In ridicule, the local people likened Prince Philip to
Esau – the son of Isaac who lost both his birthright and
his father's blessing to his twin brother Jacob (Genesis
25–27) – and they called him *Teoma* (Aramaic, 'twin'):
in Greek this name became *Thomas* and was sometimes
translated as *Didymus* (Greek, 'twin').

## (Simon) Peter and Andrew

We are dealing here with the two Apostles who are
often thought to have been the most prominent – yet in
this sequence they are placed last. Indeed, the order
in which the Apostles have been listed in this section
pretty much represents the reverse of that followed in

the Gospel lists. That is because such characters as Thaddaeus, Simon Zelotes and Judas Sicariote were far more powerful than their traditional end of the list positions indicate. But it was by no accident that the Gospel writers arranged the names as they did – for by this means they diverted Roman attention from those Apostles in the very forefront of public life.

The Apostolic tables thus usually begin with the least influential members, Peter and Andrew, who were ordinary village Essenes and held no public office. In the context of their being 'fishermen' and not 'fishers', their role at the baptism ritual was strictly as laymen: they were in charge of the nets, but performed no priestly function (such as the bestowing of blessings) as did the ordained 'fishers' James and John.

For all that, Peter and Andrew's lack of public station was of great value to Jesus. It made the two brothers more readily available to him than others who had ministerial or legislative work to accomplish. The result was that Peter became Jesus's right-hand man, and he was evidently a man of some solidity, being nicknamed *Cephas* (the Stone). In the Gospel of Thomas, Jesus refers to Peter as his 'guardian', and he was presumably Jesus's chief bodyguard. After losing his wife, Peter became a prominent evangelist and, despite the occasional disagreement with Jesus, was in time largely responsible for perpetuating the Gospel in Rome. He was martyred by crucifixion during the Emperor Nero's persecution of Christians.

## PRIESTS AND ANGELS

We have already encountered the fact that the angelic structure was maintained within the priestly hierarchy of the Qumran Community – so that the highest ranking priest was not only the Zadok dynast but was also the archangel Michael. Thus he was the Michael-Zadok (the Melchizedek). Second in ranking was the Abiathar, who was also the angel Gabriel. It is now worth taking a closer look at the angelic order, for it will shed even more light on the Apostles' social status: many of the same names recur. At the same time, various customary practices – both priestly and patriarchal – will become apparent, leading the way quite naturally to a whole new understanding of Jesus's miracles.

The first thing to note is that there is nothing spiritual or ethereal about the word *angel*. In the original Greek, *aggelos* (more usually transliterated as *angelos*, Latin *angelus*) meant no more than 'messenger'; Modern English derives the word *angel* from this via Church Latin, but the Anglo-Saxon word *engel* came originally from the old French *angele*. An 'angel of the Lord' was thus a 'messenger of the Lord', or, more correctly, an 'ambassador of the Lord'. An 'archangel' was a priestly ambassador of the highest rank (the prefix *arch-* meaning 'chief', as in archduke and archbishop).

The Old Testament describes two types of angel, the great majority of whom acted like normal human beings – as for example in Genesis 19:1 – 3, when two angels visited Lot's house, 'and [he] did bake unleavened bread, and they did eat.' Most Old Testament angels belonged to this uncomplicated category, such as the angel who met Abraham's wife Hagar by the water fountain,[17] the angel who stopped Balaam's ass in its tracks,[18] the angel who spoke with Manoah and his wife,[19] and the angel who sat under the oak with Gideon.[20]

The other class of angel seems to have been rather more than a messenger, possessing fearsome powers of destruction. This type of avenging angel features in 1

Chronicles 21:14–16: 'And God sent an angel unto Jerusalem to destroy it . . . having a sword drawn in his hand stretched out over Jerusalem.' Quite a few angels are described as wielding swords, but they are never described as divine, and there is no hint in the text of the graceful wings that are so often portrayed. (The now familiar wings were devised by artists and sculptors to symbolize the angels' spiritual transcendence above the mundane environment.)

This brings us to another category of daunting Old Testament phenomena which were said to rise above the earth by mechanical means. They were never called angels, and generally these blazing spectacles had wheels, as in Daniel 7:9: 'His throne was like the fiery flame, and his wheels as burning fire.' In Isaiah 6:1–2 there is a similar account of an airborne throne, and 'above it stood the seraphims: each one had six wings'. Yet another reference to such an apparatus occurs in Ezekiel 1, where the whole scenario – recounted at some length – is entirely in keeping with the others, including fire, wheels, and noisy, rotating rings.

Unrelated to the Bible, an ancient tractate from 3rd-century Alexandria, entitled The Origin, tells of the immortal Sophia, and of the ruler Saboath who 'created a great throne on a four-faced chariot called Cherubim . . . And on that throne he created some other dragon-shaped seraphims.'

Interestingly, it is narrated in Genesis 3:24 that the Lord stationed *cherubims* (chariots or mobile thrones) and a revolving sword of fire to protect the Garden of Eden.

The Cherubim appears again in an ancient Greek work called *The Hypostasis of the Archons*, which deals with the Rulers of Entirety and the Creation of Adam. Once more it concerns Saboath and his heavenly chariot (the *Cherubim*).

There is mention of a similar vehicle in 2 Kings 2:11, when Elijah is taken up in a chariot of fire. And there are further descriptions of a similar conveyance in the Sumerian *Epic of Gilgamesh*,[21] from the Mesopotamian Bible land of old Iraq.

It is not the purpose of this book to examine the whys and wherefores of such phenomena – simply to present them as they are depicted in the ancient texts.[22] What is certain, however, is that these flying chariots (*cherubims*) with their accompanying *seraphims* (fiery dragon-shaped auxiliaries) were never at any time described as having human form, as angels always were. It was the fearful Christian dogma of the later Roman establishment that transformed the cherubims and seraphims into adoring celestial *putti*.

Notwithstanding these spectacular devices, the angels of the New Testament were without exception all men, and their appointments to angelic office were strictly dynastic. The Book of Enoch (representing the patriarch 6th in line from Adam) was written in the 2nd century BC. It forecast a restoration of the Messianic dynasties, and laid down ground-rules for the structure of the priestly hierarchy.[23] Included was the premise that successive dynastic heads should carry the names of the traditional angels and archangels to denote their rank and position.

In the Old Testament days of King David, the senior priests were Zadok, Abiathar and Levi (in that order of precedence). The Essenes of Qumran duly preserved their priestly heritage using those names as titles – Zadok, Abiathar and Levi, as we have seen. Also in accordance with the Book of Enoch, the archangelic names were retained, under vow, as badges of priestly rank:[24] the Zadok dynast was also Michael; the Abiathar was also Gabriel, and the Levi was also Sariel.[25]

We should therefore understand that the Archangel Michael's battle with the dragon in Revelation 12:7 corresponds to the conflict between the Zadokite succession and 'the beast of blasphemy' – Imperial Rome. The 'second beast' was that of the rigidly strict regime of the Pharisees, who thwarted the ambitions of the Hellenist Jews by segregating Jews from Gentiles. This was the beast to which was attributed the number 666 (Revelation 13:8), the numerically evaluated polar opposite to the spiritual energy of water in the solar force.[26]

Those of the high orders were required to remain celibate, as detailed in the *Temple Scroll*. Trainee priests were, therefore, in limited supply, and were often raised within a monastic system from the Community's illegitimate sons. Jesus might well have become one of these trainee priests, whose mother would have been 'put away privily', were it not for the considered intervention of the angel Gabriel. Conversely, the dynastic heads of kingly and priestly successions were expressly required to marry in order to perpetuate their lines.

When procreation was embarked upon, a priestly dynast (such as the Zadok) had temporarily to suspend himself from his ordained role and pass his religious duties to another. When physical relations with his wife were completed, he would once more live apart from her and resume his celibate existence.

As we have already seen,[27] the Zadok/Michael in the early Gospel era was Zacharias (the husband of Elizabeth). His priestly deputy, the Abiathar/Gabriel, was Simeon. The story of Zacharias' procreational leave is very veiled in Luke 1:15–23, but his being rendered 'speechless in the Temple' actually means that he was prevented from speaking in his usual ordained capacity. Being concerned about his advancing age, Zacharias the Zadok transferred his priestly authority to Simeon the Abiathar, so that Elizabeth could bear a son. That son was John the Baptist who, in time, succeeded as the Zadokite head.

At the time of Jesus's early ministry, the head of the Levi priests was Jonathan Annas. As chief of the Levite dynasty he held the third archangelic rank of Sariel – and as such was the nominated King's Priest. Along with these three supreme archangels (chief ambassadors), Michael (the Zadok), Gabriel (the Abiathar) and Sariel (the Levi), there were also others with preeminent titles. These positions, however, were not dynastic, and were denoted by the representative styles, *Father*, *Son* and *Spirit*.[28] The *Father* was the equivalent of the Roman *Pope* of later times (Pope = Papa = Father) – the Roman style having been purloined directly from the original Jewish source. In essence, the *Father's* Son and Spirit were his physical and spiritual deputies. The position of *Father* was elective, and precluded its holder from certain other duties. For example, when Jonathan Annas became the *Father*, his brother Matthew (the Apostle) became his successor as the head of the Levi priests of the Succession. Hence, Matthew became the Levi of Alphaeus.

The Levi priests (Levites) operated as subordinates of the archangels. At their head, but junior to the Levi dynast, was a Chief Priest (as distinct from a High Priest). He was angelically designated Raphael. His senior priests were styled in accordance with the original sons of Levi (as given in Genesis 29:34), and they were called Kohath, Gershon and Merari. The next priest in seniority was Amram (the Old Testament son of Kohath), followed by Aaron, Moses and the priestess, Miriam. They, in turn, were senior to Nabad, Abihu, Eleazar and Ithmar – the representative sons of Aaron.

It is at this stage that the primary aspect of the Grail Code begins to emerge, for the heir to the Davidic kingly succession held no angelic title and was not in priestly service. The King was obliged to *serve* the people, and it was his express duty to champion them against establishment injustice. The very name *David* means 'beloved' – and as a beloved servitor and champion of his people, Jesus would have made a very fine king. It was this royal concept of humble *service* that the lay disciples found so hard to comprehend in their Messianic leader. This is well demonstrated in John 13:4–11, when Jesus washed the Apostles' feet. Peter queried the action, saying 'Thou shalt never wash my feet', but Jesus was insistent, replying with finality, 'I have given you an example, that ye should do as I have done to you'.

Such a charitable action is not the mark of a power-seeking dynast, but is emblematic of 'common fatherhood' in the nature of true Grail kingship.

# FIVE

# JESUS THE MESSIAH

## LOAVES AND FISHES

Although not considered to be recorded history in the traditional sense, the Gospels relate the story of Jesus by way of a continuous narrative. Sometimes they are in agreement, and sometimes they are not. On occasions, events mentioned in one or more Gospels are not mentioned in the others. In all of this, it has to be remembered that the purpose of the Gospels was to convey an imperative social message, with Jesus as the focal catalyst.

Not all of that message was delivered in an overt fashion, however. Jesus is often said to have spoken in the form of 'parables', thereby simplifying his message with allegorical discourse. To some, these moralistic tales would appear superficial, but their undertones were frequently political, being based on actual people and real situations.

The Gospels were constructed in a similar manner, and it is important to recognize that many of the stories about Jesus are themselves the equivalent of parables. Indeed, the majority of Jesus's activities were cleverly disguised within the context of diversionary stories, so that 'those with ears to hear' would understand, whereas others would not.

Since the Gospels were written in a veiled format to elude Roman scrutiny, they contain numerous symbolic elements that have distorted general understanding, even to the present day. Such veiled references include the allegorical jargon of early sectarian ritual – and have led to the complete misunderstanding of what were really very straightforward events. Some of these have even been accepted dogmatically as supernatural.

We have already encountered one example of plain misunderstanding in the nature and purpose of the 'fishers' who baptized the Gentiles after they had been hauled out of the water in large nets by the 'fishermen'. A good example of a supposedly supernatural incident occurs in John 2:1–10: the story of Jesus substituting the water for wine at the Cana wedding feast.

This well-known event was the first of many presumptuous actions by which Jesus made known his intention to circumvent tradition.

Although brought up within a strict social regime that was influenced and controlled by tradition and ancient laws, Jesus recognized that Rome could never be defeated while extremes of competitive doctrine existed within the Jewish community itself. There was no such thing as Christianity in those days – the religion of Jesus was Judaism. The Jews all worshipped one God, but even they (who presumed a special relationship with that God as his said Chosen People) were split into various factions, each with a different set of religiously based community rules. As far as they were concerned, Jehovah *belonged* to the Jews, but Jesus aspired to share Jehovah with the Gentiles. Moreover, he aspired to *share* Jehovah in a way that did not require the Gentiles to take on all the trappings of orthodox Judaism. By this means, he sought to unite the people of Palestine under one God against the might of the Roman Empire.

Jesus was a distinctly westernized Jew – a Hellenist – as opposed to the rigidly staunch Hebrews such as John the Baptist. He had little patience with the rigorous creeds of Jewish factions like the Pharisees. His attitude was unusually liberal, and his mission was one of liberation. But he knew the people could not be freed from oppression until they had freed themselves from their own uncompromising sectarianism. He was also well aware that a Saviour-Messiah had long been anticipated and, by way of a recent prophecy, was due at that very time. The coming Messiah was expected to introduce a new era of deliverance: he would necessarily be revolutionary in outlook, and would set himself apart from customary practice. As the heir to the Davidic royal throne, Jesus knew that he was qualified to be that Saviour Messiah – and that if he should emerge as such, no one would be unduly surprised.

What Jesus did not have was any officially designated social authority – he was neither reigning King nor a High Priest. For some while he was not even formally anointed, and could not have legally claimed Messianic status even if he had had all the other attributes. However, such technicalities were destined not to stand in his way, and he proceeded to implement all kinds of ritualistic changes (both religious and social) regardless of his formal deficiency.

On his first opportunity, at Cana, he hesitated, saying 'Mine hour is not yet come' (referring to the fact that he was not yet anointed). But his mother waved aside his lack of entitlement, directing the servants: 'Whatsoever he saith unto you, do it.'

The only account of this appears in John's Gospel, where the turning of water into wine is described as the first of Jesus's miracles (remarkable events). It is not stated that they *ran out* of wine at the wedding, however, as is so often misquoted. The text actually says,

'And when they wanted wine, the mother of Jesus saith unto him, they have no wine.' According to the ritual described in the Dead Sea Scrolls, the relevance of this is plain. At (the equivalent of) Communion, only fully initiated celibates (presided over by a priest) were allowed to partake of wine.[1] All others present were regarded as unsanctified and were restricted to a purifying ritual with water – these included married men, novices, Gentiles, and all lay Jews. The Gospel text continues, 'There were set there six water-pots of stone, after the manner of the purifying of the Jews'. The great significance of Jesus's action is that he took it upon himself to break with tradition: he abandoned the water entirely and allowed the 'unclean' guests to *take the sacred wine*. The 'ruler of the feast' (in Greek, the *architriclinos*) who tasted the wine 'knew not whence it was (but the servants which drew the water knew)'. He did not comment on any marvellous transformation, but simply remarked that he was surprised the *good wine* (as against the water – *poor wine*) had made its appearance at that stage of the proceedings.

As Mary declared when instructing the servants to obey Jesus, the episode 'manifested forth his glory; and his disciples believed on him.'

Communion with consecrated bread and wine was an age-old Essene tradition, not a product of later Christianity. In time, the Christian Church appropriated the original custom as its own Eucharistic sacrament symbolizing the body and blood of Jesus, in accordance with the spurious Gospel reference to its supposed institution at the Last Supper (as for instance in Matthew 26:26–28).

Represented with similar allegory in the Gospels is the episode known as the 'Feeding of the Five Thousand'. Judaic law was strict, but Jesus's new ministry was intended to be quite open-hearted. Normally,

Gentiles were afforded access to Jewish ritual only if they were committed converts, who had undertaken to observe the Jewish customs (including circumcision, if they were male). Jesus's thoughts, however, were of the uncircumcised Gentiles: why should they not also gain access to Jehovah? After all, he had already allowed Gentiles to take the consecrated wine at Cana.

The concept of a God shared by Jews and Gentiles alike became the very life-force of Jesus's mission. But it was an ideal that was more than revolutionary; to the die-hard orthodox Jews it was outrageous, for Jesus was assuming personal power over their own historical prerogative. He was making Jehovah, the God of the Chosen People, available to everyone – available, with few strings attached, to the unclean.

As we have already seen, Gentiles wishing to be baptized into Judaism underwent a ritual in which they, as 'fishes', were hauled into boats by 'fishermen', to be blessed by priestly 'fishers'. In a similar transference of imagery, the Levite officials of the Sanctuary were called 'loaves'.[2] In the rite of ordination – the ceremony of admission to the priestly ministry – the officiating Levite priests would serve seven loaves of bread to the priests, and to the celibate candidates they would administer five loaves and two fishes. There was some important legal symbolism in this, for whereas Gentiles might receive baptism as 'fishes', the Law was very firm that only Jews could become 'loaves'.

Once again, Jesus resolved to flout convention and allow 'unclean' Gentiles to partake of what was normally reserved for Jews – not just for any Jews, but for those alone who were candidates of the priesthood. In this regard, Jesus made his concession to the representatives of the uncircumcised non-Jews of the Ham fraternity (known figuratively as 'the Five Thousand'[3]). He granted their 'multitude' (governing body) symbolic access to the ministry by serving them the 'five loaves and two fishes' of the Jewish priestly candidates (Mark 6:34–44)

In the separate episode known as the 'Feeding of the Four Thousand',[4] the seven loaves of the senior priests were proffered by Jesus to the uncircumcised 'multitude' of Shem (Mark 8:1–10).

At the baptism ceremonies, the 'fishermen' who caught the Gentile 'fishes' would first take their boats out some little distance from the shore. The baptismal postulants would then wade into the water towards the boats. When everything was set, the priestly 'fishers' would leave the shore and make their own way to the moored boats along a jetty – they would thus 'walk on the water' to the boats.[5] Born into the tribe of Judah, not that of Levi, Jesus had no authority as a baptismal priest – but he nonetheless presumed to disregard the establishment and to usurp a priestly entitlement by 'walking on the sea' to the disciples' boat (Matthew 14:25–26). He even tempted Peter to arrogate to himself the same right . . . but Peter was unable to comply for fear of sinking beneath legal reprisals (Matthew 14:28–31).

Such new insight on our part, both into the veiled meaning of the Gospel wording, and into Jesus's own political motivations, does not detract from his probable skills as a healer. Being attached to the Qumran Therapeutate, he would not, however, have been unique in this regard. But then, a charismatic physician was not the anticipated image of a liberating Messiah expected to free the people from Roman oppression. What was particularly remarkable about this radical protagonist was that he applied his medical expertise to the 'unworthy' Gentiles; he did not restrict his aid to Jewish society, as the Pharisees and others would have preferred. This form of social ministry – a ministry of princely *service*, as promoted by the emergent Grail

Code – was wholly indicative of Jesus's Messianic ideal for a unified people.


## THE KING AND HIS DONKEY

Shortly after Jesus began his mission, John the Baptist was arrested because he had angered Herod-Antipas, the Governor of Galilee. Antipas had married Herodias, the divorced wife of his half-brother, Philip (Thomas), and John (the Zadok) repeatedly condemned the marriage in public, declaring that it was sinful. As a result he was imprisoned for a year, and then beheaded. On his ignoble demise, many of his followers turned their allegiance toward Jesus. Some had thought – hoped even – that the Baptist was the expected Saviour Messiah, but a number of his prophecies had not been fulfilled[6], and so he was discounted in this regard. One of the reasons why John's and other prophecies were proving inaccurate was because of the inherent differences between the commonly used solar and lunar calendars – further complicated by the Julian calendar introduced from Rome.

The Essenes were advocates of the Greek philosopher Pythagoras (c. 570–500 BC), who in his great study of arithmetical ratios searched for meaning both in the physical and metaphysical worlds through mathematical proportions. Over the centuries, using his methodology, world events were foretold with surprising accuracy. One particular event so forecast was the beginning of a new World Order, an occurrence that was in many quarters determined to be the advent of the Saviour Messiah.

The years (which we now designate BC) were thus already on a predetermined countdown long before Jesus was born. As things turned out, on the world scale of reckoning used, the forecast was actually seven years astray when applied to Jesus – which explains why he was (as far as we may be concerned) born in the year 7 BC and not in the notional year 0 (754 AUC).[7] But his brother James was actually born in the right year, and it was for this reason that so many considered James to be the legitimate heir. Much later, by way of a new Roman dating system, the notional year 0 was designated AD 1.

In the movement away from the Baptist's rigid Hebrew doctrine, even King Herod-Agrippa began to regard Jesus as the lawful heir to David, leaving James with few to champion his cause. Encouraged by this, Jesus decided to step up his campaign, but he then acted too rashly, and committed an offence that was to upset the governors and elders.

It had long been a Jewish custom to hold a Day of Atonement (*Yom Kippur*), on which day people might be absolved of their misdeeds. The solemn ritual took place in the equivalent of September, and the Essene rite was performed by the Father, in the seclusion of the Holy of Holies (inner sanctuary) of the monastery Temple at Mird. (This monastery was referred to as 'the Wilderness'.) To witness the atonement, the Father was allowed the company of one co-celebrant – a symbolic 'son'. In AD 32 the Father was Simon Zelotes, and his appointed 'son' was his immediate lieutenant Judas Sicariote. (John 13:2 gives Judas's status as Simon's 'son', but the exact relationship and its priestly significance are not made clear.)

When the act of atonement was complete, three deputies were authorized to proclaim the fact from a high location west of the Temple, symbolically spreading the word to Jews resident in other lands (the Jews of the Diaspora). On this occasion the deputies appointed were Jesus (representing King David), Jonathan Annas (representing the great mystic, Elias or

Elijah), and Thaddaeus (representing Moses), respectively corresponding to the symbolic roles of King, Priest and Prophet.[8] But when the time came for Jesus to make his proclamation, he appeared not in the apparel of a king but in the robes of a High Priest: 'And he was transfigured before them. And his raiment became shining, exceeding white as snow; so as no fuller[9] on earth can white them ... And there appeared unto them Elias with Moses: and they were talking with Jesus' (Mark 9:2–4).

Some time after this, Simon Zelotes fell foul of the civil authorities, having led an unsuccessful revolt against the Governor of Judaea, Pontius Pilate. The pretext for the revolt was that Pilate had been using public funds to have his own personal water supply improved. A formal complaint was lodged against him in court,[10] whereupon Pilate's soldiers murdered the known complainants. Armed insurrection immediately ensued, led by the prominent Zealots, Simon Zelotes, Judas Sicariote and Thaddaeus. Perhaps inevitably, the revolt failed, and Simon (Lightning) was excommunicated by edict of King Herod-Agrippa. Simon's political opponent, Jonathan Annas (Thunder), was thus enabled to accede to the supreme office of the Father.

Under the Law, excommunication (to be regarded as spiritual execution by decree) took four days for complete implementation. In the meantime, the excommunicatee was dressed in a shroud, shut away, and held to be 'sick unto death'. In view of his rank up to that point, Simon was incarcerated in the patrimonial burial chamber at Qumran known as 'the Bosom of Abraham'[11] (the original Father). Simon's 'sisters' (who were his sisters in the devotional sense only) Martha and Mary knew that his soul would be forever condemned (lost to death) if he was not reprieved (raised) by the third day, and so they sent word to Jesus that Simon was 'sick' (John 11:3).

At first, Jesus was powerless to act – for only the Father or the High Priest could perform such a raising, and Jesus held no priestly office whatever. It happened, however, that at that very time King Herod-Agrippa had an argument with the Roman authorities, losing his jurisdiction to the short-term benefit of his uncle, Herod-Antipas – a supporter of the Zealot action against Pilate. Seizing his opportunity, Antipas countermanded the order of excommunication, and instructed that Simon should be 'raised from the dead'. Jesus was in something of a quandary. Heir to the kingly line, yet with public ambitions towards becoming a High Priest, and having transgressed at the Atonement (called the Transfiguration), he wished nonetheless to come to the aid of his friend and loyal supporter. And so he did, acting on the basis that he had been Simon's appointed 'deputy' at the Atonement. Although the time of spiritual death (the fourth day following excommunication) for Simon had arrived, Jesus decided to presume a priestly function and perform the release, regardless. In so doing he confirmed the 'spiritually dead' Simon's rank as that of Abraham's Steward, Eliezer (corrupted in the Gospels to *Lazarus*), and summoned him, under that distinguished name, to 'come forth' from Abraham's Bosom.

And so it was that 'Lazarus was raised from the dead' without official sanction from the new Father, neither from the High Priest nor the Sanhedrin Council. Jesus had blatantly flouted the rules yet again. But Herod-Antipas then lent his own authority to what Jesus had done, forcing Jonathan Annas to acquiesce in the *fait accompli* – and to the people at large the unprecedented happening was indeed a 'miracle'.

Jesus had effected exactly what he wanted and, with this impressive action behind him, it remained only for him to be formally anointed and to appear before the people as their rightful Messiah in a way that would leave little room for dispute. How the Saviour Messiah was to achieve such recognition was long established, for it had been prophesied in the Old Testament book of Zechariah (9:9): 'Rejoice greatly, O daughter of Zion; shout, O daughter of Jerusalem: behold, thy King cometh unto thee: he is just, and having salvation; lowly, and riding upon an ass'.

The arrangements were made when Jesus and his disciples were in Bethany during the week before Passover, March AD 33. First, as related in Matthew 26:6–7 and Mark 14:3, Jesus was anointed by Mary of Bethany, who poured a precious boxful of spikenard[12] over his head. A suitable beast of burden was found and, in accordance with Zechariah's prophecy, Jesus rode into Jerusalem on a donkey.[13]

It has always been popularly supposed that this was a gesture of abject humility – and so it was – but it was also much more than that. From the time of King Solomon to the Jewish deportation to Babylon following the fall of Jerusalem in 586 BC, the Davidic kings had all ridden to their coronations on mules. The custom was representative of the monarch's accessibility to the lowliest of his subjects – an example, yet again, of the Messianic code of *service*.

## THE BRIDEGROOM AND THE BRIDE

It has often been said that the New Testament does not state in any forthright manner that Jesus was married. By the same token, and more importantly, however, nowhere does it state that he was unmarried. In fact, the Gospels do contain a number of specific pointers to his

*Map 4* New Testament – The Wider Scene

married status, and it would have been very surprising – if not unthinkable – if he had remained single, for the dynastic regulations were quite clear in this regard. Not only was the heir to the Davidic line obliged by law to marry, but he was also required to sire at least two sons. Marriage was both essential to the continuance of the hereditary House of David, and an integral step in the progress of the heir from initiation to full Community membership in the kingly line.

As we have already seen,[14] the rules of dynastic wedlock were no ordinary affair. Explicitly defined parameters dictated a celibate lifestyle except for the procreation of children at regulated intervals. A lengthy period of betrothal was followed by a First Marriage in September, after which physical relationship was allowed in December. If conception took place, a Second Marriage ceremony was then celebrated in March to legalize the wedlock. During that 'trial' period and until the Second Marriage, whether pregnant or not, the 'bride' was regarded in law as an *almah* (young woman or, as so often cited, *virgin*).

Among the more colourful books of the Old Testament is *The Song of Solomon*, a series of love canticles between a sovereign bridegroom and his bride. The *Song* identifies the potion symbolic of espousal as the aromatic ointment called spikenard.[15] It was the same very expensive spikenard that was used by Mary of Bethany to anoint Jesus's head at the house of Lazarus (Simon Zelotes)[16], and further investigation reveals another similar incident (narrated in Luke 7:37–38) that occurred some time earlier, when a woman anointed Jesus's feet with ointment, wiping them afterwards with her hair.

John 11:1–2 also mentions this earlier anointing – and specifically names the woman concerned as Mary. John then explains how the ritual of anointing Jesus's feet was performed yet again *by the same woman* at Bethany. When Jesus was seated at the table, Mary took 'a pound of ointment of spikenard, very costly, and anointed the feet of Jesus, and wiped his feet with her hair: and the house was filled with the odour of the ointment' (John 12:3).

In *The Song of Solomon* (1:12) there is the bridal refrain, 'While the king sitteth at his table, my spikenard sendeth forth the smell thereof.' Not only did Mary of Bethany anoint Jesus's head at Simon's house (Matthew 26:6–7 and Mark 14:3) but she also anointed his feet, and wiped them afterwards with her hair, in March AD 33. Two and a half years earlier, in September AD 30, she had performed this same ritual of foot anointing three months after the Cana wedding feast. On both occasions the anointing was carried out *while Jesus was seated at the table* (just like the king, according to the refrain in the *Song*).

This is an allusion to the ancient rite by which a royal bride prepared her bridegroom's table. To perform the rite with spikenard was the express privilege of a Messianic bride, and was performed solely at the First Marriage and Second Marriage ceremonies. Only as the full wife of Jesus, and as a priestess in her own right, could Mary have anointed both his head and his feet with the sacred ointment.

Psalm 23 – probably the best known of all the Psalms – depicts God in the male-female imagery of the era:[17] as both the Shepherd and the Bride. Of the Bride, the words say 'Thou preparest a table before me . . . thou anointest my head with oil'.[18] According to the sacred marriage rite of ancient Sumer (the land of Noah and Abraham), the Great Mother Goddess Inanna took as her bridegroom the shepherd Dumuzi (or Tammuz),[19] and it was from this union that the concept of the Matronit-and-Jehovah evolved in Canaan through the intermediate deities Asherah and El Elohim.[20]

In origin, the anointing of the king was an Egyptian custom (inherited even more anciently from Sumer in Mesopotamia), and it constituted the privileged duty of the Pharaoh's semi-divine sister-brides. Crocodile fat was the substance used in the anointing because it was associated with sexual prowess. (Indeed, the word for 'crocodile' in Egyptian was *messeh*, which corresponds to the Hebrew word *Messiah* – 'Anointed One'.[21]) It was preferred that the Pharaohs married their sisters because true dynastic inheritance was held through the female line. The Kings of Judah did not adopt this as a general practice, but they did regard the female line as a means of transferring kingship and other hereditary positions of influence (even today, one is said to be truly a Jew if one's mother is/was a Jew). David attained his kingship, for example, by marrying Michal, the daughter of King Saul. Much later, Herod the Great gained his kingly status by marrying Mariamne of the Hasmonaean royal house.

Just as the men who were appointed to various patriarchal positions took on names that represented their ancestors – such as Isaac, Jacob and Joseph – so too were the women styled according to their genealogy and rank. Their nominal styles included Rachel, Rebecca and Sarah.[22] Wives of the Zadok and David male lines held the ranks of Elisheba (Elizabeth) and Miriam (Mary) respectively. That is why John the Baptist's mother is called Elizabeth in the Gospels, and why Jesus's mother was Mary. It is also why, in compliance with this same practice, Jesus's own wife would also have been a Mary. These women underwent the ceremony of their Second Marriage only once they were three months pregnant, at which time the bride ceased being an *almah* and became a designated *mother*.

Sexual relations were permitted only in December: husbands and wives lived apart for the rest of the year.

At the outset of a period of separation, the wife was classified as a *widow* (one rank in status below an *almah*) and was required to weep for her husband. This is described in Luke 7:38, when Mary of Bethany, on the first occasion, is said to have 'stood at his feet behind him weeping, and began to wash his feet with tears'. Once the period of symbolic widowhood had been established, and during these lengthy periods of separation, the wife was given the conventual designation *sister*, just as a modern nun might be.

So who exactly was Mary of Bethany – the woman who twice anointed Jesus with spikenard in accordance with Messianic tradition?

The truth is that she never was 'Mary of Bethany'. In the Bible, she and Martha are only ever referred to as 'sisters' at the house of Lazarus (Simon) of Bethany. Mary's full title was Sister Miriam Magdala – or, as she is better known, Mary Magdalene.

Gregory I, Bishop of Rome 590–604, and St Bernard, the Cistercian Abbot of Clairvaux 1090–1153, both confirmed that Mary of Bethany was synonymous with Mary Magdalene.

At the second occasion on which Jesus was anointed with spikenard, at Simon Zelotes' house, Judas Sicariote declared his dissatisfaction at the way things were going. He stated his opposition (John 12:4–5), and thus paved the way for his betrayal of Jesus. Following the failed revolt by the Zealots against Pilate, Judas had become a fugitive. Jesus was of little political use to him, for he carried no influence with the Sanhedrin Council,[23] so Judas decided to throw in his lot with Jesus's uncontroversial brother James, who was actually a member of that Council. Judas thus not only had no interest in seeing Jesus anointed as a Messiah, but his new allegiance to James caused him to resent it once it had happened. But Jesus was adamant about the significance of his anointing by Mary (Mark 14:9): 'Verily I say unto you, Wheresoever this gospel shall be preached throughout the whole world, this also that she hath done shall be spoken of for a memorial of her.'

Apart from the fact that Jesus was said to love Mary Magdalene, there is not much in the Gospels to indicate their intimate closeness until Mary appears with Jesus's mother and Salome (the consort of Simon Zelotes[24]) at the Crucifixion. Not so, however, in the Gospel of Philip, where the relationship between Jesus and Mary is openly discussed:

> And the companion of the Saviour is Mary Magdalene. But Christ loved her more than all the disciples, and used to kiss her often on the mouth. The rest of the disciples were offended by it and expressed disapproval. They said unto him, Why do you love her more than all of us? The Saviour answered and said to them, Why do I not love you like her? . . . Great is the mystery of marriage – for without it the world would not have existed. Now the existence of the world depends on man, and the existence of man on marriage.

Notwithstanding the particular references to the importance of marriage in this passage, the reference to 'kissing on the mouth' is similarly relevant; it relates once more to the offices of the sacred bride and bridegroom, and was not the mark of extra-marital love or friendship. As a part of the royal bridal refrain, such kissing is the subject of the very first entry (after the title) in *The Song of Solomon*, which opens, 'Let him kiss me with the kisses of his mouth: for thy love is better than wine.'

There is no talk in John's Gospel of any marriage service at Cana, only of a wedding feast, and of the wine and water. The disciples were there, and the guests included Gentiles and others who were technically 'unclean'. This, then, was not the ceremony of the marriage itself but the sacred meal that preceded the betrothal. The custom was for there to be a formal host (as appears in the account); he would be in full charge as 'the ruler of the feast'. Secondary authority rested only in the bridegroom and his mother – and this is entirely relevant for, when the matter of the Communion wine arose, Jesus's mother said to the servants (John 2:5), 'Whatsoever he saith unto you, do it.' No invited guests would have had any such right of command. It is plain therefore that Jesus and the bridegroom were one and the same.

This betrothal communion (6 June AD 30) took place three months before Mary first anointed Jesus's feet at Simon's house (3 September AD 30). The rules were strictly defined, as we have seen. Only as Jesus's bride would Mary have been permitted to perform this act as laid down by Messianic tradition. With her First Marriage duly completed in the September, she would also have wept for her husband (as in Luke 7:38) before they were parted for their statutory separation. Prior to this, as a betrothed *almah*, she would have been classified as a *sinner* and ranked as a *crippled woman*.[25] The couple would not have come together for any physical union until the following December.

## SUPPRESSION OF THE MARRIAGE EVIDENCE

One of the reasons why there is no mention of Jesus's married status in the New Testament is that the evidence was deliberately removed by Church decree. This was revealed as recently as 1958, when a manuscript of the Ecumenical Patriarch of Constantinople was discovered in a monastery at Mar Saba, east of Jerusalem, by Morton Smith, Professor of Ancient History at Columbia University, USA. The extracts quoted below are from his subsequent writings.[26]

Within a book of the works of St Ignatius of Antioch was a transcription of a letter by Bishop Clement of Alexandria (c. AD 150–215), an early Father of the Christian Church. It was addressed to his colleague, Theodore. Also included was an unknown section from the Gospel of Mark. Clement's letter decreed that some of the original content of Mark was to be suppressed because it did not conform to Church requirements. The letter reads:

> For even if they should say something true, one who loves the Truth should not, even so, agree with them. For not all true things are the Truth; nor should that truth which seems true according to human opinions be preferred to the true Truth – that according to the faith.

The Gospel of Mark was the first published Gospel, and was used as a partial basis for the other Synoptic Gospels of Matthew and Luke. Bishop Clement's letter ends with an official instruction to ensure that specific original Mark texts were kept secret:

> To them one must never give way; nor, when they put forward their falsifications, should one concede that the secret Gospel is by Mark – but should deny it on oath. For not all true things are to be said to all men.

In the removed part of the Gospel is an account of the raising of Lazarus – but an account that has Lazarus (Simon Magus/Zelotes) calling to Jesus from within the tomb even before the stone was rolled back.[27] This makes it quite clear that the man was not dead in the physical sense – which, of course, quite defeated the Church's insistence that the raising should be accepted as a supernatural miracle.

Moreover the original Gospel of Mark did not include any details of the events of the Resurrection and its aftermath: it ended simply with the women fleeing from an empty sepulchre. The concluding 12 verses of Mark 16, as generally published today, were spuriously attached at a later date.[28]

The relevance of this is that the Lazarus incident was part of that same sequence of events which climaxed when Mary Magdalene anointed Jesus at Bethany. The Synoptic Gospels do not say what happened on Jesus's arrival at Simon's house, for the raising of Lazarus is not included in them. But in John 11:20–29, it is described:

> Then Martha, as soon as she heard that Jesus was coming, went and met him: but Mary sat still in the house. . . .
>
> [Martha] called Mary her sister secretly, saying, The Master is come, and calleth for thee.
>
> As soon as she heard that, she arose quickly and came unto him.

No reason is ventured for Mary's hesitant behaviour, although apart from that the passage seems straightforward enough. But the incident is described in much greater detail in the portion of Mark that was officially suppressed. It explains that Mary did actually come out of the house with Martha on the first occasion, but was then chastised by the disciples and sent back indoors to await her Master's instruction. The fact is that, as Jesus's wife, Mary was bound by a strict code of bridal practice. She was not permitted to leave the house and greet her husband until she had received his express consent to do so.[29] John's account leaves Mary in her rightful place without explanation, but the more detailed Mark text was strategically withheld from publication.

The suppression of the Lazarus story is why the accounts of anointing in the Gospels of Mark and Matthew are located at the house of Simon the leper, and not at the house of Lazarus as in John. But the description 'Simon the leper' is simply another more guarded way of referring to Simon Zelotes (Lazarus); he was classified as a 'leper' because he was rendered hideously 'unclean' by his excommunication. This in turn explains the strange anomaly by which a leper might be entertaining prestigious friends at his fine house. The symbolic description of 'leper' was used to veil the truth of the situation.

The fact was that, with his wife three months into her pregnancy, Jesus was not only a formally anointed Messianic *Christ* when he rode into Jerusalem on the donkey; he was also a father-to-be.

# SIX

# BETRAYAL AND CRUCIFIXION

## POLITICS AND THE PASSOVER

Jesus the Christ rode into Jerusalem in style; coats and palm branches were scattered in his path, and as he went along there was an amount of cheering: 'Hosanna to the Son of David' (Matthew 21:9). It has to be said, however, that this frenetic activity was mainly that of the disciples (as described in Luke 19:36–39). The strewing of the palm fronds was intended to remind the people of the triumphant entry into Jerusalem of Simon Maccabaeus – the deliverer of Palestine from the yoke of Syrian oppression – in 142 BC.[1] But Jesus's face was not well known in the city; his familiar territory was Galilee and the land around. Indeed, Matthew 21:10 states: 'And when he was come into Jerusalem, all the city was moved, saying, Who is this?'

A twice recalculated prophecy of John the Baptist[2] had determined that March AD 33 would see the proclamation of the Saviour Messiah and the restoration of the true King. Many things had been carefully prepared for this time – the anointing, the donkey, the palm leaves, and so forth. But nothing of consequence happened! According to Mark 11:11, Jesus entered the Temple, 'and when he had looked round and about upon all things, and now eventide was come, he went out unto

Bethany'. Luke 19:40 tells that the Pharisees ordered the disciples to be rebuked for creating a disturbance. Matthew 21:12 adds, 'Jesus went into the temple of God, and cast out all them that sold and bought in the temple, and overthrew the tables of the moneychangers, and the seats of them that sold doves'. He then returned to Bethany. John explains that Jesus spoke to some people in the street, following which, 'though he had done so many miracles before them, yet they believed not on him' (John 12:37).

All in all, the visit to Jerusalem was an unfortunate non-event. Jesus did not receive the acclaim he expected, and he realized that his days were numbered. The Scribes and priests 'sought how they might take him by craft, and put him to death' (Mark 14:1). His plan to create an idyllic Judaea free from the Roman shackles had failed.

It had failed because his dream of a unified people (a combination of Jews and Gentiles against the Roman oppressors) was not shared by his sectarian countrymen. In particular, the Pharisees, Sadducees and similar groups did not want to wave any banner of unification. Their sole agenda was to retain their individual laws and beliefs – and the Romans, for the most part, did not interfere with that agenda.

Also at that time, a serious rift occurred within the Apostolic group. Simon Zelotes had long been at odds with Jonathan Annas (James of Alphaeus), and their political rivalry came to a head. In their respective party roles they were styled Lightning and Thunder, and they were both contenders for the supreme position of Father. Simon was the Father from March AD 31, but lost his supremacy to Jonathan by default through his excommunication. Jonathan had been obliged to endorse the 'raising of Lazarus' (by which Simon was restored to political and social life), but he was in no mood to relinquish the power he had only just gained, especially when Simon had been 'resurrected' against the established rules.

There was also disagreement between Jonathan and Jesus over whether baptized male Gentile converts should have to submit to circumcision. Jesus was in favour of allowing the converts a choice in the matter, but Jonathan wanted circumcision made mandatory. Finally, Jonathan rejected the Zealot plan for open warfare against Rome, while Simon – fiery in word and deed – promoted the martial view. In this, Jesus was inclined to side with Simon – not that he particularly sought a military solution, but he did not like Jonathan's complacent attitude.

Trapped in the middle of all this was Judas Sicariote, who determined to side with whoever looked to be the most politically valuable. Judas had been denounced as a Zealot leader, and in the light of that his only hope was Jonathan who, as the new Father, could authorize his spiritual reinstatement and negotiate on his behalf with the Roman Governor, Pontius Pilate. As for whether Jewish converts should be circumcised, Judas was strongly opposed to Jesus and supported Jonathan. At the same time, Judas could appreciate that Simon was in a weak position: Simon stood to face criminal charges (along with Judas and Thaddaeus) for leading the Zealot revolt. It was even possible that Jesus would be charged with them, if it could be proved that he was an active supporter of the war faction. This provided a likely way out for Judas, for he could betray Jesus's sympathies and make known the whereabouts of Thaddaeus.

Soon after the debacle that was the so-called 'triumphant' entry into Jerusalem, it was time for the Jewish celebration of the Passover. Hordes of pilgrims joined the Jerusalem residents for the ritual of the Paschal Lamb, in accordance with Exodus 12:3–11.

In the course of this, Jesus and his Apostles made their way to that legendary Upper Room where they were to eat their sacred Last Supper. But there are some questionable features about this. How was it that, at such a time when all the temporary accommodation in the city was full to bursting, the Apostles were so easily able to obtain a room of some considerable size for themselves? How also could the fugitive Zealots, Simon, Judas and Thaddaeus, possibly afford to move openly in Jerusalem, while being sought for leading the recent revolt?

The answer to these questions may be found in the Dead Sea Scrolls, wherein it is quite evident that the Last Supper did not take place in Jerusalem at all, but at Qumran.[3] Indeed, Josephus explains in *The Antiquities of the Jews* that the Essenes did not observe the traditional Jewish festivals in Jerusalem,[4] and did not therefore uphold the ritual of the Paschal Lamb at the Passover.[5]

More than 160 years earlier, when the pious *Hasidim* vacated Jerusalem for Qumran in around 130 BC,[6] their new environment became a substitute Holy City for them. The custom was continued by the later Essenes and, in this context, they often referred to Qumran as 'Jerusalem'.[7] As evidenced by one of the Dead Sea Scrolls known as the *Community Rule*, the famous Last Supper corresponds in fact to the Messianic Banquet (the 'Lord's Supper'). That it occurred at the same time as the Passover celebration in Jerusalem was entirely coincidental, for the Messianic Banquet had a quite different significance. The primary hosts of the Banquet were the High Priest and the Messiah of Israel.[8] The people of the Community were represented by appointed officers who together formed the Council of Delegate Apostles. The *Rule* lays down the correct order of precedence for the seating, and details the ritual to be observed at the meal. It concludes:

> And when they gather for the Community table . . . and
> mix the wine for drinking, let no man stretch forth his hand
> on the first of the bread or the wine before the Priest, for it
> is he who will bless the first fruits of the bread and wine
> . . . And afterwards, the Messiah of Israel shall stretch out
> his hands upon the bread, and afterwards all the congre-
> gation of the Community will give blessings, each accord-
> ing to his rank.[9]

When the time came for Communion at the Banquet,
Judas left the room, ostensibly to offer alms to the poor
(John 13:28–30). Actually, he went to make the final
arrangements for Jesus's betrayal, and Jesus – who
perceived his intention – said, 'That thou doest, do
quickly' (John 13:27). There was, however, still time for
the Baptist's prophecy concerning the restoration of the
true Christ to be fulfilled – but the final deadline was
that very night, the vernal equinox of 20 March.[10] Jesus
knew that if this passed with no proclamation being
made in his favour, then his ambition was over. From
that night there would be no hope of satisfying the
Messianic prediction, and he would be denounced as a
fraud. When Judas left the room, the time was already
fast approaching midnight.

Following the Banquet, Jesus and the remaining
Apostles went to the old monastery at Qumran, customarily known as the 'Mount of Olives'. There is
some disagreement at this point between John's Gospel and the Synoptic Gospels on the precise course of
events, but one way or another Jesus foretold his fate
and outlined to his companions what their reactions
would be. He declared that even Peter 'the Stone'
would deny him in the face of the unfulfilled prophecy. While some of Jesus's disciples slept in the monastery garden, Jesus walked among them (Matthew
26:36–45), agonizing that his bid to be recognized as
the Saviour Messiah might have failed. Midnight

passed. Then Judas Sicariote arrived with the soldiers.

The ultimate success of Judas's plan relied on retaining favour with the Father, Jonathan Annas. Whether Judas took a calculated gamble or whether he and Jonathan had come to some agreement beforehand is uncertain. But when the moment of seizure came, Jonathan certainly ranged himself alongside Judas. This is not really surprising, for Jonathan's daughter was married to the Pharisee High Priest Caiaphas, and both Jonathan and Judas were politically opposed to Jesus's close friend Simon Zelotes.

With the arrest made, 'the captain and officers of the Jews took Jesus, and bound him, And led him away to Annas first; for he was father-in-law to Caiaphas, which was the high priest that same year' (John 18:12–13).

It seems more than strange that Simon Zelotes, who must surely have been present at these events, is not mentioned in any of the Gospel accounts. Yet in Mark 14:51–52 there is an equally peculiar reference in very veiled terms to a person who might very well have been Simon. 'And there followed him a certain young man, having a linen cloth cast about his naked body . . . and he left the linen cloth and fled from them naked.' For the man to 'flee naked' would have been symbolic of Simon's having been *unfrocked* from his previous high ecclesiastical rank, while for him to be described as a 'young man' relegates him to his newly demoted status as a Community novice.[11]


## CRUCIFY HIM!

Jesus's trial was hardly a trial at all, and the whole scenario, as presented in the Gospels, is full of ambiguities. Matthew 26:57–59 describes matters thus: 'They that had laid hold on Jesus led him away to Caiaphas the high priest, where the scribes and the elders were assembled . . . Now the chief priests, and elders, and all the council, sought false witness against Jesus'. The account is very much the same in Mark 14:53: 'And they led Jesus away to the high priest: and with him were assembled all the chief priests and the elders and the scribes.'

Even if it can be accepted that all these priests, scribes and elders were somehow very conveniently gathered together in the early hours at a moment's notice, the fact remains that it was quite outside the Law for the Jewish Council to sit at night. Luke 22:66 indicates that although Jesus was taken firstly to Caiaphas, the Sanhedrin did not meet until it was day. Even then, the meeting would still have been illegal, for neither was the Council allowed to sit during the Passover.[12]

The Gospels all state that Peter followed Jesus to the house in which Caiaphas was located, where he denied his master three times as predicted. The house was not in the city of Jerusalem, though: it was the Vestry house at Qumran.[13] As the current High Priest, Caiaphas would necessarily have been at the Messianic Banquet, as laid down in the *Community Rule*, and would therefore have been resident in the Community, along with other officials of the Sanhedrin, on the night before the Passover Friday.

But John's Gospel (18:15–16) introduces another character, shadowing Peter:

> And Simon Peter followed Jesus, and so did another disciple: that disciple was known unto the high priest, and went in with Jesus into the palace of the high priest.
> But Peter stood at the door without. Then went out that other disciple, which was known unto the high priest, and spake unto her that kept the door, and brought in Peter.

This other disciple, who wandered about at will, and whose acquaintance with the High Priest is accentuated, was certainly not a captive as was Jesus. In the circumstances, and with the description as given, it is likely that he was in fact Jonathan Annas (James of Alphaeus), father-in-law of the High Priest Caiaphas.

All accounts agree that Caiaphas passed Jesus over to the Roman Governor, Pontius Pilate, whose presence facilitated the immediate interrogation of Jesus during the Passover. This is confirmed in John 18:28–31, only for a further anomaly to emerge:

> Then led they Jesus from Caiaphas unto the hall of judgment: and it was early; and they themselves went not into the judgment hall, lest they should be defiled; but that they might eat the passover.
>
> Pilate then went out unto them, and said, What accusation bring ye against this man?
>
> They answered and said unto him, If he were not a malefactor, we would not have delivered him up unto thee.
>
> Then said Pilate unto them, Take ye him, and judge him according to your law. The Jews therefore said unto him, It is not lawful for us to put any man to death . . .

In this regard, the truth is that the Sanhedrin was fully empowered not only to condemn criminals but to pass and implement the death sentence if necessary.

The Gospels also claim that Pilate offered to reprieve Jesus because 'it was customary for the Governor to release a prisoner at the feast of the Passover'. Again this is simply not true – there never was such a custom.[14]

This is when Judas reappears. Repenting of his act of betrayal, he 'brought again the thirty pieces of silver to the chief priests and elders . . . And they took counsel, and bought with them the potter's field' (Matthew 27:3–7). The account is strongly reminiscent of an account in the Old Testament book of Zechariah (11:13): 'And I took the thirty pieces of silver, and cast them to the potter in the house of the Lord.' Matthew (27:5) goes on to say that once Judas had returned the bribe money to the priests he went and hanged himself. But more precisely, he set the scene for his own downfall, for his actual death is described later in Acts 1:16–18.

If both Simon and Judas are implicated in the Gospel accounts of Jesus's arrest and trial, it would appear that Thaddaeus – the third of the three leading Zealot revolutionaries – is not mentioned after the Last Supper. But he does actually come into the story at the trial. Thaddaeus 'of Alphaeus' was a deputy 'of the Succession', a deputy to the Father, and thus a devotional 'son' of the Father. In Hebrew, the expression 'son of the Father' would incorporate the elements *bar* (son) and *abba* (father) – so Thaddaeus might be described as ' Bar-abba'. And a man called Barabbas is intimately concerned with the possibility of Jesus's reprieve by Pontius Pilate.

Barabbas is described in Matthew 27:16 as 'a notable prisoner', in Mark 15:7 as one who had 'committed murder in the insurrection'; in Luke 23:19 as a man who 'for murder had been cast into prison', and in John 18:40 as 'a robber'. The John description is rather too vague, for everyday robbers were not customarily sentenced to crucifixion. However, the English word does not truly reflect the original Greek implication, for *léstés* does not mean 'robber' so much as 'outlaw'. Mark's words point far more specifically to the insurgent role of ' Barabbas' in the recent Zealot revolt against Pilate.

What seems to have happened is that when the three prisoners Simon, Thaddaeus and Jesus were brought before Pilate, the cases against Simon and Thaddaeus were clear-cut; they were known Zealot leaders, and had been condemned men since the uprising. On the other hand, Pilate found it extremely difficult to prove a case against Jesus. Indeed, he was there only because the Jewish contingent wanted him out of the way and had pushed him along to Pilate for sentencing with the others. Pilate asked the Jewish hierarchy at least to provide him with a pretext – 'What accusation bring ye against this man?' – but received no satisfactory answer. In desperation Pilate suggested they should take him and 'judge him according to your law'. At this, the Jews are said to have given the untrue excuse that 'It is not lawful for us to put any man to death'.

So Pilate then turned to ask Jesus about himself. 'Art thou the King of the Jews?' he asked – only for Jesus to answer with a retaliatory question: 'Sayest thou this thing of thyself, or did others tell it thee of me?' In utter confusion, Pilate responded, 'Thine own nation and the chief priests have delivered thee unto me: what hast thou done?' The questioning progressed, until eventually Pilate 'went out again unto the Jews, and saith unto them, I find in him no fault at all' (John 18:38).

At this point, Herod-Antipas of Galilee arrived on the scene (Luke 23:7–12). He was no friend of the Annas priests, and it suited his purposes for Jesus to be released, in order to provoke his nephew King Herod-Agrippa. Antipas therefore struck a deal with Pilate to secure the release of Jesus. The pact between Judas Sicariote and Jonathan Annas was thus superseded and overturned without involving either of them, by way of an agreement between the Herodian Tetrarch and the Roman Governor. From that moment, Judas lost any chance of a pardon for his Zealot activities, and his days were numbered.

In accordance with the new arrangement, Pilate said to the Jewish elders,

> Ye have brought this man unto me, as one that perverteth the people: and, behold, I, having examined him before you, have found no fault in this man touching those things whereof ye accuse him:

No, nor yet Herod: for I sent you to him; and, lo, nothing worthy of death is done unto him.

I will therefore chastise him, and release him.

(Luke 23:14–16)

Had the members of the Sanhedrin waited until after the Passover, they could have conducted their own trial of Jesus in perfect legality. But they had strategically passed the responsibility over to Pilate because they knew there was no true charge substantiate. They had certainly not bargained for Pilate's sense of justice, nor for the intervention of Herod-Antipas. But Pilate managed to defeat his own objective. He tried to reconcile his decision to free Jesus with the notion that it might be regarded as a Passover dispensation – and in so doing, he opened the door to a Jewish choice – Jesus or Barabbas? At this, 'they cried out all at once, saying, Away with this man, and release unto us Barabbas' (Luke 23:18).

Pilate pursued his course in favour of Jesus, but the Jews cried 'Crucify him!' Yet again Pilate asked, 'Why, what evil hath he done? I have found no cause of death in him'. But the odds were stacked against him, and giving way to his misguided commitment, Pilate released 'Barabbas' (Thaddaeus). The Roman soldiers placed a crown of thorns on Jesus's head, and wrapped a purple robe around him (so that the 'King of the Jews' should be crowned and wear the royal colour). Pilate then handed him back to the priests, saying, 'Behold, I bring him forth to you, that ye may know that I find no fault in him' (John 19:4).

## TO GOLGOTHA

At that stage things were going well for the Jewish elders: their plan had all but succeeded. The ageing

Thaddaeus (Barabbas) may have been released, but both Simon and Jesus were in custody, and so was Judas Sicariote. Undoubtedly, the greatest betrayer was the prevailing Father, Jonathan Annas, the one-time Apostle known as James of Alphaeus (or Nathanael). The three crosses were duly erected in 'the Place of a Skull', Golgotha, and were set to bear Jesus and the two Zealot guerrilla leaders Simon Zelotes and Judas Sicariote.

On the way to the Crucifixion at Golgotha, a significant event occurred when a mysterious character named Simon the Cyrene was obliged to carry Jesus's cross (Matthew 27:32). Many theories have been put forward about who the Cyrene might have been, but his real identity does not matter too much. What matters is that he was there at all. There is an interesting reference to him in an early Coptic tractate called *The Second Treatise of the Great Seth*, discovered among the books of Nag Hammadi. Explaining that there was a substitution made for at least one of the three victims of the Crucifixion, it mentions the Cyrene in this connection. The substitution apparently succeeded, for the tractate declares that Jesus did not die on the Cross as presumed. Jesus is himself quoted as saying after the event, 'As for my death – which was real enough to them – it was real to them because of their own incomprehension and blindness.'

In the event, however, Simon the Cyrene was a substitute for Simon Zelotes, not for Jesus. Clearly, the execution of two such men as Jesus and Simon could not go unchallenged, and so a strategy was implemented to outwit the Jewish authorities (even though Pilate's men may well have been party to the subterfuge). It hinged upon the use of a comatosing poison and the performance of a physical deception.

If any man could mastermind such an illusion, that man was Simon Zelotes, Head of the Samaritan Magi and renowned as the greatest magician of his day. Both *The Acts of Peter* and *The Apostolic Constitutions*[15] recount the story of how, some years later, Simon levitated himself above the Roman Forum. At Golgotha, however, things were very different: Simon was under guard and on his way to be crucified.

In the first instance it was necessary to extricate Simon from his predicament – and so a substitution was organized in the person of the Cyrene, who would have been in league with the released Thaddaeus (Barabbas). The deception began on the way to Golgotha when, by accepting Jesus's burden, the Cyrene was able to incorporate himself in the midst of the assembly. The switch itself was made at the Crucifixion site, under cover of the bustle of erecting the crosses and the general preparatory confusion. Amid this bustle, the Cyrene duly disappeared – but actually took Simon's place.[16] In the Gospels, the following sequence is carefully veiled by giving very few details about the men crucified alongside Jesus, other than describing them as 'thieves'.

And so the scene was set – Simon (Zelotes) Magus had achieved his freedom, and could stage-manage the proceedings from then on.

## PLACE OF A SKULL

Although the Crucifixion is generally portrayed as a relatively public affair, the Gospels affirm (for instance in Luke 23:49) that onlookers were obliged to watch the proceedings 'from afar off'. In Matthew, Mark and John, the site is named as Golgotha, whereas in Luke it is Calvary. But both names (Hebrew, *Gulgoleth*; Aramaic, *Gulgolta*; Latin, *Calvaria*) derive from words that mean 'skull', and the meaning of the place-name, as given in all the Gospels, is straightforward: 'a place of a skull'.

Three centuries later, as the Christian faith began to spread its influence, various sites in and around Jerusalem were renamed and dubbed with supposed New Testament significance. On many occasions it was simply a case of finding a suitable place to hang a name; sometimes quite unsuitable names were attributed – such were the demands of pilgrims and the tourist market. A suitable Calvary site was identified; a route along which Jesus carried his cross was mapped out (much later to be called the Via Dolorosa – 'the Way of Sorrows' – in, of all styles, Latin!), and a convenient sepulchre was earmarked to represent the legendary tomb.

In the context of all this creativity, Golgotha (Calvary) was said to have been located outside Herod's wall, north-west of Jerusalem. It was a barren hill, and was selected because it could be said roughly to be skull-shaped. Later tradition romanticized the place as 'a green hill far away', a theme on which many artists have produced variations. Yet for all of this fanciful idealism, not one of the Gospels makes any mention at all of a hill. According to John 19:41, the location was a *garden* in which there was a private sepulchre, identified as being owned by Joseph of Arimathea (Matthew 27:59–60). Heeding the evidence of the Gospels instead of pandering to popular folklore, it is apparent that the Crucifixion was no hill-top spectacle with enormous crosses against the skyline and an epic cast of spectators. On the contrary, it was a small-scale affair on controlled land – an exclusive garden that was, in one way or another, 'the place of a skull' (John 19:17).

The Gospels have little more to say on the subject – but (the Epistle to the) Hebrews 13:11–13 provides some very important further clues to the location:

For the bodies of those beasts, whose blood is brought into the sanctuary by the high priest for sin, are burned without the camp.

Wherefore Jesus also, that he might sanctify the people with his own blood, suffered without the gate.

Let us go forth therefore unto him without the camp, bearing his reproach.

From this we gather that Jesus suffered 'outside the gate' and 'outside the camp'. Also there is some association with a place where the bodies of sacrificed animals were burned.

Dr Barbara Thiering makes the point that this reference is particularly important because the sites at which animal remains were burned were regarded as 'unclean'. She also notes that according to Deuteronomy 23:10–14, 'without the camp' described areas set aside as cesspits, middens and public latrines which were both physically and ritually 'unclean'. By the same token, 'without the gate' defined various other 'unclean' places, including ordinary cemeteries.[17]

This is very significant, and the Dead Sea Scrolls make it clear that because it constituted an act of defilement to walk over the dead, human graveyards were identified with the sign of a *skull*. It follows, quite naturally, that the 'place of a skull' (Golgotha/Calvary) was a cemetery – plainly, a restricted cemetery garden that contained an empty sepulchre in the charge of Joseph of Arimathea.

Since we are dealing with the destined resting-place of an anointed Christ and (by implication) a high-priestly Father, the appropriate hierarchical burial-ground would only have been in one place: at or hard by the 'Bosom of Abraham' at Qumran (from which confine Simon/Lazarus had already been 'raised'). Here, indeed, south of the Vestry, was a cemetery *garden*, 'a place of a skull'.[18]

Moreover, Revelation 11:8 states that Jesus was crucified in 'the great city which spiritually is called Sodom and Egypt'. This positively identifies the location as Qumran, which was designated 'Egypt' by the ascetic order of the Egyptian Therapeutate.[19] Qumran was also geographically associated with the Old Testament centre of Sodom.

But if this was the traditional burial-ground reserved for those of the Messianic and patriarchal heritage, why was there in it a sepulchre belonging to Joseph of Arimathea?

In the Gospels, Joseph is described as an 'honourable counsellor [a member of the Sanhedrin], which also waited for the kingdom of God' (Mark 15:43). He was also 'a disciple of Jesus, but secretly, for fear of the Jews' (John 19:38). But although Joseph's allegiance to Jesus was a secret from the Jewish elders, it came as no surprise to Pontius Pilate, who accepted the man's involvement in Jesus's affairs without question. That same involvement was no surprise either to Jesus's mother Mary, or to Mary Magdalene, Mary Cleophas, or Salome. They all went along quite happily with Joseph's arrangements, accepting his authority without comment or demur.

Sometimes presumed to relate to the village of Arimeh on the plain of Gennesareth, *Arimathea* is in fact a descriptive title like so many others in the New Testament. It represented a particularly high status. Just as Matthew Annas (the brother of Jonathan) held the priestly distinction 'Levi of Alphaeus' (Levi of the Succession), so Joseph was 'of Arimathea'. However (as with the style, Levi), Joseph was not his true baptismal name, and 'of Arimathea' was yet another descriptive term. *Arimathea* is derived (like Alphaeus) from a combination of Hebrew and Greek elements, in this case Hebrew, *ram-* or *rama-* (height, top), and Greek, *theo-* (of

God), together meaning 'highest of God', and as a distinction 'Divine Highness'.

Meanwhile, we know that Jesus's father was Joseph, and that Jesus was heir to the throne of David. The patriarchal title of 'Joseph' was applied to the next in succession to the heir of the Davidic kingly line.[20] In this respect, with Jesus regarded as the 'David', then his eldest brother James was the designated 'Joseph', being his recognized successor at the time. Put another way, if Jesus was the King-God (the Divine Majesty, the Messiah – in accordance with the familiar representative Greco-Roman style, *Ichthys*: Jesus the Christ God), then James was the Crown Prince (the Divine Highness, the Joseph *Rama-Theo*, or Joseph of Arimathea). Joseph of Arimathea emerges, then, as none other than Jesus's own brother James.

It therefore comes as no surprise that Jesus was entombed in a sepulchre that belonged to his own royal family. Neither is it surprising that Pilate should allow Jesus's own brother Joseph (James) to take charge; nor that the women of Jesus's family should accept the arrangements made by 'Joseph' without question. The reason that 'Joseph' kept his personal support for Jesus a secret from the Sanhedrin is self evident, for he had his own separate following amid all ranks of the Hebrew community.

From the time the Dead Sea Scrolls were first discovered at Qumran in 1947, digs and excavations went on well into the 1950s. During this period important finds were made in a number of different caves. The archaeologists discovered that one cave in particular had two chambers (known as Caves 7 and 8) and two separate entrances quite a way apart. The access to the main chamber was through a hole in the roof path, whereas the adjoining hollow was approached from the side.[21] From the roof entrance, steps had been constructed down into the chamber, and to seal the entrance against rainfall, a large stone had to be rolled across the opening. According to the *Copper Scroll*, this sepulchre was used as a Treasury deposit, and as such it has been dubbed the 'Rich Man's Cave'. More importantly, it was the sepulchre of the Joseph Crown Prince, and it was sited directly opposite the Bosom of Abraham.

The prophecy that the Messianic King would ride into Jerusalem on an ass was not the only prediction made concerning the Messiah in the Old Testament book of Zechariah. Two other prophecies – Zechariah 12:10 and 13:6 – stated that he would be pierced and mourned in death by all Jerusalem, and that he would be wounded in the hands as a result of his friends. Jesus realized that by being crucified he would qualify in all of these respects. He might have missed the deadline as far as John the Baptist's prophecy was concerned, but the Crucifixion offered him another chance . . . if things were properly organized. So, as John 19:36 states in relation to Zechariah, 'These things were done, that the scripture should be fulfilled'.

There is no indication in the Gospels of whether Jonathan Annas was at the Crucifixion. It is likely that he was there, however, even though the disciples still recognized Simon Zelotes as the true Father (the Abraham). To them, Jonathan was instead the designated 'Elijah' (the more current name for Elijah was *Elias*). In Mark 15:34 it is stated that 'at the ninth hour Jesus cried with a loud voice, saying, Eloi, Eloi, lama sabachthani?' In Matthew 27:46, the same expression is quoted as 'Eli, Eli, lama sabachthani?' The term *Eli* in Hebrew represents the word *El* (God) with the possessive suffix -*i*, thus 'my God' (possibly *Eloi* in Aramaic), and the statement was therefore translated as meaning 'My God, my God, why hast thou forsaken me?'

But according to the Gospels, the onlookers within hearing interpreted the plea rather differently, saying, 'Behold, he calleth Elias . . . let us see whether Elias will come to take him down' (Mark 15:35–36). Those at the scene, then, were in no doubt that Jesus had called for the patriarchal Elias – the 'Elijah', Jonathan Annas – the Apostle and current Father who had truly forsaken him.

Crucifixion was both execution and punishment, death by torturous ordeal extended over a number of days. Firstly, the victim's outstretched arms were strapped by the wrists to a beam which was then hoisted into place horizontally across an upright post. Sometimes the hands were transfixed by nails as well, but nails alone would have been useless. Suspended with all his weight on his arms, a man's lungs would be compressed, and he would die fairly quickly through suffocation. To prolong the agony, chest pressure was relieved by fixing the victim's feet to the upright post. Supported in this manner a man could live for many days, possibly even a week or more. After a while, in order to free up the crosses, the executioners would sometimes break the legs of the victims, so as to increase the hanging weight and accelerate death.

On that Friday 20 March AD 33, there was no reason for any of the three men crucified to have died within the day. Nonetheless, Jesus was given some vinegar, and having taken it, he 'gave up the ghost' (John 19:30). Very soon afterwards, he was formally declared dead. At that stage, Judas and the Cyrene were still very much alive, so their legs were broken. A centurion pierced Jesus's side with a spear, and the fact that he bled (identified as blood and water) was held to indicate that he was dead (John 19:34). In reality, vascular bleeding indicates that a body is alive, not dead.

The Gospels do not say who gave the vinegar to Jesus on the cross, but John 19:29 specifies that the vessel was ready and waiting. A little earlier in the same sequence (Matthew 27:34), the potion was said to be 'vinegar mingled with gall' – that is, soured wine mixed with snake venom. Dependent on the proportions, such a mixture could induce unconsciousness or even cause death. In this case the poison was fed to Jesus not from a cup but from a sponge, and by measured application from a reed. The person who administered it was undoubtedly Simon Zelotes, who was meant to be upon one of the crosses himself, but who was actually there as the deposed (but still venerated) Father attending his Messianic King. In a true 'leap of faith' Jesus said to his trusted ally, 'Father, into thy hands I commend my spirit' (Luke 23:46).

Meanwhile, Jesus's brother James (Joseph of Arimathea) was negotiating with Pilate to remove Jesus's body before the Sabbath and put it in his sepulchre. Pilate was not unreasonably amazed that Jesus had died in so short a time (Mark 15:44): 'And Pilate marvelled if he were already dead: and calling unto him the centurion, he asked him whether he had been any while dead.' To speed matters up further, 'Joseph' quoted to Pilate a Jewish rule based on Deuteronomy 21:22–23, and confirmed in the Qumran *Temple Scroll*: 'And if a man have committed a sin worthy of death, and he be put to death, and thou hang him on a tree: His body shall not remain all night upon the tree, but thou shalt in any wise bury him that day'. Pilate therefore sanctioned the change of procedure from hanging (as manifest in crucifixion) to burial, and returned to Jerusalem leaving 'Joseph' in control.

It is perhaps significant that in Acts 5:30, 10:39 and 13:29, the references to Jesus's torture all relate to his being 'hanged on a tree'.

With Jesus apparently lifeless but actually in a coma, and with the legs of Judas and the Cyrene newly broken, the three were brought down, having been on their respective crosses for less than half a day. The fact that Judas and the Cyrene were also removed from their crosses at the same time is confirmed in John 19:31:

> The Jews therefore, because it was the preparation, that the bodies should not remain upon the cross on the sabbath day, . . . besought Pilate that their legs might be broken, and that they might be taken away.

This account does not state that the men were dead; it refers however to 'bodies' (that is live bodies as against corpses) before any mention of leg breaking. This use of the word *body* is also applicable to Jesus. Although the English language uses the word *body* quite loosely, other languages were and are rather more specific.

The Gospel accounts of what followed are not only brief, they are also vague. All agree that 'Joseph' wrapped Jesus in linen and laid him in the sepulchre, and it is related that Nicodemus arrived with an enormous quantity of myrrh and aloes. Only two Gospels state that 'Joseph' rolled a stone over the tomb's entrance, but three mention that Mary and Mary Magdalene saw the sepulchre. Otherwise, no further information is given about what happened during the rest of that Friday.

# SEVEN

# THE RESURRECTION

## THREE HOURS OF DARKNESS

The next day was the Sabbath, about which the Gospels have little to tell. Only Matthew 27:62–66 makes any mention of this Saturday, but refers simply to a conversation between Pilate and the Jewish elders in Jerusalem, following which Pilate arranged for two guards to watch Jesus's tomb. Apart from that, all four Gospels continue their story from the Sunday morning thereafter.

Yet, if any day was important to the ongoing course of events, that day was the Saturday – the Sabbath day we are told so little about. This respected day of rest and worship was the key to everything that happened. It was what occurred on the Saturday that caused the women such amazement when they found the stone rolled from its position at daybreak on Sunday. In practical terms, there was nothing startling about the displacement of the stone – anyone could have moved it. Indeed, the women would have rolled it away themselves, for they had no reason to anticipate a prevention of access. What was so unthinkable was that the stone had been moved *on the Sabbath*, a sacred day on which it was utterly forbidden to shift a burden. For the stone to have been moved on the Sabbath was quite impossible!

There is some variation between the Gospels over what actually happened on the third day – the Sunday. Matthew 28:1 tells that Mary and Mary Magdalene made their way to the tomb, while Mark 16:1 includes Salome as well. Luke 24:10 introduces Joanna, but omits Salome, whereas John 20:1 has Mary Magdalene arriving entirely alone. Mark, Luke and John claim that when the woman/women arrived, the stone had already been displaced. In Matthew, however, the two sentries were on guard, and the stone was still in position. Then – to the astonishment of the women and the sentries – 'the angel of the Lord descended . . . and rolled back the stone'.

It subsequently became apparent that Jesus was not in the tomb where he had been laid. According to Matthew 28:5–6, the angel led the women into the cave. In Mark 16:4–5, they went in by themselves, and were confronted by a young man in a white robe. Luke 24:3–4, however, describes two men standing inside. And John 20:2–12 tells how Mary Magdalene went to fetch Peter and another disciple before entering the cave with them. Then, after her companions had departed, Mary found two angels sitting within the sepulchre.

In the final analysis, it is not clear whether the guards existed or not. The number of women was either one, two, or three. Perhaps Peter was around; perhaps he was not. There was either an angel outside or a young man inside; conversely, there were two angels inside, who might have been sitting or might have been standing. As for the stone, it was possibly still in position at daybreak, or maybe it had already been moved.

There is only one potential common denominator in all of this: Jesus was no longer there. But even that is not certain. According to John 20:14–15, Mary Magdalene turned away from the angels to find Jesus standing there, whereupon she took him to be the gardener. She moved towards him, but Jesus prevented her approach, saying, 'Touch me not' (John 20:17).

These are the four accounts on which the entire tradition of the Resurrection is based – and yet they conflict in almost every detail. Because of this, hundreds of years of argument have ensued over whether it was Mary Magdalene or Peter who first saw the reappeared Jesus.

But can we trace what actually happened after 'Joseph' left Jesus in the tomb on the previous Friday?

Initially, the Cyrene and Judas Sicariote – with their legs broken, but still very much alive – had been placed in the second chamber of the tomb. Burial alive was a customary old form of execution. Jesus's body occupied the main chamber. Within the confines of the double-hollow, Simon Zelotes had already taken up his station, along with lamps and everything else required for the operation. (Interestingly, a lamp was among the items found within the cave during the 1950s.)

Then, according to John 19:39, Nicodemus arrived, bringing with him 'a mixture of myrrh and aloes, about an hundred pound weight'.[1] Extract of myrrh was a form of sedative commonly used in contemporary medical practice – but why such a vast quantity of aloes? The juice of aloes, as modern pharmacopoeias explain, is a strong and fast-acting purgative – precisely what would have been needed by Simon to expel the poisonous 'gall' (venom) from Jesus's body.

It was of great significance that the day after the Crucifixion was the Sabbath day. Indeed, the timing of the whole operation to 'raise Jesus from the dead' relied on the critical timing of the precise hour at which the Sabbath might be considered to begin. In those days there was no concept of any fixed duration for hours and minutes. The recording and measurement of time was one of the official functions of the Levites who programmed the course of hours by ground-shadows on measured areas. Also, since about 6 BC, they had been able to make use of sundials. However, neither ground markings nor sundials were of any use when there were no shadows. Hence, there were twelve designated 'hours of the day' (daylight) and, similarly, twelve 'hours of night' (darkness). The latter were measured by monastic prayer sessions (like the canonical 'hours' of the Catholic church today). Indeed, the prevailing 'Angelus' devotion – held at morning, noon and sunset – derives from the practice of the early Levite angels. The problem was however that, as the days and nights became longer or shorter, adjustments were necessary where hours 'overlapped'.

On that particular Friday of the Crucifixion, a forward adjustment of a full three hours was required and, because of this, there is a noticeable discrepancy between the accounts of Mark and John over the timing of events on that day.[2] Mark 15:24 states that Jesus was crucified at the third hour, whereas John 19:14–16 claims that Jesus was delivered for crucifixion at about the sixth hour. This anomaly occurs because Mark's Gospel relies on time as measured by Hellenist reckoning, and John's Gospel uses Hebrew time. The result of the time change was, as Mark 15:33 describes, that 'When the sixth hour was come, there was a darkness over the whole land until the ninth hour.' These *Three hours of darkness* were symbolic only; they occurred within a split second (as do changes in time today when we cross between different time-zones, or when we put clocks backward or forward by an hour). So, on this occasion, the end of the fifth hour was followed immediately by the ninth hour.

The key to the Resurrection story lies in these three missing hours (the daytime hours that became nighttime hours), for the newly defined start of the Sabbath began three hours before the old twelfth hour – that is, at the old ninth hour, which was then renamed the twelfth hour. But the Samaritan Magi (of which Simon Zelotes was head) worked on an astronomical time-frame, and did not formally implement the three-hour change until the original twelfth hour. This meant that, without breaking any of the rules against labouring on the Sabbath, Simon had a full three hours in which he could do what he had to do, even while others had begun their sacred period of rest. This was time enough to administer the medications to Jesus, and to attend to the bone fractures of the Cyrene. Judas Sicariote was dealt with none too mercifully under the circumstances: he was thrown over a cliff to his death (as obliquely related in Acts 1:16–18).

## THE EMPTY TOMB

When the Sabbath began by Magian time (three hours after the standard Jewish Sabbath), there were still a full three night hours before Mary Magdalene arrived on the first dawn of the new week. Whether or not there were sentries on guard that night is quite irrelevant; any coming and going by Simon and his colleagues would have been effected by way of the second entrance which was some distance away. Whether or not the stone was moved is equally irrelevant. The important thing is that when Jesus appeared, he was alive and well.

Concerning the angel who moved the stone for the women, Matthew 28:3 reads, 'His countenance was like lightning, and his raiment white as snow'. As we have seen, Simon (Magus) Zelotes was politically styled 'Lightning'; his vestment was white, and in rank he was indeed an angel. The sentence might thus be interpreted more literally as 'His countenance was like that of Si-mon Zelotes in his priestly vestment.' But why should this have been such a surprise to the women? Because as far as they knew, Simon had been crucified, and entombed with his legs broken.

Not only was Simon present, but so too was Thaddaeus: 'There was a great earthquake, and an angel appeared' (Matthew 28:2). Just as Simon Zelotes was styled 'Lightning' (with Jonathan Annas being 'Thunder'), Thaddaeus was, in turn, designated 'Earthquake' (in similar imagery concerning Mount Sinai as in Judges 5:4–5).[3] Simon and Thaddaeus were, therefore, the two angels encountered by Mary (John 20:11–12). Simon was also the 'young man' in the white robe (Mark 16:5), the youthful description[4] indicating his newly demoted status as a 'novice', in accordance with his portrayal at the Gethsemane arrest.

The garden in which Jesus was crucified was under the jurisdiction of 'Joseph of Arimathea' (Jesus's brother James). It was a consecrated area symbolizing the *Garden of Eden*, in relation to which James was identified with 'Adam', the man of the Garden. Thus, when Mary first saw Jesus and thought he was 'the gardener', the inference is that she believed she was looking at James. The reason that Jesus stopped Mary from touching him was that Mary was pregnant and, according to the rules for dynastic brides, she was allowed no physical contact with her husband at that time.

It is evident that Mary and most of the disciples were not party to the subterfuge of that Friday and Saturday. Indeed, it was in Simon's own interest to remain mysterious: escaping from the burial cave alive and with his legs unbroken could only add to his already great reputation. It was also in Jesus's own favour that his reappearance should be astounding to all. In the event, their joint effort, with the support of Thaddaeus, the Cyrene and brother James (Joseph), held the mission together after its near collapse, enabling the Apostles to continue their work. If Jesus had truly died, his disciples would have scattered in fear and dismay, and his cause would have died with him.[5] As it was, the mission received a whole new lease of life – the result of which was the birth of Christianity.

## RAISED FROM THE DEAD

> But if there be no resurrection of the dead, then is Christ not risen:
>     And if Christ be not risen, then is our preaching vain, and your faith is also vain . . .
>     For if the dead rise not, then is not Christ raised . . .

This is the case for the Resurrection as presented as an item of faith by St Paul in 1 Corinthians 15:13–16. It has to be said that it does not constitute much of an argument for something that is apparently so fundamental to the Christian belief. In fact, if anything it is fully self-defeating. Had Paul been speaking in spiritual terms, his contemporaries might have accepted his claim more readily – but he was not. He was talking literally, referring to the notion of corpses returning to life, in accordance with the prophecy in the book of Isaiah (26:19): 'Thy dead men shall live, together with my dead body shall they arise.'

Immortality of the soul (rather than of the body) is a concept that was around long before Jesus's time. In the ancient Greek world it was promoted by the followers of the Athenian philosopher Socrates (c. 469–399 BC). The 4th-century writer Plato maintained that mind, not matter, was the root of reality. Even earlier, Pythagoras (c. 570–500 BC) expounded the doctrine of reincarnation – the idea that upon death in one life, the soul then enters another body and starts a new life. Indeed, belief in reincarnation is common to many religions deriving from around the same time, including Hinduism and Buddhism.

But Paul was not referring to the *transmigration of souls*; he was expressing a belief in which Christianity stands alone as a major religion – the belief that a dead person came back to life *in the flesh*. The Apostles' Creed states that Jesus was 'crucified, dead, and buried; . . . The third day he rose again from the dead'. Scholars have long challenged the literal interpretation of this statement, and in recent years many churchmen have queried it too. Old doctrines die hard, however, and many feel that to dispense with the concept would be to dispense with the intrinsic ethic of Christianity itself.

Yet, if Christianity has a worthwhile base – which it surely has – then that base must rest upon the moral code and teachings of Jesus himself. This moral code and its associated teachings are what the Gospels are all about. They are the essence of the *Good News*.

It has often been pointed out that, after nearly 2,000 years, some three-quarters of the world's population does not subscribe to the idea of bodily resurrection. Many actually find the idea more disturbing than up- lifting. As a result, the Christian message is severely repressed. Few (of any religion or none) would dispute the inspiring social motive of Jesus's own Messianic ideal, an ideal of harmony, unity and service in a frater- nal society. Indeed, there is no better basis for a religion. And yet the wrap of a constraining dogma prevails – along with a constant wrangling about matters of inter- pretation and ritual. While such disputes continue, there can be no true harmony, and a divided Church society can provide no more than a limited service to itself and to others.

One of the main problems associated with the accep- tance of Jesus's bodily resurrection from physical death is that its premise is supported by little, if anything, in the Gospels. We have already noted that verses 9 to 20 of Mark 16 were spuriously attached long after the Gospel was completed and published. And if Mark was the first of the Synoptic Gospels, forming a base for the others, then legitimate doubt is cast on the authenticity of the final verses of Matthew and Luke.

If we ignore all of this, however, and accept the four Gospels as they are presented, we are faced with a very vague picture in which many details are not only confusing but conflicting. At first Mary Magdalene thought Jesus was someone else. Then Peter and Cleophas talked with him for several hours thinking he was a complete stranger. Not until Jesus sat down to eat with his Apostles did they recognize him – at which point he vanished from their sight.

What emerges is that the concept of the Resurrection as we know it today was completely unknown to those of the time. Apart from those directly concerned with the overall Crucifixion scenario, the disciples were kept in the dark. They truly believed their master had died, and would have been totally bewildered at his reappearance. These were not the high-ranking priests like Simon, Levi and Thaddaeus, but the less sophisticated Apostles like Peter and Andrew. Nonetheless, they would certainly have appreciated that Jesus's own forecast that 'his temple' would be raised 'in three days' (John 2:19) had nothing to do with a later European interpretation that completely missed the point of the *death* symbolism.

As we have seen in connection with the story of 'Lazarus',[6] a man was regarded as 'dead' when excommunicated – spiritual death by decree. The process took four days for implementation, during which period the excommunicatee was held to be 'sick unto death'. In this regard, Jesus had been formally denounced by the Sanhedrin Council of legal elders, by the High Priest,

Caiaphas, and by the new Father, Jonathan Annas. His excommunication was absolute and, from the early hours of the Crucifixion Friday, he was officially 'sick'. The only way to escape 'death' on the fourth day was to be released from the excommunication ('raised') beforehand by the Father or the High Priest. This is why Jesus made such a point of being 'raised' on the *third* day. In any other context, the period of three days had no significance whatever. But with the establishment set so firmly against him, who was there to perform the 'raising'?

The only man who might presume to undertake the rite was the deposed Father – the loyal Simon Zelotes. Irrespective of the machinations in Jerusalem, Simon's rank as the true Father was still upheld by many. But Simon had been crucified along with Jesus, or so most of the disciples believed. As it transpired, though, Simon emerged fit and well along with Jesus, whom he had 'raised from the dead' on the Sunday. On a previous occasion, Jesus had performed that very service for Simon who, as Lazarus, was resurrected from his grave.

To those who were not party to the overall scheme, the raising of Jesus was indeed a miracle. And, as the Gospel states, 'When therefore he was risen from the dead, his disciples . . . believed the scripture, and the word which Jesus had said' (John 2:22).

It was Paul (a later Hebrew convert to Hellenist ways) who established the *flesh-and-bones* Resurrection doctrine, but even his enthusiasm was short-lived. However, because he had expressed himself so excitedly on the subject, and backed his fervour with such clinching non-arguments as we saw earlier ('if there be no resurrection from the dead, then is Christ not risen . . .' and so forth) – Paul was regarded as a heretical fanatic[7] by Jesus's brother James, whose Nazarenes never preached the Resurrection. From those times of initial exaltation, the Resurrection diminished as a factor of fundamental concern. This is fully apparent in the later Epistles (letters) of Paul and other New Testament books, wherein it hardly features at all.

More important was the fact that Jesus had seen fit to suffer for the sake of his ideals, and Paul eventually sought to find a more explanatory basis for his earlier doctrine, declaring,

> There is a natural body, and there is a spiritual body.
> Flesh and blood cannot inherit the kingdom of God; neither doth corruption inherit incorruption.
> Behold, I shew you a mystery.
>
> (1 Corinthians 15:44, 50–51)

It is essential to remember that Jesus was neither a Gentile nor a Christian. He was a Hellenist Jew whose religion was radical Judaism. In time, however, his original mission was usurped and taken over by a religious movement that was named after him in order to obscure his true heirs. That movement centred on Rome, and based its self-proclaimed authority on the statement of Matthew 16:18–19, in which Jesus supposedly said, 'Thou art Peter, and upon this rock I will build my church.' Unfortunately, the Greek word *petra* (rock), relating to the 'Rock of Israel', was mistranslated as if it had been *petros* (Stone), referring to Peter[8] (who was indeed dubbed *Cephas* – a stone, as in John 1:42). Jesus was actually affirming that his mission was to be founded upon the Rock of Israel, not upon Peter. Irrespective of this, the new movement then decreed that only those who had received authority handed down directly from Peter could be leaders of the Christian Church. It was an ingenious concept which, as was intended, restricted overall control to a select, self-promoting fraternity. The Gnostic[9] disciples of Simon Zelotes called it 'the faith of fools'.

The Gospel of Mary (Magdalene) confirms that for a short time after Jesus had been 'raised from the dead', some of the Apostles knew nothing about it, and went on believing that their Christ had been crucified. The Apostles 'wept copiously, saying, How can we possibly go to the Gentiles and preach the gospel of the kingdom of the Son of Man? If they were ruthless to him, won't they be ruthless to us?' Having already spoken with Jesus at the tomb, Mary Magdalene was able to reply: 'Stop weeping. There is no need for grief. Take courage instead, for his grace will be with you and around you, and will protect you.'

Peter then said to Mary, 'Sister, we know that the Saviour loved you more than other women. Tell us all that you can remember of what the Saviour said to you alone – everything that you know of him but we do not.'[10]

Mary recounted that Jesus had said to her: 'Blessed are you for not faltering at the sight of me: for where the mind is, there is the treasure.' Then 'Andrew responded, and said to the brethren, Say whatever you like about what has been said. I for one do not believe the Saviour said that.' Peter, agreeing with Andrew, added, 'Would he really have spoken privately to a woman, and not freely to us?'

At this,

Mary wept and said to Peter . . . Do you think that I thought this all up myself, or that I am not telling the truth about the Saviour?

Levi answered, and said unto Peter . . . You have always been hot-tempered. Now I see you arguing with the woman as if you were enemies. But if the Saviour found her worthy, who are you, indeed, to reject her? The Saviour surely knows her well enough.

'Levi', as we know[11], was Matthew Annas, a priest and deputy 'of Alphaeus'. His sensible opinion was the product of intellect and education. Peter and Andrew, on the other hand, were poorly educated villagers who, despite their length of time with Jesus and the more learned Apostles, still retained old establishment views of womanhood. Eventually – as we shall discover – Peter's sexist attitude was to achieve a position of prominence in the Romanized doctrine that was founded upon his teaching.

The early bishops of the Christian Church claimed their own Apostolic succession from Peter – the handing down of episcopal authority through the personal laying-on of hands. Those same bishops were described in the Gnostic *Apocalypse of Peter* as 'dry canals'.[12] It continues,

> They name themselves bishops and deacons as if they had received their authority directly from God . . . Although they do not understand the mystery, they nonetheless boast that the secret of Truth is theirs alone.

As for the Resurrection, the matter remains a paradox – it is regarded as being of huge importance when it need not be; yet it has an express significance of which most people are quite unaware. The Gospel of Thomas quotes Jesus as saying, 'If spirit came into being because of the body, it is a wonder of wonders.'[13]

# EIGHT

---

# THE BLOODLINE
# CONTINUES

## THE TIMES OF RESTITUTION

As already mentioned, Mary Magdalene was three months pregnant at the time of the Crucifixion. She and Jesus had cemented their Second Marriage at the Bethany anointing in March AD 33. Apart from being able to derive this information directly from the Gospel sources, it is also a matter of straightforward calculation, since the rules were explicit in this regard. A male heir to a patrimonial succession was required ideally to have his first son at or close to his own 40th birthday. (Four decades was the recognized period of 'dynastic generation'.[1]) The birth of a dynastic son and heir should always have been planned to occur in September – the holiest month of the Jewish calendar. It was for this reason that sexual relations were permitted only in the month of December.

First Marriages also took place in the holy month of September – the month that included the Day of Atonement. A dynastic marriage would therefore theoretically be scheduled for the September of the bridegroom's 39th birthday, with sexual activity commenced in the December immediately following. In practice there was always the chance that the first child might be a daughter, and provision for this contingency was made by bringing the First Marriage ceremony forward to the bridegroom's 36th September. The first chance of a child then fell in his 37th September. If there was no conception in the first December, the couple would try again a year later, and so on. For a son to be born in or around the husband's 40th year was fully acceptable within the generation standard.

Once a son was born, no further sexual contact between the parents was permitted for six years.[2] On the other hand, if the child was a daughter the ensuing period of celibacy was limited to three years, until the 'times of restitution' (the return to the married state).

As we have seen, the Second Marriage was solemnized in the March following conception, at which time the bride would be three months pregnant.

In accordance with these customs and rules, Jesus's First Marriage took place in September AD 30 (his 36th September), the very occasion on which Mary Magdalene first anointed his feet (Luke 7:37–38). There was, however, no conception that December, nor in the December of the next year. But in December AD 32 Mary did conceive, and duly anointed Jesus's head and feet at Bethany (Matthew 26:6–7, Mark 14:3, and John 12:1–3), formally sanctifying their Second Marriage in March AD 33.

Jesus had been born – against the rules – on 1 March 7 BC, but in order to regularize his status, he had been allocated the official birthday of 15 September in line with Messianic requirement. (Even in later years, it has been customary for some monarchs to have both personal [real] birthdays, and separate official birthdays.) It was not until AD 314, that the Roman Emperor Constantine the Great[3] arbitrarily changed the date of Jesus's official birthday to 25 December, on which date it is still celebrated today – with many presuming it to be his real physical birthday. Constantine's reason for making this change was two-fold. Firstly, it separated the Christian celebration from any Jewish association – thereby suggesting that Jesus was himself a Christian and not a Jew. (In later times, Easter was similarly moved away from its traditional Passover connection.) Secondly, the Emperor adjusted Jesus's official birthday so that it would coincide with, and replace, the contemporary pagan Sun Festival. However, in the contemporary setting of Jesus's own time, 15 September AD 33 – six months after the Crucifixion – was his 39th official birthday, and in that month a daughter was born to Mary. She was named Tamar – *Palm tree* (assimilated in Greek to the name Damaris), a traditional Davidic family name.

Jesus was then required to enter a fully celibate state for three years until the 'times of restitution', as detailed in Acts 3:20–21:[4]

> And he shall send Jesus Christ, which before was preached unto you:
> Whom the heaven must receive until the times of restitution of all things, which God hath spoken by the mouth of all his holy prophets since the world began.

This month of September AD 33 coincided with Simon Zelotes' being formally re-established as the Father of the Community, at which juncture Jesus was finally admitted to the priesthood – a ritual in which he 'Ascended into Heaven'.

Although recognized by many as the Davidic king, Jesus had long sought entry into the priesthood, and particularly to the inner sanctum of the senior priests – the high monastery: the 'Kingdom of Heaven'. Once Simon had been reinstated, Jesus's wish was fulfilled: he was ordained and conveyed to 'Heaven' by the 'Leader of the Pilgrims' – his own brother James. In this fraternal context, James, by way of Old Testament imagery, was the designated 'Cloud'.[5] It was a cloud that had led the ancient Israelites into the Promised Land (Exodus 13:21–22), and the appearance of God to Moses on Mount Sinai had been accompanied not just by Thunder and Lightning, but also by a Cloud (Exodus 19:16). Thus (like Thunder, Lightning and Earthquake) 'Cloud' was also retained as a symbolic designation within the Community.

Jesus's elevation to the priesthood is recorded in the New Testament by the event generally known as the 'Ascension'. Not only did Jesus himself speak in parables, the Gospel writers did the same, applying allegories and parallels that were meaningful to 'those with ears to hear'. Thus, passages of the Gospel texts which seem to be straightforward narrative (no matter how apparently supernatural their contexts), are also parables. As Jesus said to the disciples (Mark 4:11-12):

> Unto you it is given to know the mystery of the kingdom of God: but unto them that are without, all these things are done in parables: That seeing they may see, and not perceive; and hearing they may hear, and not understand . . .

The Ascension, then, is another parable, as described in Acts 1:9: 'And when he had spoken these things, while they beheld, he was taken up, and a cloud received him out of their sight.' As Jesus departed into the priestly realm of Heaven, two angelic priests announced that he would eventually return in the same manner:

> Behold, two men stood by them, in white apparel, which also said, Ye men of Galilee, why stand ye gazing up into heaven? This same Jesus which is taken up . . . shall so come in like manner as ye have seen him go . . .  (Acts 1:10–11)

And so Jesus left the everyday world for three years – three years in which Mary Magdalene, the mother of his child, would have no physical contact with him.

From her sixth month of pregnancy, Mary had the right to call herself *Mother*,[6] but once her daughter was born and the three years of celibacy commenced, she would have been ranked as a *widow*. Dynastic children were brought up and educated at a monastic community centre, in which their mothers (those designated *widows* or *crippled women* – wives in celibacy) also lived. It was because Jesus had himself been brought up in such enclosed conventual surroundings that so little is said about his childhood in the Gospels.

## TO MARY A SON

Jesus's three-year period of monastic separation expired in September AD 36, following which physical relations with his wife were permitted once more in the December.

One very clear property of the language used in the New Testament is that words, names and titles which have a cryptic meaning[7] are used with that 'same meaning' throughout – not only do they have the same meaning every time they are used, but they are used every time that same meaning is required. Undoubtedly the most thorough studies to date in this field of research have been conducted by Dr Barbara Thiering, based on information contained in the Dead Sea Scrolls *commentaries* on Old Testament books. These *commentaries* hold the secrets of the *pesharim* (the routes to vital clues), and they were produced by the learned Scribes at Qumran.

In some cases, individual derivations of coded names or titles may be complex or obscure, but more often they are straightforward, though rarely obvious. Frequently, cryptic information in the Gospels is heralded by the statement that it is intended 'for those with ears to hear' – this phrase is an inevitable precursor to a passage with a hidden meaning for those who know the code. The governing rules of the code are fixed, and the symbolism remains constant – as in the case of Jesus himself.

By way of the *pesher* (singular of *pesharim*, and meaning 'explanation/solution') Jesus is defined as 'the Word of God' – as established from the very outset in the Gospel of John:

> In the beginning was the Word, and the Word was with God . . .
> And the Word was made flesh, and dwelt among us, and we beheld his glory, . . .
>
> (John 1:1, 14)

There are no variables in the Gospel texts: whenever the phrase 'the Word of God' is used (with or without a capital 'W'), it means that Jesus either was present or is the subject of the narrative – as in Luke 5:1, when 'the word of God' stood by the lake.

The phrase was also used in Acts to identify Jesus's whereabouts after the Ascension. So when we read that 'the apostles which were at Jerusalem heard that Samaria had received the word of God' (Acts 8:14), we may immediately understand that Jesus was in Samaria.

It follows, therefore, that when we read 'the word of God increased' (Acts 6:7), we should apprehend at once that Jesus 'increased',[8] as symbolized through the *pesher* in the parable of the Sower and the Seed (Mark 4:8): 'And other [seed] fell on good ground, and did yield fruit that sprang up and increased . . .' In short, the Acts reference means that Jesus [yielded fruit and] 'increased' – that is to say, he had a son.

As required by the Messianic rules, the birth took place in AD 37 – the year after Jesus returned to his marriage at 'the times of restitution'. Following the birth of a son, however, Jesus was now destined for no less than six more years of monastic celibacy.

In the Russian Church of St Mary Magdalene, Jerusalem, there is a wonderful portrayal of Mary, which depicts her holding a red egg up to the viewer. This is the ultimate symbol of fertility and new birth. In a similar vein, *Sacred Allegory* by Jan Provost – a 15th-century esoteric painting – shows a sword-wielding Jesus together with his wife Mary, who is crowned and wearing the black garb of a Nazarite, while releasing the dove of the Holy Spirit.

Perhaps not surprisingly, the first son of Jesus and Mary was named Jesus – to whom we shall return.

## PAUL'S MYTHOLOGICAL JESUS

During the years of Jesus the Christ's monastic separation (the 'heavenly state'), his Apostles continued to preach – but they had no concept of founding a new religion. Albeit their message was radical, they were still Jewish, and sought only to be reformers within Judaism, with Peter at the evangelical forefront of operations.

In direct opposition to the evolving movement was Saul of Tarsus, a staunchly orthodox Hebrew who was tutor to King Herod-Agrippa's son. Saul had no time for the liberal Hellenist views of Jesus. He believed that Jews were superior to all Gentiles, and considered James to be the rightful Messiah.

The year AD 37 was one of administrative change throughout the Roman Empire, and especially in Palestine. Emperor Tiberius had died, and the new Emperor, Gaius Caligula, sacked Pontius Pilate to install his own man, Felix, as Governor in Judaea. Also ousted from their positions were Caiaphas the High Priest, and Simon Zelotes the Father. Theophilus, the brother of

Jonathan Annas, took over as High Priest. A whole new administration was in place, and it was more answerable to Rome than any before.

In AD 40 Jesus was in Damascus, where the leading Jews attended a conference to discuss their position in relation to Rome. Just as Jesus knew that the Jews could never defeat Rome while divided from the Gentiles, Saul of Tarsus was equally sure that association with Gentiles represented a weakness that left the Jews vulnerable and exposed. Saul was particularly incensed when a statue of Caligula was set up within the Temple of Jerusalem – an outrage for which he put the blame squarely on Jesus and the Hellenists, whom he regarded as having split the Jewish nation. He too made his way to Damascus to state his case.

The account in Acts suggests that Saul went to Damascus with a mandate from the High Priest in Jerusalem, but that cannot have been the case. The Jewish Sanhedrin had no jurisdiction whatever in Syria.[9] It is much more likely that Saul, who was attached to the House of Herod, was in fact operating for the Roman administration in an attempt to suppress the Nazarenes.[10]

Before Saul had a chance to make his presence felt at the conference, Jesus confronted him in the monastery buildings. When Saul entered at noon, the sun was at its height immediately above the vestry skylight.[11] Jesus was there, ready to face his accuser:

> . . . Suddenly there shined round about him a light from heaven:
> And he fell to the earth, and heard a voice saying unto him, Saul, Saul, why persecutest thou me?
>
> (Acts 9:3–4)

Having listened to Jesus's persuasive sermon, Saul realized that he had hitherto been 'blinded' by sectarian dogma (Acts 9:8).

Jesus then instructed the disciple Ananias to further enlighten Saul, but Ananias hesitated, believing Saul to be an enemy agent: 'Lord, I have heard by many of this man, how much evil he hath done to thy saints at Jerusalem' (Acts 9:13). Nonetheless, the disciple obeyed, saying, 'Brother Saul, the Lord, even Jesus, that appeared unto thee in the way as thou camest, hath sent me, that thou mightest receive thy sight' (Acts 9:17). The use in the passages of the words 'sight' and 'the way' are again cryptic for, as previously related, the doctrinal theme of the Community was called 'the Way'. After a course of instruction on Hellenist thinking, Saul was initiated so that he could clearly 'see' the path to salvation in unity with the Gentiles: 'There fell from his eyes as it had been scales: and he received sight forthwith, and arose, and was baptized' (Acts 9:18).[12]

From this experience, Saul emerged as a fully-fledged Hellenist. At once, he began preaching in Damascus – but there was a problem, for the people could not believe that the man who had come hotfoot to challenge the Messiah was now promoting him instead. The Jews were confused, distrustful and, within a short time, angry: Saul's life was threatened, and the disciples had to spirit him out of the city. Nonetheless, by AD 43 Saul was a fervent evangelist, well enough known under his new name, Paul, to be associated in the popular mind with Peter.

However, a much more insidious problem remained. His conversion had been so traumatic, his change of heart so far-reaching, that Paul regarded Jesus not as an earthly Messiah with an inspiring social message, but as the manifest Son of God – a heavenly power-lord.

Paul's missionary journeys took him to Anatolia (Asia Minor) and the Greek-speaking areas of the eastern Mediterranean. But his dramatically revised version of the *Good News* was that an awesome Saviour would soon establish a worldwide regime of perfect righteousness – and in this he was aided by ambiguous Old Testament writings, such as from the book of Daniel 7:13–14:

> I saw in the night visions, and, behold, one like the Son of man came with the clouds of heaven . . .
> And there was given him dominion, and glory, and a kingdom, that all people, nations, and languages, should serve him . . .

When written, these texts had nothing whatever to do with Jesus, but they were inspiring enough for Paul, and provided the necessary inspiration for his fiery invective.[13] In his excitement he proclaimed 'the Wrath of the Lord' with all the zeal of an Old Testament prophet – making outrageous claims that gained him unprecedented attention.

In 1 Thessalonians 4:16–17, he stated:

> For the Lord himself shall descend from heaven with a shout, with the voice of the archangel, and with the trump of God: and the dead in Christ shall rise first:
> Then we which are alive and remain shall be caught up together with them in the clouds, to meet the Lord in the air: and so shall we ever be with the Lord.

Through Paul's imaginative teaching, a whole new concept of Jesus arose. No longer was he simply the long-awaited 'Anointed One', the Messiah who would reinstate the Davidic line and free the Jews from oppression in Palestine. He was now the heavenly Saviour of the World!

> . . . the image of the invisible God, the firstborn of every creature:
> For by him were all things created, that are in heaven, and that are in earth, visible and invisible . . .

> And he is the head of the body, the church: . . . that in all
> things he might have the preeminence.
>
> For it pleased the Father that in him should all fullness
> dwell . . .
>
> (Colossians 1:15–19)

While James and Peter were individually preaching
their less imaginative message, Paul had strayed into
the unfathomable realm of pure fantasy. In his unbri-
dled enthusiasm, he invented an inexplicable myth, and
uttered a string of self-styled prophecies that were
never fulfilled.

Yet for all that, it is Paul – not Peter, not James – who
dominates the bulk of the New Testament beyond the
Gospels. Such was the power of Paul's teaching that
the ministering Jesus of the Gospels was transformed
into an aspect of Almighty God . . . and Jesus the
dynastic Christ, the royal heir to the House of Judah,
was lost to religious history altogether.

Paul's allotted task was to further Hellenic-Jewish
instruction among the Gentiles of the Mediterranean
coastal lands, and to take Jesus's message to those Jews
who lived outside the Near East. Instead he ignored the
root objective and – as was perhaps inevitable – he
contrived his own cult following. For Paul, the veneration and outright worship of Jesus was sufficient to
ensure redemption and entry into the Kingdom of
Heaven. All the social values professed and urged by
Jesus were cast aside in Paul's attempt to compete with
a variety of pagan beliefs.

Throughout the ancient Mediterranean world, there
were many religions, whose gods and prophets were
supposedly born of virgins and defied death in one way
or another. They were all of supernatural origin and had
astounding powers over ordinary mortals. To be fair to
Paul, he certainly encountered problems that James and

Jesus never faced in their native environment. Paul's route to success against such odds was to present Jesus in a way that would transcend even these paranormal idols. But in so doing, he created an image of Jesus so far removed from reality that Jewish society regarded him a fraud. Notwithstanding any of this, however, it was the transcendent Jesus of Paul's invention who later became the Jesus of orthodox Christianity.[14]

## THE GRAIL CHILD

During the early AD 40s, Peter and Paul linked up in Antioch, Syria, while James and his Nazarenes remained operative in Jerusalem. A further division in the ranks became apparent when Simon (the Magus) Zelotes set up a separate base for his esoteric Gnostic sect in Cyprus.[15]

Peter had been Jesus's right-hand man and, as such, he should have become Mary Magdalene's guardian during the years of her separation (symbolic widowhood) – but Peter had a low opinion of women, and was not prepared to be at the beck and call of a priestess.[16] Paul's opinion of women was even less flattering, and he strongly objected to their involvement in matters of religion.[17] The two men, therefore, deliberately excluded Mary from any standing in their new movement, and to ensure her total alienation, they publicly declared her a heretic because she was a close friend of Simon Zelotes' consort Helena-Salome.

In the course of all this, Jesus and Mary once more resumed their married state in December AD 43, six years after the birth of their son. Jesus was not too concerned about Peter and Paul's attitude towards Mary, for he knew Peter well, and he was aware of Paul's fanaticism. He was in fact perfectly happy for his wife to be associated with the Gnostic faction of Simon and Helena (or with the Nazarenes of James) rather than with the new style of sexist ministry that was being promoted by Peter and Paul. After all, Mary (along with Martha) had been the devotional 'sister' of Simon/Lazarus in Bethany, and they were well acquainted.

It was at this time that Mary once more conceived. By the spring of AD 44, Jesus had embarked on a mission to Galatia (in central Asia Minor) with the Chief Proselyte (Head of the Gentile converts), John Mark.

While they were away, James and his Nazarenes became an increasing threat to Roman authority in Jerusalem. As a direct result, the Apostle James Boanerges was executed by Herod of Chalcis in AD 44 (Acts 12:1–2). Simon Zelotes took immediate retaliatory action and had Herod-Agrippa poisoned,[18] but was then obliged to flee. Thaddaeus, however, was not so fortunate: in trying to escape across the Jordan, he was seized by Chalcis and summarily executed. This placed the expectant Mary in a precarious situation, for Chalcis knew that she was a friend of Simon. She appealed for protection from Paul's one-time student, young Herod-Agrippa II (then aged 17). He duly arranged her passage to the Herodian estate in Gaul, where Herod-Antipas and his brother Archelaus had been sent into exile.

Later that year, Mary gave birth to her second son in Provence – and there is a specific reference to this in the New Testament: 'The word of God grew and multiplied' (Acts 12:24).[19] This son was the all-important 'Grail Child', and he was called Joseph.


## HIDDEN RECORDS AND THE *DESPOSYNI*

Having fulfilled his dynastic obligation to father two sons, Jesus was duly released from restrictions, and able to lead a normal life once more. From AD 46,[20] his elder son, the 9-year-old Jesus, was schooled in Caesarea. Three years later, he underwent the ceremony of his 'Second Birth' in Provence. In accordance with custom, he would have been symbolically 'born again' from his mother's womb at the age of 12 – his designated 'First Year' as an initiate. In attendance was his uncle James (Joseph of Arimathea), who afterwards took his nephew to the West of England for a time.

In AD 53 Jesus junior was officially proclaimed Crown Prince at the synagogue in Corinth, and duly received the Davidic Crown Prince's title of 'Justus' (*the Righteous* or *the Just* – Acts 18:7).[21] He thereby formally succeeded his uncle, James the Just, as the kingly heir. Having reached the age of 16, Jesus Justus also became the Chief Nazarite that year, gaining entitlement to the black robe of that office – as worn by the priests of Isis, the universal Mother Goddess.[22]

His father, Jesus the Christ, went to Rome, via Crete and Malta, in AD 60. Meanwhile, Paul returned to Jerusalem, having travelled extensively with the physician Luke. Once there, however, he was accused of conspiracy against Jonathan Annas, who had been murdered by Governor Felix. The Governor was sent for trial before Emperor Nero in Rome, and Paul was obliged to follow. Then, after some time, Felix was acquitted – but Paul remained in custody because of his association with ex-pupil Herod-Agrippa II, whom Nero detested. During this period, Jesus Justus was also in the city (Colossians 4:11).

At about the same time, but far from the perils of Rome, Jesus Justus's younger brother Joseph had finished his education at a Druidic college, and was settled in Gaul with his mother. They were later joined by young Joseph's uncle James, who came permanently to the West, having been hounded out of Jerusalem in AD 62. His Nazarenes had been subjected to brutal harassment by the Romans, and the Sanhedrin Council charged James with illegal teaching.[23] He was consequently sentenced to stoning, and was excommunicated – to be declared spiritually 'dead' by the Jewish elders.[24] The once 'honourable councellor' of the Sanhedrin, and prospective Messiah of the Hebrews, thus fell from the very pinnacle of civil and religious grace – an event which has been symbolically portrayed in the past as if he fell bodily from the Temple roof itself.

Having lost all spiritual credibility in the eyes of the law, James reassumed his hereditary style, Joseph of Arimathea, and made his way westward to join Mary Magdalene and her colleagues in Gaul.

Back in Nero's Rome, Peter had arrived to assume responsibility for the Pauline sect – who were by then known as 'Christians'. Nero had developed a passionate hatred for the Christians and, to lessen their number, he instituted a fanatical regime of persecution. His favourite torture was to tie them to stakes all around his palace gardens, and to fire them as human torches at night.[25] This led to a major revolt by the Christians in AD 64, during the course of which Rome was engulfed by fire. The unbalanced Emperor was the suspected instigator, but he blamed the Christians, and had both Peter and Paul put to death.

Before he died, Paul managed to relay a message to Timothy that Jesus the Christ was in a place of safety,[26] but he did not say where. It has been suggested by some that Jesus traced Thomas the Apostle's footsteps to India, and he is reckoned to have died at Srinagar, Kashmir, where a tomb is attributed to him.[27]

Once James (Joseph of Arimathea) had settled permanently in the West, it was not long before Simon Zelotes led most of the Nazarenes out of Jerusalem in AD 65. He took them east of the Jordan (to where his late colleague Thaddaeus had been headed), and they spread into the region of old Mesopotamia.

Nero's regime had caused considerable political nervousness, and temperatures were raised to dangerous heights in the Holy Land. Early in AD 66, sporadic fighting broke out in Caesarea between Zealots and Romans. The hostility quickly moved to Jerusalem, where the Zealots gained a number of strategic positions. They held the city for four years ... until a massive Roman army led by Flavius Titus arrived in AD 70, laying Jerusalem to waste. As Jesus had so rightly predicted many years before, the Temple fell, and everything fell with it. Most of the inhabitants were slaughtered; the survivors were sold into slavery, and the Holy City was an empty ruin for the next six decades.

In the wake of this destruction, the Jewish nation was in a state of turmoil. Not only did Jerusalem fall, but so did Qumran and, in time, the famous last bastion was the mountain fortress of Masada, south-west of the Dead Sea. There, fewer than a thousand Jews withstood repeated sieges by a mighty Roman army, but they were gradually deprived of all supplies and provisions. By AD 74 their cause was hopeless, and the garrison commander, Eleazar Ben Jair, organized a programme of mass suicide. Only two women and five children survived.[28]

Various waves of Nazarene refugees fled the Holy Land to perpetuate their tradition in the northern reaches of Mesopotamia, Syria and southern Turkey. The chronicler Julius Africanus, writing in around AD 200 while resident in the city of Edessa (now Urfa, in Turkey, as opposed to Edessa in Greece), recorded details of the exodus.[29] At the onset of the revolt, the Roman governors had caused all the public records in Jerusalem to be burned so as to prevent future access to the details of Jesus's family genealogy. During the

Jewish Revolt itself, all records were fair game to the Roman troops, who were ordered to destroy private records as well – indeed to destroy any relevant documentary evidence they could find. But, for all that, the destruction was not complete, and certain papers remained successfully hidden.

Writing about this purposeful eradication of Messianic documentation, Africanus stated: 'A few careful people had private records of their own, having committed the names to memory or having recovered them from copies, and took pride in preserving the remembrance of their aristocratic origins.' He described these royal inheritors as the *Desposyni* ('heirs of [or belonging to] the Lord [or the Master]').[30] Throughout the early centuries AD, various Desposyni branches were hounded by Roman dictate – first by the Roman Empire, and later by the Roman Church. Eusebius confirmed that in Imperial times the Desposyni became the heads of their sects by way of a 'strict dynastic progression'. But, wherever possible, they were pursued to the death – hunted down like outlaws,[31] and put to the Roman sword by Imperial command.

The full truth about this selective Inquisition was certainly concealed, but its mythology and tradition have survived. They have survived by way of Grail lore, the Tarot cards, Arthurian romance, the songs of the Troubadours, Unicorn tapestries, esoteric art, and a continued veneration for the heritage of Mary Magdalene. So potent has been the tradition, that even today the 'Holy Grail' remains the ultimate relic of Quest. But all of this – no matter how enthralling or romantic – is deemed heretical by the orthodox ecclesiastical establishment. Why? Because the ultimate object of the enduring Quest still poses a daunting threat to a Church that dismissed the Messianic succession in favour of a self-styled alternative.

# NINE

# MARY MAGDALENE

## ROYAL BRIDE AND MOTHER

Mary Magdalene died in AD 63, aged 60, at (what is now) St Baume in southern France,[1] far from her native home and far from where her husband is thought to have met his end.

We have examined Jesus's life and significance in some considerable detail over the last few chapters. We have also traced the events of Mary's life chronologically in relation to Jesus. But we have not yet explored the significance of Mary to contemporary or later ecclesiastical events.

During the Qumran era, *Mary* was not simply a name but a distinguished title, being a form of *Miriam* (the name of the sister of Moses and Aaron).[2] Miriams (Marys) participated in a formal ministry within spiritual orders such as the ascetic and healing community of the Therapeutae.

While the 'Moses' would lead the liturgical ceremonies of the men, the 'Miriam' would similarly lead the women – an arrangement that interpreted Miriam with her timbrel (tambourine) in Exodus 15:20.

Mary Magdalene is first described in the New Testament as a woman 'out of whom went seven devils' (Luke 8:2), and later in the same Gospel is said to be 'a sinner'. But in addition to this, she is portrayed in all the Gospels as a favourite and loyal companion of Jesus. Luke's descriptions of Mary are yet again a matter of cryptic coding.

Prior to marriage, Marys were under the authority of the Chief Scribe who, in Mary Magdalene's time, was Judas Sicariote. The Chief Scribe was also the Demon Priest *Number 7*,[3] and the 'seven demon priests' were established as a formal opposition group to those priests who were the 'seven lights of the Menorah' (the seven-branched candlestick familiar in Jewish symbolism). It was their duty to supervise the Community's female celibates. Upon her marriage, Mary Magdalene was naturally released from this arrangement. Hence, 'the seven demons went out of her', and she was permitted sexual activity on the regulated basis detailed earlier. As mentioned, her marriage was no ordinary one, and Mary was subject to long periods of marital separation from her husband – periods during which she was ranked not as a wife, but as a *sister* (in the devotional sense – as a nun might be). In her capacity as a *sister*, Mary was attached to the Father, Simon Zelotes (Lazarus). Also a *sister* of the Father was Martha, whose name was similarly titular. Martha meant *Lady*, and the difference between Marthas and Marys was that Marthas were allowed to own property, whereas Marys were not. In society, *sisters* held the same community status as *widows* (*crippled women*),[4] a rank below that of *almah*. Thus, an *almah* (virgin) would marry and move up to the rank of *mother*, but during her periods of marital separation she would be demoted to below her original unmarried rank.

Mary Magdalene's father was the Chief Priest (subordinate to the High Priest) Syrus the 'Jairus'. The Jairus priest officiated at the great marble synagogue at Capernaum, and was ranked quite separately from the

Zadok and the Abiathar. It had been a hereditary post from the time of King David, restricted to the descendants of Jair (Numbers 32:41). As 2 Samuel 20:25–26 confirms: 'And Sheva was scribe: and Zadok and Abiathar were the priests: and Ira also the Jairite was a chief ruler about David.'

The first mention of Mary in the New Testament is actually the story of how she was raised from death as Jairus' daughter in AD 17.[5] Being 'raised' (symbolically, from eternal darkness) related either to elevation of status within the 'Way' or, as we have seen, to release from spiritual death by excommunication. The term is still used in modern Freemasonry. However, since women were not excommunicated, Mary's event was plainly an initiatory raising.

First 'raisings' for boys were at the age of 12, and for girls at 14. Given that Mary was raised from darkness in AD 17, this means that she was born in AD 3, and she was therefore nine years younger than Jesus – making her 27 when she first married him in AD 30.[6] Having conceived in December AD 32, Mary was aged 30 at her Second Marriage, during which year (AD 33) she bore her daughter Tamar. Four years later she gave birth to Jesus the younger, and in AD 44, when she was 41 years old, her second son, Joseph, was born. By that time Mary was in Marseilles (Massilia), where the official language was Greek until the 5th century.[7] A fact not generally recognized, but which should perhaps be emphasised, is that the language of Jesus, the Apostles, and all concerned with Hellenic Judaism was heavily influenced by Greek. The Hebrews, of course, used their own specifically Semitic tongue. This is why words such as *Alphaeus* and *Rama-Theo* are combined from both Greek and Hebrew elements. In addition, having been under Roman occupation for so long, this other linguistic culture was to some degree incorporated.

Adjustments were also made in respect of the Gentiles (non-Jews) and the Proselytes (Gentile converts to Judaism) so that, within all the variables, there was a general cross-understanding.

According to Gnostic tradition, Mary Magdalene was associated with Wisdom (*Sophia*), represented by the sun, moon, and a halo of stars. The female gnosis of Sophia was deemed to be the *Holy Spirit*, thus represented on Earth by the Magdalene, who fled into exile bearing the child of Jesus. John, in Revelation 12:1–17, describes Mary and her son, and tells of her persecution, her flight into exile, and of the continued Roman hounding of the 'remnant of her seed' (her descendants).

And there appeared a great wonder in heaven; a woman clothed with the sun, and the moon under her feet, and upon her head a crown of twelve stars:

And she being with child cried, travailing in birth, and pained to be delivered.

And there appeared another wonder in heaven; and behold a great red dragon, having seven heads and ten horns, and seven crowns upon his heads.

And . . . the dragon stood before the woman which was ready to be delivered, for to devour her child as soon as it was born.

And she brought forth a man child . . .

And the woman fled into the wilderness, where she hath a place prepared of God . . .

And there was war in heaven: Michael and his angels fought against the dragon; . . .

And the great dragon was cast out, that old serpent, . . .

And they overcame him by the blood of the Lamb, and by the word of their testimony; . . .

And when the dragon saw that he was cast unto the earth, he persecuted the woman which brought forth the man child.

And to the woman were given two wings of a great eagle, that she might fly into the wilderness, into her place . . .

> And the dragon was worth with the woman, and went
> to make war with the remnant of her seed, which keep the
> commandments of God, and have the testimony of Jesus
> Christ.

In addition to Mary, other migrants to Gaul in AD 44 included Martha, and her maid Marcella. There were also Philip the Apostle, Mary Jacob (the wife of Cleophas) and Mary-Salome (Helena). Their point of disembarkation in Provence was Ratis, which later became known as Les Saintes Maries de la Mer.[8] Despite Mary and Martha's prominence in the Gospel texts, there is no mention at all of them in Acts, nor in any of St Paul's letters (epistles) following their westward departure in AD 44.

*The Life of Mary Magdalene* by Raban Maar (776–856), Archbishop of Mayence (Mainz) and Abbé of Fuld, incorporates many traditions about Mary dating back well beyond the 5th century. A copy of the Maar manuscript was unearthed at Oxford University in the early 1400s, and inspired the founding of Magdalen College there by William of Waynflete in 1448. The work had also been quoted earlier in the *Chronica Majora* of Matthew Paris, in around 1190, and is listed in the *Scriptorum Ecclesiasticorum Historia literaria Basilae* at Oxford. Louis XI of France (ruled 1461–1483) was insistent on Mary's dynastic position in the royal lineage of France. *Saint Mary Magdalene*, by the Dominican friar Père Lacordaire (published after the French Revolution), is a particularly informative work, as is *La Légende de Sainte Marie Madeleine* by Jacobus de Voragine, Archbishop of Genoa (b.1228). Both de Voragine and Maar state that Mary's mother Eucharia was related to the royal house of Israel. (This is the Hasmonaean royal house rather than the Davidic House of Judah.)

Another important work by Jacobus de Voragine is the famous *Legenda Aurea* (Golden Legend), one of the earliest books printed at Westminster by William Caxton in 1483. The text was previously published in French and Latin, and had been partly translated into English before, but some important sections had been omitted. Caxton was persuaded by William, Earl of Arundel, to produce a complete version from the European manuscripts. It is a collection of ecclesiastical chronicles detailing the lives of selected saintly figures. Highly venerated, the work was given public readings on a regular (often daily) basis in medieval monasteries and churches in continental Europe.

One particular narrative from the *Legenda* is about St Martha of Bethany and her sister Mary Magdalene. The following corresponds to a résumé in modern English:

> St Martha, hostess to Lord Jesus Christ, was born into a royal family. Her father's name was Syro, and her mother's Eucharia; the father came from Syria. Together with her sister by inheritance through their mother, Martha came into possession of three properties: the castle Magdalene, and Bethany, and a part of Jerusalem. After the Ascension of our Lord, when the disciples had departed, she, with her brother Lazarus and her sister Mary, also St Maxim, embarked in a ship, on which – thanks to its preservation by our Lord – they all came safely to Marseilles. They thereafter proceeded to the region of Aix, where they converted the inhabitants to the faith.

The name *Magdalene* (or Magdala) derives from the Hebrew noun *migdal* (tower). In practical terms, the statement that the 'sisters' possessed three castles is a little misleading – particularly since Marys (Miriams) were not allowed to own property. The joint heritage actually related to personal status – that is to say they inherited high community stations (castles/towers) of guardianship, as in Micah 4:8[9] – the Magdal-eder (watchtower of the flock).

The most active Magdalene cult was eventually based at Rennes-le-Château in the Languedoc region.[10] Elsewhere in France there were many shrines set up to Ste Marie de Madeleine. These included her burial place at St Maximus, where her sepulchre and alabaster tomb were guarded by Cassianite monks from the early 400s.

The Cassianite Order has an interesting history. Although St Benedict is customarily regarded as the 'father of western monasticism', he was actually preceded by John Cassian, who founded his Cassianite monastery in about 410 (albeit following innovatory communal endeavours by Martin, Bishop of Tours and Honoratius, Archbishop of Arles). The significant advance in monastic discipline made by Cassian (to be followed by Benedict and others) was its separation and independence from the organization of the episcopal Church. Cassian denounced the taking of holy orders as a 'dangerous practice', and declared that monks should 'at all costs avoid bishops'. Initially an ascetic hermit in Bethlehem, John Cassian established his twin schools near Marseilles – one for men, and one for women. Marseilles became a recognized conventual centre, the birthplace of the Candlemas ritual which succeeded the earlier torchlight procession of Persephone of the Underworld. Similarly, the Feast of the Madonna originated at St Victor's Basilica in Marseilles.

Another important seat of the Magdalene cult was that of Gellone, where the Academy of Judaic Studies (the monastery of St Guilhelm le Désert) flourished during the 9th century. The church at Rennes-le-Château was consecrated to Mary Magdalene in 1059, and in 1096 (the year of the First Crusade) the great Basilica of St Mary Magdalene was begun at Vézelay. It

was here that St Francis of Assisi founded the Franciscan Friars Minor (later the Capuchins) in 1217.[11] It was
also at Vézelay in 1146 that the Cistercian abbot St
Bernard of Clairvaux preached the Second Crusade to
King Louis VII, Queen Eleanor, their knights, and an
assembled congregation of 100,000. Indeed, the enthusiasm of the Crusades was intimately allied to the
veneration of the Magdalene.

The Cistercians, Dominicans, Franciscans, and various other monastic Orders of the era thus all followed
a lifestyle separate from the episcopacy of the Roman
Church. But they shared a common interest in Mary
Magdalene. In drafting the Constitution for the Order
of Knights Templars in 1128, St Bernard specifically
mentioned a requirement for 'the obedience of Bethany,
the castle of Mary and Martha'. It is evident, then, that
the great *Notre Dame* cathedrals of Europe, which were
wholly Cistercian-Templar instigated, were dedicated
not to Jesus's mother Mary, but to 'Our Lady' Mary
Magdalene.

## SCARLET WOMAN – BLACK MADONNA

Early Christian texts describe Mary Magdalene as 'the
woman who knew the All'; she was the one whom
'Christ loved more than all the disciples'. She was the
apostle 'endowed with knowledge, vision and insight
far exceeding Peter's'; and she was the beloved bride
who anointed Jesus at the Sacred Marriage (the *Hieros
Gamos*) at Bethany.

Disregarding all of this, the Roman Church chose in
due course to discredit Mary Magdalene in an attempt
to exalt her mother-in-law, Jesus's mother Mary. To
accomplish this, they made use of ambiguous comments in the New Testament – comments that originally
described the unmarried Magdalene as a 'sinner'

(which actually meant that she was a celibate *almah* undergoing assessment in betrothal).

The duplicitous bishops decided, however, that a sinful woman must be a whore, and Mary was thereafter branded as a harlot! Even today, one definition of the word *Magdalene* in the Oxford Dictionary is 'reformed prostitute'. Many artists have nonetheless been careful to counter this Church-promoted slur by depicting Mary wearing a white blouse or a cloak lined with the white silk of purity.

There is a fascinating parallel between Mary and one of her fellow-migrants to Gaul in terms both of aspersions cast on her character, and of coloration in depiction by later artists. The migrant in question is Helena-Salome.

Because of his dislike for women – and especially educated women – Peter had always regarded Helena-Salome as a witch. He paid no heed to the fact that she was close to Jesus's mother, and had accompanied her at the Crucifixion. As the consort of Simon Zelotes (Zebedee), Helena had in fact also been the conventual 'mother' of the Apostles James and John Boanerges. Unlike Mary Magdalene, who was attached to the regional Order of Dan, Helena belonged to the Order of Asher, an order wherein the women were allowed to own personal property,[12] and in which the priestesses were known, in Greek, as *hierodulai* ('sacred women'). Helena was indeed a High Priestess of the Order in Ephesus (holding the title of 'Sarah') and as such was entitled to wear a red robe (much as today's Roman Catholic cardinals are dressed from head to toe in red). Such highly-ranked women were greatly feared by Peter, for the likes of Helena were a constant threat to his own position. The Roman Church inherited that same dislike and that same fear: outside conventual orders, there are no Roman Catholic female clergy today. Thus the once venerated image of the 'scarlet women' – the *hierodulai* – was transformed and (via medieval French into English) they became *harlots*. Prostitutes still use this perverted Church imagery by perhaps wearing red or by displaying themselves in red light.

The women of the Order of Dan were lay Nazarites. Mary Magdalene, as a 'Miriam', was a Head Sister of the Order (the equivalent of a senior bishop) and was entitled to wear black, like the Nazarites[13] and the priests of Isis. It is also a fact that in parallel with the early reverence for Mary Magdalene, a cult known as that of the 'Black Madonna' emanated from Ferrières in AD 44.[14] Among the many Black Madonna representations that still exist, one of the finest statues is displayed at Verviers, Liège: she is totally black, with a golden sceptre and crown, surmounted by Sophia's halo of stars. Her infant child also wears a golden crown of royalty.

In contrast to the blackness of the Black Madonna image, it was also common for Mary Magdalene to be portrayed wearing a red cloak – often over a green dress (the green representing fertility).[15] An example is the famous *Saint Mary* fresco by Piero della Francesca, of about 1465, in the Gothic cathedral of Arezzo, near Florence. She is similarly clothed in Botticelli's *Mary at the Foot of the Cross*. The red is intended (like the red of the cardinals' robes) to signify Mary's perceived high clerical status.

The concept of red-caped women of religious rank actively infuriated the Vatican hierarchy. Despite the Church's separate veneration of Jesus's mother (especially following the Council of Ephesus in 431), Catholic bishops were determined that artists should not dignify her with the same privileged posterity accorded to the Magdalene. In 1659, Rome felt obliged to go as far as to issue a decree that all images of Jesus's mother (the

'White Madonna') should depict her wearing 'blue and white' only.[16] This had the desired effect that Jesus's mother Mary, although exalted – even adulated – by the Church, was nonetheless denied any ecclesiastical recognition within the establishment.

Women were barred from ordination in the Catholic domain. And the relegation of women other than Jesus's mother from any venerable status pushed Mary Magdalene ever further into the background. By the same strategy, Jesus's own physical heirs were totally eclipsed, and the bishops were enabled to reinforce their claim to holy authority by means of a self-devised male 'succession'. It was not a Messianic descent from Jesus, as should have been the case, nor even a descent from the *Rama-Theo* (Arimathea) prince, James the Just (brother of Jesus), but a contrived 'succession' from Peter, the headstrong rustic Essene who despised women.

At the same time, the early Church was having also to battle with veneration for the Universal Goddess, a veneration that was particularly strong in the contemporary Mediterranean world, and that was actually to heighten during this period of clerical squabbling over sexist issues. From prehistoric times, the Universal Goddess had appeared in many guises and had been known by many names, including Cybele, Diana, Demeter, and Juno. But however personified, she was always identified with Isis 'the Universal Mother, mistress of all the elements, primordial child of time, sovereign of all things, and the single manifestation of all'.

To the ancient Egyptians, Isis was the sister-wife of Osiris, who was the founder of civilization and the judge of souls after death. Isis was the Universal Goddess, specifically a maternal protectress, and her cult spread far and wide. She was frequently portrayed holding her child, Horus, whose incarnations were the

pharaohs themselves. It is a well established fact that
the familiar image of the 'White Madonna' is founded
upon the depictions of Isis as the nursing mother. It is
she too who inspired the mysterious Black Madonna, of
whose image there were nearly 200 in France by the 16th
century. Some 450 representations have now been discovered worldwide.[17] Even the cherished patron goddess of France, *Notre Dame de Lumière* (Our Lady of
Light), has her origins in the Universal Mother.

The image of the Black Madonna and her child has
presented a constant dilemma for the Church – particularly those statues at notable churches and shrines in
continental Europe. In some cases they are black all
over, but many have only black faces, hands and feet. It
is not a question of discoloration, as some disconcerted
clerics have suggested. A few have been overpainted in
pale flesh tones to conform to the standard Madonna
representation; some have simply been removed from
the public gaze altogether. The features of the Black
Madonna are in no way negroid in racial characteristics,
but are quite simply black in colour. Some Black Madonnas are modestly garbed (much in the fashion of
traditional White Madonnas) but others are displayed
in various degrees of prestige and sovereignty, having
ornately decorated clothing and crowns.

The Black Madonna has her tradition in Queen Isis
and her roots in the pre-patriarchal Lilith. She thus represents the strength and equality of womanhood – a
proud, forthright, and commanding figure – as against
the strictly subordinate image of the conventional White
Madonna as seen in Church representations of Jesus's
mother. It was said that both Isis and Lilith knew the
secret name of God (a secret held also by Mary Magdalene, 'the woman who knew the All'). The Black
Madonna is thus also representative of the Magdalene
who, according to the Alexandrian doctrine, 'transmitted

the true secret of Jesus'. The long-standing Magdalene cult was in fact particularly associated with Black Madonna locations. She is black because Wisdom (*Sophia*) is black, having existed in the darkness of Chaos before the Creation. To the Gnostics of Simon (Magus) Zelotes, Wisdom was the *Holy Spirit* – the great and immortal Sophia who brought forth the First Father Yaldaboath from the depths. Sophia was held to be incarnate as the *Holy Spirit* in Queen Mary Magdalene, and it was she who bore the ultimate observance of the Faith.

## MARY AND THE CHURCH

Regardless of the prominence of the Goddess ideal, it transpired that during the rise of orthodox Christianity all venerators of the female principle were regarded as heretics. Early Church Fathers such as Quintus Tertullian set the scene long before the days of Constantine the Great. Tertullian upheld the ruling:

> It is not permitted for a woman to speak in church, nor is it permitted for her to baptize, nor to offer the Eucharist, nor to claim for herself a share in any masculine function – least of all in priestly office.

Tertullian was himself only following opinions expressed by Church leaders before him, notably Peter and Paul.

In the Gospel of Mary,[18] Peter challenges Mary's relationship with Jesus, saying, 'Would he really have spoken privately to a woman, and not freely to us? Why should we change our minds and listen to her?' Again in the Coptic tractate called *Pistis Sophia* (The Wisdom of Faith),[19] Peter complains about Mary's preaching, and asks Jesus to silence her, to stop her undermining his supremacy. Jesus instead rebukes Peter, and Mary later confides, 'Peter makes me hesitate. I am afraid of him because he hates the female race.' To this Jesus replies, 'Whatsoever the Spirit inspires is divinely ordained to speak, whether man or woman.' Mary had good reason to be wary of Peter, for his attitude was made perfectly obvious on many occasions – as in the Gospel of Thomas.[20] Objecting to Mary's presence among the disciples, 'Simon Peter said unto them, Let Mary leave us, for women are not worthy of life'.

In the Gospel of Philip[21], Mary Magdalene is regarded as 'the symbol of divine wisdom'. All such texts were, however, censored and excised by the Bishops of Rome because they undermined the dominance of the male-only priesthood. Paul's New Testament teaching was expounded instead:

> Let the woman learn in silence with all subjection.
>   But I suffer not a woman to teach, nor to usurp authority over the man, but to be in silence.
>
> (1 Timothy 2:11–12)

Such authoritative directions were especially useful because they actually masked the real issue. The point was that women had to be excluded at all costs. If they were not, the Magdalene's lingering presence would be seen to prevail. As the wife of Jesus she was not only the Messianic Queen but also the mother of the true heirs. For centuries after her death, Mary's legacy remained the greatest of all threats to a fearful Church that had by-passed Messianic descent in favour of Apostolic succession.

In general, the faiths that opposed Roman Christianity, and that were described by Rome as pagan and heretical, were not hideous, savage or satanic. To the Roman Church, however, they were all of these things because they accepted the female principle along with the male. To Gnostic believers, the *Holy Spirit* was essentially the female element that bound the Father to the Son. But Rome decreed that the Trinity was 'One God'. And for this reason, although Jesus's mother Mary was afforded some concession as the Mother of God, she was not a part of the divine Trinity which remained defined in wholly masculine terms.

Christianity adopted the God of Israel as a result of Jesus's mission, as did the Gnostics and the Nazarenes, whose women members acted quite freely as teachers, healers, evangelists and priestesses. Within the Romanized Christian environment, however, all trace of female opportunity rapidly disappeared. One of the most prominent matriarchal sects of the 2nd century preached a faith inherited directly from Mary Magdalene, Martha and Helena-Salome. Tertullian angrily denounced the group:

> These heretical women! How dare they! They are brazen enough to teach, to engage in argument, to undertake exorcisms, to effect cures, and (it may be) even to baptize!

In sectarian Jewish communities women had long been excluded from many aspects of everyday life – education, public worship, and indeed any social or political activity outside the family environment. But this had not been the case for those in Hellenist communities, whose ideals were conversely inspired by cultural thought in Greece and Asia Minor, where women were involved equally with men in the veneration of Isis. In Jesus's time, women were in a particularly advanced state of emancipation in Egypt. Likewise, Roman women of the wealthy classes were equally involved in business, politics, literature, mathematics, and philosophy. It was the Roman Church that was the exception – and it was different for one overriding reason: to curtail Jesus's dynastic royal legacy as embodied in Mary Magdalene.

Many of the learned women who led the groups that were formally described as heretical promoted a teaching based on the instruction from the ascetic Therapeutate at Qumran. Such teaching was inclined to be spiritually-based (whereas the Roman form of Christianity was very materialist), and the spiritual teaching was accordingly perceived as an enormous threat. Rome's strategy against the women teachers was straightforward: they were to be considered sinners and subordinates on the authority of St Paul:

> For Adam was first formed, then Eve.
> And Adam was not deceived, but the woman being deceived was in the transgression.
>
> (1 Timothy 2:13–14)

It was at this time that such women teachers were first described intentionally as *harlots*, with its revised connotation for 'scarlet women'.[22] The Church decreed that they were all whores, and the malicious redefinitions have prevailed to this day.

By the early 2nd century AD, a process of segregation had commenced in Christian churches: the men performed the rite, the women worshipped in silence. At the end of the century even this level of involvement had gone – women's participation in religious worship was forbidden altogether. Any female known to take part in religious practice was denounced as 'a whore and a sorceress'.

According to The Gospel of Mary, Levi (Matthew Annas) argued with Peter over the rights of Mary Magdalene: 'But if the Saviour found her worthy, who are you, indeed, to reject her? The Saviour surely knows her well enough – that is why he loved her more than us.' In contrast to Peter and his brother Andrew, the other disciples are said to have agreed with Levi, for they were encouraged by what Mary had said, and readily accepted her teaching. Gospels that showed Mary in such a light were, in the event, simply not selected for inclusion in the canonical New Testament. Furthermore, the four that were chosen were edited to suit Church requirement. But people were generally aware of Mary's importance even before any form of official Bible was produced. The tradition that retained the knowledge remained current in Britain and France, through the Dark Ages, to medieval times when the Magdalene was the inspirational *Notre Dame* of the early Crusades and the great Gothic cathedrals.

That being the case, then, how did the Church manage to remove her from the forefront of its Apostolic structure?

What happened in the first instance was that the Roman Church drew specific attention to two passages in the the Bible: Genesis 3:16 and 1 Corinthians 11:3. Both had been quoted in the Church's original 4th-century *Apostolic Constitutions*. The first described how the Lord God said to Eve of Adam, 'He shall rule over thee.' The second (a quotation of St Paul's words) stated, 'The head of the woman is the man.'

A special new document was then produced, setting out what the Church reckoned to be the position of Mary Magdalene. Called *The Apostolic Order*, it was effectively the transcript of an imagined discussion between the Apostles after the Last Supper. Quite incidentally, it claimed (as the Gospels do not) that both Mary and Martha were present, thereby defeating part of its own objective. An extract from the supposed debate reads:

> John said: When the Master blessed the bread and the cup, and assigned them with the words, This is my Body and Blood, he did not offer them to the women who are with us.
>
> Martha said: He did not offer them to Mary because he saw her laugh.

On the basis of this purely imaginary story, the Church decreed that the first Apostles had clearly stated that women were not to be permitted to become priests because they were not serious-minded! The essence of this fabricated conversation was then adopted as formal Church doctrine, and Mary Magdalene was thereafter pronounced a disbelieving recusant.

Much earlier, in about AD 180, Bishop Clement of Alexandria had written something that amounted to the exact opposite. A prominent Father of the Church, he declared:

> Men and women share equally in perfection, and are to receive the same instruction and the same discipline. For the word 'humanity' applies equally to both men and women, and for us in Christ there is neither male nor female.

In justification of his words Clement listed a number of women who had been significant in past history, especially in terms of academic learning. His view was widely supported by contemporary educated society. Even so, the Pope later ruled that Clement had been in error: it was declared with thunderous authority that 'a woman cannot be a priest because our Lord was a man'!

## THE LADY OF THE LAKE

In 633 a mysterious little boat sailed into the harbour of Boulogne-sur-Mer in northern France. There was no one aboard, just a 3-foot (approx. 1 metre) statuette of the Black Madonna and child, together with a copy of the Gospels in Syriac.[23] Wherever the boat had come from, it caused quite a stir on its arrival. The strange Madonna – known as *Our Lady of the Holy Blood* – became the insignia of the cathedral of *Notre Dame* at

Boulogne, an object of considerable veneration until it was destroyed in the French Revolution.

The Black Madonna of Boulogne reinforced the connection between Mary and 'the sea' (Latin, *mare*) in the popular mind. The 'Madonna of the Sea' emblem (derived from the subsequent Boulogne insignia) was used on pilgrims' badges before the time of Charlemagne, and a version of the same device found its way into Scotland before armorial seals were common in Britain.[24] In 11th-century Scotland, Edinburgh's Port of Leith incorporated its own official emblem – a depiction of 'Mary of the Sea' and her Grail Child in a sailing boat protected by a cloud (a reference to James, [Joseph of Arimathea], who was once the 'Cloud' – the Leader of the Pilgrims).[25]

For some reason, scholars of heraldry have largely seen fit to ignore the importance of such feminine devices, in just the same way that compilers of family trees

The Edinburgh Port of Leith *Madonna of the Sea* device

and peerage registers have been guilty of dismissing female lineages. This was particularly so during the Georgian and Victorian eras in Britain, the volumes of which provide the basis for much of the unsatisfactory information available today. Maybe the current onset of the Age of Aquarius will see an end to male-dominated history, but for the time being the majority of such works are published in the old style and format. Very little research is required, however, to discover that the concept of *noblesse uterine* (matrilineal inheritance of nobility) was a concept thoroughly embraced throughout the Dark and early Middle Ages.

It is generally stated that the notion of heraldry (of bearing arms and of family escutcheons) began in the 12th century. This may well be so in Britain – but the British did not invent the idea, as the heralds would once have had us believe.[26] The reputed authorities on the subject, the College of Heralds and the College of Arms, were both established sometime in the late 1300s to control the registers of armsbearers. It was necessary then for a knight to bear a decorated escutcheon so that he might be recognized despite being dressed from head to toe in chain mail and armour. The use of flags and other emblems indicating family or region emanated from earlier times in Flanders and northern France. However, in spite of this, few in Britain have ever seen an insignia dating from before the 12th century, particularly one that is not of feudal origin. The emblem of the Port of Leith is thus unique in respect of its date, and in respect of its non-feudal, female association.

Archbishop Raban Maar's richly illuminated manuscript of *The Life of Mary Magdalene*[27] comprises 50 chapters bound into six volumes. It tells, among other things, of how Mary, Martha, and their companions left the shores of Asia, and favoured by an easterly wind they travelled on across the [Mediterranean] Sea between Europe and Africa, leaving the city of Rome and all the land of Italy to the right [north]. Then, happily changing course to the right [north], they came to the city of Marseilles in the Gaulish province of Vienne, where the River Rhone meets the coast. There – once they had called upon God, the Great King of all the world – they parted.

The libraries of Paris contain a number of ancient manuscripts even older than Maar's, some of which bear witness to the same period in Mary's life. Her mission in Provence is specifically mentioned in a hymn of the 600s (republished in the researched records called the *Acta Sanctorum*, first popularly issued during the 17th century by the Jesuit Jean Bolland).[28] Mary's companions Mary-Salome (Helena) and Mary Jacob (the wife of Cleophas) are said to be buried in the crypt of *Les Saintes Maries* in the Camargue. Long before the 9th-century church was built, the original church on the spot was called *Sanctae Mariae de Ratis*; near the present main nave is the remains of a sculpture showing the Marys at sea.

Mary Magdalene's association with Gaul has been artistically depicted in two distinct ways: representative and mystical. In some cases she is shown *en voyage* to Marseilles, as in the documented accounts. The most important example of this style of portrayal is perhaps that which has been exhibited at the 9th-century church of *Les Saintes Maries*: a painting by Henri de Guadermaris. It depicts the Marys' arrival in a boat off the coast of Provence, and was shown at the Salon de Paris in 1886. Another famous picture on similar lines is *The Sea Voyage* by Lukas Moser, which forms part of the gold- and silver-leafed altarpiece (*Der Magdalenenaltar*) at the Katholisches Pfarramt St Maria Magdalena, Tiefenbrohn, in southern Germany.

She is alternatively portrayed moving above the Earth to receive heavenly enlightenment (as apocryphal romance had her doing on a daily basis), or being carried westward as in the Revelation. A fine example of this style of representation is *Mary Magdalene Carried by the Angels*. This work of around 1606, by Giovanni Lanfranco, at the *Galleria Nazionale di Capodimonte* in Naples, shows the naked Magdalene together with three putti soaring above an empty European landscape.

Martha's remains lie buried at Tarascon, in the French province of Vienne. Letters patent of Louis XI dated 1482 refer to a visit by the Merovingian King Clovis to this tomb back in the late 5th century. Mary Magdalene's own remains were preserved at the Abbey of St Maximus, some 30 miles (c. 48 kilometres) or so from Marseilles. Charles II of Sicily, Count of Provence, disinterred Mary's skull and humerus (upper arm bone) in 1279 in order to have them set in gold and silver display casings, in which they remain today.[29] Some of Mary's other bones and ashes were kept in an urn, but these were vandalized during the French Revolution.

Mary's 'cave of solitude' is to be found nearby at La Sainte Baume. It was this cave that the Sire de Joinville visited in 1254 on returning from the 7th Crusade with King Louis IX. Afterwards he wrote that they

> came to the city of Aix in Provence to honour the Blessed Magdalene who lay about a day's journey away. We went to the place called Baume, on a very steep and craggy rock, in which it was said that the Holy Magdalene long resided at a hermitage.

Three centuries earlier, Wuillermus Gerardus, Marquis of Provence, made a pilgrimage to the cave. The lofty grotto church at La Sainte Baume – with its various

altars and its sculpture of Mary Magdalene – has long
been a noted place of pilgrimage.

Aix-en-Provence, where Mary Magdalene died in
AD 63, was the old town of Acquae Sextiae.[30] It was the
hot springs at Aix (Acqs) which gave it its name – *acqs*
being a medieval corruption of a derivative of the Latin
*aquae* (waters), sometimes, *aquense*. In the Languedoc
tradition, Mary is remembered as *la Dompna del Aquae*
'Mistress of the Waters'. Alternatively, as we have seen,
she might be called 'Mary of the Sea'. But the association
is always with water. To the Gnostics (as indeed to the
Celts), females who were afforded religious veneration
were often associated with lakes, wells, fountains and
springs. Gnosis (knowledge) and Wisdom were connected with the female *Holy Spirit* which 'moved on the
face of the waters' (Genesis 1:2). This was the Holy
Spirit of *Sophia* held to be incarnate in Mary Magdalene.

In an earlier chapter,[31] the baptismal priests of the
Gospel era were described as 'fishers'. From the moment Jesus was admitted to the priesthood[32] in the
Order of Melchizedek (Hebrews 5, and as we have seen
in Acts), he too became a designated 'fisher'. The dynastic line of the House of Judah was thus uniquely
established as a dynasty of Priest-Kings – or, as his
descendants became aptly known in Grail lore, 'Fisher
Kings'.

The lines of descent from Jesus and Mary which
emerged through the Fisher Kings preserved the maternal Spirit of Aix, to become the 'family of the waters' –
the House del Acqs.

The family was prominent in Aquitaine – an area
with a name that also has its roots in *aquae* 'waters' or
*acqs*, as indeed does the town name of Dax, west of
Toulouse, which stems from *d'Acqs*.[33] Here, Merovingian[34] branches of the family that descended from
Jesus through the Fisher Kings became Counts of

Toulouse and Narbonne, and Princes of the Septimanian Midi (the territory between France and Spain).[35] Another family branch, related through the female line, was granted the Celtic Church heritage of Avallon, with Viviane del Acqs acknowledged as the hereditary High Queen in the early 6th century. In Brittany, a corresponding male branch of the Provençal House del Acqs became the Comtes (Counts) de Léon d'Acqs in descent from Viviane I's granddaughter Morgaine.

From the time that Chrétien de Troyes wrote his 12th-century tale of *Ywain and the Lady of the Fountain* – in which 'the Lady corresponds to *la Dompna del Aquae* – the heritage of Acqs has persisted in Arthurian literature.

The legacy remained central to the theme, and was also directly related to the 'sacred waters' associated with *Genesis*, Sophia and the Magdalene. In 1484, Sir Thomas Malory's *Morte d'Arthur* marginally adjusted the distinction by way of phonetic assimilation from *del Acqs* to *du Lac* – with the result that, in translation, Viviane II (*Lady of the Fountain*, and the mother of Lancelot del Acqs) became the *Lady of the Lake*.

As this book continues, the various lines of descent from Jesus and his brother James will gradually unfold. We shall also discover why Arthurian romance and Grail lore have prevailed despite the charges of heresy persistently levelled at them by the Church.

It is, however, with Jesus's brother, James the Just, that we should begin – except that in this context he is better known as Joseph of Arimathea.

# TEN

# JOSEPH OF ARIMATHEA

## JOSEPH (JAMES) AT GLASTONBURY

In the 1601 *Annales Ecclesiasticae*, the Vatican librarian Cardinal Baronius recorded that Joseph of Arimathea first came to Marseilles in AD 35. From there, he and his company crossed to Britain to preach the Gospel. This was confirmed much earlier by the chronicler Gildas III (516–570), whose *De Excidio Britanniae* stated that the precepts of Christianity were carried to Britain in the last days of Emperor Tiberius Caesar, who died in AD 37. Even before Gildas, such eminent churchmen as Eusebius, Bishop of Caesaria (260–340),[1] and St Hilary of Poitiers (300–367) wrote of early apostolic visits to Britain. The years AD 35–37 are thus among the earliest recorded dates for Christian evangelism. They correspond to a period shortly after the Crucifixion – prior to the time when Peter and Paul were in Rome, and earlier than the New Testament Gospels.

An important character in 1st century Gaul was St Philip.[2] He was described by Gildas and William of Malmesbury as being the inspiration behind Joseph's assignment in England. The *De Sancto Joseph ab Arimathea* states, 'Fifteen years after the Assumption [that is to say in AD 63], he [Joseph] came to Philip the Apostle among the Gauls.' Freculphus, 9th-century

*Map 5* The Roman Empire

Bishop of Lisieux, wrote that St Philip then sent the mission from Gaul to England, 'to bring thither the good news of the word of life, and to preach the incarnation of Jesus Christ'.

Upon their arrival in the West Country, Joseph and his twelve missionaries were viewed with some scepticism by the native Britons, but were greeted with some cordiality by King Arviragus of Siluria, brother of Caractacus the Pendragon. In consultation with other chiefs, he granted Joseph twelve hides of Glastonbury land. A hide is an area of land reckoned agriculturally to support one family for one year with one plough, equal in Somerset (the Glastonbury area) to 120 acres (c. 48.5 hectares). Here they built their unique little church in a scale of the ancient Hebrew Tabernacle.[3] These grants remained holdings of free land for many centuries thereafter, as confirmed in the *Domesday Book* of 1086: 'The Church of Glastonbury has in its own ville twelve hides of land which have never paid tax.' In Joseph's era, Christian chapels were hidden underground in the catacombs of Rome – but once the wattle chapel of St Mary was built at Glastonbury, Britain could boast the first above-ground Christian church in the world.[4]

A monastery was subsequently added to the chapel, and the Saxons rebuilt the complex in the 8th century. Following a disastrous fire in 1184, Henry II of England granted the community a Charter of Renovation in which Glastonbury was referred to as 'the mother and burying place of the saints, founded by the disciples of our Lord themselves'.[5] A stone Lady Chapel was constructed at that time. Later, the whole grew to become a vast Benedictine abbey, second in size and importance only to Westminster Abbey. Prestigious figures associated with Glastonbury included St Patrick, who was the first Abbot in the 5th century, and St Dunstan, who was Abbot from 940 to 946.

In addition to the accounts of Joseph of Arimathea at Glastonbury, others tell of his association with Gaul and the Mediterranean tin trade. John of Glastonbury (14th-century compiler of *Glastoniencis Chronica*) and John Capgrave (Principal of the Augustinian Friars in England 1393 – 1464) both quote from a book found by the Emperor Theodosius (ruled 375–395) in the Pretorium in Jerusalem. Capgrave's *De Sancto Joseph ab Arimathea* tells how Joseph was imprisoned by the Jewish elders after the Crucifixion. This is also described in the apocryphal *Acts of Pilate*. The historian Bishop Gregory of Tours (544–595) similarly mentions the post-Crucifixion imprisonment of Joseph in his *History of the Franks*. And in the 12th century it was recounted yet again in *Joseph d'Arimathie* by the Burgundian Grail chronicler Sire Robert de Boron.

The *Magna Glastoniensis Tabula* and other manuscripts go on to say that Joseph subsequently escaped and was pardoned. Some years later he was in Gaul with his nephew, Joseph, who was baptized by Philip the Apostle. Young Joseph (Jesus and Mary's second son) is traditionally referred to as '*Josephes*' – the name that we shall continue to use in this book in order to distinguish him from his uncle, Joseph of Arimathea.

A good many valuable writings and relics were destroyed in the Glastonbury fire of 1184. More were lost in the ravages of the Tudor dissolution of the monasteries. In the course of this latter destructive episode, Abbot Richard Whiting of Glastonbury was murdered (1539) by the brutal henchmen of Henry VIII. Fortunately, copies of some important manuscripts were salvaged. One of these (attributed to Gildas III) refers to Joseph of Arimathea as a '*noble decurio*'. The 9th-century Archbishop Raban Maar likewise described him as a '*noblis decurion*'. A *Decurio* was an overseer of mining estates, and the term originated in Spain, where

Jewish metalworkers had been operative in the celebrated foundries of Toledo since the 6th century BC.[6] It
is not unlikely that Joseph's mining interest was one
reason for the generous land grant by King Arviragus.[7]
Joseph was after all a well-known metal merchant and
artificer in metals (as were the Old Testament characters
Tubal-cain and Hiram Abiff – both remembered in
modern Freemasonry).

The *De Sancto Joseph* states that Joseph of Arimathea's wattle church of St Mary was dedicated 'in the
31st year after our Lord's Passion' (that is, AD 64). This
conforms to AD 63 as its date of commencement, as
given by William of Malmesbury. But with regard to
the fact that the dedication was to St Mary, it has long
been a point of some debate that a church should have
been consecrated (apparently) to Jesus's mother Mary
some 15 years after her Assumption, and still centuries
before there was anything approaching a Virgin Mother
cult. Many have suggested that such an early chapel
would more likely have been dedicated to an archangel,
or even to Jesus himself. But (as confirmed in the
12th/13th-century *Chronicles* of Matthew Paris) AD 63
was the very year in which the other Mary – Mary
Magdalene – died at St Baume.

Among the visits Joseph made to Britain, two were
of great importance to the Church and were cited later
by a number of clerics and religious correspondents.
The first (as described by Cardinal Baronius) followed
Joseph's initial seizure by the Sanhedrin after the Crucifixion. This visit in AD 35 ties in precisely with an
account of St James the Just's being in Europe – which
is hardly surprising, since Joseph of Arimathea and St
James were one and the same person. The Revd Lionel
S Lewis (Vicar of Glastonbury in the 1920s) also confirmed from his annals that St James was at Glastonbury
in AD 35. The second of Joseph's visits followed the AD

62 stoning and excommunication (spiritual death) of James the Just in Jerusalem.[8]

Cressy, the Benedictine who lived shortly after the Reformation, wrote,

> In the one-and-fortieth year of Christ [that is, AD 35], St James, returning out of Spain, visited Gaul, Brittany and the towns of the Venetians, where he preached the Gospel, and so came back to Jerusalem to consult the Blessed Virgin and St Peter about matters of great weight and importance.

The 'weighty matters' referred to by Cressy concerned the necessity for a decision on whether to receive uncircumcised Gentiles into the Nazarene Church. As Jerusalem's first bishop, Jesus's brother James presided at the Council meeting which handled the debate.

A number of old traditions relate to St James in Sardinia and Spain, but they are often attributed to the wrong St James. This is mainly because the Apostle James Boanerges (sometimes called St James the Greater, as distinguished from James of Alphaeus – the Lesser) disappears from the New Testament for an unwarranted period.

Misunderstandings, caused by apparent anomalies and duplicated entries concerning Joseph of Arimathea and St James the Just, provoked some argument between the bishops at the Council of Basle in 1434. As a result, individual countries decided to follow their different traditions. It is 'St Joseph' who is most remembered in connection with Church history in Britain, whereas it is as 'St James' that he is revered in Spain. Even so, the English authorities compromised when linking him with the monarchy, and the royal court in London became the Palace of St James.

The bishops' debate followed an earlier dispute at the Council of Pisa in 1409 on the subject of the seniority, in age, of national Churches in Europe. The main contenders were England, France and Spain. The case was ruled in favour of England – because the church at Glastonbury was founded by Joseph/James *'statim post passionem Christi'* (shortly after the Passion of Jesus). Henceforth, the monarch of France was entitled 'His Most Christian Majesty', while in Spain the appellation was 'His Most Catholic Majesty'. The bitterly contested title of 'His Most Sacred Majesty' was reserved for the King of England.[9] Records of the debate – *Disputatio super Dignitatem Angliae et Galliae in Concilio Constantiano* – state that England won her case because the saint was not only granted land in the West Country by Arviragus, but was actually buried at Glastonbury. The possibility that the other Saint James (Boanerges, James the Greater) might have visited Spain at some stage was not relevant to the debate.

Having established that Joseph/James was buried at Glastonbury, we ought to look into how it is that the Cistercian *Estoire del Saint Graal* claims that he was buried 'at the Abbey of Glais in Scotland'. This is not as contradictory as it seems, for at the time of Joseph's death the Scots Gaels had not settled in the Western Highlands (Dalriada) but constituted a tribal population of Northern Ireland (Ulster) who had infiltrated the south-west of Britain. The West Country areas settled by the early Scots were often referred to as 'Scotland' (land of the Scots), when the far north of Britain was called 'Caledonia'. Furthermore, the word *glais* – so common in old Scots names – comes from the Irish (Goidelic) Celtic, and means 'stream', 'rivulet'. *Douglas*, for example, derives from *dubh glais* (dark stream). Early Glastonbury was set amid watery marshland, and was called the Isle of Glais. Thus, Joseph's said burial place at the 'Abbey of Glais' actually referred quite correctly to the Abbey of Glastonbury.[10]

In the 1st century, mainland Britain (England, Wales and Scotland) was generally known as *Albion*. The Irish called it *Alba* – a name which was later restricted to the Scottish north after the Irish Scots had settled in the Western Highlands of Dalriada. By the 900s *Alba* had been adapted to *Albany*, and the alternative name, *Scotland* (or *Scotia*),[11] emerged about a century later.

## LORDSHIP OF THE GRAIL

The 'Joseph' distinction (Hebrew, *Yosef*, meaning 'he shall add') was conferred on the eldest son of each generation in the Davidic succession. When a dynastic son of the House of Judah (by whatever personal name) succeeded to become the 'David', his eldest son (the Crown Prince) became the 'Joseph' (with the meaning 'he shall add' denoting his royal heirship). If there was no son at the time of a Davidic accession (or if the son was under 16 years old), then the eldest brother of the 'David' would temporarily hold the 'Joseph' distinction. It would be relinquished to the senior line if and when a son was of age to inherit the style.

Within the Judaean kingly, priestly, angelic and patriarchal successions, there were numerous dynastic and hereditary titles, along with various distinctions of office and appointment. Thus it was possible for any senior individual to be known by a series of different names according to the context of the moment. As we have seen, Matthew was also Levi in his official capacity. Zacharias was the Zadok and was, therefore, angelically Michael. Jonathan Annas (sometimes called Nathanael) was also James of Alphaeus (the Jacob of the Succession) but, additionally, he was the Elias. It is simply by virtue of this hierarchical and patriarchal structure that James the Just,[12] brother of Jesus, came also to be known as Joseph of Arimathea (*Rama-Theo*) – the Joseph (he shall add) of 'Godly Highness'. At different times there were, of course, other Josephs of Arimathea. Now, with other related facts to hand, we should look at the situation from a different perspective – that of pure chronology.

Apart from a few very vague descriptive terms, the New Testament gives no clue to what the ' Arimathea' element had to do with Jesus's family; nor do the Gospels mention Joseph's age. Outside the scriptures, however, Joseph is popularly conceived as Jesus's mother Mary's uncle (Jesus's great-uncle). Paintings and picture-books consequently portray him as already rather elderly in the AD 30s. That apart, a great number of written accounts from a variety of sources record him as coming to Glastonbury 30 years later in AD 63. Cressy's *Church History*, which incorporates the records of Glastonbury Monastery, asserts that Joseph of Arimathea died on 27 July AD 82.

If Jesus's mother Mary was born in about 26 BC, as is generally reckoned, she would have been aged 19 (or thereabouts) when Jesus was born. By the time of the Crucifixion she would have been in her middle fifties. If Joseph had been her uncle, he would have been, say, 20 years older than Mary – putting him somewhere in his middle seventies at that point in time. But then, 30 years afterwards (apparently at over 100 years of age) he is reputed to have begun a whole new life as an evangelist and *decurio* in the West! If that were not enough, the records then show him dying 20 years later!

Clearly, none of this makes any sense, and the hereditary aspect of the 'Joseph of Arimathea *distinction* has to be applied. And so, as established, the Joseph of the Crucifixion era was James the Just, born in AD 1. He died in AD 82, having been formally excommunicated in Jerusalem 20 years earlier.

It is also apparent that Jesus's mother Mary's background and family are not accounted for in the Bible. This is not surprising since the Church interpretation of Mary's heritage is that she was a product of Immaculate Conception. The main sources concerning Mary are not the canonical Gospels but the apocryphal scriptures: *The Gospel of Mary* and the *Protevangelion*. Many of the great artistic depictions of Mary's life and family are based on these, like Albrecht Dürer's famous *The Meeting of Anna and Joachim* (Mary's parents). The most comprehensive work on the subject is customarily accepted to be *La Leggenda di Sant' Anna Madre della Gloriosa Vergine Maria, e di San Gioacchino* (The Story of Saint Ann, Mother of the Blessed Virgin Mary, and of Saint Joachim). This comprehensive work links her parents with the Royal House of Israel, but it does *not* mention Joseph of Arimathea as her uncle.

It was by way of a 9th-century Byzantine concept that the Church first promoted the idea that Joseph was Mary's uncle. There is no mention of him in that role beforehand. The concept arose at a time when the cautiously fearful Church Councils were ruling on what should be the approved content of the New Testament. So long as Joseph of Arimathea could be contained as a sideline character in the Davidic structure, and was not associated with the key Messianic line, his royal descendants could not embarrass the self-styled Apostolic structure of the Roman bishops.

By this strategy the existence of Jesus and Mary's son Josephes was also conveniently disguised in the West. He was generally portrayed as Joseph of Arimathea's son, or sometimes as his nephew (which of course he was). In either role he was no threat to the orthodox scheme of things, and indeed both definitions of his relationship (son and nephew) had genuine foundation, for he was Joseph of Arimathea's heir to the *Rama-*

*Theo* (Arimathea) distinction. When Jesus became the 'David', his brother James became the 'Joseph' (and thus, the 'Joseph of Arimathea'). This only changed when Jesus the younger was of an age to inherit the title. After the death of Jesus the Christ, his eldest son Jesus the Justus took over the role of the 'David', the Davidic king. His younger son Josephes (the new David's brother) then became the 'Joseph' and the Crown Prince – the designated *Rama-Theo* (Arimathea). But until that time, while his brother Jesus II Justus (called Gais or Gésu in Grail lore) was abroad in Rome and Jerusalem, Josephes' foster-father and legal guardian was his uncle James (the 'Joseph of Arimathea').

Later, the first-born son of Jesus Justus was Galains (called Alain in the Grail tradition).[13] In accordance with the custom of dynastic wedlock (see Chapter 3, p 45–6f), Jesus Justus would have first married in September AD 73; his wife was a granddaughter of Nicodemus. The legacy of Davidic kingship (which was to become represented as *Lordship of the Grail*), was promised to Galains, and was in time formally passed to him by his uncle and guardian, Josephes. But Galains became a committed celibate and died without issue. Hence, the Grail heritage reverted to Josephes' junior line – to be inherited by his son Josue,[14] from whom the Fisher Kings (Priest-Kings) descended.[15]

As we have seen,[16] Joseph of Arimathea had been to Britain with Mary's elder son, the 12-year-old Jesus Justus, in AD 49. This event is well remembered in West Country tradition, and is evidenced in William Blake's famous song *Jerusalem*. The stories tell of how young Jesus walked upon the Exmoor coast, and went to the Mendip village of Priddy. Because those royal feet did indeed 'walk upon England's mountains green' (albeit the son's feet rather than the father's), a stone in memory of his parents, Jesus and Mary Magdalene, was eventually set into the south wall of St Mary's Chapel, Glastonbury. This stone, which remains on the site of the original 1st-century wattle chapel, is inscribed '*Jesus Maria*' and in due course, as one of the most venerated relics of the Abbey, it became a 'station of prayer' for pilgrims in the Middle Ages. The original chapel was begun in AD 63 immediately after Mary Magdalene's death, and the old annals[17] all state that Jesus consecrated the chapel 'personally, in honour of his mother'. It was, therefore, to the Magdalene (not to Jesus the Christ's mother Mary) that the Glastonbury chapel was dedicated by her eldest son, Jesus Justus, in AD 64.

## THE SHIELD OF THE MOST WORTHY

By the time of Mary Magdalene's death in AD 63, her son Josephes had become Bishop of Saraz. In Malory's *Morte d'Arthur*, Saraz (Sarras) features as the realm of King Evelake, as mentioned in the story of Lancelot's son Galahad. The tale begins when Galahad inherits a supernatural shield of the Christ, and encounters the mysterious White Knight:

> Then within a while came Galahad thereas the white knight abode him by the hermitage, and every each saluted other courteously.
>
> 'Sir,' said Sir Galahad, 'by this shield be many marvels fallen?'
>
> 'Sir,' said the knight, 'it befell after the passion of Our Lord Jesu Christ thirty-two year, that Joseph of Arimathea, the gentle knight, the which took down Our Lord off the holy Cross, at that time he departed from Jerusalem with a great party of his kindred with him. And so he laboured till that they came to a city that hight Sarras. And at that same hour that Joseph came to Sarras there was a king that hight Evelake, that had great war against the Saracens, and in especial against one Saracen, the which was King

> Evelake's cousin, a rich king and a mighty, which marched nigh this land, and his name was called Tolleme le Feintes. So on a day these two met to do battle. . . .'

Sarras (Saraz) was Sahr-Azzah on the Meditteranean coast.[18] It was and is better known as Gaza – the once Philistine centre where Samson met his fate (Judges 16).

There is no record of a King Evelake as such, but the name is a literary variant of the title *Avallach*, as found in quite a number of sovereign and saintly genealogies. It was subject to many different forms – such as *Abalech*, *Arabach* and *Amalach* – but all were ultimately corruptions of the Egyptian-Greek word *Alabarch*. Again it does not represent a 'name' (neither a forename nor a family name) but a title. St Jerome (*c.*340–420), translator of the Bible into Latin, stated that Tiberius Alexander, the Procurator of Judaea from AD 46, was the son of Alexander Lysimachus, *Alabarch* of Alexandria. In essence (although politically applied to magistrates responsible for justice among the Jews), the word *Alabarch* indicated a community headman (a chief).

The White Knight's tale recounted (as above) that Evelake's Saracen enemy was Tolleme le Feintes (Tholomy the 'feigned', thus the False), who is also mentioned in the *Antiquities* of Josephus:

> Tholomy the arch robber, was after some time brought to him bound, and slain; but not till he had done a world of mischief to Idumaea and the Arabians.

The person to whom Tolleme/Tholomy was brought from Saraz was the Procurator of Judea, Cuspius Fadus (the predecessor of Tiberius Alexander), who had Tolleme executed in around AD 45.

The White Knight went on to tell how Bishop Josephes informed King Evelake that he would inevitably be killed by Tolleme unless he 'left his belief of the old law and believe upon the new law. And then there he showed him the right belief of the Holy Trinity'. Evelake was immediately converted, and the *Shield of the Most Worthy* was presented to him, whereupon he defeated Tolleme.[19] Josephes later baptized King Evelake before setting out to preach the Gospel in Britain.

The strength of the white shield lay in its red cross, and in a mystic veil that went before it bearing the image of Jesus. This is reminiscent of the conversion of Emperor's son, Vespasian. As narrated in the *Vindicta Salvatoris*, he was cured of leprosy by an ethereal shroud which bore an effigy of the Messiah.[20]

In conclusion, the White Knight related that following Josephes' instruction the shield was placed for safe keeping with the holy hermit Nacien. It lay with him in the abbey after his death, to be retrieved eventually by Sir Galahad. 'Thereafter' (in the dying words of Bishop Josephes), 'the last of my lineage shall have it about his neck, that shall do many marvellous deeds'. In the *De Sancto Joseph* and elsewhere, Nacien (or Nacion) is described not as a hermit, but as a Prince of the Medas. Historically, Prince Nascien of the Septimanian Midi was the 5th-century ancestor of the Merovingian kings of the Franks, and his descendants also included the 11th-century Seneschals (Stewards) of Dol and Dinan. These powerful major-domos of Brittany were descended from Lancelot's mother, Viviane II del Acqs, dynastic Queen of Avallon, and were progenitors of the most influential of all *Desposynic* strains – the Scots Royal House of Stewart.

## APOSTOLIC MISSIONS TO THE WEST

A most supportive colleague of Mary Magdalene in Provence was her husband Jesus's great friend Simon Zelotes who, no longer the Father (the 'Abraham'), assumed the style given to him by Jesus at his 'raising' – that of Abraham's steward Eliezer (or Lazarus). Under this name he became the first Bishop of Marseilles, and his statue is at St Victor's church. A doorway from the nave of the church leads to a subterranean chapel built by Cassianite monks in the 4th century, an old crypt that was deliberately located on the site of Lazarus's residence, and was fiercely guarded by the monks in the early days. It was Lazarus – also known as the 'Great One', or '*Maximus*' – who buried Mary Magdalene in her original alabaster sepulchre at St Maximin in AD 63. Prior to this he had been in Jerusalem and Antioch for a time, and after Mary's death he went again to Jerusalem and Jordan, before returning to join Joseph of Arimathea.

In Britain, Lazarus remained better known by his Apostolic name, Simon Zelotes. Nicephorus (758–829), Patriarch of Constantinople and Byzantine historian, wrote that,

> St Simon, surnamed Zelotes . . . travelled through Egypt and Africa, then through Mauritania and all Libya, preaching the Gospel. And the same doctrine he taught to the peoples of the Occidental Sea and the islands called Britannia.

Nearly five centuries earlier, Bishop Dorotheus of Tyre wrote in his *Synopsis de Apostole* in 303 that 'Simon Zelotes preached Christ through all Mauritania, and Afric the less. At length he was crucified in Britannia, slain, and buried'. The 1601 *Annales Ecclesiasticae* of Cardinal Baronius confirm Simon's martyrdom in Britain. He was crucified by the Romans under Catus Decianus at Caistor, Lincolnshire. By the saint's own request, however, his mortal remains were later placed with those of the Magdalene in Provence.

Also associated with Joseph of Arimathea in Britain was Herod-Agrippa's uncle Aristobulus, who had been

Mary Magdalene's particular ally when she was afforded protection by the Herodian establishment at Vienne, outside Lyon.[21] Some commentators have suggested that a younger Aristobulus (the second husband of the deadly dancer Salome) was Mary's confederate, but he was acting as regent for the king in Lesser Armenia at the time. The correct Aristobulus is described in the writings that name him in Britain; they duly refer to him as *Arwystli Hen* ('Aristobulus the Old') and the town of Arwystli in Powys was named after him. He was the brother of Herod-Agrippa I, Herod of Chalcis, and Herodias (the mother of Salome).

The writings of the Roman churchman Hippolytus (born about AD 160) list Aristobulus as a Bishop of the Britons. Cressy maintains that he was a bishop in Britain ordained by St Paul himself. The Greek Church *Martyrology* claims that Aristobulus was martyred in Britain 'after he had built churches and ordained deacons and priests for the island'. This is further confirmed by St Ado (800–874), Archbishop of Vienne, in the *Adonis Martyrologia*. Earlier (AD 303), St Dorotheus, Bishop of Tyre, wrote that Aristobulus was in Britain when St Paul sent greetings to his household in Rome: 'Salute them which are of Aristobulus' household' (Romans 16:10). And the Jesuit *Regia Fides* additionally states, 'It is perfectly certain that before St Paul reached Rome, Aristobulus was away in Britain.' He was in fact executed by the Romans at Verulamium (modern St Albans)[22] in AD 59.

In addition to being known as 'Joseph of Arimathea', St James the Just was called *Ilid* by the chroniclers of Wales. He was the patron of Llan Ilid in Gwent, having founded a mission at Cor-Eurgain. The *Cwydd to St Mary Magdalene* in the *Gestyn Ceriog* refers to Joseph as *Ilid*, as does the manuscript of *The Sayings of the Wise*. The name *Ilid* is thought to be a variant of the Hebrew

*Eli* (meaning 'my God' or 'raised up'). The *Achan Sant Prydain* (Genealogy of the Saints of Britain) states that 'there came with Brân the Blessed from Rome to Britain Arwystli Hen, Ilid, Cyndaf [meaning an elder] – men of Israel, and Maw or Mawan, son of Cyndaf'. The *Iolo Manuscripts* recount that Ilid was summoned to Britain by Eurgain, the wife of King Caractacus of Camulod, and states, 'This same Ilid was called Joseph in the lections of his life.'

The Silurian Archdruid Brân the Blessed ( Bendi-geidfran) was married to Joseph of Arimathea's daughter Anna (Enygeus),[23] who is sometimes loosely referred to as a *consabrina of the Blessed Mary* (that is Jesus the Christ's mother Mary). Because Joseph has sometimes been wrongly portrayed as Mary's uncle, the word *consabrina* has been taken to denote a 'cousin', and is often given as such. In practice, the definition, *consabrina*, was very obscure, and denoted no more than a junior kinswoman of inferior status. It was the perfect word to use when a genealogical rela-tionship was unspecific – or when it was deemed necessary for it to remain unspecified, as was precisely the case here.

In AD 51, Brân was taken hostage to Rome along with Caractacus the Pendragon. (Pendragons were overlords of Celtic Britain, as we shall see in a later chapter.[24]) Resident in Rome, Gladys, the younger daughter of Caractacus, married the Roman senator Rufus Pudens,[25] and thus became Claudia Rufina Bri-tannica (as confirmed by the Roman poet Martial in about AD 68). Caractacus' other daughter was St Eur-gen of Llan Ilid (the wife of Salog, Lord of Salisbury). His famed son Prince Linus became the first appointed Bishop of Rome.[26] In 2 Timothy 4:21 (New Testament), Paul writes: 'Eubulus greeteth thee, and Pudens and Linus, and Claudia, and all the brethren'. Eubulus (*eu-boulos* 'well-advised', 'prudent') was a variation of Aristobulus (*aristo-boulos* 'best-advised', 'noblest in counsel').

While in Britain, Joseph of Arimathea's enterprise was maintained by a close circle of twelve celibate anchorites. Whenever one died, so he was replaced by another. In Grail lore these anchorites were referred to as 'the brethren of Alain (Galains)', who was one of their number, and as such they were symbolic sons of Brân, the *Elias* patriarch of Hebron (the 'Father' in the old order – as against the newly styled 'Bishop of Rome'). This is why, in some literature, Alain is defined as the son of Brân (Bron). After Joseph's death in AD 82 the group disintegrated – mainly because Roman control had altered the character of England.

We have already seen that an amount of confusion reigned because of the various names attributed to Joseph (Joseph of Arimathea, St James the Just, Ilid, and so forth), but it is clear that certain works of popular folklore have done much to further confuse the issue of descendant lines after his time. These works include the *Bruts*, the *Triads*, the *Mabinogion*, and *Cycles of the Kings*. Historically they are all important because they are not entirely fictional. Most traditions are, by their very nature, based on ancient facts. But the tales are purposefully romantic in construction and, as a result, many sceptical historians have attacked them mercilessly. Equally regrettable is the fact that other writers have been guided rather too wilfully by these semi-fanciful works. Consequently, a good deal of genealogically impossible information is contained in books that appear to stem from unimpeachably authoritative sources.

Unfortunately too, romantic literature pays little heed to correct chronology, and the players concerned are scattered willy-nilly in the adventurous texts. The

*High History of the Holy Grail* (of around 1220) provides a good example in claiming that Perceval (a 6th-century adherent of King Arthur) was the grandnephew of the 1st-century Joseph of Arimathea: 'Good knight was he of right, for he was of the lineage of Joseph of Arimathea, and this Joseph was his mother's uncle.' The basis of the lineage is correct – but the relationship as given is impossible.

# ELEVEN

## RELIGION AND THE BLOODLINE

### GOOD KING LUCIUS

In the mid-2nd century, King Lucius, the great-grand-son of Arviragus, revived the spirit of the early disciples in Britain. In so doing, he was popularly held to have 'increased the light' of Joseph's first missionaries, and accordingly became known as *Lleiffer Mawr* (the Great Luminary). His daughter Eurgen forged the first link between the two key Davidic successions – that from Jesus and that from James (Joseph of Arimathea) – when she married Aminadab, the great-grandson of Jesus and Mary Magdalene (in the line from Bishop Josephes).

Lucius openly confirmed his Christianity at Winchester in AD 156, and his cause was heightened in AD 177 by a mass Roman persecution of Christians in Gaul. This was enforced especially in the old Herodian regions of Lyon and Vienne, where St Irenaeus and 19,000 Christians were put to death 30 years later. During the persecution, a good many Gaulish Christians fled to Britain – and especially to Glastonbury, where they sought the aid of Good King Lucius. He decided to approach Eleutherius, the Bishop of Rome, for advice – this was of course before the days of the formal Roman Church. Lucius wrote earnestly to Eleutherius, requesting instruction in Christian government.

The letter in reply, as contained in the *Sacrorum Conciliorum Collectio*, is still extant in Rome. Eleutherius suggested that a good king was always at liberty to reject the laws of Rome – but not the law of God. The following is an extract from it in translation:

> The Christian believers, like all the people of the kingdom, must be considered sons of the king. They are under your protection . . . A king is known by his government, not by whether he retains his power over the land. While you govern well, you will be a king. Unless you do this, the name of the king endures not, and you will lose the name of king.[1]

John Capgrave (1393–1464), the most learned of Augustinian friars, and Archbishop Ussher, in his *De Brittanicarum Ecclesiarum Primordiis*, both recount that Lucius sent the missionaries Medway and Elfan, together with his request for advice, to Rome. They eventually returned with the bishop's emissaries Faganus and Duvanus, whom the Welsh annals name as Fagan and Dyfan, and whose journey was confirmed by Gildas in the 6th century. The Venerable Bede of Jarrow (673–735) also wrote about the king's appeal, which is likewise mentioned in the *Anglo-Saxon Chronicle*.

Fagan and Dyfan reinstated the old order of 'anchorites' (reclusive devotees) at Glastonbury, and have since been credited with the second foundation of Christianity in Britain. Following this, the fame of Lucius spread far and wide. He was already celebrated as the builder of the first Glastonbury tower on St Michael's Tor in AD 167, and now the church at Llandaff was dedicated to him as Lleurwgg the Great.[2]

Even more impressively, he was responsible for founding the first Christian archbishopric in London. A Latin plaque above the vestry fireplace at St Peter's, Cornhill, in the old City of London, reads:

In the year of our Lord 179, Lucius, the first Christian king of this island now called Britain, founded the first church in London, well known as the Church of St Peter in Cornhill; and founded there the archiepiscopal seat, and made it the metropolitan church and the primary church of his kingdom. So it remained for the space of four hundred years until the coming of St Augustine. . . Then, indeed, the seat and pallium of the archbishopric was translated from the said church of St Peter in Cornhill to Dorobernia, which is now called Canterbury.

The advice given by Bishop Eleutherius in response to Good King Lucius' plea is fascinating, for it is fully in keeping with the underlying principle of *service* that permeates the Messianic Grail Code. Kings of the Grail dynasties in Britain and France always operated on this basis: they were 'common fathers' to the people, never rulers of the lands. (The latter was a particularly feudal and imperial concept that completely undermined the Code.) They understood, for example, the important difference in being 'Kings of the Franks' as against being kings of France, or in being 'Kings of Scots' as against being kings of Scotland. By virtue of this, the Grail monarchs were able to champion their nations rather than champion the clerics and politicians. From the moment that a nation's monarch becomes regulated by Acts of Parliament and Church decree, the title King or Queen becomes worthless. Under such circumstances there is no one left with authority enough to equal that of Church or Parliament, and therefore no one to act solely on the people's behalf. Grail Kings were defined as 'Guardians of the Realm'. In this regard, Bishop Eleutherius' advice to Lucius was both profound and enlightened: '. . . all the people of the kingdom must be considered sons of the king. They are under your protection.'

## THE RISE OF THE ROMAN CHURCH

In AD 66, the Hasmonaean, Flavius Josephus, had been appointed Commander in the defence of Galilee. He had previously trained for the Pharisee priesthood, but accepted military service when the Jews rose up against their Roman overlords. Josephus subsequently became the foremost historian of the era, and his writings, *The Wars of the Jews* and *The Antiquities of the Jews*, provide a comprehensive insight into the long and complex history of the nation from the time of the early patriarchs to the years of Roman oppression. In the context of his work it is interesting to note his one and only reference to Jesus.[3] It locates Jesus firmly within the historical fabric of the time, but without any reference to his divinity or to any scriptural motive:

> Now it was at around this time that Jesus emerged – a wise man, if he may be called a man, for he was a worker of marvels. A teacher of such men as receive the truth with pleasure, he drew to him many of the Jews in addition to many of the Gentiles. He was the Christ, and when Pilate – at the suggestion of the principal men among us – had him condemned to be crucified, those that had loved him from the first did not forsake him, for he appeared to them alive again on the third day – just as the godly prophets had foretold about him, and ten thousand other wonderful things about him besides. And the sect of Christians – named after him – are still very much in existence even today.

Josephus' scholarly opus, comprising some 60,000 manuscript lines, was written during the AD 80s when Josephus was in Rome, from where the Gospel of Mark also emerged a short while before. Although Peter and Paul were executed under Nero's regime, the Gospel writings of the era were not, on the face of it, anti-Roman. Indeed, the early Christians were more inclined to blame the Jews (rather than Pilate) for the persecution of Jesus. And because the Jewish uprising of AD 66–70 had failed, they firmly believed that God had switched allegiance from the Jews to themselves.

Notwithstanding this, the position of Christians within the expanding Roman Empire was hazardous; they were very much a minority group with no legal status. From Nero's crucifixion of Peter to the Edict of Milan in 313 (when Christianity was officially recognized), there were no fewer than 30 appointed Christian Bishops of Rome. The first Bishop, installed during Peter's lifetime by Paul in AD 58,[4] was Britain's Prince Linus, the son of King Caractacus. (Linus is sometimes portrayed as if he had been a slave – but this was later Church propaganda, and we shall return to it because it is of particular importance.) By about AD 120, individual appointments had become the prerogative of group election, and candidates had to be citizens of Rome. By the time of Bishop Hyginus (from AD 136), there was little or no connection between the Pauline Christians and the Nazarene followers of Jesus's own Judaic doctrine. The latter had settled mainly in Mesopotamia, Syria, southern Turkey and Egypt – apart from the established movements in Britain and Gaul. In the meantime, the Christians of Rome had been constantly suppressed because their beliefs were thought to challenge the traditional divinity of the Caesars (Emperors). As time passed, the suppression became even more severe, until it once more reached the proportions of Nero's reign and became outright persecution.

The prevailing religion of Imperial Rome was polytheistic (observing many gods) and had emanated largely from the worship of natural deities such as those of the woods and waters. As Rome grew to statehood, the gods of her Etruscan and Sabine neighbours had been incorporated. These included Jupiter (the sky god)

## EARLY EMPERORS AND BISHOPS OF ROME *44 BC – AD 337*

| ROMAN EMPERORS | TERM | BISHOPS | TERM |
|---|---|---|---|
| AUGUSTUS | 44 BC - AD 14 | | |
| TIBERIUS | AD 14-37 | | |
| GAIUS CALIGULA | 37-41 | | |
| CLAUDIUS | 41-54 | | |
| NERO | 54-68 | | |
| GALBA | 68-69 | Linus<br>*First Bishop of Rome*<br>*(appointed by Paul before death of Peter)* | 58-78 |
| OTHO (joint)<br>+ VITELLIUS | 69<br>69 | | |
| VESPASIAN | 69-79 | Anacletus | 78-89 |
| TITUS | 79-81 | | |
| DOMITIAN | 81-96 | | |
| NERVA | 96-98 | Clement I | 89-98 |
| TRAJAN | 98-117 | Evaristus<br>Alexander I<br>Sixtus I | 99-106<br>107-115<br>116-125 |
| HADRIAN | 117-138 | Telesphorus<br>Hyginus | 125-136<br>136-140 |
| ANTONINUS PIUS | 138-161 | Pius I<br>Anicetus | 140-154<br>155-165 |
| MARCUS AURELIUS | 161-180 | Soter | 165-174 |
| COMMODUS | 180-192 | Eleutherius<br>Victor I | 174-189<br>189-198 |
| PERTINAX (joint)<br>+ DIDIUS JULIANUS | 193<br>193 | | |
| LUCIUS SEVERUS | 193-211 | Zephyrinus | 199-217 |
| CARACALLA | 211-217 | | |
| MACRINUS | 217 | Callixtus I | 217-222 |
| HELIOGABALUS ↓ | 218-222 | ↓ | |

| | | | |
|---|---|---|---|
| ALEXANDER SEVERUS | 222-235 | Urban I | 222-230 |
| | | Pontianus | 230-235 |
| MAXIMINUS | 235-238 | Anterus | 235-236 |
| | | Fabian | 236-250 |
| GORDIAN I (joint) + GORDIAN II | 238 | | |
| PUPIENUS (joint) + BALBINUS | 238 | | |
| GORDIAN III | 238-244 | | |
| PHILIP (the Arabian) | 244-249 | | |
| DECIUS | 249-251 | | |
| GALLUS | 251-253 | Cornelius | 251-253 |
| AEMILIAN | 253 | | |
| VALERIAN (joint) | 253-260 | Lucius | 253-254 |
| + GALLIENUS | 253-268 | Stephen I | 254-257 |
| | | Sixtus II | 257-258 |
| | | Dionysius | 259-268 |
| CLAUDIUS | 268-270 | Felix I | 269-274 |
| AURELIAN | 270-275 | | |
| TACITUS | 275 | | |
| PROBUS | 276-282 | Eutychianus | 275-283 |
| CARUS | 282-283 | | |
| CARINUS (joint) | 284 | Gaius | 283-296 |
| + NUMERIANUS | 284 | | |
| DIOCLETIAN (joint) | 284-305 | | |
| + MAXIMIANUS | 286-305 | Marcellinus | 296-304 |
| CONSTANTIUS CHLORUS | 305-306 | | |
| MAXENTIUS | 306-312 | Marcellus I | 308-309 |
| | | Eusebius | 309 |
| | | Miltiades | 310-314 |
| CONSTANTINE THE GREAT (Britain and Gaul) | 306- | | |
| (West) | 312- | Silvester I | 314-335 |
| (Overall) | 324-337 | *(First Imperial Bishop of Rome)* | |

*Map 6* Merovingian Gaul

and Mars (the god of war). Grecian cults were also embraced, and from 204 BC the orgies of Cybele (the Asiatic earth goddess) were evident, soon emulated by the hedonistic rituals of Dionysus/Bacchus (the god of wine). As the Roman Empire spread eastward, so the esoteric cult of Isis, the Universal Mother, was introduced, along with the mysterious Persian veneration of Mithras (god of light, truth and justice). Eventually, the Syrian religion of Sol Invictus (the Unconquered and Unconquerable Sun) became the all-encompassing belief. Its vision of the sun as the ultimate giver of life enabled all other cults to be subsumed within it, and it supported the Emperor as the incarnation of the god-head.

By the middle of the 2nd century, the original Naz-arenes (the followers of Jesus and James' teachings) were unpopular not only with Rome, but were being severely harassed by the Pauline Christians – particu-larly by Irenaeus, Bishop of Lyon (born about AD 120). He condemned them as heretics for claiming that Jesus was a man and not of divine origin as ruled by the new faith. In fact, he even declared that Jesus had himself been practising the wrong religion, and that he was personally mistaken in his beliefs! Irenaeus wrote of the Nazarenes, whom he called *Ebionites* (the poor), that

> They, like Jesus himself, as well as the Essenes and Zadokites of two centuries before, expound upon the pro-phetic books of the Old Testament. They reject the Pauline epistles, and they reject the apostle Paul, calling him an apostate of the Law.

In retaliation, the Nazarenes of the *Desposynic* Church denounced Paul as a 'renegade' and a 'false apostle', claiming that his 'idolatrous writings' should be 're-jected altogether'.

In AD 135 Jerusalem was again crushed by Roman armies, this time under Emperor Hadrian, and the sur-viving Jews were scattered. Those who remained in Palestine were content (in their despair at such final military defeat) to concern themselves solely with rab-binical law and religion. Meanwhile, the Pauline sect (now quite divorced from its Judaic origins) was be-coming ever more troublesome to the authorities.

Having reached the height of its glory in Hadrian's era (AD 117–138), Roman imperialism began to decline under Commodus. His ineffective rule (AD 180–192) prompted a good deal of disunity which led to many decades of civil war, pitting various generals against each other and against the central government. A conflict arose over who should wear the crown, and opposing sections of the army began to elect their own sovereigns. Emperor Lucius Severus (ruled AD 193-211) managed to restore some order by judicious use of the Praetorian Guard (the Emperor's personal body-guard, drawn from elite infantry regiments), but his discipline did not last for long. Throughout the 3rd century, internal disputes left the borders of the Empire open to attack by Sassanians from Persia and Goths from the Black Sea regions.

In AD 235 the Emperor Maximinus decreed that all Christian bishops and priests should be seized, their personal wealth confiscated, and their churches burned. The captives were sentenced to various forms of punishment and slavery, including penal servitude at the lead mines in Sardinia. On arrival, each captive would have one eye removed, and the left foot and right knee damaged to restrict movement. The men were also castrated. If that were not enough, they were chained from their waists to their ankles so they could not stand upright, and the fetters were permanently welded. Not surprisingly, the majority did not live for more than a few months. In those days, being a Christian was in itself dangerous, but to be a known leader was tanta-mount to signing a personal death warrant.

By the time of Emperor Decius (AD 249), the Chris-tians had become so rebellious that they were proclaimed criminals, and mass persecution began on an official basis. This continued into the reign of Dio-cletian, who became Emperor in AD 284. He dispensed with any vestige of democratic procedure and insti-tuted an absolute monarchy. Christians were required to offer sacrifices to the divine Emperor – and they suffered the harshest punishments for disobedience. It was ruled that all Christian meeting-houses be demolished. Disciples who convened alternative assemblies were put to death. All Church property was confiscated by the magistrates, and all books, testaments and written doctrines of the faith were publicly burned. Christians of any prominent or worthy birthright were barred from public office, and Christian slaves were denied any hope of freedom. The protection of Roman law was withdrawn, and those who argued with the edicts were roasted alive over slow fires or eaten by animals in the public arena.

Diocletian attempted to counter the persistent aggressions of barbarian invaders by decentralizing control and establishing two separate divisions of the Empire. From AD 293 the West was managed from Gaul, and the East was centred at Byzantium in (what is now) north-western Turkey. Still the assaults continued, in particular new western invasions by the Germanic tribes of Franks and Alamanni, who had previously been held across the Rhine. No longer were the Romans an invading power; they were now themselves the constant victims of insurgency from all sides.

One of the most ruthless of the persecutors under Diocletian was Galerius, governor of the eastern provinces. He ordered that anyone who did not worship the Emperor above all others would be painfully executed. Just before his death in 311, however – and much to everyone's surprise – Galerius issued a decree of relaxation, giving Christians the right to 'assemble in their conventicles without fear of molestation'. After some two and a half centuries of dread and suppression, the Christians entered a new age of conditional freedom.

From 312, Constantine became Emperor in the West – ruling jointly with Licinius in the East. By then Christianity had increased its following considerably and was flourishing in England, Germany, France, Portugal, Greece, Turkey, and all corners of the Roman domain. In fact, Christian evangelists were having more success in subduing the barbarians than were the legions of Rome – even in places as far afield as Persia and Central Asia. It took little imagination for Constantine to realize that, while his Empire was falling apart at the seams, there could be some practical merit in his harnessing Christianity. He perceived in it a unifying force which could surely be used to his own advantage.

Although Constantine had succeeded his father, he had a rival for the supreme imperial rank in the person of his brother-in-law, Maxentius. Their armies met at Milvian Bridge (a little outside Rome) in 312, and Constantine was victorious. This campaign was the prime moment of opportunity to establish his personal affiliation with Christianity. He announced that he had seen the vision of a cross in the sky, accompanied by the words 'In this sign conquer'. The Christian leaders were most impressed that a Roman Emperor had ridden to victory under their banner.

Constantine thereupon summoned the ageing Bishop Miltiades. The Emperor's purpose was not to join the faith under the authority of the Bishop of Rome, but to take over the Christian Church in its entirety. Among his first instructions was that the nails from the Cross of Jesus be brought to him – one of which he would have affixed to his crown. His pronouncement to the bewildered Miltiades was destined to change the structure of Christianity for all time: 'In the future, We, as the Apostle of Christ, will help choose the Bishop of Rome.' Having declared himself an apostle, Constantine proclaimed that the magnificent Lateran Palace was to be the Bishops' future residence.

When Miltiades died in 314, he was the first Bishop of Rome in a long succession to die in natural circumstances. Quite suddenly, Christianity had become respectable, and was approved as an Imperial religion. Constantine became Caesar of all the Roman Empire in 324, thereafter to be known as Constantine the Great.

To replace Miltiades, Constantine (in breach of traditional practice) chose his own associate, Silvester, to be the first Imperial Bishop. He was crowned with great pomp and ceremony – a far cry from the shady backroom proceedings customary to previous Christian ritual. Gone were the days of fear and persecution. But the high price for this freedom was veneration of the Emperor – precisely what the Christian forebears had struggled so hard to avoid. The rank and file had no choice in the matter, and the existing priests were quite simply instructed that their Church was now formally attached to the Empire. It was now the Church of Rome.

Silvester was too overwhelmed to perceive the trap into which he was leading the disciples of St Peter. He saw only the route to salvation offered by Constantine. Although this monumental step gained Christians the right to move openly in society, their hierarchy was now to be encased in gold, ermine, jewels, and all the trappings that the Christ himself had decried. Many followers of the faith were outraged, for their leaders had been seduced and corrupted by the very regime that had been the bane of their ancestors. They declared that the new-found status of acceptability was in no way a victory of conversion. It was an evil cloud of absolute defeat – a profanation of all the principles they had so long held sacred.

Up to that point the Christian message had been gaining support in all quarters. Those spreading the Gospel knew that Constantine and his predecessors were sorely weakened in the face of the Church's evident gradual success. It was, after all, one of the reasons why Constantine's father had married Britain's

Christian Princess Elaine (Helena). Silvester and his colleagues in Rome may have considered the new alliance to be a politically sound manoeuvre, but the emissaries in the field viewed it for precisely what it was: a strategic buy-out by the enemy. They claimed that the spiritual message of St Peter had been subverted by the idolatry of a self-seeking power striving to prevent its Imperial demise. In real terms, the very purpose of Christianity was nullified by the new regime. After nearly three centuries of strife and struggle, Jesus's own ideal had been forsaken altogether – handed over on a plate to be devoured by his adversaries.

Apart from various cultic beliefs, the Romans had worshipped the Emperors in their capacity as gods descended from others like Neptune and Jupiter. At the Council of Arles in 314,[5] Constantine retained his own divine status by introducing the omnipotent God of the Christians as his personal sponsor. He then dealt with the anomalies of doctrine by replacing certain aspects of Christian ritual with the familiar pagan traditions of sun worship, together with other teachings of Syrian and Persian origin. In short, the new religion of the Roman Church was constructed as a 'hybrid' to appease all influential factions. By this means, Constantine looked towards a common and unified 'world' religion ('Catholic' meaning *universal*) with himself at its head.

## THE *DESPOSYNI* AND THE EMPEROR

From the content of many books about early Christianity, it could easily be imagined that the Roman Church was the true Church of Jesus, whereas other Christ-related beliefs were heretical and ungodly. This is far from the truth; many branches of Christianity were actually far less pagan than the politically-contrived

Church of Rome. They despised the idols and opulent trappings of the Roman ideal – and for their pains were accordingly outlawed by imperial decree. In particular, the esoteric Gnostics were condemned as heathen for insisting that the *spirit* was good, but that *matter* was defiled. This distinction certainly did not suit the highly materialistic attitudes of the new Church. In the same way, Manichaeism (which was of Gnostic origin) was denounced for teaching that materialism was an evil invasion of the sacred spirit.

And then there were still those of the Nazarene tradition, who upheld the original cause of Jesus rather than the eccentric and embellished teachings of Paul that were so expediently misappropriated by Rome. These Judaic-Christians of the traditional school controlled many of the principal churches of the Near East during the reign of Constantine. Moreover, they were led by none other than the bloodline descendants of Jesus's own family – the *Desposyni* ([heirs] of the Lord).

In 318 a *Desposyni* delegation sailed to Ostia, and then journeyed by donkey to Rome where, at the newly commissioned Lateran Palace, the men were given audience by Bishop Silvester. Through their chief spokesman Joses (said to be a descendant of Jesus's brother Jude), the *Desposyni* argued strongly that the Church should rightfully be centred in Jerusalem, not in Rome. They claimed that the Bishop of Jerusalem should be a true hereditary *Desposynos*, while the bishops of other major centres – such as Alexandria, Antioch and Ephesus – should be at least related. Not surprisingly, their demands were in vain, for Silvester was hardly in a position to countermand the decrees of the Emperor. He informed the delegation that they had no place in the new Christian order. The teachings of Jesus had been superseded by a doctrine that had been amended to be more amenable to imperial requirement.

In no uncertain terms, Silvester informed them that the power of salvation rested not in Jesus the Christ but in Emperor Constantine!

In that Emperors had for centuries been accorded due reverence as deities on Earth, and that Constantine had officially claimed apostolic descent, there was still one significant door left to close. After the visit of the *Desposyni*, he dealt with this very expediently at the Council of Nicaea in 325. The Pauline Christians had been expecting a Second Coming of their Messiah sooner or later, and so Constantine had to demolish this expectation. The mission of Jesus to throw off Roman dominion had failed because of disunity among the sectarian Jews. Constantine took advantage of this failure by sowing the seed of an idea – perhaps Jesus was not the awaited Messiah as perceived! Furthermore, since it was the Emperor who had ensured the Christians' freedom within the Empire, then surely their true Saviour was not Jesus but Constantine! After all, his royal mother, Helena, was of Arimatheac descent. The Emperor knew, of course, that Jesus had been venerated by Paul as the *Son of God*, but there was no room for such a concept to persist. Jesus and God had to be merged into one entity, so that the Son was identified with the Father. It thus transpired at the Council of Nicaea that God was formally defined as Three Persons in One God: a deity comprising three coequal and coeternal parts – the Father, Son and Holy Spirit (or Holy Ghost).

These aspects (persons) of the Trinity bore an uncanny resemblance to the three priestly designations, the *Father*, *Son* and the *Spirit*, as used so long before by the Essenes at Qumran.[6]

There were nonetheless some bishops who opposed this new dogma. Many of the delegates were Christian theologians of the old school who averred that Jesus was the Son, and, furthermore, that the Son had been

created in the flesh by God – but he was not himself
God. The leading spokesman for this faction was an
aged Libyan priest of Alexandria named Arius. But
when Arius rose to speak, Nicholas of Myra punched
him in the face – and that swiftly dealt with the opposition! The Nicene Creed of the Trinity of God was
established as the basis for the new, reformed, orthodox
Christian belief. The followers of Arius (thereafter
known as Arians) were banished. Some delegates, including Bishop Eusebius of Caesaria, were prepared to
compromise in the matter, but this was not acceptable,
and they were compelled to relent fully in favour of the
new Creed. And so it was that with God designated as
both the Father and the Son, Jesus was conveniently
bypassed as a figure of any practical significance. It was
the Emperor who now was regarded as the Messianic
godhead – not only from that moment, but as of right
through an inheritance deemed reserved for him 'since
the beginning of time'.

Within its revised structure, the Roman Church was
presumed safe from the emergence of any alternative
Christian champion. Indeed, once the historical Jesus
had been strategically sidelined, the Christian religion
was said to have been named after a man called Chres-
tus who, in AD 49, had led the early riots which caused
a large number of Jews to be expelled from Rome. There
were now only two official objects of worship: the Holy
Trinity of God, and the Emperor himself – the newly
designated Saviour of the World. Anyone who dis-
puted this in any way was at once declared a heretic.
Christians who attempted to retain loyalty to Jesus as
the Messianic Christ were discounted by the Imperial
Church as heathens.

Meanwhile, it had been customary (through generations of leaders since Prince Linus) for the prevailing
Bishop of Rome to nominate his own successor before

he died. This naturally changed once Constantine proclaimed himself God's Apostle on Earth. It became the
Emperor's right to ratify appointments, and the candidates, with their adherents, came physically to blows
with one another on occasions, giving rise to a good deal
of bloodshed in the streets. The theory of Apostolic
Succession was retained, but the candidature was in
practice a farce. Bishops of Rome were thereafter generally selected from the Emperors' own nominees.

In 330, Constantine declared Byzantium the capital
of the Eastern (Byzantine) Empire, and renamed it Constantinople. In the following year he convened a
General Council in that city to ratify the decision of the
earlier Council of Nicaea. On this occasion the doctrine
of Arius (which had gained a significant following in
the interim) was formally declared blasphemous. The
Emperor's management of the Church was very much
a part of his overall autocratic style. His rule was absolute, and the Church was no more than a department of
his Empire. Silvester might well have been the appointed senior bishop as the Bishop of Rome, but his
name barely featured in a sequence of events that were
dictated by Constantine, and that forever changed the
nature and purpose of Christianity.

Once this form of Roman Christianity had been established as the new imperial religion, an even more
totalitarian edict was to come at the behest of Emperor
Theodosius the Great (ruled 379–395). In 381 a second
Ecumenical Council of Constantinople was convened
with the purpose of ending the Arian dispute. Theodosius found it difficult to implement his sole divine
right of Messianic appointment while the Arians still
preached that the Son (Jesus) had been created by God,
and that the Holy Spirit passed from the Father to the
Son. This concept had to be crushed, and Jesus had to
be removed entirely from the reckoning.

It was therefore decreed by the Church that the doctrine of the Trinity of God must be upheld by all: God was the Father, God was the Son, God was the Holy Spirit – and there was to be no more argument! Ten years later, Theodosius contrived a way to end the Arian dispute once and for all. This was facilitated by a challenge to his authority in the Macedonian port of Thessalonica, as a result of which he judicially murdered 7,000 citizens. Following this, in 391 he banned all forms of religion and any kind of religious rite other than that of the Roman Church, on pain of death. He especially forbade the assembly of unorthodox Christian groups.

## DECLINE OF THE EMPIRE

Through all of this, however, the Nazarene tradition was upheld. From the days of the early Jewish revolts the Nazarenes had retained their religion under the leadership of the *Desposyni*. They flourished in Mesopotamia, eastern Syria, southern Turkey and central Asia. Entirely divorced from the fabricated Christianity of the Roman Empire, their faith was closer to the original teachings of Jesus than any other, and had an essentially Jewish base rather than any idolatrous entanglement with sun worship or other mystery cults. In fact the Nazarenes were the purest of true Christians. Their approach to the Trinity was a simple one: God was God, and Jesus was a man – a hereditary human Messiah of the Davidic succession. They were absolutely emphatic about this, and repudiated any notion that Jesus's mother Mary was a physical virgin.

At the same time, there were others who, although prepared to accept the doctrine of the Triune God, still retained a belief in the divinity of Jesus. Their views differed considerably from that of the Nazarenes, for they believed what Paul had said – that Jesus was the Son of God. This gave rise to yet another Creed, which emerged in about 390 to become known as the Apostles' Creed. It began, 'I believe in God the Father Almighty, and in Jesus Christ his only begotten Son, our Lord.'

This front-line reintroduction of Jesus was hardly conducive to the Saviour status of the Emperor – but within a few years Rome was sacked by the Goths, and the Western Empire fell into decline.

At that point a new protagonist emerged in the dispute over the Trinity – he was Nestorius, Patriarch of Constantinople from 428. In accord with the Nazarenes, Nestorius maintained that the argument over whether Jesus was God or the Son of God was totally irrelevant, for it was plain to all that Jesus was a man, born quite naturally of a father and mother. From this platform Nestorius stood against his Catholic colleagues, who had brought Jesus back into the picture now that the Empire was failing. They referred to Mary as the *Theotokas* (Greek, 'bearer of God') or *Dei Genitrix* (Latin, 'conceiver of God'). As a result, the Nazarene/Nestorian notion that Mary was a woman like any other was condemned by the Council of Ephesus in 431, and she was thereafter venerated as a mediator (or intercessor) between God and the mortal world. As for Nestorius, he was declared a heretic and banished – but soon found himself among friends in Egypt and Turkey, establishing the Nestorian Church at Edessa in 489. It was here that Julius Africanus had previously recorded the Romans' purposeful destruction of the *Desposynic* papers of royal heritage, and had also confirmed the existence of continuing private accounts of lineage – describing the Davidic family sect as controlled by a 'strict dynastic succession'.

From the mid-5th century, the Church of Rome continued in the West while the Eastern Orthodox Church emerged from its centres at Constantinople, Alexandria, Antioch and Jerusalem. The unresolved debate over the Trinity had driven a wedge firmly between the factions, and each claimed to represent the true faith. The Church of Rome was reformed under the management of an appointed city administration – the cardinals (a title derived from Latin *cardo* [pivot], thus 'key [man]'), of whom there were 28 appointees, all stationed at the Vatican.

While the Church of Rome was being restructured, the Western Empire collapsed – demolished by the Visigoths and Vandals. The last Emperor, Romulus Augustulus, was deposed by the German chieftain Odoacer, who became King of Italy in 476. In the absence of an Emperor, the prevailing High Bishop Leo I[7] duly inherited the title of *Pontifex Maximus* (Chief Pontiff or 'bridge-builder'). In the East, however, the story was different, and the Byzantine Empire was destined to flourish for another thousand years.

As the might of Rome crumbled, so too did Roman Christianity subside. The Emperors had themselves been identified with the Christian God – but the Emperors had failed. Their religious supremacy had been switched to the Chief Pontiff, but his was now a minority religion in a Christ-related environment of Gnostics, Arians, Nazarenes, and the emergent Celtic Church.

## THE MEROVINGIAN SORCERER KINGS

During the latter years of the declining Empire, the greatest of all threats to the Roman Church arose from a *Desposynic* royal strain in Gaul. They were the Merovingian dynasty – male line descendants of the Fisher Kings, corresponding also to a Sicambrian female heritage. The Sicambrians took their name from Cambra, a tribal queen of about 380 BC. They were originally from

Scythia, north of the Black Sea, and were called the *Newmage* (New Kindred).

The Bibliothèque Nationale in Paris contains a facsimile (produced by the monk Lucerius) of the highly reputed *Fredegar's Chronicle* – an exhaustive 7th-century historical work of which the original took 35 years to compile. A special edition of Fredegar's manuscript was presented to the illustrious Nibelungen court and was recognized by the state authorities as a comprehensive, official history. Fredegar (who died in 660) was a Burgundian scribe, and his *Chronicle* covered the period from the earliest days of the Hebrew patriarchs to the era of the Merovingian kings. It cited numerous sources of information and cross-reference, including the writings of St Jerome (translator of the Old Testament into Latin), Archbishop Isidore of Seville (author of the *Encyclopedia of Knowledge*), and Bishop Gregory of Tours (author of *The History of the Franks*).

Fredegar's *Prologue* asserts that his own researches were if anything even more painstaking than those of other writers he quotes. He says,

> I have judged it necessary to be more thorough in my determination to achieve accuracy . . . and so I have included . . . (as if source material for a future work) all the reigns of the kings and their chronology.

To achieve such accuracy Fredegar, who was of high standing with Burgundian royalty, made use of his access to a variety of Church records and State annals. He tells how the Sicambrian line of 'Franks' – from whom France acquired its name – were themselves first so called after their chief Francio (a descendant of Noah) who died in 11 BC. Prior to their Scythian days, Francio's race originated in ancient Troy (in what is now north-western Turkey), after which the French city of Troyes was named. The city of Paris (established by

6th-century Merovingians) likewise bears the name of Prince Paris (the son of King Priam of Troy) whose liaison with Helen of Sparta caused the Trojan War.

In the 4th century the Sicambrian Franks were in the Rhineland, to which they had moved from Pannonia (west of the Danube) in 388 under their chiefs Genobaud, Marcomer and Sunno. Settling into the region of Germania, they established their seat at Cologne. Over the next century, their armies invaded Roman Gaul and overran the area that is now Belgium and northern France. It was at this stage that Genobaud's daughter Argotta married the Fisher King Faramund (or Pharamond, reigned 419–430), who is often cited to have been the true patriarch of the French monarchy. Faramund was the grandson of Boaz (Anfortas – to whom we shall return) in the direct Messianic succession from Josue's son Aminadab (Christine line), who married King Lucius' daughter Eurgen ( Arimatheac line).

Faramund, however, was not the only marital partner with a Messianic heritage. Argotta was herself descended from King Lucius' sister Athildis, who married the Sicambrian chief Marcomer (8th in descent from Francio) in about AD 130. Thus the Merovingian succession which ensued from Faramund and Argotta was dually *Desposynic*.

Argotta's father, Genobaud, Lord of the Franks, was the last male of his line, and so Faramund and Argotta's son Clodion duly became the next Guardian of the Franks in Gaul.

Clodion's son Meroveus was in due time proclaimed Guardian (Lord) at Tournai in 448, and it was after him that the line became noted as the mystical dynasty of Merovingians, as they rose to prominence as Kings of the Franks. They reigned not by coronation or created appointment, but by an accepted tradition that corresponded to the Messianic right of past

**SICAMBRIAN FRANKS AND THE FIRST MEROVINGIANS**
*4th to 6th century*

Dagobert d. 317
[ See Chart: SICAMBRIAN DESCENT ]

Chiefs of Sicambrian Franks

| | | |
|---|---|---|
| Clodius d. 319 | Clodomir d. 337 | Genebaud d. 358 |
| | Richemir d. 350 | Dagobert d. 379 |
| | Theodomir d. 360 | Clodius d. 389 |
| | Clodius d. 378 | Marcomer d. 404 |

Dagobert d. 389    Marcomer d.s.p. 393

**Messianic Descent**
[ See Chart: BLOODLINE OF THE GRAIL ]

FROTMUND
c. 400

Genobaud d. 419    Marcomer    Sunno
Lord of the Franks    d.s.p. 414    d.s.p. 414

Marcomer
Lord of the East Franks
d. 423

FARAMUND (Pharamond) . . . . . . . . . = . . . . . . . . *Princess Argotta*
Lord of the West Franks 419-430    *(Sicambrian heiress)*

CLODION of Tournai    Fredemundus    Frotmund
(Clodius Crintus)
Salian Chief & Neptunis d'Arcadie
Lord of West Franks 430-446
= *Queen Basina I*
*widow of King Weldephus of Thuringia*

East Franks descend to
Counts of Rattenburg

MEROVEUS    Nascien I    Saracint    Sires of France,
King of the Franks    Prince of the Septimanian    Comtes de Toulouse
d. 456    Midi    & the House del Acqs
= *Merira*

Celedoin    Eliezer

KING CHILDERIC
of Franks d. 481
= *Basina II, ex-wife of*    Nascien II
*King Basin of Thuringia*

King Chilperic    Gondebaut    Galains    Godefil
of Burgundy d. 504    King of Burgundy    Prince of the Midi    d. 504
(Succeeded Gundioch, son of Tabica)    d. 508

KING CLOVIS . . . . . . = . . . . *Clotilde*    Jonaans
of Franks d. 511    d. 550
                    (492)

Counts of    Counts of    Counts of
Brittany    Liege    Ardennes

MEROVINGIAN
KINGS

generations, through the succession of Fisher King (Priest-King) Faramund.

Despite the carefully listed genealogies of his time, the heritage of Meroveus was strangely obscured in the monastic annals. Although the rightful son of Clodion, he was nonetheless said by the historian Priscus to have been sired by an arcane sea creature, the *Bistea Neptunis* (as discussed in the next chapter). There was evidently something very special about King Meroveus and his priestly successors, for they were accorded special veneration and were widely known for their esoteric knowledge and occult skills.[8] The 6th-century Gregory of Tours stated that the Frankish chiefs in the Sicambrian female line of their ancestry were not generally known for their ascetic culture, yet this learned dynasty – from what he called 'the foremost and most noble line of their race' (the descendants of Argotta and Faramund) – emerged in the ancient Nazarite tradition to become the 'long-haired Sorcerer Kings'.

In the Old Testament (Numbers 6:1–13 and elsewhere), Nazarites were Jews such as Samson and Samuel who were bound by strict vows of obligation:

> He shall separate himself from wine and strong drink . . .
> All the days of the vow of his separation there shall no razor come upon his head: until the days be fulfilled, in the which he separateth himself unto the Lord, he shall be holy, and shall let the locks of the hair of his head grow . . .
> And this is the law of the Nazarite .
>
> (Numbers 6:3, 5, 13)

Nazarite vows were binding for specified terms. In the Essene tradition, periods of absolute celibacy were also implemented. The rank of Chief Nazarite was traditionally held by the Davidic Crown Prince, who wore ceremonial black. In this capacity, the royal head of the

**MEROVINGIAN KINGS**
*House of Meroveus – 5th to 8th century*

Clodion of Tournai d. 446
= *Queen Basina*

(3)       (1)       (2)

Sigimer
= *Dau. of Roman
Senator, Ferreolus*

MEROVEUS
Founder of Merovingian Dynasty
d. 456
= *Meira*

Alberic
Lord of Moselle
= *Arotta of the
Ostrogoths*

Ferreolus
Lord of Moselle
= *Dinteria (Roman)*

CHILDERIC = *Basina II - Queen of Thuringia*
d. 481     *ex-wife of King Basin*

Vaubert
d. 528
= *Lucilla (Roman)*

CLOVIS I (1) .............. (2)
d. 511   = *Evochild*   = *Clotilde of Burgundy*

Clotilde
= King Almaric
of the Visigoths

THEUDERIC I   CHLODOMER   CHILDEBERT I
d. 534       d. 524       d. 558

THEUDEBERT   THEUDEBALD
d. 548       d. 555

LOTHAR I (1) (sisters) (2)
d. 561   = *Ingund*   = *Aregund*

Ansbert ... = ... *Blitildis*
d. 570

Carloman
of Brabant

CHARIBERT
d. 567

GUNTRAM
d. 593

SIGEBERT I
d. 575
= *Brunhilde
(Visigoth)*

CHILPERIC
d. 584
= *Fredegund*

Arnoald
of Scheldt
d. 601
= *Princess Dua
of Swabia*

Pepin I
Lord of Brabant
Mayor of Palace
of Austrasia d. 647

CHILDEBERT II
d. 595
= 1. *(Mistress)* = 2. *Faileuba*

LOTHAR II
d. 629

Arnulf
Bishop of Metz
d. 641
= *Dobo (Saxon)*

THEUDEBERT
d. 612

THUDERIC II
d. 613

DAGOBERT I
( the Great ) d. 638
= *Raintrude*
= *Nanthilda*

Ansegis ......... = *Begga
of Brabant*
Lord of Brabant
Margrave of Scheldt
d. 685

Grimoald
Lord of Brabant
Mayor of Palace
of Austrasia
d. 656

*Map 7* England, Ireland and Wales – Celtic and
Anglo-Saxon Lands

order had once been Jesus's brother James the Just, and the successive *de jure* Crown Princes of Judah retained the status and its responsibilities.

Regardless of their ultimately Jewish descent, the Merovingians were not practising Jews, but neither were other non-Roman Christians whose beliefs had sprung from Judaic origins. The Catholic Gregory of Tours described them as 'followers of idolatrous practices', but the priestly Merovingians were not pagan in any sense of being unenlightened. Their spiritual cult was not dissimilar to that of the Druids, and they were greatly revered as esoteric teachers, judges, faith-healers and clairvoyants. Although closely associated with the Burgundians, the Merovingians were not influenced by Arianism, and their unique establishment was neither Gallo-Roman nor Teutonic. Indeed, it was said to be 'something entirely new': the culture seemed to appear from out of nowhere.

The Merovingian kings did not rule the land, nor were they politically active; governmental functions were performed by their 'Mayors of the Palace' (chief/prime ministers). The kings were more concerned with military and social matters. Among their primary interests were education, agriculture and maritime trade. They were avid students of proper kingly practice in the ancient tradition, and their model was King Solomon,[9] the son of David. Their disciplines were largely based on Old Testament scripture – but the Roman Church nevertheless proclaimed them irreligious.

Not only were the Merovingians akin to the early Nazarites, but they retained other customs from Biblical times. According to Essene tradition, boys were 'reborn' at the age of 12 when, dressed in a simple robe, they would undergo a ritual re-enactment of birth – a Second Birth (as was mentioned earlier in relation to Jesus

Justus). The boy would thus symbolically be 'born again from his mother's womb', and installed in his community position. Merovingian royalty followed a similar practice: kings' sons were granted a hereditary right to dynastic kingship by initiation on their twelfth birthday. There was no need for later coronation. The dynasty was not one of *created* kings but a succession of *natural* kings, whose entitlement to the crown was automatic by virtue of hallowed appointment. As we have seen, the Merovingians were not only of Christine descent, but were descended from James (Joseph of Arimathea) through both the sister and daughter of King Lucius.[10]

The Essene custom of 'Second Birth' is evidenced in the Gospels, although in a very obscure manner that was completely misunderstood in translation. In Luke 2:1–12, Jesus's own ceremony of 'Second Birth' was chronologically confused with his actual birth.[11] As in the other Gospels, Luke dates the Nativity (the First or actual birth of Jesus) during the latter reign of Herod the Great, who died in 4 BC. But Luke also states that Cyrenius (Quirinius) was Governor of Syria at the time, and that the Emperor Caesar Augustus had instituted a national census. In reality Cyrenius was never Governor of Syria while Herod was alive; he was appointed to the office in AD 6 when, according to Josephus in the *Antiquities*, there was a head-count in Judaea conducted by Cyrenius at the behest of Caesar. This is the only recorded census for the region; there was none in Herod's time. The census was held 12 years after Jesus's 'First (actual) Birth' – precisely in the year of his 'Second (initiatory) Birth'.

This error was in turn responsible for the chronological confusion that surrounds the story of how Jesus was delayed at the Temple when in Jerusalem with his parents (Luke 2:41–50). The event is reported as occurring when Jesus was aged 12 – but it should actually relate to his designated 'twelfth year' – that is, not twelve years after his birth into the world, but twelve years after his 'birth into the Community'. At the Passover of that year, Jesus would actually have been 24 (or 23 in accordance with his 'official' September birthday). At that time, he would have been raised from initiate to manhood, but instead of accompanying his parents to the related celebrations, he stayed behind to discuss his 'Father's business'. His spiritual 'Father' at that time was the priest Eleazer Annas.

Throughout his childhood Jesus had been associated with brilliant teachers and astronomers – in particular the philosophical Magi, who were so admired by the Merovingians. In Merovingian times, the three wise Magi of the Nativity became the patron saints of Frankish Cologne, having in the meantime been spuriously dubbed Caspar, Melchior and Balthazar.

The Merovingian kings were noted sorcerers in the manner of the Samaritan Magi, and they firmly believed in the hidden powers of the honeycomb. Because a honeycomb is naturally made up of hexagonal prisms, it was considered by philosophers to be the manifestation of divine harmony in nature.[12] Its construction was associated with insight and wisdom – as detailed in Proverbs 24:13–14:

> My son, eat thou honey, because it is good . . .
> So shall the knowledge of wisdom be unto thy soul . . .

To the Merovingians, the bee was a most hallowed creature. A sacred emblem of Egyptian royalty, it became a symbol of Wisdom. Some 300 small golden bees were found stitched to the cloak of Childeric I (the son of Meroveus) when his grave was unearthed in 1653. Napoleon had these attached to his own coronation robe in 1804. He claimed this right by virtue of his descent from James de Rohan-Stuardo, the natural son (legitimated

1667) of Charles II Stuart of Britain by Marguerite, Duchesse de Rohan. The Stuarts were in turn entitled to this distinction because they, and their related Counts of Brittany, were descended from Clodion's brother Fredemundus – thus (akin to the Merovingians) they were equally in descent from the Fisher Kings through Faramund. The Merovingian bee was adopted by the exiled Stuarts in Europe, and engraved bees are still to be seen on some Jacobite glassware.

When Meroveus' son Childeric died in 481, he was succeeded by his son Clovis, the most prominent of all Merovingian kings and the essential founder of the French monarchy. In the first instance, Clovis (whose mother was the Thuringian ex-Queen Basina) succeeded his father in the region of Tournai at the age of 15. During the next five years, however, he led his armies southward from the Ardennes, pushing out the Gallo-Romans, so that by 486 his realm included such centres as Reims and Troyes. The Romans managed to retain a kingdom at Soissons, but Clovis defeated their forces, and the ruler, Syagrius, fled to the Visigoth court of King Alaric II. At this, Clovis threatened war against Alaric, and the fugitive was handed over for execution. By his early twenties, with both the Romans and the Visigoths at his feet, Clovis was destined to become the most influential figure in the West.

At that time the Roman Church greatly feared the increasing popularity of Arianism[13] in Gaul. Catholicism was dangerously close to being overrun in Western Europe, where the majority of active bishoprics were Arian. Clovis was neither Catholic nor Arian. It therefore occurred to the Roman hierarchy that the rise of Clovis could be used to their advantage. As it transpired, Clovis aided them quite inadvertently when he married the Burgundian Princess Clotilde. The couple were first united at the Black Madonna centre of Ferrières.[14]

Although the Burgundians were traditionally Arian in their beliefs, Clotilde was herself a Catholic, and she made it her business to evangelize her version of the faith. For a time she had no success in promoting the doctrine to her husband, but her luck changed in 496. King Clovis and his army were then locked in battle against the invading Alamanni tribe near Cologne. For once in his illustrious military career, the Merovingian was losing. In a moment of desperation he invoked the name of Jesus at much the same instant that the Alaman king was slain. On the loss of their leader, the Alamanni faltered and fell into retreat. Clotilde afterwards wasted no time in claiming that Jesus had caused the Merovingian victory. Clovis was not especially convinced of this, but his wife sent immediately for St Rémy, Bishop of Reims, and arranged for Clovis to be baptized.[15]

In due allegiance to their leader, around half of the Merovingian warriors followed Clovis to the font. Word soon spread that the high potentate of the West was a Catholic, and this was of enormous value to Bishop Anastasius in Rome. A great wave of conversions followed, and the Roman Church was effectively saved from almost inevitable collapse. In fact, were it not for the baptism of King Clovis, the ultimate Christian religion of Western Europe might well now be Arian rather than Catholic. Nevertheless, the royal compliance was not a one-way bargain; in return for the king's agreement to be baptized, the Roman authorities pledged an allegiance to him and his descendants. They promised that a new 'holy empire' would be established under the Merovingians. Clovis had no reason to doubt the sincerity of the Roman alliance – but he unwittingly became the instrument of a bishops' conspiracy against the Messianic bloodline. With the blessing of the Church, Clovis was empowered to move his troops into Burgundy and Aquitaine. It was calculated that by virtue of this, the Arians would be obliged to accept Catholicism. But the Romans also had a longer-term plan in mind: in time the Merovingians could be strategically manoeuvred out of the picture, to leave the Bishop of Rome supreme in Gaul.[16]

Following a succession of military conquests, King Clovis died in Paris at the age of 45. He was succeeded by his sons Theuderic, Chlodomir, Childebert and Lothar. At that time, in 511, the Merovingian domain was divided into separate kingdoms. Theuderic succeeded in Austrasia (from Cologne to Basle) based at Metz. From Orléans in Burgundy, Chlodomir supervised the Loire Valley and the west of Aquitaine around Toulouse and Bordeaux. Childebert succeeded in the region from the Seine across Neustria to Armorica (Brittany) with his capital at Paris; and Lothar inherited the kingdom between the Scheldt and the Somme, with his centre at Soissons. Their decades of combined rule were tempestuous; conflicts continued against the Gothic tribes and eventually afforded Merovingian penetration into eastern Aquitaine, with Burgundy being fully absorbed into the realm.

Lothar was the last of the four to die, in 561, having previously become overall king. His sons Sigebert and Chilperic succeeded, with the line from Chilperic settling four generations later on Dagobert II, who became King of Austrasia in 674. By then a council of leading bishops had extended the authority and immunities of the Church, while also reducing the powers of taxation and general administration by the royal house. In consequence, the key provinces of the Merovingian realm were under the immediate supervision of the Mayors of the Palace, who were themselves closely allied to the Catholic bishops. The Roman dismantling of Merovingian supremacy had begun.

# TWELVE

# ELEMENTS OF ARTHURIAN LORE

## ANFORTAS, ST MICHAEL AND GALAHAD

The Sicambrian Franks, from whose female line the Merovingians emerged, were associated with Grecian Arcadia before migrating to the Rhineland. As we have seen, they called themselves the *Newmage* – 'People of the New Covenant', just as the Essenes of Qumran had once been known.[1] It was the Arcadian legacy that was responsible for the mysterious sea beast – the *Bistea Neptunis* – as symbolically defined in the Merovingian ancestry.[2] The relevant sea-lord was King Pallas, a god of old Arcadia. His predecessor was the great Oceanus.

The immortal sea-lord was said to be 'ever incarnate in a dynasty of ancient kings' whose symbol was a fish – as was the traditional symbol of Jesus. Among the early Hellenized Jews, a word for 'fish' was the Greek *ichthys*. Its image was used as a memorable acronym representing *Iesus Christos Theos* (Jesus the Christ, God: in Greek and Latin the letter *J* was identical with *I*).

The fish was an emblem of the Merovingian kings, along with the Lion of Judah. The *fleur-de-lys* was also introduced in the late 5th century by King Clovis to denote the royal bloodline of France. Prior to this, the familiar Judaic trefoil had been emblematic of the covenant of circumcision. Both the lion rampant and the *fleur-de-lys* were incorporated in the later arms of the Royal House of Scots. As shown in medieval seals and watermarks, moreover, the lion and the fish were often amalgamated with the *fleur-de-lys* – indicative of the conjoined royal strains of France and Judah. In Arthurian lore, the Davidic sovereign lineage was represented by the Fisher Kings of the Grail Family, and the patriarchal line was denoted by the name *Anfortas*, a symbolic name corrupted from *In fortis* (Latin for 'in strength'). It was identified with the Hebrew name *Boaz* (the great-grandfather of David, who is remembered in modern Freemasonry), similarly meaning 'in strength'.

The name *Boaz* was given to the left-hand pillar of King Solomon's Temple (1 Kings 7:21 and 2 Chronicles 3:17). Its capitals – and those of the right-hand pillar, Jachin ('He shall establish') – were decorated with brass pomegranates (1 Kings 7:41–42), a symbol of male fertility, as identified in the *Song of Solomon* 4:13. It is not by chance that Botticelli's famous paintings, *The Madonna of the Pomegranate* and *The Madonna of the Magnificat*, both show the infant Jesus clutching a ripe, open pomegranate.[3] Indeed, from 1483 to 1510, Botticelli (more correctly, Sandro Filipepi) was Helmsman of the Priory Notre Dame de Sion, an esoteric society with Grail connections. In the Grail tradition of Botticelli's time, the Arcadian sea-lord, Pallas, was manifest in King Pelles: 'My name is Pelles, king of the foreign country, and cousin nigh to Joseph of Arimathea.' It was his daughter, Elaine, who was the Grail Bearer of le Corbenic (*Cors Beneicon*, the Blessed Body) and the mother of Galahad by Lancelot del Acqs.

The Chapel of St Michael, Glastonbury, was established by King Lucius on an ancient pagan site. To this place, the St Michael ley line runs from St Michael's Mount, Marazion – through St Michael's Church, Brentor; St Michael's church, Burrowbridge Mump; St Michael's Church, Othery – onwards to Stoke St Michael.[4]

St Michael, to whom so many churches were dedicated, was not a traditional clerical or martyred saint, but corresponds to the Archangel Michael, who is mentioned only once in the New Testament (Revelation 12:7). In his 1st-century work *The Wars of the Jews*, Flavius Josephus confirmed that the Essenes of Qumran vowed to preserve the names of the angels within their priestly hierarchy.[5] The holder of the angelic style 'Michael' was the Zadokite priest. In descent from the original Zadok of King David's era, the 'Michael' at the time of Jesus was John the Baptist, who had inherited the office from his father Zacharias.[6]

Up to that point, the *de jure* Davidic king always had been ranked separately from the angelic priests Michael, Gabriel, Sariel and Raphael. However, both the Zadok and David lines were strictly dynastic, and when John the Baptist died he left no successor. Jesus tried on many occasions to gain recognition as a priest – he even promoted himself visibly as such at what came to be called the *Transfiguration*.[7] But it was not until the *Ascension* that his priesthood was formalized, on being 'carried to the Kingdom of Heaven' (the high monastery) to become a High Priest (Hebrews 3:1) in the Order of Melchizedek (Hebrews 5:6). His dynastic role then became dually Messianic – that of a Priest-King (or, as related in Grail lore, a 'Fisher King'). For the first time since the era of David and Zadok, the kingly and angelic titles were conjoined: Jesus became both the 'David' and the 'Michael':

Whither the forerunner is for us entered, even Jesus, made
an high priest for ever after the order of Melchizedek.

(Hebrews 6:20)

Fragments of the *Prince Melchizedek Document* found
among the Dead Sea Scrolls indicate that Melchizedek
and Michael were one and the same. It is this representation which features in the Revelation when the
Archangel Michael (the descending Zadokite power of
the Messiah) fights with the Roman dragon of oppression.

Hebrews 7:14 totally dismisses the Gospel-inter-
preted notion of the Virgin Birth in order to confirm
that Jesus's real father was Joseph. It states: 'it is evident that our Lord sprang out of Judah, of which tribe
Moses spake nothing concerning priesthood'. It is also
explained that the Law concerning priesthood was
changed to accommodate Jesus's new archangelic distinction (Hebrews 7:12).

From that time, the dynastic Melchizedek (Melchi-
Zadok) succession lay with Jesus's own male line –
descending through the Fisher Kings. This was the line
of the Davidic *Sangréal* – the Blood Royal of Judah, more
romantically known as the 'Grail Family'. In the early
days, they were not actual (*de facto*) monarchs but were
Priest-Kings by right (*de jure*). Not until the 5th century
– when the descendant Fisher King, Faramund, married
Princess Argotta, heiress of the Sicambrian Franks – did
the Christine line begin its impressive rise to prominence. It was by no coincidence that St Michael's presence was recorded in Cornwall in around 495, and in
Gaul in about 580. Each senior descendant in the Grail line
was the dynastic 'Michael', and the Cornish town of
Marazion had Judaic origins, its name (meaning Market
Zion) being synonymous with Jerusalem. Across the
low-tide causeway from Marazion stands St Michael's

Mount – the location of an early Celtic monastery. This became a Benedictine priory in the 8th century, and was a designated cell of the Abbey of St Michel in Brittany.

Within the traditional Grail stories there is a consistency of names with Jewish or apparently Jewish implications: names such as Josephes, Lot, Elinant, Galahad, Bron, Urien, Hebron, Pelles, Joseus, Jonas, Ban, and so on. In almost all of the legends, including Sir Thomas Malory's later 15th-century accounts, accentuated digressions constantly occur to tell of the Fisher Kings. In addition, there are many references to Joseph of Arimathea, King David and King Solomon. Even the priestly Judas Maccabaeus (who died in 161 BC) is featured. His Hasmonaean warriors were the champions of Jerusalem against the Syrians. Over the years, many have thought it strange that this well-born Judaean hero is treated with such high esteem in a seemingly Christianized Grail story:

> 'Sir Knight,' saith he to Messire Gawain, 'I pray you bide . . . and conquer this shield, or otherwise I shall conquer you . . . for it belonged to the best knight of his faith that was ever . . . and the wisest.'
> 'Who then was he?' saith Messire Gawain.
> 'Judas Machabee was he . . .'
> 'You say true,' saith Messire Gawain, 'and what is your name?'
> 'Sir, my name is Joseus, and I am of the lineage of Joseph of Abarimacie. King Pelles is my father, that is in the forest, and King Fisherman is my uncle.'[8]

It is known that some of the knights attributed to King Arthur were based on real characters – particularly Lancelot, Bors and Lionel, who were connected to the del Acqs branch of the Grail Family. But what of the others? The indications are that many had factual origins, although not necessarily from the Arthurian era. When the majority of Grail romances were written in the Middle Ages there was little love for the Jews in Europe. Dispersed from Palestine, many had settled in various parts of the West, but owning no land to cultivate they turned to trade and banking. This was not welcomed by the Christians, and so money-lending was prohibited by the Church of Rome. In the light of this, King Edward I had all Jews expelled from England in 1209 – except for skilled physicians. In such an atmosphere, it is quite apparent that medieval writers (whether in Britain or continental Europe) would not have found it natural or politically correct to use a string of Jewish-sounding names for local heroes, knights and kings. Yet the names persist, from those of the early protagonists such as Josephes to that of the later Galahad.

In the early Grail stories, Galahad was identified by the Hebrew name *Gilead*. The original Gilead was a son of Michael, the great-great-grandson of Nahor, brother of Abraham (1 Chronicles 5:14). *Gilead* means 'a heap of testimony'; the mountain called Gilead was the 'Mount of Witness' (Genesis 31:21–25), and *Galeed* was Jacob's cairn, the 'Heap of the Witness' (Genesis 31:46–48). In the footsteps of Bernard de Clairvaux, the Lincolnshire Abbot Gilbert of Holland equated the Arthurian Galahad directly with the family of Jesus in the Cistercian *Sermons on the Canticles*. Christian writers would not have exalted men of Jewish heritage to high positions in a chivalric environment unless their names were already known and well established. Evidently the characters were real enough, even though their individual time-frames were brought into common alignment for the romances.

**THE HOLY FAMILIES OF BRITAIN** *Saints and Sovereign Houses – 1st to 6th century*

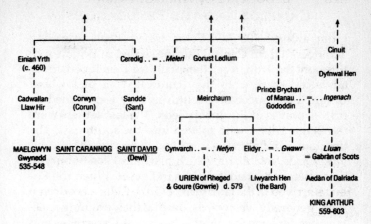

## CAMELOT AND THE PENDRAGONS

From around 700 BC, Celtic tribes (*Keltoi* meaning 'strangers') from Central Europe settled in Britain and, through the Iron Age, their culture developed to an advanced stage until they controlled all of lowland Britain. Over successive centuries they were joined by further waves of European Celts. The last settlers were the Belgic tribes, who moved into the south-east. The previous inhabitants spread northwards and westwards, establishing such places as Glastonbury in Somerset, and Maiden Castle in Dorset. When the Romans arrived in the later years BC, the Celts were driven more generally westwards, despite their ongoing resistance under such formidable leaders as Caractacus and Boudicca (Victoria). The Romans called the ancient Britons *Pretani*, a name that derived from the Cymric language of old Wales in which the whole mainland island was called *B'rith-ain*, meaning 'Covenant Land'.[9]

The Romans had considerable success in their conquest of Britain, but they could never defeat the Celts of Caledonia – those of the far north. Because of this, Emperor Hadrian (ruled AD 117–138) had built a great wall across the entire country to separate the cultures. A majority of Celts south of the wall adopted the Roman way of life, but their fiery northern cousins kept on fighting. The mountainous highlands and islands of Caledonia were inhabited by the Picts (Latin, *Picti* 'the painted men'), and the north of Ireland was then the province of the *Scots* Gaels.

In Wales, the early rulers of Powys and Gwynedd descended from Avallach in the line of Beli Mawr (sometimes called Bili, Billi or Heli). Beli the Great (*Mawr*) – a 1st-century BC overlord of the Britons – is a good example of a character whose time-frame is often confused because of the fables that have grown around him. His grandson was the Archdruid Brân the Blessed (son-in-law of James/Joseph of Arimathea). By virtue of their historical association, Beli and Brân are often muddled with the earlier brothers Belinus and Brennus (the sons of Porrex) who contended for power in northern Britain in around 390 BC, and were regarded as gods in the old Celtic tradition.

More potential confusion arises in that Brân the Blessed is often cited as the 'father' of Caractacus. They were indeed contemporaries in the 1st century AD, but Caractacus' father was Cymbeline of Camulod. The persistent anomaly has fostered no end of complications in books dealing with lineage in the Dark Ages, but the cause is easily explained. Brân's father, in descent from Beli Mawr, was King Llyr (Lear). Some generations later, in a succession from King Lucius, the names were repeated during the 3rd and 4th centuries. The later Welsh chief Llyr Llediath was the father of another Brân, father of Caradawc (a variant of the name Caractacus or Caratacus). A further cause of confusion lies in the fact that, as the Archdruid, Brân was the designated 'patriarchal' *Father*. In symbolic terms, therefore, Brân would indeed have been the 'father' of Caractacus, just as Eleazer Annas and Simon Zelotes were Jesus's spiritual 'fathers' in Judaea.

From the name *Beli* or *Billi* London's Billingsgate is partly derived. His descendant, Avallach, was the grandson of Joseph of Arimathea's daughter Anna, the wife of Archdruid Brân the Blessed. Joseph's own wife was also called Anna (meaning grace).[10] As previously discussed, *Avallach*[11] was a descriptive title and, in the same way, the name *Beli* was also titular – denoting a 'sovereign lord'. As such, it too was historically repetitive. Another descendant of Beli Mawr was King Llud (after whom London's Ludgate is partly named). He was the progenitor of the kingly houses of Colchester, Siluria, and Strathclyde, and his family celebrated key marriages into the lineage of Joseph of Arimathea (St James the Just). From among the Welsh princes in the Arimatheac succession emerged the founders and local rulers of Brittany (Little Britain), a Frankish region that had previously been called Armorica ([land] facing the sea). Another very early Davidic line, which progressed through Ugaine Már (4th century BC), maintained the lordship of Ireland as High Kings (Ard Rí) of Tara.

King Llud's grandson, the mighty Cymbeline (father of Caractacus), was the 'Pendragon' of mainland Britain during Jesus's lifetime. The Pendragon, or 'Head Dragon of the Island' (*Pen Draco Insularis*) was the King-of-Kings and 'Guardian of the Celtic Isle'. The title was not dynastic; Pendragons were appointed from Celtic royal stock by a Druidic council of elders. Cymbeline governed the Belgic tribes of the Catuvellauni and Trinovantes from his seat at Colchester – the most impressive Iron Age fort in the land. Colchester was then called Camulod (or Romanized, Camulodunum) – from the Celtic *camu lot* meaning 'curved light'. This fortified settlement became the later model for the similarly named court of *Camelot* in Arthurian romance.[12] North of Cymbeline's domain, in Norfolk, the people known as the Iceni were ruled by King Prasutagus, whose wife was the famous Boudicca (or Boadicea). She led the great, but unsuccessful, tribal revolt against Roman domination from AD 60 – yelling her famous war-cry '*Y gwir erbyn y Byd*' ('The Truth against the World'). It was immediately after this that Joseph of Arimathea came from Gaul to set up his Glastonbury church in the face of Roman imperialism.

The concept of the dragon in Celtic mythology emerged directly from the holy crocodile (the *Messeh*) of the ancient Egyptians.[13] The Pharaohs were anointed with crocodile fat, and thereby attained the fortitude of

**DESCENT TO THE RULERS OF WALES AND BRITTANY**
*Arimatheac descent – 1st to 10th century*

JOSEPH OF ARIMATHEA (Saint James the Just) d. AD 82

*Anna* = Brân (Bron)
[See Chart: ARTHURIAN DESCENT]

**ARVIRAGUS** **CARACTACUS** *Gladys*
= *Genuissa* = *Eurgain* = Aulus Plautius
Roman Commander

Beli *Penardun* = Marius

Linus *St. Eurgen* *Gladys (Claudia)*
Bishop of Rome *of Llan Ilid* b. AD 36
AD 58-78 = Salog, Lord = (AD 53) Rufus Pudens
of Salisbury Roman Senator d. AD 96

Avallach Coel I

Eugein Lleiffer Mawr (King Lucius)

Brithguein Eudelen Keribir *Gladys*
= Cadvan of Cumbria

Duvun Endos Parar

Onmum Ebiud Llyr Llediath Coel II of Colchester

Anguerit Outigar Brân *ST. HELENA (Elaine)*
248-328
= Constantius I Chlorus

Angouloyb Oudecant

Gur Dumn Retigern Caradawc Vreichvras CONSTANTINE THE GREAT
(Caratacus Strong-arm) Roman Emperor 312-337
Ruler of Gwent and Archenfield

Dumn Jumutel

Guiocein Grat Eudes (Euidaf)
Dur Gewissorum (Warlord of the Gewissi)
= Dau. of Count Carausius II of the Saxon Shore

Cein Urban

Tacit Teuhant Cynan of Ewyas *Elen (Oriene)*
= Magnus Maximus
Imperial Guletic of Britain
383-388
[See Chart: HOUSE OF AVALLON]

Patern Pesrut Techmant Caradawc II

Octern Guorepauc

COEL HEN GODEBOG of Rheged CONAN MERIADOC (Cynan)
Gwyr-y-Gogledd seat at Carlisle Duke of the Armorican Frontiers
b.c. 380 = *Ystrafael* First King of the Bretons d. 421
= St. Dererca, grand niece of
St. Martin of Tours

**CUNEDDA WLEDIG of Manau** = *Gwawl*
b.c. 395
[See Charts:
<u>RULERS OF STRATHCLYDE</u>
and
<u>ARTHURIAN DESCENT</u>]

Urbien

St. Salomon
= *Patricia Flavia*

Aldroenus
= *Sister of St. Germannus d'Auxerre*
*Duke of the Armorican Tract.*
*Dau. of Decimus Junius Rusticus, Prefect of Gaul*

Einian Yrth (Enniaun Girt) c.460

King Urien of Rheged & Goure
= *Morgaine (half-sister of Arthur)*
*Dau. of Gwryllieu, Dux Caruele,*
*and Ygerna del Acqs*

Owen Danwyn
(Owain Ddantgwyn)
Ruler of Powys
d.c. 520

Cadwallan Llaw Hir
(The Longhanded)

Buidic I (Emyr Llydaw)
King of the Bretons d. 513

Cuneglasus
Ruler of Powys
d.c. 550

Maelgwyn Gwynedd
Ruler of Gwynedd
c. 535-548

Hoel I (Rivallous)
King of the Bretons
Founded Dumnonia 520. d. 545
= *St. Pompeia*
*Dau. of Count Eusebius*

*Alienor* . . . . . = . . . . . . . . Ywain
Founder of the
House of Léon d'Acqs
c. 530

Run
Ruler of Gwynedd
c. 548

*Rimo* . . . . . = . . . . . . Hoel II
(Vychan)
King of the Bretons
d. 546

Withur
Comte de Léon d'Acqs

Beli
Ruler of Gwynedd

Alain I
King of the Bretons d. 580
= *Dau. of the Lord of Brest*

Ausoch
Comte de Léon d'Acqs

Jacob (Iago)
Ruler of Gwynedd
d. 616

Hoel III . . . . . . . . . . . . . . . = . . . . . . . . . . *Pritelle*
King of the Bretons

**KING CADFAN of Gwynedd**
616-625
= *Acha, dau. of King*
*Aelle of Deira*

Salomon II
King of the Bretons
d. 632

Saint Judicael
King of the Bretons
d. 658
= *Morone (maternal cousin)*

Cadwallon II
King of Gwynedd d. 634
= *Helen, dau. of Wibba*

*Map 8* Early Scotland – Caledonia, Dalriada and
Gwyr-y-Gogledd

the Messeh (thus *Messiah* – Anointed One). The image
of the intrepid *Messeh* evolved to become the Dragon,
which in turn became emblematic of mighty kingship.
The Imperial Romans displayed a purple dragon on

their standard, and it is this symbol that is depicted in Revelation 12:3, when Michael confronts the 'dragon with seven heads'. As we have seen earlier,[14] the dragon in this instance was Rome: known historically as the *City of the Seven Kings* (or heads – the number of kings before the Republic was formed).

The Celtic kings in Britain were called 'dragons' in the ancient *Messeh* tradition as intrepid guardians. But there were many separate kingdoms in those days before England gained an overall monarch in Saxon times. It was therefore necessary to appoint a King-of-Kings – a High King to preside overall, and to lead combined armies from different tribal areas. The first Pendragon (Head Dragon/High King) was Cymbeline.

Following the Romans' withdrawal from Britain in 410, regional leadership reverted to tribal chieftains. One of these was Vortigern of Powys in Wales, whose wife was the daughter of the previous Roman governor, Magnus Maximus. Having assumed full control of Powys by 418, Vortigern was elected Pendragon of the Isle in 425, and took to himself the dragon emblem – the emblem which became the red dragon on the national flag of Wales.

By that time, various kingly branches had emerged in the Arimatheac lines from Anna and Brân the Blessed. Among the most prominent of these local kings was Cunedda, the northern ruler of Manau, by the Firth of Forth. In a parallel family branch was the wise Coel Hen who led the 'Men of the North' (the *Gwyr-y-Gogledd*). Fondly remembered in nursery-rhyme as *Old King Cole*, he governed the northern regions of Rheged from his Cumbrian seat at Carlisle. Another noted leader was Ceretic, a descendant of King Lucius.[15] From his base at Dumbarton he governed the regions of Clydesdale. Together with Vortigern, these three kings were the most powerful overlords in 5th-century

Britain. Theirs were the families who also bore the most
famous Celtic saints, and were accordingly known as
the 'Holy Families of Britain'.

In the middle 400s, Cunedda and his sons led their
armies into North Wales to expel unwanted Irish settlers at the request of Vortigern. In so doing, Cunedda
founded the Royal House of Gwynedd in the Welsh
coastal region west of Powys. The Picts of Caledonia in
the far north then took advantage of Cunedda's absence, and began a series of border raids across
Hadrian's Wall. An army of Germanic Jute mercenaries,
led by Hengest and Horsa, was swiftly imported to
repel the invaders – but when they had succeeded, the
mercenaries turned their attentions to the far south, and
seized the kingdom of Kent for themselves. Other Germanic Saxon and Angle tribes subsequently invaded
from Europe. The Saxons took the south generally,
developing the kingdoms of Wessex, Essex, Middlesex
and Sussex. The Angles occupied the rest of the land
from the Severn estuary to Hadrian's Wall, comprising
Northumbria, Mercia and East Anglia. The whole became known as 'England' (*Angle-land*), and the new
occupants called the Celtic western peninsula 'Wales'
(*Weallas* – [land of] foreigners).

Because Ireland was separated by sea from the tempestuous British mainland, it became a perfect haven
for monks and scholars. (*Eireland* is said by some to
mean 'land of peace' – but the ancient name derived
more directly from Eire-amhon, father of Eochaid I of
Tara, who married the daughter of King Zedekiah
of Judah, in about 586 BC.) A unique and indigenous
culture thus developed in the form of Celtic Christianity. It derived primarily from Egypt, Syria and
Mesopotamia, and its precepts were distinctly Nazarene. The liturgy was largely Alexandrian and, because
Jesus's own teachings formed the basis of the faith, the

Mosaic content of the Old Testament was duly retained. The old Jewish marriage laws were observed, together with the celebrations of the Sabbath and Passover, while the divinity of Jesus and the Roman dogma of the Trinity played no part in the doctrine. The Celtic Church had no diocesan bishops but was essentially under the direction of abbots (monastic elders). The whole was organized on a clan structure, with its activities focused on scholarship and learning.

Cunedda remained in North Wales and, after Vortigern's death in 464, he succeeded as Pendragon, also becoming the supreme military commander of the Britons. The holder of this latter post was called the *Guletic*. When Cunedda died, Vortigern's son-in-law Brychan of Brecknock became Pendragon, and Ceretic of Strathclyde became the military Guletic. Meanwhile, Vortigern's grandson Aurelius – a man of considerable military experience – returned from Brittany to lend his weight against the Saxon incursion. In his capacity as a Druidic priest, Aurelius was the designated 'Prince of the Sanctuary', the sanctuary in question being a holy chamber called the *Ambrius* that was symbolically modelled on the ancient Hebrew Tabernacle (Exodus 25:8, 'And let them make me a sanctuary; that I may dwell among them'). The Guardians of the Ambrius were individually styled 'Ambrosius', and wore scarlet mantles (cloaks). From his fort in Snowdonia, Aurelius the Ambrosius maintained the military defence of the West, and succeeded as the Guletic when Brychan died.

## Saint Columba and Merlin

In the early 500s Brychan's son (also Brychan) moved to the Firth of Forth as Prince of Manau. There he founded another region of Brecknock in Forfarshire, which the Welsh people thereafter referred to as 'Breichniog of the North'. His father's seat had been at Brecon in Wales, and so the northern fortress was likewise called Brechin. Brychan II's daughter married Prince Gabràn,[16] of Scots Dalriada (the Western Highands), as a result of which Gabràn became Lord of the Forth, inheriting a castle at Aberfoyle.

Ousted from Gwynedd, the Northern Irish under King Cairill of Antrim launched a revenge assault on Scots Manau in 514. The invasion was successful, and the Forth area was brought under Irish rule. Brychan duly called for assistance from his son-in-law Prince Gabràn, and from the Guletic commander Aurelius. Rather than attempt to remove the Irish from Manau, the leaders decided to launch a direct sea offensive against Antrim. In 516, Gabràn's Scots fleet sailed from the Sound of Jura with the Guletic troops of Aurelius. Their objective was the castle of King Cairill, the formidable hill-fort at Dun Baedan (Badon Hill). The Guletic forces were victorious, and Dun Baedan was overthrown.[17] In 560, the chronicler Gildas III (516–570) wrote about this battle in his *De Excidio Conquestu Britanniae* ('The Fall and Conquest of Britain'), and the great battle featured in both the Scots and Irish records.[18] Some years after the Battle of Dun Baedan, Gabràn became King of Scots in 537. His West Highland court was at Dunadd, near Loch Crinan.

At that time the Pendragon was Cunedda's great-grandson, the Welsh king Maelgwyn of Gwynedd. He was succeeded in this appointment by King Gabràn's son, Aedàn of Dalriada. Aedàn became King of Scots in 574, and was the first British king to be installed by priestly ordination, when anointed by St Columba.

Born of Irish royal stock in 521, Columba was eligible to be a king in Ireland but abandoned his legacy to become a monk, attending the ecclesiastical school at

Moville, County Down. He founded monasteries in Derry and around, but his greatest work was destined to be in the Western Highlands and Islands of Scots Dalriada, having been banished from Ireland in 563. Columba had mustered an army against the unjust King of Sligo, following which he was imprisoned at Tara, and then exiled at the age of 42. With twelve disciples, he sailed to Iona and established the famous Columban monastery. Later, further north in Caledonia, Columba's royal heritage was well received by King Bruide of the Picts, and he attained prominence as a political statesman for the Druidic court. With a fleet of ships at his disposal, Columba visited the Isle of Man and Iceland, setting up schools and churches wherever he went – not only in Caledonia and the islands but also in English Northumbria (Saxonia).

At that time, the Scottish Lowlands (below the Forth) comprised thirteen separate kingdoms. They bordered on the Northumbrian realm to the south and the Pictish domain to the north. Although geographically outside Wales, the regions of Galloway, Lothian, Tweeddale and Ayrshire were all governed by Welsh princes. One of these dynastic regions above Hadrian's Wall was that of the *Gwyr-y-Gogledd* (Men of the North), whose chief was King Gwenddolau.

Shortly before Aedàn's kingly ordination by Columba, King Rhydderch of Strathclyde had killed King Gwenddolau in battle near Carlisle. The battlefield sat between the River Esk and Liddel Water, above Hadrian's Wall. (It was here, at the Moat of Liddel, that the Arthurian tale of *Fergus and the Black Knight* was set.) Gwenddolau's chief adviser (the *Merlin*) had been Emrys of Powys, the son of Aurelius. On Gwenddolau's death, the Merlin fled to Hart Fell Spa in the Caledonian Forest, and then sought refuge at King Aedàn's court at Dunnad.

The title 'Merlin' – Seer to the King – was long established in Druidic tradition. Prior to Emrys, the appointed Merlin was Taliesin the Bard, husband of Viviane I del Acqs. At his death in 540, the Merlin title passed to Emrys of Powys, who was the famous *Merlin* of Arthurian tradition. Emrys was an elder cousin of King Aedàn, and was therefore in a position to request that the new king take action against Gwenddolau's killer. Aedàn complied, and duly demolished Rhydderch's Court of Alcut at Dumbarton.

In those days the most important urban centre in the north of the British mainland was Carlisle. It had been a prominent Roman garrison town, and by 369 was one of Britain's five provincial capitals. In his *Life of St Cuthbert*, Bede refers to a Christian community in Carlisle long before the Anglo-Saxons penetrated the area. A little south of Carlisle, near Kirkby Stephen in Cumbria, stands the ruin of Pendragon Castle. Carlisle was also called *Cardeol* or *Caruele* in Arthurian times, and it was here that Grail writers such as Chrétien de Troyes located Arthur's second royal court. *The High History of the Holy Grail* refers specifically to Arthur's court at 'Cardoil'. Carlisle features additionally in the French *Suit de Merlin*, and in the British tales, *Sir Gawain and the Carl of Carlisle* and *The Avowing of King Arthur*.

The supreme office of Pendragon endured for 650 years – but throughout all that time the one Pendragon who never existed was Uther Pendragon, the legendary father of King Arthur. He certainly did not exist under that name, at least, although Arthur's father was indeed a renowned Pendragon, as we shall see.

## THE HISTORICAL KING ARTHUR

It is often claimed that the first quoted reference to Arthur comes from the 9th-century Welsh monk

Nennius, whose *Historia Brittonum* cites Arthur at numerous identifiable battles. But Arthur was recorded long before Nennius in the 7th-century *Life of St Columba*. He is also mentioned in the Celtic poem *Gododdin*, written in about 600.

When King Aedàn of Dalriada (Western Highlands) was ordained by Columba in 574, his eldest son and heir (born in 559) was Arthur. In the *Life of St Columba*, Abbot Adamnan of Iona (627–704) related how the saint had prophesied that Arthur would die before he could succeed his father. Adamnan further confirmed that the prophecy was accurate, for Arthur was killed in battle a few years after St Columba's own death in 597.

The name *Arthur* is generally reckoned to derive from the Latin name *Artorius*, but this is quite incorrect. In fact, the reverse is the case. The Arthurian name was purely Celtic, emerging from the Irish *Artúr*. The 3rd-century sons of King Art were Cormac and Artúr. Irish names were not influenced by the Romans, and the root of *Arthur* can be found as far back as the 5th century BC, when Artu mes Delmann was King of the Lagain.

In 858 Nennius listed various battles at which Arthur was victorious. The locations included the Caledonian Wood north of Carlisle (*Cat Coit Celidon*), and Mount Agned – the fort of Bremenium in the Cheviots, from which the Anglo-Saxons were repelled. Also featured by Nennius was Arthur's battle by the River Glein (Glen) in Northumbria, where the fortified enclosure was the centre of Northumbrian operations from the middle 500s. Other named Arthurian battlegrounds were the City of the Legion – Carlisle, and the district of Linnuis – the old region of the Novantae north of Dumbarton, where Ben Arthur stands above Arrochar at the northern head of Loch Long.

To place Arthur in his correct context it is necessary to understand that such apparent names as *Pendragon* and *Merlin* were actually titles. They applied to more than one individual over the course of time. Arthur's father, King Aedàn mac Gabràn of Scots, became Pendragon by virtue of the fact that he was Prince Brychan's grandson. In this line, Aedàn's mother, Lluan of Brecknock, was descended from Joseph of Arimathea. There never was an Uther Pendragon, even though he was much later grafted into English charts of the era. The name *Uther Pendragon* was invented in the 12th century by the romancer Geoffrey of Monmouth (later Bishop of St Asaph). The Gaelic word *uther* (or *uthir*) is simply an adjective meaning 'terrible'. There was only ever one Arthur born to a Pendragon – he was Arthur mac Aedàn of Dalriada.

On his sixteenth birthday in 575, Arthur became sovereign Guletic (commander). The Celtic Church accepted his mother, Ygerna del Acqs, as the true High Queen of the Celtic kingdoms. Her own mother (in the hereditary lineage of Jesus) was Viviane I, dynastic Queen of Avallon. The priests therefore anointed Arthur High King of the Britons following his father's ordination as King of Scots.[19] At the time of her conception of Arthur by Aedàn, Ygerna (sometimes called Igraine) was still married to Gwyr-Llew, Dux of Carlisle. The *Scots Chronicle* records the event thus:

> Becaus at ye heire of Brytan was maryit wy tane Scottis man quen ye Kinrik wakit, and Arthure was XV yere ald, ye Brytannis maid him king be ye devilrie of Merlynge, and yis Arthure was gottyn onn ane oyir mannis wiffe, ye Dux of Caruele.

In the *Historia Regum Britanniae* ('History of the Kings of Britain') by Geoffrey of Monmouth (*c.*1147), Gwyr-Llew, the Dux of Caruele (Warlord of Carlisle) was literally spirited away to the southern West Country to become Gorlois, Duke of Cornwall.[20] This adjustment

**RULERS OF SCOTS DALRIADA (ARGYLL)**
*AD 500 – 841*

ERC [See Chart: DESCENT FROM UGAINE MAR]

FERGUS MOR
*Kingdom of Alba*
d. 501

LOARN
*Kingdom of N. Argyll*

AENGUS
*Kingdom of Islay*

**HIGH KINGS OF DALRIADA**

Muiredach

*Tribe of Angus*

DOMANGART
501-506

Eochaid

COMGALL
506-537

GABRÀN
537-559

Baetan (Baodan)

CONALL
559-574

AEDÀN MAC GABRÀN
574-608

Colum (Colman)

*House of Ulster*

CONNAD
d. 630

EOCHAID BUIDE
608-630

Nechtan

Eoganan
d. 659

*Ferchar*
643-651

Fergus

Duncan
d. 680

DONALD BRECC
630-643

CONALL CRANDOMNA
651-659

Feradach

DOMANGART
659-673

MAELDUIN
673-688

DONALD DOND
688-695

FERCHAR – the Long
696-697

Ossene

EOCHAID
695-696

AINFCELLACH
697-698

SELBACH
701-723

FIANNAMAIL
of Antrim
698-701

EOCHAID
726-733

ALPIN
736-740

MUIREDACH
733-736

DUNGAL
723-726

INDRECHTACH
741

AED FIND
748-778

FERGUS
778-780

EOGAN
741-747

EOCHAID

EOCHAID
781
= Unuisticc of Fortrenn

Constantine

**Descent to House of Moray**
*11 generations to Macbeth*

ALPIN – KING OF SCOTS
839-841

DONALD
781-805

**Other Houses:**

CONALL 805-807  CONALL 807-811  CONSTANTINE 811-820

ANGUS 820-834  AED  834-836  EOGANNAN 836-839

of the facts was necessary because Geoffrey's Norman patron was Robert, Earl of Gloucester. The *Historia* was funded by Norman money, with an express requirement to cement King Arthur into English tradition, even though he did not feature in England's *Anglo-Saxon Chronicle*.

Although presented as a factual history, Geoffrey's work was known to be inaccurate in many respects. The historian William of Malmesbury called it 'dubious stuff', and William of Newburgh went even further, stating, 'Everything that the man took pains to write concerning Arthur and his predecessors was invented.'

Many were particularly baffled by Geoffrey's Duke Gorlois of Cornwall, because there were no Dukes in 6th-century England. The early title *Dux* was quite different from that of the later ducal nobility: it was a strictly military title, and held no feudal tenure of land ownership. Another anomaly was the assertion by Geoffrey that the 6th-century Arthur had been born at Tintagel Castle. There was no castle at Tintagel until the 1st Earl of Cornwall built one in the early 1100s. Previously there had been only a ruined Celtic monastery on the site.

A different misappropriation of the Pendragon's son, King Arthur, was manifest in Wales, and the tradition persists today. There actually was an Arthur in 6th-century Wales – in fact, he was the only other royal Arthur of the era. But he was not the son of a Pendragon, and he was not the Arthur of Grail lore. This other Arthur was installed as Prince of Dyfed by St Dubricius in 506, even though he and his forebears were enemies of the native Welsh. He was in fact descended from disinherited Déisi royalty expelled from Ireland in the late 4th century. When the Roman troops left South Wales in 383, the Déisi leaders came over from Leinster to settle in Dyfed (Demetia). Arthur, Prince of Dyfed, features as a notorious tyrant in *The Lives of the Saints* – in the tales of Carannog and others – and he is generally portrayed as a troublesome regional interloper.

In Arthurian romance, the confusion between the Scots and Welsh Arthurs arose mainly because of the Merlin connection. As we have seen, Merlin Emrys was the son of Aurelius. But Aurelius' wife was Arthur of Dyfed's sister, Niniane. Aurelius had married her in an effort to curtail the Déisi invasions of Powys, but his strategy was short-lived. This, of course, meant that Merlin Emrys was Arthur of Dyfed's nephew . . . while at the same time he was a cousin to the Pendragon, Aedàn mac Gabràn, and was the appointed guardian of Aedàn's son, Arthur of Dalriada.[21]

According to the 10th-century *Annales Cambriae* (Annals of Wales), Arthur perished at the Battle of Camlann. But to which Arthur do the annals refer? The answer is that, being composed so long after the event, they actually refer to a composite Arthur – a character forged from both the Dyfed and Dalriadan princes.

The 15th-century *Red Book of Hergest* (a collection of Welsh folk-tales) states that the Battle of Camlann was fought in 537. If this location relates to Maes Camlan, south of Dinas Mawddwy, it is quite possible that Arthur of Dyfed fought there. He was renowned for leading incursions into both Gwynedd and Powys. What is certain, however, is that Arthur of Dalriada fought a later battle at Camelon, west of Falkirk. The *Chronicles of the Picts and Scots* refer to this northern conflict as the 'Battle of Camelyn'. He also fought at Camlanna (or Camboglanna), by Hadrian's Wall – the battle which led to his demise.

As for Geoffrey of Monmouth, he decided to ignore all geographical indications, siting his fanciful battle instead by the River Camel in Cornwall. Geoffrey also associated the Irish battle of Badon Hill (Dun Baedan) with a battle at Bath, because the latter place had conveniently once been known as Badanceaster.

In *The Life of Saint Columba*, Abbot Adamnan related that, in the late 500s, King Aedàn of Scots had consulted St Columba about his due successor in Dalriada, asking, 'Which of [my] three sons is to reign – Arthur, or Eochaid Find, or Domingart?' Columba replied,

> None of these three will be ruler, for they will fall in battle, slain by enemies; but now if thou hast any other younger sons, let them come to me.

A fourth son, Eochaid Buide, was summoned, and the saint blessed him, saying to Aedàn, 'This is thy survivor.' Adamnan's account continues:

> And thus it was that afterwards, in their season, all things were completely fulfilled; for Arthur and Eochaid Find were slain after no long interval of time in the Battle of the Miathi. Domingart was killed in Saxonia; and Eochaid Buide succeeded to the kingdom after his father.

The *Miathi*, as mentioned by Adamnan, were a tribe of Britons who respectively settled in two separate groups north of the Antonine and Hadrian Walls. The Antonine Wall extended between the Firth of Forth and the Clyde estuary. Hadrian's Wall traversed the lower land between the Solway Firth and Tynemouth. In 559, the Angles had occupied Deira (Yorkshire) and had driven the Miathi northwards. By 574, the Angles had also pushed up into Northumbrian Bernicia. Some of the Miathi decided to stay by the lower Wall and make the best of it, while others moved further north to settle beyond the upper Wall.

The main stronghold of the northern Miathi was at Dunmyat, on the border of (modern) Clackmannanshire, in the district of Manau on the Forth. Here, they had cast their lot in with the Irish settlers, which made

**ARTHURIAN DESCENT**
*Houses of Siluria, Camulod, Dalriada and Gwynedd*

BELI MAWR (the Great) – Sovereign Lord of the Celtic Britons 132-72 BC

Casswallan (Cassivellaunos) 62-48 BC
(Seat at Wheathampstead, Herts)

King Llud (Lud) of the Britons 72-62 BC

JOSEPH OF ARIMATHEA
(Saint James the Just)
AD 1-82

King Llyr (Lear) ...... = ...... *Penardim*
20 BC – AD 10

Tenantius (Tasciovanus) 48-20 BC
King in S.E. (Seat at Colchester, Essex)

*Anna*
*(Enygeus)* .. = .. Arch Druid BRÂN THE BLESSED (Bron) of Siluria

Cymbeline (Cunobelinus) AD 10-17 Pendragon
Court at Camulod

Beli (Heli)

King Guiderius
AD 17-44

ARVIRAGUS, King of Siluria AD 44-74
= (AD 45) Genuissa, dau. of Emp. Claudius

CARACTACUS
Pendragon
AD 46-54

Avallach (Abalach/Amalech)

*Penardun*
*(protégée of Boudicca)* ...... = ...... King Marius of Siluria AD 74-125

Eugein (Iougueb/Owain)

Coel I of Camulod (Colchester) 125-170

Owain

Brithguein (Brithwein/Brychwn)

Lleiffer Mawr (KING LUCIUS) 170-181

Merchoin

Duvun (Dwhwn/Dwfnn)

*Gladys*
= Cadwan, Prince of Cumbria

*Athildis*
= Marcomer of Franks

Gorig

Onwed (Onwydd/Onum)

Sicambrian descent
to the
Merovingian Kings

Gorddwin

Anguerit (Enwerydd/Anweryd)

King Coel II of Camulod d. 262

Eunydd

Angouloub (Angoloit/Arnguloi)

Arthfael

Gur Dumn (Gorddwfn/Gwordwfn)

*EMPRESS HELENA 248-328*
= Constantius I

Cunedd

Gwrgon-frych

Dumn (Dwfn/Dyfn)

CONSTANTINE
THE GREAT

CONFER of Strathclyde

Merchion

Guiocein (Gwrgain)

Fer

Meirig

Cein (Cain/Kain)

Cursalen

Brechrwy

Tegid (Tacit) Pies Rudawg

Cluim (Clemens)

Edrig

Patern Pesrut (Padarn Pesrud)
(of the Red Mantle)

Cinhil (Quintillius)

Octern (Edeyrn/Edern)
|
CUNEDDA WLEDIG of Manau b.c 395
= Gwawl, dau. of Coel Hen Godebog
|
Einian Yrth (Enniaun Girt) c. 460
|
Cadwallan Llaw Hir (the Long-handed)
|
Maelqwyn Gwynedd c. 535-548
|
Rhun c. 548-
|
Beli (late 6th c.)
|
Iago (Jacob) d. 616
|
KING CADFAN OF GWYNEDD 616-625

Cynloyp
|
CERETIC GULETIC of Allt Clud
(Dumbarton) c. 450
|
Cinuit
|
King Dyfnwal Hen of Strathclyde
|
Inganach
= Brychan II of Manau Gododdin ‡
|
Princess Lluan of Brechin
= King Gabràn of Scots
|
Aedàn mac Gabràn of Dalriada
(Guletic and Pendragon)
|
ARTHUR Ard Rí and Warlord 559-603

Urban
|
Mynon (Nynio)
|
Tischfallt (Teudfall) c. 430
|
Tewdrig
(Regulus of Garth Madrun)
|
Marchell
‡ (G. mother of Prince Brychan II)
Mother of Brychan of Breichniog

**ARTHUR AND THE HOUSE OF AVALLON DEL ACQS**
*Merlin, Vortigern and Aurelius – 4th to 6th century*

*Map 9* Route of the 1st-century Metal Traders

them none too popular with the Scots and Welsh. Despite King Cairill's 516 defeat in Antrim, the Irish remained boisterously obstructive in Manau. The Guletic forces consequently made another incursion into Ulster in 575. This second assault at Dun Baedan is

**RULERS OF STRATHCLYDE AND GWYR-Y-GOGLEDD**
*Supplement to Arthur and Avallon chart*

[See Chart: ARTHURIAN DESCENT]

**CERETIC GULETIC**
of Allt Clud, Strathclyde
Seat at Dumbarton
(Ceretic Guletic/Coroticus)

Cinuit

**DYFNWAL HEN**
(Dumnagual Hen)

__STRATHCLYDE__

Cormac
of Man and Galloway

Teithfallt
= *Gratiana*

Anlach
= *Marchell of Garth Madrun*

Saint Brychan of Breichniog
= *Ribwast, dau. of Vortigern*

[See Chart: RULERS OF WALES AND BRITTANY]

**COEL HEN GODEBOG**
Old King Coel of Rheged  b.c. 380
__Gwyr-y-Gogledd__ seat at Carlisle
= *Ystrafael, dau. of Conan Meriadoc*

Keneu                    **Gwawl**
                         = CUNEDDA WLEDIG
                         of Manau Gododdin
                         b.c. 395

Gorust Ledlum    Mar        ↓
                         House of Gwynedd

Meirchaum Gul

__GWYR-Y-GOGLEDD__

*Ingenach* = Brychan II
           of Manau
           Gododdin

__RHEGED__

Garthwys

Clinoch      Guipno                                                              Keidau

Tutagual     Neithon        *Lluan*         Cynvarch = *Nefyn*      *Guar* = Elidyr
                            = *Gabràn of Scots*                              Lydanwyn

**RHYDDERCH HEN**   Beli    King Aedàn              **GWYR-LLEW**        **GWENDDOLEU**
(Hael) d. 603               of Dalriada (Pendragon Insularis)   Dux Caruele (Carlisle)    of Gwyr-y-gogledd
Chief of Cumbria           = *Ygerna* ◊ (2nd husband)   = *Ygerna del Acqs* ◊    k. 574 at Arderydd

                 Eugein    **ARTHUR** (Artúr)   URIEN of Rheged    = *Morgaine II*    **LLWYARCH HEN**
**BRUDE**        c. 645    Ard Rí and Guletic   (Llyn Catraeth)       *del Acqs*        The Bard
Pictish King 672-693       d. 603               d.c. 579
[See Chart: KINGS OF PICTS]  Elfin    = *Morgaine II*
                                    *d'Avallon del Acqs*

                 Beli     **MODRED**           **YWAIN** (Owain)
                 d. 722   (filius Regis Scotii)   Lord of Llwyfenydd
                                               Comte de Léon d'Acqs
Theudebur d. 752                               = *Alienor, dau. of*
                                               *Buidic I of the Bretons k. 513*
Dyfnwal II
                         **Gwithur** (Witúr)          **Garthwys**
Eogan                    2nd Comte de Léon            = *Danyw, dau. of Lot*
                         d'Acqs                       (Llawddyn Lleuddawg)
Rhydderch
[See Chart: EARLY KINGS OF SCOTS]   Ausoch             Cynderyn
                                    3rd Comte de Léon   Bishop of Strathclyde
                                    d'Acqs             (Saint Kentigern)

the one mentioned by Nennius, who rightly described Arthur's presence, whereas the Gildas account relates to the earlier 516 battle, and correctly gives Ambrosius Aurelius as the commander. Nennius gives Arthur rather more credit than his due, however, for this time the Scots were defeated, and Arthur's father, King Aedàn, was obliged to submit to Prince Baedan mac Cairill at Ros-na-Rig on Belfast Lough.[22]

Following King Baedan mac Cairill's death in 581, Aedàn of Scots finally managed to expel the Irish from Manau and the Forth. Later, in 596, Arthur's cavalry drove the Irish out of Scots Brecknock. King Aedàn was present at the battles, but Arthur's younger brothers Brân and Domingart were killed at Brechin on the Plain of Circinn.

In confronting the Irish at Manau, the Guletic troops also had to face the Miathi Britons. They were successful in driving many of them back to their southern territory, but those who remained – when the Guletic troops departed – had to contend with the Picts, who promptly moved into their domain. By the end of the century the Picts and Miathi were united against the Scots, whom they met at the *Battle of Camelon* north of the Antonine Wall. Once again the Scots were victorious, and the Picts were driven northwards. Afterwards, a nearby ironworks foundry building was dubbed *Furnus Arthuri* (Arthur's Forge) to mark the event. It was a long-standing attraction, and was not demolished until the 18th-century Industrial Revolution.

Three years after Camelon, the Scots faced the southern Miathi and the Northumbrian Angles. This confrontation was a protracted affair over two battle-grounds – the second resulting from a short-term Scots retreat from the first. The forces initially met at Cam-lanna, an old Roman hill-fort by Hadrian's Wall. Unlike the previous encounter, the *Battle of Camlanna* was a complete fiasco for the Scots. Falling for a diversionary tactic by the Miathi, the Scots allowed the Angles to move behind them in a concerted north-westerly push towards Galloway and Strathclyde. The unlucky definition of a 'Cath Camlanna' has been applied to many a lost battle thereafter.

Only a few months earlier, the Angle king, Aethelfrith of Bernicia, had defeated King Rhydderch at Carlisle, thereby acquiring new territory along the reaches of the Solway. The Dalriadan forces under Aedàn and Arthur were thus under some pressure to intercept and halt the Angles' northward advance. They were said to have assembled immense forces drawn from the ranks of the Welsh princes, and they even gained support from Maeluma mac Baedàn of Antrim, the son of their erstwhile enemy. By that time the Irish were themselves daunted at the prospect of an Anglo-Saxon invasion.

## MODRED AND THE CELTIC CHURCH

It is important to note that King Aedàn was a Celtic Church Christian of the Sacred Kindred of St Columba. Indeed, the Dalriadans were generally associated with the Sacred Kindred, which was distinctly grounded in the Nazarene tradition, but incorporated some customary Druidic ritual.

Arthur, however, became obsessed with Roman Christianity, to the extent that he began to regard his Guletic cavalry as a holy army. This disposition led to considerable disturbance within the Celtic Church – Arthur was, after all, destined to be the next King of Scots. The elders were particularly worried that he might try to inaugurate a Romanized kingdom in Dalriada, and it was on this account that Arthur made an enemy of his own son Modred, who was Archpriest of the Sacred Kindred.[23] Modred was an associate of the

Saxon King Cerdic of Elmet (the West Riding of York-shire), and Cerdic was allied to Aethelfrith of Bernicia. It was not difficult therefore to persuade Modred to oppose his father on the battlefield, and to ally himself with the Angles in his bid to save the Scots kingdom from losing its ancient Druidic heritage.

And so it was that, when the Scots faced the Angles and Miathi at Camlanna in 603, Aedàn and Arthur found themselves not only against King Aethelfrith but also against their own Prince Modred. The initial affray at Camlanna was short-lived: the Celtic troops were obliged to chase after the Angles, who had swept past them. They caught up with them again at Dawston-on-Solway (then called Degsastan in Liddesdale – the *Chronicles of Holyrood* and *of Melrose* refer to the battle site as Dexa Stone). Archpriest Modred's appearance with the invaders severely downcast the Celtic spirits, and it was here that Arthur (aged 44) fell alongside Maeluma mac Baedan.

The battle, which began at Camlanna and ended at Dawston, was one of the fiercest in Celtic history. The *Tigernach Annals* call it 'the day when half the men of Scotland fell'. Although Aethelfrith was victorious, heavy losses were sustained by all. His brothers Theobald and Eanfrith were slain, along with all their men, and King Aedàn fled the field having lost two sons, Arthur and Eochaid Find, along with his grandson, Archpriest Modred.

Aethelfrith never reached Strathclyde, but his success at Dawston enabled the Northumbrian territory to be extended northwards to the Firth of Forth, incorporating the Lothians. Ten years later, in 613, Aethelfrith besieged Chester and brought Cumbria fully under Angle control. This drove a permanent geographical wedge between the Welsh and the Strathclyde Britons. The Mercian Angles thereafter pushed westward, forcing the Welsh behind what was eventually to be the line of Offa's Dyke. The Wessex Saxons then encroached beyond Exeter, annexing the south-west peninsula.

In time, the once conjoined Celtic lands of Wales, Strathclyde and Dumnonia (Devon and Cornwall) were totally isolated from each other – and the Kindred of St Columba blamed it all on Arthur. He had failed in his duties as Guletic and High King. His father, King Aedàn of Dalriada, died within five years of the Camlanna disaster, which was said to have opened the door to the final conquest of Britain by the Anglo-Saxons. The days of Celtic lordship were done and, after more than six centuries of tradition, Cadwaladr of Wales (26th in line from Joseph of Arimathea) was the last Pendragon.

In the wake of Arthur's defeats at Camlanna and Dawston (jointly called *di Bellum Miathorum* – Battle of the Miathi), the old kingdoms of the North existed no more. The Scots, physically separated from their former allies in Wales, perceived that their only route towards saving the land of *Alba* (Scotland) was to become allied with the Picts of Caledonia. This they achieved in 844, when Aedàn's famed descendant, King Kenneth MacAlpin, united the Picts and Scots as one nation.[24] The records of Kenneth's coronation support his truly important position in the family line by referring to him as a descendant of the Queens of Avallon.

Had Modred survived he would undoubtedly have become Pendragon, for he was a great favourite of the Druids and the Celtic Church. Arthur's mother, Ygerna, was the elder sister of Morgause, who married Lot of Lothian, the ruler of Orkney. Lot and Morgause were the parents of the Orkney brothers Gawain, Gaheries, and Gareth. Morgause was also, like Ygerna, a younger sister of Viviane II, the consort of King Ban le Benoic[25] (Ban [of] the Blessed Body – a *Desposynic* descendant of

Faramund and the Fisher Kings). Viviane and Ban were the parents of Lancelot del Acqs. On the death of her first husband, the Dux of Carlisle, Ygerna married Aedàn of Dalriada, thereby legitimating Arthur before his titles were granted. By way of this union, the lineages of Jesus and James ( Arimathea) were combined in Arthur for the first time in about 350 years.

Arthur's maternal grandmother, Viviane I, was the dynastic Queen of Avallon, a kinswoman of the Merovingian kings. His aunt Viviane II was the official Keeper of Celtic Mysticism, and this heritage in due course fell to Ygerna's daughter, Morgaine.[26] Arthur was married to Gwenhwyfar of Brittany, but she bore him no children. On the other hand he did father Modred by Morgaine. Registers such as the *Promptuary of Cromarty* suggest that Arthur also had a daughter called Tortolina, but she was actually his granddaughter (the daughter of Modred). Morgaine (alternatively known as Morganna or Morgan le Faye) was married to King Urien of Rheged and Gowrie (Goure),[27] who in Arthurian romance is called Urien of Gore. Their son was Ywain, founder of the Breton House de Léon d'Acqs (holding the rank of Comte [Count] – or Earl). In her own right, Morgaine was a Holy Sister of Avallon and a Celtic High Priestess.

Writers have sometimes deemed Arthur's sexual relationship with his half-sister Morgaine to be incestuous – but this is not the way it was regarded in Celtic Britain. At that time, the anciently perceived dual nature of God[28] prevailed, as did the equally ancient principle of the 'sacred sister-bride' – so revered in the holy ritual of old Mesopotamia. In this regard, the Prayer of the Celts began, 'Our Father-Mother in the heavens'. In conjunction with this, specifically defined rites were performed to denote the mortal incarnation of the 'dual male-female entity'. As the earthly manifestation of the goddess Cerridwin (Ceridwen), Morgaine represented the female aspect of the duality. Arthur was her true male counterpart in the established royal tradition of the Pharaohs.[29] On the festival of Beltane (the spring equinox), Arthur was apprehended as a god in human form and obliged to participate in a ritual of sacred intercourse between the twin aspects of the incarnate Father-Mother. In view of Arthur and Morgaine's supposed divinity during this rite, any male offspring from the union would be deemed the 'Celtic Christ', and would be duly anointed as such. By virtue of this, although Arthur was destined to become the prominent subject of romantic history, it was his son Modred who held the highest spiritual position: he was the designated Christ of Britain; the ordained Archpriest of the Sacred Kindred, and an anointed Fisher King.

In his maturity Arthur upheld the Roman tradition – but it was the Archpriest Modred who strove to amalgamate the old Celtic teachings with those of the Christian Church, treating both Druids and Christian priests on an equal basis. It was this essential difference between father and son that drove them against each other. Arthur became completely Romanized, whereas Modred upheld religious toleration in the true nature of a Grail King. Despite the extraordinary success of Arthur's early career, his Catholic fanaticism caused him to betray his Celtic Oath of Allegiance. As High King of the Britons he was supposed to be the *Defender of Faiths*, but instead he imposed specific ritual upon the people. When he and Modred perished in 603, Arthur's death was not mourned by the Celtic Church. But he will never be forgotten. Arthur's kingdom fell because he forsook the codes of loyalty and service. His ultimate neglect facilitated the completion of the Saxon conquest, and his knights will roam the wasteland until the Grail is returned. Contrary to all myth and legend, it was the dying Archpriest Modred (not Arthur) who was carried from the field by his mother Morgaine's Holy Sisters.

## THE ISLE OF AVALON

As indicated in Geoffrey of Monmouth's romance, Avalon was traditionally associated with the magical Otherworld. It was here that the legendary Arthur was tended by the maidens in his eternal abode. Morgan le Faye promised to heal Arthur's wounds if he would remain on the Isle, and nothing was ever said of his death. The implication was, therefore, that Arthur might one day return.

When Geoffrey wrote his story, he was clearly unaware of the furore it would cause. Not only was the story inaccurate in many respects, but he had suggested a possible 'Second Coming of the King'. This, along with the sacred powers he attributed to women, was quite unacceptable to the Roman Church. In later times, Thomas Malory took a route of compromise. He simply had Bedevere place the wounded Arthur in a barge full of women who would transport him to Avalon. Then Bedevere walked through the forest and came upon a chapel in which Arthur's body had been interred.

Although Geoffrey's *Avalon* was based on the 'Otherworld' of Celtic tradition (A-val or Avilion), his interpretation was more related to Classical writings about the Fortunate Islands, where the fruit was self-tending and the people immortal. In mythological terms, such places were always 'beyond the western sea'. At no point did any of the early writers identify a location for the mystic Isle, for it did not have to be anywhere in particular – certainly not in the mortal domain. Its enchantment was that of an eternal paradise.

All of this changed in 1191 when the Isle of Avalon suddenly became identified with Glastonbury in Somerset. The definition of this inland location as an island was justified on the basis that Glastonbury stood amid watery marshland, and the nearby lake-villages of Godney and Meare dated from about 200 BC. Because of the geographical anomaly, however, the name 'Vale of Avalon' became a popular alternative. Prior to this date, there had been no recognized connection between Arthur and Glastonbury, except for a passing mention by Cardoc of Llancarfan,[30] who wrote, in 1140, that the Abbot of Glastonbury had been instrumental in Gwynefer's release from King Melwas of Somerset. But he did not suggest that Glastonbury was Avalon – and nor did anyone else.

What happened in 1191 was that the monks of Glastonbury made use of Arthurian tradition in a manner that would truly impress today's marketing specialists. Some writers have since labelled their actions an outright fraud, while others have tried to make the case that the monks were themselves deluded by circumstance. Whatever the truth of the matter, they not only saved their abbey from extinction, but gave birth to a whole new Glastonbury tradition. The Abbey had been badly damaged by fire in 1184, and Henry II began to fund the reconstruction. When he died in 1189, his son Richard I came to the throne, but he was more concerned with applying Treasury resources to the Holy Land Crusade, and so the Glastonbury funding was cut off. The Abbot and his monks were left penniless – so what did they do but dig a hole between a couple of Saxon monuments south of the Lady Chapel, where (to the amazement of all) they found the remains of King Arthur and Queen Guinevere!

Some 16 feet (c4.8 metres ) below ground, in a hollowed oak canoe, they unearthed the bones of a tall man, along with some smaller bones and a tress of golden hair. Such a find was of little consequence in its own right, but the monks were in luck, for not far above the log coffin was a leaden cross embedded in a stone. Upon the cross was inscribed *Hic Iacet Sepultus Inclytus Rex Arthurius In Insula Avallonia Cum Uxore Sua Secunda Wenneveria* (Here lies interred the renowned King Arthur in the Isle of Avalon with his second wife Guinevere). Not only had they found Arthur's grave but they had also found written proof that Glastonbury was the Isle of Avalon!

The Church was not at all happy that Guinevere was described as the king's 'second' wife, and it was asserted that the inscription was obviously incorrect.[31] Soon afterwards, the legend reappeared miraculously changed in spelling and format, this time dispensing with Guinevere altogether. It was now far more in keeping with requirement: *Hic Iacet Sepultus Inclitus Rex Arturius In Insula Avalonia* (Here lies interred the renowned King Arthur in the Isle of Avalon).

Quite why the monks should have dug in that particular spot is unclear. And even if they did find the bones as stated, there was nothing to associate them with King Arthur. The identification came only from the inscription on the leaden cross, yet the Latin was plainly of the Middle Ages, differing from Arthurian Latin to the extent that today's English differs from that of Tudor times.

Whatever the facts, the monks' purpose was well served and, following a successful publicity campaign, pilgrims flocked in their thousands to Glastonbury. The Abbey was substantially enriched with their donations, and the complex was rebuilt as planned. As for the alleged bones of Arthur and Guinevere, they were deposited in two painted chests, and placed in a black marble tomb before the high altar.

The entombed remains proved to be such a popular attraction that the monks determined to benefit further from their new-found tourist trap. It was apparent that if Arthur's bones created such a stir, then the relics of a saint or two would have a significant impact. So they took to their spades once more and, lo and behold! – other discoveries were soon announced: the bones of St Patrick and St Gildas, along with the remains of Archbishop Dunstan, which everyone knew had lain at Canterbury Cathedral for 200 years!

By the time of Henry VIII's dissolution of the monasteries, Glastonbury Abbey was boasting dozens of relics, including a thread from Mary's gown, a sliver from Aaron's rod, and a stone that Jesus had refused to turn into bread. At the dissolution, though, the Abbey's days of monastic activity were done, and the said relics disappeared without trace. Since that time, no one has seen the supposed bones of Arthur and Guinevere; all that remains is a notice marking the site of the tomb. To many people, nonetheless, Glastonbury will always be associated with Avalon. Some prefer Geoffrey's idea of Tintagel, while others stake their claims on Bardsey or Holy Island. Yet apart from the reality of Avallon in Burgundy, it is plain that the Celtic 'Otherworld' was a mythical realm, with a tradition dating back beyond record.

If the mystic Isle existed within the mortal plane, then it was akin to that eternal paradise which the pre-Goidelic Fir-Bolg tribe called Arúnmore. From Connacht in Ireland, the Fir-Bolg installed their king, Oengus mac Umóir, on the timeless island haven in the ancient days BC. It was to this place that the warriors fled after their defeat by the Tuatha Dé Danann at the legendary battle of Magh Tuireadh.[32] The Enchanted Isle was said to lie in the sea between Antrim and Lethet (the stretch of land between the Clyde and the Forth).

Arúnmore was the Isle of Arran, the traditional home of Manannan, the sea-god. Arran was also called Emain Ablach (the place of apples),[33] and this association was perpetuated in the *Life of Merlin*, which referred specifically to the *Insula Pomorum* (the Isle of Apples).

## MORGANNA AND THE CHURCH

In Geoffrey of Monmouth's *Historia*, Morgan le Faye was the head of nine Holy Sisters who were guardians of the Isle of Avalon. As far back as the 1st century, the geographer Pomponius Mela had similarly written of nine mysterious priestesses living under vows of chastity on the Isle of Sein, off the Brittany coast near Carnac. Mela told of their powers to heal the sick and foretell the future, in much the way that Morgaine del Acqs was a Celtic High Priestess with prophetic and medicinal powers. The Roman Church, however, would not tolerate such attributes in a woman, and because of this, the Cistercian monks were obliged to transform Morgan le Faye's image in the Arthurian *Vulgate Cycle*.

The Cistercians were closely identified with the Knights Templars of Jerusalem, and Grail lore was born directly from the Templar environment. The Counts of Alsace, Champagne and Léon (with whom writers like Chrétien de Troyes were associated) all had affiliations with the league, but the Catholic Church still held sway in the public domain. For publications to be issued in Europe, certain rules had to be acknowledged. The *Prophecies of Merlin* were specifically black-listed and outlawed by the Council of Trent in 1545, and women were afforded no rights to fulfil any ecclesiastical or sacred function. To this end, from the middle 1200s, Morgaine (dynastic heiress and Celtic holy sister of Avallon) was portrayed as Morganna, the malevolent sorceress. In the English poem *Gawain and the Green*

*Knight* (written in around 1380), it is the jealous Morganna who transforms Sir Bercilak into the Green Giant in order to frighten Guinevere.

In a manner similar to the matriarchal practice of the Picts, Morgaine's honorary Avallonian dynasty was perpetuated in the female line. The difference was that the Queens' daughters held supreme position rather than their sons – thus the honour was eternally female in concept. Morgaine's mother was Ygerna, the daughter of Queen Viviane I del Acqs. Originating from the same lineage of Jesus, the Celtic nominal Queens of Avallon emerged alongside the Merovingian kings. Other important genetic offshoots were the lines of the Septimanian and Burgundian royal successions. Morgaine's son Ywain (Eógain) founded the noble house of Léon d'Acqs in Brittany, and the later arms of Léon bore the black Davidic Lion on a gold shield (in heraldic terms: *or, a lion rampant, sable*). The province was itself so named because *leon* was Septimanian-Spanish for 'lion'. The English spelling, *lion*, appeared in the 12th century as a variant of the Anglo-French *liun*. Until the 14th century, the Scots Lord Lyon, King of Arms, was still called the *Léon Héraud*.

In some books it is suggested that Ywain's son Comte Withur de Léon d'Acqs (often corrupted to d'Ak) is identical with Uther Pendragon because of the similarity of first name. But actually *Withur* was a Basque name, derived from the Irish *Witúr*; its Cornish equivalent was *Gwythyr*. The Comité (County) of Léon was established in about 530 at the time of the Breton King Hoel I. He was of Welsh Arimatheac descent, and his sister Alienor was Ywain's wife.

At that time, there were two levels of authority in Brittany. In the course of a protracted immigration from Britain, Breton Dumnonia had been founded in 520, but it was not a kingdom as such. There emerged a line of kings such as Hoel – but they were not Kings of Brittany, they were kings (governors) of the immigrant Bretons. Throughout this period, the region remained a Merovingian province, and the local kings were subordinate to Frankish authority by appointed Counts – the *Comites non regis*. The supreme Frankish Lord of Brittany 540–544 was Chonomore, a native of the Frankish State with Merovingian authority to oversee the development of Brittany by the settlers. Chonomore's forebears were Mayors of the Palace of Neustria, and he was the hereditary Comte de Pohor. In time, the descendants of Ywain's aunt Viviane II became overall Counts of Brittany.

Brittany features prominently in Arthurian romance. At Paimpont, about 30 miles (c. 48 kilometres) from Rennes, is the enchanted *Forest of Brocéliande*. Stretching from here is the *Valley of No Return*, where Morganna confined her lovers. Also to be found are the magic *Spring of Barenton* and Merlin's *Garden of Joy*. Actually though, most of the stories of Brocéliande were transposed from much earlier accounts of the historical Merlin Emrys in the Caledonian Forest of Scotland.

# THIRTEEN

# INTRIGUE AGAINST THE BLOODLINE

## THE AGE OF SAINTS

Having been separated from the Byzantine Church, the Church of Rome developed the theme of the Apostles' Creed sometime after the year 600. Passages were incorporated that are still familiar today: God became 'the maker of heaven and earth' and, in a thoroughly non-Biblical portrayal, Jesus (having 'suffered under Pontius Pilate') 'descended into hell', before rising on the third day. The Creed also at this time introduced the concept of the 'Holy Catholic Church and the Communion of Saints'.

During the 6th and 7th centuries, the supposedly heretical Nestorian belief[1] spread into Persia, Iraq and southern India – even as far east as China, where missionaries arrived at the Imperial Court of the T'ang Emperor T'ai-tsung in 635. He was so inspired by the new doctrine that he had the Nestorian Creed translated into Chinese, and sanctioned the building of a commemorative church and monastery. Nearly a century and a half later, in 781, a monument in honour of Nestorius was erected at Sian-fu.

In the meantime, the Arians – who also denied Jesus's divinity – had gained a very strong foothold in European society. Catholic-based history generally uses the term 'barbarian' to describe Arians such as the Goths, Visigoths (West Goths), Ostrogoths (East Goths), Vandals (Wends), Lombards and Burgundians, but the description refers to no more than cultural differences. It does not mean these peoples were heathen ruffians. The open hostility of the said barbarians towards Rome and Byzantium was no more barbaric than the Romans' own savage empire-building. Although once wholly pagan (as indeed were Romans themselves), these tribes had, in large measure, become followers of Arius during the 4th century. From Spain and southern France through to the Ukraine, most of Germanic Europe was Arian Christian in the 600s.

Another doctrine that had to some extent become associated with the Nestorians and Arians was a remnant of the 4th century cult of Priscillian of Avila. His alternative Christian movement had begun in north-western Spain and had made significant inroads into Aquitaine. Fundamental to the Priscillian belief – which came out of Egypt, Syria and Mesopotamia – was the ordinary mortality of Mary (the mother of Jesus), as against her semi-divine image in the Roman Church. Priscillian had been executed in 386 at Trier (north of Metz) although his body was later transferred for burial in Spain.[2]

In view of these widespread alternatives to orthodox Christianity, it is quite apparent that the Catholic Church was far from paramount in the Christian West. Catholicism was surrounded and infused with various other forms of Christianity which individually upheld many different sectarian banners. However, they were together generally based on Judaic traditions rather than on the Pauline concept which had been adopted and revised by Rome. With the exception of some spiritually-based factions within the Gnostic movement, they retained beliefs akin to the *Desposyni* tradition, promoting the Nazarene doctrine of Jesus's own genuine humanity, and preaching his message rather than venerating his person.

In parallel with the ceremonial structure of the Roman Church, a scholarly sect evolved on the fringe of Catholicism. It was a monastic movement which denied the episcopacy, and it was based on ancient Egyptian and generally Eastern concepts. The Essene society at Qumran had lived a solemn, regulated existence – a style of religious discipline that had been perpetuated in the desert regions. This same austere seclusion, essential to the monastic existence whether applied to small communities or ascetic hermits (*eremoi*), was entirely appropriate to a life of study and contemplation.

The monastic pioneer, Saint Martin (*c*.316–397), is perhaps best remembered for dividing his cloak to share it with a naked beggar. Originally from Pannonia, Martin was a successful soldier in the Imperial Army before he settled in Poitiers and established Gaul's first great monastery at Marmoutier. In about 371 he was appointed Bishop of Tours, but continued his monastic existence. Later he was to become a patron saint of France.

One of the early missionaries from Europe to the British Isles was St Germannus d'Auxerre, who visited Britain in the 5th century and was the teacher of Ireland's St Patrick. The son of a Celtic Church deacon, Patrick had been captured as a boy by pirates. After some time in slavery, he had escaped to Gaul, where he was trained as a missionary at the monasteries of Lérins and Auxerre. In 431 he returned to Britain, and began his mission in Northumbria.

Patrick's teachings were different in many respects from those of Rome, and his writings indicate a distinct tendency towards Arian and Nestorian tradition. He was not at all popular with the Catholic Church –

indeed, its governors at one time stated definitively that he was quite unsuited to the priesthood. Patrick relied solely on the scriptures for his teaching. He had no time for the contrived authority of Roman bishops, for he was much more concerned with the Orders of the Celtic Church.

One of the foremost figures in the establishment of European monasteries was St Benedict (c.480–544). Initially a native of Spoleto in Italy, Benedict took up residence in a remote forest-cave near Rome. He later found a far more congenial retreat on the beautiful Monte Cassino (a prominent hill between Rome and Naples), at what was in fact an old temple site of Apollo. The pagan location was hardly to the liking of the Catholic bishops, but Benedict was soon joined by a large following of disciples, from whose number emerged Gregory the Great, Bishop of Rome 590–604.[3] In a fairly short space of time, the Benedictine group attained some considerable influence in political affairs – especially in their efforts to reconcile the Goths with the warlike Lombards of Italy.

The Order of St Benedict promoted pious reverence, the strict observance of set times for prayer, and common ownership within an environment of work and learning. Benedict's monastic rule provided for government by a resident abbot. In due course he founded twelve monasteries each housing twelve monks, and is generally regarded as 'the father of monastic Orders in Western Christendom'. From those early times, the Benedictines were largely responsible for maintaining high standards of education, and of sacred art and music, in Europe.

This era of the evolving Benedictine monastic Order marks the beginning of what is sometimes called 'the Age of Saints' – an age which, in the Roman Catholic tradition, may be said still to be in progress.

But, while the Roman Church was busily concerned with dogma and ecclesiastical structure, the Celtic Church was showing an interest in the hearts and minds of ordinary people. By 597, Celtic Christianity was so widespread that Bishop Gregory of Rome sent the Benedictine monk, Augustine, to England specifically to establish the Roman Church more firmly in that country. His arrival was deliberately timed to follow the death that year of the prominent 'Father of the Sacred Kindred', the gentle saint of the Celts, St Columba. Augustine began his work in south-eastern England, in Kent to be precise, where the local King Aethelbert's wife was already a Catholic. In 601, Augustine was proclaimed the first Archbishop of Canterbury, and two years later he attempted to become Primate of the Celtic Church as well. However, such an endeavour could not but fail against an establishment that remained far more Nazarene than Roman. Indeed, Augustine's plan was not for a unification of Churches, but for the strategic subjugation of a traditional Church which Rome had declared more or less heretical.

It was not until 664, at the Synod of Whitby in north Yorkshire, that Rome achieved the first doctrinal victory over the Celtic Church. The main debate concerned the date of Easter, for the Chief Pontiff of the day had decided that Easter should no longer be formally associated with the Jewish Passover. Against all prevailing custom, and against all Celtic tradition, the Catholic bishops succeeded in getting their own way – so displacing for all time the historic Jewish and Celtic ties. Traditionally, however, England's Easter festival was not a Passover celebration in the Jewish style – nor was it anything to do with Jesus. Easter actually represented the Celtic goddess of Spring, *Eostre*, whose feast-day was observed long before any association with Christianity.

Following the Synod, the Catholic Church increased its strength in Britain – but the Celtic Church could not be suppressed without an open declaration of war against Ireland. However, the days of Roman imperialism were over, and the armies which the Roman Church might call upon could never defeat the fierce troops of the Irish kings. The Celtic Church consequently remained very active in Britain, and the Sacred Kindred of St Columba became the *ecclesiastical seat* of the Kings of Scots.

Through all of this, the Bishop of Rome's biggest problem was his inability to gain supremacy over the royal houses of Celtic Britain. Rome had seen a measure of potential success with the conversion of King Arthur, but Arthur had been killed, and the Druidic-Nazarene heritage remained firm through the successors of his half-brother, Eochaid Buide. Shortly after Eochaid's accession, Bishop Boniface IV adopted the new Roman style of *Pope* (papa) in 610, as an alternative to being called a 'bridge-builder' (Pontiff). This was a blatant and positive attempt to compete with the long-standing Celtic distinction of 'Father', inherited from Nazarene and Essene traditions. But when the new papal supremacy was tested on Dianothus, Abbot of Bangor, he responded that neither he nor his colleagues recognized any such authority. They were prepared, he said, to acknowledge the Church of God, 'but as for other obedience, we know of none that he whom you term the Pope (or Bishop-of-Bishops) can demand'. A Celtic letter written to the Abbot of Iona in 634 referred unequivocally to St Patrick (the prevailing 'Father') as '*Our Pope*'.

Through the centuries, various attempts were made to deny the priestly and patriarchal heritage of the Celtic Church (which was more than authoritative enough to cause concern in the Vatican[4]). Roman

Catholic holy orders were supposed to rely on Apostolic Succession, but no such succession could be proved, for the Apostle Peter (on whom the succession supposedly hinged) had never actually been a bishop. The first appointed Bishop of Rome was Britain's Prince Linus (son of Caractacus the Pendragon) and, as recorded in the *Apostolic Constitutions*, Linus began the true succession, having been installed by Paul during Peter's lifetime in AD 58. Later, in AD 180, Irenaeus, Bishop of Lyon, wrote, 'The Apostles having founded and built up the Church at Rome, committed the ministry of its supervision to Linus'. In attempts to veil the royal heritage of Linus, he has often been portrayed as if he were a lowly slave, but this has not removed the thorn from the Church's side and, because of it, the papal doctrine has to be considered 'infallible'. If not, then the whole concept of a structured progression of High Bishops in Apostolic succession from Peter collapses, since Peter was never a Bishop of Rome, nor of anywhere else.

Bishop Theodosius attempted to forge an Apostolic link in 820, when he announced that the remains of St James Boanerges (St James the Greater) had been unearthed at Compostela in Spain. In 899 the resultant shrine (to *Sant Iago*, 'St James') became a great cathedral, later to be destroyed by the Moors in 997, and rebuilt in 1078. But it was common knowledge from the New Testament that James Boanerges (the brother of John) was executed in Jerusalem by Herod of Chalcis in AD 44 (Acts 12:2). Therefore, the bones that had been discovered, if genuinely belonging to a 'James' at all, were more likely those of the disciple James Cleophas (Cleopas), who came to the West with his wife, Mary Jacob, on the Magdalene voyage. Even this is something of a remote possibility, however, and it has been not unconvincingly suggested that the relics and the later Santiago heritage more likely belong to Priscillian of Avila.

## SCHISM IN CHRISTIANITY

Rome's final split with the Eastern Orthodox Church occurred in 867, when the latter announced that it upheld the true Apostolic succession. The First Vatican Council disagreed, and so Photius, Patriarch of Constantinople, excommunicated Pope Nicholas I.

This led to a whole new round of argument about the definition of the *Trinity*. The Catholics of Western Christendom decided to ratify what was called the 'Filioque Article', which had been introduced at the Council of Toledo in 598. It declared that the Holy Spirit proceeded 'from the Father *and from the Son* (Latin, *filioque*)'. The Eastern Orthodox Church claimed otherwise, stating that the Spirit proceeded 'from the Father *through the Son* (Greek, *dia, tou huiou*)'. It was a somewhat intangible and quite extraordinary point of theological dispute, but it was apparently good enough to split formal Christianity down the middle. In reality, of course, it was simply a trivial excuse to perpetuate the debate over whether the Church should be politically managed from Rome or from Constantinople.

The final result was the formation of two quite distinct Churches from the same original.[5]

Over the course of time, the Orthodox Church changed relatively little. From its primacy at Constantinople, it continued to adhere strictly to scriptural teachings, and its focus of worship became the Eucharist (*thanksgiving*) Communion ritual with bread and wine.

Catholicism, on the other hand, underwent numerous changes: new doctrines were added, and old concepts were amended or further substantiated. The disciplinarian notion of 'Purgatory', for example, was instituted to represent the place (or state) in which souls were held after death before being purified for entry into Heaven. The length of time a soul remained in Purgatory was directly related to the person's obedience to the Church while alive – those who were disobedient were inevitably doomed to Hell! From the 12th century, seven 'sacraments' were deemed to embody the grace of God in a person's physical life (though not all were necessary for individual salvation). They were: baptism, Holy Communion (Mass), confirmation, confession and penance, ordination to holy orders, the solemnization of matrimony, and the anointing of the seriously ill and dying ('extreme unction' or 'the last rites'). It was further decreed that the bread and wine of the Eucharist were respectively transformed, upon consecration, into the body and blood of the Christ (the doctrine of Transubstantiation).

Inasmuch as Constantine's Roman Church had commenced as a 'hybrid' religion, so too was the structure to remain composite. New methods and ideologies were introduced to maintain efficient control of congregations from a distance in an expanding Catholic society. In this way Roman Catholicism evolved in a strictly regulated fashion, and some doctrines that seem today to be traditional are actually quite recently implemented features. It was not until Victorian times that certain aspects of the Catholic creed, hitherto only implied, were determined as explicit items of faith. The doctrine of the 'Immaculate Conception', for instance, was not formally expressed until 1854, when Pope Pius IX decreed that Mary the mother of Jesus was herself conceived 'free from Original Sin'. Mary's 'Assumption' (into Heaven) was not defined until the 1950s by Pope Pius XII; and Pope Paul VI did not proclaim her 'Mother of the Church' until 1964.

Such decrees were themselves rendered possible by the ultimate assertion of authority – that of 'papal infallibility'. The dogma to this effect was proclaimed at the

First Vatican Council in 1870, and stated, in a way that brooked no opposition, that 'the Pope is incapable of error when defining matters of Church teaching and morality from his throne'!

## CONTROL OF RELIGIOUS ART

The Roman Catholic Church was not concerned only with retaining control over historical records[6] and romantic literature.[7] Indeed, the bishops set their sights against anything that appeared contrary to their dogmatic notions, and to this effect an orthodox correctness was implemented and regulated throughout the creative sphere. That the Madonna should be depicted only in blue and white has already been mentioned,[8] but there were other rules which governed sacred art in general. Some artists, such as Botticelli and Poussin, successfully introduced symbolic elements into their works – elements that the uninitiated would not comprehend, but in general the art of much of Europe was constrained by strict Vatican guidelines.

From the earliest days of the Roman Catholic Church, the male relatives of Jesus had posed a problem. But this was successfully countered when they were pushed into the background of Church tradition while Mary, the mother of Jesus, was brought to the fore. The unfortunate Joseph, father of Jesus and James – actually the true link in the royal succession – was deliberately sidelined while the cult of the 'Virgin Mother' grew out of all proportion. By way of this considered strategy, public knowledge of the continuing bloodline of Judah was conveniently suppressed.

Rules were laid down by the Church as to who might be portrayed in art, and how.[9] Anne (Anna), the mother of Mary, was seldom introduced into paintings with her daughter because her presence would detract from

From Taddeo Gaddi's *Joachim Rejected from the Temple*

Mary's divine status. If Anne's visible attendance was essential, she was placed in a subordinate position. Francesco da San Gallo's *Saint Anne and the Madonna* provides a good example of how the mother is seated behind her daughter. Cesi's *The Vision of Saint Anne* shows Anne kneeling before a vision of Mary. Leonardo

From *The Nativity* by Lorenzo di Credi

da Vinci's *The Virgin and Child with Saint Anne* is cleverly contrived to position the adult Mary on her mother's knee, thereby keeping the Madonna to the fore. Anne duly stands behind her daughter in Pietro Perugino's *The Family of the Virgin*.

Mary's husband Joseph, and her father Joachim, were generally confined to inferior or background positions within pictorial artwork. Both characters created problems because their paternal functions were contrary to the purported Immaculate Conception and Virgin Birth. As early as in the fresco paintings of Taddeo Gaddi (died 1366), it was preferred to reduce Joachim's status by showing him at his least dignified. He was often therefore portrayed being ejected from the Temple by the High Priest Issachar, having presumed to offer a feast-day lamb although he was not yet a father. In Michelangelo's *The Holy Family*, Mary is raised on a central throne, while her husband Joseph leans over a background balustrade, seemingly contemplating some unrelated matter.

The Church would gladly have denied that Mary ever married, but artists could not escape the directness of the Gospels. Nevertheless, there was no room for any suggestion of physical attachment between Joseph and Mary. Joseph was for that reason generally depicted as being considerably older than his wife, balding, and taking little interest in the rest of his family, as in Ghirlandaio's *The Adoration of the Shepherds* (c.1485). The famous *Doni Tondo* by Michelangelo (1504) similarly features a very bald and white-bearded Joseph, as does Caravaggio's *The Rest on the Flight into Egypt*. Indeed, Joseph was not infrequently shown as positively infirm, leaning uncomfortably on a crutch, while Mary remained always beautiful and serene, as in Paolo Veronese's *The Holy Family*.

When Joseph was advanced to sainthood in his own right in 16th-century Spain, things changed a little to his benefit. Yet by means of subtle symbolism he was still portrayed only as Jesus's foster-father, and held a white lily to express the purity of his relationship with Mary. Raphael's renowned *Lo Sposalizio* falls into this category – displaying a lily atop Joseph's baton, even though allowing him to be a younger man than was usual.

Just as the lily was the accepted symbol of Mary's virginity, so the rose was the symbol of her beauty. She was often depicted holding a rose, or in a rose garden, as in the *Madonna* of Cesare di Seso, and *The Madonna of the Rose Bush* by Martin Schoen. The two concepts both derive from *The Song of Solomon* 2:1 – 'I am the rose of Sharon and the lily of the valleys'. From very early on the lily was called the 'fleur de Marie', and it was for this reason that the gladiolus lily ( in its Judaic *fleur de lys* form) was adopted by the Merovingian kings to signify their Messianic descent in France.

Joseph's necessary presence was a cause of some difficulty for artists depicting the Nativity. But the difficulty was overcome in such paintings as Alessandro Moretto's 16th-century *The Nativity* by showing him as elderly with a supportive staff. Sometimes Joseph even appears to be in his dotage, or asleep, as in Lorenzo di Credi's portrayal. One way or another, this kingly descendant of the House of David was, time after time, reduced to being a superfluous onlooker (as in Hans Memling's *The Adoration of the Magi*), and he was seldom permitted to be a part of any relevant action. Moreover, in such pictures as Van Dyck's *Repose in Egypt*, Joseph seems hardly capable of any action – being more ready to collapse at Mary's feet, and to join her father Joachim on the official road to oblivion.

## FROM MEROVINGIAN TO CAROLINGIAN

By 655, Rome was in a position to begin dismantling the Merovingian succession in Gaul. At that time, the Mayor of the Austrasian Palace (akin to a Prime Minister) was firmly under papal control. When King Sigebert II died, his son Dagobert was only five years old – at which point Mayor Grimoald took action. First, he kidnapped Dagobert and had him conveyed to Ireland, to live in exile among the Scots Gaels. Then, not expecting to see the young heir again, Grimoald told Queen Immachilde that her son had died.

Prince Dagobert was educated at Slane Monastery, near Dublin, and he married the Celtic Princess Matilde when he was fifteen. Subsequently, he went to York under the patronage of St Wilfred. But then Matilde died, and Dagobert decided to return to France – where he appeared much to the amazement of his mother. In the meantime, Grimoald had placed his own son on the Austrasian throne, but Wilfred of York and others spread word of the mayoral treachery, and the House of Grimoald was duly discredited. Having married Gizelle de Razès, a niece of the Visigoth king, Dagobert was reinstated in 674, after an absence of nearly 20 years, and the Roman intrigue was thwarted – but not for long.[10]

Dagobert II's reign was short but effective: his major success was in centralizing the Merovingian sovereignty. But the Catholic movement set itself firmly to negate his Messianic heritage because it overshadowed the supremacy of the Pope. Dagobert's jealous enemies included his own powerful Mayor, Pepin the Fat of Heristal (or Herstal). Two days before Christmas 679, Dagobert was hunting near Stenay in the Ardennes when he was confronted by one of Pepin's men and lanced to death – impaled to a tree. The Church of Rome was quick to approve the assassination, and immediately passed the Merovingian administration in Austrasia to the ambitious Mayor.

Pepin the Fat was in due course succeeded by his illegitimate son, the well-known Charles Martel ('the Hammer') who gained recognition by turning back the Moorish invasion near Poitiers in 732. He then sustained the Roman endeavour by gaining control of other Merovingian territories. When Martel died in 741, the only Merovingian of any notable authority was Dagobert II's nephew, Childeric III. Martel's son, Pepin the Short, was the Mayor of Neustria. Up to that point (except for the Grimoald affair), the Merovingian monarchy had been strictly dynastic – hereditary succession was an automatic and sacred right, a matter in which the Church had no formal say whatsoever. But that tradition was destined to be overturned when Rome grasped the opportunity to create kings by papal authority. In 751 Pepin the Short, in league with Pope

Zachary, secured Church approval for his own coronation as King of the Franks in place of Childeric. The
Church's long-awaited ideal had come to fruition –
and from that time onwards kings were endorsed and
crowned only by self-styled Roman prerogative.

So Pepin became king, with the full blessing of the
Pope, and Childeric was deposed. The pledge of allegiance made by the Roman Church in 496 to King Clovis
and his descendants was broken. After two and a half
centuries, the Church was suitably geared to usurp the
ancient legacy of the Merovingian bloodline, and to
take control of the Frankish realm  by appointing its
own kings. Childeric was publicly humiliated by the
bishops. His hair, kept long by Nazarite tradition, was
cut brutally short, and he was incarcerated in a monastery, where he died four years later.

Thus began a new dynasty of French kings, the
'Carolingians' – so named after Pepin's father, Charles
(Carolus) Martel.[11]

The 'official' histories of the era were, not surprisingly, compiled by Vatican scribes, or by others who
operated by Vatican authority. The inevitable result
was that accounts of Dagobert's life were suppressed to
the point of his non-existence in the chronicles. Not for
another thousand years were the true facts of his existence to be made public once more. And only then did
it become apparent that Dagobert had a son called
Sigebert, who was rescued from the mayoral clutches
in 679. Following his father's murder he was removed
to his mother's home at Rennes-le-Château in Languedoc. By the time of Childeric's deposition, Sigebert
(effectively Sigebert III) had become the Count of Razès,
succeeding his maternal grandfather, the Visigoth, Bera
II. In time, the deposed Merovingian line from Sigebert
included the famous crusader, Godefroi de Bouillon,
Defender of the Holy Sepulchre.

**THE CAROLINGIANS**
*House of Charlemagne – 8th to 10th century*

*HOLY ROMAN*
*EMPERORS AND*
*KINGS OF FRANCE*

PEPIN (the Short)
(Mayor of Merovingian Palace) King of France 751-768
= *Princess Bertha (Bigfoot)*

CHARLEMAGNE (the Great)
King of France 771-814 Emperor Charles I   800-814
= *(4th wife) Hildegarde*

Pepin
King of Italy d. 810

*LOUIS I (the Pious) 814-840*
Emperor 814-840
= (1) *Irmengarde*
= (2) *Judith of Bavaria*

Charles
King of Franconia
d. 811

*Bertha*

Descent to Counts
of Boulogne

Lothair I
Middle Emperor
(Italy, etc) from 840
Ruler of Western Franks
843-855

Pepin
King of
Aquitaine
d. 838

Emperor Charles II (the Bald)
CHARLES I of France 843-877
Western Emperor (France) from 840
Overall Emperor 876-877

*Louis II (the German)*
Eastern Emperor
(Germany) from 840
Ruler of Eastern Franks
843-876

Louis II
Emperor of
Italy
855-875

Charles
King of
Provence
855-863

Lothair II
King of
Lorraine
855-869

LOUIS II
(the Stammerer)
877-879

Carloman
of Bavaria
876-880

Louis
(Younger)
of Saxony
876-882

Charles III
Emperor 875
CHARLES II of
France 885-887

Arnulf 887-899
Ruler of E. Franks

Robert the Strong

LOUIS III
879-882   -joint-

CARLOMAN
879-885

Louis (the Child)
of E. Franks 899-911

EUDES
888-893

ROBERT I
922-923

*Irmingarde*
= Count Boso of Vienne
Bouquet VIII of Provence

CHARLES III (the Simple)
893-dep.922 (d. 929)
= *Eadgifu*

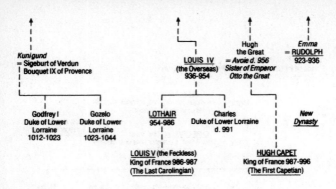

## THE KING OF THE JEWS

After their defeat by Charles Martel in the 730s, the
Moors (or Mohammedans – the forces of Islam) re-
treated to the city of Narbonne in the south of France,
which became their base for further military resistance.
This posed a difficult and prolonged problem for Pepin
the Short, who duly sought assistance from the Jews
who lived in Narbonne. He finally gained their support
– but at a price. The Jews agreed to deal with the
problem if Pepin guaranteed the setting up of a Jewish
kingdom within the territory of Burgundy: a kingdom
that would have at its head a recognized descendant of
the Royal House of David.[12]

Pepin agreed to the condition, and the Jews defeated
the Moors and ousted them from within the city.

The Jewish kingdom of Septimania (The Midi) was
then established in 768, from Nimes to the Spanish
frontier, with Narbonne as its capital. The previous
governor of the region was the Merovingian, Theuderic
IV (Thierry), who had been ousted from power in Neustria and Burgundy by Charles Martel in 737. Theuderic
(known to the Moors as Makir Theodoric) was married

**GUILHELM DE GELLONE AND GODEFROI DE BOUILLON**
*Merovingian descent – 7th to 12th century*

DAGOBERT I
King of Austrasia
King of the Franks 630-638

[See Chart: MEROVINGIAN KINGS]

= (1) Raintrude    = (2) Nanthilda

SIGEBERT II
King of Austrasia 632-656
= Immachilde

CLOVIS II
633-656
= Batilde

DAGOBERT II
King of Austrasia 674-679
= 671 (2) Gisèlle, dau. of
Bera II Comte de Razès

BLICHILDE … = … CHILDERIC II
651-674

THEUDERIC III
King of Neustria & Burgundy 673
King of Austrasia 679-691

SIGEBERT III
Comte de Razès
d. 758
= Magdalene

CLOVIS III
691-695

CHILDEBERT III
695-711

SIGEBERT IV
Comte de Razès
758-769

CHILDERIC III
Deposed 751 by
Pepin the Short

DAGOBERT III
711-715
= Saxon princess

BERA III
Comte de Razès
769-770
= Alba

Princess
BLANCHE FLEUR
= Flora of
Hungary

CHARLES MARTEL
Mayor of the Palaces
of Austrasia, Neustria
& Burgundy d. 741

GUILHELM I
Comte de Razès
770-c.795

Princess … = PEPIN III (the Short)
BERTHA          Mayor of the Palace
(Big-foot)      of Neustria d. 768

ALDA … = …. THEUDERIC IV
(Thierry)
King of Neustria
& Burgundy from 720
deposed 737  d. 741
Lord of Septimania
[Makir-Theodoric]

BERA IV
Comte de Razès
c. 795-813
= Romille

GUILHELM de TOULOUSE de GELLONE
b. 752 Master of Aquitaine. Davidic Sovereign
of Jewish State of Septimania. 2nd Comte de Toulouse
(succeeded 1st Comte Chorfin/Thursin)
Peer of France. Founded Judaic Academy at Gellone:
Saint Guilhelm-le-Désert 791  d. 828
= Guibourg

ARGILA
Comte de Razès
813-836
= Reverge

BERA V
Comte de Razès
836-860

CHARLEMAGNE THE GREAT
Carolingian King of France 771-814
Emperor Charles I  800-814
= (4th wife) Hildegarde

824

HILDERIC I
Comte de Razès
860-867

BERNARD
Comte de Razès
867-877

*Princess*
*BERTHA*
= Angilibert
de Ponthieu
(Poet Courtier)

LOUIS I ( the Pious)
King and Emperor
814-840
= (1) Irmengarde
= (2) Judith of Bavaria

*Princess ...*
*DHUADA*

= .. PRINCE BERNARD
of Septimania
Imperial Chamberlain
to Carolingian Court
Master of Aquitaine

Nithard

Helgaud

CHARLES II ( the Bald)
Western Emperor from 840
King of France from 843
Overall Emperor 867-877

LOTHAIR I
Middle Emperor from 840
King of West Franks
843-855

GUILHELM
d'Aquitaine
d.s.p.

BERNARD
Master of Aquitaine

SIGEBERT V... =
Comte de Razès
877-885

*ROTILDE*
*dau. of*
*Charles II*
*( the Bald)*

Herlouin

Roget

LOUIS II ( the Stammerer)
King of France 877-879

LOUIS II
Emperor of Italy
855-975

GUILHELM II
d. 914 England
= *Idoine*

WILLIAM
Comte de Ponthieu c. 878
Champion of Louis II of France

GUILHELM III
d. 936

CHARLES II ( the Simple)
King of France 893-dep.922
= *Eadgifu*

ARNAUD
d. 952

ERNICULE I
Comte de Ponthieu from 965
Comte de Boulogne by grant of
Lothair, son of Louis II of France
= *Adéline , Heiress of Boulogne*

LOUIS IV ( the Overseas)
King of France 936-954
= *Gerberga, dau. of*
*Henry I ( the Fowler)*
*of Germany*

*IRMENGARDE*
= Count Boso of Vienne
(Bouquet VIII of Provence)

**BERA VI**
( the Architect )
d. 975

**SIGEBERT VI**
d. 980

**HUGUES I**
d. 971
= *Anna*

**JEAN I**
d. 1020
= *Isabel*

*MAUD (Mahaut)*
= Adolphe Comte de Guisnes

**GUY** (Blanc-barbe)
Comte de Guisnes & Boulogne
*= Widow of uncle, Arnoul Comte
de Boulogne (1st son of Ernicule)*

**BALDWIN**
Compte de Boulogne
d. 1033
*= Adèle de Gand (Ada of Ghent)
Sister of Ralph, Lord Alost (S. Brabant)*

**CHARLES**
Duke of Lower Lorraine
d. 991

*GERBERGA*
= Lambert de Louvain

*KUNIGUND*
= Sigebert of Verdun
( Bouquet IX of Provence )

**GOZELO I** (Gotheion)
Duke of Lower Lorraine
1023-1044

(1) <            > (2)

**HUGUES** .... = *AGNES* .... = .... **ERNICULE II**
(des Plantard)     *de Jumièges*     Comte de Boulogne
d. 1015                                          d. 1041

**EUSTACE I** ..... = .... *MAUD (Matilde)*     **HENRY**
Comte de Boulogne     *de Louvain*     of Brussels
d. 1049

**GODFREY II** ( the Bearded )
Duke of Upper Lorraine
d. 1069
= *Doda*

> (2)

**EUSTACE II** ...... = ........ *IDA*
( Aux Grenons )     *(Saint Ide d'Ardennes)*
Comte de Boulogne     *1040-1113*
d. 1081

Malcolm III
King of Scots
1058-1093

*Mary* .... = .... **EUSTACE III**
Comte de Boulogne

*Mathilde*
= Stephen de Blois

**GODEFROI DE BOUILLON**
c. 1060-1100 Crusader
Duke of Lower Lorraine
King of Jerusalem 1099

**BALDWIN I**
King of Jerusalem
d. 1118

to Pepin the Short's sister Alda. It was their son, Count Guilhelm de Toulouse, who then acceded to the new throne as the King of Septimania in 768. Guilhelm was not only of Merovingian lineage, but was a recognized Potentate of Judah, holding the distinction of 'Isaac' in the patriarchy.

Pepin's son Charles was the ruler who became known as Charlemagne. The King of the Franks from 771, and Emperor of the West from 800, Charlemagne was pleased to confirm Guilhelm's entitlement to dynastic sovereignty in Septimania. The appointment was also upheld by the Caliph of Baghdad and, reluctantly, by Pope Stephen in Rome. All acknowledged King Guilhelm of the House of Judah to be a true bloodline successor of King David. Guilhelm was particularly influential at the Carolingian Court, and had an illustrious military career. In spite of his prominent position, Guilhelm was greatly influenced by St Benedict's monastic asceticism, and founded his own monastery at Gellone. In 791 he instituted his famous Judaic Academy of St Guilhelm, and was later featured by the Holy Grail chronicler Wolfram von Eschenbach.

By his wife Guibourg, Guilhelm's eldest son and heir was Prince Bernard of Septimania; his other sons were Heribert, Bera and Theodoric. Bernard became Imperial Chamberlain, and was second in authority to the Carolingian Emperor. He was the leading Frankish statesman from 829, and married Charlemagne's daughter Dhuada at the Imperial Palace of Aix-la-Chapelle in June 824. They had two sons: William (born November 826) and Bernard (born March 841). William became a prominent military leader, and Bernard II held the reins of Aquitaine, to rival King Louis II in power and influence within the region.

More than 300 years later, the Davidic succession was still extant in the Spanish Midi, although the kingdom, as such, had ceased to function as a separate State within a State. In 1144 the Cambridge monk Theobald stated (when initiating a charge of ritual murder against the Jews of Norwich),

> The chief men and rabbis of the Jews who dwell in Spain assemble together at Narbonne, where the Royal Seed resides, and where they are held in the highest esteem.

In 1166 the chronicler Benjamin of Tudela reported that there were still significant estates held by the prevailing Davidic heirs:

> Narbonne is an ancient city of the Torah[13] . . . Therein are sages, magnates and princes, at the head of whom is Kalonymos, son of the great Prince Todros of blessed memory, a descendant of the House of David, as stated in his family tree. He holds hereditaments and other landed properties from the rulers of the country, and no one may dispossess him.

## THE HOLY ROMAN EMPIRE

King Charlemagne greatly expanded the Frankish territories, and by harassing the Saxons also became King of the Lombards. In 800 he was crowned Emperor of the West by Pope Leo III. By this strategy the Church of Rome inaugurated a new imperial dominion – a dominion in control of territory that comprised much of western and central Europe. Charlemagne's successor was Louis I (the Pious), at whose death in 840 the unity of the Empire was undermined by his rebellious sons. Then, after three years of strife, the kingdom was split into three at the Treaty of Verdun (843). The middle kingdom included Italy, Lorraine and Provence. In the west was France, and in the east Germany.

Apart from Charlemagne – who established France as an imperial and cultural domain – the Carolingians were largely incompetent rulers. Their nobles became semi-independent, while the Norsemen (Normans) were allowed to invade northern France and establish Normandy. The last Carolingian king was Louis V (the Feckless). He was succeeded by Hugh Capet, the Duke of France, in 987, and thus began the new 'Capetian' dynasty, which was to rule until 1328.

When the Capetians succeeded to the throne of France, the elective imperial title passed to the German kings of Saxon lineage; from the 11th century onward, the Emperors were mainly of the Hohenstaufen succession. In due course they became so powerful that they were contending with the papacy for overall supremacy in Europe. The main dispute began in 1075 as an argument – called the Investiture Controversy – over exactly who had the primary right to invest bishops in return for their pledges of loyalty.

In the context of this ongoing struggle against Vatican domination, the supporters of the anti-Roman Hohenstaufens became known as *Ghibellines* (after their castle at Waiblingen). Their pro-Roman rivals were known as Guelfs (or Guelphs, after Welf, Duke of Bavaria). The Ghibellines held their position of prominence until the Hohenstaufens were militarily defeated by a papal alliance in 1268. From that time the Empire became the Holy Roman Empire, and the emergent Emperors were invariably Habsburgs – a family that originated in 10th century Switzerland. From 1278, the Habsburgs were the rulers of Austria, and from 1516 they also inherited the Spanish crown. For five centuries they were the most prominent of all European houses, and they governed the Holy Roman Empire, almost continuously, until it was abolished in 1806.

# FOURTEEN

# TEMPLE OF THE GRAIL

## LEGACY OF THE HOLY RELIC

Of all Arthurian themes, the most romantic is that of the Holy Grail. Yet because of the Grail's enduring tradition, there is a lingering uncertainty about its place in time. Its champions have been portrayed in the 1st century, in the Arthurian period, and in the Middle Ages. In essence, the Grail is timeless.

The Grail has been symbolized by many things: a plate or dish, a chalice, a stone, a casket, an aura, a jewel, and a vine. It is sought by some, and seen by others. It is sometimes tangible, with appointed guardians and maidenly bearers, but is often ethereal, appearing in a variety of guises including that of the Christ himself. Either way, it has a genuine purpose, and a heritage that prevails with the Grail Family. Rarely alone, the Grail is generally accompanied by a blood-tipped spear. Its powers include those of rejuvenation, knowledge and provision; just as Jesus was a healer, teacher and provider, so too is the Grail. In name it has been the *Graal*, the *Saint Graal*, the *Seynt Grayle*, the *Sangréal*, the *Sankgreal*, the *Sangrail*, the *Sank Ryal* and the *Holy Grail* – but however defined, its spirit remains at the very centre of achievement.

The Grail legacy is a relic of early Judaic Christianity, but the Christian Church has never recognized the fact. Despite a background that is both romantic and sacred, Grail lore remains an unproclaimed heresy. It has been associated with pagan tradition, blasphemy, and unholy mysteries. Moreover, the Roman Church has openly condemned the Grail because of its strong female associations – particularly its association with the ethos of Courtly Love (*Amour Courtois*) in the Middle Ages. The romantic notions of Chivalry and the songs of the Troubadours were despised by Rome because they placed womanhood on a pedestal of veneration, contrary to Catholic doctrine. To a far greater extent, though, the Church's reluctance to accept Grail tradition derived from the Grail Family's specifically defined Messianic lineage.

*Map 10*  Medieval France

In its most popular role, the Holy Grail is identified as the cup used by Jesus at the Last Supper. After the Crucifixion it was supposedly filled with Jesus's blood by Joseph of Arimathea. This concept first arose in the 12th century, but its perpetuation was largely due to Alfred Tennyson's *Holy Grail*, published in 1859, and by Richard Wagner's 1882 opera *Parsifal*.

It was Sir Thomas Malory who first used the words *Holy Grayle* in his 15th-century adaptation of the French *le Saint Graal*. Malory referred to 'the holy vessel', but also wrote of the *Sankgreal* as being 'the blessed blood of Christ', and both definitions appeared in the same story. Apart from such mentions, Malory gave no description of the Grail – only that it appeared at Camelot 'covered in white samite' (fine silk). It was seen by Lancelot in a vision, and eventually achieved by Galahad. In Malory's account, the Grail champions are Bors, Perceval, Lancelot, and his son Galahad. The last was described as 'a young knight of kings' lineage, and the kindred of Joseph of Arimathea, being the grandson of King Pelles'.

Medieval tradition related that Joseph of Arimathea brought the Holy Grail to Britain. Even earlier European lore told how Mary Magdalene originally brought the *Sangréal* into Provence. It is a significant fact that, prior to the 15th century, the majority of Grail romances came out of continental Europe. Even such tales as the Welsh *Peredur* derived from European texts. The Celtic legends of Ireland and Wales featured magic cauldrons, and it was partly because of these that the Grail came to be perceived as a cup or chalice. However, the notion was not inappropriate, for it was only to be supposed that the royal blood must have been conveyed in a vessel of some kind.

The earliest written account of *Le Seynt Graal* comes from the year 717, when a British hermit called Waleran

saw a vision of Jesus and the Grail. Waleran's manu-
script was referred to by Heliand, a French monk of the
Abbey of Fromund, in around 1200; also by John of
Glastonbury in the *Cronica sive Antiquitates Glastoniensis
Ecclesie*, and later by Vincent of Beauvais in his 1604
*Speculum Historiale*. Each of these texts relates how Jesus
placed a book in Waleran's hands. It began:

> Here is the Book of thy Descent;
> Here begins the Book of the Sangréal.

In the public domain, the Grail did not appear in
writing until the 1180s, at which stage it was described simply as a 'graal'; it was neither a holy relic
nor associated with the blood of Jesus. In his *Le Conte
del Graal – Roman de Perceval*, Chrétien de Troyes
states:

> A damsel came in with the squires, holding between her
> two hands a graal . . . And as she entered . . . there was such
> a brilliant light that the candles lost their brightness. After
> her came a damsel holding a dish of silver. The graal which
> preceded her was of refined gold, and it was set with
> precious stones of many kinds . . . The youth [Perceval]
> watched them pass, but he did not dare to ask concerning
> the graal and whom one served with it.

On this first occasion, at the castle of the wounded
Fisher King, the graal is not described as a cup, neither
is it associated with blood. But later in the story
Chrétien explains:

> Do not think that he [the Fisher King] takes from it a pike
> or a lamprey, or a salmon; the holy man sustains and
> refreshes his life with a single mass wafer. So sacred a thing
> is the graal, and he himself is so spiritual, that he needs no
> more for his sustenance than the mass wafer which comes
> with the graal.

**BLOODLINE OF THE GRAIL** *The Messianic descent: Britain and Europe – 1st to 7th century*

1 *Lilith – consort of Adam before Eve* (Terra-cotta relief carving from ancient Sumer c2000 BC). Lilith was the symbolic handmaiden to Matronit, the female counterpart of God. She left Adam because he tried to dominate her.

2 *The Goddess Astarte* (Syrian gold pendant c1450 BC). In Canaan, the Goddess was called Ashtoreth, and in Sumer she was Ishtar.

3 *'I have given you an example that ye should do as I have done to you'* (19th Century engraving). Jesus washes the Apostles' feet at the Last Supper (John 13).

4 *Sacred Allegory* by Jan Provost (15th century depiction of Jesus and Mary Magdalene). Jesus is armed with a sword, whilst Mary is crowned and wears the black robe of a Nazarite priestess. The upturned 'M' of the hands below identifies the bride who frees the dove of the Holy Spirit.

5 (left) *Merovingian Seal Ring of King Childeric* (Plaster cast from an impression of the 5th century ring).

6 (below) *Nazarite Bishop Josephes passes the Grail to King Alain* (French manuscript illustration of the Middle Ages). A strategic move by the black bishop secures the heritage of the Holy Grail.

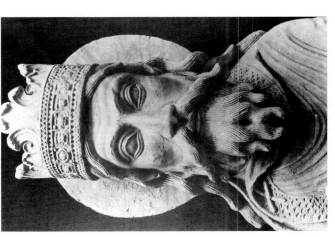

7 *The Merovingian King Clovis and Queen Clotilde* (Statues at the Notre Dame de Corbeil near Paris). Clovis reigned in Gaul AD 481–511.

8 *Madonna of the Magnificat* by Botticelli (1445–1510). Jesus clutches the ripe open pomegranate of fertility.

9 *The Birth of Venus* by Botticelli c1486. Signifies the Aphrodite status of Mary Jacob, with a distinctive engrailed scallop shell bearing her upon the sea foam.

10 *Mary Magdalene Carried by the Angels* by Giovanni Lanfranco (1582–1647). This 16th century portrayal relates to *The Revelation* story of the expectant Mary's flight into exile.

11 *Mary Magdalene holding the red egg of fertility and new birth* (Portrayal at the Russian Church of Saint Mary Magdalene, Jerusalem). Serge Ivanov's 19th century mural depicts Mary displaying the egg before Emperor Tiberius. Coloured eggs have long been associated with Eostre (Easter), the ancient goddess of Spring.

12 *The Ruins of the Great Synagogue at Capernaum.* The synagogue was governed by Mary Magdalene's father, the Jairus priest Syrus.

13  (left) *The Sea Voyage* by Lucas Moser c1432 (At the Katholisches Pfarramt St Maria Madgalene, Tiefenbronn, Black Forest). The altar panel depicts Mary Magdalene's arrival in Provence. It is significant because it is set in the artist's own era, thereby denoting the Church's acceptance of Mary's Western history in those days.

14  (right) *Mary Magdalene from the 1490 Sforza Book of Hours.* (Depicting her AD 44 arrival on the shore of Provence).

15 *Leap of Faith* by Peter Robson. (Signifies the Resurrection of the virile Christ, emblematic as the Unicorn of Cathar allegory). Below, the fox of the Roman establishment threatens the Vine of the Grail bloodline.

16 *Truth Against the World* by Peter Robson. The day of fulfilment when the dragon is slain and the Phoenix shall rise. (*Y gwir erbyn y Byd* was the war-cry of Queen Boudicca). Wearing the black garb of the esoteric church, the triumphant woman carries the therapeutic serpent of wisdom and healing.

17 (left) *The Ruin of Pendragon Castle*
Near Kirkby Stephen in Cumbria.

18 (below) *Carlisle Castle in Cumbria*
Carlisle was a centre of northern
British operations in Arthurian times.

19 (left) *Sophia* (From the 16th century *Book of Wonders*). The immortal Spirit of Faith and Wisdom brings light to the darkness of Chaos.

20 (right) *The Black Madonna of Verviers*. Both mother and son are crowned, while the Madonna bears the sceptre of royalty and wears Sophia's halo of stars.

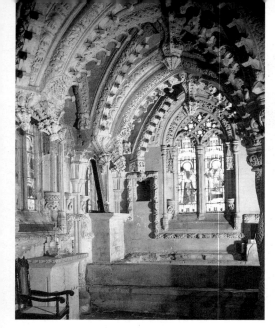

**21** *The south and east interior of Rosslyn Chapel* Hundreds of stone carvings adorn the walls and ceiling of the Chapel. They tell stories from the Bible within an array of Templar and Masonic symbols.

**22** *South exterior of Rosslyn Chapel* (The Templar Church of the Holy Grail near Edinburgh). The chapel was built in the 15th century by the Sinclair Barons of Roslin.

23 (left) *Jacobite chalice bearing the Merovingian Bee emblem.* Representing the bloodline of Judah, the bee was a symbol of royal wisdom from before the time of Solomon.

24 (below) *The 'Jesus Maria' Stone* (In the south wall of the Lady Chapel, Glastonbury).

25 *The Achieving of the Sangréal* (Illustration by Aubrey Beardsley 1893).
From *The Birth, Life and Acts of King Arthur.*

If Chrétien's graal was big enough to accommodate a large fish, it was clearly not a cup in this context, but a sizable tureen. Its mystery lay in the fact that it served 'a single mass wafer'. Elsewhere in Chrétien's work there is mention of 'a hundred boars' heads served on graals', and the Abbot of Froidmont (in around 1215) described a *graal* as a deep dish used by the rich.

Up to that point there was no link between the Fisher King's *graal* and the traditional *Sangréal*. In the 1190s, however, the Burgundian writer, Sire Robert de Boron, changed this with his poem *Joseph d'Arimathie – Roman de l'Estoire dou Saint Graal*. He redefined Chrétien's Fisher King (previously contemporary with King Arthur) as Bron, a kinsman by marriage of Joseph of Arimathea, and reclassified the graal dish/platter as the *Saint Graal* – a 'chalice of holy blood'.

According to de Boron, Joseph obtained the Passover cup from Pilate, and collected Jesus's blood when removing him from the cross. He was imprisoned by the Jews, but managed to pass the cup to his brother-in-law Hebron, who travelled to the 'Vales of Avaron'. There he became Bron, the 'Rich Fisher'. Bron and his wife Enygeus (Joseph's sister) had twelve sons, eleven of whom married, while the twelfth, Alain, remained celibate. Meanwhile, Joseph joined the family abroad, and constructed a table to honour the Graal. At this table there was a particular seat called the 'Siege Perilous'. It represented the seat of Judas Iscariot, and was reserved especially for Alain. In later stories it was to be the virgin knight Galahad for whom the 'Siege Perilous' was reserved at the Round Table of Camelot.

At about the same time as de Boron's *Joseph d'Arimathie*, another related work appeared by a writer known as Wauchier. It was very much a continuation of Chrétien's account, and in this tale the Graal takes on a very different aspect, performing a physical role:

> Then Gawain saw entering by the door the rich Graal,
> which served the knights and swiftly placed bread before
> each one. It also performed the butler's office – the service
> of wine, and filled large cups of fine gold, and decked the
> tables with them. As soon as it had done this, without delay
> it placed at every table a service of food in a large silver
> dish. Sir Gawain watched all this, and marvelled much
> how the Graal served them. He wondered sorely that he
> beheld no other servant, and hardly dared to eat.

In some respects, Wauchier's version brought the
Chrétien and de Boron stories together. King Arthur's
knights were featured, but the author also recounted
the tradition of Joseph of Arimathea. He explained that
Joseph's lineal descendant was Guellans Guenelaus,
the deceased father of Perceval, and that – in keeping
with previous texts – Perceval's mother was a widow.

The story known as the *Perlesvaus* or the *High History
of the Holy Grail* is a Franco-Belgian work that dates from
about 1200. It is very specific about the importance of
Grail lineage, asserting that the *Sangréal* is the repository of royal heritage – thereby reiterating the important dynastic principle of Waleran's 8th century
manuscript. In the *Perlesvaus*, the Grail is not defined as
a material object, but as a mystic aura that comprises
various images of Christian significance. In this work,
the *Corpus Christi* of Chrétien's mass-wafer emerges as
the continuing presence of the Christ.

In respect of the cup symbolism, the *Perlesvaus* states:

> Sir Gawain gazes at the Grail, and it seems to him that there
> is a chalice within it, although at the same time there is not
> one.

Gawain, Lancelot and Perceval are all featured in the
*Perlesvaus*, and the paramount question is, '*Whom does
the Grail serve?*' Only by asking this question can Perceval heal the groin wound of the Fisher King and

return the barren Wasteland to fertility. In the *Perlesvaus*, the Fisher King (Priest-King) is called Messios, denoting his Messianic standing. Other accounts refer to the Fisher King Anfortas (effectively the same name as Boaz, thus 'in strength' – so identifying the Davidic lineage). Alternatively, the Fisher King is sometimes Pelles (from Pallas, the ancient *Bistea Neptunis* of the Merovingian ancestry).[1]

Not the least important feature of the *Perlesvaus* is its evident reference to the Knights Templars. On the 'Island of the Ageless', Perceval comes to a Glass Hall, to be met by two Masters. One acknowledges his familiarity with Perceval's royal descent. Then, clapping their hands, the Masters summon 33 other men who are 'clad in white garments' each bearing 'a red cross in the midst of his breast'. Perceval also carries the red cross of the Templars upon his shield. The tale is basically Arthurian, but it is set in a later period at a time when the Holy Land is in the hands of the Saracens.

Also from the early 1200s comes a most important Grail romance called *Parzival*, by the Bavarian knight Wolfram von Eschenbach. Once again a Templar association is evident, for the Knights of the *Templeise* are portrayed as guardians of the Temple of the Grail – located on the Mount of Salvation (or *Munsalvaesche*). Here, the Fisher King officiates at the Grail Mass, and is specifically depicted as a Priest-King in the style of Jesus, the Merovingians, and the Kings of Scots. Munsalvaesche has long been associated with the mountain fortress of Montségur in the Languedoc region of southern France.

Wolfram stated that Chrétien's Grail story was wrong. He gave his own source as being Kyôt le Provenzale, a Templar attaché who wrote of an early Grail manuscript from Arabia. It was by the learned Flegetanis, a scholar of nature, descended from Solomon, and born of a family which had long been Israelite until baptism became our shield against the fire of hell.

As with the *Perlesvaus*, Wolfram's *Parzival* lays great stress on the importance of Grail lineage. Wolfram also introduced Perceval's son, Lohengrin, the Knight of the Swan. In the Lorraine tradition, Lohengrin was the husband of the Duchess of Brabant (Lower Lorraine). *Parzival* explains that Perceval's father was Gahmuret (as against Guellans in the Wauchier account), and that the Fisher King of Perceval's day was Anfortas, son of Frimutel, son of Titurel. The Fisher King's sister, Herzeylde, was Perceval's mother – the widow-lady of tradition. Expounding at length on the various mystical attributes of the Grail, the text names its bearer as the Queen of the Grail Family, Repanse de Schoye, declaring:

> She was clad in the silk of Arabia, and she bore, resting on a green silk cloth, the perfection of earthly paradise, both roots and branches. It was a thing men call the Grail, which surpassed every earthly ideal.

Despite the reference to roots and branches, the Grail is said to be a 'stone of youth and rejuvenation'. It is called *Lapsit Exillis* (sometimes *Lapis Elixis*) – a variant of *Lapis Elixir*, the alchemical Philosophers' Stone. Wolfram explains:

> By the power of that stone the Phoenix burns to ashes, but the ashes speedily restore him to life again. Thus doth the Phoenix moult and change its plumage, after which he is bright and shining as before.

At the Fisher King's sacrament of the Eucharist, the Grail Stone records the names of those called to its service. But it is not possible for everyone to read those names:

Around the end of the stone, an inscription in letters tells the name and lineage of those, be they maids or boys, who are called to make the journey to the Grail. No one needs to erase the inscription, for as soon as it has been read it vanishes.

In very similar terms, the New Testament (Revelation 2:17) states:

To him that overcometh will I give to eat of the hidden manna [divine food, as in the Eucharist], and will give him a white stone, and in the stone a new name written, which no man knoweth saving he that receiveth it.

Wolfram (who also wrote of Guilhelm de Gellone, King of Septimania) said that the original Flegetanis manuscript was held by the House of Anjou, a noble house that was closely allied with the Templars. He also claimed that Perceval was himself of Angevin blood. In *Parzival*, King Arthur's Court is firmly set in Brittany; in another work, Wolfram located the Grail Castle in the Pyrenees. He also made specific mention of the Countess of Edinburgh (Tenabroc) as being the Grail Queen's retinue.

The Cistercian 'Vulgate Cycle' of around 1220 contains the *Estoire del Graal*, the *Queste del Saint Graal*, and the *Livres de Lancelot*, as well as other tales of Arthur and Merlin. In these, the descriptions of the Grail are largely influenced by Chrétien and de Boron, and the earlier '*Graal*' spelling is reinstated. In the *Estoire*, the story of Joseph of Arimathea is extended to include his time in Britain, while his heir, Bishop Josephes of Saraz, is identified as head of the Grail fraternity. Bron (de Boron's *Rich Fisher*) reappears as the *Estoire*'s Fisher King. The Graal, meanwhile, has become the miraculous *escuele* (dish) of the Paschal Lamb. In both the *Estoire* and the *Queste*, Grail Castle is symbolically called 'le Corbenic' (the Body Blessed).[2] The *Queste* identifies Galahad as being 'descended from the high lineage of King David'; more importantly, the *Queste* notes his descent in the succession from King Solomon.

The *Books of Lancelot* (which feature Gawain in the first instance) go on to expand the story of Galahad, detailing him as the son of Lancelot by the daughter of Pelles. She is the Grail Princess, Elaine le Corbenic. Here, too, Pelles is the son of the wounded Fisher King (whereas in Malory's later account, Pelles is himself the King).

King Arthur certainly received mentions in the early Grail literature, but it was not until the 13th-century 'Vulgate Cycle' that he was fully established in this regard. However, after the Holy Land fell in 1291, the Grail legends slipped from the public arena. It was not until the 15th century that Sir Thomas Malory revived the theme with his tale of *The Sangréal – the blessed blood of Our Lord Jesus Christ*.

## THE ROD OF JESSE

In the meantime, references to the Holy Grail became purely emblematic. Even the inventive monks of Glastonbury did not produce anything purporting to be the Grail – if only because it had never been defined as a Christian relic prior to their digging escapades. Although de Boron was soon to identify the *Saint Graal* as the chalice of the Last Supper, the monks had never heard of it as such; there was no Holy Grail mentioned in the Bible, nor in any other orthodox scripture. Moreover, because the Grail legends emanated mainly from outside England, there was nothing of substance to link the Grail with Glastonbury . . . apart from the connection with Joseph of Arimathea.

And so, not to be outdone, the monks announced the discovery of a pair of cruets that were said to have been

buried with Joseph. They had previously been mentioned (in around 540) by King Maelgwyn of Gwynedd,
the uncle of St David, who wrote:

> Joseph had with him in his sarcophagus two white and
> silver cruets filled with the blood and sweat of the prophet,
> Jesus.

The cruets are portrayed in stained-glass windows at St
John's Church, Glastonbury, at Langport Church in
Somerset, and in a rood-screen portrait at Plymtree,
Devon.

But the cruets were never put on public display, and
this lack of visible accreditation gave rise a few centuries later to a new Glastonbury tradition – one that was
more amenable to the common gaze – the enchanted
thornbush.[3] In 1520, local literature described a bush on
Wearyall Hill that bore fresh leaves and blossoms at
Christmastime as well as in May. The bush was destroyed during the Cromwellian Civil War (1642–1651),
but shoots from it were replanted in the area, and each
plant flowered again in the same way. Botanical experts
discerned that the shrub was not native to England, and
seemed to be of Levantine origin. And so a new Somerset mythology began.

In 1716 a local innkeeper asserted that the unusual
thorn plant sprang from the staff of Joseph of Arimathea, which he had planted to blossom at Christmas
(not that the December festival had been relevant in
Joseph's day. It was nearly 300 years later that Constantine adjusted the date of Jesus's birthday). The notion
that Joseph's 'rod' should burst into flower in this way
derived originally from a prophetic verse in Isaiah
(11:1), which reads: 'And there shall come forth a rod
out of the stem of Jesse [the father of David], and a
Branch shall grow out of his roots'. In some Church
artwork and apocryphal writings, the budding staff of

the royal bloodline is depicted in the hand of Jesus's father, Joseph.

It was not until Alfred Tennyson's 19th-century *Idylls of the King* that Glastonbury was specifically linked with the Holy Grail. The unusually reddish water of Glastonbury's Chalk Well (actually tinted red because of the presence of iron oxide) was ready-made for association with the blood of Jesus. It was duly renamed Chalice Well, and the water's colour was said to derive from the contents of the Grail chalice which Joseph had buried nearby. The famous lid of the well shaft, complete with Celtic-style ironwork, was designed by the architect Frederick Bligh Bond after World War I. Notwithstanding the assortment of saintly and Arthurian mementoes at Glastonbury (some real and some contrived), Joseph of Arimathea's personal association with Britain remained historically much better attested. It was a subject of debate at various European Church Councils, with the English able to claim a Christian connection long before any at Rome. At the Council of Pisa in 1409 there was even an argument about whether Joseph or Mary Magdalene had come to the West first. These days it would be astonishing if the Church was to admit that Mary or Joseph ever came at all.

## DRUIDIC TRADITION AND THE PHILOSOPHERS' STONE

We have already seen that Jesus and Mary Magdalene's younger son Josephes attended a Druidic college.[4] Educational institutions of the kind were internationally renowned: there were no fewer than 60 such colleges and universities in Europe, boasting a total attendance of more than 60,000 students. The Druid priests were not part of the Celtic Church but were an established, cohesive element in the structure of Celtic society in Gaul, Britain and Ireland. They were described by the writer Strabo, in the 1st century BC, as 'students of nature and moral philosophy'.[5] He continued,

> They are believed to be the most just of men, and are therefore entrusted with judgements in decisions that affect both individuals and the public at large. In former times they arbitrated in war, able to bring to a standstill opponents on the point of drawing up in line of battle; murder cases have very frequently been entrusted to their adjudication.

The Sicilian, Diodorus, another writer of the time, described the Druids as great 'philosophers and theologians, who are treated with special honour'.

The Druids were in addition said to have been both exceptional statesmen and divine seers.[6] One ancient text states that

> The Druids are men of science, but they are also men of God, enjoying direct intercourse with the deities and able to speak in their name. They can also influence fate by making those who consult them observe positive rules or ritual taboos, or by determining the days to be chosen or avoided for any action that is contemplated.

In later times the Roman Church sought the slightest excuse to denounce the Druid priests and the monks of the Celtic Church, finding the mark of sin even in their hairstyles. Both priests and monks wore long, flowing hair from the back of their heads, with their hair at the front shaved across from the temples – sometimes leaving a separate band of hair above the forehead. The emergent Roman clergy adopted an alternative tonsure: a circlet of short hair around an otherwise cleanshaven head, representative of a holy crown. According to Rome, the Celtic hairstyle was the heretical symbol of the Magians, and they condemned it as 'the tonsure of Simon Magus'.[7]

When Diodorus wrote of the Britons in the 1st century BC, he referred to the works of the Greek writer Hecataeus from three centuries before, and accordingly called them *Hyperboreans* (people from beyond the North Wind). He told how the god Apollo visited a Hyperborean temple 'every 19 years – the period over which the return of the stars to the same place in the heavens is accomplished'. This 19-year astronomical cycle was used by the Druids for calendar calculation, as confirmed by the 'Calendar of Coligny' found in the French Department of Ain, north of Lyon, in 1897.[8]

The Calendar – a fragmented bronze tablet – dates from the 1st century AD and is the longest document to be unearthed in Gaul. It gives a table of 62 consecutive months (about five solar years), each month having either 29 or 30 days. Also intercalated is the alternative lunar calendar of thirteen months per solar year. The days of each month are related to each other, with inherent dark and light periods, and annotated as to auspicious and inauspicious days. Altogether, the Coligny Calendar indicates a significant competence in astronomical science, akin to that of the ancient Babylonians.

Astronomy was of prime importance to the Druids, who were said to 'have much knowledge of the stars and their motions, of the size of the world and of the earth, and of natural philosophy'. They believed also in reincarnation (the transmigration of souls) – an aspect of ancient Pythagoreanism. As long ago as the 6th century BC, Pythagoras founded one of the earliest mystery schools. Within this environment was developed a model of the universe that was correctly based on the fact that the Earth revolves around the Sun (the heliocentric principle). But even as long afterwards as the

16th century AD, the Polish astronomer Nicholas Copernicus was threatened with excommunication and worse for his belief in this concept. On presenting his theory, Copernicus suffered an onslaught of abuse from the Catholic Church, which insisted that the Earth was the centre of the universe. To the earlier Druids, with their advanced knowledge of heavenly bodies, the very idea of an Earth-centred universe would have been unthinkable.

In common with the Samaritan Magi of the Qumran era, the Druids were practitioners of advanced numerology and healing. During the Gospel period, the Essenes of Qumran were especially interested in the mathematics which governed the order of the cosmos. Their culture was to a large extent dominated by Pythagorean thought, inherited through the Magi of West Manasseh – a sect founded by Menahem in 44 BC. A successor of Menahem as head of the Magi was, as we have seen, Mary Magdalene's colleague Simon (the Magus) Zelotes, whose Gnostics were said to possess a unique and esoteric wisdom (called *sapientia*) that transcended Christianity.

A Gnostic document, found at Chenoboskion in Egypt and known as the *Treatise of Hermes Trismegistus* (or *Trimegistos*), states:

> It is thus by degrees that the adepts will enter into the way of immortality, and will attain to a conception of the Ogdoad, which in turn reveals the Ennead.

The Ogdoad ('eightfold') corresponds to the heaven of the stars, outside the individual heavens of the planets, and the Ennead ('ninefold') refers to the great outer heaven of the universe. The separate heaven of Earth itself was called the Hebdomad ('sevenfold'). To the Gnostics the heavens were strictly stratified areas of space surrounding the Earth, the planets and the stars.

Even though the heavens were subject to their own mythology, the logical understanding of the Gnostics bore little relation to the cosmological principle of the later Roman Church, which for centuries insisted that the Earth was flat, and that Heaven was simply 'above'.[9] (Some schools even suggested that Heaven – also flat – was supported above the Earth by invisible pillars.)

Hermes Trismegistus was the Greek Neoplatonists' name for Thoth, the Egyptian god revered as the founder of alchemy and geometry. Following the teachings of Plato (429–347 BC), the Neoplatonists[10] claimed that the human intellect was not related to the material world, and that individual spirituality would increase in relation to one's contempt for earthly values. The relevance of Hermes was that his special knowledge was held to represent the 'Lost Wisdom of Lamech' (Lamech was seventh in succession from Adam's son Cain – Genesis 4:18–22). Just as Noah saved various life forms from the great Flood, so Lamech's three sons, Jabal, Jubal and Tubal-cain, preserved the ancient wisdoms of creative science, carved upon two stone monuments – the 'Antediluvian Pillars'. One son was a mathematician, the second a mason, and the third a metalworker. Hermes discovered one of the pillars, transcribing its sacred geometry onto an emerald tablet that was inherited by Pythagoras, who also discovered the second pillar.

The association of the sacred knowledge of the cosmos with an emerald tablet is reminiscent of Wolfram's *Parzival*, in which the Grail is identified as a stone and likened to 'an emerald jewel'. Moreover, an inscription from the emerald tablet of Hermes appears on some Temperance Tarot cards:

> Visit the interior parts of the earth; by rectification thou shalt find the hidden stone.

Through association with the enigmatic Stone, the Grail has been identified with alchemy – the science of concentrating vital currents and life forces. At the time of the Catholic Inquisition, alchemists were careful to veil their art behind symbols of metallurgy – claiming they were attempting only to turn base metals into gold. In philosophical and metaphysical terms, the alchemists were rather more concerned with the transformation of the worldly person (lead) into a spiritually illuminated person (gold). Just as gold was tried and tested in the fire, so the human spirit was tried in the crucible of life – and the agent for this illumination was perceived as the *Holy Spirit*.[11]

Not surprisingly, this doctrine of human perfectibility through 'enlightenment' was deemed heretical by the Church whose teachings it superseded. Although founded on a Judaeo-Christian base, the Grail tradition was likened to alchemy, and was therefore itself regarded as a heresy. The 'hidden stone' was described in the alchemic *Rosarium Philosophorum* in terms of geometry:

> Make a round circle of the man and the woman, and draw out of this a square, and out of the square a triangle. Make a round circle, and you will have the stone of the philosophers.

Like the Philosophers' Stone, the Grail has been identified as the key to knowledge and the sum of all things. In its nominal form as the *Graal*, the etymological root is the Celtic word *gar*, meaning 'stone', so that *gar-al* is the 'cup of the stone'.[12] As we have seen, the priesthood of Jesus was that of Melchizedek (Hebrews 5:6–7),[13] who is portrayed in the north doorway of Chartres Cathedral. Here, at the Door of the Initiates, Melchizedek is the host of Abraham in accordance with Genesis 14:18–20, and he bears a *cup* which holds the hidden *manna* (spiritual nourishment/daily bread) of the sacred *stone*.

The Guild of Masons, who built Chartres and other French cathedrals, were called the 'Children of Solomon'. Hiram Abiff, the architect of King Solomon's Temple, was a Hermetic alchemist – described as 'an artificer in metals'. His ancient forerunner was Tubalcain (Genesis 4:22), the son of Lamech, and the teacher of all who followed. In Freemasonry, Hiram Abiff is identified as the 'Son of the Widow' – and in Grail lore, the constant epithet of Perceval is precisely the same. The original 'widow' of the Grail bloodline was Ruth the Moabite (heroine of the book of Ruth), who married Boaz to become the great-grandmother of David. Her descendants were called *Sons of the Widow*.

The underlying principle of Hermes Trismegistus was 'As above, so below', which denotes that the harmony of earthly proportion is representative of its universal equivalent – in other words, that earthly proportion is the mortal image of cosmological structure.[14] From the smallest cell to the widest expanse of the galaxies, a repetitive geometric law prevails, and this was understood from the very earliest of times.

## THE VESSEL AND VINE OF THE SANGRÉAL

In its representation as a stone or jewel, the Holy Grail is the repository of spiritual wisdom and cosmological knowledge (signifying *fulfilment*). As a graal-dish (escuele) or platter, it carries the mass-wafer of the Eucharist or the Paschal Lamb, and symbolizes the ideal of *service*. Its identity as a chalice containing the blood of Jesus is a purely female image, denoted by the receptacle figure V. Although the Grail supports a Christian ideal, it was its concept as a sacred vessel which led the Church to remove Grail lore from a centre-stage position. To the Church, sacred vessels had pagan associations, and Grail imagery was thus moved into the convenient wings of mythology.

In the pagan tradition, the Grail was likened to the mystical cauldrons of Celtic folklore – the Horns of Plenty, which held the secrets of provision and rebirth. The father of the Irish gods, Dagda of the Tuatha Dé Danaan, had a cauldron that would cook only for heroes. Likewise, the horn of Caradoc would not boil meat for cowards. The pot of the goddess Ceridwen contained a potion of great knowledge, and the Welsh gods Matholwch and Brân possessed similar vessels.[15] The similarity of the name Brân to that of Bron the Rich Fisher has often been cited, along with the suggestion that perhaps one derived from the other.

The 'vessel of mystery' to the ancient Greeks was the *Krater*. (In mundane contexts a *crater* was a stone bowl for mixing wine.[16]) In philosophical terms, the krater contained the elements of life; Plato referred to a krater which contained the light of the sun. Alchemists similarly had their own vessel from which was born Mercurius (Mercury), the *filius philosophorum* ('son of the philosophers'), a divine child who symbolized the wisdom of the *vas-uterus*, while the Hermetic vessel itself was called the *womb of knowledge*. It is this 'uterine' aspect of the mysterious vessel that is so important in Grail science. The medieval *Litany of Loretto* went so far as to describe Jesus's mother Mary as the *vas spirituale* (spiritual vessel). In esoteric lore, the womb was identified as the 'vessel of life' and was represented by the female symbol V – the *chalice*. Prehistoric shrines dating from 3500 BC associate the figure V with the womb of the Mother Goddess.[17] The reverse male symbol Λ was a blade or horn, ordinarily symbolized as a sword, although its most powerful representation was in the fabulous mythology of the Unicorn. In Psalm 92:10 we read, '*My horn shalt thou exalt like the horn of an unicorn*'. Along with the Lion of Judah, the legendary Unicorn remained synonymous with the anointed kingly line of Judah – to emerge in the heraldic arms of Scotland.

The Holy Grail became likened to a vessel because it was said to carry the sacred blood of Jesus. Just as the kraters and cauldrons had contained their various secrets, so too was the blood of Jesus (the *Sangréal*) held to be contained within a cup. But it was the *Chalice* (V) of Mary Magdalene which carried the Sangréal *in utero*. It was she who inspired the *Dompna* (Great Lady) of the Troubadours, who were so callously treated by the Inquisition – and they called her the 'Grail of the World'.

In *Parzival*, it is said of the Grail Queen that 'she bore . . . the perfection of earthly paradise, both roots and branches'. According to the New Testament Gospel of John 15:5, Jesus said, 'I am the vine, ye are the branches'. Psalm 80:8 reads, 'Thou hast brought a vine out of Egypt: thou hast cast out the heathen, and planted it.'

The lineage of the Merovingian kings was called *The Vine*. The Bible classifies the descendants of Israel as a 'vine', the line of Judah being described at some length as the Lord's cherished plant (Isaiah 5:7). Some medieval portrayals of Jesus show him in a wine-press, accompanied by the statement 'I am the true vine' (John 15:1). Some Grail emblems and watermarks depict a chalice containing clusters of grapes – the fruit and seeds of the vine.[18] From the grape comes wine – and the wine of the Eucharist is the eternal symbol of the blood of Jesus.

In the original Grail legends there were constant references to the Grail Family, the Grail dynasty, and the custodians (or guardians) of the Grail. Quite apart from legend, the Knights Templars of Jerusalem were the Guardians of the *Sangréal*. The associated Priory of Notre Dame de Sion became allied to the Merovingian bloodline in particular, and it was the Merovingian descendant Godefroi de Bouillon, Duke of Lower Lorraine, who was installed as 'Defender of the Holy Sepulchre' and King of Jerusalem in 1099.

Cups and stones aside, the importance of the Grail exists in its definition as the *Sangréal*. From this came *San Gréal* = *San Graal* = *Saint Grail* = *Holy Grail*. More correctly, it was the *Sang Réal* – the Blood Royal, carried by the uterine Chalice of Mary Magdalene. As detailed in medieval literature, the Grail was identified with a family and a dynasty. It was the *Desposynic* 'Vine of Judah', perpetuated in the West through the blood of the Messiah. The lineage of Jesus included the Fisher Kings and Lancelot del Acqs. It descended to the Merovingian Kings of France and the Stewart Kings of Scots, and included such reputed figures as Guilhelm de Gellone and Godefroi de Bouillon.

In descent from Jesus's brother James (Joseph of Arimathea), the Grail Family founded the House of Camulod (Colchester) and the Princely House of Wales. Notable in these lines were King Lucius, Coel Hen, Empress Helena, Ceredig Gwledig and King Arthur. The divine legacy of the *Sangréal* was perpetuated in the sovereign and most noble houses of Britain and Europe – and it is still extant today.

Having established that the *Vine* represents the Messianic bloodline, it follows that the *Vineyard* is the place where that Vine will flourish. About two centuries after the Council of Constance in 1417, Archbishop Ussher of Armagh (the 17th-century compiler of Bible chronology) commented on the Council records. From these he quoted, 'Immediately after the passion of Christ, Joseph of Arimathea . . . proceeded to cultivate the Lord's Vineyard, that is to say, England.'[19]

It is apparent from the annals of saintly genealogy and bardic pedigree that the Messianic line of the

*Sangréal* came into Britain from 1st-century Gaul. In the 'Lord's Vineyard', the line flourished to become the Princely House of Wales, and from this early root stemmed the Gwyr-y-Gogledd chiefs of the northern regions.

In parallel, another branch of the *Vine* conjoined with the great kings of Camulod and Siluria. It was by no chance that Prince Linus, son of Caractacus, became the first Bishop of Rome. Neither was it a fluke of circumstance that Helena (Princess Elaine of Camulod), daughter of Britain's Coel II, married Emperor Constantius.[20] By way of this alliance, Rome was attached to the Judaean royal succession which it had tried so hard to suppress by other means. St Helena's son was Constantine the Great. Having a Celtic Christian mother[21] of a *Desposynic* line, Constantine was not slow to proclaim himself the true Messiah, even though his father's predecessors had been savage persecutors of the Christian movement.

## THE GRAIL HALLOWS AND THE TAROT

The mysterious blood-tipped, white lance that generally accompanied the Grail was said to be the weapon that pierced the hips of the Fisher King. It was identified with the Biblical spear of Longinus, which drew the blood of Jesus. The lance, along with a cup, sword and dish, constituted the 'Hallows' of the Grail Castle.[22] Following Pope Gregory IX's first Catholic Inquisition of 1231, Grail lore was condemned by the Church. It was not denounced outright as a heresy, but all material related to it was suppressed. As a result, the tradition moved towards underground symbolism – particularly that of the Tarot cards.[23] These emerged from northern Italy, Marseilles and Lyon in the 1300s. Some of the most refreshing work to emerge in recent years concerning the Tarot, and concerning graphic symbolism in general, comes from the American author, Margaret Starbird. Her writings in this regard are fully in accord with the precepts of Grail tradition.

The four suits of the Tarot's minor arcana (56 cards, including the court cards: King, Queen, Knight and Page) were the Swords, Cups, Pentacles and Batons or wands. These corresponded with the sword, cup, dish and lance of the Grail Hallows. Eventually they became redefined as the Spades (♠), Hearts (♥), Diamonds (♦), and Clubs (♣) that are used today. The Spade was originally a Blade (the male symbol); the Heart was the Chalice of the alternative Church (the female symbol V); the Diamond was a valuable Pentacle disc (also representing a dish or platter of *service*), and the Club (denoting the continuing Davidic lineage) was depicted as the sprouting Rod of Jesse.

From the earliest times, the symbols Λ and V had been used to identify the sacred unity of the bridal chamber. The male Blade and female Chalice (gender opposites) were brought together (one above the other) in the familiar X sign. This was the original holy Sign of the Cross, and was used as the mark of baptism and initiation long before the time of Jesus. As confirmed in the Dead Sea Scrolls, it was placed on the foreheads of those who cried for Jerusalem (Ezekiel 9:4), and was granted at the highest degree of Community initiation into the Sanctuary.

By way of later Roman influence, a new cross was devised – the upright Latin cross of Peter's Church, with its high crosspiece. The esoteric Christians retained their former X, however, perceiving the Latin cross as representative of Roman torture. And so the original X became a sign of heresy in the eyes of Rome. This heretical image has been perpetuated to this day as being associated with flesh and the devil – as in X-rated movies. Indeed, its anti-establishment significance has been indoctrinated in schools through the simple process of using 'x' to mean 'wrong'.[24]

Even though St Peter's cross was Latinized, the tradition of his brother Andrew was maintained by the original X – the St Andrew's cross. Andrew was crucified at Patras near the Black Sea, where he had worked among the Scythians before they began their westward movement to Caledonia. As a result, he later became the patron saint of Scotland, and his cross became the famous national *Saltire*. Rome was not happy about the reappearance of this ancient esoteric device, and a covering story was contrived to the effect that Andrew himself perished on an X-shaped cross.

A compromise cross was later devised – the familiar non-cruciform, non-esoteric, upright-centred cross. This became the cross of Saint George, whose cult was brought to the West by the Crusaders. Following the 1864 Geneva Convention, it became the symbol of the International Red Cross agency – a colour reversal of the Swiss flag.

The powers of the Pope's inquisitors were increased in 1252, when torture, secret trials, and death by burning were authorized. In Spain, the persecution of heretics was aimed particularly at apostate Jews and Muslims from 1478. Pope Paul III's Roman Inquisition against Protestants began in 1542. The Christians' *underground stream* retained its identity by way of secret watermarks and outline symbols. Because of its simplicity, the X-symbol was widely used – sometimes very openly and cleverly. In Botticelli's *Madonna of the Pomegranate*, an angel wears a red ribboned X on his chest. In his *Madonna of the Book* (1483), Mary wears a red X on her bodice, while the baby Jesus holds three miniature golden arrows. These were the esoteric

Tarot Cards – The World and The Tower

symbols of the 'Three Shafts of Enlightenment' – a motif of Hermetic alchemists.

The secrets of the Tarot were held in the 22 trump cards – the *major arcana*. The word *trump* in this context derives from the Old French, *trompe*, corresponding to the trumpet that figuratively split Peter's Church. The trumps have been called *The Book of Thoth*, an expression of the secret wisdom. The Church of Rome condemned the minor suits, but expressly banned the trumps because they were deemed blasphemous. In truth there was nothing anti-Christian about the playing-cards, although they were undoubtedly anti-establishment. The Christianity of the Tarot was that of Grail lore, not that of Catholicism. The fact that gypsies subsequently used the Tarot cards for divination was quite incidental to their original purpose – but it was through this secondary use that Church propaganda managed to foist an abiding sinister image onto the Tarot deck.

Modern playing-cards retain only one from the Tarot deck – the *Joker*. He is a fool but, even so, the *Joker* always wins. His legacy is from 1 Corinthians:

> The Lord knoweth the thoughts of the wise, that they are vain. Therefore, let no man glory in men . . . (3:20–21)
> We are fools for Christ's sake (4:10)

A literary representation of the *Joker* is apparent in Perceval, the simple man who succeeds where the accomplished fail. Other Tarot figures have made their mark in the world at large. Not the least of these is the female symbol of *Justice*. She is the star-maiden Virgo, with her two-edged sword and the scales of Libra. The portrayal actually has more to do with discrimination than with justice – showing Nature's balance and harmony on the one hand, while the other wields the spike of judicial authority. The original card depicted the tenuous position of the Grail Church against the severity of the Roman Inquisition, and it was known as the 'Magdalene Card'.

Other cards associated with Mary Magdalene were *The Tower*, *The World*, and *Strength*. In the Grail tradition, *The Tower* (or the *House of God*) represented the *Magdal-eder* (the 'Tower of the Flock', as in Micah 4:8) and was not unlike a chess-game castle (rook). Being struck by lightning, or otherwise mysteriously assaulted, it symbolized the plight of the esoteric Church against the merciless Roman establishment.

The spirit of Mary was also manifest in *The World*. Standing or dancing within an oval wreath, and either naked or clothed, the woman held a sceptre or other mark of sovereignty. Some cards showed her above an encircled landscape. The portrayal was similar to the soaring, hair-enveloped Magdalene in the Sforza *Book of Hours* of 1490.

The *Strength* card normally depicted a woman in charge of a lion, or supporting a broken pillar. Some cards had both images. The former was the Lion of Judah, and the latter was the Pillar of Boaz ('in strength') from Solomon's Temple. Either way, the woman was the governess and mainstay of the royal succession:

> And thine house and thy kingdom shall be established for ever before thee: thy throne shall be established for ever.
>
> (2 Samuel 7:16)

In some early decks, a Grail design was incorporated within this card, and the woman was identified with Mary Magdalene. The depiction represented the continuation of the Davidic line as in Psalm 89:4: 'Thy seed will I establish for ever, and build up thy throne to all generations.'

# FIFTEEN

# GUARDIANS OF THE GRAIL

## THE CRUSADER KNIGHTS

By the time of the Norman conquest of Britain in 1066, the Merovingians of France had been formally ignored for some 300 years. They were far from extinct, but they had certainly been manoeuvred out of the picture as far as the Church and its dutiful historians were concerned. During their reign, however, the Merovingians had established a number of customs which prevailed even though the general administration had become feudal. One of the Merovingian innovations was a system of regional supervision by chief officers called *Comites* (Counts). As deputies of the Kings, the Counts acted as chancellors, judges and military leaders. They were not unlike the Celtic Earls of Britain, although the nature of both titular groups became changed to incorporate land tenure during feudal times.

In the 11th century, the Counts of Flanders and Boulogne emerged at the very forefront of Flemish society. Given Godefroi de Bouillon's Davidic inheritance,[1] through the Merovingians, it was fitting enough that he (a brother of Count Eustace III of Boulogne) should become the designated King of Jerusalem after the First Crusade. This military venture was sparked in 1095 by the Muslim seizure of Jerusalem, and it was particularly inspired by Peter the Hermit who led an ill-fated Peasants' Crusade of men, women and children across Europe to regain the Holy Land. The majority did not reach their destination; thousands were massacred *en route* by outlaws and wayward soldiers of the Byzantine Empire. In the esoteric Tarot cards, the Hermit (an allusion to Peter) is portrayed with a lantern lighting the way.

In the wake of the Hermit's misfortune, Pope Urban II raised a formidable army, led by the best knights in Europe. They were coordinated by Adhemar, Bishop of Le Puy, and in the vanguard was Robert, Duc de Normandie, together with Stephen, Comte de Blois, and Hugh, Comte de Vermandois. The Flemish contingent was led by Robert, Comte de Flandres, and included Eustace, Comte de Boulogne, with his brothers Godefroi de Bouillon and Baldwin. The south of France was represented by Raymond de Saint Gilles, Comte de Toulouse.

At that point Godefroi de Bouillon was Duke of Lower Lorraine. He had succeeded to the title through his famous mother, St Ida, who was responsible for the rebuilding of the great cathedral at Boulogne. From Ida, Godefroi gained the castle and lands of Bouillon, but he mortgaged his entire inheritance to the Bishop of Liège in order to fund his Holy Land campaign. By the time the First Crusade was underway, Godefroi had become its overall commander, and on its eventual success in 1099 he was proclaimed King of Jerusalem. In the event, he preferred not to use the title 'King', assuming instead the alternative distinction, 'Guardian of the Sacred Sepulchre'.

Of the eight Crusades, which persisted until 1291 in Egypt, Syria and Palestine, only Godefroi's First Crusade was to any ultimate avail. But even that was marred by the excesses of some irresponsible troops who used their victory as an excuse for wholesale slaughter of Muslims in the streets of Jerusalem. Not only was Jerusalem important to the Jews and Christians, but it had become the third Holy City of Islam, after Mecca and Medina. As such, the city sits at the heart of continuing disputes today.

The Second Crusade to Edessa, led by Louis VIII of France and the German Emperor Conrad III, failed miserably. Then, around 100 years after Godefroi's initial success, Jerusalem fell again to the mighty Saladin in 1187. This prompted the Third Crusade, under Philip Augustus of France and Richard the Lionheart of England, but they did not manage to win back the Holy City. The Fourth and Fifth Crusades centred on Constantinople and Damietta. Jerusalem was reclaimed briefly after Emperor Frederick II's Sixth Crusade, but was finally conceded to the Sultan of Egypt in 1244. Loius IX then led the Seventh and Eighth Crusades, but fell short of reversing the situation. By 1291, Palestine and Syria were firmly under Muslim control, and the Crusades were over.

During this crusading era, various knightly Orders emerged, including the Ordre de Sion (Order of Sion)[2] founded by Godefroi de Bouillon in 1099. Others were the Knights Protectors of the Sacred Sepulchre and the Knights Templars.

Godefroi de Bouillon died in 1100, soon after his Jerusalem triumph, and was succeeded as king by his younger brother, Baldwin of Boulogne. After 18 years, Baldwin was followed (in 1118) by his cousin, Baldwin II du Bourg. According to the orthodox accounts, the Knights Templars were founded in that year as the 'Poor Knights of Christ and of the Temple of Solomon'. They were said to have been established by a group of nine French knights, who took vows of poverty, chastity and obedience, and swore to protect the Holy Land.

The Frankish historian Guillaume de Tyre wrote at the height of the Crusades (in around 1180) that the function of the Templars was to safeguard the highways for pilgrims. But, given the enormity of such an obligation, it is inconceivable that nine poor men succeeded without enlisting new recruits until they returned to Europe in 1128. In truth, there was a good deal more to the Order than is conveyed in Guillaume's account. The Knights were in existence for some years before they were said to have been founded by Hugues de Payens, and their function was certainly not highway patrol. They were the King's front-line diplomats in a Muslim environment, and in this capacity they endeavoured to make due amends for the actions of unruly Crusaders against the Sultan's defenceless subjects. The Bishop of Chartres wrote about the Templars as early as 1114, calling them the *Milice du Christi* (Soldiers of Christ). At that time the Knights were already installed at Baldwin's palace, which was located within a mosque on the site of King Solomon's Temple. When Baldwin moved to the domed citadel on the Tower of David, the Temple quarters were left entirely to the Order of Templars.

Hugues de Payens, the first Grand Master of the Templars, was a cousin and vassal of the Comte de Champagne. His second-in-command was the Flemish knight Godefroi Saint Omer, and another recruit was André de Montbard, a kinsman of the Count of Burgundy. In 1120, Fulk, Comte d'Anjou (father of Geoffrey Plantagenet) also joined the Order, and he was followed in 1124 by Hugues, Comte de Champagne. The Knights were evidently far from poor, and there is no record of these illustrious noblemen policing the Bedouin-infested highways for the benefit of pilgrims. The King's chronicler, Fulk de Chartres, certainly did not portray them in that light.

The task of ministering to the pilgrims was actually performed by the Hospitallers of St John of Jerusalem. The separate Knights Templars were a very select and special unit. They had sworn a particular oath of obedience – not to the King, nor to their leader, but to the Cistercian Abbot, St Bernard de Clairvaux (died 1153).[3] St Bernard was related to the Comte de Champagne and, through him, to Hugues de Payens. Indeed, it was on land donated by the Count that Bernard built the Cistercian monastery of Clairvaux in 1115. Bernard's mother was Aleth, the sister of André de Montbard, and the other Knights of the Order were his own hand-picked Flemings. They included Archambaud de Saint Amand, Geoffrey Bisol, Rosal, Gondemare, Godefroi, and Payen de Montdidier.

It was St Bernard who rescued Scotland's failing Celtic Church, and rebuilt the Columban monastery on Iona.[4] It was St Bernard who (from 1128) first translated the 'sacred geometry' of King Solomon's masons, and it was St Bernard who preached the Second Crusade at Vézelay to King Louis VII and a congregation of 100,000. At Vézelay stood the great Basilica of St Mary Magdalene, and St Bernard's Oath of the Knights Templars required the 'Obedience of Bethany – the castle of Mary and Martha'.[5]

There is no coincidence in the fact that Chrétien de Troyes' 12th-century work, *Le Conte del Graal*, was dedicated to Philippe d'Alsace, Comte de Flandres. Nor was it by chance that Chrétien was sponsored and encouraged in his undertaking by Countess Marie and the Court of Champagne. Grail lore was born directly out of this early Templar environment, and the *Perlesvaus* portrayed the Knights as the wardens of a great and sacred secret. Wolfram's *Parzival* defined them as the Guardians of the Grail Family.

## THE SECRETS OF THE ARK

Deep beneath the Jerusalem Temple site was the great stable of King Solomon, which had remained sealed and untouched since Biblical times. The enormous underground shelter was described by a Crusader as 'a stable of such marvellous capacity and extent that it could hold more than 2,000 horses'.[6] To find and open up this capacious store-room was the original secret mission of the Knights Templars, for it was known by St Bernard to contain the Ark of the Covenant which, in turn, held the greatest of all treasures – the Tables of Testimony.[7]

One might well ask why these relics from the time of Moses became the objects of such a guarded mission fronted by a Cistercian abbot and the flower of Flemish nobility. Today's Church-approved writings state that the tablets of Moses bore the Ten Commandments etched into stone by God Himself – yet the substance of these well-known decrees of moral discipline hardly constituted any sort of secret. In fact, the tablets sought by the Knights were uniquely important, for they bore far more than the familiar Commandments. Inscribed on them were the Tables of Testimony – the Cosmic Equation: the divine law of number, measure and weight. The mystical art of reading the inscriptions was achieved by the cryptic system of the Cabbala.

The Ten Commandments were something else altogether. They were the precepts that God first delivered to Moses and the people on Mount Sinai (Exodus 20 to 23), accompanied by a series of verbal ordinances. Then, God said to Moses (Exodus 24:12),

> Come up to me into the mount, and be there: and I will give thee tables of stone, and a law, and commandments which I have written; that thou mayest teach them.

There are three quite separate items listed here: tables of stone; a law; commandments. God further stated, 'And thou shalt put into the ark the testimony which I shall give thee' (Exodus 25:16). Later, in Exodus 31:18, 'he gave unto Moses . . . two tables of testimony, tables of stone . . .'

The original tablets were broken by Moses when he cast them to the ground (Exodus 32:19). Afterwards, God said to Moses (Exodus 34:1),

> Hew thee two tables of stone like unto the first: and I will write upon these tables the words that were in the first tables, which thou brakest.

Subsequently, God verbally reiterated the Commandments, and said to Moses, 'Write thou these words', whereupon Moses 'wrote . . . the words of the covenant, the ten commandments' (Exodus 34:27–28).

There was a positive distinction made between the 'Tables of Testimony', written by God, and the 'Ten Commandments', which were separately written by Moses. For centuries the Church has implied that the Covenant of the Ten Commandments was the important part of this package, in consequence of which the truly important Tables of Testimony have been strategically ignored.

Onwards from Exodus 25, precise instructions for the Ark's construction are set down in great detail. Similarly, the methods for its transportation are given, along with the specifications for clothes and footwear to be worn by the bearers and overseers. The design and materials for the Tabernacle, in which the Ark was to be kept, are in addition thoroughly described, as is the composition of the altar within. Notwithstanding all of this, Exodus 37 to 40 continues to give a full account of how these instructions were followed to the letter, so repeating everything again. There was no room for any mistakes, nor any deviation from the blueprints laid down. All the building work was entrusted to Bezaleel, the son of Uri ben Hur of Judah.

When constructed precisely in compliance with the Old Testament descriptions, the Ark is discovered to be not only an elaborate coffer but an electrical condenser – built of resinous wood, and double-plated inside and out with gold. The facts have been stated many times by scientists and theologians alike. The individual plates when negatively and positively charged can produce several hundred volts – sufficient even to kill a man. Uzzah discovered this to his cost when he touched the Ark (2 Samuel 6:6–7 and 1 Chronicles 13:9–10). Moreover, the Ark also emerges as an effective transmitter of sound, with its two magnetic cherubim and the Mercy Seat between, where Moses communicated with God (Exodus 25:22).

The Ten Commandments were, and are, written, spoken, discussed and taught. They have never been a secret to anyone – unlike the Tables of Testimony. These precious tabulations were placed in the self-protecting Ark, to be guarded by the Levites. Following the Ark's dramatic transportation across Jordan and through Palestine (Joshua and 1 Samuel), it was taken to Sion (Jerusalem) by David. His son, King Solomon, had the Temple built by the Master-Mason Hiram Abiff, and the Ark was lodged in the Holy of Holies. Access was forbidden, except for ritual inspection by the High Priest alone once a year. Apart from a few items of passing reference, that is the last the Bible has to tell about the Ark of the Covenant. Rumour suggested that the Ark was removed to Ethiopia (Abyssinia), but Revelation 11:19 indicates that it remained in the Temple of Heaven. Undoubtedly, the Ark and the Tables were the prized possessions of Jerusalem – but when Nebuchadnezzar destroyed the

Temple (in around 586 BC), neither was listed in the schedule of plunder.

By 1127, the Templars' search was over. They had retrieved not only the Ark and its contents, but an untold wealth of gold bullion and hidden treasure, all of which had been safely stowed below ground long prior to the Roman demolition and plunder of AD 70. It was not until very recently, in 1956, that confirmatory evidence of the Jerusalem hoard came to light at Manchester University. The deciphering of the Qumran *Copper Scroll* was completed that year. It revealed that an 'indeterminable treasure', along with a vast stockpile of bullion and valuables, had been buried beneath the Temple.

In the light of the Templars' overwhelming success, Hugues de Payens received a summons from St Bernard to attend a forthcoming Council at Troyes. It was to be chaired by the papal ambassador, the Cardinal Legate of France. Hugues and a company of knights duly left the Holy Land with their auspicious find, and St Bernard announced that the Templars' mission had been fulfilled. He wrote,

> The work has been accomplished with our help, and the Knights have been sent on a journey through France and Burgundy, under the protection of the Count of Champagne, where all precautions can be taken against all interference by public or ecclesiastical authority.[8]

The Champagne Court at Troyes was well prepared for the cryptic translation work to follow. In readiness, the Court had long sponsored an influential school of Cabbalistic and esoteric studies. The Council of Troyes was held as planned in 1128, at which time St Bernard became the official Patron and Protector of the Knights Templars, using a beehive as his personal emblem. In that year, international status as a Sovereign Order was

The Conventual Blood Cross of the Knights Templars

conferred upon the Templars, and their Jerusalem headquarters became the governing office of the capital city. The Church established the Knights as a religious Order, and Hugues de Payens became the first Grand Master.

As a mark of particular distinction, the Templars were classified as Warrior-Monks, granted the right to wear the white mantles of purity – a privilege not given to any other military group – and obliged to grow their beards to separate them from lesser fraternities in which the knights were clean-shaven. In 1146, the Templars were awarded their famous conventual blood cross by the Cistercian Pope Eugenius III.

As distinct from the Templars' Cross (red on white), the Hospitallers of Saint John used a different colour scheme (silver on black) in the same design. Their pilgrims' hospital in Jerusalem was founded before the Crusades, in about 1050. After the fall of Acre, which ended the Crusades in 1291, the Hospitallers were forced to leave Palestine. They went to Rhodes and Cyprus, adding secular and military ventures to their activities. From 1530 they were established as the Knights of Malta. An offshoot, chartered in 1888, created Britain's St John Ambulance Association, which still uses the same badge.

After the Council of Troyes, the Templars' rise to international prominence was remarkably swift. They became engaged in high-level politics and diplomacy throughout the western world, and were advisers to monarchs and parliaments alike. Just eleven years later, in 1139, Pope Innocent (another Cistercian) granted the Knights international independence from obligation to any authority save himself. Irrespective of kings, cardinals or governments, the Order's only superior was the Pope. Even prior to this, however, they were granted vast territories and substantial property across the map from Britain to Palestine. The *Anglo-Saxon Chronicle* states that when Hugues de Payens visited England's Henry I, 'the King received him with much honour, and gave him rich presents'. The Spanish King, Alfonso of Aragon, passed a third of his kingdom to the Order, and the whole of Christendom was at their feet.

## NOTRE DAME

When news spread of the Templars' incredible find, the Knights became revered by all, and – notwithstanding their Jerusalem wealth – large donations were received from all quarters. No price was too high to secure affiliation, and within a decade of their return the Templars were probably the most influential body the world has ever known. Nonetheless, despite the prodigious holdings of the Order, the individual Knights were still bound to a vow of poverty. Whatever his station in life, every Templar was obliged to sign over title to his possessions. Even the Grand Master, Hugues de Payens, had done so. Yet still the sons of nobility flocked to join the Order, either as warriors in the Crusades or as travelling ambassadors and political consultants. Being so well funded, the Templars established the first

The Virgo Constellation and Notre Dame Cathedrals. Based
on a diagram by Louis Charpentier

international banking network, becoming financiers for
the Levant and for practically every throne in Europe.

Just as the Order grew to high estate, so too did the
Cistercians' fortune rise in parallel. St Bernard had built
the monastery at Clairvaux in 1115, and a few more
Cistercian centres were established in the following

decade. Then, within 25 years of the Council of Troyes, the Cistercians could boast of more than 300 abbeys. But that was not the end of it, for the people of France then witnessed the most astounding result of the Templars' knowledge of the universal equation. City skylines began to change as the great *Notre Dame* cathedrals, with their majestic Gothic arches, rose from the earth. The architecture was phenomenal – impossible, some said. The pointed ogives reached incredible heights, spanning hitherto insurmountable space, with flying buttresses and thinly ribbed vaulting. Everything pulled upwards and, despite the thousands of tons of richly decorated stone, the overall impression was one of magical weightlessness.

By reference to the Tables of Testimony, the Cosmic Law and its sacred geometry were applied by the Templar masons to construct the finest holy monuments ever to grace the Christian world. At the northern door of *Notre Dame de Chartres* (the Gate of the Initiates), a relief carving on a small column depicts the Ark of the Covenant undergoing transportation. The inscription reads *Hic amititur Archa cederis* 'Here, things take their course – you are to work through the Ark'.[9]

Both concept and formula for the *Notre Dame* programme were entirely Templar-Cistercian. The word *Gothic* as applied to the architectural design had nothing whatever to do with the Goths, but derives instead from the Greek *goetik* – 'magical [action]' (which is possibly cognate with the old Celtic word *goatic* 'plant lore'). The cathedrals were all built at much the same time, even though some took more than a century to complete in their various stages.[10] *Notre Dame* in Paris was begun in 1163, Chartres in 1194, Reims in 1211, and Amiens in 1221. Others of the same era were at Bayeux, Abbeville, Rouen, Laon, Evreux and Etampes. In accordance with the Hermetic principle 'As above, so below',[11] the combined ground-plan of the *Notre Dame* cathedrals replicates the Virgo constellation.[12]

Of all these, the *Notre Dame* at Chartres is said to stand on the most sacred ground. Notable among the authorities on the history of Chartres Cathedral is Louis Charpentier, whose research and writings have done much to increase the understanding of Gothic architecture in general. At Chartres the telluric earth currents are at their highest, and the site was recognized for its divine atmosphere even in Druidic times. So venerated is the location of Chartres that it is the only cathedral not to have a single king, bishop, cardinal, canon, or *anyone* interred in the soil of its mound. It was a pagan site, dedicated to the traditional Mother Goddess – a site to which pilgrims travelled long before the time of Jesus. The original altar was built above the *Grotte des Druides*, which housed a sacred dolmen,[13] and was identified with the 'Womb of the Earth'.

One of the greatest mysteries of Cistercian Gothic architecture is the stained glass used in the cathedral windows. It first appeared in the early 12th century, but disappeared just as suddenly in the middle of the 13th century. Nothing like it had ever been seen before, and nothing like it has been seen since.[14] Not only is the luminosity of truly Gothic stained glass greater than any other, but its light-enhancement qualities are far more effective. Unlike the stained glass of other architectural schools, its interior effect is the same whether the light outside is bright or dim. Even in twilight, this glass retains its brilliance way beyond that of any other.

Gothic stained glass also has the unique power to transform harmful ultra-violet rays into beneficial light, but the secret of its manufacture was never revealed. Although it is known to have been a product of Hermetic alchemy, no modern scientific process or chemical analysis has yet managed to penetrate its mystery. Those employed to perfect Gothic glass were Persian philosophical mathematicians such as Omar Khayyam, and the adepts claimed their method of staining incorporated the *Spiritus Mundi* – the cosmic breath of the universe. In modern language this corresponds to high-energy penetrative radiation.

Throughout the Gothic cathedrals, works of art abound in stone and glass, depicting Biblical history and the Gospel stories, in which much attention is given to the life of Jesus. Some of the work currently visible was added after the 1300s, but during the true Gothic era there was not one portrayal of the Crucifixion. On the basis of pre-Gospel writings which they found in Jerusalem, the Templars denied the Crucifixion sequence as described in the New Testament, and for that reason never depicted the scene. The 12th-century window in the West front of Chartres includes a medallion of the Crucifixion, but this was transferred from elsewhere at a later date – probably from St Denis, just north of Paris. There are similarly inherited windows at other *Notre Dame* cathedrals.

In addition to the Jerusalem bullion, the Templars also found a wealth of ancient manuscript books in Hebrew and Syriac. As mentioned above, many of these predated the Gospels, providing first-hand accounts that had not been edited by any ecclesiastical authority. It was widely accepted that the Knights possessed an insight which eclipsed orthodox Christianity, an insight that permitted them the certainty that the Church had misinterpreted both the *Virgin Birth* and the *Resurrection*. They were nevertheless highly regarded as holy men, and were firmly attached to the Cistercian popes of the era.

In times to follow, however, the once revered knowledge of the Templars caused their persecution by the savage Dominicans of the 14th-century Inquisition. It was at that point in the history of Christianity that the last vestige of free thinking disappeared. Neither special knowledge nor access to truths counted for anything against the hard new party line of Rome. So too did all traces of the female aspect disappear, with only Mary the mother of Jesus left to represent all womankind. In practice, her semi-divine Virgin-Madonna status was so far removed from any reality that she represented no one. But for all that, a ray of hope has prevailed through the centuries – for another female light shines from the cathedrals of *Notre Dame*. The age-old cult of Mary Magdalene, the embodiment of the *Pistis Sophia*, remains fully central to the theme, and the beautiful Magdalene window at Chartres has an inscription which reads 'Donated by the Water-carriers' (the Aquarians). Mary was the bearer of the Holy Grail, and she will undoubtedly become ever more prominent as the great new 'Inspiration' of the Aquarian Age – the age of renewed intellect, wisdom and the Universal Law of the Ark.

## THE BROTHERHOOD OF THE THIRD DEGREE

The *Notre Dame* cathedrals and major Gothic constructions were mainly the work of the *Children of Solomon* – a guild of masons instructed by St Bernard's Cistercian Order. St Bernard had translated the secret geometry of King Solomon's masons who, under their own master, Hiram Abiff, were denoted by degrees of knowledge and proficiency. Solomon had specifically approached King Hiram of Tyre for the assistance of Hiram Abiff, an architect and metalworker skilled in sacred geometry.[15] Even though Tyre was a renowned centre of Goddess worship, Hiram Abiff became the chief designer and Master Mason for the Temple of Jehovah. By virtue of this, he was destined to become a key symbolic figure in later Freemasonry.

Other masonic brotherhoods of medieval France were the *Children of Father Soubise*, and the *Children of Master Jacques*.[16] When the 14th-century Dominican-led Inquisition against the Templars was in full swing, these guilds were equally at risk. Being practitioners of the Masonic Craft, they held privileged information concerning the workings of sacred geometry and Universal Law according to their attained degrees. There were three such degrees: Apprentice Companion, Attained Companion, and Master Companion – just as there are now three degrees in the mainstream of modern speculative Freemasonry. This is why, following the Inquisition of the Templars, a severe interrogation to extract the most vital or the most secret information is often called the 'third degree'.

Although modern Freemasonry is said to derive from the medieval guilds of Europe, the Craft had far more distant origins. Carvings on the Egyptian obelisk in Central Park, New York, have been identified as masonic symbols from the time of Pharaoh Tuthmosis III (c. 1468–1436 BC)[17] – the great-great-grandfather of Moses. Tuthmosis (heir of Tuth/Thoth) was the founder of an influential secret society of scholars and philosophers, whose purpose was to preserve the sacred mysteries. In later times, the Samaritan Magi were members of the Order, being attached to the Egyptian Therapeutate, an ascetic community at Qumran. It was from Egypt that Moses (Akhenaten[18]) introduced the concept of temple worship to the Israelites when he created the Tabernacle at Sinai. Similarly, the very notion of priesthood was Egyptian – inherited originally from ancient Sumer. Prior to the Tabernacle of Moses, the Jewish patriarchs had used simple outside stone altars as places of reverence and sacrifice – such as those erected by Noah (Genesis 8:20) and Abraham (Genesis 22:9).

A second Egyptian obelisk from the Temple of the Sun (known for some obscure reason as Cleopatra's Needle – relating to Cleopatra VII – although it pre-dated her by more than a thousand years) stands on the Thames Embankment in London. It is 68 feet 6 inches (20.88 metres) high[19] and weighs 186 tons (tonnes). The two granite obelisks were originally entrance pillars to the Temple at Heliopolis, but were moved to Alexandria in 12 BC, then to London and New York in 1878 and 1881 respectively.

In line with the Egyptian practice of placing free-standing pillars at temple entrances, Hiram Abiff introduced the same theme at the porch of King Solomon's Temple in Jerusalem. The pillars, with their rounded capitals, were akin to the designs of Tyre goddess worship, and were also similar to the fertility symbols dedicated to Astarte in Canaan. The Jerusalem pillars were called *Jachin* and *Boaz* (1 Kings 7:21 and 2 Chronicles 3:17). They were built hollow in order to serve as repositories for the archival and constitutional rolls of Masonry. Moreover, although the Temple was dedicated to Jehovah and designed primarily to house the Ark of the Covenant, its construction was not limited to the Hebrews' masculine principle of God: it was constructed largely in keeping with traditional custom, and incorporated both the male and female geometric energies.

The Temple was completed in seven years, at the end of which time Hiram was murdered and placed in a shallow grave. His death is said to have come about through his refusal to impart the Master Mason's secrets to the unenlightened workers. Today, the symbolized slaying of Hiram features significantly in the Third Degree ceremony of Freemasonry: the candidate is struck down and raised again from the darkness of his grave by use of the Master Mason's secret grip.

Modern Freemasonry is speculative rather than operative, but even in Hiram's day the society of artificers to which he belonged had its own lodges, symbols and passwords. One evident symbol was the *ascia*, the mason's trowel, an emblem used by the Pythagoreans and Essenes. It is also found in the catacombs of Rome, where portrayals of masonic initiation were painted in the tombs of the persecuted *Innocenti*.

## SLAUGHTER IN LANGUEDOC

West-north-west of Marseilles, on the Golfe du Lion, stretches the old province of Languedoc where, in 1208, the people were admonished by Pope Innocent III for unchristian behaviour. In the following year, a papal army of 30,000 soldiers descended on the region under the command of Simon de Montfort. They were deceitfully adorned with the red cross of the Holy Land Crusaders, but their purpose was immeasurably different. They had in fact been sent to exterminate the ascetic *Cathari* sect (the Pure Ones) who resided in Languedoc, and who – according to the Pope and King Philippe II of France – were heretics. The slaughter went on for 35 years, claiming tens of thousands of lives, culminating in the hideous massacre at the seminary of Montségur, where more than 200 hostages were set up on stakes and burned alive in 1244.[20]

In religious terms, the doctrine of the Cathars was essentially Gnostic; they were notably spiritual people, and believed that the *spirit* was pure but that physical *matter* was defiled. Although their convictions were unorthodox in comparison with the avaricious pursuits of Rome, the Pope's dread of the Cathars was actually caused by something far more threatening. They were said to be the guardians of a great and sacred treasure, associated with a fantastic and ancient knowledge. The

Languedoc region was substantially that which had formed the 8th-century Jewish kingdom of Septimania, under the Merovingian scion Guilhelm de Gellone. The whole area of Languedoc and Provence was steeped in the early traditions of Lazarus (Simon Zelotes) and Mary Magdalene, and the inhabitants regarded Mary as the 'Grail Mother' of true Western Christianity.[21]

Like the Templars, the Cathars were expressly tolerant of the Jewish and Muslim cultures, and they also upheld the equality of the sexes.[22] They were nonetheless condemned and violently suppressed by the Catholic Inquisition (formally instituted in 1233), and were charged with all manner of blasphemies.

Contrary to the charges, the witnesses brought to give evidence spoke only of the Cathars' *Church of Love*, and of their unyielding devotion to the ministry of Jesus. They believed in God and the Holy Spirit, recited the Lord's Prayer, and ran an exemplary society with its own welfare system of charity schools and hospitals. The Cathars even had the Bible translated into their own tongue – the *langue d'oc* (hence the regional name) – and the non-Cathar population equally benefited from their altruistic efforts.

The Cathars were not heretics; they were simply non-conformists, preaching without licence, and having no requirement for appointed priests, nor the richly adorned churches of their Catholic neighbours. St Bernard had said that 'No sermons are more Christian than theirs, and their morals are pure.' Yet still the papal armies came, in the outward guise of a holy mission, to eradicate their community from the landscape.

The edict of annihilation referred not only to the mystical Cathars themselves but to all who supported them – which included most of the people of Languedoc. To add weight to the Holy Inquisition, the citizens of the region were accused by the Dominican monks of unnatural sexual practices. This charge has led to all sorts of later guesswork as to the nature of such deviations. In fact, what the enlightened people of Languedoc practised was nothing more than birth control. By most standards of accomplishment and learning, the Cathars were probably the most cultured people in Europe, with both boys and girls having equal access to education.

At that time, Provençal Languedoc was not part of France but an independent state. Politically, it was more associated with the northern Spanish frontier, having the Count of Toulouse as its overlord – a remnant of the Septimanian kingdom. Classical languages were taught, along with literature, philosophy and mathematics. The area was generally quite wealthy and commercially stable – but all this was to change in 1209 when the papal troops arrived in the foothills of the Pyrenees. In allusion to the Languedoc centre at Albi, the savage campaign was called the 'Albigensian Crusade'.

Of all the religious cults that flourished in medieval times, Catharism was the least menacing. The fact that the Cathars were associated with a particular ancient knowledge was in itself no new revelation; Guilhelm de Toulouse de Gellone, King of Septimania,[23] had established his Judaic Academy more than four centuries earlier. But the Cathars were known also to be adepts of the occult symbolism of the Cabbala, an expertise that would have been of significant use to the Knights Templars who were thought to have transported the Ark and their Jerusalem hoard to the region. These things (along with the premise that the Cathars held an unsurpassed treasure more historically meaningful than the root of Christianity) led Rome to only one conclusion: the Tables of Testimony and the Jerusalem manuscripts of the Gospel era must be hidden in Languedoc.

Over and above this, the traditions of Provence from the 1st century included the lore of the Grail bloodline. The church at Rennes-le-Château had been consecrated to Mary Magdalene in 1059, and the people of the region declared that Rome's interpretation of the Crucifixion was a fraud. In common with the Templars, the Cathars would in no way support the claim that Jesus died on the cross. Although the Cathar ritual was not in itself threatening, the sect was presumed to hold enough information of substance to blow the lid off the fundamental concept of the orthodox Roman Church. There was only one solution for a desperate and fanatical regime, and the word went out: 'Kill them all!'

The people were bloodily killed in their thousands, and their towns demolished, but the treasure was never found. The Church wondered whether it had perhaps been removed during the onslaught, or whether it was still there, as yet undiscovered. Either way, its curse hung over the Pope, and the danger prevailed. The Knights Templars would have known the answer, and in the wake of the Languedoc carnage they were destined to suffer a similar victimization.

## PERSECUTION OF THE KNIGHTS TEMPLARS

The mock Crusade ended in 1244, but it was to be another 62 years before Pope Clement V and King Philippe IV were in a position to harass the Knights Templars in their bid for the arcane treasure. By 1306 the Jerusalem Order was so powerful that Philippe IV of France viewed them with trepidation; he owed a great deal of money to the Knights but was practically bankrupt. He also feared their political and esoteric might, which he knew to be far greater than his own. With papal support, King Philippe persecuted the Templars in France and endeavoured to eliminate the Order in other countries. Knights were arrested in England, but north of the border in Scotland the papal Bulls were ineffective. This was because King Robert the Bruce and the whole Scottish nation had been excommunicated for taking up arms against Philippe's son-in-law, king Edward II of England.[24]

Until 1306, the Knights had always operated without papal interference, but Philippe managed to change this. Following a Vatican edict forbidding him to tax the clergy, the French king arranged for the capture and murder of Pope Boniface VIII. His successor, Benedict XI, also met his end in very mysterious circumstances soon afterwards, to be replaced in 1305 by Philippe's own candidate, Bertrand de Goth, Archbishop of Bordeaux, who duly became Pope Clement V. With a new Pope under his control through financial indebtedness to him, Philippe drew up his list of accusations against the Knights Templars. The easiest charge to lay was that of heresy, for it was well established that the Knights did not hold to the orthodox view of the Crucifixion, and they would not bear the upright Latin cross. It was also known that the Templars' diplomatic and business affairs involved them with Jews, Gnostics and Muslims.

On Friday 13 October 1307, Philippe's henchmen struck, and Templars were seized throughout France. Captured Knights were imprisoned, interrogated, tortured, and burned. Paid witnesses were called to give evidence against the Order, and some truly bizarre statements were obtained. The Templars were accused of a number of assorted practices deemed unsavoury, including necromancy, homosexuality, abortion, blasphemy, and the black arts. Once they had given their evidence, under whatever circumstances of bribery or duress, the witnesses disappeared without trace. Despite all this, the King did not achieve his primary objective, for the Ark and the treasure remained beyond his grasp. His minions had scoured the length and breadth of Champagne and Languedoc – but all the while the hoard was hidden away in the Treasury vaults of Paris.

At that time, the Grand Master of the Order was Jacques de Molay. Knowing that Pope Clement V was a pawn of King Philippe, de Molay arranged for the Templar treasures to be removed in a fleet of eighteen galleys from La Rochelle. The majority of these treasure ships sailed to Scotland,[25] but Philippe was quite unaware of this and negotiated with other monarchs to have the Templars generally pursued outside France. Subsequently, Philippe forced Pope Clement to outlaw the Order in 1312 and, two years later, Jacques de Molay was burned at the stake.

Edward II of England was reluctant to turn against the Knights but, as Philippe's son-in-law, he was in a difficult position. Thus, on receiving an outright instruction from the Pope, he complied with the rule of the Inquisition. Many Templars were arrested in England, while their lands and preceptories were confiscated and subsequently passed to the Hospitallers of St John.

In Scotland, however, the story was very different: the papal Bull was totally ignored. Long before, in 1128, Hugues de Payens had first met King David I of Scots soon after the Council of Troyes, and St Bernard de Clairvaux had integrated the Celtic Church with his wealthy Cistercian Order. King David granted Hugues and his Knights the lands of Ballantradoch, by the Firth of Forth (now the village of Temple), and they established their primary seat on the South Esk. The Order was then promoted and encouraged by successive kings, particularly William the Lion. Considerable tracts of land were passed to the Knights – especially around the Lothians and Aberdeen – and the Templars also took possession of property in Ayr and western Scotland. A large contingent fought at Bannockburn in 1314, following which they became very prominent in Lorne and Argyll. From the time of Robert the Bruce, each successive Bruce and Stewart heir was a Knight Templar from birth and, by virtue of this, the Scots royal line comprised not only Priest-Kings but Knight-Priest-Kings.

These days, history books and encyclopedias are almost unanimous in declaring that the Knights Templars became extinct in the 1300s. They are quite wrong. The Chivalric Military Order of the Temple of Jerusalem (as distinct from the later contrived Masonic Templars) is still flourishing in continental Europe and Scotland.

# SIXTEEN

# RISE OF THE HOUSE OF STEWART

## ANTECEDENTS: BANQUO AND LADY MACBETH

We shall soon be entering the world of the Royal House of Stewart who, from the time of the usurped Merovingians, emerged as the most significant reigning dynasty in the *Desposynic* succession. Beforehand, however, we must backtrack just a little in order to set the scene for them in Scotland. The Stewart heritage was part Scots and part Breton, and in respect of their Scottish ancestry one of the most important characters in their history was Banquo, 11th-century Thane of Lochaber.

From the time that Kenneth MacAlpin united the Picts and Scots in 844, the individual Kings of Scots inherited their crowns by way of *Tanist* descent, in accordance with Pictish custom. Although the Scots maintained their kingship by succession through the male line, the Pictish tradition had been matrilinear. An arrangement was therefore devised by which Pictish princesses married Scots Kings, thus maintaining the status quo, but the descent was not set in one family line. Kings were selected in advance from sons, nephews and cousins in parallel lines of descent from a common source. In this particular case, the common

**EARLY KINGS OF SCOTS**
*Carolingian contemporaries – 8th to 10th century*

ALPIN
King of Scots 839-841

[See Chart: RULERS OF STRATHCLYDE]

Rhydderch

KENNETH I
King of Picts & Scots
844-859

DONALD I
859-863

Dyfnwal III

Artgal d. 872

CONSTANTINE I
863-877

AEDH
877-878

Daughter = King Run of
Strathclyde

DONALD II
889-900

CONSTANTINE II
900-942

EOCHAID
878-889

5th century descent from
Niall High King of Ireland

MALCOLM I
942-954

INDULPH
954-962

Family of Tir Conaill

DUBH (Duff)
962-967

CUILEAN
967-971

[Priests of Dull from c.850]

Duncan, Priest of Dull

KENNETH III
997-1005

KENNETH II
971-995

CONSTANTINE III
995-997

Duncan MacDonachadh
Abbot of Dunkeld
(d. 965)

Boede
Chief of
Clan Duff

MALCOLM II
MacKenneth
1005-1034

Duncan MacDonachadh
Abbot of Dunkeld
Hereditary Priest & Abthane of Dull

Olith = Sigurd II
Jarl of Orkneys

Donada = Finlaech
Mormaer of Moray
d. 1057

Bethoc = Crinan
Abbot of Dunkeld
Thane of the Isles
k. 1045

THORFINN II
Jarl of Orkneys
d. 1057

– (joint kings) –    MACBETH
1040-1057
*Slain by Malcolm, son of Duncan*

DUNCAN I
1034-1040
*Slain by Macbeth*

source was King Kenneth. The Chart: Early Kings of Scots, indicates how the *Tanist* system worked, with kingship moving back and forth between one line and another. The great advantage of this selective arrangement was that minors never achieved the crown, as happened (to Scotland's detriment) in later times after the system was discarded.

Following nearly 200 years of alternating Tanist succession in the Scots descent, a furious dispute arose when the tradition was broken by Malcolm II. Instead of correctly affording the kingship to his younger cousin, Boede of Duff (Dubh), he decided that his own offspring should inherit the crown. The problem was that Malcolm had no son. But he did have three daughters, and Bethoc, the eldest, was married to Crinan, Archpriest of the Sacred Kindred of St Columba.[1] Alike to St Columba himself, Crinan was descended from the Tir Conaill royalty of Ireland. Malcolm's second daughter, Donada, was married to Findlaech MacRory, Mormaer of Moray; while Olith, the youngest, was married to Sigurd II, Norse Prince and Jarl (Earl) of the Orkneys. An additional complication was caused because King Malcolm's sister Dunclina was married to Kenneth of Lochaber who, through the structure of Tanistry, had a secondary claim to the crown as a cousin of Boede, in descent from Kenneth MacAlpin.

The sons of these various marriages were each and all in the running for kingship when Malcolm II died in 1034 and, among these sons, the heir with the closest right to succession was Dunclina's son, Banquo, Thane of Lochaber. Yet, in accordance with Malcolm's wishes, the son of his eldest daughter, Bethoc, succeeded as King Duncan I. Being also the son and hereditary heir of Archpriest Crinan (who was murdered by Vikings in 1045), Duncan became Scotland's first Priest-King, in the style of the earlier Merovingians of Gaul. This concept of the monarch as both the sovereign and the religious patriarch remained at the core of Scots culture thereafter.

Prior to Malcolm's death, a revolt against the planned succession had been instigated by Gruoch, daughter of the logical Tanist, Boede of Duff. As a consequence of this revolt, King Malcolm slew Boede, thereby leaving his heiress, the Lady Gruoch, with a significant sovereign claim by the rule of Tanistry. She mustered fierce opposition against the King, who responded by killing her husband, Gillacomgen of Moray. Gruoch (who was pregnant at the time) fled to the protection of her cousin-in-law Macbeth, the son of Donada and Findlaech. Shortly afterwards, in 1032, she married her protector – and was henceforth Lady Macbeth.

When Malcolm II died in 1034, Lady Gruoch persuaded Macbeth to challenge his cousin Duncan's succession. She was not alone in her resentment of Duncan, and a series of riots ensued, led by various clan chiefs. Not even Banquo, a captain in Duncan's army, could contain the riots. A military council was therefore convened, at which Macbeth gained control of the King's troops, managing where others had failed to subdue the revolt. He thus became more popular than the King himself, further elevating the ambitions of Lady Macbeth, who knew the crown was within her husband's grasp. But what of King Duncan? The truth of his demise in 1040 is still uncertain. History relates that he was killed in an affray at Bothnagowan (Pitgaveny, near Elgin), whereas romantic literature tells that he was murdered in Macbeth's castle. Whatever the case, Macbeth became King south and west of the Tay, while his cousin Thorfinn of Caithness (the son of Olith and Sigurd) ruled the rest of Scotland.

For 17 years Macbeth ran an orderly realm, while his wife ran a popular court. At the beginning, however,

Thane Banquo of Lochaber endeavoured to regain the crown for Duncan's son, Malcolm Canmore, Prince of Cumbria. In the course of the dispute, Macbeth slew two of Banquo's sons and arranged for Banquo and his eldest son, Fleance, to be ambushed. Banquo was killed in the ensuing fight, but Fleance escaped to the castle of Prince Gruffyd ap Llewelyn of Gwynedd (north-west Wales). There he became the first husband of Gruffyd's daughter Nesta (or Nest), with whom he remained in Wales for some time. Then, following his eventual death, Nesta married Osbern Fitz Richard de Léon.

Throughout Macbeth's reign, Malcolm persisted with his claim, gaining the support of Thorfinn, and in 1057 their combined armies forced Macbeth's retreat at Lumphanan. Conceding absolute defeat, Lady Gruoch Macbeth committed suicide, and soon afterwards Macbeth was slain. Thorfinn was also killed in the battle, and his widow Ingibjorg was obliged to marry Malcolm Canmore. Despite his victory, Malcolm did not accede to the crown immediately, for the Macbeth party was still in control and placed Lady Gruoch's son Lulach (by her first husband Gillacomgen) on the throne. A few months later, however, Lulach was slain at Strathbogie – and in 1058 Malcolm III Canmore was proclaimed King of Scots.[2]

The accounts of Macbeth, Lady Macbeth and Banquo have been treated very sparingly by historians, but their legendary status lives on in William Shakespeare's popular play – which was based on the *Chronicles of Englande, Scotlande, and Irelande* by Raphael Holinshed (died 1580). Shakespeare's *Macbeth* was written nearly six centuries after the historical event. Therefore, when constructing the prophecies of the three *Weird Sisters*, the playwright already knew precisely what had followed in history. On consulting their auguries early in the play, the witches inform Macbeth that he will be

King. They also tell Banquo that, although he will never reign, he will beget future kings – as indeed he did.

## THE FIRST STEWARTS

The name *Stewart* derives from the distinction, *Steward*, as used in 13th-century Scotland. The early Stewarts became Kings of Scots in 1371, and the royal branch later adopted the French corruption, *Stuart* (as did some other branches also). From their earliest days it was known that the Stewarts were descended from Banquo of Lochaber, and their descent through this noble Thane, ultimately from King Alpin (the father of Kenneth I), was listed in all relevant genealogies (a matter to which we shall return in a later chapter). It was also known, however, that the Stewarts emerged from the 11th-century Seneschals of Dol in Brittany.[3] In sovereign terms, their conjoined legacies were of enormous significance, for their Scots lineage was of the Arimathea succession, and their Breton inheritance was that of the Christ himself, through the Fisher Kings.

The pre-Scotland forebear of the Breton line was Alan, Seneschal of Dol and Dinan, a contemporary of Banquo and Macbeth in the second quarter of the 11th century. Alan's sons were Alan and Flaald (hereditary Stewards of Dol), and Rhiwallon (Lord of Dol). The senior son, Alan (Alanus Siniscallus), was a commander in the First Crusade, and appears in the *Cartulary of St Florent* as a benefactor of the Abbey. His brother Flaald (Fledaldus) was the Baron of St Florent, and married Aveline, the daughter of Arnulf, Seigneur de Hesdin of Flanders. The third brother, Lord Rhiwallon, became Abbot of St Florent de Saumur in 1082.

Certain peerage registers cite Aveline as the wife of Flaald's son, Alan, but such entries are incorrect.[4] Alan Fitz Flaald was born with the *de Hesdin* title inherited

*Map 11*  Scotland

from his mother, Aveline (Ava). She is described in the *Cartulary of St George, Hesdin* as being of an age to consent to her father's gifting of English estates to the Priory in 1094. When Seigneur Arnulf (the brother of Count Enguerrand de Hesdin) joined the Crusade in 1090, Aveline became his deputy and heiress in

## ORIGINS OF THE STEWARTS
*Scottish and Breton descents*

Kenneth b. 960 d. 1030
= *Dunclina*
*dau. of Kenneth II*

Lachlan
|
Phaetus

ALAN
SENESCHAL OF DOL & DINAN
DAPIFER OF DOL c. 1045
Dapifer Dolensis Brittany

BANQUO .... = .... *Muldivana*
k. by Macbeth        *(Maud)*
b. 990 d. 1043

MACBETH
k. by Malcolm 1057
[See Chart: MACBETH TO THE STEWARTS]

FLEANCE
b. 1020
= *(1st husband of)*
*Nesta (Mary) dau. of*
*Prince Gruffyd*
*son of King Llewelyn*
*of Gwynedd and first wife*
*Guerta of Deheubarth*

ALAN
Hereditary Steward of Dol
Commander in First Crusade
b.c. 1050 d. 1097

FLAALD (Fledaldus)
Hereditary Steward of Dol
Baron of St. Florent c. 1101
= *Aveline (Ava, Domina de Norton)*
*dau. of Arnulf, Seigneur*
*de Hesdin, Picardy*

Rhiwallon
Lord of Dol
Abbot of St. Florent
de Saumur 1082

William
Abbot of St. Florent
1102

John
Monk of
St. Florent

WALTER  =  *Emma*
Thane of      *b.c. 1070*
Lochaber
b.c. 1045
d. 1093 at
Alnwick

William Fitz Alan
Baron of Oswestry
Sheriff of Shropshire
Castellan of Shrewsbury 1138
b. 1105 d. 1160
= (1) *Christian (niece of*
*Robert Fitzroy of Gloucester)*
= (2) *Isabel (dau. of Elias*
*de Say, Lord of Clun)*

Jordan Fitz Alan
Hereditary Steward of Dol
c. 1130
= *Mary*

ALAN FITZ FLAALD DE HESDIN
Sheriff of Shropshire
Baron of Oswestry d.c. 1122
= *Adeliza, dau. and heiress of*
*Sheriff Warine of Shropshire*

Jordan
Fitz Jordan
d.s.p.

Alan Fitz Jordan
Seneschal of Dol
d.c. 1167
= *Joan*

ALAN OF LOCHABER  =  *ADELINA OF OSWESTRY*
b.c. 1088           *b.c. 1095*
d. 1153

William (Fitz William) Fitzalan
Baron of Oswestry, Sheriff of Shropshire
b. 1090 d. 1211

Jordan Fitz Alan
d.s.p.

*Olive*
of Tuxford
& Sharrington
c. 1227

*Alice*
= *William Epine*
Steward of Dol

William
d. 1216

John Fitzalan
Baron of Oswestry
= *Isabel d'Aubigny* d. 1240
*dau. of William*
*3rd Earl of Arundel*

Fitzalan Earls of
Arundel (1289-1580)
Descend

WALTER FITZ ALAN ...... = ...... *Eschyne de Molle*
1st HIGH STEWARD        *Dau. of Thomas de Lundins*
OF SCOTLAND             *Maternal granddaughter*
(THE GREAT STEWART)     *of Uhtred de Molle*
d. 1177

STEWARTS DESCEND

England. She was styled *Domina de Norton* (Lady of Norton), and her son was Alan Fitz Flaald de Hesdin, Baron of Oswestry, in the reign of King Henry I. Alan married Adeliza, the daughter of Sheriff Warine of Shropshire,[5] thereby in due course inheriting that same office. He also founded Sporle Priory in Norfolk as a cell of St Saumur.

Alan the Steward's sons were William and Jordan Fitz Alan. William succeeded to the Oswestry and Shropshire titles after the death of his cousin, Alan, and from him the Fitzalan Earls of Arundel descended. Jordan inherited the hereditary Stewardship of Dol, and also the lands of Tuxford, Burton and Warsop in England. Alan also had a daughter, Emma, who married Walter, Thane of Lochaber – the son of Fleance (son of Banquo) and Princess Nesta of Gwynedd. Their son, Alan of Lochaber, married his cousin, Adelina of Oswestry, the daughter of Alan Fitz Flaald. They, in turn, were the parents of Walter Fitz Alan (died 1177), who became the first High Steward of Scotland.

Some published charts of Stewart genealogy mistakenly identify Walter the High Steward with his grandfather, Walter, Thane of Lochaber. The mistake arose because an alternative form of the name Alan was Flan, and this became confused with Fleance, the name of the son of Banquo.[6]

It was actually the latter Walter Fitz Alan who was appointed to the Scots Grand Stewardship of King David I (1124–1153). Walter arrived in Scotland in about 1138, and was granted lands in Renfrewshire and East Lothian by King David I. On becoming the High Steward of Scotland, Walter gained the highest of conferred positions, and was also made Chancellor of Treasury Revenues. This latter office gave rise to the *Fesse Chequey* in the armorial bearings of the Stewarts: the 'chequey' represents the chequered (or checked) table that was used for monetary calculation, and from this derived the term *Exchequer*, as applied to the State Treasury Department.

During the reign of David's grandson, Malcolm IV, Walter founded the Cluniac Paisley Priory, and was appointed Commander of the King's Army. In 1164 the Renfrew coastline was invaded by 160 Norse warships of the mighty Somerled, Thane of the Isles. The ships contained more than 6,000 warriors bent on conquest, but once ashore they were defeated by a much smaller force under the command of Walter's Household Knights. In the Library of Corpus Christi College, Cambridge, there is a manuscript by the monk William of Glasgow that gives an eyewitness account of the 1164 Battle of Renfrew. He states that Somerled was killed early in the fight, following which the invaders were routed with heavy slaughter. The battle is also described in the *Chronicles of Man*, *of Holyrood* and *of Melrose*.

Of all the Scots kings, young Malcolm IV (known as 'the Maiden') was the weakest, as he proved by giving away the long-prized territories of Cumbria to Henry II of England. He then went to Toulouse at the age of 14, and spent most of his remaining ten years abroad. It was just as well for Scotland that Walter the Steward was there to manage political, military and financial affairs in the king's stead. Malcolm IV was succeeded by his brother William in 1165; he was a much stronger character, nicknamed 'the Lion'. A while after his accession, William sought to regain Northumberland and Cumberland from Henry II at Alnwick in 1174. By that time, King Henry of England was married to Eleanor of Aquitaine (the former wife of Louis VII of France), but their sons (with Eleanor's approval) sided with William of Scots in the Cumbrian dispute, standing against their father on the battlefield. In the event, William was

defeated and captured, following which he was obliged
to sign the *Treaty of Falaise*, recognizing the English King
as Lord Paramount of Scotland. William was thereafter
held in custody and, once more, Walter the High Steward took the reins.

Walter Fitz Alan died in 1177 and was succeeded by
his son, Alan, as the Second High Steward. In 1189, Alan
joined the Third Crusade with Henry II's son and successor, Richard I Coeur de Lion (the Lionheart). Before
leaving for the Holy Land with Alan, King Richard
declared the *Treaty of Falaise* null and void, and reaf-
firmed Scotland's right to independence. Alan the
Steward died in 1204, and his son Walter became Third
High Steward to William's son and heir, Alexander II.
This Walter was the first to use the name *Stewart*, and it
was he who raised Paisley Priory to the status of an
Abbey in 1219. By 1230 he was Justiciar north of the
Forth as well as Chancellor.

The Fesse Chequey of the High Stewards of Scotland

The succeeding king, Alexander III, became one of Scotland's most impressive rulers although, in the early days, his reign was subject to the partial regency of the Fourth High Steward, Walter's son Alexander. At that time the Norse invaders were proving troublesome once more, and in 1263 the fleet of the Norwegian King Haakon arrived at Clydeside. They were defeated at the Battle of Largs by Scots forces under the command of Alexander Stewart, who was rewarded with the lordship of Galloway.

King Alexander III married Margaret, the daughter of Henry III Plantagenet of England, and to keep the peace with the King of Norway, their daughter, Princess Margaret of Scotland, was married to the future King Eric II. Unfortunately, she died in childbirth soon afterwards – two years before the death of her father, who left no surviving sons. This meant that the sole heiress to the Kingdom of Scots was Alexander's granddaughter, the 'Maid of Norway' – who was then only 3 years old. And so the Fifth High Steward, Sir James (Alexander Stewart's son), became Regent in Scotland.

The Scots were then concerned that their nation might come under rule from Norway. The Bishop of Glasgow approached the Maid's uncle, King Edward I of England, for advice in the matter – but in view of Plantagenet aspirations towards control of Scotland, Edward's response was predictable. He suggested that Margaret, Maid of Norway, should be married to his own son, Edward Caernarvon, and further that she should be brought up at the English Plantagenet court. From that moment, Edward I considered his suggestion to be a positive betrothal, but the Scots did not take the matter as settled in this way and certainly did not think of it as a binding agreement. Four years later, it was decided to bring the young heiress to Scotland in any event.

In September 1290, Margaret, the 7-year-old Queen of Scots, set sail for her sovereign land – only to die suddenly and mysteriously when her ship reached Orkney. In the aftermath of this tragedy Sir James Stewart endeavoured to keep the peace, but the emergent Wars of Succession and Independence were destined to plague Scotland for many years.

## ROBERT THE BRUCE

The three main contenders for Margaret's inheritance were John Comyn (in descent from King Donald Ban), John Balliol (in descent from Prince David, Earl of Huntingdon), and Robert Bruce, Lord of Annandale (in another descent from Prince David). Bruce was the initial favourite, but Edward I of England proclaimed himself Lord Paramount of Scotland in view of the supposed betrothal of his son. He gained permission from a few Scots nobles to adjudicate, and by political manoeuvre took control of the nation's key fortresses. Then, with a specially appointed committee, whom he called 'the wisest in England', Edward made his selection. The Plantagenet council was insistent that the new King of Scots must be prepared to rule under the King of England. Robert Bruce was the Scots' own choice, but he refused to submit to Edward, stating,

> If I can get the aforesaid kingdom by means of my right and a faithful assize, well and good. But if not, I shall never, in gaining that kingdom for myself, reduce it to thraldom.

John Balliol, on the other hand, agreed to the requirement, and thereupon became the appointed King, swearing the necessary oath:

> I, John, King of Scotland, shall be true and faithful to you, Lord Edward, by the grace of God, King of England, the

noble and superior Lord of the Kingdom of Scotland, the which I hold and claim to hold of thee.

Balliol gained the throne in 1292, at which time the High Steward was still Sir James Stewart. Sir James was himself a supporter of Robert Bruce and a stern opponent of King Edward and Balliol. Edward compelled Balliol to provide money and troops for the English army – a move that stirred many to form a martial resistance movement under the Paisley-born knight Sir William Wallace. With the support of James Stewart, Wallace achieved some initial successes, and so Edward deposed Balliol in 1296 and began to rule Scotland himself. Wallace won a good victory at Stirling in 1297, after which he was proclaimed Warden of Scotland, but in the following year he was defeated by Edward's longbowmen at Falkirk. In 1305 he was captured and executed by the English, who impaled his head on London Bridge and sent the rest of his body in pieces to cities in Scotland and the north.

From that time, a new leader took up the Scots cause. He was Robert the Bruce, the eldest son of Robert Bruce the contender. Irrespective of the presumed Plantagenet interest, the Scots crowned Robert I Bruce in 1306. Then, when Edward II invaded Scotland in 1314, Bruce defeated him at Bannockburn and declared his nation's independence.

## THE ROYAL HOUSE OF STEWART

Sir James Stewart died within three years of Bruce's coronation, and was succeeded by his son Walter Stewart, the Sixth High Steward. Walter had commanded the left wing of the Scots army at Bannockburn, and been knighted by Bruce on the battlefield. In 1315 Walter Stewart married King Robert's daughter Marjorie.

Some months later Robert went to Ireland, leaving Walter as Regent in Scotland, but Marjorie then died in a riding accident, still within a year of her marriage. At the time of her death she was pregnant, but her unborn son was saved by caesarian operation and in time this son, Robert, became the Seventh High Steward. By the age of 19 he was the Regent for Bruce's son, King David II, holding the office until David was of age in 1341.

Soon afterwards, Edward III Plantagenet began the Hundred Years' War with France. David decided to take up the French cause, but was defeated and captured by the English at Nevill's Cross in 1346. He was held in custody for eleven years, during which time Robert the High Steward took charge in Scotland. King David was eventually freed in 1357, but not before he had come to an arrangement with Edward III. Addressing the Scottish Parliament, David announced that, should he die without issue, the crown of Scotland would pass to the King of England. The response was clear enough: 'So long as one of us can bear arms, we will never permit an Englishman to reign over us'. From that moment, David was disregarded by the Scots, and when he died without an heir in 1371 the people decided to make their own choice for his successor.

There was only one man who could possibly succeed – the man who had been running Scotland for years, and whose ancestors had been deputy kings for six generations. He was Robert Stewart, the Seventh High Steward.

On 26 March 1371, the Royal House of Stewart was founded by King Robert II. For the first time since the 6th-century Arthur mac Aedàn of Dalriada, the key Grail successions of Britain and Europe had conjoined in Scots royalty, and the Stewarts' ancient legacy of kingship was fulfilled.

# SEVENTEEN

# THE AGE OF CHIVALRY

## WAR AND THE BLACK DEATH

The 14th century was a period of great strife and general disorder in Britain and continental Europe. It was a century not only of continual wars but also of plagues, one of which claimed the lives of nearly one-third of England's population. During the later 1200s the Scots had been continually harassed by the House of Plantagenet, but in 1314 Robert the Bruce defeated the English invaders at Bannockburn. Subsequently, in 1328, Scotland's independence was formally recognized by Edward II at the *Treaty of Northampton*.

Soon afterwards, England was at war with France. The struggle was sparked by a dispute between Edward II and the French king, to whom Edward (who was also the Duke of Aquitaine) was technically a vassal in respect of certain properties in France. Edward refused to acknowledge the primary authority of the French crown in this regard, whereupon (in 1324) King Charles IV of France seized some of Edward's territories in Gascony. In retaliation, Edward threatened to cease trading with Flanders, and formed an alliance with the Duke of Burgundy. The irony was that Edward II was married to the French king's sister, Isabella, who became so unpopular in England because of the dispute that in 1325 she returned to France. There, she and her English lover, Roger Mortimer, Earl of March, plotted the overthrow and murder of Edward II in 1327.

The following year, Charles IV (the last of the Capetian succession) died, and a new dynasty began under his cousin the Duke of Valois, who became Philip VI. But Philip's inheritance was challenged by the new King of England, Edward III. In consequence of his father's assassination (instigated by his own mother), Edward declared that he was himself the true King of France, being the grandson of Isabella's father, Philip V. In 1330 Edward III had Mortimer executed, and confined Isabella to a convent. Then in 1346 he took his bowmen to Crécy and mowed down the serried ranks of French knights with a hail of arrows. So began the Hundred Years' War, which had hardly got under way when England was struck by the *Black Death* in 1348.

In that very same year – amid the general turmoil of battle and plague – the 'Age of Chivalry' was born. Tradition has it that in 1348 King Edward noticed some of his courtiers laughing when the Countess of Salisbury dropped her garter in their presence. Apparently, Edward picked up the item and affixed it to his own leg, saying, '*Honi soit qui mal y pense* (Shame to him who sees wrong in it)'. From this small beginning emerged the Order of the Garter, taking the King's chance comment as its motto (alternatively, and badly, translated as 'Evil to him who evil thinks'). Edward, whose jousting tournaments became widely renowned, selected twenty-four knights with whom to inaugurate the Order. The romantic tradition of King Arthur's Round Table was his model for knightly equality, and a Code of Chivalry was drawn up whereby knights were required to serve God and the King, to do battle for their good names, and to respect and defend the honour of ladies.

Edward III's eldest son was Edward, Prince of Wales (designated by later historians the Black Prince because of the colour of his armour). At Crécy he won three plumes (feathers), along with the motto *Ich dien* ('I serve'), and these have since become emblems of the Princes of Wales. For eight years, the Black Prince ruled Aquitaine, where he was ruthless and greatly feared. In England, however, he was a noted exponent of chivalry, and his reputation introduced an element of high romance into a bleak period of long-term war and disease.

## ARTHURIAN ROMANCE

The legends of King Arthur, which provided the model for the 'Age of Chivalry', had little to do with the historical Arthur – a Celtic Ard Rí (High King) and warlord, whose Guletic warriors gained a fearsome reputation in the 6th century. Nevertheless, Grail lore had brought Arthur into the public domain of the Middle Ages, and the stories of his questing knights were widely known. So when the Order of the Garter was founded, Arthur's knights were updated to become gallant armoured champions of the day. The great oak Round Table of the Plantagenet era (18 feet/5.5 metres in diameter and weighing 1.25 tons/tonnes) now hangs in Castle Hall, Winchester. It has been carbon-dated to about the reign of Henry III (1216–1272), but its symbolic Arthurian paintwork was a later addition, probably designed in the Tudor reign of King Henry VIII.

We have already considered the historical Arthur in a previous chapter,[1] but it is appropriate now to look at the legendary Arthur who so inspired the 'Age of Chivalry' – the Arthur whose story was born when Geoffrey of Monmouth produced his romantic *Historia Regum Britanniae* in about 1147. Commissioned by the Norman Earl of Gloucester, Geoffrey transposed Arthur mac

Aedàn of Dalriada into a West Country environment; transformed Gwyr-Llew, Dux of Caruele, into Gorlois, Duke of Cornwall; invented Uther Pendragon; and introduced various other themes to suit the feudal requirement. Amid all of this, one of Geoffrey's most romantic introductions was Arthur's magical sword, Caliburn, which had been forged on the Isle of Avalon.

In 1155 the Jersey poet Robert Wace composed *Roman de Brut* (the Romance of Brutus). This was a poetical version of Geoffrey's *Historia* based on a traditional notion that civilization in Britain was founded in around 1130 BC by Brutus[2] and a colony of Trojan exiles. A copy of Wace's poem, which included the very first reference to the Knights of the Round Table, was presented to Eleanor of Aquitaine. In this notable work, Geoffrey's Queen Guanhumara[3] appeared more correctly as Gwynefer (from the Celtic *Gwen-hwyfar* 'fair spirit'), and Arthur's sword, *Caliburn*, was renamed *Excalibur*.[4]

In about 1190, the Worcestershire priest Layamon compiled an English version of Wace's poem, but prior to this a more exciting romance emerged from France. Its author was Chrétien (Christian) de Troyes, whose mentor was Marie, Countess of Champagne. Chrétien transformed Arthur's already colourful tradition into thoroughly romantic legend, and gave Gwynefer the more poetic name Guinevere. His five related tales appeared in about 1175, and it was in his tale of Lancelot – *le Chevalier de la Charrette* – that Camelot first appeared as the royal court. Chrétien moved in aristocratic circles, and such stories of his as *Yvain – le Chevalier au Lion* were based on a number of noble characters from 6th to 11th-century Léon. The distinctive heraldic arms of the Comtes de Léon d'Acqs (or d'Ak) comprised a black lion on a golden shield, and they were accordingly known as 'Knights of the Lion'.

It was at this stage that continental European writers began amalgamating Arthurian literature with the lore of the Holy Grail. At the request of Count Philippe d'Alsace, Chrétien commenced his famous tale of Perceval in *le Conte del Graal* (the Story of the Grail). But Chrétien died during the course of this, and the work was concluded by other writers.

Next on the Arthurian scene was the Burgundian poet Robert de Boron. His verses of the 1190s included *Joseph d'Arimathie – Roman l'Estoire dou Saint Graal*. However, unlike Chrétien's story of the Sangréal, de Boron's was not contemporary with King Arthur. In essence it was more concerned with the time-frame of Joseph of Arimathea.

From about the same era came an anonymous manuscript entitled *Perlesvaus*. This work had Templar origins, and declared that Joseph of Arimathea was Perceval's great-uncle. Then, in about 1200, emerged the tale of *Parzival*, a detailed and expanded story of the Grail Family by the Bavarian knight Wolfram von Eschenbach.

King Arthur was brought more fully into the picture by a series of five stories from the period 1215–1235 which became known as the *Vulgate Cycle*. Written by Cistercian monks, these works featured Lancelot's son Galahad, whose mother was the Fisher King's daughter, Elaine le Corbenic. Arthur's greatest knight, Perceval, also remained a central character. The *Vulgate Cycle* retained Wace's *Excalibur* as Arthur's sword, and established the theme of his obtaining it from the Lady of the Lake. At this stage, the story of Arthur's drawing a sword from an anvil-stone had nothing whatever to do with *Excalibur*. This stemmed from a quite separate incident in Robert de Boron's *Merlin*. It was not until the 19th century that *Excalibur* and the stone were brought together.

Throughout this period of Franco-European lore, King Arthur had little prominence in Britain except for brief appearances in such works as the 13th-century *Black Book of Carmarthen*. Geoffrey of Monmouth had claimed that the Welsh town of Carmarthen was named after Merlin (as *Caer Myrddin* 'the seat of Merlin'). In fact the name had nothing whatever to do with Merlin but derived from the Roman name for the settlement, *Castra Maridunum*.

The English poem *Arthour and Merlin* appeared in the latter 1200s. From Wales (in around 1300) came the *Book of Taliesein*, which featured Arthur in the supernatural 'Otherworld'. He also made appearances in the *White Book of Rhydderch* (c.1325) and the *Red Book of Hergest* (c.1400). The Welsh *Triads* included some Arthurian references, as did the *Four Branches of the Mabinogi* which, in the 19th century, were translated into English by Lady Charlotte Guest under the revised title of *The Mabinogion*.

Not until the 15th century – around 800 years after the time of the historical Arthur – did all the legends consolidate into the general format that we know today. This occurred in the collected writings of Sir Thomas Malory of Warwickshire. They were printed in 1485 under the title *Le Morte d'Arthur* (The Death of Arthur). Being one of the first books published in print by William Caxton, Malory's Arthurian cycle was acknowledged as the standard work on the subject – although it has to be said that it was not an original account of anything. The work was commissioned by Margaret Beaufort of Somerset, the mother of the man who in that very year became King Henry VII Tudor. It was also during that same period that Uther and Arthur began to appear in newly assembled genealogies – and there was an express reason for this. When Henry VII (son of Edmund Tudor of Richmond) usurped the Plantagenet throne of Richard III, his only claim to succession was through his mother, who was a great-great-granddaughter of Edward III. In order to present his own Tudor heritage in a favourable light, Henry commissioned new genealogies showing his impressive descent from the princely House of Wales. However, in preparing these generally accurate charts the genealogists sought also to add a spark of intrigue, and so, for good measure, the names of Uther Pendragon and Arthur were introduced into a Cornish line.

Malory's famous tales were a compilation of the most popular traditions from various sources. All the familiar names were brought into play, and to content Henry Tudor, Camelot was located at Winchester in Hampshire. In addition, the old tales were greatly enhanced and many new story lines were conceived. Not the least of these was the love affair between Lancelot and Guinevere. Chivalric principles were central to Malory's portrayal even though he was himself a criminal of some renown – imprisoned for theft, rape, cattle rustling, debt, extortion, and the attempted murder of the Duke of Buckingham. At various stages between 1451 and 1470, he was held under lock and key in the cells of Coleshill, Colchester Castle, Ludgate, Newgate, and the Tower of London.

Malory settled Arthur firmly into the Middle Ages, and his characters forsook their Celtic garb for suits of shining armour. He entitled his inspired work *The Whole Book of King Arthur and his Noble Knights of the Round Table*, but it was the title of the last account which came to embody the collection. In all, there were eight interlaced stories: The Tale of King Arthur, The Noble Tale of King Arthur and Emperor Lucius, The Noble Tale of Sir Lancelot du Lake, The Tale of Sir Gareth, The Book of Sir Tristram de Lyonesse, The Tale of the

Sangréal, The Book of Sir Lancelot and Queen Guinevere, and The Most Piteous Tale of the Morte Arthur.

From the days of Thomas Malory, the Arthurian legends became an integral part of British heritage. They achieved a great revival with the birth of 19th-century Romanticism – a largely nationalistic movement which appealed to the Victorians' nostalgia for a lost Golden Age. The Poet Laureate Alfred, Lord Tennyson, wrote his famous *Idylls of the King*, and Arthurian themes were apparent in the striking paintings of the Pre-Raphaelite Brotherhood.

## MERRIE ENGLAND

The turbulent medieval times have often been referred to as the age which saw the flowering of 'Merrie England', a tag that persists despite the severe hardships of the era. In truth, the description had little to do with the fact that England was 'merry'. The description derives rather more precisely from *Mary* Jacob (St Mary the Gypsy), who had come to western Europe with Mary Magdalene in AD 44. Alongside veneration for the Magdalene, the cult of Mary the Gypsy was widespread in England during the Middle Ages. The name *Mary* is an English form (based on a Greek variant) of the Hebrew *Miriam*, and as we have seen the name had long been associated with the sea (Latin *mare*), and with water in general. As a result, Mary the Gypsy was identified with the goddess Aphrodite, who was born 'from the foam'.

St Mary Jacob (the wife of Cleophas according to John 19:25) was a 1st-century priestess, and is sometimes referred to as Mary the Egyptian. Her Oath of Wedlock was called the '*Merrie*' – partly derived from the Egyptian name Mery (which meant *beloved*). Hence, probably, derives the English verb *to marry*. Outside Catholic doctrine, the Holy Spirit was considered to be female, and was always associated with water. Often depicted with a fish-tail, St Mary was the original *merri-maid* (mermaid), and given the attributive name *Marina*. She is portrayed alongside Mary Magdalene (*la Dompna del Aquae*) in a window at the Church of St Marie in Paris. As *Maid Marian*, her cult is incorporated in the Robin Hood legends, while Mary Magdalene's incarnation appears in the Celtic tradition as the Morrigan (Great Queen) of Fate – Morgan le Faye. The individual identification of the two Marys is often confusing because both are associated with Provence and the sea.

In the early days of Christianity, the Emperor Constantine banned the veneration of Mary the Gypsy, but her cult continued, and it was introduced into England from Spain. Mary (Cleophas) Jacob had landed at Ratis (later, Saints Maries de la Mer) together with Mary Magdalene and Mary (Helena) Salome – as detailed in *The Acts of Magdalene* and the ancient *MS History of England* in the Vatican archives. Her most significant emblem was the scallop shell, depicted so effectively along with her Aphrodite status in Botticelli's *The Birth of Venus*. Even today, the Compostela pilgrims carry the shells of the aphrodisiac fish to the supposed St James's tomb at Santiago. Mary the Gypsy – sacred harlot and love cultess – was ritually portrayed by the Anglo-Saxons as the 'May Queen', and her dancers, *Mary's Men*, still perform their rites under the corrupted name of 'Morris Men' in English rural festivities. Another reference to *Mary's Men* is found in the rebellious 'Merrie Men' of the greenwood.

## SCOTLAND AND THE GRAIL

Many of the Scottish families so often credited with Norman descent are actually of Flemish origin.[5] Their ancestors were actively encouraged to emigrate to Scotland during the 12th and 13th-century reigns of

David I, Malcolm IV, and William the Lion. A policy of purposeful settlement was implemented because the Flemings were very experienced in trade, agriculture and urban development. It was quite unlike the unwanted Norman invasion of England. Such families as Balliol, Bruce, Comyn, Douglas, Fleming, Graham, Hay, Lindsay, and many others all have their heraldic origins in Flanders. In recent years some excellent in-depth research has been conducted in this field by the heraldic historian Beryl Platts.

There were few Normans of note in medieval Scotland, but one Norman family who did achieve great prominence from the 11th century was that of St Clair. Henri de St Clair was a Crusader with Godefroi de Bouillon. More than two centuries later, his descendant – also Henri de St Clair – was a commander of the Knights Templars at the Battle of Bannockburn. The St Clairs (who eventually become the Sinclair Earls of Caithness) were of dual Viking heritage through both the Dukes of Normandy and the Jarls (Earls) of Orkney. Following the Inquisition of the Templars, and their settlement in Scotland, the St Clairs became Scots Ambassadors to both England and France. Henry de St Clair (son of Henri the Crusader) was a Privy Councillor. His sister Richilde married into the de Chaumont family, who were kin to Hugues de Payens, the original Grand Master of the Templars.[6]

The Templar legacy of the St Clairs is particularly apparent at Roslin, just south of Edinburgh, near to the original Templar centre at Ballantradoch. Here, in the village of Roslin, stands the 15th-century Rosslyn Chapel. At first glance it resembles a miniature Gothic cathedral, with its pointed-arch windows and climbing buttresses topped with elaborate pinnacles. Closer inspection reveals, however, that it is actually a strange combination of Nordic, Celtic and Gothic styles.

The St Clairs received the Barony of Roslin from Malcolm III Canmore in 1057, and in the following century they built their castle in the vicinity. Deep beneath this fortress, it is said that the sealed vaults still contain some of the Templar treasure brought from France during the Catholic Inquisition.[7] When the Templar Fleet left the coast of Brittany in 1307, the majority of the ships and their valuable cargo went to Scotland via Ireland and the Western Isles.[8] Some went to Portugal, where the Templars became reincorporated as the Knights of Christ. The famous Portuguese navigator Vasco da Gama, who pioneered the Cape route to India in 1497, was a Knight of Christ. Earlier, Prince Henry the Navigator (1394–1460) was the Order's Grand Master.

In addition to the French evacuees, Scotland also received the Templars who escaped from England. Until then, their headquarters from 1185 had been at Temple, south of Fleet Street, in London. Since their 14th-century proscription, the site has been occupied by two Inns of Court – the Inner Temple and Middle Temple. Nearby stands the 12th-century round church of the Templars. Temple Bar, the Westminster gateway to the City, stood between Fleet Street and the Strand.

From the time that Roslin came into St Clair possession, prominent family members were buried there – with the exception of Rosabelle, the wife of Baron Henri the Crusader. She was drowned off the coast, to leave a haunting memory, as recalled by Sir Walter Scott during the 19th century. In his *The Lay of the Last Minstrel*, he wrote,

> And each Sinclair was buried there,
> With candle, book and knell;
> But the sea-caves rung,
> And the wild winds sung
> The dirge of lovely Rosabelle.

Throughout their early years, the St Clair Barons of Roslin were of the highest ranking Scots nobility, and they were numbered among the closest confederates of the kings. In the 13th century, Sir William de St Clair was Sheriff of Edinburgh, Lothian, Linlithgow and Dumfries, while also appointed Justiciar for Galloway. King Alexander III additionally selected him as foster-father to the Crown Prince of Scotland.

Following the death of Robert the Bruce in 1329, a later Sir William de St Clair, Bishop of Dunkeld, set out with Bruce's heart in a silver casket.[9] Along with Sir James Douglas and two other knights, he was to bury the casket in Jerusalem. On reaching Andalusia in southern Spain, however, the party was confronted by the Moorish cavalry. Seeing no way out, the four men charged the invincible foe and were duly slain. The Moors were nonetheless so impressed with the knights' courage that they returned the casket to Scotland. Bruce's heart was later buried at Melrose Abbey, which is itself steeped in Templar and Cistercian tradition.

It was a descendant William Sinclair, Earl of Caithness, Grand Admiral and Chancellor of Scotland, who founded Rosslyn Chapel in 1446. The family of St Clair (having adapted their name to Sinclair in the late 1300s) were by then the eminent guardians of the Kings – the Sangréal (Blood Royal) – in Scotland. Five years earlier, King James II Stewart had also appointed William to the post of Hereditary Patron and Protector of Scottish Masons. These were not speculative freemasons but operative, working stonemasons, proficient in the application of mathematics and architectural geometry. William was thus able to call upon the finest craftsmen and builders in the country. Once the Rosslyn foundations were laid, building work started in 1450. The Chapel was completed in 1486 by William's son Oliver.

It was meant to be part of a larger collegiate church but the rest was never built, although the foundations are still discernible.

In spite of its age the Chapel is in remarkable condition and is still in regular use. The building is 35 feet x 69 feet (c. 10.7 metres x 21 metres), with a roof height of 44 feet (13.4 metres). Many hundreds of stone carvings adorn the walls and ceilings. They tell stories from the Bible and depict numerous Masonic symbols and examples of Templar iconography. There are swords, compasses, trowels, squares and mauls in abundance, along with various images of King Solomon's Temple. Rosslyn Chapel provides such an unusually stimulating visual and spiritual experience as to commend itself to visitors. The historian and biographer Andrew Sinclair has written at length about the history of Rosslyn and the Sinclairs, imparting a detailed account of the Sinclair fleet's transatlantic voyage in 1398 – long before the supposed discovery of America by Christopher Columbus.

Apart from the Judaic and esoteric carvings, the Christian message is also evident, with an assortment of related depictions in stone. Amid all this there are constant traces of Islam, and the whole is strangely bound within a pagan framework of winding serpents, dragons and woodland trees. Everywhere, the wild face of the Green Man peers from the stone foliage of the pillars and arches – symbolizing the constant earth forces and the life-cycle. And all of this is enveloped in a vast array of fruits, herbs, leaves, spices, flowers, vines, and the emblematic plants of the garden paradise. Inch for inch, Rosslyn is probably the most extravagantly decorated church in the country – although not one crafted image can be construed as being art for art's sake. Every carving has a purpose, and each purpose relates to the next, while despite the seeming ambiguity of the scene, an almost magical harmony reigns throughout.

Above all else, Rosslyn is the ultimate Chapel of the Holy Grail, and the mystical quest is paramount in its imagery. The Knights Templars were the Guardians of the Grail Family, and the shield of St Clair bore an engrailed black cross upon silver to denote its bearer as a Knight of the Grail. The name *Saint-Clair* is derived from the Latin *Sanctus Clarus*, meaning 'Holy Light'. As we have seen earlier, the esoteric female symbol V represents the 'Chalice' of life, whereas its male counterpart Λ symbolizes the 'Blade' of virility. When conjoined one above the other (X) they indicate Unity, and their indented ᢦᢦᢦ or engrailed sequence ᔧᔧ denotes Generation. An en*grail*ed cross is therefore indicative of Holy Generation.

In Grail imagery, just as in graphic symbolism, the Messianic succession is denoted by the female Chalice accompanied by the male Blade. At Rosslyn and elsewhere in Scotland, wall carvings and tombs of the Grail Knights bear this dual emblem. It is portrayed as a tall-stemmed Chalice, with the bowl face-forward. In its bowl, the Rosy Cross (with its *fleur-de-lys* design) signifies that the *vas-uterus* contains the blood of Jesus. Alongside, the Blade is shown in the form of a sword.

## THE STONE OF DESTINY

Not only were the Grail Knights and Templars appointed Guardians of the Stewart Sangréal in Scotland, they also became protectors of the Stone of Destiny (the Stone of Scone). This most sacred of Scots treasures had been brought to Scotland from Ireland by Fergus Mór mac Erc, the first King of Dalriada, in the 5th century, having originally been carried to Ireland from Judah in

The Engrailed Cross of St Clair

about 586 BC. The venerated holy relic was said to be the Stone of the Covenant, known as 'Jacob's Pillow' (Genesis 28:18–22), on which Jacob laid his head and saw the ladder reaching up to Heaven at Beth-el. In a dream God promised Jacob that his seed would generate the line of kingship to follow – the line which in due course became the Davidic succession.

When the Jews were persecuted by Nebuchadnezzar of Babylon, Mattaniah, the son of King Josiah (and a direct descendant of David), was installed in Judah. Known as King Zedekiah, he acceded to the throne of Jerusalem in 598 BC. Twelve years later Jerusalem fell to Nebuchadnezzar, whereupon Zedekiah was taken to Babylon and blinded (Jeremiah 39:6–7, 52:10–11). His sons were murdered, but his daughter Tamar was removed to Ireland (via Egypt and Spain) by the prophet Jeremiah. He also brought the anointed Stone of the Covenant, which became known as *Lia Fáil* (Stone of Destiny).[10] In Latin it was the *Saxum Fatale*.

Princess Tamar (Teamhair) gave her name to Tara, the seat of the High Kings of Ireland, and she married Ard Rí (High King) Eochaid, ancestor of Ugaine Már (Ugaine the Great). Subsequently, over a millenium, Eochaid's successors were crowned in the presence of

The Sword and Chalice of the Holy Grail

the sacred Stone. The Irish heritage then progressed into Scotland, where the relic of Judah became synonymous with the Kings of Dalriada. King Kenneth I MacAlpin (844–859) later moved the Stone to Scone Abbey when he united the Scots and the Picts. By the time of William the Lion (d. 1214), the Stone of Destiny bore witness to nearly a hundred coronations in sovereign descent from King Zedekiah.

On declaring himself Overlord of Scotland in 1296, Edward I of England stole what he thought was the Stone of Destiny. What he actually got was a piece of sandstone from a monastery doorway, which has since rested beneath the Coronation Throne at Westminster Abbey. This piece of rubble is 26 inches long by 11 inches deep (c. 66 x 28 cm) and weighs about 335 lbs (c. 152 kg). Royal seals of the early Scots kings depict a much larger installation rock, but this rock was not the sacred Stone of Destiny – no more than is the medieval masonry prize of King Edward. The real Stone of Destiny is said to be smaller, more naturally rounded, and is of inscribed black basalt, not of hand-cut sandstone. It was hidden by the Cistercian Abbot of Scone in 1296, and it has remained hidden ever since. The Columban tradition tells that, on secreting the Stone, the Abbot prophesied that one day 'The Michael' would return to his inheritance. It is of importance to note that the X sign, which became so hated by the Roman Church,[11] was identified with the archangel Michael (Melchizedek)[12] onwards from Old Testament times. The heritage of St Michael was the dynasty of high Zadok priests[13] – a heritage that prevailed in the continuing Messianic line.[14] The relationship of St Andrew with the *saltire* was a later development.

It is hardly surprising that the Scots authorities never attempted to retrieve the bogus stone from England. Even Robert the Bruce declined to accept it in 1328 at the Treaty of Northampton. After some young Scots removed the Westminster stone across the border on Christmas Day 1950, it was duly returned to London without any undue excitement. In relation to the real Stone, the Revd J. MacKay Nimmo of St Columba's Church, Dundee, has since stated, 'When Scotland achieves self-government, the Stone will reappear...Until then, we will continue to guard this ancient symbol of our national identity'.[15]

The current Parliamentary decision to return the sham artefact to Scotland is, therefore, of no consequence whatever. Furthermore, even if one accepts the *symbolism* of the Westminster stone as being emblematic of Scottish nationhood, the proposal is not to return it to Scots ownership. It is intended simply that the Crown officers will keep it in Scotland instead of London, with the proviso that it will be carried back for future Westminster coronations. In short, this constitutes a thoroughly 'empty gesture'. Indeed, it openly perpetuates the coercive ideal of King Edward I by confronting the Scots with a daily reminder of their subjugated historical position.

## JOAN OF ARC

During the 1400s when Rosslyn Chapel was being built, the Grand Helmsman of the Priory de Sion was René d'Anjou (*b*.1408). René was the Count of Bar, Provence, Piedmont and Guise, and Duke of Calabria, Anjou and Lorraine. He was also titular King of Jerusalem, being a scion of Godefroi de Bouillon's House of Lorraine. In his capacity as Helmsman, René was succeeded by his daughter Yolande, whose successors included Botticelli and Leonardo da Vinci. René's other daughter, Margaret, married King Henry VI of England.

It is from René d'Anjou that the familiar 'Cross of Lorraine' derives. The cross -- with its two horizontal bars -- became the lasting symbol of Free France, and was the emblem of the French Resistance during World War II. Among René's most prized possessions was a magnificent Egyptian cup of red crystal, which he obtained in Marseilles. It was said to have been used at the wedding of Jesus and Mary Magdalene at Cana, and it bore the inscription (translated),

> He who drinks well will see God. He who quaffs at a single draught will see God and the Magdalene.[16]

René d'Anjou's literary work, entitled *Battles and the Order of Knighthood, and the Government of Princes*, exists today in the translation of the Rosslyn-Hay Manuscript in the library of Lord William Sinclair. It is the earliest extant work of Scottish prose and its leather-bound, oak cover bears the names *Jhesus – Maria – Johannes* (Jesus – Mary – John). Similarly, a mason's inscription at Melrose Abbey reads, *Jhesus – Mari – Sweet Sanct John.*[17]

St John (Jesus's 'beloved disciple') was greatly venerated by the Grail Knights and Templars. He was the inspiration for the Hospitallers of Saint John of Jerusalem, and the later St John Ambulance Association. It is significant that the New Testament Gospel of John (compiled in around AD 37) makes no mention of the Virgin Birth, only of Jesus's Davidic descent. More importantly, it gives the New Testament's only account of the historically significant wedding at Cana (John 2:1–11). The Rosslyn manuscript symbolizes St John by way of a Gnostic serpent and a Grail emblem.

Among René d'Anjou's subjects was the famous 'Maid of Orléans', Jeanne d'Arc (Joan of Arc). Born in 1412, Joan was the daughter of a Domrémy farmer in the Duchy of Bar. In the following year Henry V became King of England. Probably the most power-crazed of all English monarchs, Henry was described by his own nobles as a cold, heartless warmonger – even though historical propaganda has since conferred upon him the mantle of a patriotic hero. At the time of his accession, the Plantagenet war against France had subsided, but Henry decided to revive Edward III's claim to the kingdom of France. This he did on the basis that Edward's mother of a whole century before was the daughter of Philippe IV.

Henry V, with 2,000 men-at-arms and 6,000 archers, swept through Normandy and Rouen, defeating the French at Agincourt in 1415. He was proclaimed Regent of France at the Treaty of Troyes. With the aid of the faithless French Queen Isabau, Henry then married the French king's daughter, Katherine de Valois, and set a course toward overthrowing her brother, the Dauphin, who was married to René d'Anjou's sister, Mary. As fate would have it, Henry V died two years later, and so did King Charles VI of France. In England the heir to the throne was Henry's infant son, whose uncles – the Dukes of Bedford and Gloucester – became Overlords of France. The French people were somewhat concerned about their future prospects – but all was not lost, for along came the inspired Joan of Arc. In 1429 she appeared at the fortress of Vaucouleurs, near Domrémy, announcing that she had been commanded by the saints to besiege the English at Orléans.

At the age of 17, Joan departed for the Royal Court at Chinon, along with the Dauphin's brother-in-law, René d'Anjou. Once at Chinon on the Loire, she proclaimed her divine mission to save France from the invaders. At first the Court resisted Joan's military ambitions, but she gained the support of Yolande d'Aragon, who was the Dauphin's mother-in-law and the mother of René d'Anjou. Joan was entrusted with the command of more than 7,000 men, including the prestigious Scots Royal Guard of the *Gendarmes Ecossais* and the most prominent captains of the day. With René d'Anjou at her side, Joan's troops destroyed the blockade at Orléans and overthrew the English garrison. Within a few weeks the Loire Valley was again in French hands, and on 17 July 1429 Charles the Dauphin was crowned at Reims Cathedral by Archbishop Regnault of Chartres.

Less than a year after her success, the Maid of Orléans was captured while besieging Paris. The Duke of Bedford arranged for her trial by Pierre Cauchon, Bishop of Beauvais, who condemned her to life imprisonment on bread and water. When Joan refused to submit to rape by her captors, the Bishop pronounced her an ungrateful sorceress and a heretic, and without further trial she was burned alive in the Old Market Square at Rouen on 30 May 1431.

When the Dauphin was crowned at Reims, the brave shepherdess of Lorraine had stood alongside the new king with her banner. The banner bore the names *Jhesus – Maria*, the same as on the sacred stone at the Glastonbury Chapel (*Jesus – Maria*),[18] and as repeated (along with St John) in the Rosslyn-Hay manuscript (*Jhesus – Maria*), and as etched at Melrose Abbey (*Jhesus – Mari*) – the names which at all times relate to the wedding at Cana and the perpetual *Bloodline of the Holy Grail*.

# EIGHTEEN

# HERESY AND
# INQUISITION

## THE HAMMER OF WITCHES

Following the persecution of the Knights Templars
and their allies, the 'Holy Office' of the Catholic Inquisition continued its work mainly in France and Italy.
The Pope's appointed Inquisitors were essentially
Franciscan Grey Friars and Dominican Black Friars.
Their power was considerable, and they gained a
terrible reputation for their cruelty. Torture had been
granted papal sanction in 1252, and trials were all held
in secret. Victims who confessed to heresy were
imprisoned and burned; those who made no such
confession were given exactly the same punishment
for their disobedience.

By the 15th century the Inquisition had lost some of
its momentum, but new impetus was gained in Spain
from 1480, when the wrath of the Spanish Inquisition
was largely directed against Jews and Muslims. The
Grand Inquisitor was the brutal Dominican Tomâs de
Torquemada, senior confessor to Ferdinand II and
Queen Isabella. A few years after its implementation,
however, the Spanish Inquisition set its sights toward
another apostate cult. The resultant oppression was to
last for more than two centuries – not only in Spain, but
throughout Christian Europe. The unsuspecting prey

were described as the most diabolical heretics who ever conspired to overthrow the Roman Church.

In 1484 two Dominicans, Heinrich Kramer and James Sprenger, published a book called the *Malleus Maleficarum* (the *Hammer of Witches*). This evil but imaginative work gave full details of what was perceived to be the hideous new threat posed by practitioners of satanic magic. The book was so persuasive that two years later Pope Innocent VIII issued a Bull to authorize the suppression of this blasphemous sect.[1] Up to that point, the cult known as witchcraft had not really constituted a threat to anyone; it rested mainly in the continuation of pagan ritual and fertility rites by the peasant classes. In real terms it was little more than the vestige of a primeval belief in the divine power of natural forces, focused above all on Pan – the mischievous Arcadian god of the shepherds. Pan was traditionally portrayed with the legs, ears and horns of a goat – but the creative Dominicans had other ideas about the pipe-playing 'Horned One'. They blackened his image so that he was seen to correspond to the Devil himself, and the friars invoked a passage from the ordinances of Exodus 22:18–19, which stated,

> Thou shalt not suffer a witch to live. Whosoever lieth with a beast shall surely be put to death.

Then, by means of a blatant misapplication of the Biblical text, they condemned the Pan cultists firstly as witches and secondly as people who performed hideous revels with a 'familiar' animal. Since the Inquisitors were all men, it was determined that witchcraft must be a form of depravity essentially linked to the insatiable wantonness of women!

The word *witch* derives from an ancient variant of *willow*, from which also come *withy*, *wicker* (and probably *wicked*). The willow was the tree of the 'triple moon

goddess' (maiden, woman and hag). Willow worshippers (*witchers*) were said to possess supernatural powers
of divination (as graphically portrayed by the three
*Weird Sisters* – the Triple Hecate of Shakespeare's *Macbeth*) – and this enabled the Church to include all manner
of magicians and fortune-telling gypsies within its loose
classification of 'witchcraft'. Indeed, the revised definition was so all-embracing that just about anybody who
did not conform precisely to the orthodox dogma was
under suspicion as a practitioner of the black arts.

Numerous anti-establishment figures were inevitably caught in the ever-widening net, and the charge of
sorcery became an expedient substitute for criminal
and political indictments. In fact the flexible accusation
was often used to circumvent courtroom trial altogether. That apart, organized witch-hunts were more
generally directed against the defenceless rural classes.
The unfortunate victims were either strangled,
drowned, or burned alive, having been accused of venerating the Devil at nocturnal orgies, and of consorting
with evil spirits. Meanwhile, those of the privileged
class who possessed true esoteric skills and Hermetic
knowledge were obliged to conduct their business in
the secrecy of their lodges and underground clubs.


## THE PROTESTANT REVOLT

During the early years of this persecution, the Dominican monk Johann Tetzel institutionalized a lucrative
scheme to replenish the Vatican coffers. The scheme
concerned the forgiveness of sins, which had generally
been expiated by means of penances such as fasting,
repetition of the rosary, and other acts of sincere repen-
tance. Tetzel's concept replaced these traditional
penalties with Indulgences – formal declarations of
guaranteed absolution which were available for cash

(as was mentioned in the *General Prologue* and the *Pardoner's Tale* of Geoffrey Chaucer's *The Canterbury Tales*, compiled in the latter 1380s). Approved by papal decree, the sale of Indulgences soon became a source of considerable revenue for the Church.

For centuries the orthodox clergy and its associated monastic Orders had suffered a series of outrageous measures imposed by an avaricious hierarchy that was becoming ever more corrupt. Through it all, they had nonetheless upheld successive Vatican dictates with as much loyalty as they could muster – but the trading of Christian salvation for money was more than some could tolerate. The practice, therefore, was openly challenged. In October 1517, an Augustinian monk and professor of theology at the University of Wittenberg, Germany, nailed his written protest to the door of his local church – an act of formal objection that was destined to split the Western Church permanently in two. When he received a papal reprimand, he publicly set fire to it – and was excommunicated for his pains. His name was Martin Luther, and his fellow protesters became known as Protestants.

Luther's attempt to reform a particular Church practice in effect gave rise to a much larger-scale Reformation movement, and the establishment of an alternative Christian society outside Vatican control. In England the most significant consequence of the ensuing Reformation was the formal rejection of the Pope's authority, and his replacement as Head of the English Church by the Tudor King Henry VIII. This was in due course followed by the establishment of the independent 'Church of England' under Queen Elizabeth I, who was excommunicated by Rome in 1570. Scotland's secession from papal control occurred in 1560, under the influence of the Protestant reformer John Knox. It was by no chance that Martin Luther's protest gained support in some very influential circles, for Rome had many enemies in high places. Not the least of these enemies were the Knights Templars, and the underground Hermetic societies whose esoteric crafts had been condemned by the Catholic Inquisition. The truth was not so much that Luther gained the support of others, but that he was the willing instrument of an already active movement which endeavoured to dismantle the rigid international domination of the Pope.

The Protestant split with Rome facilitated an environment of democratic free-thinking which culminated in the achievements of Britain's Royal Society. It fuelled the cultural and intellectual ideals of the Renaissance (the true 'rebirth' of civilization). Indeed, the High Renaissance movement of 1500–1520 set the perfect scene for Luther's stand against the  politically motivated bishops. This was the age of the individual and of human dignity; it was the age when Leonardo da Vinci, Raphael and Michelangelo developed the harmony of classical art to its highest form; it was the age in which the excitement of pagan-orientated scholarship re-emerged in a burst of colour to cross new frontiers of science, architecture and design. Above all else, the Reformation countered aspirations to recreate the supreme lordship of Imperial Rome.

Ever since the Catholic Church had ousted the Merovingian kings in the 8th century there had been a calculated move to reflect earlier glories through the contrived Holy Roman Empire. But the Reformation undermined all of this as the nations of Europe polarized and divided. Germany, for instance, separated into a predominantly Protestant north and a Roman Catholic south. As a result, the Spanish Inquisition against Jews and Muslims was extended to include Protestants as well. Initially, they were hounded mainly in the Low Countries, but then in 1542 an official Roman by the succeeding House of Bourbon, to whom the Scots Guard had no formal commitment.

From the early days of the Frankish kings, the papal administrators had managed to displace any powerful institution that threatened the evolving Holy Roman Empire. But, quite suddenly, it had been confronted by an unforeseen opponent – a revised and generally more acceptable image of itself – a parallel, independent Christian Church. Moreover, this opposition movement was upheld by the same victims of persecution and proclaimed heresy that the Vatican had thought suppressed. In the newly enlightened 'Age of Reason' the Protestants emerged under the unified banner of the Red (Rosy) Cross – an emblem incorporated even in Martin Luther's own personal seal.

The *Rosicrucians* (as they were styled) preached liberty, fraternity and equality, and they were the constant challengers of tyrannical oppression. In time they were destined to be instrumental in both the American and French Revolutions. Following the Reformation, the Rosicrucian Order was largely responsible for the establishment of a new spiritually aware environment. People discovered that the Apostolic history of the Roman bishops was an outright fraud, and that the Church had deliberately sabotaged the story of Jesus. It also became apparent that the Rosicrucians (like the Cathars and Templars before them) had access to an ancient knowledge which held more substance than anything promulgated by Rome.

Against the weight of this onslaught, Rome's only defence was to continue with its well-tried declarations of heresy. Threats of violence were issued against anyone who opposed the Catholic doctrine. In fact, a new charge had to be found – a charge that was not so lightweight as that of heresy, which had sufficed in the past. The opposers of Catholicism, in whatever form, were therefore specifically defined as 'devil worshippers', and the *Hammer of Witches* Inquisition was implemented against an imagined satanic conspiracy fronted by sorcerers and witches. The problem was that nobody really knew who these presumed witches were. And so a series of ludicrously tragic trials and tests was devised to root them out. In the midst of all of this, the Puritan sect became politically allied to the Roman strategy, implementing their own witch-hunts in England and America. Over a period of some 250 years, around a million innocent men, women and children were murdered by the delegated authority of the witch-finders.

## THE ORDER OF THE ROSY CROSS

In 1614 and 1615 two tracts known as the 'Rosicrucian Manifestos' emerged from Germany. They were the *Fama Fraternitatis* and the *Confessio Fraternitatis*. These were followed in 1616 by an associated romance called *The Chemical Wedding*, written by the Lutheran pastor Johann Valentin Andreae. The earlier *Manifestos* were by related authors, if not also by Andreae, who was a senior official of the Priory Notre Dame de Sion. The publications announced a new age of enlightenment and Hermetic liberation in which certain universal secrets would be unlocked and made known. In view of the advent of the Stuart Royal Society a few decades later, the prophecies were correct enough, but at the time they were veiled in allegory. The writings centred on the travels and learning of a mysterious character named Christian Rosenkreutz – a Brother of the Rosy Cross. His name was plainly designed to have Rosicrucian significance, and he was depicted wearing the apparel of the Templars.

The action of *The Chemical Wedding* takes place in the magical Castle of the Bride and Bridegroom – a palace filled with lion effigies, where the courtiers are students of Plato. In a setting worthy of any Grail romance, the Virgin Lamplighter arranges for all present to be weighed on the scales, while a clock tells the motions of the heavens and the Golden Fleece is presented to the guests. Music from strings and trumpets is played throughout, and all is cloaked in an atmosphere of chivalry while knights in Holy Orders preside. Beneath the castle stands a mysterious sepulchre bearing strange inscriptions, and outside in the harbour lie twelve ships of the Golden Stone flying their individual flags of the Zodiac. Amid this curious reception, a fantasy play is conducted to tell the compelling story of an unnamed princess who, cast ashore in a wooden chest, marries a prince of similarly obscure background and thereby causes a usurped royal heritage to be restored.

When combined with the two earlier publications, *The Chemical Wedding*'s Grail significance was blatantly obvious. The Church therefore wasted no time in bringing the full weight of its condemnation against the *Manifestos*. The setting was mythical, but to illustrate the scene the Rosicrucians only ever used one actual castle in their depictions: the castle of Heidelberg, the abode of the Palatine Lion – the home of Prince Friedrich of the Rhine and his wife Princess Elizabeth Stuart, the daughter of King James VI of Scots (I of England).

Notwithstanding the Rosicrucian awakening of the Reformation, the Brotherhood of the Order of the Rosy Cross had a very ancient history, dating back to the Egyptian Mystery School of Pharaoh Tuthmosis III (*c.*1468–1436 BC).[4] The ancient teachings (documented in the *Wisdom of Lamech* and the *Tablet of Hermes*) were furthered by Pythagoras and Plato. Later they found their way into Judaea through the ascetic Egyptian Therapeutate which presided at Qumran in the days before Jesus. Allied to the Therapeutate were the Samaritan Magi of West Manasseh, at whose head was the Gnostic leader Simon (Magus) Zelotes, a lifelong confederate of Mary Magdalene, who was his appointed devotional sister. The Samaritan Magi, whose representatives were prominent at the Nativity, were founded in 44 BC by Menahem, a Diaspora Essene and the grandfather of Mary Magdalene. Menahem's descent was from the priestly Hasmonaeans – the family of Judas Maccabaeus, who is so revered in Arthurian legend and Grail lore, as we have seen in the story of Gawain.

The 'beloved disciple' John Mark (sponsor of the Gospel of John, and also known as Bartholomew) was a specialist in curative healing and remedial medicine, attached to the Egyptian Therapeutate (cognate in name with the English adjective *therapeutic*). It was because of this that John became the revered saint of the Knights Hospitallers of Jerusalem. John Mark was the disciple to whom Jesus entrusted the care of his mother at the Crucifixion: 'And from that hour the disciple took her unto his own' (John 19:27). Some Bibles – including even the Authorized Version – erroneously add an extra word, '. . . unto his own *home*', but that last word *home* (usually in italics) was not applicable to the original text of the Gospel. John was, in fact, appointed Mary's *paranymphos* (personal attendant), and those defined as *his own*, unto whom he took Mary, were the nurses of the Therapeutate. A *paranymphos* was, strictly speaking, one who ceremonially conducted a bride to her bridegroom.

The symbol of the Therapeutate healers was the serpent – the same as is shown (along with the Rosy Cross Grail emblem) to denote St John in the Rosslyn-Hay Manuscript of René d'Anjou. The Gnostic Serpent of Wisdom is used as part of the caduceus[5] insignia of today's British Medical Association. It was because of John's particular closeness to Jesus's family that he recognized the true significance of the sacred wedding at Cana. The kingly dynasty of Jesus was of great merit, but so too was the Hasmonaean and royal heritage of Mary Magdalene. She was the original *Notre Dame des Croix*, the bearer of the Messianic vase, the 'Lady of the Light', and it is in her Chalice that the Rosy Cross of the Sangréal is always found.

Among the notable Rosicrucian Grand Masters was the Italian poet and philosopher Dante Alighieri, author of *The Divine Comedy* in around 1307.[6] One of Dante's most avid students was Christopher Columbus who, in addition to his patronage by the Spanish court, was sponsored by Leonardo da Vinci, a member of René d'Anjou's Order of the Crescent (a revival of an earlier crusading Order established by Louis IX). Another prominent Grand Master was Dr John Dee, the astrologer, mathematician, Secret Service operative, and personal adviser to Queen Elizabeth I. Also the lawyer and philosophical writer Sir Francis Bacon, Viscount St Albans, was Grand Master in the early 1600s. Under James VI (I) Stuart, Bacon became Attorney General and Lord Chancellor. Because of the continuing Catholic Inquisition, he was greatly troubled by the prospect of large-scale Spanish settlement in America – and so he became particularly involved with Britain's own transatlantic colonization, including the famous *Mayflower* voyage of 1620. Among Bacon's Rosicrucian colleagues was the noted Oxford physician and theological philosopher Robert Fludd, who assisted with the English translation of the King James (Authorized Version of the) Bible.

In the Stuart era, the Rosicrucians were inextricably linked with early Freemasonry and the Royal Society. Such academics as Robert Boyle and Christopher Wren were therefore prominent within the Order of the Rosy

Cross. The aims and ambitions of the Order were straightforward – to advance the study and application of ancient science, numerology and cosmic law. Rosicrucians also undertook to encourage the ideals of the Egyptian Therapeutate by promoting international medical aid for the poor. It is not in the least coincidental that the most influential agency in the field of emergency relief throughout the world (as established by the Geneva Convention of 1864) is identified by its familiar Red Cross.

By the time of King Charles I, the Rosicrucian Order was well established in a number of countries, including Britain, France, Germany and Holland. The work of the Order progressed very well for a time, irrespective of papal condemnation issued by way of decrees from the Vatican. Against this background of progress, however, a new enemy was setting its sights towards the scholarly fraternity – an enemy whose pernicious endeavour was to blight spiritual and technological advancement for a good time to come. The Puritans had arrived.

It is a sad fact that often when the actions of one malicious regime are suppressed, another of equal iniquity is created in its stead. Such was the case with the separation of Henry VIII's English Church from Rome. It took little time for Henry to close the monasteries and sell their land to the merchant classes – but it was not as if the cultured monks of England bore any real affinity to the episcopal Catholic Church. Similarly, in establishing the Protestant Anglican Church (the Church of England), Elizabeth I was quick to force her absolute control on the Catholics of Ireland. She sold Ulster to the London Guilds, whose merchants compelled the Irish to become their servants or leave their homeland.

Henry VIII did not himself become a Protestant as is often suggested; in fact he had expressly denounced

Martin Luther in his writings. What he did was to sever the English branch of the Church from papal control. This facilitated his divorce from Catherine of Aragon (the daughter of Ferdinand and Isabella of Spain). It also enabled him to gain access to Church wealth and property in England. When the Council of Protestant Reformists took the reins after his death, the people were not happy – but they were even less happy when Mary Tudor married Philip of Spain and began to burn Protestants in England. *Bloody Mary* died before a great public revolt could take place, and her half-sister Elizabeth calmed the furore by creating the Protestant Anglican Church. It was her fear that Ireland might be used to launch a Spanish invasion of England that prompted her actions in that country. But a short-term end rarely justifies a long-term means, and the sad repercussions of Elizabeth's assault are still being felt today. Whatever the motives of Henry and Elizabeth, their efforts greatly increased the power of the merchant classes, who joined forces with the Dutch Protestants to suppress Spain's international commercial pretensions. King Philip II's response was the great Armada, but this was successfully repelled with the considerable help of inclement weather. England emerged as a religiously independent nation with the Anglican Church firmly at its helm – but a good deal had changed since Martin Luther had made his stand well over a century before.

The Anglican Church, with its own episcopal structure, became no more tolerant of other denominations than had been the Church of Rome. By the time of Charles I (reigned 1625–1649) it had become positively antagonistic towards anyone who dared to question its dogma. Catholic believers had at least retained a single shred of female recognition in the form of their reverence for Jesus's mother Mary, but the Protestants discarded even this last vestige of womanhood in religion.

As an ironic repeat of Templar history, the Rosicrucian scientists, astronomers, mathematicians, navigators and architects became victims of the pernicious Protestant establishment. The Anglican clerics called them pagans, occultists and heretics, just as the Roman Church had done before. In truth, the downfall of King Charles I had far more to do with his religious toleration and his association with these great men of advanced learning than orthodox history books will ever tell.

If the occult scientists of high society were persecuted by their own national Church, there was little hope for the practitioners of old lore in the lower strata – those who had been called witches by the Inquisition. They lived in fear of the Protestant extremists just as they had lived in fear of the Catholics. And the Protestant sect that came closest to the Inquisition's fanaticism was the very sect which split from the Anglican episcopacy in order to become more religiously 'pure'. What these Puritans achieved, however, was to become intolerant bigots, devoid of any spiritual intellect. Indeed, they were so undemocratic in their beliefs that their parliamentary head was a brutal despot who put even Tomás de Torquemada in the shade. It was during the years of Oliver Cromwell's savage Protectorate, from 1649, that the Royal Society was forced to go underground as the 'Invisible College'. Not until after the 1660 Stuart Restoration did the brilliant Rosicrucians appear openly once more, with King Charles II as the Society's patron and sponsor.

# NINETEEN

## HOUSE OF THE UNICORNS

### THE UNION OF CROWNS

Scotland's Royal House of Stewart arose from a marital union of the hereditary lines of Jesus and his brother James – springing from the Merovingians' own source on the one hand, and from the Celtic Kings of Britain on the other. The Stewarts emerged, therefore, as a truly unique Grail dynasty and have long been known as the 'House of Unicorns'. We have already seen that the 'Horn' of the Unicorn was equivalent to the 'Blade' in Grail lore, and both were represented by the male symbol $\Lambda$.

Along with the Davidic Lion of Judah and the Franco-Judaic *fleur-de-lys*, the *Desposynic* Unicorn was incorporated in the Royal Arms of Scotland. The Unicorn was considered to correspond to the virile Jesus, and was related to the anointing (Messianic) imagery of Psalm (sacred song) 92:10. The mystic beast was among the foremost symbols of the Albigensian Cathars, who were so hideously persecuted by the Inquisition. In medieval legend the Unicorn was always associated with fertility and healing, and Renaissance tapestries portray his head in the lap of the Bride. This alludes to the ancient ritual text of the

Sacred Marriage (the *Hieros Gamos*), 'The king goes with lifted head to the holy lap,'[1] as originally expressed in the poetic rite of old Sumerian Mesopotamia – the land of Noah and Abraham.

The Cathars believed that only the Christine horn of the Unicorn could purify the false doctrines that flowed from the Roman Church, and in this regard the revered creature was often portrayed with his horn dipped into a stream or a fountain. Other depictions show the Unicorn trapped within an enclosed garden – confined, but very much alive. The seven tapestry panels of *la Dame à la Licorne* at the Cluny Museum in Paris were originally from medieval Lyon. The seven Flemish *Hunt of the Unicorn* panels in the cloisters of the Metropolitan Museum, New York, come from 16th-century Languedoc, and show the Unicorn being chased and persecuted. When captured, he is sacrificed, but is then seen alive and well in the garden of the Bride. This is a direct replication of the story of Jesus.

The mythological symbolism of the Unicorn was central to the so-called heresies of Provence that were so brutally condemned by the Church. It was by no chance that the fabulous beast of the Grail bloodline found his place as guardian of the Lion in the Arms of Scotland, along with the early Christian sign of male and female unity ($\Lambda$ + $V$ = $X$) – the well-known Saltire, popularly identified as the cross of St Andrew.

When Robert II Stewart (grandson of Robert the Bruce) founded the Scottish Royal House in 1371, the succession was entailed on his heirs in the Scots Parliament. The Plantagenet Houses of York and Lancaster subsequently battled for dominion in England, but lost out to the Tudors. In France, the Valois dynasty fought constant wars against rival claimants, and were succeeded by the Bourbons. But through all of this the Stewarts maintained their uninterrupted dynastic position.

Before the High Stewards became Kings of Scots, their family branches were well positioned in terms of noble status, and as time progressed they acquired titles in Lorne, Innermeath, Atholl, Lennox, Doune, Moray and elsewhere. By the late 16th century the name *Stewart* had become *Stuart* in the royal line, a change that occurred by way of French association through the Stewart Seigneurs d'Aubignie and Mary Queen of Scots' first marriage to the Dauphin.

Following the childless death of Elizabeth Tudor of England, the Scottish and English Crowns were united in 1603. James VI of Scots was the great-grandson of James IV, and Henry VIII's sister Margaret. He was therefore deemed to be Elizabeth's closest living relative, and was invited to succeed. In fact, England had a suitable heir to the throne in Edward Seymour, Lord Beauchamp, by descent from Henry VII's daughter Mary. Nevertheless, although many were happy enough to recognize a legitimate parallel succession from Henry VII, others were far from content that the King of Scots had become King of England. They did not object to the crowns being united, but they would have preferred a reverse situation, so that an English monarch governed Scotland. As a result, one of history's greatest political conspiracies was set against James and the Stuart kings.

When James VI of Scots arrived in London to become also James I of England, he was confronted by two immediate problems. The first was related to religion. Both Scotland and England were established as Protestant nations, but James had experienced a Presbyterian upbringing whereas England was Anglican. The second difficulty was that the Westminster administration was wholly English, and Scots born before James's 1603 accession were debarred from government office.

After many failed attempts to gain control of Scotland, the English Parliament had discovered a strategic route to Scottish possession – one that may well have been devised before James was invited to succeed. Once James was settled on the united thrones, a solution to the longstanding ambition was in place: (a) future Kings of Britain would remain based in London, thereby restricting Scottish influence even in the affairs of Scotland; (b) Westminster could eventually dissolve the traditional Scottish Three Estates Parliament; (c) at an appropriate time, the Stuarts could be discredited and deposed, and (d) a puppet monarch of Westminster's own choosing could then replace the Scottish succession. The perceived outcome of this strategy would be Scotland's overall subjection to English rule – an ambition which had prevailed since the Plantagenet days of Edward I. And that is precisely what happened from 1688 when King James VII (II) was usurped and sent into exile by Church and parliamentary conspirators.

Earlier, in 1560, the austere Presbyterian Kirk (regulated by elders rather than bishops) had become the National Church of Scotland. South of the border, the Anglican Church had existed since Elizabeth I authorized the *Thirty-Nine Articles* of the English doctrine in 1563. So when the Stuarts succeeded as overall monarchs of Britain, they were expected to uphold two major Churches, each without offence to the other. It was an impossible task – particularly since the king was supposed to be Head of the Church of England. In order to achieve a compromise, the Stuarts founded the Scottish Episcopal Church, which introduced a like structure of Protestant bishops in parallel with the Anglican equivalent. But the kings then had a third Church to uphold, and this made things even more difficult. Over and above this, there was another complication. In addition to being Kings of Britain, the Stuarts were also Kings of Ireland (the Irish Free State was not established until 1921), and therefore had responsibilities towards the Irish people, who were traditionally Catholic.

Elizabeth I had ruled without much parliamentary consultation, and had put the crown into considerable debt. King James was in consequence obliged to implement higher taxation. However, in approving this measure, Parliament insisted that he could not rule in the autocratic Elizabethan style. In fact they put forward a series of restrictions which left the King with hardly any individual powers at all. James responded, declaring that by Scots tradition he was not answerable to Parliament but to God and the nation. It was his duty, he maintained, to uphold Scotland's Written Constitution on behalf of the people, and to take constitutional stands against Parliament and the Church if and when the need arose. But unlike Scotland, England had no Written Constitution (as is still the case), and the people had nothing to protect their rights and liberties. All that existed was a feudal tradition which vested the power of the land in the wealthy upper classes.

Throughout the Stuart era, religious differences between rival factions of the Christian Church were very much to the fore. In enforcing the Acts of Uniformity in respect of the *Book of Common Prayer*, James VI (I) upset the Catholics and prompted the Gunpowder Plot. Conversely, in introducing his Authorized Version of the Bible, he caused the Protestants to assert that he was siding with Rome. There was no way in which the Stuart king could satisfy the Anglicans, the Presbyterians, the Episcopalians and the Catholics without being thoroughly tolerant of them all. The problem was that the Anglican Parliament did not react well to such toleration, especially when it was extended to include Jews as well.

When James's son Charles I acceded to the throne, his immediate concern was the discriminatory nature of the Westminster Parliament. The ministers were so wrapped up in religious and territorial wrangling that they had forgotten all about managing the country. Charles therefore dissolved the troublesome Parliament in 1629 and instituted his own new administration. By so doing he gained considerable popularity; he also managed to balance the national budget for the first time in centuries. Within six years he was more favourably accepted than any monarch since Henry VII (1485–1509) – but as the dogmatic Puritans rose to power, so Charles's reign collapsed.

The high-minded doctrines of the Anglican bishops had become thoroughly disliked by large sectors of the community. Not surprisingly, the people were quick to follow instead their local Puritan preachers who denounced the episcopacy altogether. King Charles did all he could to salvage the Anglican reputation, but succeeded only in alienating many potential supporters. During the ongoing struggle with Spain, Charles allied himself with France by marrying Henri IV's daughter, Henrietta Maria, and this upset both the Anglican Church and the Puritans, for Henrietta Maria was a Catholic.

## CIVIL WAR

After eleven years of self-sufficiency, Charles was obliged to recall his Parliament in 1640. This followed severe problems with the Scottish Kirk, whose non-episcopal elders had been offended by the Archbishop of Canterbury's attempt to enforce the Anglican Prayer Book in Presbyterian Scotland. At Westminster the Puritan ministers promptly impeached Archbishop Laud for treason, and he was subsequently beheaded along with King Charles's deputy, Viscount Strafford. The Puritans then set about abolishing the King's council of the *Star Chamber*, and drew up the 'Grand Remonstrance' – a list of complaints against the King himself.

Having smoothed over the Scottish problem, Charles was then confronted by further troubles the following year in Ireland. There the Catholics were reacting violently against the presence of British Protestants who were being encouraged to migrate in their thousands to Ulster. King Charles endeavoured to raise an army to quell the insurgency, but Parliament refused him the finance, thinking that Charles might turn his army upon themselves. Then in 1642, when Charles tried to arrest five MPs for obstructive behaviour, the gates of London were locked firmly against him – and the result was civil war.

In Nottingham the King mustered a force of Royalist Cavaliers, while Oliver Cromwell – an ambitious country MP – assumed command of the Parliamentary forces. His cavalry met the Royalists at Edgehill, but the battle ended indecisively. Unlike the colourful Cavaliers, the Westminster party were indeed puritanical, especially with their severely short haircuts which caused them to be dubbed 'Roundheads'. Cromwell's breast-plated troopers were given the nickname 'Ironsides'.[2]

Following Edgehill, the Roundheads established the *Solemn League and Covenant* with the Scottish Kirk: they promised to introduce Presbyterianism into England if the Kirk would supply additional soldiers. This, along with a fee of £30,000 a month (equivalent to around £2,000,000 a month in today's terms), was sufficient to win the Kirk's support – and it was as a direct result that Cromwell defeated the Royalists at Marston Moor in 1644.

In the following year, Parliament's *New Model Army* defeated Charles again at Naseby. Only at this stage, however, did the Kirk's soldiers discover the true nature of their fellow Puritans. They had previously seen them simply as other non-episcopal Protestants, akin to their own Presbyterian society, but now their eyes were opened. It was reported that the Roundheads slaughtered all the Irish women found in the Royalist camp after the Battle of Naseby, and they mutilated the English women with knives. They took the Scotsmen prisoners, gouged out their eyes, cut off their ears, and nailed down their tongues. In the South, people had supported the Puritan cause in large numbers, but now this seemingly temperate sect was seen in a new light as an army of fanatical persecutors – to rival the savage Catholic Inquisitors of the 'Holy Office'. These same Puritan fanatics were soon destined to pursue their own erstwhile supporters with a vengeance, in their effort to root out witches and sorcerers!

It was only a matter of time before King Charles was forced to surrender, and in 1646 he was handed into Parliamentary custody at Newark. Later the same year he began negotiations with the sorely embarrassed Presbyterian Kirk. The elders recognized that in siding with the Puritans they had actively assisted in the downfall of their own royal dynasty (unlike the Scots Episcopalians who had stayed loyal to the Crown). But it was too late to make amends, and although a Scots army was despatched against Cromwell, he defeated it at Preston in August 1648. Early in the following year, King Charles I was tried at Westminster Hall, and beheaded in Whitehall on 30 January 1649. The Puritan army thereafter swept through Ireland, killing thousands of innocent citizens – an atrocity for which the unfortunate English people as a whole were blamed.

With no king to consider, Parliament established an interim period of 'Commonwealth', and in 1650 Cromwell defeated the late king's son, Charles, Prince of

Wales, at Dunbar. Irrespective of this, the Scots crowned Charles II at Scone on 1 January 1651, and he faced Cromwell's troops again at Worcester. He lost once more, however, but managed to escape to France.

Some two years later, in 1653, Oliver Cromwell terminated both his Parliament and the Commonwealth. Appointing himself 'Lord Protector', he then ruled by military force alone, and his Protectorate was far more severe than any regime that had ever gone before. At his order, the Anglican Prayer Book was forbidden, along with any form of celebration at Christmas or Easter. Property was sequestrated, education was constrained, and freedom of speech was terminated. Adultery was punished by death, and single mothers were imprisoned. Sports and entertainment were pronounced blasphemous, inns were closed, meetings were prohibited, and punitive fines were imposed at will by the soldiers. Those who dared to pray at all prayed for 'a speedy return to the protection of the Common Law'.

When Oliver Cromwell died in 1658, his despotic legacy fell to his son Richard. Fortunately, he was not possessed of his father's ambition, with the result that it was not long before Charles II was invited back to his kingdoms. The 'Restoration' of Charles Stuart to the throne thus occurred in 1660, eleven years after the execution of his father.

Charles proved to be a skilful and popular king. He reformed the Anglican Church, and maintained a society wherein all religious denominations were equally accepted. Yet despite these achievements, the Anglican politicians and clergy pursued their imperious course. No matter what the king thought, they had no intention of showing any forbearance towards other religious persuasions, particularly not to the Jews or the Catholics. Moreover, because Charles was married to the

Portuguese Catherine of Braganza, they insisted that he must have leanings toward the Church of Rome. Parliament therefore passed the restrictive 1673 and 1678 *Test Acts*, precluding anyone other than Anglicans from holding governmental or public office.

## THE INVISIBLE COLLEGE

It is no secret – although perhaps not the most widely known fact – that the early development of Masonic lodges in Britain was directly allied to the House of Stuart. Emanating from the archetypal grading of medieval stonemasons by degrees of proficiency, a symbolic concept of ritualized Masonry evolved during the reign of Charles I. The earliest inductions into Free (or speculative) Masonic lodges were recorded in about 1640. The movement was largely concerned with the structured acquisition of knowledge in unexplained science, much of which had been preserved in Scotland since the time of the original Templars and Cistercian monks.

In Stuart England, the early Freemasons of Charles I and Charles II were men of philosophy, astronomy, physics, architecture, chemistry and generally advanced learning. Many were members of the country's most important scientific academy, the Royal Society, which had been styled the *Invisible College* after it was forced underground during the Cromwellian Protectorate.[3] The Society was established under Charles I in 1645, and incorporated under Royal Charter by Charles II in 1662 after the Restoration. Early members included Robert Boyle, Isaac Newton, Robert Hooke, Christopher Wren and Samuel Pepys.

One only has to consider the accomplishments of the Royal Society to realize that, like the early Templars, they were endowed with very special knowledge. The natural philosopher Robert Boyle (1627–1691) was a noted alchemist, a student of Nostradamus, and a leading authority on Grail lore. Boyle supported the mathematical astrologer Galileo Galilei in his avowal of the Copernican heliocentric principle of the solar system. He made many discoveries concerning the properties of air, and formulated the notable *Boyle's Law*.[4] His colleague, the physicist Robert Hooke (1635–1703), invented the hair-spring, the double air-pump, the spirit level, and the marine barometer. Also in the fraternity was the astronomer and geometrician Edmund Halley, who calculated the motion of celestial bodies and accurately predicted the future regular reappearances of *Halley's Comet*.

Isaac Newton (1642–1727) was one of the greatest scientists of all time, renowned in particular for announcing the *Law of Gravity* and the definitions of orbital force. He was a noted alchemist, a refiner of the calculus, deviser of the *Laws of Motion*, and inventor of the reflecting telescope. One of Newton's foremost studies concerned the structure of the ancient kingdoms, and he claimed the pre-eminence of the Judaic heritage as an archive of divine knowledge and numerology. Newton was wholly conversant with Universal Law, sacred geometry, and Gothic architecture. Although he was a deeply spiritual man, and an authority on early religion, he openly rejected the *Trinity* dogma and the divinity of Jesus, maintaining that the New Testament had been distorted by the Church before its publication. Not only was Newton the President of the Royal Society but he was also a Grand Helmsman of the Priory Notre Dame de Sion.

The original Order of Sion had been inaugurated by the Knights Templars to accommodate Jews and Muslims within their Christian organization, and until 1188 they shared the same Grand Master. Although the early

Templars had a Christian affiliation, they were noted exponents of religious toleration, which enabled them to be influential diplomats in both the Jewish and Islamic communities. However, their liberal association with Jews and Muslims was denounced as 'heresy' by the Catholic bishops, and was instrumental in the Knights' excommunication by the Church of Rome in 1306.[5]

From 1188, the Order of Sion had been restructured, and evolved to pursue a more specific course of loyalty to the Merovingian lineage of France. The Templars, on the other hand, were especially concerned with supporting the emergent Stewart succession. In practice, the two operated in close association because they were essentially concerned with the same root bloodline.

Another prominent Royal Society member was Sir Christopher Wren (1632–1723) – the architect of St Paul's Cathedral, the Royal Exchange, Greenwich Hospital (the Royal Naval College), the Royal Greenwich Observatory, and numerous other churches, halls and monuments. He was also an acclaimed mathematician and a professor of astronomy. Wren was Grand Master of the esoteric Order of Rosicrucians. So too had been Robert Boyle and the Lord Chancellor, Sir Francis Bacon. Other Rosicrucian Grand Masters included Benjamin Franklin (1706–1790), who distinguished between positive and negative electricity, and Thomas Jefferson, the third President of the United States of America (term of office 1801–1809).

Modern historians have an unfortunate habit of extolling certain virtues of such great and learned men while paying no attention to the root sources of their wisdom. They are explicitly described as artists, scientists, politicians or whatever, but from Leonardo to Newton, and from Newton to Franklin, their common interests were Hermetic alchemy and the Sacred Craft.

In fact their various revelations were not necessarily first-time discoveries; they were more the products of studying cosmic laws and equations of very ancient origin. As an organized group, the men were able to assist each other with translation, experiment and development. The story of Newton and the falling apple may well add a little memorable humour to the *Law of Gravity*, but Newton admitted the true source of this inspiration to be Pythagoras' 'Music of the Spheres', a concept dating from the 6th century BC.

In Britain, and during their later exile, the Stuart kings were at the very forefront of Scottish Rite Freemasonry, which was founded on the most ancient of all arcane knowledge and Universal Law. Their Breton heritage was closely allied to the noble families of Boulogne and Jerusalem, and their background was largely Templar-inspired. It should come as no surprise, therefore, that it was under Charles I and Charles II (who posed such a problem to the narrow-minded Puritans and the Anglican Church) that the *Invisible College* of the Royal Society emerged – a college that within a brief period of Stuart patronage revealed some of the greatest scientific discoveries of all time.

## THE JACOBITES

In religious terms it is quite impossible to classify the early Stuarts within any specific denomination; they were simply Christians. Yet, one by one, they were the victims of individual Church jealousies, with each opposing faction seeking to further its own ambition against the others. Not until King Charles II's brother and successor James VII (II) declared his personal Catholicism could any Stuart king be individually labelled in such a way. Nonetheless, despite his personal leaning, it is quite apparent that King James was the most religiously tolerant king in the history of Britain. He not only refrained from imposing his persuasion but did quite the opposite – he issued a written *Declaration for Liberty of Conscience*, proposing the ideal of religious freedom for all:

> It is our constant sense of opinion that Conscience ought not to be constrained, nor people forced in matters of mere religion. It has ever been contrary to our inclination – as we think it is to the interest of governments which it destroys, by spoiling trade, depopulating countries and discouraging strangers. And finally, that it never obtained the end for which it was employed . . .
>
> We do likewise declare that it is our royal will and pleasure that, from henceforth, the execution of all, and all manners of, penal laws (in matters ecclesiastical) for not coming to the Church, or not receiving the sacrament, or for any other nonconformity to the religion established, or by reason of the exercise of religion in any manner whatsoever, be immediately suspended; and the further execution of the said penal laws is hereby suspended . . . And to the end that, by the Liberty hereby granted, the Peace and Security of our Government in the practice thereof may not be endangered, we have thought fit, and do hereby straitly charge and command all our loving subjects, that we do freely give them leave to meet and serve God after their own way and manner . . .

In issuing this Declaration on 4 April 1687 James endeavoured to dispel all bigotry in favour of sympathetic indulgence. What he failed to recognize was that neither he nor the people were at liberty to make decisions in this regard. By that time, two operative political groups (parties) had evolved at Westminster, and they were each denoted by a 'nickname' foisted by the other. They were the Whigs (rustlers) and the Tories (thieves) – the latter of whom were the natural inheritors of the

Royalist position. The Whigs were essentially those of the wealthy land-owning establishment, and when James issued his Declaration the Whigs were in the majority. They not only condemned the King but had him formally deposed for daring to acknowledge the alternative faiths of the Catholics, Presbyterians, Jews, Quakers and others. They centred their argument on James's toleration of Catholics although his forbearance in relation to the Jewish faith would realistically have been a more likely target for committed Anglican Christians. It is evident therefore that his persecution had little to do with matters of religion: it was more precisely concerned with the fact that the King challenged the right of Parliament to impose its will upon the people.

This, of course, brings us back to where our book began – with the notion of *service*. In essence, King James was acting fully in accordance with the Grail Code – a code that obliges those in authority, whether in elected or hereditary positions, to concern themselves not with the 'powers' of their positions but with the 'duties' of those positions.

In attempting to grant religious equality, King James endeavoured to override the restrictive 1673 and 1678 *Test Acts*, which bound those in public office to communion with the Church of England. The *Test Acts* were eventually repealed in 1828–29 to the benefit of Catholics. Later, in 1858, the clauses were also relaxed in favour of Jews. In Britain today, all religious denominations (Christian or otherwise) are afforded the right to worship according to their conscience – precisely as King James VII (II) conceived over 300 years ago. Few would now claim that James was wrong in his tolerant outlook; he was simply ahead of his time.

Not all of the Anglican hierarchy were in opposition to King James, however. His supporters included

Archbishop Sancroft of Canterbury, and the Bishops of Bath and Wells, Ely, Gloucester, Norwich, Peterborough, Worcester, Chichester, and Chester. When James was deposed, they were all deprived of their sees and incumbencies. History has since been manipulated to suggest that James was displaced because he was a Catholic. In truth he was deposed to guarantee power to a Parliament that was not elected by a democratic vote.

On James's departure, the throne was jointly offered to the Dutch Stadholder (chief magistrate), William of Orange, and his wife (James's daughter) Mary. But at this stage, strict new rules were introduced. The 1689 *Bill of Rights* stated that future monarchs could reign only with 'Parliamentary consent', and that MPs should be freely elected. In fact, MPs of the era were certainly not freely elected. Only a very limited number of male property-owners who enjoyed high incomes were allowed to vote, and the House of Commons was far from characteristic of the populace it was supposed to represent.

Although Queen Mary was a Protestant, the ministers were concerned about William's own relationship with Rome. Holland was the chief northern province of the then independent Netherlands, but had previously been attached to the Holy Roman Empire, and it was known that William's army largely consisted of Catholic mercenaries. It was for this reason that in 1701 the *Act of Settlement* was passed to secure the throne of Britain for Protestants alone – an Act that remains binding today, even though it was passed in the Commons by a majority of only *one* vote!

After King James's deposition, the House of Lords determined that because there was a legal compact between the king and the people, the throne was 'not vacant' (although not technically occupied either). It was suggested that a regency was the best way to preserve the kingdom during the remainder of James Stuart's lifetime.

But William of Orange assembled a London Convention Parliament on 26 December 1688. With his armed guards stationed in and around the House, he declared that he had no intention of becoming a Regent – neither would he consent to sharing in government. His declaration was so forceful that there was an immediate fear of war, and many thought he would seize the crown regardless. A panic conference ensued between the Lords and the Commons, resulting in a revised decision that perhaps the throne was vacant after all![6]

At the time of writing, the present Prince of Wales is faced with a personal dilemma in matters of religion and the Church. Ever since Tudor times English monarchs have been designated 'Defenders of the Faith' – that is the Anglican Protestant faith. HRH Prince Charles has stated that as a prospective king in these cosmopolitan times, he would prefer to be classified simply as a 'Defender of Faith' – meaning faith in general, of whatever persuasion. There are significant echoes here of the unfortunate King James VII (II) and his *Declaration for Liberty of Conscience*. Yet very little has changed in the past 300 years. British monarchs are still invested as Heads of the Church of England, and the current Anglican hierarchy are as protective and separatist as their 17th-century predecessors. Despite the fact that the United States of America and other Western nations have formal Written Constitutions to uphold individual rights and liberties, the British have no such protection. By virtue of this, Parliament and the Church retain ultimate dominion over the monarchy (and thus over the people) as long as the *Bill of Rights* and the *Act of Settlement* prevail.

When William III and Mary II acceded jointly to the British throne, an ambiguous Stuart legacy was inherent. Mary was the daughter of King James VII (II) by his first wife, Anne Hyde of Clarendon. William (whose father was William of Nassau) was the son of King Charles I's daughter Mary. However, despite these apparent links, the Scots were not satisfied at the loss of their rightful dynastic king. In 1689 (the year after James's deposition) there came the first Jacobite Rising. Viscount Graham of Claverhouse, Grand Prior of the Knights Templars in Scotland (and known as *Bonnie Dundee*), led a force of Highlanders against government troops at Killiecrankie on 27 July. Although the Scots' attempt was successful, Viscount Dundee was mortally wounded in the battle. On 18 August the Highlanders were less fortunate at Dunkeld. Then on 1 July 1690 King William's *Orangemen* defeated James VII's restitutional troops at the Battle of the Boyne in Ireland.

Amid all this, the Campbells and some other Scottish clans decided to win favour with the new monarchs by aiding the government's suppression of the Jacobite loyalists (they were called *Jacobites* because the name *James* derives from the Latin *Jacobus/Jacomus*, being originally *Jacob* in Hebrew – hence they were *Jacob-ites*). King William instructed that all Highland Chiefs should swear an Oath of Allegiance to him, but the majority were reluctant to comply; their kings had always sworn 'fealty to the nation', rather than the reverse. In order to force the issue, Sir John Dalrymple, Secretary of State for Scotland, was empowered to persecute one reluctant clan as an example to the others. He chose the MacDonalds of Glencoe, who had failed to meet the Oath of Allegiance deadline of 1 January 1692. The ageing MacDonald chief, MacIain, had actually tried to swear his

Oath at Fort William on 30 December, but no Crown officer was present, and as a result he did not manage to comply until 6 January – almost a week late.

Unlike some other clans, the MacDonalds had no military strength and were easy prey. Their settlement nestled between the towering mountains of Glencoe, which constituted more of a geographical trap than a natural fortress. On 1 February Dalrymple sent two companies of Argyll's Regiment, under Robert Campbell of Glenlyon, to exterminate the unsuspecting clan. Arriving in the guise of a peaceful mission, the soldiers took lodging with the hospitable families for many days. Then, on the bitter morning of 13 February, they cut down every MacDonald they could find, sparing neither the women, the elderly, nor the young. Not surprisingly, the dreadful 'Glencoe Massacre' had an effect opposite to that intended. Instead of intimidating the clans into supporting the new regime, it caused them to form a strong Jacobite confederacy against the ruthless Dutchman and his government.

## THE TREATY OF UNION

When Queen Anne succeeded William III in 1702, the majority of Scots showed no enthusiasm, even though she was the late Queen Mary's sister. Anne had openly deserted her father, King James, to support her brother-in-law William of Orange. She was anathema to the Stuarts, and had never visited Scotland. In 1706, Anne announced her intention to dissolve the Scottish Parliament. On receipt of the declaration, however, the Scots ministers responded that such an action was illegal under Scots law. They cited their Written Constitution, the 1320 *Declaration of Arbroath*, which stated that, if a monarch should make us or our kingdom subject to the King of England or the English, we should exert ourselves at once to drive him out as our enemy and a subverter of his own rights and ours, and make some other man, who was well able to defend us, our King.

It was clear that Anne's plan would fully subject the realm to English domination from Westminster. But although the Scots could not 'drive out' the English Queen, they were afforded the legal right to introduce a *Bill of Security* (1706), by virtue of which, in accordance with the Constitution, they were not bound to accept Anne's chosen heir. In this they retained the liberty to elect a Scots sovereign from a royal line other than one chosen by England. That Anne would have to choose an heir, rather than give birth to one, was meanwhile becoming ever more apparent. She actually conceived eighteen times, but only five children were born alive, of whom one alone survived infancy, and even he died at the age of 11. Her own nominated choice of successor was the German Electress, Sophia.

In the event, Anne got her way despite the *Bill of Security*. She proposed commercial restrictions on the Scots, and threatened a large-scale military invasion. In March 1705 Westminster passed the *Alien Act*, which stated that the Scots must accept Sophia of Hanover as Anne's nominated successor or all trade between the north and the south would cease: the importation of Scottish coal, linen and cattle into England would be forbidden, and there would conversely be no continued export of English goods into Scotland.

From 1 May 1707 the Scottish Parliament was adjourned, and the crowns of Scotland and England became one as Westminster took control of the newly conjoined kingdom of Great Britain under the terms of the *Treaty of Union*. Regardless of this, the Scottish

Covenanters ignored the imposed regime; they formally renounced Queen Anne, and proclaimed her half-brother, James Francis Edward Stuart, the true King of Scots. He was the son and heir of James VII (II) by his second wife Mary d'Este de Modena. James VIII (like his father before him) was a Catholic, but the Presbyterian Covenanters cared nothing for the individual religion of their king. Unlike the English system, the Scots monarchs were not Heads of the national Church. Both the Presbyterians and Episcopalians were far more concerned with preserving their traditional royal house outside English supremacy.

Following the *Treaty of Union*, the Scots were allowed to keep their own Kirk, along with their separate legal system. However, various Parliamentary measures were introduced to disadvantage the Scots in relation to the English.[7] But the Scots were not alone at the mercy of the regulatory powers; the English people had suffered William and Mary's rapacious taxing of light and air since 1695. This taxing of each individual window above six in every house worth more than five pounds a year was retained for 156 years. Even today the bricked-up windows of many old houses are still to be seen, particularly in rural areas.

By the time of Queen Anne's death in 1714, her nominee Sophia of Hanover had also died. The Whig ministers therefore installed Sophia's son George, Elector of Hanover, on the throne of Britain – in spite of loud protests from the Tory benches. Much to the convenience of the Whig oligarchs, King George I spoke only German, and spent most of his time abroad. The reins of national administration were held mainly by his Lord of the Treasury, Robert Walpole. He became the first effective Prime Minister, and developed the undemocratic idea of the Cabinet (an inner circle of ministers who meet privately outside the House to control

Government policy). From that time, not only did the people have no say in matters of their own government, but nor did the majority of MPs, who were subsequently regulated by the Whips (so named after the deputies of Hunt Masters) in accordance with Cabinet (or Shadow Cabinet) requirement.

Outside Scotland, many Westminster Tories and their supporters had sought to replace Anne with James Francis Edward Stuart. He was the rightful heir to the Scots succession, and had been their titular King James VIII since 1707. Nevertheless, the Whigs strategically ignored James because he refused to be tied to the Anglican Church. Scottish and English royalists made an attempt to gain the crown for James Stuart in 1715, but their limited revolt was unsuccessful, and so James returned across the water to continue his French exile at St Germain-en-Laye, near Paris.

## BONNIE PRINCE CHARLIE

In 1727 George II of Hanover succeeded his father. The next significant Jacobite Rising took place eighteen years later, in 1745, when the 'Bonnie Prince' Charles Edward Stuart challenged Britain's German succession. The Scottish clergy were wholly supportive. On Sunday 24 September of that year, the Episcopal Church symbolically crowned King Charles III at the Abbey of Holyrood House. Representatives of the Catholic and Presbyterian Churches were also present to witness and approve the event.

Despite the fact that James VIII was still alive, he had formally transferred his interests to his son by Declaration on 23 December 1743:

> We esteem it for our service, and for the good of our kingdoms and dominions, to nominate and appoint, as we

hereby nominate, constitute and appoint, our dearest son, Charles, Prince of Wales, to be sole Regent of our kingdoms of England, Scotland and Ireland, and of all our other dominions during our absence.

Prince Charles was eager to restore Parliament and the Constitution. He was similarly determined that the English should be afforded identical rights of political and religious freedom. In his first Proclamation, issued in Edinburgh on 9 October 1745, Charles Edward stated,

With respect to the pretended Union of the two nations, the King cannot possibly ratify it since he has had repeated remonstrances against it from each kingdom.

Soon after his figurative coronation, Charles was invested as Grand Master of the Order of the Temple of Jerusalem. On taking his vow, he declared,

You may be sure that when I truly come into my own I will raise the Order to what it was in the days of William the Lion.

From successful beginnings at the Battle of Prestonpans, the Scots marched southward. Having advanced at speed all the way to Derby, they were quite unaware of the panic that had seized London and the House of Hanover. George II had even loaded the Crown Jewels onto a Thames barge ready for a quick getaway to Germany. The politicians hastily put out a barrage of propaganda to convince English and Welsh Jacobites that Charles would never reach the capital – and it worked. The Prince's anticipated reinforcements did not materialize.

Because the Scots had not yet confronted King George's main force under the Duke of Cumberland, Lord George Murray persuaded the Clan chiefs that a strategic retreat was in order. Back in Scotland they could regroup, and meet Cumberland on their own territory. After a few skirmishes on the way, and a Jacobite success at Falkirk, the Scots finally met Cumberland's massive army on Culloden Moor, near Inverness, on 16 April 1746. But despite all their previous success, the Scots were too tired and hungry to perform well. Bad judgements were made, and they were thoroughly defeated.

Ironically, had it not been for the ministerial propaganda in the south, the Highlanders could actually have marched from Derby and seized the capital with ease. 'Your ancestor was quite wrong,' said the later King George V to Murray, Duke of Atholl. 'The Jacobite army should have continued straight on to London, and a Stewart would be today's King of Scotland and England, with each country having its own Parliament.'

## CHARACTER ASSASSINATION

For the majority of people in Britain, James VII's objective of religious freedom for all was a very welcome innovation. It appealed greatly to their sense of individual liberty. It was therefore seen as imperative by the Whigs that, to preserve their own dominion, they should denigrate the memory of King James and the Stuarts. Their attack was launched on a thoroughly personal level, and aimed first at James's wife, Queen Mary d'Este. She was the daughter of Alfonso IV, Duke of Modena, but the Hanoverians decided to portray her as an illegitimate child of the Pope!

There was not much that could be said against James's brother and immediate predecessor, Charles II – he was too well regarded in the popular mind – but James VI (I) and Charles I were other good targets. The Cromwellian annals were scoured for suitably critical content. James VI had been known to all as the 'British Solomon', but the Whigs renamed him the 'wisest fool in Christendom'. His unfortunate intestinal illness was used to create the impression that he was a vulgar glutton, and the most common of all Puritan witch-hunting charges was laid against him: sexual deviancy.

These things apart, the widespread popularity of Prince Charles Edward Stuart was an enormous threat to George II, and so he became the main object of the Hanoverian thrust. While the Duke of Cumberland pursued his violent subjugation of the Highlands after Culloden, the *Bonnie Prince* was portrayed in England as a treacherous warmonger, and labelled as a danger-ous usurper – even though it was his own family that had been usurped. Before long, the whole scene was set against the Scots King *de jure*. He was described as a drunk and a woman-hater; his various offspring (apart from Charlotte of Albany) were excluded from the Brit-ish history books, as indeed were his numerous lady companions, except for one childless marriage to Prin-cess Louise de Stolberg and his relationship with Char-lotte's mother, Clementina Walkinshaw. Indeed, his later fits of asthma and epilepsy made it very easy for the image of drunkenness to be sustained.

Establishment-based history in England still por-trays the Prince as a troublesome pawn of Rome, but he was certainly not that. His rapport with the Pope was far from amicable, and he formally converted to the Anglican Protestant faith at the age of 29. Subsequently, he wrote,

> In order to make my renunciation of the Church of Rome the most authentic . . . I went to London in the year 1750, and in that capital did then make a solemn abjuration of the Romish religion, and did embrace that of the Church of England.

Following Charles Edward's death in 1788, various accounts of his life were compiled from Hanoverian sources. There are now any number of published biographies, in large measure adapted from one another. Whether intentionally or otherwise, these biographies are generally founded on the contrived reports of the Hanoverian propaganda machine. Scotland, however, has retained her own legacy of pride in the *Bonnie Prince*. The registers of Europe similarly convey a very different image of Charles Edward and his legitimate descendants; they depict a resolute royal bloodline that was strategically veiled by the British Government until recent times.

The English now await the prospect of HRH Charles Windsor, Prince of Wales, becoming their King Charles III. At the same time, many Scots pursue a dogged course towards renewed independence. The first step in this latter regard will doubtless be a reinstatement of the Scottish Parliament. Scotland already has a traditional Written Constitution which could be re-implemented, if not bettered, and that Constitution gives the nation the right to 'choose' its own monarch while also rejecting overlordship from England.

If Charles, Prince of Wales, does become King of Britain, it is unlikely that nationalist Scots would readily accept a second Charles III. Following the coronation of Queen Elizabeth II, the Scots rightly protested that they never had an Elizabeth I – Elizabeth Tudor had reigned in England but not in Scotland.

The prevailing Royal House is therefore faced with a considerable dilemma. Just as it once changed its German family name from Saxe-Coburg-Gotha to Windsor in order to appease the British nation during World War I, might it perhaps be obliged to consider taking a further such diplomatic step? Just as Prince Charles's grandfather Albert, Duke of York, became

King George VI, might it be that Britain's next king is crowned not as Charles III but as George VII? Alternatively, given that Parliament and the Church hold the 'trump cards', might Prince Charles somehow be by-passed altogether – particularly if he does not satisfy Anglican requirements with regard to his marital status and the Defence of the Faith? These are, of course, speculative notions . . . but it will be interesting to see what happens.

# TWENTY

# THE SANGRÉAL TODAY

## THE BLOODLINE CONSPIRACY

These days it is generally understood that establishment history is largely based on recorded propaganda. It was originally compiled to suit the political needs of the era when written rather than necessarily being an accurate record of events. In short, it is generally a 'slanted' version of the truth. For example, the English historical version of the 1415 Battle of Agincourt understandably differs from that of the French viewpoint. Similarly, the Christian perception of the Crusades is not necessarily shared by the Muslims. There are at least two sides to most stories.

In 1763 the journalist John Wilkes accused George III's government of misrepresenting facts in the king's speech. Today such challenges are common enough, but Wilkes was seized and flung into the Tower of London. In those days there was no freedom of speech or opinion, yet during that same period of constraint, a vast amount of Government-approved 'history' was produced.

Gradually, over the years of the 20th century, the official registers of nobility have been revised to correct a multiplicity of errors in past editions. But many of the errors (some still not fully corrected) were not *mistakes*

**COUNTS OF ALBANY (SCOTLAND)**
de jure *Princes and Lord High Stewards of Scots to date*

HENRY BENEDICT STUART
Cardinal Duke of York
*de jure* HENRY I (IX)
d.s.p.

PRINCE CHARLES EDWARD STUART ( *m. Nov 1785* ) MARGUERITE O'DEA d'AUDIBERT
1st Count of Albany ............... = ............... de Lussan, Comtesse de Massillan
1720-1788 *de jure* CHARLES III                                    1749-1820
= (Declared 1746 – Annulled 1766)
Clementina Walkinshaw of Borrowfield
Comtesse d'Alberstoff

Charlotte
de Johnstone Douglas
Duchess of Albany 1753-1789
= (w/m) Ferdinand de Rohan Guenéné
Archbishop of Bordeaux

PRINCE EDWARD JAMES STUART (Count Stuarton)
2nd Count of Albany 1786-1845 *de jure* JAMES IX (IV)
= (1809) Maria Emmanuella Pasquini 1789-1854
Dau. of Edouardo Guiseppe Pasquini (Italy)
and Leonora, Comtessa di Vaglio

Marie Beatrice
1783-1823
= Philippe d'Auvergne
g.g-son of Godefroid
Duc de Bouillon

Aglae Clementine
1781-1825
= (1812) Jehan de
la Tour d'Auvergne
Son of Jacques
Prince de Bouillon

PRINCE HENRY EDWARD BENEDICT STUART
3rd Count of Albany 1809-1869 *de jure* HENRY II (X)
= (1829) Agnes Beatriz de Pescara 1810-1878
Dau. of Conte Anselmo Bernardo de Pescara
and Aliena Gabrielle Barberini-Colonna
Principessa di Palestrina

Charlotte Marie
d'Auvergne
1806-1865
= Prince Louis Xavier
de Bourbon, son of
Charles, Duc de Berri
son of KING CHARLES X

Marie Louise
de Bouillon
1812-1870
= Jean de Jaeghere

PRINCE CHARLES BENEDICT JAMES STUART
4th Count of Albany 1829-1887 *de jure* CHARLES IV
= (1864) Louise Jeanne Francoise Dalvray
1839-1906 Dau. of Jean Francois Louis
Dalvray (France), and Jeanne Amélie de Valois

Victorine
1829-1911
= Baron Fernand
Lafosse de Chatry

Prince Louis
Duc d'Aquitaine
1827-1918
= Princess Dona
Mariana de Forano

Armand Godefroid
de Jaeghere
1837-1904
= Elize Van Achelen

PRINCE JULIUS ANTHONY HENRY STUART
5th Count of Albany 1874-1941 *de jure* HENRY III
(HENRY XI *d.j.* of England until relinquished in 1913)
= (1898) Marie Joanna Vandenbosch of Flanders
1873-1942 Dau. of Claude Philippe
Vandenbosch de Monpertigen, and Marie
Jeanne Philippe, Comtesse de Lannoy

Clement Joseph
Lafosse de Chatry
d. 1928
= Jeanne de Blois

Renee Adelaide
de France
1854-1906
= Baron Gerault
Despardons

Suzanne Marie
Théodose
1878-1935
= Henri Jean Baptiste
Segers d. 1931

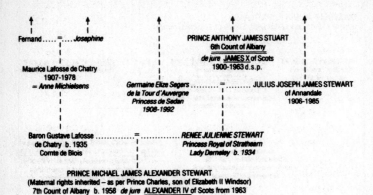

Fernand ..... = ..... *Josephine*

Maurice Lafosse de Chatry
1907-1978
= *Anne Michielsens*

**PRINCE ANTHONY JAMES STUART**
6th Count of Albany
*de jure* <u>JAMES X</u> of Scots
1900-1963 d.s.p.

*Germaine Elize Segers* .......... = .......... JULIUS JOSEPH JAMES STEWART
*de la Tour d'Auvergne*                                                of Annandale
*Princess de Sedan*                                                    1906-1985
*1908-1992*

Baron Gustave Lafosse .............. = .............. *RENEE JULIENNE STEWART*
de Chatry  b. 1935                                          *Princess Royal of Strathearn*
Comte de Blois                                              *Lady Derneley  b. 1934*

**PRINCE MICHAEL JAMES ALEXANDER STEWART**
(Maternal rights inherited – as per Prince Charles, son of Elizabeth II Windsor)
7th Count of Albany  b. 1958  *de jure*  <u>ALEXANDER IV</u> of Scots from 1963

as such in the first place – they were purposeful misrep-
resentations.[1] As a direct result of Hanoverian
(Georgian and Victorian) policy, for instance, it has long
been claimed in Britain that the Stuart succession became extinct while in exile. British history books are
pretty well unanimous in stating that Charles Edward
Stuart had no wife at his death, and no legitimate male
offspring. But they are quite wrong, and the continental
European records tell a very different story.

According to doctrinal English opinion, the present
heir to the Royal House of Stuart is Prince Franz of
Bavaria who is said to inherit the Scottish honours by
virtue of the Last Will and Testament of Charles Edward's younger brother, Cardinal Henry, *de jure* Duke
of York. This Will supposedly nominated Charles Emmanuel IV of Sardinia as the Stuart successor. By way
of marriages in the female line of descent from Charles
Emmanuel's brother, Victor Emmanuel I, the present
Franz of Bavaria succeeds his father, the late Prince
Albrecht, relying in this on a somewhat tenuous ancestry back to Henrietta, a daughter of Charles I. The fact
is, however, that Cardinal Henry Stuart's Will did *not*
name Charles Emmanuel as his successor. This is a
complete fantasy that has made its way into the history
books, but was originally a purposely-contrived deception on the part of Georgian politicians – a deception
perpetuated by the later Victorian ministers.

From the time that the Elector of Hanover began his
reign as King George I of Britain in 1714, it became
politically expedient to suppress or veil a good deal of
information about certain families while enhancing the
lineage of others. The House of Stuart came under
particular attack in order to justify the incoming German succession. Even today, history books repeat the
nonsense contrived contemporarily and afterwards to
discredit the Scots dynasty and its associated families.

The fabrications are so well ingrained that they are destined to prevail for as long as historical authors continue to copy from one another.

Charles Edward Stuart was married in 1772 to Princess Louise Maximilienne, the daughter of Gustavus, Prince de Stolberg-Guedern. In 1784, however, papal dispensation for divorce was obtained following Louise's affair with the Italian poet Vittorio, Count Alfieri. Louise had been declared barren by the doctors, and after a few years of marriage she left Charles in 1780 to take up residence with her lover. The divorce is frequently described as the end of married life for Charles Edward – but it was not.

The Stuart archives in Rome and Brussels reveal that in November 1785 Charles was married again, to the Comtesse de Massillan at the Santi Apostoli in Rome. She was Marguerite Marie Thérèse O'Dea d'Audibert de Lussan – a cousin by descent from Charles's granduncle, King Charles II. Until 1769 she had been a ward of her own granduncle, Louis Jacques d'Audibert, Archbishop of Bordeaux. Marguerite's paternal grandmother Theresa, Marchesa d'Aubignie, was the daughter of James de Rohano Stuardo, Prince of Boveria, Marquis d'Aubignie. He was the natural son (legitimated 1667) of King Charles II and Marguerite, Duchesse de Rohan. On her mother's side, Marguerite de Massillan was descended through the Comtes de Lussan.

In November 1786 the 37-year-old Countess gave birth to a son, Edouard Jacques Stuardo (Edward James Stuart), who became known as 'Count Stuarton'. Although no secret in Europe, news of Charles Edward's legitimate son and heir was immediately suppressed by the Hanoverian government at Westminster. He has consequently since been totally neglected by academic historians in Britain. In that same month, Charles

Edward's daughter Charlotte of Albany (born 1753 by Clementina Walkinshaw of Borrowfield) met King George III's brother William, Duke of Gloucester, at the house of Prince Santa Croce in Rome. Concerned about the strength of her own position as Charles Edward's 'legitimated' offspring, she informed Gloucester of the royal birth and sought his advice. The Duke confided that Charlotte's status was probably safe enough, but his main concern was a letter that had been sent to her father by King George III in 1784. It suggested that Charles Edward could return to Britain from exile as the *Count of Albany* (Scotland). Charles had declined the invitation, but the matter was now complicated by the new-born son who might well choose otherwise on becoming the Second Count in due course.

When Charles Edward died, a contrived substitution of Wills enabled knowledge of both the marriage and the birth to be concealed from the British public, a concealment that was perpetuated through the Hanover – Saxe-Coburg era until the truth finally emerged in the 1970s.

In 1784 Charles had made a Will nominating his brother Cardinal Henry, *de jure* Duke of York, as his royal heir. Charlotte of Albany was to be the sole estate beneficiary. This is well enough documented in the historical biographies – but what those accounts fail to mention is that this was not Charles's final Testament. It was superseded by another before his death. Not only was the fact of this later Will concealed by the Georgian Parliament, but so too was the reason for its existence. In order to stabilize King George III's position, his politicians thought it expedient to end the problem of Stuart popularity in Britain by having the Scottish line declared extinct – particularly since the Jacobites had been so instrumental in the American War of Independence (1775–1783). An enormous number of deprived Scots had emigrated to America following the subjugation of the Highlands after Culloden. They had not managed to regain their independence at home, but continued their Cause from across the Atlantic, thereby aiding their fellow Americans to secure their own freedom from Hanoverian constraint.

On 30 January 1788 the *de jure* King Charles III (fondly remembered as *Bonnie Prince Charlie*) died, aged 67, at the Mutti Palazzo in Rome. Shortly before his death he wrote his Last Will and Testament. This was witnessed on 13 January 1788 by the Dominican Father O'Kelly and the Abbé Consalvi, both of whom were executors. The Will stated that Charles's offspring, Edward James and Charlotte, were to be co-heirs of the estate; his son Edward was to succeed to the Royal Honours on his 16th birthday, and Cardinal Henry was to be temporary Regent in the meantime.

Following Charles Edward's demise, his ambitious brother Henry wasted no time in proclaiming himself King Henry I *de jure* of Scots (IX of England). To support this claim he produced not Charles's Will of 1788 but his earlier Will of 1784 – which suited Britain's Government since the Cardinal was not likely to have any children. Both O'Kelly and Consalvi were party to the intrigue in return for rapid promotion within the Church. Soon afterwards, the former became Dominican Procurator, while the Abbé was raised to the Cardinalate. Charlotte of Albany was provided with a home in Frascati, and the Mutti Palazzo was retained for Marguerite de Massillan and Prince Edward. Also involved in the scheme was the Abbé James Placid Waters, Procurator of the Benedictines in Rome.

By declaring himself King *de jure*, Henry sought to nullify the immediate Regency clause in his brother's Will. But in January 1789 Henry made his own Will in which he redressed his selfish strategy for the future: all his possessions and heritable status were bequeathed to Prince Edward James – that is, 'to my nephew, Count Stuarton'. Both Cardinal Ercole Consalvi and Cardinal Angelo Cesarini were privy to the Will and were executors, as attested in their memoirs.

As it happened, Henry subsequently lost a great deal of his wealth in the French Revolution and during the Napoleonic advance into the Papal States. In 1799 he became a pensioner of the British Crown at the rate of £5,000 per annum (about £250,000 in today's terms) – but in return he was required to rewrite his Will. At a joint meeting between Prince Edward, Comtesse Marguerite, and the Pope, a suitable rewording was agreed. The new Will was made in 1802, but the inheritance still rested with Prince Edward. The revised document simply substituted the words 'to my nephew, Count Stuarton' with 'in favour of that Prince to whom it descends by virtue of *de jure* blood relationship'.

When Henry Stuart died in July 1807, King George and the British Parliament decided that the second Will was actually less appropriate than the former. They therefore ignored the 1802 document and reverted to Henry's original Will of 1789 – and the press reported that Henry had made his bequest to his 'relation Count Stuarton' (meaning, of course, Edward James). However, no one in England thought to enquire who this relation, Count Stuarton, might be.

Having dealt with the first hurdle, the Hanoverian ministers then produced Henry's amended 1802 Will. By virtue of its malleable nature, the wording ('in favour of that Prince to whom it descends by virtue of *de jure* blood relationship') was strategically implemented in favour of Charles Emmanuel IV, ex-King of Sardinia. He had recently abdicated to join the Jesuit Order, and so the Stuart legacy passed to a potentially childless monk. Charles Emmanuel duly wrote to King George's

Parliament denouncing the nomination because he knew the Stuarts to be alive and well. Indeed, having lived with him in Sardinia from 1797, Marguerite and her son Edward were then resident at his house by the Corso in Rome. The correspondence was ignored at Westminster, and the whole issue was put under wraps in Britain. History now records the 'diverted succession' as having progressed from Sardinia, through Modena, into Bavaria. The reality is that the legitimate Royal House of Stuart (Stewart) exists today, and has long been actively interested in European constitutional management.

In 1809 a dispute over sovereign loyalties arose between two sons of George III. It became known as the 'War of the Brothers'. Prince Edward, Duke of Kent (the father of Queen Victoria), was a Freemason, while his brother Prince Augustus Frederick, Duke of Sussex, was a Knight Templar. Edward's problem was that his brother's Templar colleagues were Stuart supporters. He therefore endeavoured to sway their allegiance to the reigning House of Hanover. In the event he failed, but compromised by creating a Templar-styled branch within the existing Masonic structure. This fell under the protectorate of Kent, and followed the English *York Rite* of Freemasonry. The chivalric Templars pursued the *Scottish Rite* under the protectorate of Prince Edward James Stuart, Second Count of Albany.

While the exiled Stuarts were in France and Italy, they were deeply involved with the general growth and dissemination of Freemasonry, and they were the instigators of the exported *Scottish Rite*, which had higher degrees and held more profound mysteries than other Masonic systems. Prominent in this movement was Charles Edward's cousin and mentor, the Comte de St Germain. The Stuarts' involvement was firmly based on established rights and privileges, with a desire to initiate brethren into the true antiquity and pedigree of the Craft. In England, the inherent secrecy of the club-like lodges provided the perfect facility for undercover intrigue against the Whigs and the German succession. Throughout the land, the Jacobite societies and Tory lodges became closely entwined – as a result of which they became prime targets for Whig Intelligence, whose high-ranking Secret Service operatives duly infiltrated the fraternities. In later years English Freemasonry dispensed with political intrigue to become more concerned with allegorical representation and the codes of brotherly love, faith and charity. In Europe, however, many scientifically-based intellectual lodges of the traditional style are still extant.

In 1817 a Dr Robert Watson purchased in Rome some of Cardinal Henry's documents concerning the Stuart dynasty. He paid £23 sterling (equivalent to about £610 today), and prepared to publish the contents. But, before he had a chance to do this, the files were seized by the papal police and passed to London so that their contents would not become known. Some time later, the doctor received a payment from Westminster for having been deprived of his property. Not content with this, Watson pursued his right to the papers – only to be found dead, supposedly having committed suicide, in 1838. The papers have never since appeared in the public domain.

Along with Cardinal Henry, the Abbé Waters also lost his possessions and became a pensioner of King George. Waters, an executor for Charlotte of Albany, was the custodian of various other Stuart papers – his guardianship of which constituted the route to his future Hanoverian income. In 1805 the Abbé was obliged to pass them over to the British Government. At length, some were deposited at Windsor Castle, where they remain today. As for the rest, their whereabouts are conveniently unknown.

By virtue of these documentary acquisitions, the way was deemed clear for Prince Edward James to be totally excluded from historical records in Britain. But this was not the case in continental Europe, where he is well documented in papers held by the Stuart Trustees, and features in the writings of René, Vicomte Chateaubriand, Abbé James Waters, Princess Caroline Murat, and others. Although the Stuarts have been ignored by the British authorities since the death of Cardinal Henry, the descendants of Prince Edward James, Count Stuarton, Second Count of Albany, have been actively engaged in social, political, military and sovereign affairs for the past two centuries. They have often advised governments on constitutional and diplomatic matters in an effort to promote the ideals of *public service* and *religious toleration*, as upheld by their own reigning house, and they have been particularly concerned with matters of trade, welfare and education.

In 1888 Prince Edward's grandson, Charles Benedict James Stuart, Fourth Count of Albany, was scheduled to visit Britain. He was due to attend a grand Stuart Exhibition at the New Gallery, London. It was sponsored by the Order of the White Rose, and the main organizers were Bertram, Earl of Ashburnham, and Melville Massue, Marquis de Ruvigny. But the Exhibition was wholly undermined by Hanoverian agents, and Prince Charles Benedict was found dead (presumed murdered) in Italy. There was no display in 1888 after all. A rather different Exhibition was held the following year. Instead of being in honour of the Stuarts, as was planned, it was promoted to celebrate the bicentenary of the *Whig Revolution* which had deposed James VII (II) and the Stuarts in 1688! The Exhibition's new patron was Queen Victoria herself, and the event was used as a cover to obtain even more valuable documents of Stuart heritage. Having been ousted from their patronage, Lord Ashburnham and the Marquis de Ruvigny directed their future interests towards the chivalric societies of Europe – the Order of the Realm of Sion, the Knights Protectors of the Sacred Sepulchre, and the Order of the Sangréal.

In spite of Queen Victoria's efforts to suppress Stuart popularity, there was a significant Jacobite revival in the late 1800s. The Queen's advisers therefore sought to emphasize her tenuous claim to Stuart descent to the exclusion of the Stuarts' own Scottish heritage. As a result, Thane Banquo and the Scots line from King Alpin disappeared from the Hanoverians' readjusted Stuart registers. The Lord Lyon, King of Arms, subsequently wrote, 'The traditional account of the descent of the family from Banquo, Thane of Lochaber, and through him from the ancient Kings of Scotland, is now generally discredited.' From that time, the Stuarts' Breton line was brought wholly to the fore – but why anyone should have to discredit one line of a descent in order to promote another is beyond ordinary understanding. Everyone has at least two lines of immediate descent, and the Stuarts were no exception.

Subsequent members of the Scots Royal Family were prominent in the Belgian Resistance during World War II. Hubert Pierlot, Prime Minister of Belgium, was a close friend of the Stewarts, who had reverted to the original spelling of their name in 1892. In that year they had moved to the Château du Moulin in the Belgian Ardennes, where they lived until 1968. This castle had originally been given to the family in 1692 by King Louis XIV. As recently as 1982, the City of Brussels honoured the Stewarts with a grand reception. Then, on 14 December 1990, the Brussels Registrars signed, sealed and authenticated an updated Charter of the Royal House of Stewart, detailing the complete family descent from the time of Robert the Bruce down to date.

Today, there are several lines descended from Prince Edward James, Second Count of Albany. They include the Counts of Derneley and the Dukes of Coldingham. Foremost, however, in the main line of legitimate descent from Charles Edward Stewart and his son Edward James is the present Seventh Count of Albany: Prince Michael James Alexander Stewart, Duc d'Aquitaine, Comte de Blois, Head of the Sacred Kindred of St Columba, Knight Grand Commander of the Order of the Temple of Jerusalem, Patron Grand Officer of the International Society of Commission Officers for the Commonwealth, and President of the European Council of Princes. Prince Michael's own compelling book *Scotland – The Forgotten Kingdom?* (a thoroughly detailed and politically corrected history of the Scots royal descent) is now in the course of preparation.

This senior Stewart descent goes all the way back to King Arthur's father, King Aedàn of Scots, on the one hand and to Prince Nascien of the Septimanian Midi on the other. The Scots descent traces further back through King Lucius of Siluria to Brân the Blessed and Joseph of Arimathea (St James the Just), while the Midi succession stems from the Merovingians' male ancestral line through the Fisher Kings to Jesus and Mary Magdalene. Conjoining the lines from their 1st-century points of departure, the descent is in the succession of the Royal House of Judah. This is a truly unique line of sovereign lineage from King David in one of the key descents which comprise the *Bloodline of the Holy Grail*.


## THE CROWN OF AMERICA

Beneath the streets of Rome, the catacombs of the pagan era hold the remains of more than 6 million Christians. Laid in a single row the passages would extend for 550 miles (880 kilometres). Ironically, the later fanaticism of the Inquisitions accounted for more than a million additional lives because the victims were supposedly *not* Christian! Through the centuries, millions of Jews have been persecuted and killed as a result of anti-Semitism initiated by the early Christian Church. This was managed mostly under cover of the accusation of deicide – it ran completely out of control during the holocaust of the early 1940s – but anti-Semitism still lingers. Tens of millions of Soviet Russian lives were lost during Stalin's brutal dictatorship, an autocratic totalitarianism that despised religion in any form. Vast numbers such as these are beyond the bounds of practical imagination, but their memory cannot be confined to savage regimes of the past. Worldwide religious feuds continue just as in the days of old, and the *ethnic cleansing* of the Inquisition is still apparent today.

In theory, Communism was introduced to fulfil a socialist ambition, but the dream soon died as the giant machine rose to power by military oppression. Capitalism, on the other hand, is equally ruthless because it venerates balance-sheets above the welfare of people; as a result millions are condemned to starve to death in the poorer regions while vast food mountains stockpile elsewhere. Even in the United States, where the Constitution promotes the ideal of *liberty* and *equality*, we see an ever-widening gap between the privileged and subordinate groups. Rich communities are now barricading themselves within walled environments, while the welfare systems of the West are crumbling into bankruptcy.

History has proved many times over that absolute rule by monarchs or dictators is a road to social disparity. Yet the democratic alternative of elected government has often proved similarly inequitable. Even elected parliaments can become egotistic and dictatorial in a world where those entrusted to *serve* may regard themselves instead as the masters. Additionally, in countries such as Britain that have a multi-party political structure, the people are regularly faced with the rule of ministers empowered by a minority vote. In such circumstances who is there to champion the rights of individuals? Trade unions, some might say – but quite apart from being politically biased in themselves, such organizations are still subject to governmental control. Although they may have a weight of membership, they have no final authority to equal that of Parliament. As far as the judicial system is concerned, its purpose is to uphold legal justice, not moral justice.

Others in Britain may cite the Queen as the people's guardian – but Britain has a Parliamentary monarchy in which the sovereign reigns only by consent of Westminster. Given the lack of any Written Constitution, British monarchs are quite powerless to champion individual rights and liberties to any effect. The present heir to the throne has genuinely sought to bypass the restrictions by speaking out from time to time, only to suffer recriminations from the establishment. Like a Victorian child he is supposed to be 'seen and not heard', while bankers and industrialists control the fate of the nation.

So often one hears politicians quoting the British Constitution as if it actually exists by way of a documentary privilege – but it does not. It is simply an accumulation of old customs and precedents concerning parliamentary sanctions, together with a number of specific laws defining certain aspects. Since Scotland's 1320 *Declaration of Arbroath* was nullified by England's Treaty of Union in 1707, the oldest Written Constitution now in force is that of the United States of America. It was adopted in 1787, ratified in 1788, and effected in 1789. In that same year began the French Revolution, which abolished feudalism and 'absolute' monarchy in France, thereby influencing politics in much of Europe.

In close to 200 years since the Revolution, France and other European States (with Britain as a noticeable exception) have adopted Written Constitutions to protect the rights and liberties of individuals – but who champions these Constitutions on behalf of the people?

A popular alternative to absolute monarchy or dictatorship has been found in Republicanism. The Republic of the United States was created primarily to free the emergent nation from the despotism of Britain's House of Hanover. Yet its citizens tend still to be fascinated by the concept of monarchy. No matter how Republican the spirit, the need for a central symbol remains. Neither a flag nor a president can fulfil this unifying role, for by virtue of the 'party system' presidents are always politically motivated. Republicanism was devised on the principle of fraternal status, yet an ideally classless society can never exist in an environment that promotes displays of eminence and superiority by degrees of wealth and possession.

For the most part, those responsible for the United States' morally inspired Constitution were Rosicrucians and Freemasons, notable characters such as George Washington, Benjamin Franklin, Thomas Jefferson, John Adams and Charles Thompson. The last, who designed the *Great Seal* of the United States of America, was a member of Franklin's American Philosophical Society – a counterpart of Britain's Invisible College. The imagery of the *Seal* is directly related to alchemical tradition, inherited from the allegory of the ancient Egyptian Therapeutate. The eagle, the olive branch, the arrows, and the pentagrams are all occult symbols of opposites: good and evil, male and female, war and peace, darkness and light. On the reverse (as repeated on the dollar bill) is the truncated pyramid, indicating the loss of the Old Wisdom, severed and forced underground by the Church establishment. But above this are the rays of ever-hopeful light, incorporating the 'all-seeing eye', used as a symbol during the French Revolution.

In establishing their Republic, the Americans could still not escape the ideal of a parallel monarchy – a central focus of non-political, patriotic attachment. George Washington was actually offered kingship, but declined because he had no immediately qualifying heritage. Instead he turned to the Royal House of Stuart. In November 1782 four Americans arrived at the San Clemente Palazzo in Florence, the residence of Charles III Stuart in exile. They were Mr Galloway of Maryland, two brothers named Sylvester from Pennsylvania, and Mr Fish, a lawyer from New York. They were taken to Charles Edward by his secretary, John Stewart. Also present was the Hon Charles Hervey-Townshend (later Britain's ambassador to The Hague) and the Prince's future wife, Marguerite, Comtesse de Massillan. The interview – which revolved around the contemporary transatlantic dilemma – is documented in the US Senate archives and in the Manorwater Papers. Writers such as Sir Compton Mackenzie and Sir Charles Petrie have also described the occasion when Charles Edward Stuart was invited to become 'King of the Americans'.

Some years earlier, Charles had been similarly approached by the men of Boston, but once the War of Independence was over George Washington sent his own envoys. It would have been a great irony for the House of Hanover to lose the North American colonies to the Stuarts. But Charles declined the offer for a number of reasons, not the least of which was his lack of a legitimate male heir at the time. He knew that without a due successor the United States could easily fall to Hanover again at his death, thereby defeating the whole Independence effort.

## PRECEPT OF THE SANGRÉAL

Since those days, many other radical events have taken place: the French Revolution, the Russian Revolution, two major World Wars, and a host of changes as countries have swapped one style of government for another. Meanwhile, civil and international disputes continue just as they did in the Middle Ages. They are motivated by trade, politics, religion, and whatever other banners are flown to justify the constant struggle for territorial and economic control. The Holy Roman Empire has disappeared, the German Reichs have failed, and the British Empire has collapsed.

The Russian Empire fell to Communism, which has itself been disgraced and crumbled to ruin, while Capitalism teeters on the very brink of acceptability. With the Cold War now ended, America faces a new threat to her superpower status from the Pacific countries. In the meantime, the nations of Europe band together in what was once a seemingly well conceived economic community, but which is already suffering from the same pressures of individual custom and national sovereignty that beset the Holy Roman Empire.

Whether nations are governed by military-style regimes or elected parliaments, by autocrats or democrats, and whether formally described as monarchist, socialist or republican, the net product is always the same: the few control the fate of the many. In situations of dictatorship this is a natural experience – but it should not be the case in a democratic institution based on the principle of majority vote. True democracy is government *by* the people *for* the people, in either direct or representative form, ignoring class distinctions and tolerating minority views. The American Constitution sets out an ideal for this form of democracy ... but, in line with other nations, there is always a large sector of the community that is not represented by the party in power.

Because presidents and prime ministers are politically tied, and because political parties take their respective turns at individual helms, the inevitable result is a lack of continuity for the nations concerned. This is not necessarily a bad thing, but there is no reliable ongoing institution to champion the civil rights and liberties of people in such conditions of ever-changing leadership. Britain does, at least, retain a monarchy, but it is a politically constrained monarchy, and as such is ineffectual in performing its role as guardian of the nation. The United States, unlike Britain, has a Written Constitution – but has no one with the power to uphold its principles against successive governments who determinedly pursue their own politically vested interests.

Is there an answer to the anomaly – an answer that could bring not just a ray of hope but a shining light for the future? There certainly is, but its energy relies on those in governmental service appreciating their roles as 'representatives' of society rather than presuming to stand at the head of society. Alongside the political administration, an appointed Constitutional champion would be empowered to keep check on any potential disparities and infringements of the Constitution that might occur. This can be achieved in the manner first envisaged by George Washington and the American Fathers. Their original plan was for a democratic Parliament combined with a working Constitutional Monarchy bound not to Parliament or the Church but to the people and their Written Constitution. In such an environment, sovereignty would ultimately rest with the people, while the monarch (as an operative Guardian of the Realm) would pledge an 'Oath of Fealty to the Nation' – not the reverse, as in Britain's case, whereby the nation pays homage to the sovereignty of Parliament and the monarchy.

The unfulfilled ambition of the American Fathers was that government ministers should be elected by the majority vote of the people, but that their actions be directed within the boundaries of the Constitution. Because that Constitution belongs to the people, its champion – as George Washington perceived – should be a monarch whose obligation is not to politics or religion but to the sovereign nation. Through the natural system of heredity (being born and bred to the task), such a Constitutional guardian would provide an 'ongoing continuity' of public representation through successive governments. In this regard both monarchs and ministers would be servants of the Constitution on behalf of the Community of the Realm. Such a concept of moral government lies at the very heart of the Grail Code, and it remains within the bounds of possibility for every civilized Nation State.

A leading British politician recently claimed that it was not his job to be popular! Not so – a popular minister is a trusted minister, and holding a deserved electoral trust facilitates the democratic process. No minister can honestly expound an ideal of equality in society when that minister is deemed to possess some form of prior lordship over society. Class structure is always decided from above, never from below. It is therefore for those on self-made pedestals to be seen to kick them aside in the interests of harmony and unity. Jesus was not in the least humbled when he washed his Apostles' feet; he was raised to the realm of a true Grail King – the realm of *equality* and *princely service*. This is the eternal 'Precept of the Sangréal', and it is expressed in Grail lore with the utmost clarity: only by asking 'Whom does the Grail serve?' will the wound of the Fisher King be healed, and the Wasteland returned to fertility.

# NOTES AND REFERENCES

## Chapter 1: Origins of the Bloodline

1 As also mentioned in Hugh Schonfield, *The Passover Plot*, Element Books, Shaftesbury, 1985, ch 5, p 245.

2 Eusebius of Caesarea, *Ecclesiastical History* (translated by C F Crusé), George Bell, London, 1874, III, 11.

3 Malachi Martin, *The Decline and Fall of the Roman Church*, Secker and Warburg, London, 1982, p 43.

4 Massue, Melville Henry, 9th Marquis of Ruvigny and Raineval, *The Jacobite Peerage, Baronetage, Knightage, and Grants of Honour*, 1904, Introduction.

5 The date of 4004 was calculated by Archbishop James Ussher of Armagh in his *Annales Veteris Testamenti* of 1650. Adam's creation has been separately dated at 5503 BC by means of Alexandrian texts and at 5411 BC based on the Greek Septuagint. The standard Jewish reckoning for Creation (on which the Judaic calendar relies for its emergent year) is 3760 BC.

   Ussher's date provides a satisfactory mean, and is often used in today's chronologies. The *Universal History*'s error was in confusing Adam's date (see note 7) with the world's Creation.

   The Septuagint was produced by 72 translators of Old Testament texts in around 270 BC.

6 Darwin was not the first in the field of evolutionary research. The French naturalist Comte George de Buffon, Keeper of the Jardin du Roi, published the *Epochs of Nature*

in 1778; the Scottish physician James Hutton (sometimes known as 'the founder of geology') published his *Theory of the Earth* in 1785; the French anatomist Baron Georges Cuvier (the 'father of palaeontology') published his *Tableau elementaire de l'histoire naturelle des animaux* in 1798, in turn followed by his great work *Le regne animal*; the French naturalist le Chevalier Jean Baptiste de Monet Lamarck, Professor of Zoology at the University of Paris, published his *Philosophie zoologique* in 1809, and followed it with the *Histoire naturelle des animaux sans vertebres*; and the Scotsman Sir Charles Lyell published his *Principles of Geology* in the early 1830s.

7   For Adam to have appeared somewhere around Ussher's mean year of 4004 BC (see note 5) would put him notionally in the tribal Bronze Age of his locality. By that time, Sumer had been civilized for at least 2,000 years. From around 6000 BC there were villages and organized farming communities. By 5000 BC there were what passed for genuine cities, complete with civic councils run by the Halafans of Tel Halaf. In Jordan, Jericho was an established urban residential centre from about 6000 BC, and in China the Yangtze Basin (the basin of the Chang Jiang) was developed in the same era.

By the time of Adam, therefore, the plough, the wheel, and the sailing ship were all in widespread use.

8   Prior to *The Descent of Man*, Darwin's *On the Origin of the Species by Means of Natural Selection . . .* was published in 1859.

9   The Hebrew language at the time the books of the Pentateuch (the first five books of the Old Testament) were written did not distinguish between past tenses as we do in English. There was only one past tense and it referred to events that 'happened', 'have happened' and 'had happened' with equal relevance – linguistically, there was no difference between what took place a thousand years ago and what occurred yesterday. Moreover, the Hebrew words for 'day' and 'year' were used with total flexibility, which made translation into languages with more concrete ideas of time very difficult. See Mary Ellen Chase,

*Life and Language in the Old Testament,* Collins, London, 1956, ch 3, pp 32–9.

10  One very possible derivation of the name Israel is from *ysra* 'ruler' 'lord', plus the element *El* 'God' (found in many forenames, such as Michael and Elizabeth): thus 'God [is] ruler' – see Ahmed Osman, *The House of the Messiah,* Harper Collins, London, 1992, ch 17, p 96. But see note 11 below.

11  Jacob was renamed Israel (Genesis 32:28, 35:10) following his 'wrestling' with God, a name that may or may not celebrate that feat, for an alternative translation of *Israel* is 'God wrestles'. The descendants of Jacob were defined as Israelites.

12  *Oxford Concordance to the Bible,* ref. Rameses (2).

13  Ahmed Osman, *The House of the Messiah,* p 11.

14  *Ibid,* ch 12, p 67.

15  The Tabernacle of the Congregation (also translated as the Tent of Meeting) was a wooden-framed rectangular tent or booth covered with cloth and skins. It was used as a portable place of worship during the wanderings in the Wilderness. (See the *Oxford Concordance to the Bible.*)

## Chapter 2: In the Beginning

1  The subject is fully covered by Dr Raphael Patai, a noted authority on historical Judaic culture, in *The Hebrew Goddess,* Wayne State University Press, Detroit, 1967.

2  Some of the Old Testament, however, derived directly from the 'Book of the Law' that was discovered in the Temple at Jerusalem (2 Kings 22:8–13) some 35 years before the Babylonian Exile during the reign of King Josiah of Judah (640–609 BC). The existing Hebrew text of the Old Testament corresponds to that produced by the Massoretic scholars in around AD 900 (although it is based on much earlier manuscripts, some from the 1st century BC).

3  Eridu (modern Abu Shahrein) was the most sacred city of ancient Mesopotamia, a jewel within a green and fertile land that to the inhabitants of the very different Canaan

seemed a veritable paradise. In acknowledgement of its lush surroundings the city was dedicated to the water deity Enki (or Enkidu or Ea), and has often been identified with the Garden of Eden.

4 According to Sir Charles Leonard Woolley (one-time Director of the British Museum and of the University of Pennsylvania's archaeological expedition to Mesopotamia) in *Ur of the Chaldees* (1, 21–32), the Flood as narrated in Genesis took place before the reign (*c.* 2372–2326 BC) of Sargon the Great of Mesopotamia. Cuneiform clay tablets relating the history of Sumeria from about 3000 BC and stored at Nippur (modern Nuffar), suggest confirmation.

5 The Tower of Babel, a huge ziggurat, was constructed on the Babylonian Plain of Shinar. Such richly decorated, multi-levelled ziggurats (the word is Babylonian for 'high place' or 'tower') were features of Sumerian cities, each of them surmounted by a small temple to the primary deity of the region. The Great Ziggurat was sited at the city of Uruk (from which the modern state of Iraq derives its name); its temple was consecrated to the goddess Ishtar.

6 To the Jews the Underworld was known as Sheol. It was an equivalent to the Graeco-Roman kingdom of Hades, the infernal region in which souls dwelt in mournful darkness separated from their earthly bodies.

7 The first five Books of Moses correspond to the first five books of the Old Testament (also called the Pentateuch): Genesis, Exodus, Leviticus, Numbers and Deuteronomy.

8 The Books of the Prophets are technically those written by or about the Jewish prophets, and named after them, as opposed to books that are narrative histories, although the general definition also includes some historical books such as Judges, Samuel and Kings. The balance of the Old Testament is called the Hagiographa ('Holy Writings').

9 Other Jewish holy writings are the *Mishnah* and the *Talmud*.

The Mishnah ('Repetition') is an early codification of Jewish Law, based on ancient compilations and edited in

Palestine by the Ethnarch (Governor) Judah I in the early 3rd century AD. It consists of traditional law (*Halakah*) on a wide range of subjects, derived partly from old custom and partly from Biblical law (*Tannaim*) as interpreted by the rabbis (teachers).

The Talmud is basically a commentary on the Mishnah, compiled originally in Hebrew and Aramaic, and deriving from two independently important streams of Jewish tradition, the Babylonian and the Palestinian.

10 See the Revd John Fleetwood, *The Life of Our Lord and Saviour Jesus Christ*, William MacKenzie, Glasgow, c. 1900, ch 1, p 3: the entry by Dr G Redford.

11 The Hasmonaeans, or Asmoneans, were a distinguished priestly family prominent in Jerusalem during the 2nd century BC. At the time of Antiochus IV, the head of the household was the high priest Mattathias, who initiated the Jewish revolt. Just before he died he nominated his third son Judas (nicknamed Maccabaeus or Maccabee, 'the appointed [one]' or possibly 'the hammerer') to be the movement's military commander. Judas was in turn succeeded by his brothers Jonathan and Simon, and not only they but all their followers were thereafter known as the Maccabees.

12 See Baigent, Leigh and Lincoln, *The Holy Blood and the Holy Grail*, Jonathan Cape, London, 1982, ch 12, p 285.

13 See Baigent, Leigh and Lincoln, *The Dead Sea Scrolls Deception*, ch 9, p 141.

14 Twelve other works dating from and related to the last part of the Old Testament era constitute what is called the Apocrypha ('Hidden things'). Included in the Greek Septuagint, they were nonetheless not contained in the Hebrew canon. They originated in the Hellenist Judaism of Alexandria but are not accepted by orthodox Jews. The books are, however, included in St Jerome's Latin Vulgate (*c.* AD 385) as an extension to the Old Testament, and are recognized by the Roman Catholic Church, although they are omitted by almost all Protestant Bibles, having been sidelined by the prime reformer Martin Luther (1483–1546) and largely therefore ignored by translators. The

twelve books are: Esdras, Tobit, Judith, the Rest of Esther, the Wisdom of Solomon, Ecclesiasticus (of Jeremiah), Baruch with the Epistle of Jeremy, the Song of the Three Holy Children, the History of Susanna, Bel and the Dragon, the Prayer of Manasses, and Maccabees.

15 J T Milik, *Ten Years of Discovery in the Wilderness of Judaea* (translated by J Strugnell), SCM Press, London, 1959, ch 1, pp 11–19.

16 In the New Testament, 2 Corinthians 4:3, 7 similarly states: 'If our Gospel be hid, it is hid to them that are lost . . . But we have this treasure in earthen vessels'.

17 See James Robinson and the Coptic Gnostic Project, *The Nag Hammadi Library*, E J Brill, Leiden, Netherlands, 1977.

18 *Bedouin* is used in English as a singular adjective whereas it is technically a plural noun in Arabic: *bedu* is 'desert' and the *bedu'een* are the 'people of the desert'.

19 Josephus, *Antiquities of the Jews* (translated by W Whitson), Thomas Nelson, London, 1862, XV, ch 5, p 2.

20 J T Milik, *Ten Years of Discovery in the Wilderness of Judaea*, ch 3, pp 51–3.

21 John Allegro, *The Dead Sea Scrolls*, Penguin, Harmondsworth, 1964, ch 5, p 94.

22 *Ibid*, ch 5, p 93.

23 See Barbara Thiering, *Jesus the Man*, Doubleday/Transworld, London, 1992, ch 4, pp 20–1.

24 *Eschatology*: the study (or branch of theology) that has to do with the end of the world, the Last Things – that is, death, or judgement.

25 John Allegro, *The Dead Sea Scrolls*, ch 6, p 104.

26 *Pesharim*: 'Interpretations', thus 'Commentary' or 'Exegesis'; the singular is *pesher*.

27 See Barbara Thiering, *Jesus the Man*, *passim*.

28 *Ibid*, Appendix III, p 339.

29 Josephus, *The Jewish Wars*, II, ch 8, p 6.

30 See Barbara Thiering, *Jesus the Man*, ch 12, p 65; Appendix III, p 344.

31 During the earlier era of polytheistic religions, Zoroaster (or Zarathustra) modified the faith he had grown up with and devised the world's first genuinely dualist creed. He

became the archpriest and prophet of Ahura Mazda (Or-
muzd), god of life and light, who was opposed by Ahri-
man (Angra Mainyu), the evil lord of death and darkness.
These ancient deities were destined to wage a continual
war, Light against Darkness, until Light won in the Final
Judgement. At that time, Ahura Mazda would resurrect
the dead to create a Paradise on Earth.

Over the centuries thereafter, and as the tradition
altered with the differing cultural influences, much of
the legend nonetheless remained fixed. At the time of the
Essenes of Qumran (as the years BC drew to a close),
the story of the dualist war was very much current,
although generally as an allegory related to the hoped-for
overthrow of Roman imperialism.

Later still, Christianity retained the basic idea (as
adopted by the Romans), with the result that many Christians believe there is still a Final Judgement to come.

## Chapter 3: Jesus, Son of Man

1 See the Revd John Fleetwood, *The Life of Our Lord and
Saviour Jesus Christ*, ch 1, pp 21–2. For the various interpretations of the prophecy, see *Dr Smith's Bible Dictionary*.
2 It has been suggested that the first element of the name
Emmanuel is in fact Egyptian, corresponding to the name of
the god Amun (the 'Hidden One'), and that the name thus
combines Hebrew and Egyptian in a statement that
*Amun-u-El* 'Amun is God' (or 'The Hidden One is God').
See Ahmed Osman, *The House of the Messiah*, ch 31, pp
166–7.
3 See A N Wilson, *Jesus*, Sinclair Stevenson, London, 1992,
ch 4, p 79.
4 See Nancy Qualls-Corbett, *The Sacred Prostitute*, Inner
City Books, Toronto, 1988, ch 2, p 58.
5 The concept that Mary was 'ever-virgin' was established
at the Council of Trullo in AD 692.
6 A N Wilson, *Jesus*, ch 4, p 83.
7 An old monastic complex stood on the outskirts of the Qumran Community. Among its buildings was the house where

Essene children were born out of wedlock. The Community referred to this house as 'Bethlehem of Judaea' (as opposed to the quite separate town of Bethlehem, south of Jerusalem). Matthew 2:5 states that Jesus was born 'in Bethlehem of Judaea'. See Barbara Thiering, *Jesus the Man*, ch 9, pp 50–2.

The Gospel narratives were geared to comply with the prophecy of Micah 5:2, which dates from about 710 BC: 'But thou, Bethlehem Ephratah, though thou be little . . . yet out of thee shall he come forth unto me that is to be ruler in Israel'.

8  *Dr Smith's Bible Dictionary* says that the Hebrew word translated as 'inn' in English more literally signifies a 'lodging-place': inns, in the way we think of them, were unknown in the ancient Near East, where it was more common to invite travellers into one's home, and regarded as a pious duty to do so.

9  A N Wilson, *Jesus*, ch 4, p 80.

10 See Ahmed Osman, *The House of the Messiah*, ch 5, p 31. *Robinson's Bible Researches*, on the other hand, gives the Arabic name as *en-Nusara* (see the Revd John Fleetwood, *The Life of Our Lord and Saviour Jesus Christ*, ch 1, p 10).

11 The Old Testament does not refer to Nazareth either. Neither does the Hebrew Talmud, and nor does Josephus mention the town in his 1st-century *The Antiquities of the Jews* and *The Jewish Wars* (according to *Robinson's Bible Researches*). Nazareth became a place of pilgrimage only from the 6th century AD (Ahmed Osman, *The House of the Messiah*, ch 5, pp 30–2).

12 The Revd John Fleetwood, *The Life of Our Lord and Saviour Jesus Christ*, 1, 4, confirms the information in *Dr Smith's Bible Dictionary* that the name *Gabriel* in this context represents a title corresponding to 'angelic' office.

13 Josephus, *The Jewish Wars*, II, ch 8, p 7.

14 Barbara Thiering, *Jesus the Man*, Appendix III, pp 335–8. The name *Gabriel* means 'Man of God'.

15 Barbara Thiering, *Jesus the Man*, Appendix III, p 340. The name *Michael* means 'Who [is] like God'.

16 Luke 1:5 – Elizabeth was herself a daughter of the priestly house of Aaron.

17  Luke 2:25.
18  The Revd John Fleetwood, *The Life of Our Lord and Saviour Jesus Christ*, ch 1, pp 10–11; an extract by Dr Paxton outlines the customary rules of Jewish matrimony as distinct from the more restrictive dynastic regulations.
19  Barbara Thiering, *Jesus the Man*, p 8; Appendix I, p 177.
20  Josephus, *The Jewish Wars*, II, ch 8, p 13.
21  Barbara Thiering, *Jesus the Man*, ch 7, p 42: Appendix I, p 209.

It was not until AD 314 that the Emperor Constantine the Great arbitrarily changed the date of Jesus's birthday to 25 December to coincide with the pagan sun festival (see Chapter 7, Raised from the dead, and Chapter 11, The Rise of the Roman Church).

Meanwhile it will be noticed that the dates of some New Testament events as given in this book do not conform to the traditional ones. The year of Jesus's birth, for example, is often considered to have been 5 BC, but herein is 7 BC. The date of the Crucifixion is similarly often shown as AD 30 whereas it is given here as AD 33. The first published sequence of Biblical dates appeared in AD 526 and expressed the calculations of the monk Dionysius Exiguus. By his reckoning Jesus was born in the Roman year 754 AUC (*Anno Urbis Conditae* 'years after the founding of the city [of Rome]') – equivalent to AD 1. But Herod the Great died four years before this, in 750 AUC ( = 4 BC). Because it was known that Herod was still alive at the time of Jesus's birth, the monk's chart was arbitrarily adjusted to set the Nativity a year before Herod's death – in the year 749 AUC ( = 5 BC). This became the accepted date, and the rest of the Gospel time-frame was recalculated accordingly.

In the light of information currently available, a more accurate chronology has become possible. The early reckonings took no account of the calendar variables of the era (the solar, lunar and Julian), but adjustments for these have now been made by Scrolls interpreters. In recent years the most exacting work on New Testament chronol-

ogy has been conducted by Dr Barbara Thiering (see her
*Jesus the Man*). Interesting Old Testament discoveries in
this field have been made by David Rohl (see his *A Test of
Time*).

22  Barbara Thiering, *Jesus the Man*, ch 8, p 47 and Appendix I.

23  In 1380 the Yorkshire reformer John Wycliffe (a Past Master of Balliol College, Oxford, and Rector of Lutterworth)
supervised the first Bible translation from Latin into English. But the Synod of Blackfriars banned the book in 1382
and Wycliffe was declared a heretic. The first printing of
the New Testament in English (1525) was a translation by
William Tyndale, who for his pains was seized in Ant-
werp and executed in 1535. Miles Coverdale, a friar at
Cambridge, published a clerically acceptable Bible under
the aegis of Thomas Cromwell, who had supervised the
separation of the English Church from the Roman Church
on behalf of King Henry VIII. This work led to the Great
Bible of 1539, made compulsory in all churches; Coverdale was made Bishop of Exeter.

A further English translation was effected in Geneva by
Puritan exiles who, in 1560, introduced the verse pattern.
This was followed by another edition, known as the Douai
Bible (1582–1609), which was translated by Roman Catholic scholars who had fled from Oxford to continental
Europe in the reign of Elizabeth I. Then, in 1611, came the
amalgamated work upon which many of today's Bibles
are based: the Authorized Version of King James (James
VI of Scotland, James I of England). This richly worded
work was not a 'direct' translation from anything, but it
was a fair and well conceived compromise responsibly
derived from original texts.

24  In relating Jesus's lineage, Matthew and Luke do not agree
precisely on the genealogical list purportedly showing the
direct line of heredity from King David. Matthew charts
the kingly line from Solomon, whereas Luke details a
descent from another of David's sons, Nathan. This
segment of the genealogical list in Matthew contains 22
ancestors, against 20 in Luke. However, both lists eventually coincide at Zerubbabel, who they agree was the direct

and immediate heir of Shealtiel. Even this is subject to some further debate, though, for whereas the Old Testament books of Ezra (3:2) and Haggai (1:1) confirm that Zerubbabel was born into Shealtiel's family, there could apparently have been a generation between the two, constituted by a possible son of Shealtiel named Pedaiah who would then have been Zerubbabel's father. The account in 1 Chronicles 3:19 is confusing in this regard.

The main difference between Matthew and Luke is thus the list of ancestors that spanned the generations from the time of David's sons to the era at about the time of the return from the Babylonian captivity. For this term the equivalent list in 1 Chronicles is in general accord with Matthew's genealogy. Unhappily, having converged on Zerubbabel, the genealogies of Matthew and Luke then diverge again: Matthew traces Jesus's descent through a son named Abiud, and Luke takes a course through a son called Rhesa (which may have been a title rather than a name, since it means 'Chieftain').

Jesus's paternal grandfather is called Jacob according to Matthew 1:16, but in Luke 3:23 he is Heli. Both versions are correct, however, for Joseph's father Heli actually held the title of 'Jacob' in his patriarchal capacity (see Barbara Thiering, *Jesus the Man*, ch 5, p 29).

The genealogical list in Matthew, from David to Jacob-Heli (spanning about 1,000 years), thus contains 25 generations at 40 years each. Reversing the direction in which the relations are listed, and reversing also the proportions of generations and lifespans, Luke gives 40 generations at 25 years each. In this way, Luke places Jesus in the 20th generation from Zerubbabel whereas Matthew places him in the 11th. Through this latter period of around 530 years, the Matthew list supports a 53-year generation standard; the Luke is more comprehensible with its 28-year standard.

See Appendix I.

25  Barbara Thiering, *Jesus the Man*, Appendix III, p 348.
26  *Ibid*, ch 12, p 65; Appendix I, p 216, although the reference here should read 'Luke 13:11 – in the paperback edition this is on p 292.

27 The original Zadok was the High Priest who anointed
David's son King Solomon in around 1015 BC (1 Kings
1:38–40), as celebrated by Handel in the anthem sung at
British coronations since the 18th century.

## Chapter 4: The Early Mission

1 Barbara Thiering, *Jesus the Man*, Appendix II, p 299.

2 *Ibid*, Appendix I, pp 325–30.

3 The Revd John Fleetwood, *The Life of Our Lord and Saviour
Jesus Christ*, ch 1, pp 11–12; extract from *Dr Smith's Bible
Dictionary*.

4 See Chapter 2, Heritage of the Messiah.

5 The Samaritans believed that Simon (Zelotes) Magus represented the 'power of God' (Acts 8:9–10).

6 Steve Richards, *Levitation*, Thorsons, Wellingborough,
1980, ch 5, pp 66–7.

7 Barbara Thiering, *Jesus the Man*, ch 15, p 80.

8 Judas the Galilean died in AD 6.

9 The Syrian Semitic verb *skariot* was an equivalent of the
contemporary Hebrew *sikkarti* 'to deliver up'. It has been
suggested that Judas Iscariot was therefore 'Judas the
Deliverer', referring to his betrayal of Jesus. (See Ahmed
Osman, *The House of the Messiah*, ch 15, p 81.)

10 *Jacob* is synonymous with *Jacobus*, of which there was a
Latin variant *Jacomus*, from which in turn (via the Norman
French) English now has the variant nominal form of
*James*. The connection between the forms has never been
forgotten, and is of course the reason that, from the 17th
century, adherents of the Stuart King James VII of Scot-
land (James II of England) were known as Jacobites, (ie
Jacob-ites).

11 Barbara Thiering, *Jesus the Man*, ch 5, p 28.

12 Despite his religious background, Matthew was regarded
with considerable hostility by the Pharisees. Their strict,
orthodox Jewish outlook caused them to be petty in the
extreme about the observance of laws that predated
the Books of Moses (the Pentateuch or Torah), to the

extent that they believed Israel could not be redeemed until all Jews were 'purified'. To them, such essential purification was incompatible with monetary affairs or political intrigues, and someone who was involved in both – like a publican, and especially one who collected taxes – could only be regarded as a sinner.

13 The Proselytes were Gentile converts to the Jewish faith.

14 Shem was a son of Noah and an ancestor of Abraham: he represents the ancient lineage of the S(h)emitic peoples.

15 The name *Bartholomew* derives from *Bar-Ptolemy* (Aramaic 'servant of Ptolemy') and thus has its own Egyptian connotations. See Barbara Thiering, *Jesus the Man*, Appendix III, p 361.

16 Thomas was born Philip, the son of Herod the Great and Mariamne II. In due course he became the first husband of Herod's granddaughter Herodias (see Barbara Thiering, *Jesus the Man*, ch 15, p 81), with whom he had a daughter, Salome – that very Salome who requested the head of John the Baptist from Herod-Antipas of Galilee. Well known for her 'dance of the seven veils', Salome is not mentioned by name in the New Testament, but features in Flavius Josephus's *The Antiquities of the Jews*, XVIII, ch 5, sect 4.

17 Genesis 16:7–12.

18 Numbers 22:21–35.

19 Judges 13:3–19.

20 Judges 6:11–22.

21 The twelve clay tablets recounting the Epic of Gilgamesh, ruler of Uruk, derive from the 7th century BC. They were discovered among the effects of King Ashurbanipal of Assyria (ruled 669–626 BC) at Nineveh. Among the myriad other events described in the Epic is the story of Enkidu who, like the prophet Elijah, was confronted by a roaring from the heavens. He was seized and transported upwards in the brazen talons of an eagle, with a vertical speed that made his body feel as heavy as an enormous boulder.

Reference of this kind to an eagle occurs in the *Moses Apocalypse*, in which Eve sees a chariot of light drawn by shining eagles.

Flaming seraphims also appear with regularity in the ancient documents. That they are fiery is at least consistent with the etymology of the word *seraph*, which is related to an old Hebrew stem meaning 'flame'. But they sometimes have awesomely destructive properties, as in Numbers 21:6, when a large proportion of Israel died after the Lord sent fiery serpents (*seraphims*) among them.

Such stories are not confined to the countries of North Africa and the Near East. From that same period similar accounts come from Tibet, India, Scandinavia, and even North America. The writings all tell of heavenly chariots that spout fire and quicksilver (mercury), and of thunderbirds with brazen wings.

22 The subject is well covered in Erich von Däniken, *Chariots of the Gods* Souvenir, 1969.

23 1 Enoch 4:9; also the Qumran *War Scroll* 9, 15–17. See also A Dupont-Sommer, *The Essene Writings From Qumran* (translated by G Vermes), Basil Blackwell, Oxford, 1961, V, p 183 (the angelic shields).

24 Josephus, *The Jewish Wars*, II, ch 7, p 7.

25 Tabulated details of the angelic and priestly structures are quoted in Barbara Thiering, *Jesus the Man*, Appendix III.

26 The spiritual energy of springs and streams was numerically represented in the 'solar force' as 1080: see John Michell, *Dimensions of Paradise*, Thames and Hudson, London, 1988, ch 1, p 18.

27 In Chapter 3, Dynastic wedlock.

28 Barbara Thiering, *Jesus the Man*, Appendix III, p 339.

## Chapter 5: Jesus the Messiah

1 The Qumran *Manual of Discipline* (the *Scroll of the Rule*), ch 6, pp 4–5; annex 18–20.

2 Barbara Thiering, *Jesus the Man*, ch 18, p 91.

3 *Ibid.*, Appendix III, p 357. There were not actually 5,000 people at this symbolic feeding: 'the Five Thousand' was a name applied to a body of non-Jews native to Palestine (not Romano-Greeks) and who thus could be described as 'the sons of Ham' (Ham was the son of Noah, regarded

as the founder of the Hamitic tribes of the area). The Community's 'liaison officer' with 'the Five Thousand' was Jesus's Apostle John Boanerges.

4  Again there were not 4,000 recipients involved: this 'Four Thousand' (the Men of Shem) was another particularized group of Gentiles. Together with the Proselytes (converts to Judaism) called 'the Three Thousand', the Five Thousand and the Four Thousand were held to comprise part of the especially cosmopolitan tribe of Asher.

5  Barbara Thiering, *Jesus the Man*, ch 18, p 92; Appendix II, pp 325–31.

6  There was a good deal of popular confusion over whether John the Baptist was the awaited Messiah, and later, over whether Jesus was. John was after all 'the Zadok' and anointed as such, thereby holding Messianic status (*Messiah* 'anointed'). But when asked directly about the Saviour Messiah, John 'confessed, and denied not; but confessed, I am not the Christ' (John 1:20). The Qumran Scrolls indicate that the Community lived in expectation of *two* important Messiahs. One was to be of the priestly caste, whom they called 'the Teacher of Righteousness'; the other would be a Prince of the line of David – a warrior who would restore the kingdom of his people.

John the Baptist made it quite clear that, anointed or not, he was not the Kingly Messiah (John 3:28): 'I said, I am not the Christ, but that I am sent before him.'

For the Qumran notion of the two Messiahs, see also John Allegro, *The Dead Sea Scrolls*, ch 13, pp 167–72.

7  The Hebrew calendar is lunar in origin, and its 12 months in the year thus total 354 days, although to make up for the deficiency of 11 days in relation to the solar calendar year it adds a complete calendar month (II Adar) in seven years out of a 19-year cycle. The Hellenists in Palestine adopted the Romans' Julian (365-day) calendar in 44 BC, a system that suited the Samaritan Magi, who made astronomical calculations according to the solar calendar, which added 10 days per year to the lunar calendar.

It is suggested that the difference in calendars over a number of centuries might account for a displacement of seven years in a forecast relating to a time sufficiently far ahead.

8 Barbara Thiering, *Jesus the Man*, 19, 94–6; Appendix III, 340–1.

9 A fuller was a person who beat and scoured the textiles of the washed clothes (using a special grease-absorbent clay and certain herbs) so that the material fluffed up, with an effect much like that provided by today's fabric conditioners. On white garments, the result was an extra lustrous sheen. (Modern English Bibles tend to translate the original Greek word – which may be an adjective, not an agent noun – as 'bleacher'.)

10 Josephus, *The Antiquities of the Jews*, XVIII, ch 3, p 2.

11 Barbara Thiering, *Jesus the Man*, ch 20, pp 97–100.

12 Spikenard is the name of the fragrant, sweet-smelling ointment compounded from the nard plant, which in those days grew only in the Himalayan mountains at heights of around 15,000 feet (c. 4,570 metres) and was extremely expensive.

13 In the Gospels of Matthew and Mark, Jesus's entry into Jerusalem occurs *before* the anointing at Bethany. A political motivation lies behind this textual switch of events in their accounts. In John, the anointing is correctly related in conjunction with the 'raising of Lazarus' – and for Jesus to be accredited as the Messiah it was imperative that he be anointed beforehand.

14 See Chapter 3, Dynastic wedlock.

15 Spikenard was also used as an unguent in funerary rites: it was customary for a grieving widow to place a broken vial of the ointment in her late husband's tomb. (See Margaret Starbird, *The Woman With the Alabaster Jar*, Bear, Santa Fe, New Mexico, 1993, ch 2, pp 40–1.)

16 See Chapter 5, The King and his Donkey.

17 See Chapter 2, Jehovah and the Goddess.

18 Margaret Starbird, *The Woman With the Alabaster Jar*, ch 11, pp 35–6.

19 Of the academic works on the subject of sacred marriage, Samuel Kramer's *The Sacred Marriage Rite* (see especially ch 3, p 63) is worthy of particular recommendation. From

the female standpoint, however, nowhere is the story of 'the Lost Bride' more compassionately conveyed than in the writings of Margaret Starbird.

20  See Chapter 2, Jehovah and the Goddess.
21  Ahmed Osman, *The House of the Messiah*, ch 28, p 152.
22  Barbara Thiering, *Jesus the Man*, Appendix III, pp 366–71.
23  The Sanhedrin was the Jewish assembly that held supreme authority in all religious and civil matters: it was made up of priests, scribes and elders, who together formed the Supreme Court of Judicature (*Oxford Concordance to the Bible*).
24  Salome's baptismal name was Helena. As the spiritual adviser to Salome, daughter of Herodias, she too was called Salome in accordance with custom. Helena-Salome was the spiritual foster-mother of the Apostles James and John Boanerges (see Barbara Thiering, *Jesus the Man*, Appendix III, p 334).
25  Barbara Thiering, *Jesus the Man*, Appendix III, 366–71.
26  Morton Smith, *The Secret Gospel*.
27  *Ibid*, ch 7, p 51.
28  In the 4th century AD, when the New Testament was first collated, the Gospel manuscripts of Mark ended at the present Chapter 16 verse 8, before the narration of the Resurrection events. These shorter manuscripts are part of the *Codex Vaticanus* and the *Codex Sinaiticus*. (See Baigent, Leigh and Lincoln, *The Holy Blood and the Holy Grail*, ch 12, pp 282–3; notes, p 432.)
29  Baigent *et al.*, ch 12, p 296.

# Chapter 6: Betrayal and Crucifixion

1  See Chapter 2, Heritage of the Messiah.
2  John the Baptist had initially supported a prediction known as the *Prophecy of Enoch*, which gave a date for the restoration of both the Zadokite and Davidic hereditary lines as 'the end of the eighth World Week' – that is, 3,920 years after the supposed Creation. This had been calculated to occur in the year now defined as 21 BC . . . but nothing had happened. Calendar revision allowed for an

extension to AD 29, but judicious recalculation further extended the deadline date to AD 31 (see Barbara Thiering, *Jesus the Man*, ch 13, pp 67–8). John's whole reputation, with all its wild mystique, hung on this prediction. Following John's execution the prophecy was recalculated yet again to fall on the vernal equinox of AD 33.

3  Barbara Thiering, *Jesus the Man*, ch 22, p 105.
4  Josephus, *The Antiquities of the Jews*, XVIII, ch 1, sect 3.
5  Barbara Thiering, *Jesus the Man*, Appendix I, p 195.
6  See Chapter 2, Secret Codes of the New Testament.
7  Barbara Thiering, *Jesus the Man*, ch 22, p 106.
8  John Allegro, *The Dead Sea Scrolls*, ch 7, p 131; ch 12, p 164; ch 13, p 168.
9  The Scroll of *The Rule*, Annex II, 17–22.
10  Barbara Thiering, *Jesus the Man*, ch 21, p 102.
11  *Ibid.*, ch 23, p 109.
12  Baigent, Leigh and Lincoln, *The Holy Blood and the Holy Grail*, ch 12, p 309.
13  Barbara Thiering, *Jesus the Man*, ch 22, p 105.
14  Baigent, Leigh and Lincoln, *The Holy Blood and the Holy Grail*, ch 12, p 309; notes, p 433.
15  *The Apostolic Constitutions*, VI, sect 9. See Clement (Cults and Religions) in bibliography.
16  Gnostic tradition has it that Simon the Cyrene was crucified 'in the place of Jesus'. This does not mean 'instead of Jesus', but 'in what should have been Jesus's location' – because, understanding Jesus to represent the kingly Davidic heritage and Simon to represent the priestly line (and therefore Judas to represent the line of the prophets), the positioning of the three crosses should have been made to observe the formal hierarchical ranks. According to this scheme, the position of the King should have been to the west (on the left); the position of the Priest should have been in the centre; and the position of the Prophet should have been to the east (on the right). But the Gospels state that Jesus's cross was in the middle. If, though, the Cyrene was crucified in this place instead of Simon (as the Priest), Jesus (as the King) would have been correctly

positioned to the west. See Barbara Thiering, *Jesus the Man*, Appendix II, p 324.

17 Barbara Thiering, *Jesus the Man*, ch 24, p 113.
18 *Ibid*, Appendix II, p 324.
19 *Ibid*, Appendix II, p 312.
20 *Ibid.*, Appendix III, p 353.
21 *Ibid*, ch 26, p 122.

## Chapter 7: The Resurrection

1 The translation 'pound' in this case represents the Greek *litra* (a variant of the Roman *libra*), a measure of weight equal to one ninetieth of a *talantaios* 'talent', which in modern terms approximates to 330 grams or 12 ounces avoirdupois; 100 'pounds' is thus roughly equal in modern terms to 33 kilograms or 75 pounds (more than 5 stone) avoirdupois – a considerable quantity for one man (Nicodemus) to manage alone.

2 Barbara Thiering, *Jesus the Man*, Appendix I, pp 238–42.
3 See Chapter 4, Who Were the Apostles? – sections entitled *James and John* and *Thaddaeus, James and Matthew*.
4 See Chapter 6, Politics and the Passover.
5 Christianity did survive, although for many the Crucifixion was seen as a blow that should have snuffed out the flame once and for all. Senator Cornelius Tacitus (born *c.* AD 55), referring to the Crucifixion, wrote ruefully that 'in spite of this temporary setback, the deadly superstition [Christianity] had broken out afresh, not only in Judaea where the mischief had started, but even in Rome' (Tacitus, *The Annals of Imperial Rome*, XIV, ref. AD 64).
6 See Chapter 5, The King and his Donkey.
7 Baigent, Leigh and Lincoln, *The Messianic Legacy*, ch 6, p 68.
8 Gladys Taylor, *Our Neglected Heritage*, Covenant Books, London, 1974, Vol.1, p 42.
9 The Gnostics were so called because they were accredited with *gnosis* (Greek 'knowledge', especially esoteric insight). The Gnostic movement originated in Samaria, where Simon Zelotes – in this context better known as Simon (the) Magus – was head of the Magi (men of

wisdom) of West Manasseh. Later, it was further developed in Syria, again with Simon as its principal proponent. The cult was identified particularly with the
spiritual ideals of the Samaritan community.

In other respects, the Magi were renowned for their
astronomical knowledge, which was a direct result of the
fact that the first magians were the priests of Zoroaster (or
Zarathustra), the founder of Zoroastrianism, whom some
ancient texts define as a pupil of Abraham in the study of
astrology.

10  Nag Hammadi *Codex* BG 8502, 1.
11  See Chapter 4, Who Were the Apostles? *Thaddaeus, James and
Matthew.*
12  Nag Hammadi *Codex* VII, 3.
13  Nag Hammadi *Codex* II, 2.

# Chapter 8: The Bloodline Continues

1  Barbara Thiering, *Jesus the Man*, Appendix I, p 177 and
p 196.
2  *Ibid.*, Appendix III, p 177.
3  See Chapter 11, The Rise of the Roman Church.
4  The fact that Jesus is mentioned in connection with the
'times of restitution' (Acts 3:21) indicates that he had
become a parent and was obliged therefore (for the time
being) to lead a celibate existence. There is no suggestion
that this child was a son, which means that the child was
a daughter. See also Barbara Thiering, *Jesus the Man*, ch
33, p 151; Appendix I, p 251.
   Note that 'Damaris' is mentioned in Acts 17:34.
5  Barbara Thiering, *Jesus the Man*, Appendix I, p 297 and
p 299; Appendix III, pp 363–4.
6  *Ibid.*, Appendix III, p 367.
7  See Chapter 2, Secret Codes of the New Testament.
8  Barbara Thiering, *Jesus the Man*, ch 29, p 133.
9  A N Wilson, *Jesus*, ch 2, p 26.
10  Baigent, Leigh and Lincoln, *The Messianic Legacy*, ch 6,
p 67.
11  Barbara Thiering, *Jesus the Man*, ch 30, p 139.

12 As we have seen (in Chapter 2, Secret Codes of the New Testament), the doctrinal theme of the Qumran Community was 'the Way', and those who followed 'the Way' were 'the Children of Light'. It was in this context that those who were unsympathetic to the Community's doctrine were 'blind to the Way', as was Saul, to whom Jesus appeared 'in the Way', (Acts 9:17). Symbolically, his instruction in Hellenist principles enabled him to 'see the Way' and, as the English metaphor has it, also to 'see the Light'.

13 A N Wilson, *Jesus*, ch 2, pp 18–19.

14 *Ibid*, ch 2, pp 22–3.

15 Simon is honoured as the first missionary priest in Cyprus. The main church in Larnaca is dedicated to him – under the New Testament name he is generally better known by: St Lazarus. He is sometimes said to have been the first Bishop of Larnaca.

16 See Chapter 9, Scarlet Woman – Black Madonna.

17 See Chapter 9, Mary and the Church.

18 Barbara Thiering, *Jesus the Man*, ch 31, pp 143–4.

19 *Ibid*, ch 31, p 141.

20 *Ibid*, Appendix I, p 264.

21 *Ibid*, Appendix I, p 268.

22 There is some confusion from this early date over the colour black as used for ecclesiastical garb. It would certainly seem to have some associations that are much older than Christianity.

The tall black statue of Isis at the Church of St Germain, Paris, was identified as 'the Virgin of Paris' until the 16th century. The original abbey on the site was built for Childebert I on top of a Temple of Isis. It housed Childebert's relics from the Treasures of Solomon, and was a burial-place for the Merovingian kings (see Ean C M Begg, *The Cult of the Black Virgin*, Arkana, London, 1985, ch 2, p 66). The Benedictine monks of St Germain-des-Prés wore black cassocks in the Nazarite tradition.

A statue of St Genevieve was erected in the Benedictine chapel. In her way she was a successor to Isis in France, and she was a close friend of King Clovis.

23 It was in AD 62 that Ananus the Younger, a brother of Jonathan Annas and himself a Sadducee, became High Priest. Such a background meant that he was distinctly predisposed towards furthering the Sanhedrin's opposition to James and his Nazarene ideals.

24 The stoning took place in AD 62, according to Josephus' 1st-century *The Antiquities of the Jews*, XX, ch 9, p 1.

25 Tacitus, *The Annals of Imperial Rome*, XV, 43: ref. AD 64.

26 Barbara Thiering, *Jesus the Man*, ch 35, p 159; note the words of 2 Timothy 2:9: 'The word of God is not bound . . .'

27 Andreas Faber-Kaiser, *Jesus Died in Kashmir*, Abacus/Sphere, London, 1978.

28 The only time that Jewish forces ever again dented Roman military pride was when, in AD 132, they revolted once more, under the leadership of Simon Ben Kochba, Prince of Israel. Simon assembled a large army comprising native volunteers together with professional mercenary soldiers from abroad. His battle plan included many strategic operations, some of which made use of a series of tunnels and underground chambers beneath Jerusalem. Within one year, Jerusalem was recaptured from the Romans. Jewish administration was established and was maintained for two years. But outside the city the struggle continued, and the final strategy depended on military assistance from Persia. Unfortunately, just when the Persian forces were meant to be setting out for the Holy Land, Persia itself was invaded. Its troops had to stay and defend their own territory – with the result that Simon and his gallant band were not able by themselves to counter the advance of the twelve Roman legions who had regrouped in Syria at the command of the Emperor Hadrian. They were eventually overwhelmed at Battin, west of Jerusalem, in AD 135.

29 Julius Africanus made his reputation by translating into Latin a series of works written by the 1st-century disciple Abdias, the Nazarene Bishop of Babylon. The *Books of Abdias* amounted to ten volumes of firsthand Apostolic

history. Like so many other important eyewitness accounts of the era, however, they were rejected outright for inclusion in the eventual New Testament.

30 See Chapter 1, Whom does the Grail serve?

31 Malachi Martin, *The Decline and Fall of the Roman Church*, p 44.

## Chapter 9: Mary Magdalene

1 John W Taylor, *The Coming of the Saints*, Covenant Books, London, 1969, ch 7, p 138.

2 Barbara Thiering, *Jesus the Man*, ch 17, p 89.

3 *Ibid.*, ch 17, p 88; also ch 15, pp 80–1.

As Chief of the Scribes, Judas Sicariote also held the post of 'the Tempter'. It was thus with Judas that Jesus debated when he was 'led up of the Spirit into the wilderness to be tempted of the devil' (Matthew 4:1). Judas was at that time seeking to become the 'Father' in the place of John the Baptist. The gist of his negotiation with Jesus was that if Jesus would aid him to priestly eminence, he would assist him to become king. 'All this power I will give thee, and the glory of them: for that is delivered unto me; and to whomsoever I will give it. If thou therefore wilt worship me, all shall be thine' (Luke 4:6–7).

See also Chapter 2, Secret Codes of the New Testament.

4 *Ibid*, Appendix III, p 367.

5 *Ibid*, Appendix I, p 215.

6 *Ibid*, ch 17, p 89.

7 Gladys Taylor, *Our Neglected Heritage*, Vol I, p 17.

8 Ean Begg, *The Cult of the Black Virgin*, ch 4, p 98.

9 Margaret Starbird, *The Woman With the Alabaster Jar*, ch 3, p 50.

10 Henry Lincoln, *The Holy Place*, Jonathan Cape, London, 1991, ch 7, p 70.

11 Ean Begg, *The Cult of the Black Virgin*, Gazetteer, p 234.

12 Barbara Thiering, *Jesus the Man*, Appendix III, p 367.

13 *Ibid*, p 368.

14 Ean Begg, *The Cult of the Black Virgin*, Introduction, p 20.

15 Margaret Starbird, *The Woman With the Alabaster Jar*, ch 6, p 123.

16 *Ibid*, ch 6, p 123.

17 Ean Begg, *The Cult of the Black Virgin*, Introduction, p 3.

18 *Nag Hammadi* Codex BG 8502-1.

19 Elaine Pagels, *The Gnostic Gospels*, Weidenfeld and Nicolson, London, 1980, ch 3, p 65.

20 *Nag Hammadi* Codex II, 2.

21 *Ibid*., II, 3.

22 See Chapter 9, Scarlet Woman – Black Madonna.

23 Ean Begg, *The Cult of the Black Virgin*, ch 2, p 68.

24 Beryl Platts, *Origins of Heraldry*, Proctor Press, London, 1980, ch 1, p 33.

25 See Chapter 8, The Times of Restitution.

26 The whole much misunderstood subject is refreshingly well covered in Beryl Platts' *Origins of Heraldry*, which sets many heraldic myths to rights.

27 See above, Mary Magdalene – Royal Bride and Mother.

28 John W Taylor, *The Coming of the Saints*, ch 6, p 103.

29 The Revd Père Lacordaire, *St Mary Magdalene*, Thomas Richardson, Derby, 1880, chs 106–8.

30 *Dictionnaire étymologique des noms de lieux en France*.

31 See Chapter 4, Who Were the Apostles? *Peter and Andrew*.

32 See Chapter 8, The Times of Restitution.

33 *Dictionnaire étymologique des noms de lieux en France*.

34 The Merovingians were the dynasty of Frankish kings in the 5th to 8th centuries who founded and established what became the monarchy of France. See Chapter 11, The Merovingian Sorcerer Kings.

35 See Chapter 13, The King of the Jews.

## Chapter 10: Joseph of Arimathea

1 In *De Demonstratione Evangelii* Eusebius wrote: 'The Apostles passed over the ocean to the islands known as Britain.' See The Revd Lionel Smithett Lewis, *Joseph of Arimathea at Glastonbury*, A R Mobray, London, 1927, p 54.

2 Archbishop Isidore of Seville (600–636) wrote: 'Philip of the city of Bethsaida, whence also came Peter, preached Christ to the Gauls, and brought barbarous nations and

their neighbours . . . into the light of knowledge. . . . Afterwards he was stoned and crucified, and died in Hierapolis, a city of Phrygia.' This information is confirmed by Freculphus, 9th-century Bishop of Lisieux.

3 The Tabernacle of the Hebrews is described in Exodus 26 and 36.

4 The Revd Lionel Smithett Lewis, *Joseph of Arimathea at Glastonbury*, pp 15–16.

5 Writing in about AD 600, St Augustine describes how 'There is on the western confines of Britain a certain royal island called in ancient speech Glastonia . . . In it, the earliest Angle neophytes of the Catholic doctrine – God guiding them – found a church not made by any man, they say, but prepared by God Himself for the salvation of mankind, which church the Heavenly Builder Himself declared (by many miracles and mysteries of healing) he had consecrated to Himself and to Holy Mary, Mother of God.' See William of Malmesbury, *The Antiquities of Glastonbury*, Talbot/JMF Books, Llanerch, 1980, p 1.

6 The route used by the Jewish tin traders was described by Diodorus Siculus in the days of the Emperor Augustus (63 BC – AD 14): 'The tin ore is transported from Britain into Gaul, the merchants carrying it on horseback through the heart of Celtica to Marseilles and the city called Narbo[nne].' It was then taken by ship across the Mediterranean to any of several destinations. See John W Taylor, *The Coming of the Saints*, ch 8, p 143.

7 Tin is essential to the production of bronze – and the most important tin mines were in south-western England, an area also rich in copper and lead, for which there was a great market in the expanding Roman Empire. The British Museum contains two splendid examples of lead from the Mendip mines near Glastonbury, dated AD 49 and AD 60 respectively. One bears the name of 'Britannicus, son of the Emperor Claudius', and the other is inscribed (in Latin) 'British lead: property of the Emperor Nero'.

8 It is important to note here that stoning was not necessarily a method of execution. It was more often simply a way of

hounding a denounced victim out of one area of the city, or out of the city altogether.

9 The Revd Lionel Smithett Lewis, *Joseph of Arimathea at Glastonbury*, p 15. Following the union of Scotland with England and Wales, the king's title was adjusted to the less pious 'His Britannic Majesty'.

10 It has to be said, however, that in *Glastonbury*, earlier *Glastonia*, there may just be an etymological connection with the blue vegetable dye woad instead. An Old British element *glaist-* means 'woad' (and modern Scots/Irish Gaelic *glas* means 'translucent blue', 'blue-green'). Many commentators have supposed that 'the Isle of Glais' might in time have been misconstrued as 'the Isle of Glass', and for that reason in due course come to be translated by the Old British (Welsh) as *Ynys Witrin* (as recorded in the early 600s). Yet the British/Welsh *witrin* 'glass' is evidently cognate with the Latin *vitrum* which means 'glass' but also means 'woad'. Or it may well be that all the meanings are connected anyway – that these ancient people considered that glass was translucent blue, the colour of woad.

11 The Gaelic term *Scotia* (from which *Scots* and *Scotland* are essentially derived) is taken from the name of Princess Scota, daughter of Pharaoh Nechonibus (Nekau I) of Egypt (610–555 BC). The wife of Galamh of Scythia (known also as Milidh), she moved to Ireland with her sons after Galamh died in Spain. It was Nial Noighiallach and the Dal Riata who gave the name *Scota* to Alba during the 4th century AD. See Geoffrey Keating, *The History of Ireland* (translated by David Comyn and The Revd P S Dinneen), Irish Texts Society, London, 1902–14, I, p 102; II, p 44, p 46, p 58, p 78, p 372 and p 374.

12 See Chapter 6, Place of a Skull.

13 Professor Roger Sherman Loomis, in *The Grail: From Celtic Myth to Christian Symbolism*, University of Wales Press, Cardiff, 1963, makes the point that proper names in manuscript transmission sometimes lose their initial letter (although mutation of the initial letters of names is a feature of the Celtic languages). By this process, Morgaine

is sometimes found as Orguein and, with specific relevance to the present case, Galains (Galaain) became Alain (Alaain).

14 The *Grand Saint Grail* confirms that on the death of Alain the Lordship of the Grail passed to Josue – although defining him as Alain's brother rather than his cousin.

15 This is also confirmed in the *Grand Saint Grail*.

16 See Chapter 8, Hidden Records and the *Desposyni*.

17 Including for example *De Sancto Joseph ab Arimathea* and William of Malmesbury's *De Antiquitate*.

18 Professor W A S Hewins, *The Royal Saints of Britain*, Chiswick Press, London, 1929, p 18.

19 Sir Thomas Malory, *Morte d'Arthur*, Book XIII, Chapter 10.

20 The shroud was known as 'Veronica's veil': St Veronica was said to have wiped the sweat from Jesus's face with it as he walked to his Crucifixion. His image was left imprinted on the veil. For centuries this story has also been bound up with the length of cloth known as the Turin Shroud, although of course the Turin Shroud contains the imprint of a complete body. The name *Veronica* would itself seem to be a corruption of the Latin words *vera icona* 'true image'. See Nancy Qualls-Corbett, *The Sacred Prostitute*, ch 5, p 151.

21 Herod-Antipas, the Tetrarch of Galilee, was banished by Rome to Lyon in Gaul following his beheading of John the Baptist.

It was also at Lyon, from 28 June AD 208, that 19,000 Christians were put to death at the personal direction of the Emperor Septimius Severus.

22 Verulam or Verulamium was renamed St Albans after a 4th-century martyr: the Roman soldier Alban, beheaded by his military superiors in AD 303 (the Diocletian era) for sheltering a Christian priest. He is often referred to as 'the first Christian martyr in England' – which of course he most certainly was not. Modern St Albans is a compact, bustling market-city in Hertfordshire: it has a spectacular abbey-cathedral.

23 *Genealogies of the Welsh Princes*, Harleian MS 3859, confirm that Anna was the daughter of Joseph of Arimathea.

24 See Chapter 12, Camelot and the Pendragons.
25 Gladys Taylor, *Our Neglected Heritage*, I, p 33.
26 See Chapter 11, The Rise of the Roman Church. Peter was never formally appointed Bishop of Rome. Linus – appointed by Paul in AD 58 (during Peter's lifetime: *Apostolic Constitutions*) – was therefore the first pope. See Gladys Taylor, *Our Neglected Heritage*, I, pp 40–5.

# Chapter 11: Religion and the Bloodline

1 A transcript of Eleutherius' reply to King Lucius in AD 177 is given in John W Taylor, *The Coming of the Saints*, Appendix K.

2 Lucius died on 3 December 201 and was buried at St Mary le Lode in Gloucester. His remains were later reinterred at St Peter's, Cornhill. References in Roman martyrology to the burial of Lucius at Chur in Switzerland are inaccurate on two counts: they actually relate to King Lucius of Bavaria, not Lucius the Luminary of Britain; also the Bavarian Lucius died at Curia in Germany not at Chur in Switzerland.

3 The reference to Jesus in the *Antiquities of the Jews* (XVIII, ch 3, p 3) is regarded by some commentators as a later interpolation, an assumption based on the fact that the entry expresses more Christian than Jewish sympathies. Origen, writing before AD 245, does not mention the passage, although Eusebius in his *Demonstration of the Gospel*, written in around AD 320, does. It may therefore be held to have been interpolated after Origen but before Eusebius (see Ahmen Osman, *The House of the Messiah*, ch 3, pp 19–20). But the basis of such a claim is tenuous, to say the least. The reference in the passage is not really Christian in sentiment at all: it defines neither Jesus's status as the 'Messiah, nor his relationship to God. In effect, it states simply that he was 'the Christ' a 'wise man', a 'worker of marvels' and a 'teacher' . . . in much the way that the Jews of the era would indeed have perceived him. (See A N Wilson, *Jesus*, ch 4, p 89.)

4  George F Jowett, *The Drama of the Lost Disciples*, Covenant Books, London, 1961, ch 12, pp 125–6.

5  Three British bishops attended the Council of Arles in 314: those of London, York, and Lincoln.

6  See Chapter 4, Priests and Angels.

7  In 452 Bishop Leo I of Rome and an unarmed body of monks confronted the fearsome Attila the Hun and his army by the River Po in northern Italy. At that time, Attila's barbarian empire stretched from the Rhine right across into Central Asia. His well-equipped hordes were ready with chariots, ladders, catapults and every martial device to sweep on towards Rome. The conversation lasted no more than a few minutes, but the outcome was that Attila ordered his men to vacate their encampments and retreat northwards. What actually transpired between the men was never revealed, but afterwards Leo the Great was destined to wield supreme power. Some time earlier, in 434, an envoy sent by the Byzantine Emperor Theodosius II had met the dreaded Hun in similar circumstances by the Morava River (south of modern Belgrade). He had given Attila the contemporary equivalent of millions of dollars as a ransom for peace in the East. Bishop Leo's arrangement was probably much the same. See Malachi Martin, *The Decline and Fall of the Roman Church*.

And for further reading on the subject, see also Norman J Bull, *The Rise of the Church*, Heinemann, London, 1967.

8  The word *occult* is today often associated with sinister magic. It actually means no more than 'hidden' or 'obscure' (and thus 'esoteric'). Initiates of the occult during the Middle Ages revered the planet Venus as representative of Mary Magdalene, who was regarded as a medium of secret revelation. Over its regular 8-year cycle, Venus traces a precise pentangle (a five-pointed star) in the night sky. This same figure is formed by the five mountain peaks around the Magdalene centre at Rennes-le-Château in the Languedoc. See Henry Lincoln, *The Holy Place*, ch 7, pp 65–70.

9 The esoteric tradition of Solomon spanned the centuries to the era of Gnostic Christianity which preceded the Merovingian age. The Gnostics, whose texts referred to the *Book of Solomon*, were the inheritors of the early Jewish sects of Babylonia: their form of Christianity was thus closely allied to the metaphysical doctrines of Plato and Pythagoras; their creeds were largely founded on astrology and on cosmic awareness. In addition they claimed a particular insight (*Gnosis* 'knowledge') into Jesus's teaching that was unknown to the Church of Rome.

10 See Chapter 11, Good King Lucius, p 189.

11 Barbara Thiering, *Jesus the Man*, ch 12, pp 63–5.

12 The hexagon is formed by dividing the circumference of a circle by chords equivalent to its radius, so producing a figure of six equal straight sides – as found in the cells of some forms of organic life. For this reason, bees were held to be endowed with special geometrical forethought, employing strength with economy of space as their guiding principles. King Solomon's Seal (which is made up of two intersecting equilateral triangles within a circle) incorporates a natural hexagon. And as two intersecting equilateral triangles, the hexagram symbolically denotes the unity (if not the harmony) of opposites: male and female, fire and water, earth and air, hot and cold, and so on. Prominently used in alchemy, the symbol in outline remains specific to the Jews as the Star of David.

13 See Chapter 11, The *Desposyni* and the Emperor.

14 The town of Ferrières was destroyed by Attila the Hun in AD 461 but was substantially rebuilt by the Merovingians. See Ean Begg, *The Cult of the Black Virgin*, Introduction, pp 20–1.

15 What traditional history makes of this baptism is that the pagan Clovis became a Christian; what actually transpired was that the already Christian Clovis became a Roman Catholic.

16 The whole subject of the relationship between Clovis and the Vatican is well covered in Baigent, Leigh and Lincoln, *The Holy Blood and the Holy Grail*, ch 9, p 209 and elsewhere.

# Chapter 12: Elements of Arthurian Lore

1  John Allegro, *The Dead Sea Scrolls*, ch 7, p 110.

2  See Chapter 11, The Merovingian Sorcerer Kings.

3  Some art historians maintain that the pomegranates in these paintings denote the Resurrection through classical associations with the story of Persephone. She was the ancient Greek goddess (a daughter of Zeus and Demeter) who was carried off to the Underworld by Hades (Pluto). A condition of her eventual rescue was that she could spend only part of each year thereafter on the Earth's surface. But her annual return is marked by the regeneration of natural life that characterizes the spring. The story is an allegory of the growth-and-decay cycle of vegetation, and has nothing whatever to do with bodily resurrection from the dead. Such a connotation was conferred on Botticelli's paintings by a fearful establishment wishing to conceal the facts. Botticelli was a Grail student, a leading esotericist and a designer of Tarot cards. His pomegranate seeds represent fertility in accordance with the pomegranates of the Song of Solomon, and the pillar capitals of Solomon's Temple, built around one thousand years before Jesus was crucified.

4  Geoffrey Ashe, *Avalonian Quest*, Methuen, London, 1987, ch 7, p 126.

5  See Chapter 3, Dynastic wedlock.

6  Barbara Thiering, *Jesus the Man*, Appendix III, p 338.

7  See Chapter 5, The King and his Donkey.

8  From *The High History of the Holy Grail*, compiled in around 1220 from an earlier manuscript by the clerk Josephus.

9  George F Jowett, *The Drama of the Lost Disciples*, ch 6, pp 45–6.

10  The 13th-century French work *Sone de Nansai* identifies Joseph's wife as a Nordic princess.

11  See Chapter 10, The Shield of the Most Worthy.

12  Henry VIII's antiquary, John Leland, in 1542 identified the Iron Age hill-fort at South Cadbury in Somerset as Camelot, mainly on the grounds that a couple of villages nearby

included the river-name Camel. Excavations at Cadbury during the 1960s unearthed the remains of a Dark Age feasting-hall, but appealing as it was to the tourist industry, there was nothing there to associate the camp with Arthur. Indeed, more than 40 constructions of similar age and type have been found in the south-west of England alone, and there are many more elsewhere in the country. See Michael Wood, *In Search of the Dark Ages*, BBC Books, London, 1981, ch 2, p 50.

13 See Chapter 5, The Bridegroom and the Bride.

14 See Chapter 12, Anfortas, St Michael and Galahad.

15 See Chapter 11, Good King Lucius. Note that Lucius was the grandson of Brân's daughter Penardun of Siluria. She is sometimes held to have been the daughter instead of Beli Mawr, or sometimes his sister. She was, however, the sister of the later Beli, son of Brân. Penardun was a protégée of Queen Boudicca.

16 Gabràn was a grandson of Fergus mac Erc, who was born of Gaelic Scots royalty in descent from the High King Conaire Mór of Ireland. Fergus left Ireland in the latter 5th century in order to colonize the Western Highlands, taking with him his brothers Loarn and Angus. Loarn's family occupied the region of northern Argyll thereafter known as Loarna (or Lorne), based at Dunollie, Oban.

17 Individual annals cite various different names for this conflict and/or its location. Names for the location include Mount Badon, Mons Badonicus, Dun Baedàn and Cath Badwn (in which *mount* and *mons* imply a hill, *dun* implies either a hill or a hill-fort, and *cath* represents a stronghold) while names for the battle include *Bellum Badonis* and *Obsessio Badonica* (the first suggesting a war and the second a siege).

18 The battle is cited in the Bodleian Manuscripts, the *Book of Leinster*, the *Book of Ballymote* and the *Chronicles of the Scots*: all give the date as 516. The Scots commander is generally named as Aedàn mac Gabràn of Dalriada – but Aedàn had not yet been born at that time. The leader was actually his father, Gabràn, who became King of Dalriada in 537. Aedàn and his eldest son Arthur fought

at the second battle of Dun Baedan, which took place in 575. Despite the definitive date of 516 quoted in the chronicles, there has been a great deal of speculation about this (first) battle, much of which has arisen because researchers have been directed to the wrong historian Gildas. All too often it is Gildas II who is mistakenly identified as the author of *De Excidio*. But he lived 425–512, and was thus already dead when Gildas III was born in 516 – the very year of the battle, as he himself says.

Other selected reading on the subject of Britain in the Dark Ages should include Myles Dillon and Nora K Chadwick, *The Celtic Realms*; Hector Munro Chadwick *et al.*, *Studies in Early British History*; Hector Munro Chadwick, *Early Scotland*; W F Skene, *Celtic Scotland*; R Cunliffe Shaw, *Post-Roman Carlisle and the Kingdoms of the North-West*; Eoin Macneill, *Celtic Ireland*; and Peter Hunter Blair, *The Origins of Northumbria*.

19  Tenets of the Sacred Kindred of St Columba: the Scots royal ecclesiastical seat of the Celtic Church.

20  In the time of Arthur, the south-west peninsula of the British mainland was called Dumnonia (from which *Devon* derives); the name *Cornwall* did not emerge until the 9th century.

21  Tenets of the Sacred Kindred of St Columba.

22  *Tract on the Tributes Paid to Baedan, King of Ulster* in the *Chronicles of the Picts and Scots*.

23  Tenets of the Sacred Kindred of St Columba.

24  This was at a time when there was as yet no unified nation of England. It was not until 927 that Alfred the Great's grandson Aethelstan was recognized as overall king by the majority of Anglo-Saxon territorial groupings.

25  'le Benoic' derives ultimately from Latin *ille benedictum* 'the blessed'.

26  Tenets of the Sacred Kindred of St Columba.

27  Urien is most famous for effecting a coalition of Strathclyde rulers against the Northumbrian Angles of Bernicia.

28  See Chapter 2, Jehovah and the Goddess.

29  See Chapter 1, The Bloodline Begins.

30 Geoffrey Ashe, *Avalonian Quest*, ch 3, sect 2, p 48.
31 The tradition that Arthur had two wives is yet another manifestation of the confusion caused by the convergence in mythology of two separate Arthurs described as one in the *Annales Cambriae*. Arthur of Dalriada and Arthur of Dyfed both had wives.
32 Thomas F O'Rahilly, *Early Irish History and Mythology*, Dublin Institute for Advance Studies, 1946, ch 6, 145.
33 William J Watson, *The History of the Celtic Place Names of Scotland*, William Blackwood, Edinburgh, 1926, ch 3, p 97.

## Chapter 13: Intrigue against the Bloodline

1 See Chapter 11, Decline of the Empire.
2 Some useful information on Priscillian is to be found in Baigent, Leigh and Lincoln, *The Messianic Legacy*, ch 8, pp 99–101.
3 It was Gregory who in 600 determined that Latin was, and should remain, the sole official language of the Roman Catholic Church – an edict that was effectively repealed only in the early 1960s.
4 For further information about the Celtic Church, see Nora K Chadwick, *The Age of Saints in the Celtic Church*, Oxford University Press, 1961: Dom Louis Gougaud, *Christianity in Celtic Lands*; and E G Bowen, *The Settlements of the Celtic Saints in Wales*, University of Wales Press, Cardiff, 1956.
5 Notwithstanding the practicalities of the break between Rome and Constantinople, the fact that it resulted in two separate and independent Churches was not formalized by the denominations concerned until 1945.
6 See Chapter 12, Anfortas, St Michael and Galahad.
7 See Chapter 12, Morganna and the Church.
8 See Chapter 9, Mary and the Church.
9 Anna Jameson, *Legends of the Madonna*, Houghton Mifflin, Boston, 1895.
10 Literature on the subject of this latter period of Merovingian history is fairly scant in the English language.

Gregory of Tours' 6th-century *History of the Franks* does not extend to this era. It is covered, up to a point, in J M Wallace Hadrill, *The Long-Haired Kings*. But the best overview of the story of Dagobert II is recounted in various chapters of Baigent, Leigh and Lincoln, *The Holy Blood and the Holy Grail*. There is also a useful summary of the late Merovingian situation in Margaret Deanesley, *A Medieval History of Europe 476 to 911*, Methuen, London, 1956, 15.

11 The transference of power from the Merovingians to the Carolingians is well narrated in R H C Davis, *A History of Medieval Europe*, Longmans Green, London, 1957, ch 6, pp 120–53. Unlike the Dagobert intrigue, which is outside the scope of conventional history books, the rise of the Carolingians is widely documented as a historical subject in its own right.

12 The most comprehensive account to date of the Septimanian kingdom is to be found in Arthur J Zukerman, *A Jewish Princedom in Feudal France*, Columbia University Press, New York, 1972.

13 The Jewish faith represented here by the collective term (Torah) for the first five scriptural books of the Jewish Bible.

## Chapter 14: Temple of the Grail

1 See Chapter 12, Anfortas, St Michael and Galahad.

2 Corbenic = Cors Beneicon = *corpus benedictum* 'body blessed', thus the Blessed Body. Accordingly, 'Château du Corbenic' = the Castle of the Consecrated Body.

3 Geoffrey Ashe, *Avalonian Queste*, ch 5, sect 4, pp 93–7.

Other selected reading on the subject of the Holy Grail should include Sebastian Evans, *In Quest of the Holy Grail*; Roger Sherman Loomis, *The Grail: From Celtic Myth to Christian Symbolism*; John Matthews, *The Grail: Quest for the Eternal*; David Nutt, *Studies on the Legend of the Holy Grail*; D D R Owen, *The Evolution of the Grail Legend*; and Arthur E. Waite, *The Hidden Church of the Holy Grail*.

4 See Chapter 8, Hidden Records and the *Desposyni*.

5 Myles Dillon and Nora K. Chadwick, *The Celtic Realms*, Weidenfeld and Nicolson, London, 1967, ch 1, p 7.

6 Henri Hubert, *The Greatness and Decline of the Celts*, Kegan Paul, London, 1934, III, ch 2, p 229.

7 Dom Louis Gougaud, *Christianity in Celtic Lands* (translated by Maud Joynt), Four Courts Press, Dublin, 1932. 6, ch 2, p 204.

8 Myles Dillon and Nora K. Chadwick, *The Celtic Realms*, ch 1, p 15.

9 As late as in 1632, the Italian scientist Galileo Galilei was summoned to Rome to explain his public confirmation of Copernicus's heliocentric principle of cosmology; his explanation was not accepted, and he was duly condemned by the Catholic Inquisition.

10 Neoplatonism emerged in about AD 250.

11 Margaret Starbird, *The Woman With the Alabaster Jar*, ch 5, p 102.

12 Louis Charpentier, *The Mysteries of Chartres Cathedral*, Research into Lost Knowledge Organization/Thorsons, Wellingborough, 1992, ch 14, p 113.

13 See Chapter 9, The Lady of the Lake.

14 Nigel Pennick, *Sacred Geometry*, Turnstone, Wellingborough, 1980, Introduction, p 8.
     Other selected reading on the subject of sacred geometry should include John Michell, *The Dimensions of Paradise* and *Ancient Metrology*; and Henry Lincoln, *The Holy Place*.

15 John Matthews, *The Grail: Quest for the Eternal*, Thames and Hudson, London, 1981, p 8.

16 *Ibid*, p 9.

17 Riane Eisler, *The Chalice and the Blade*, Harper and Row, New York, 1987, p 72.

18 Harold Bayley, *The Lost Language of Symbolism*, Williams and Norgate, London, 1912, which contains comprehensive details of medieval watermarks in Provence.

19 Lionel Smithett Lewis, *Joseph of Arimathea at Glastonbury*, p 35.

20 George F Jowett, *The Drama of the Lost Disciples*, ch 18, p 212.

21 Gladys Taylor, *Our Neglected Heritage*, II, pp 47–8.
22 John Matthews, *The Grail: Quest for the Eternal*, p 6.
23 Margaret Starbird, *The Woman With the Alabaster Jar*, ch 5, pp 104–16: an excellent synopsis of the *major arcana*.
24 *Ibid.*, ch 6, pp 128–9.

## Chapter 15: Guardians of the Grail

1 See Chapter 13, The King of the Jews.
2 The original Order of Sion was established so that eligible Muslims, Jews, and others similar could be allied to the Christian Order that became the Knights Templars.
3 Cistercian ideals were far removed from the concerns of the curia at the Vatican: they pertained to education, agriculture and the sacred arts.
4 The original Columban mission on Iona was destroyed by Norse pirates in 807. St Bernard's new monastery on the site was Cistercian rather than Columban.
5 Ean Begg, *The Cult of the Black Virgin*, ch 4, p 103.
6 Louis Charpentier, *The Mysteries of Chartres Cathedral*, ch 7, p 55.
7 *Ibid*, ch 7, p 56.
8 *Ibid*, ch 8, p 69.
   Other selected reading on the subject of the Templars and the Crusades should include John C Andressohn, *The Ancestry and Life of Godfrey de Bouillon*; Baigent, Leigh and Lincoln, *The Temple and the Lodge*; Desmond Seward, *The Monks of War*; and Steven Runciman, *A History of the Crusades*.
9 Louis Charpentier, *The Mysteries of Chartres Cathedral*, ch 9, p 70.
10 The Notre Dame ground-plan made use of ley lines and 'Mother Earth' locations in which the terrestrial forces were heightened by deep underground caverns or wells.
11 See Chapter 14, Druidic Tradition and the Philosopher's Stone.
12 Louis Charpentier, *The Mysteries of Chartres Cathedral*, ch 2, p 29.

13 A dolmen usually comprises two upright stones with a horizontal capstone across the top, as at Stonehenge. From prehistoric times dolmens were used as gigantic resonators (much like sound-boxes used to amplify acoustic musical instruments) to boost the properties of the Earth's telluric current.

14 Louis Charpentier, *The Mysteries of Chartres Cathedral*, ch 17, pp 137–43.

15 Numerical values have often been employed to disguise the use of sacred geometry, as in the Old Testament descriptions of King Solomon's Temple (1 Kings 6 and 2 Chronicles 3, 4).

16 Louis Charpentier, *The Mysteries of Chartres Cathedral*, ch 18, pp 144–51.

17 Michael Howard, *The Occult Conspiracy*, Rider/Century Hutchinson, London, 1989, ch 1, pp 9–10.

18 See Chapter 1, The Bloodline Begins, p 12.
    Other selected reading on the subject of early Freemasonry should include R F Gould, *Gould's History of Freemasonry*; Alexander Horne, *King Solomon's Temple in the Masonic Tradition*.

19 The system of measurement that is by far to be preferred is that which counts in feet and inches rather than in metres. Indeed, adepts in sacred geometry and metrology tend to regard the metre as nothing more than a 'fashionable folly' because of its determined adherence to tens and hundreds. The decimal base of 10 leads to inevitable inaccuracies and such nonsenses as recurring decimals. Universal Measurement is much more accurately founded on a base of 12, which of course is divisible by five of the first six numbers and provides a more flexible foundation for numerical calculation than does 10. Similarly, geometry that is founded upon a decagon is inherently unstable. The cardinal factors in sacred mathematics are 3, 4 and 12. (See John Michell, *The Dimensions of Paradise*.)

20 The subject is well covered in Baigent, Leigh and Lincoln, *The Holy Blood and the Holy Grail*, ch 2, pp 19–34. Similarly, *The Temple and the Lodge* by the same authors, ch 3, pp

51–62 and ch 4, pp 63–76, is informative on the Inquisition of the Templars and the Templar Fleet.

21  A good overview of Provence as a 'cradle of awakening' is given in Margaret Starbird, *The Woman With the Alabaster Jar*, ch 4, pp 67–78.

22  Eleanor of Aquitaine (1122–1204) is an excellent example of female equality in the region. Her importance and influence were a constant embarrassment to the Roman Church bishops.

23  See Chapter 13, The King of the Jews.

Other selected reading on the subject of the Albigensian Crusade should include Zoe Oldenburg, *Massacre at Montségur*; and J Sumption, *The Albigensian Crusade*.

24  The excommunication of Scotland as a nation was not repealed until 1323, following Robert the Bruce's defeat of Edward II at Bannockburn in 1314 and the drawing up of the Scottish Constitution – the Declaration of Arbroath – in 1320. Subsequently, in 1328, the Treaty of Northampton confirmed Scotland's independence under King Robert I.

25  See Chapter 17, Scotland and the Grail.

## Chapter 16: Rise of the House of Stewart

1  Although there were enclaves of celibate monks within the Celtic Church, the priests were permitted to marry. Their clerical ordination was strictly hereditary, passing from father to son. Crinan's ancestors had maintained the hereditary priesthood of Dull for more than five generations (from around 850). By the late 900s Crinan was Seneschal (Steward) of the Isles, Abthane of Dull (Dule, near Aberfeldy, Perthshire) and Abbot of Dunkeld.

2  At the time of Malcolm III Canmore's installation, the Celtic Church prevailed. But this was destined to change. Malcolm's wife Margaret (the last Saxon heiress, and a great-granddaughter of Aethelred the Unready) had been raised at the Roman Catholic Court of her grandfather, King Stephen of Hungary. She also spent time at the court of

Edward the Confessor in England. When she married Malcolm, Margaret had no knowledge of the Gaelic language used by the Celtic priests, but her son became King David I of Scots and, accordingly, head of the Sacred Kindred of St Columba. Margaret (later St Margaret) ignored the Celtic heritage and pursued her Catholic endeavour, so that the two cultures became firmly integrated.

The historical content of this section of the chapter derives from the family archives of the Royal House of Stewart and the records of the Head of the Sacred Kindred of Columba.

3 The monastery at Dol was founded by the Celtic saint, Samson, who first sailed to Brittany from Cornwall in the early 500s during the reign of the Merovingian King Childebert. Dol is on the Brittany coast, near Dinan, not far from Saint Michel. The spear-carrying Samson, with his long hair and Druidic frontal tonsure, had been educated by the Welsh abbot Illtyd. He was installed as Bishop of Dol in about 530. The bishopric was elevated to become an archbishopric in 845. Later still, the ancient town of Dol (in which the main street was subsequently named la Grande Rue des Stuarts) became prominent in sovereign history. It was from here that the closely related major-domos of the royal house – the Seneschals of Dol and Dinan – emerged through the female line to found the Royal House of Stewart in Scotland.

4 This error originated in *The History of Shropshire*, 1858.

5 This marriage is correctly recorded in Chalmers' *Caledonia*, 1807.

6 This error was an element of the 1895 book *The Isle of Bute in the Olden Time* by J K Hewison, in which he quite wrongly averred that 'Walter, the son of Fleadan, son of Banchu, is identical with Walter, son of Alan.'

The historical content of this section of the chapter is extracted from the Royal House of Stewart Jacobite Records of Saint Germain.

# Chapter 17: The Age of Chivalry

1  See Chapter 12, The Historical King Arthur.

2  Brutus (*d*.1103 BC) was the grandson of Ascanius Julius, son of Aeneas and Creusa (daughter of King Priam of Troy). After the fall of Troy (in about 1184 BC), the royal house of Dardanos was scattered. The *Trojan Cycle*, as listed by Proclus in the 2nd century AD, records that Aeneas went to Italy with 88,000 Trojans in a fleet of 332 ships. Brutus led another party to Britain, where – according to Nennius' *Historia* — he founded London, calling it Trinovantium. The Brutus Stone, from which royal accessions were traditionally proclaimed, is at Totnes, Devon. See Gladys Taylor, *Our Neglected Heritage*, III, ch 4, pp 28–9.

3  Guanhumara of Ireland was the wife of Arthur of Dyfed, whereas Gwenhwyfar of Brittany married Arthur of Dalriada.

4  The historical Sword of Avallon was passed to Lancelot by his mother, Viviane del Acqs. He was to hold it in trust for the son of the dynastic heiress Morgaine. This son was Modred, Archpriest of the Celtic Kindred. But Lancelot instead gave the sword to Modred's father, Arthur, thereby – so it was reckoned – causing the downfall of the kingdom. In the event, both Arthur and Lancelot were denounced by the Celtic Church (Records of the Columban Kindred).

5  Beryl Platts, *Scottish Hazard*, Proctor Press, London, 1985–90: various entries throughout.

6  The Sinclair records of Roslin.

7  Friends of Rosslyn Chapel and Sinclair genealogist H S 'Pete' Cummings, Jr.

8  See Chapter 15, Persecution of the Knights Templars.

9  Baigent, Leigh and Lincoln, *The Temple and the Lodge*, Jonathan Cape, London, 1989, ch 8, p 113.

10  Andrew Sinclair, *The Sword and the Grail*, Crown, New York, 1992, ch 7, p 73.

11  See Chapter 14, The Grail Hallows and the Tarot.

12  Barbara Thiering, *Jesus the Man*, Appendix III, p 351.

13 See Chapter 3, Dynastic wedlock.
14 See Chapter 12, Anfortas, St Michael and Galahad.
15 *Dundee Courier*, 12 April 1991.
16 Baigent, Leigh and Lincoln, *The Holy Blood and the Holy Grail*, ch 6, p 108.
17 Andrew Sinclair, *The Sword and the Grail*, ch 7, pp 77–8.
18 See Chapter 10, Lordship of the Grail.

## Chapter 18: Heresy and Inquisition

1 Michael Howard, *The Occult Conspiracy*, ch 3, p 43.
2 Lorraine as a name derives from *Lotharingia*, in turn so called after the Carolingian King Lothair II.
3 There is a highly informative section on the Scots Guard in Baigent, Leigh and Lincoln, *The Temple and the Lodge*, ch 7, pp 103–10.
4 Michael Howard, *The Occult Conspiracy*, ch 3, p 44.
5 The caduceus corresponds to the winged staff of Mercury, borne by him as messenger of the gods.
6 Michael Howard, *The Occult Conspiracy*, ch 4, pp 73–4.
  Other selected reading on the subject of the Rosicrucians should include Frances A Yates, *The Rosicrucian Enlightenment*; and Arthur E Waite, *The Real History of the Rosicrucians*.

## Chapter 19: House of the Unicorns

1 The quoted verse refers to the marriage of the Sumerian deities Inanna and Dumuzi (Tammuz): Samuel Kramer, *The Sacred Marriage Rite*, Indiana University Press, Bloomington, 1969, ch 4, p 84.
2 The sobriquet 'Ironsides' was conferred on Cromwell's troopers by the Rosicrucian general Prince Rupert of Heidelberg, son of Friedrich of Palatine and Elizabeth Stuart.
3 See Chapter 18, The Order of the Rosy Cross.
4 Boyle's Law: at a constant temperature the volume of a (perfect) gas varies inversely in relation to its pressure.

5  See Chapter 15, Persecution of the Knights Templars.
6  An account of this sequence of events is given in Marquis
   de Ruvigny et Raineval, *The Jacobite Peerage, Baronetage,
   Knightage, and Grants of Honour*, Appendix II.
7  The tax imposed on the manufacture of linen provides a
   good example: it was of little consequence in the south, but
   linen was a major industrial product in Scotland.
       The contents of this section of the chapter are drawn
   in part from the Royal House of Stewart Jacobite Records
   of St Germain, and from archives of the Chivalric Military Order of the Temple of Jerusalem.

## Chapter 20: The Sangréal Today

1  J Horace Round, in his *Studies in Peerage and Family History*,
   Constable, London, 1901, referred to these contrived entries
   in 1902, stating, 'For the source . . . we have to penetrate
   behind Burke to the authors of these fabrications – the
   heralds and antiquaries.'
       The contents of this chapter are drawn from the Royal
   House of Stewart Jacobite Records of St Germain; from the
   records of Melville Henry Massue, Marquis de Ruvigny et
   Raineval 1868–1921; the Stewart Family Papers in Edinburgh and Brussels; the archives of the Stewart Trustees in
   Rome; and the Presidential files of the European Council of
   Princes.

# APPENDIX I

## THREE TABLES OF THE GRAIL

Tradition relates that *'Three Tables bore the Grail; they were round, square and rectangular. Each had the same perimeter, and the number of the Three was Two-One.'* This ambiguous description of Tables has served to perpetuate the image of the Grail being an object, such as a cup or platter. The Tables have been likened to those of King Arthur, Grail Castle, and the Last Supper. However, the 2–1 specification is an inherent tabular proportion of the *Golden Mean*, and has little to do with tables in the utility sense.

The *Golden Mean* is a geometric progression employed by the Greek mathematician, Euclid, in the 1st century BC. In practice, however, it dates back far beyond Euclid to the time of Plato. The *Golden Mean* has been used as an architectural standard for proportionment, and is used today in sophisticated artwork, framing and design. Roughly speaking, it is a proportion of 5:8, but the precise mathematical ratio is .618:1. The subject is fully covered in Nigel Pennick's *Sacred Geometry* ch 2, pp 25–28.

The *Golden Mean* is based on the division of space by root rectangle derivatives, and it needs no form of measurement. Root rectangles can be produced from a square with compasses only. A square is simply a √1 rectangle. A √2 rectangle is produced from a square by

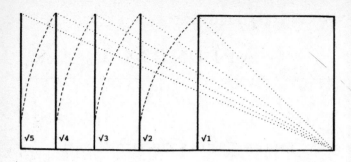

The Golden Mean. Based on a diagram by Nigel

setting the compasses at the length of the diagonal, and extending the base line to meet the arc. A √3 rectangle is produced from the diagonal of the second, and so on. A √5 rectangle (double-square) has the Grail proportion of 2:1.

Although not measured with numbers, such rectangles are not irrational because they can be measured in terms of the squares produced from them. Calculation in terms of area instead of length was the basis of ancient geometry. The *Pythagoras Theorem* is understandable only in terms of square measure. For instance, the area of a √1 square is exactly one-fifth of the area of a square on the long side of its extended √5 rectangle. Hence, the relationship between the end and side of the √5 rectangle may be used as an expression of area.

Rectangles with strictly numerical ratios such as 3:2, 5:4, etc. have been defined as *Static*, but root rectangles are *Dynamic*. They establish a particular harmony by virtue of their related proportion. The *Static* and *Dynamic* attributes are both inherent in the square (1 = 1:1 = √1:1) and in the extended double-square (2 = 2:1 = √4:1).

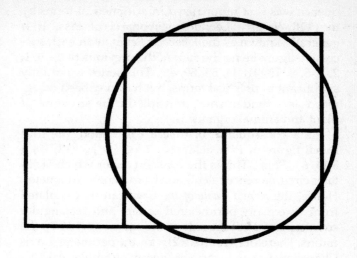

The Three Tables of the Grail

The diagonal of the double-square (which is itself √5) has been widely used for constructing temples and sacred enclosures. It relates directly to the *Golden Mean* proportion of (√5 + 1) ÷ 2 = 1.618.

The *Golden Mean* exists when the ratio between the larger and the smaller quantity is equal to the ratio between the sum of the two and the larger. The *Golden Number* 1.618 is mathematically symbolized by the Greek letter Φ. Numerically, it possesses exceptional mathematical properties: 1.618 ÷ 0.618 = (1 + 1.618) = (1.618 × 1.618) = 2.618. Thus $Φ^2$ = 2.618.

In any increasing progression where Φ is the ratio between the successive terms, each term is equal to the sum of the two preceding. This uniqueness affords the simple calculation of a series.

From any two successive terms, all others may be defined by the use of compasses. This additive sequence was first rationalized in arithmetical terms by the 12th-century Leonardo Fibonacci of Pisa. It is generally known as the *Fibonacci Series*, with each successive figure being the sum of the previous two – ie 1, 2, 3, 5, 8, 13, 21, 34, 55, 89, etc. This series is not only significant in practical terms, but has long been recognized as a fundamental principle in the structure of plant and animal organisms.

As a consequence of *Golden* calculation, the irrational figure of *Pi* is achieved: $2.618$ $[\Phi^2] \times (12/10) = 3.1416 = Pi$ $[\pi]$. This is the constant factor which facilitates circumference calculation from a known diameter. Hence, the *Round Table of the Grail* can be calculated from its equally perimetered square and rectangular counterparts: Half the side of the square $\times \sqrt{1.618}$ = the radius. Therefore, (radius $\times 2) \times \pi$ = the perimeter. Louis Charpentier covers various aspects of tabular calculation in *The Mysteries of Chartres Cathedral*, ch 12, pp 83–90, ch 13, pp 91–111 and ch 15, pp 118–27.

The symbolic *Round Table of the Grail* had its origin in the *Circle* – the ancient representation of wholeness. The famous figure of the *Vitruvian Man* is that of a circle encompassing man emblematic as a five-pointed star. From this, with a square and compasses, derive all other geometrical figures, each in precise relation to the others. From the earliest times, hut-circles, fairy rings and megalithic temples were all *Round Tables* of cosmic unity.

Allegorically, the *Round Table* is the table of *Intuition*; the *Square Table* is that of *Intellect*, and the *Rectangular Table* is that of *Mysticism*. It was by no chance that the Knights Templars built their churches on round tables.

# APPENDIX II

## MUSIC OF THE GRAIL

The most impressive and awe-inspiring use of Grail geometry exists in Gothic architecture. The name, *Gothic*,
had nothing whatever to do with Goths; it was dually
derived from the Greek, *Goetic* (magical action), and
the Celtic, *Goatique* (the plant lore related to organisms).
The main visual aspect of Gothic building is the pointed
arch – the *Ogive* – which first emerged in about 1130
directly after the Knights Templars returned from the
Holy Land Crusade. The Templars, and their allied Cistercians under Bernard de Clairvaux, were wholly
instrumental in the introduction and advancement of
Gothic construction. In terms of location, they made
express use of *Earth Goddess* sites, where the *Telluric
Current* (earth force) was strong. In megalithic times,
such sites were reinforced by the use of artificial stone
caverns called *Dolmens* (uprights and a cap stone, as
at Stonehenge). Being natural accumulators and sound
amplifiers, they became charged with telluric
resonance.

In Gothic architecture, the *Ogive* substitutes as a
dynamic sound vibrator. Unlike other styles of construction, its cosmic force pulls upwards, carrying the
telluric current vertically through the people beneath.
The action of sound waves within an Ogive can be
controlled, as can the sound from organ pipes of

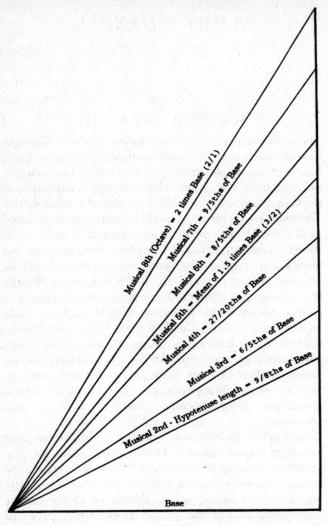

Musical Scale in Architecture. Based on a diagram by
Louis Charpentier

differing length or from the varied keys of a xylophone. The degrees of resonance alter with the specification of individual Ogives, and Gothic buildings were often tuned in the same manner as, say, a piano. This subject is no better covered than in Louis Charpentier's *The Mysteries of Chartres Cathedral*, ch 16, pp 128–36. The *Crossed-Ogive*, as used in ceilings and flying buttresses, affords an even greater degree of fine tuning by pulling the building's energy further upwards, all of which serves to elevate people to a more upright posture. Within such a calculated environment, certain musical sounds can heighten the rising terrestrial force, just as the Gregorian Chant was devised for this purpose in heavier, less tensile confines.

Given that Grail geometry was inherent in cathedral construction, it is interesting to note that the multiplication factor of 12/10 (as applied to $\Phi^2$ to achieve $\pi$) is also the interval of a *Third* in music (6/5) – the interval between relative minor and major keys (eg A minor and C major). Music is essentially geometry in the form of sound. It incorporates the same harmonies that appear in sacred architectural proportion. Just as there are *scales* in geometry, so there are *scales* in music. These can be plotted as right-angled triangles, with the top hypotenuse intersections relating to the tonal frequencies of the verticals. If one transposes such musical figures to the base and high-points of building interiors, then the relevant notes of a scale can be plotted on the uprights. Thereby, an interior space can be constructed musically in accordance with any given scale, and its harmonic qualities will be directly related to the design. This concept was expounded long ago by Pythagoras. He stated that numerical scales which agree with the ear are the same as delight the eye and mind. Plato also used musical example as a measure of harmonious proportion in all things.

# APPENDIX III

## GRAIL CARDS OF THE TAROT MAJOR ARCANA

In Chapter 14, the Grail significance of the Tarot cards was discussed, and certain cards from the Major Arcana were detailed. They were *The Joker, Justice, The Tower, The World,* and *Strength.* Having mentioned these few individual cards, it is worth putting them into context with the rest of the deck in terms of their Grail significance. A very good background to the Tarot's Grail symbolism is given in Margaret Starbird's *The Woman With the Alabaster Jar,* ch v, pp 104–16.

NO. VIII: JUSTICE – The symbol of this *Female Virtue* card is well known outside the Tarot. She is the star-maiden, *Virgo,* with her two-edged sword, and the scales of *Libra.* The portrayal has rather more to do with discrimination than justice. It denotes that Nature's balance and harmony have been destined to the one hand, while the other wields the spike of judicial authority. The original card denoted the tenuous position of the Grail Church against the severity of the Inquisition. It is known in esoteric circles as the *Magdalene Card.*

NO. II: THE HIGH PRIESTESS (Popess) – She identifies the higher aspects of the *feminine principle,* and relates to the status achievable by women such as Helena/

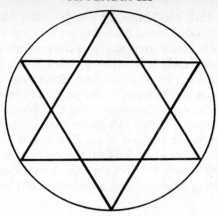

The Seal of King Solomon

Salome in the Gnostic Church. Associated with *Isis*, this card was often confiscated in the early days.

NO. III: THE EMPRESS – With the subject generally pregnant, this card personifies the love of *Venus*. It was another confiscated card, and was deemed heretical by the establishment.

NO. XI: STRENGTH – This *Female Virtue* card normally depicts a woman in charge of a lion, or supporting a broken pillar. Some cards have both images. The former is the *Lion of Judah*, and the latter is the *Pillar of Boaz* (In Strength) from Solomon's Temple. Either way, the woman is the governess and mainstay of the royal succession: *'And thine house and thy kingdom shall be established for ever before thee'* (2 SAMUEL). In some early decks, a Grail design was incorporated, and the woman was identified with Mary Magdalene. The card represents the continuation of the Davidic line as in PSALM 89.

NO. XXI: THE WORLD – The spirit of Mary Magdalene is manifest once more, standing or dancing within an oval wreath. Sometimes naked and sometimes clothed, the woman holds a sceptre or other mark of sovereignty. Some cards show her above an encircled landscape, and others depict the physical world by way of Ezekiel's *Living Creatures* – the Ox, Man, Lion and Eagle (EZEKIEL 1: 5–10). Whatever the case, the woman is content. Being the last of the Trumps, the card conveys eventual success through the mysteries and hazards of the others. It is not dissimilar in concept to the soaring, long-haired Magdalene in the 1490 Sforza *Book of Hours*.

NO. XVII: THE STAR – The naked Star-woman is steeped in the cult of Mary the Gypsy. Crowned with the stars of *Sophia*, she pours the waters of life and truth from two vessels into a stream – emphasising the female source of fertility and wisdom. The union represents the esoteric *Stream* which was forced *Underground*.

NO. XIV: TEMPERANCE (Prudence) – The subject of this *Female Virtue* card is often winged. She is the heavenly alchemist, pouring quicksilver from one vessel into another. Sometimes two streams flow in opposite directions. In this context the image is associated with *mingling the opposites*. In some cases, she pours Water onto a Lion (the *House of David*), and Fire onto an Eagle (*Rome*). She is nourishing the line of one Church, while assaulting the ferocity of the other. It is the card of the Grail Church in opposition to Catholicism.

NO. VI: THE LOVERS (Two Paths) – This card links the female and male aspects. It depicts a couple or couples, and has embraced portrayals from Adam and Eve to various other sweethearts. *Cupid* generally appears as well. Occasionally the male stands between two women – one older than the other. They are his mother and his bride. The outward significance of the card is apparent, but its variations identify the *Two Paths* of love – the sexual and the spiritual – often referred to as *Vice and Virtue*. In Grail terms, the card is indicative of partnership and procreation. Its esoteric name is *The Vine*.

NO. XIX: THE SUN – The sun shines on high from beyond a wall or perhaps a row of sunflowers. In the foreground, two naked children embrace or frolic on the ground. Alternatively, one child plays with a responsive pet. The overall sentiment is that of joy and freedom. Some early cards portrayed *Briar Rose* (Sleeping Beauty) with the spindle on which she pricked her finger. She fell asleep until the Prince arrived to break the spell. It is the *Card of Liberation*.

NO. 0: THE JOKER (Jester) – He is a fool but, even so, he always wins. His legacy is from 1 CORINTHIANS – *'The Lord knoweth the thoughts of the wise, that they are vain. Therefore, let no man glory in men . . . We are fools for Christ's sake.'* The Grail representation is Perceval, the simple man who succeeds where the accomplished fail.

NO. I: THE MAGICIAN (Juggler) – Here is an illusionist and mathematician, performing his table-top wonders before the eyes of the beholder. Often his props are entirely alchemic. He is associated with *Hermes Trismegistus*, whose subtlety could always trump another's trick.

NO. V: THE HIGH PRIEST (Pope) – Representing the masculine Roman Church, the subject is pictorially identified with *Aries*.

NO. IV: THE EMPEROR – Another male card representing Roman authority. Here, the pictorial association is with *Taurus*.

NO. IX: THE HERMIT (Wise Man) – He is the man who seeks the truth – commonly depicted with a lantern, and perhaps the *Seal of Solomon*. He is *Peter the Hermit*, who preached the First Crusade, incarnate in the hermit, *Trevrizent*. He told Perceval the secrets of the Grail, advising him to substitute his pride with humility.

NO. XII: THE HANGED MAN – Trevrizent also told of the maimed *Fisher King*, whose plight is symbolized. He hangs upside-down by one leg, depicting his physical constraint. In each hand is a bulging bag to which he clings despite his predicament. The portrayal is of the Grail Church retaining its purpose despite persecution.

NO. VII: THE CHARIOT (Sphinxes) – Pulled by a pair of horses or sphinxes, it is rather more of a draped coffer than a wagon. The lone charioteer is generally a knight or kingly figure, and various emblems of geomancy appear in the designs. Not the least of the early symbols was the Judaic *fleur-de-lys* of the Merovingian bloodline. The Grail significance is that of triumph over adversity.

NO. XV: THE DEVIL – This male card depicts a hideous demon or gigantic ogre. Unlike the *Magician*, he uses his wiles for evil ends. He is the awesome representation of the iniquitous regime.

NO. XIII: DEATH – Also a male card, it generally portrays a skeleton (sometimes clothed or armoured) on horseback. He wields a scythe or cudgel. In the famous *Charles VI Deck*, the characters trampled by the skeletal horseman were the Pope and his cardinals. The card signifies the demise of the repressive establishment.

NO. X: THE WHEEL OF FORTUNE – A non-gender card with a self-evident meaning. The wheel denotes fate or fortune, and spun against the esoteric Church during the Roman and Spanish Inquisitions. The Knights Templars were excommunicated in 1307 because their esoteric might was greater than that of the Pope.

NO. XVI: THE TOWER (House of God) – Though not characterized, the card is feminine, being another *Magdalene* representation (*Magdal-eder*: Tower of the Flock). The depiction is not dissimilar to a chess *Castle*. Being struck by lightning, or otherwise mysteriously assaulted, it symbolizes the plight of the Grail Church against the merciless Roman establishment.

NO. XX: THE JUDGEMENT (Judgement Day) – The portrayal is of a trumpeting angel (or angels) hovering above a naked group who rise from their sepulchres. This is not the Last Judgement of THE REVELATION, but a *Day of Awakening*. Mankind transcends the darkness of orthodoxy, and emerges into the light of truth.

NO. XVIII: THE MOON (Crisis) – Generally a crescent moon, this card has achieved an unwarranted sinister image. This came from the moon's *Gothic novel* association with the dark side of the occult, but that was not the way it began. The moon's traditional relationship was with the *Great Mother Goddess*. Some cards show wailing dogs, and a scorpion or crayfish, with the moon above a pool of still water. An early deck from the 1300s shows a different scene: two geometricians, with dividers and compasses, translate the scale of the moon to their architectural drawing below. The representation is Hermetic, based on the principle, *'As above, so below'* – ie in the proper order of things, the nature of mortality reflects the nature of the cosmos. It is through the geometry of this principle that the great sacred monuments were constructed – from Stonehenge to the Gothic cathedrals of Europe. It is the principle by which the *Notre Dame* churches of Northern France plot a ground replication of the constellation of *Virgo* and her associated stars.

# APPENDIX IV

## AMERICA BEFORE COLUMBUS

It was mentioned in Chapter 18 that Christopher Columbus was sponsored by Leonardo da Vinci, whose connection with prominent families such as the Medicis facilitated high level financial patronage. However, there was a good deal more to Columbus' own family background than the history books generally tell. He is, of course, best known as the official discoverer of America, but he was not the first to make the voyage.

Columbus (the son of Domenico Colombo and Suzanna Fontanarossa) was born in Genoa, Italy, in 1451. Having entered service with the Captain of Porto Sancto in Madeira, he married the Captain's daughter, Felipa Perestrello, in 1478. Subsequently, he approached the Portuguese Court with the concept of reaching Asia by sailing westwards. His appeal for funding was rejected by King John II, who contracted Ferman Dulmo to explore the Atlantic in accordance with Columbus' suggestion. A good account of Columbus' personal family background is given in Rosslyn Chapel's *The Sinclair Genealogist* by H S 'Pete' Cummings, Jnr.

Columbus made a secondary approach to the Spanish monarchs, King Ferdinand II of Aragon and his wife, Queen Isabella of Castile. However, since the Portuguese scheme was under way, Columbus was rejected yet again. In 1492, Dulmo returned, but with no report of any new lands. Columbus then confronted Ferdinand and Isabella once more and, this time, he won their support. On August 3rd 1492, he set sail from Palos with three small ships – the *Niña*, the *Pinta* and the *Santa Maria*.

Eight months later, Columbus returned to Barcelona, but not with the anticipated silks and spices from the East. Instead, he was accompanied by six brown-skinned natives bearing pearls, strange fruits, gold, and exotic birds. He had discovered an exciting *New World* across the sea, and the Pope declared that these rich lands belonged to Spain. The name *America* did not emerge for another five years. It derived from the Florentine navigator, Amerigo Vespucci, who sailed to the south continental mainland in 1497.

Upon his return, Columbus related that he had landed on Watling Island (now San Salvador in the Bahamas). He had also visited Hispaniola (Haiti and the Dominican Republic) and Cuba. Ferdinand and Isabella were delighted, and their hero was offered a seat at the Spanish Court. His second voyage (1493–96) took him to Guadeloupe, Antigua, Puerto Rico and Jamaica. The third voyage, of 1498, saw Columbus in Trinidad, and on the mainland of South America. Then, in 1499, the colonists of Haiti revolted against his command. Consequently, a new Spanish governor was installed, and Columbus was shipped back to Europe in chains. His last voyage, in 1502–04, concerned the coastal exploration of Honduras and Nicaragua but, despite his hour of glory, he died in poverty two years later at Valladolid. Columbus was buried at Seville and, in 1542, his remains were removed to Hispaniola.

This exciting piece of maritime history is well enough known. What is not so well known is the fact that the *New World* discovery was no accident.

Columbus was fully armed with detailed navigational charts before he set sail. They had been drawn up on previous Atlantic crossings, and were vouched for at the Spanish Court by John Drummond, whose grandfather had been to America in 1398. Drummond was related to the Drummond Earls of Perth, where the records confirm that he was with Ferdinand and Isabella in 1492. Both Columbus and Drummond had lived on the Island of Madeira. Drummond's father, John (The Scot) Drummond, had settled there in 1419, along with Columbus' father-in-law, Bartholomew Perestrello.

John the Scot's father was Sir John Drummond of Stobhall, Justiciar of Scotland. Sir John's sister, Anabella, was the wife of King Robert III Stewart of Scots. Sir John's own wife was Elizabeth Sinclair, whose nephew, William Sinclair, was the founder of Rosslyn Chapel. Elizabeth's father, Henry Sinclair, Baron of Roslin, Earl of Orkney, led a successful transatlantic expedition nearly a century before Columbus – and even he was not the first.

Henry Sinclair's Norse ancestors had explored the Atlantic as far back as the 10th century. In *Hauk's Book* of the *Icelandic Saga* (extant copy dated 1320), Leif Ericsson is detailed as having crossed the Atlantic to *Wineland the Good* in 999. Indeed, the Orkney sailors had reached land to the West within Henry's own lifetime. Their reports claimed that the natives of a far away place called *Estotilands* sowed corn, and exported furs and sulphur to Greenland.

Estotilands was the place eventually called Nova Scotia (New Scotland) in Canada. The Orkney sailors also told of a southern country called *Drogio*. The natives of Drogio ran naked in the hot winds but, across the sea, the people were very refined. Their land was rich in gold, and they had cities and great temples to their gods. These various accounts were all confirmed when voyagers travelled to the Caribbean Islands, and onwards to Florida, and Mexico – the home of the Aztec indians. In complete disregard of these early discoveries, tradition has it that the Aztec empire was not explored until the Spanish conquistador, Hernán Cortéz, arrived there in 1519.

From 1391, the master of Sinclair's fleet was the Venetian sea captain, Antonio Zeno. The Zenos were among the oldest families of Venice and were noted Admirals and Ambassadors from the 8th century. Before Sinclair and Zeno made their own passage across the ocean, Henry drew up a contract with his daughter, Elizabeth, and her husband, Sir John Drummond. The Deed was sealed at Roslin on May 13th 1396. It empowered Sir John and Elizabeth to claim Henry's Norwegian lands if he and his sons should perish in the expedition. As given in Chapter 17, an account of the Sinclair-Zeno voyage is to be found in Andrew Sinclair's *The Sword and the Grail*, pp 108–50.

In May 1398 the Sinclair fleet set sail. There were twelve warships and a hundred men – some of whom had made the voyage before. Their first port of call was Nova Scotia, where they landed at Cape Blomidon in the Bay of Fundy. Even today, the Micmac indians tell of the incoming ships of the great god, *Goolscap*, who taught them about the stars, and how to fish with nets. On his return home to Venice, Antonio Zeno wrote that, at this place, he had seen streams of pitch running into the sea and a mountain that issued smoke from its base. Nova Scotia is certainly very rich in coal, and there are exposed coastal seams of pitch where the coal brooks run at Asphalt. Nearby, the greasy underground residues often smoulder beneath the hills of Cape Smokey. At Louisburg on Cape Breton, there is a primitive cannon, found in 1849. It is of the Venetian type used by

Zeno, and of a style that was quite obsolete by the time of Columbus.

From Nova Scotia, Sinclair continued south towards the land of Drogio. Evidence of the journey can be seen at Massachusetts and Rhode Island. At Westford, Massachusetts, where one of Henry's knights died, the grave is still discernible. Punched into a rock ledge is the seven-foot effigy of a 14th-century knight wearing a basinet, chain-mail and a surcoat. The figure bears a sword of the 1300s, and a shield with Pentland heraldry. The knight's sword is broken below the hilt – indicative of the customary broken sword that would have been buried with the knight – the same as was laid before Perceval in Grail lore.

At Newport, Rhode Island, is a well preserved two-storey medieval tower. Its construction (an octagon within a circle, and eight arches around) is based on the circular model of the Templar churches. Similar remains are to be found at the 12th century Orphir Chapel on Orkney. The Newport architecture is Scottish, and its design is reproduced at the St. Clair Church, Corstorphine, where Henry Sinclair's daughter has her memorial. Rhode Island was not officially founded until 1636, but its founding was no chance event. At the Public Records Office in London, a text dated four years earlier describes the *rounde stone towre* at Newport. It proposed that the tower be used as a garrison for the soldiers of Sir Edmund Plouden, who colonized the area.

More than fifty years after the Sinclair expedition, Christopher Columbus was born into the high *Age of Discovery* in Europe. In Portugal, he became a *Knight of Christ* in the revised Templar Order, as did his famous contemporaries, Vasco da Gama, Bartolomeu Dias and Ferdinand Magellan. He also belonged to the *Order of the Crescent* (founded by René d'Anjou) – also known as the *Order of the Ship*. The Crescent knights were particularly concerned with matters of navigation, but had been condemned by the Church for insisting that the World was round!

Through John Drummond and others, Columbus knew precisely where he was heading – and it was not to Asia. Maps of the trans atlantic *New World* were already in existence within his Templar circle. In particular, he had access to the new *Globe of the World*, which was completed in 1492 – precisely the year that he set sail. This was produced by the Nuremberg cartographer, Martin Behaim. He was a navigational business partner of John Affonso Escorcio – better known as John Drummond.

# APPENDIX V

Additional Genealogical Charts

**BIBLE CHART – A**
*From Adam to Abraham*

**BIBLE CHART – B**
*From Abraham to David*

ADAM
= *Eve*

SHETH (Seth)

ENOSH (Enos)

KENAN (Cainan)

MAHABEEL (Mahalaleel)

JARED (Jered)

ENOCH (Henoch)

METHUSELAH (Mathusala)

LAMECH

NOAH (Noe)

SHEM (Sem)

ARPHAXAD (Arpachshad)

SHELAH (Sala)

EBER (Heber)

PELEG (Phalec)

REU (Ragau)

SERUG (Saruch)

NAHOR (Nachor)

TERAH (Tara)

ABRAHAM (Abram)

ABRAHAM
= *Sarah (Sarai)*

ISAAC
= *Rebechak (Rebecca)*

JACOB
= *Leah*

JUDAH (Juda/Judas)
= *Tamar*

PHAREZ (Phares)

HEZRON (Esrom)

RAM (Aram)

AMMINADAB (Aminadab)

NAHSHON (Naasson)

SALMA (Salmon)
= *Rachab (Rahab)*

BOAZ (Booz)
= *Ruth*

OBED

JESSE

DAVID
King of Israel 1048-1015 BC

BIBLE CHART – C
*From David to Zerubbabel*

**DAVID** – King of Israel 1048 BC
= *Bathsheba – widow of Uriah the Hittite*

**SOLOMON** – King of Israel 1015 BC
= *Naamah the Ammonitess*

**REHOBOAM (Roboam)** – King of Judah 975 BC
= *Maachiah – daughter of Ureil of Gibeah*

**ABIJAH (Abia)** – King of Judah 957 BC

**ASA** – King of Judah 955 BC
= *Azubah – daughter of Shilhi*

**JEHOSHAPHAT (Josaphat)** – King of Judah 917 BC

**JEHORAM (Joram)** – King of Judah 893 BC
= *Athalia – daughter of Omri*

**AHAZIAH** – King of Judah 885 BC
= *Zibiah of Beersheba*

**JOASH** – King of Judah 878 BC
= *Jehoaddan of Jerusalem*

**AMAZIAH** – King of Judah 840 BC
= *Jecoliah of Jerusalem*

**UZZIAH (Oziah)** – King of Judah 811 BC
= *Jerushah – daughter of Zadok*

**JOTHAM (Joatham)** – King of Judah 759 BC

**AHAZ (Achaz)** – King of Judah 742 BC
= *Abija – daughter of Zechariah*

**HEZEKIAH (Ezekias)** – King of Judah 726 BC
= *Hephzibah*

↓

**MANASSEH** (Manasses) – King of Judah 697 BC
= *Meshullemeth – daughter of Haruz of Jotbah*

**AMON** – King of Judah 642 BC
= *Jedidah – daughter of Adaiah of Boscath*

< 1     **JOSIAH** (Josias)     2 >
*Zebudah*    =    King of Judah 640 BC    =    *Hamutal*
*daughter of*                       *daughter of*
*Pediah of Rumah*                *Jeremiah of Libnah*

**JEHOAHAZ**        **JEHOIAKIM** [ELIAKIM] (Jechonais)        **MATTANIAH**
King of Judah          King of Judah 609 BC             <u>**KING ZEDEKIAH**</u>
609 BC             ( Taken hostage to Babylon )          King of Judah
                   = *Nehushta , dau. of*            598 BC
                   *Elnathan of Judaea*

**JECHONIAH** [JEHOIAKIN]
King of Judah 598 BC
( Taken hostage to Babylon )

**SHEALTIEL** (Salathiel)
[ I asked God ]

**PEDAIAH**
[ Jehovah distinguished ]

**ZERUBBABEL** (Zorobabel)
King *de jure* of Judah
[ Born in Babylon ]

## NOTES TO BIBLE CHART – C

1) Bible Chart C is based on the 1650 chronology prepared by Bishop James Ussher of Armagh. Possible alternative dates for accessions prior to Amon in 642 are: David 1000 BC, Solomon 962 BC, Rehoboam 922 BC, Abijah 915 BC, Asa 908 BC, Jehoshaphat 867 BC, Jehoram 849 BC, Ahaziah 842 BC, Joash 835 BC, Amaziah 800 BC, Uzziah 791 BC, Jotham 739 BC, Ahaz 732 BC, Hezekiah 715 BC, and Manasseh 686 BC.

2) Prior to becoming King of Israel, David had been King of Judah, having succeeded King Saul – the first king from 1055 (or 1021) BC. Although David and Solomon were overall rulers of Israel and Judah, the combined kingdom was divided on Solomon's death, to become Judah and Israel. Solomon's son, Rehoboam, became King of Judah, while Jeroboam, son of Nebat, became King of Israel. The two kingdoms ran parallel – each with its own succession. Samaria (capital of Israel) fell in 721 BC to the Assyrians (passing to Babylonian control in 650 BC). Jerusalem (capital of Judah) fell in 586 BC to Nebuchadnezzar of Babylon.

3) King Ahaziah was murdered in 884 (or 842) BC by Jehu, son of Nimshi. His mother, Athaliah, ruled in his stead for six years until his son, Joash, succeeded.

4) Following the death of King Josiah in 609 BC, his eldest son, Jehoahaz, took the throne. He was forced out of Judah by the Pharoah of Egypt, and his brother Jeoiakim (Jechonais) succeeded him in that same year. Eleven years later, Jehoiakim was captured and taken to Babylon by Nebuchadnezzar. Jehoiakim's son, Jechoniah (Jehoiakin), duly took over as King, but he too was seized and removed to Babylon. His uncle, Mattaniah (half-brother to Jehoahaz and Jehoiakin), succeeded as King Zedekiah in 598 BC. When Jerusalem fell entirely to Nebuchadnezzar in 586 BC, Zedekiah was also taken to Babylon and blinded. His sons were murdered, but Jeremiah the Prophet removed Zedekiah's daughter, Tamar Tephi, to safety in Ireland (see Chapter 17 - The Stone of Destiny).

**BIBLE CHART – D**
*From Zerubbabel to Jesus*

ZOROBABEL [Zerubbabel]

RHESA (ABIUD)

JOANNA [Jehohanen/Johanan]

JUDA [Judah/Judas]

JOSEPH

SEMEI [Shimei]

MATTATHIAS [Mattithiah]

MAATH

NAGGE [Nogah]

ESLI [Azaliah]

NAUM [Nahum]

AMOS

MATTATHIAS

JOSEPH

JANNA [Johanan]

MELCHI

LEVI

MATTHAT

HELI (JACOB)

JOSEPH

JESUS [Joshua]

## SICAMBRIAN DESCENT  *Early Franks from 5th century BC*

**ANTENOR (d. 443 BC)**
Trojan royal descendant – King of the Cimmerians of Scythia on the Black Sea

**MARCOMER (d. 412 BC)**
Moved Cimmerians from the Black Sea to West-Friezland, Gelders and Holland
Crossed the Rhine and conquered Northern Gaul

**ANTENOR (d. 385 BC)**
= *Cambra (from whom the SICAMBRI tribe were named)*

**PRIAMUS (d. 358 BC)**
Introduced the New Covenant *(Newmage)* and the Saxon language

**HELENUS (d. 339 BC)**
Priest of the Arcadian sea-god, Pallas

**DIOCLES (d. 300 BC)**
Aided Saxons against the Goths and Southern Gauls

**BASSANUS MAGNUS (Priest-King d. 250 BC)**
Built the city of Bassanburg (Aix la Chapelle)
= *Norwegian princess*

**CLODOMIR (d. 232 BC)**
Allied with Saxons and Thuringians against the Gauls

**NICANOR (d. 198 BC)**
= *Daughter of the British Chief, Elidure*

**MARCOMER (d. 170 BC)**
Defeated Romans, Gauls and Goths. Set the *Acts of the Gauls* to rhyme

**CLODIUS (d. 159 BC)**
Withstood further invasions by Romans and Gauls

**ANTENOR (d. 143 BC)**
Concluded a Peace Treaty with the Gauls

**CLODOMIR (d. 123 BC)**
Gauls broke treaty, but their further incursions were repelled

**MEROVACHUS (d. 95 BC)**
Led army of 22,000 against Roman centres in Italy, and overthrew Bohemia

↑

**CASSANDER (d. 74 BC)**
Allied militarily with King Harnecus of Thuringia and King Arabius of Saxony

**ANTHARIUS (d. 39 BC)**
Withstood invasions by Julius Caesar

**FRANCUS (Francio d. 11 BC)**
Issued an edict changing the tribal name from Sicambri to FRANKS (Franci)
Led a Frankish-Saxon-Thuringian army of 300,000 against the Romans
Made a perpetual league with the German princes

**CLODIUS (Clogio d. AD 20)**
Continued to withstand Roman incursions

**MARCOMER (d. AD 50)**

**CLODOMIR (d. AD 63)**
Drove Nero's legions out of Metz and Trier

**ANTENOR (d. AD 69)**

**RATHERIUS (d. AD 90)**
Ratified league with Germans and Saxons. Built Rotterdam

**RICHEMER (d. AD 114)**
Continued wars against Romans and Goths. Founded Brandenburg

**ODOMAR (d. AD 128)**
Established a Peace Treaty with the Romans and Goths

**MARCOMER (d. AD 169)**
Built Marpurg in Hesse
= *ATHILDIS of Camulod – elder sister of British King Lleiffer Mawr (Lucius)*
[See Chart: ARTHURIAN DESCENT]

**CLODOMIR (d. AD 180)**
= *Basilda – dau. of King of the Rugij*

**FARABERT (d. AD 186)**
Renewed league with the Germans

↓

**SUNNO (d. AD 213)**
Perpetual wars with Romans and Goths after Romans ignored earlier treaty

**HILDERIC (d. AD 253)**
Built Hildeburg Castle on the Rhine

**BARTHERUS (d. AD 272)**
Led armies into Italy as far as Ravenna. Razed Aragon

**CLODIUS (d. AD 298)**
Built Orleans in AD 275

**WALTER (d. AD 306)**

**DAGOBERT (d. AD 317)**

SCOTS IMPERIAL DESCENT *Supplement to Chart : The Holy Families of Britain*

Julia (sister of Julius Caesar)
= Senator Atius Balbus

Atia = **Emperor Augustus Caesar**
(Octavian)
63 BC – AD 18

*Octavia*
= Marcus Antonius (Mark Antony)

*Antonia Minor*
= Nero Claudius Drusus

Emperor Claudius Caesar AD 41-45
= *Valeria Messalina*

**King Gwenivyth ( ARVIRAGUS ) of Siluria** = *Genuissa (Venus Julia)*
( brother of Caractacus )

**King Marius of Siluria**

Coel I                Eugein

**LLEIFFER MAWR**          = *Gladys*
(King Lucius)  c. AD 180

Keribir          *Gladys*          *Eurgen*
= Cadwan of Cumbria          = Aminadab
[See Chart: BLOODLINE OF THE GRAIL]

Parar          Coel II of Colchester

Llyr Llediath

Brân          *SAINT HELENA (Elaine)*          Cunedd
= Constantius I

**CARADAWC**          **CONSTANTINE I**          **CONFER**
(Caractus)          (the Great ) 312-337          of Strathclyde
of Archenfield          Constantius II
337-361

Neithon          Fer

Eudes (Eudaf)          *Constantia*          Eubre Gwydel          Cursalen
= Dau. of Carausius II          = Gratianus          of Ayr
(Augustus) of the Saxon Shore          Western Emperor

## THE HOUSE OF TIR CONAILL
*Irish royal descent of Saint Columba*

**UGAINE MÁR** (the Great)
High King of Ireland (4th century BC)

[See Chart: DESCENT FROM UGAINE MÁR]

**MUIRDACH TIRECH**
(4th century AD)

**EOCHU MUIGEMEDÓN**
King of Ireland
= *Carien Chasdub*
*(dau. of Sachell Balb, King of Saxons)*

**NÍALL NOÍGALLAH** (of the Nine Hostages)
King of Ireland (379-405)
Head of Goidelic Dynasty – Died in Scotland

**EOGAN**
King of Dál n'Araide
of Tyron Tir Eógain
d. 465

**CONALL GULBAN**
of Tir
Conaill

**ENDA**

**LOEGAIRE**
King of Tara
Succeeded Níall
(427-463)
(Era of St. Patrick)

**FERGUS** (Longhead)
of the Northern Uí Néill

**FEDHLIMIDH** (Phelim)
Chieftain of Clan O'Donnell
= *Eithne of Leinster*

**SAINT COLUMBA**
(Crimthann O'Donnell)
Columcille = Dove of the Church
Went to Scottish Dál Riata
Founded Iona Monastery
b. 521 Donegal d. 597

**EOGAN**   **CONALL**

Northern Uí Néill
of Ailech

Kings of
Tyrone

**CRIMTHANN**

Southern Uí Níell
of Tara

Dynasty of
Tara

**KINGS OF THE PICTS**
*Caledonian rulers AD 555 – 843*

BRUDE *(son of Maelchon)* : 555-584
GARTNAIT *(son of Domelch)* : 584-601
NECHTAN *(g.son of Verb)* : 601-621
KENNETH *(son of Luchtren)* : 621-633
GARTNAIT *(son of Foith)* : 633-637
BRUDE *(son of Foith)* : 637-642
TALORC *(son of Foith)* : 642-653
TALORCAN *(son of Eanfrith)* : 653-657
GARTNAIT *(son of Donald)* : 657-663
DRUST *(son of Donald)* : 663-672
BRUDE *(son of Beli)* : 672-693
TARAIN *(son of Ainftech)* : 693-697
BRUDE *(son of Derile)* : 697-706
NECHTAN *(son of Derile)* : 706-724
DRUST *(son of Derile)* : 724-726
ALPIN *(son of Derile)* : 726-728
NECHTAN *(son of Derile)* : 728-729
ANGUS *(son of Fergus)* : 729-750
BRUDE *(son of Maelchon)* : 750-752
ANGUS *(son of Fergus)* : 752-761
BRUDE *(son of Fergus)* : 761-763
KENNETH *(son of Feradach)* : 763-775
ALPIN *(son of Wroid)* : 775-780
DRUST *(son of Talorcan)* : 780
TALORCAN *(son of Drostan)* : 780-782
TALORCAN *(son of Angus)* : 782-784
CONALL *(son of Tade)* : 784-789
CONSTANTINE *(son of Fergus)* : 789-820
ANGUS *(son of Fergus)* : 820-834
DRUST *(s. Constantine)* + TALORCAN *(s. Wthoil)* : 834-836
EOGANAN *(son of Angus)* : 836-839
WRAD *(son of Bargoit)* : 839-842
BRED *(son of Eoganan)* : 842-843
KENNETH *(SON OF ALPIN OF SCOTS)* SUCCEEDED TO SCOTS AND PICTISH THRONES IN 844

## NORTHUMBRIAN KINGS
### Bernicia and Deira AD 547 – 873

**Bernicia – Forth to Tees**

IDA : 547-559
CLAPPA : 559-560 *(son of Ida)*
ADDA : 560-568 *(son of Ida)*
AEDILRIC : 568-572 *(son of Ida)*
THEODRIC : 572-575 *(son of Ida)*
FRITHWEALD : 575-581 *(son of Ida)*
HUSSA : 581-588 *(grandson of Ida)*
AETHELRIC : 588-593 *(grandson of Ida)* ◆
AETHELFRITH : 593-617 *(son of Aethelric)* ▼
EANFRITH : 633-634 *(son of Aethelfrith)*
OSWALD (Saint) : 634-642 *(son of Aethelfrith)*
OSWIU : 642-670 *(son of Aethelfrith)* ▲

**Deira – Tees to Humber**

AELLE : 559-588 *(son of Yffi)*
*Aelle's daughter, Acha, married*
*Aethelfrith of Bernicia*

AETHELRIC of Bernicia : 588-593 ◆
AETHELFRITH of Bernicia : 593-617 ▼
EDWIN : 617-633 *(son of Aelle)*
OSRIC : 633-634 *(son of Edwin)*
OSWALD (Saint) of Bernicia : 634-642 ▮
OSWINE : 642-651
AETHELWEALD : 651-655 *(son of Oswald)*
EALHFRITH : 655-864 *(son of Aethelweald)*
OSIWU of Bernicia : 664-670 ▲

**All Northumbria**

ECGFRITH : 671-685 *(son of Oswiu)*
EALDFRITH : 685-704 *(son of Oswiu)*
EADWULF : 704-705
OSRED I : 705-716 *(son of Ealdfrith)*
COENRED : 716-718
OSRIC : 718-729 *(son of Ealdfrith)*
CEOLWULF : 729-737 *(son of Coenred)*
EADBEORHT : 737-758
OSWULF : 758-759 *(son of Eadbeorht)*
AETHELWEALD MOLL : 759-765
EALHRED : 765-774
AETHELRED I : 774-779 *(son of Aethelweald Moll)*
AELFWOLD I : 779-789 *(son of Oswulf)*
OSRED II : 789-790 *(son of Ealhred)*
AETHELRED I : (restored) 790-796
OSBEALD : 796
EARDWULF : 796-806
AELFWOLD II : 806-808
EARDWULF : (restored) 808-810
EANRED : 810-841 *(son of Eardwulf)*
AETHELRED II : 841-844 *(son of Eanred)*
REDWULF : (usurper) 844
AETHELRED II : (restored) 844-848
OSBEORHT : 848-863
AELLE II : (usurper) 863-868

[Danish Control from 873]

EARLY ENGLISH KINGS  *East Anglia, Mercia, Wessex & Kent – 6th to 10th century*

| East Anglia | Mercia | Wessex | Kent |
|---|---|---|---|
| WEHHA | EOMAER | CERDIC 519-534 | |
| WUFFA (son of Wehha) | ICIL (son of Eomar) | CYNRIC (g. son of Cerdic) 534-560 | AETHELBERT I 560-616 |
| TYTTLA (son of Wuffa) | CREODA (son of Icil) d. 593 | CEAWLIN (son of Cynric) 560-591 | |
| RAEDWALD (son of Tyttla) 593-617 | PYBBA (son of Creoda) 593-606 | CEOLRIC (g. son of Cealwin) 592-597 | |
| ENI (son of Tytta) 617 | CEARL (son of Creoda) 606-626 | CEOWULF (brother of Ceolric) 597-611 | EADBALD 616-640 |
| EORPWALD (son of Raedwald) 618-628 | PENDA (son of Pybba) 626-655 | CYNEGILS (son of Ceolwulf) 611-643 | |
| RAEGENHARE (son of Raedwald) 628-631 | PEADA (son of Pybba) 655-656 | CENWEALH (son of Cynegils) 643-645 + 648-672 | EARCONBERT 640-664 |
| SIGEBERT (son of Raedwald) 631-634 | WULFHERE (son of Penda) 657-674 | *Anarchy* 645-648 | LOTHERE 673-685 |
| EGRIC (son of Eni) 634-635 | BERTHWALD (bro. of Wulfhere) 675-685 (joint + Aethelred) | SEAXBURH (Queen of Caenwealh) 672-674 | EADRIC 685-686 |
| ANNA (nephew of Raedwald) 635-654 | AETHELRED (son of Wulfhere) 675-704 | AESCWINE (line of Ceowulf) 674-676 | *Anarchy* 686-693 |
| AETHELHERE 654-655 | COENRED (son of Wulfhere) 704-709 | CENTWINE (son of Cynegils) 676-685 | |
| AETHELWOLD (brother of Anna) 655-664 | COELRED (son of Aethelred) 709-716 | CAEDWALLA (line of Ceawlin) 685-688 | |

| | | | |
|---|---|---|---|
| EALDWULF 664-713 | AETHELBALD (son of Alweo) 716-757 | INE (line of Ceawlin) 688-726 | WIHTRAED 694-725 |
| AELFWALD (line of Egric) 713-749 | BEORNRED (line of Cenwealh) 757 | AETHELHEARD 726-740 | EADBERT I 725-762 |
| BEORNA 749- | OFFA (son of Thingfrith, son of Eanulf) 757-796 | CUTHRED (kin of Aethelheard) 740-756 | AETHELBERT II 748-762 |
| AETHELRED | ECGFRITH (son of Offa) 796 | SIGEBERHT 756-757 | Mercian Rule 762-796 |
| AETHELBERHT -793 | COENWULF (line of Cenwealh) 796-821 | CYNEWULF 757-786 | EADBERT II 796-798 |
| Rule from Mercia 793-829 | CEOWULF I (line of Cenwealh) 821-823 | BEORHTRIC 786-802 | CUTHRED 798-805 |
| | BEORNWULF (line of Beornred) 823-825 | EGGBERT 802-839 | BALDRED 805-823 |
| AETHELSTAN 829-839 | LUDECAN 825-827 | | Wessex Rule from 825 |
| | WIGLAF 827-828 & 830-839 Rule from Wessex in 829 | | |
| AETHELWEARD 839-854 | BEORHTWULF 840-852 | AETHELWULF (son of Egbert) 839-858 | |
| OSWALD 854-856 | BURGHRED (line of Beornwulf) 852-874 Married Aethelswith, dau. of Aethelwulf of W. Saxons | → | |
| EDMUND (Saint) 856-870 | CEOWULF II (line of Ceowulf I) 874-880 | [Continued in Chart: THE HOUSE OF WESSEX] | |
| 870 – East Angles conquered by Vikings | 874 – Mercians conced to to West Saxons | 880 – West Saxon House of Egbert succeeds as Kings of the English | |
| 920 – Submit to West Saxons | | | |

THE ENGLISH HOUSE OF WESSEX
*AD 802 – 1066 : Including Danes and Norman descent*

**MONARCHS FROM THE NORMAN CONQUEST**
*England, Scotland and France – 11th to 14th century*

| ENGLAND | SCOTLAND | FRANCE |
|---|---|---|
| | | **CAPETIANS** |
| | **SCOTS** | ROBERT II    996-1031<br>Son of Hugh Capet<br>= Constance of Provence |
| | LULACH of Moray    1057-1058<br>Step-son of Macbeth | |
| **NORMANS** | | |
| WILLIAM I (Conqueror)    1066-1087<br>Duke of Normandy<br>= Matilda of Flanders | MALCOLM III Canmore    1058-1093<br>Son of Duncan I<br>= 1. Ingibjorg of Orkney<br>= 2. Margaret the Saxon | HENRI I    1031-60<br>Son of Robert II<br>= Anne of Kiev |
| WILLIAM II (Rufus)    1087-1100<br>Son of William I<br>Unmarried | DONALD BAN    1093-1094<br>Brother of Malcolm II    (dep.) | PHILIP I    1060-1108<br>Son of Henri I<br>= (1) Bertha of Holland |
| | DUNCAN II    1094<br>Son of Malcolm III<br>and Ingibjorg | |
| | DONALD BAN (Restd.)    1094-1097 | |
| | EDGAR    1097-1107<br>Son of Malcolm III<br>and (Saint) Margaret | |
| HENRY I (Beauclerk)    1100-1135<br>Brother of William II<br>= Maud, daughter of<br>Malcolm III of Scots | ALEXANDER I    1107-1124<br>Brother of Edgar<br>= Sybilla, natural dau.<br>of Henry I of England | LOUIS VI    1108-1137<br>(the Fat) Son of Philip I<br>= 1. Lucienne de Rochefort |
| STEPHEN Count of Blois    1135-1154<br>Grandson of William I<br>= Matilda of Boulogne | DAVID I (the Saint)    1124-1153<br>Brother of Alexander<br>= Matilda of Huntingdon | LOUIS VII    1137-1180<br>(the Young)<br>Son of Louis VI<br>= 2. Alix of Champagne |
| **PLANTAGENETS** | | |
| HENRY II (Curtmantle)    1154-1189<br>Grandson of Henry I<br>= Eleanor of Aquitaine<br>Ex 1st wife of Louis VII of France | MALCOLM IV (Maiden)    1153-1165<br>Grandson of David I<br>Unmarried | |
| RICHARD I (Lionheart)    1189-1199<br>Son of Henry II<br>= Berengaria of Navarre | WILLIAM (the Lion)    1165-1214<br>Brother of Malcolm IV<br>= Ermengarde of Bellomont | PHILIP II    1180-1223<br>(Augustus) Son of Louis VII<br>= Isabella of Hainault |

**JOHN** (Lackland)    1199-1216
Brother of Richard I
= *Isabel of Angoulême*

**HENRY III**    1216-1272
Son of John
= *Eleanor of Provence*

**ALEXANDER II**    1214-1249
Son of William I
= *Mary of Picardy*

**LOUIS VIII**    1223-1226
(Lionheart)
Son of Philip II
= *Blanch of Castile*

**LOUIS IX**    1226-1270
(Saint Louis)
Son of Louis VIII
= *Margaret of Provence*

**ALEXANDER III**    1249-1286
Son of Alexander II
= *Margaret, dau. of
Henry III of England*

**PHILIP III**    1270-1285
(the Bald)
Son of Louis IX
= *Mary of Brabant*

**EDWARD I** (Longshanks) 1272-1307
Son of Henry III
= *Eleanor of Castile*

**MARGARET**    1286-1290
(The Maid of Norway)
Granddaughter of
Alexander III, Daughter of
Eric II of Norway
*Unmarried*

**PHILIP IV**    1285-1314
(the Fair)
Son of Philip III
= *Joan of Navarre*

**JOHN BALIOL**    1292-1296
Gt. grandson of Earl of
Huntingdon (bro. of
William the Lion)

**LOUIS X**    1314-1316
(the Headstrong)
Son of Philip I

**EDWARD I OF ENGLAND**    1296-1306
*(Scots Crown Usurped)*

**PHILIP V**    1316-1322
(the Tall)
Son of Philip IV

**EDWARD II** (Caernarvon) 1307-1327
Son of Edward I
= *Isabella of France
Daughter of Philip IV*

**ROBERT I** (the Bruce)    1306-1329
Gt.g-grandson of Earl
of Huntingdon (bro.
of William the Lion)
= 1. *Isabel of Mar*
= 2. *Elizabeth of Ulster*

**CHARLES IV**    1322-1327
Son of Philip IV

**VALOIS**

**PHILIP VI**    1328-1350
Nephew of Philip IV
Son of Count Charles
de Valois
= (1) *Joan of Burgundy*

**EDWARD III** (Windsor)    1327-1377
Son of Edward II
= *Philippa of Hainault*

**DAVID II**    1324-1371
Son of Robert I
and Elizabeth

**JOHN**    1350-1364
(the Good)
Son of Philip VI
= (2) *Blanch of Boulogne*

## STONE OF DESTINY DESCENT TO UGAINE MAR
*Early High Kings of Ireland – descent from 586 BC*

### High Kings of Ireland

EOCHAID I
= *Tamar c.586 BC*
*dau. of King Zedekiah of Judah*

IRIAL FAIDH (Jairol)

EITHRIALL (Etheoir)

FOLLAIN (Fallaig)

TIGHERNMAS (Tigernaig)

EANBOTHA (Enmocha)

SMIORGUIL (Smirnai)

FIACHACH LABHRUINE (Fiachrach-laibrinne)

AONGUS OILBHUAGAH (Oengussa-olmochada)

MAOIN (Ogmain)

ROTHEACHTA (Rodchada)

DEIN (Dem)

SIORNA SAOGHALACH (Sirna)

OILIOLLA OLCHAOIN (Elchada-olchaim)

NUADHA FIONN FAIL (Noethach-fail)

GIALLCHADH (Glachs)

SIMON BREAC (Semoin-bricc)

MUIRIADHACH BOLGRACH (Muredaich-bollgreaich)

FIATHADH TOLGRACH (Fiacgraig-tollgreich)

DUACH LAIGHRACH (Duach-iographich)

EOCHAIDH BUILLAIG (Ecdaig-buadaig)

UGAINE MÁR – THE GREAT (Hugune-Mor)
[See Chart: DESCENT FROM UGAINE MAR]

**SCOTS & WELSH DESCENT FROM UGAINE MAR**
*4th century BC to 9th century AD – detailing Arthur of Dalriada and Arthur of Dyfed*

UGAINE MÁR (THE GREAT) OF IRELAND
(4th century BC)

Cobhtach Caolbreag

Meilage

Jaran Gleofathach

Conla Cruaich

Cealgach

Oiliolla Caisfhiaclach

Eochaid Foltleathan

Aonghus Tuirimheach

| Eanda Aignach | Fiachra-firmara |
| Labrha Luire | Feradaig |
| Blathachta | Fergus I |
| Eamhna | Maine |
| Easamhuin Eamhna | Dornadil |
| Roighneim Ruadh | Rowein |
| Finlogha (Finlochu) | Reuther |
| Finn | Eders |
| Eochaid Fiedhlioch | CONAIRE MOR (the Great) |
| Bias Fineamhnas (Bria) | Admoir |
| Lughaid Riab n'Derg | |
| Criomthann Niadhnar (Crimthann) | Corbred I (Coirbre-findmor) |
| Fioraidhach Fionfachtnach (Feradach) | Dare-dommoir |

Fiachadh Fionchudh

TUATHAL TEACHTMAR (c. AD 100)

Feidhlimhioh Reachtmar (Fedlimid)

**Irish Descent into South Wales**

Corbred II
(Coirbre-crungen)

Luigdig-ellatig

Modha Lamha

Fiachu Suidge
(Fiachaidh Swighde)

CONN CEADCHADHACH (of 100 Battles)

Aonghus

Art Aonfhir

*Saraid* = Conaire II

CORMAC ULFHADA MAC ART

Corbred of Dal Riata

Cairbre Liffeachaire (Coirpre)

Eochaid

Arttchuirp
(Artcharp)

Athirco

Echach (Eochaid)
( Moved to Demetia (Dyfed) )

Fiachadh Streabhthuine
(Fiachu Srobtine)

Findacher

Thrinklind

Corath
(Corach/Cyndwr)

Waegdaeg

Muiredach Tirech

Romaich

Ada Brose
(Ewen-vreise)

Sigegart

Eochu Mugmedón – King of Ireland

Angus

Trestin
(Tryphun)

Saebald

NIALL NOÍGIALLAH – King of Ireland
379-405

Eochaid Muin-remor

Alchoil
(Aircol/Alcon)

Siggoth

Conall Gulban

Erc

Gartbuir
(Erbin/Gwrdeber)

Saebald

LOARN OF ARGYLL   FERGUS MOR
d. 501

Saefugel (Zegulf)

Fergus (Longhead) ···· = ···· *Erca*

[See Chart:
RULERS OF SCOTS DALRIADA]

Congair
(Kyngar)

Sudrtha

Fedhlimidh
[See Chart:
HOUSE OF TIR CONAILL]

Soernil

Retheoir
(Petuir/Peder)

Westers (Westerfalca)

Wilgils (Guilglis)

SAINT COLUMBA
521-597

SCOTS CLANS

Domangart
of Dalriada
501-506

__ARTHUR OF DYFED__
Regulus 506-537
Installed by
Saint Dubricius
= *Guanhumara*
*of Ireland*

*Niniane*
= *Ambrosius*
*Aurelius*

Wyse-frea (Uxfrea)

Yffe (Iffi)

PRINCELY HOUSE OF WALES
[See Chart: ARTHURIAN DESCENT]

King Gabràn
537-559

King Aedàn
574-608

Noé
(Naiee)

KING AELLE OF DEIRA (Northumbria)
(Elle/Ulli) 559-588

__ARTHUR of DALRIADA__
b. 559    d. 603
High King of Britons
= *Gwenhwyfar of Brittany*

Ciotenn
(Caitlenn)

Merlin Emrys

Edgum (Edwin) 617-633
Slain at Battle of Hatfield
by Mercians, along with sons
Osfird and Eadfrith
( No Succession )

*Acha* ........ = ..... CADFAN OF GWYNEDD
*(widow of Aethelfrith*                      d. 625
*of Bernicia)*

Eochaid Buide
608-630

Donald Brec
630-643

Caitien
(Catacuind)

Cadwallon II – King of Gwynedd d. 634
= *Helen, dau. of Wibba* (son of Angle chieftain Crida)

< Usurper: Cadafael 634-654

Domangart
659-673

Rigind
(Regin)

CADWALADR THE BLESSED 654-664
( The last Pendragon )
= *Widow of Alain II King of the Bretons*

Eochaid
695-696

King Edwal of Gwynedd 664-

Aed Find
748-778

Tauloder
(Twalador)

Rhodri Molwynog d. 754

Eochaid
781

Cinan Tindaethwy  754-816
(Succeeded by brother, Hywel 816-825)

ALPIN
King of Scots
839-841

Gwynedd

*Esylth*

Merfyn Vrych 825-844

Hyfaidd (Hemeid)
Deposed by sons of
Rodri Mawr in late 9th c.

RODRI MAWR (The Great)
of Gwynedd 844-878

## BISHOPS OF ROME AND POPES FROM CONSTANTINE
*AD 336 – 1061*

| BISHOP/POPE | TERM | POPE | TERM | POPE | TERM |
|---|---|---|---|---|---|
| Mark | 336 | Eugene I | 654-657 | Theodore II | 898 |
| Julius I | 337-352 | Vitalian | 657-672 | John IX | 898-900 |
| Liberius | 352-366 | Adeodatus | 672-676 | Benedict IV | 900-903 |
| Damasus I | 366-384 | Donus | 676-678 | Leo V | 903 |
| Siricius | 384-399 | Agatho | 678-681 | Sergius III | 904-911 |
| Anastasius | 399-401 | Leo II | 682-683 | Anastasius | 911-13 |
| Innocent I | 401-417 | Benedict II | 684-685 | Lando | 913-914 |
| Zozimus | 417-418 | John V | 685-686 | John X | 914-929 |
| Boniface I | 418-422 | Conon | 686-687 | Leo VI | 929 |
| Celestine | 422-432 | Sergius I | 687-701 | Stephen VIII | 929-931 |
| Sixtus III | 432-440 | John VI | 701-705 | John XI | 931-936 |
| Leo I | 440-461 | John VII | 705-707 | Leo VII | 936-939 |
| Hilarus | 461-468 | Sisinnius | 708 | Stephen IX | 939-942 |
| Simplicius | 468-483 | Constantine I | 708-715 | Marinus II | 942-946 |
| Felix III | 483-492 | Gregory II | 715-731 | Agapitus II | 946-955 |
| Gelasius I | 492-496 | Gregory III | 731-741 | John XII | 955-963 |
| Anastasius II | 496-498 | Zachary | 741-752 | Leo VIII | 963-964 |
| Symmachus | 498-514 | Stephen II | 752 | Benedict V | 964 |
| Hormisdas | 514-523 | Stephen III | 752-757 | John XIII | 965-972 |
| John I | 523-526 | Paul I | 757-767 | Benedict VI | 973-974 |
| Felix IV | 526-530 | Stephen IV | 768-772 | Benedict VII | 974-983 |
| Boniface II | 530-532 | Adrian I | 772-795 | John XIV | 983-984 |
| John II | 533-535 | Leo III | 795-816 | John XV | 985-996 |
| Agapitus | 535-536 | Stephen V | 816-817 | Gregory V | 996-999 |
| Silverius | 536-537 | Paschal I | 817-824 | Silvester II | 999-1003 |
| Vigilius | 537-555 | Eugene II | 824-827 | John XVII | 1003 |
| Pelagius I | 556-560 | Valentine | 827 | John XVIII | 1003-1009 |
| John III | 561-578 | Gregory IV | 827-844 | Sergius IV | 1009-1012 |
| Benedict I | 575-579 | Sergius II | 844-847 | Benedict VIII | 1012-1024 |
| Pelagius II | 579-590 | Leo IV | 847-855 | John XIX | 1024-1033 |
| Gregory I | 590-604 | Benedict III | 855-858 | Benedict IX | 1033-1044 |
| Sabinianus | 604-606 | Nicholas I | 858-867 | Silvester III | 1045 |
| Boniface III | 607 (First styled *Pope*) | Adrian II | 867-872 | Benedict | 1045 |
| Boniface IV | 608-615 | John VIII | 872-882 | Gregory VI | 1045-1046 |
| Deusdedit | 615-618 | Marinus | 882-884 | Clement II | 1046-1047 |
| Boniface V | 619-625 | Adrian III | 884-885 | Benedict IX | 1047-1048 |
| Honorius I | 625-638 | Stephen VI | 885-891 | Damascus II | 1048 |
| Severinus | 640 | Formosus | 891-896 | Leo IX | 1049-1054 |
| John IV | 640-642 | Boniface VI | 896 | Victor II | 1055-1057 |
| Theodore I | 642-649 | Stephen VII | 896-897 | Stephen X | 1057-1058 |
| Martin I | 649-655 | Romanus | 897 | Nicholas II | 1059-1061 |

**THE FIRST HIGH STEWARDS OF SCOTLAND**
*Kings' Commissioners – 12th to 14th century*

WALTER FITZ ALAN .............. = .................. *Eschyne de Molle*
1st HIGH STEWARD OF SCOTLAND          *Daughter of Thomas de Lundins*
(Dapifer Regis Scotiae)               *Sister of Malcolm, 1st Doorward of Scotland*
Benefactor of the Knights Templars    *Widow of Robert le Croc, Snr.*
Founder of Paisley Priory 1164
Received Grant of Lands from David I
Ratified by Malcolm IV                [See Chart: ORIGINS OF THE STEWARTS]
d. 1177

ALAN FITZ WALTER ........... = ................ *Eve*
2nd HIGH STEWARD OF SCOTLAND      *dau. of Swein of Crawford*
Crusader with Richard Coeur de Lion  *(ancestor of Ruthvens of Gowrie)*
d. 1204

WALTER STEWART ............ = ....... *Beatrix*
3rd HIGH STEWARD OF SCOTLAND       *dau. of Gilchrist*
(Walter of Dundonald)              *3rd Earl of Angus*
Justiciar of Northern Scotland
Raised Paisley Prior to an Abbey
d. 1241

ALEXANDER STEWART ........ = ........ *Jean*
4th HIGH STEWARD OF SCOTLAND      *g.dau. of Angus, Lord of Bute*
Crusader and Co-Regent            *and Arran (son of Somerled of the Isles)*
Lord of Garlies, Galloway
Commander at 1263 Battle of Largs
against King Haakon of Norway
d. 1283

SIR JAMES STEWART ............ = ............ *Jill de Bourg*
5th HIGH STEWARD OF SCOTLAND      *dau. of Walter, 1st Earl of Ulster*
Supporter of Robert Bruce
Co-Regent & Guardian of the Realm
d. 1309

1315
SIR WALTER STEWART ....... = ....... *Margorie Bruce*
6th HIGH STEWARD OF SCOTLAND           *d. 1316*
Commander at Bannockburn 1314          *dau. of Robert I*
Regent of Scotland                     *(the Bruce)*
d. 1326

KING ROBERT II STEWART
7th HIGH STEWARD OF SCOTLAND
r. 1371-1390

# APPENDIX V

531

**KINGS OF SCOTS FROM MACBETH TO THE STEWARTS**
*1040 – 1371*

**ENGLISH DOMINATION**

↑ 1233
*Devorguilla* ... = ... *John*
*d. 1290*          *de Balliol*
                   *d. 1269*

↑
*Robert Bruce* ... = ... *Isabel*
*of Annandale*        *dau. of Gilbert*
*d. 1294*             *le Clare, Earl*
                      *of Gloucester*

↑ 1251
**ALEXANDER II** ... = ... *Margaret*
*1249-1286*              *dau. of*
                         *Henry III*
                         *of England*

*Margaret* = *Eric III*
            *of*
            *Norway*

**JOHN BALLIOL**
Ruled 1292-1296
Selected by
Edward I of England.
Deposed by Edward who
ruled 1296-1306
= *Isobel, dau. of*
*John de Warenne*
*Earl of Surrey*

*Robert Bruce* ... = ... *Marjorie*
*of Annandale*        *dau. of Neil*
*Earl of Carrick*     *Earl of Carrick*

**_MARGARET_**
(Maid of Norway)
1286-1290
Died at sea
aged seven.
Crown seized by
Edward I of England

**SCOTTISH INDEPENDENCE**

(1)
1295
*Isabel* ... = ... **ROBERT I (the Bruce)** ... = ... *Elizabeth*
*dau. of*              1306-1329                *du Bourgh*
*Donald*            Seized Throne from          *dau. of*
*Earl of Mar*       Edward of England.          *Richard,*
                    Defeated English at         *Earl of*
                    Bannockburn 1314 to         *Ulster*
                    achieve Scottish
                    Independence

(2)
1302

**Edward Balliol**
Crowned by English
in 1332, but fled
Scotland

**_DAVID II_**
1329-1371
Opposed Edward III
at Halidon Hill 1333
d.s.p.

**ROYAL HOUSE OF STEWART**

1315
*Marjorie Bruce* ... = ... *Walter Stewart*
*d. 1316*                6th High Steward
                         of Scotland
                         (1291-1326)

**_ROBERT II STEWART_**
1371-1390

**NORSE DESCENT TO SOMERLED AND ST. CLAIR**
*7th to 14th century – with Norman descent also*

Ragnhild ......... = ......... **SOMERLED**
Thane of Argyll & South Isles
d. 1164

**KING DUGALL**
Lord of Argyll

**HOUSE OF LORNE Descends**

**NORMAN DESCENT OF ST. CLAIR**

For Norse Descent of Dukes of Normandy
[See Chart: ENGLISH HOUSE OF WESSEX]

**RICHARD II (the Good)**
Duke of Normandy  d. 1026

**PAYENS & CHAUMONT**

Tibault        Hugues        Robert
de Payens    de Chaumont    de Chaumont
d. 1064      d. 1067        d. 1075

**MAUGER LE JEUNE**
Comte de St. Clair
Archbishop of Rouen
= Dau. of House of St. Clair
de Basseneville (St. Clair-en-Auge)

**PAUL**
d. 1103
20th Jarl of Orkney
= dau. of Magnus II
King of Norway

**ERLAND II**
d. 1103
21st Jarl of Orkney
= Thora of Iceland

**HAAKON**
(the Imperious)
d. 1122
23rd Jarl of Orkney
= Helga of Thurso

**MAGNUS I**
(the Martyr)
d.s.p. 1115
22nd Jarl of Orkney
(Slain by Haakon)

Adelaide = Hugues
de Chaumont
d. 1075

**WALDERNE DE ST CLAIR**
d. 1047

Tibault        Tibault
de Payens
d. 1094

Osmon
de Chaumont
c. 1100

**WILLIAM DE ST. CLAIR**
Baron of Roslin 1057
= Dorothy of Raby

**HARALD I**
(the Orator)
d. 1127
24th Jarl of Orkney
Earl of Caithness

**MARGARET**
Countess of Orkney
= Madoch of Atholl

Hugues

**HUGUES
DE PAYENS**
d. 1131
Grand Master of
Knights Templars

Guillaume
de Chaumont
c. 1120

**HENRI DE ST. CLAIR**
Baron of Roslin
Crusader with
Godefroi de Bouillon
= Rosebelle Forteith

**PAUL**
(the Silent)
d.s.p. 1136
25th Jarl
of Orkney

**ERLEND II**
(the Younger)
d. 1156
26th Jarl of Orkney
= Gormlath of Moray

Robert        =   Richilde
de Chaumont

**HENRI DE ST. CLAIR**
Baron of Roslin
Scots Privy Councillor
= Margaret Gratney

**RANALD III**
d. 1158
27th Jarl of Orkney

**JEAN DE GISORS**
d. 1220
Helmsman of
*Prieuré de Sion*

**WILLIAM DE ST. CLAIR**
Baron of Roslin 1180
= Agnes Dunbar, dau. of
*Patrick 1st Earl of March*

*INGEGERD*
= Eric Slagbriller
of Norway

**HARALD III**
(the Younger)
d.s.p. 1198
28th Jarl of Orkney

**HARALD III**
(the Wicked)
d. 1206
29th Jarl of Orkney
= *Havraflode of Ross*

**HENRI DE ST. CLAIR**
Baron of Roslin
= *Katherine* - dau. of
*Earl of Strathearn*

**DAVID**
d.s.p. 1214
30th Jarl
of Orkney

**JOHN I**
d. 1232
31st Jarl
of Orkney

**MAGNUS II** d. 1239
32nd Jarl of Orkney

**GILBERT I** d. 1256
33rd Jarl of Orkney

**HENRI DE ST. CLAIR**
Baron of Roslin
d. 1270
= *Margaret*
dau. of Earl of Mar

**GILBERT II** d. 1267
34th Jarl of Orkney

**MAGNUS** d. 1273
35th Jarl of Orkney

**WILLIAM DE ST. CLAIR** = *Matilda*
Ambassador to France

**MAGNUS IV**
d.s.p. 1284
36th Jarl of Orkney
Earl of Tunsberg

**JOHN II**
d. 1310
37th Jarl of Orkney
= *(1300) dau. of King*
*Eric of Norway*

**MAGNUS V**
d. 1321
38th Jarl of Orkney
= *Katherine, Countess*
*of Caithness*

**MALISE I**
d. 1333
39th Jarl of Orkney
Earl of Strathearn
= *Isabella of Caithness*

**HENRY DE ST. CLAIR**
Baron of Roslin
Commander of Knights Templars
at Bannockburn 1314
= *Alicia de Fenton*

WILLIAM DE ST. CLAIR
d. 1330 in Spain

MALISE II d. 1345
40th Jarl of Orkney
= *Marjorie of Ross*

WILLIAM DE ST. CLAIR ....... = ...... *ISABEL*
Baron of Roslin
d. 1358

HENRY SINCLAIR
Baron of Roslin
Earl of Orkney  d. 1400
(Sailed to America in 1398)

Sinclair Earls of Caithness Descend

**GERMAN KINGS AND EMPERORS**
*Saxons, Salians and Hohenstaufens : 919 – 1250*

HOHENSTAUFEN HOUSE

[GHIBELLINES]

GERTRUDE = HENRY (the Proud) — WELF VI — JUDITH = FREDERICK — CONRAD III — LEOPOLD IV — HENRY

**GERTRUDE = HENRY (the Proud)**
Duke of Bavaria
1126-1139
Duke of Saxony
1137-1139

**WELF VI**
Marquis of
Tuscany
Duke of
Spoleto
d. 1191

**JUDITH = FREDERICK (the One-eyed)**
Duke of Swabia
1105-1147

**CONRAD III**
King & EMPEROR
Founder of
HOHENSTAUFEN
DYNASTY
1138-1152
[Opposed
Lothair II ‡]

**LEOPOLD IV**
Duke of
Bavaria
1139-1141

**HENRY**
Duke of
Bavaria
1141-1156
First Duke
of Austria

**HENRY (the Lion)**
Duke of Saxony
1142-1180
Duke of Bavaria
1156-1180  d. 1195
= Matilda, dau. of
Henry I of England

**WELF VII**
d.s.p. 1167

**FREDERICK I
BARBAROSSA
EMPEROR**
1152-1190
= Beatrice
of Burgundy

**FREDERICK VON
ROTHENBURG**
Duke of Swabia
1152-1167

**OTTO IV
EMPEROR**
1198-1218

**HENRY VI
King & EMPEROR**
1190-1197
[Imprisoned Richard I
of England]
= Constance
of Sicily

**PHILIP**
of Swabia
King 1198-1208

**FREDERICK II
King & EMPEROR**
( The Last of Hohenstaufen)
1212-1250
[Leader of 5th Crusade]
FREDERICK I of Sicily

## HOLY ROMAN EMPERORS *House of Habsburg and others 1273 – 1806*

| EMPEROR | HOUSE | EMPEROR | HOUSE |
|---|---|---|---|
| **RUDOLPH I** 1273-1291<br>of Habsburg (Rudolph I of Austria) | Habsburg | **RUDOLPH II** 1576-1612<br>(Son of Maximillian II) | Habsburg |
| **ADOLPH** 1291-1298<br>Son of Walram II of Nassau | Nassau | **MATTHIAS** 1612-1619<br>King of Bohemia & Hungary<br>(Bro. of Rudolph II) | Habsburg |
| **ALBERT I** 1298-1308<br>(Son of Rudolph I) | Habsburg | **FERDINAND II** 1619-1637<br>King of Bohemia & Hungary<br>(Nephew of Matthias) | Habsburg |
| **HENRY VII** 1308-1313<br>of Luxembourg | Luxembourg | **FERDINAND III** 1637-1657<br>(Son of Ferdinand II) | Habsburg |
| **LOUIS III** 1314-1346<br>(G-son of Rudolph I - via dau.<br>Matilde, and Louis II, Duke of Bavaria) | Wittelsbach | **LEOPOLD I** 1657-1705<br>(Son of Ferdinand III) | Habsburg |
| **CHARLES IV** 1346-1378<br>King of Bohemia (G-son of Henry VII,<br>via son, John, and *Elizabeth of Bohemia*) | Luxembourg | **JOSEPH I** 1705-1711<br>(Son of Leopold I) | Habsburg |
| **WENCESLAS** 1378-1410<br>King of Bohemia (Son of Charles IV) | Luxembourg | **CHARLES VI** 1711-1740<br>(Bro. of Joseph I) | Habsburg |
| **SIGISMUND** 1410-1437<br>King of Bohemia (Bro. of Wenceslas)<br>= *Mary of Hungary* | Luxembourg | *MARIA THERESA* 1740-1742<br>*(Dau. of Charles VI)*<br>= Francis of Lorraine | Habsburg |
| **ALBERT V** 1438-39<br>(Gt.Gt.g-son of Albert I)<br>= *Elizabeth, dau. of Sigismund* | Habsburg | **CHARLES VII** 1742-1745<br>Elector of Bavaria<br>(Contested inheritance of *Maria Theresa*) | Wittelsbach |
| **FREDERICK III** 1440-1493<br>Archduke of Austria (Cou. of Albert V<br>Last H.R. Emperor crowned by Pope | Habsburg | **FRANCIS I** 1745-1765<br>Francis of Lorraine<br>= *Express Maria Theresa* | Habsburg-Lorraine |
| **MAXIMILLIAN I** 1493-1519<br>(Son of Frederick III)<br>= *Mary of Burgundy* | Habsburg | **JOSEPH II** 1765-1790<br>(Son of Francis I)<br>[Joint Emperor with mother to 1780] | Habsburg-Lorraine |
| **CHARLES V** 1519-1558<br>(G-son of Maximilian via Philip of<br>Burgundy and *Joanna of Castile*) | Habsburg | **LEOPOLD II** 1790-1792<br>Son of Francis I | Habsburg-Lorraine |
| **FERDINAND I** 1558-1564<br>(Bro. of Charles V) | Habsburg | **FRANCIS II** 1792-1806<br>Emperor of Austria (Son of Leopold II)<br>Last Holy Roman Emperor | Habsburg-Lorraine |
| **MAXIMILLIAN II** 1564-1576<br>(Son of Ferdinand I) | Habsburg | | |

**THE SPANISH SUCCESSION**
*León, Castile, Navarre & Aragon : 970 – 1931*

ALBERT II
Habsburg Duke
of Austria 1330-1358

JOHN I = ELEANOR
King of Castile    of Aragon
1379-1390

LEOPOLD III
Duke of Austria
1358-1386

HENRY III
King of Castile
1390-1406

FERDINAND I
King of Aragon
and Sicily
1412-1415

ERNST
Duke of Austria
1406-1424

JOHN II
King of Castile
1406-1454

ALFONSO V
King of Aragon
Sicily and Naples
1416-1458

JOHN II
King of Aragon
and Sicily
1458-1479

FREDERICK III
Duke of Austria
1424-1493

HENRY IV
King of Castile
1454-1474

FERRANTE
King of Naples
1459-1494

MAXIMILIAN I
of Austria
Holy Roman Emperor
1493-1519
= Mary of Burgundy

ISABELLA
Queen of Castile
1474-1504

FERDINAND II
(the Catholic)
King of Aragon
1479-1516
FERDINAND V
of Castile
1474-1504

Spanish Inquisition
from 1480

PHILIP OF BURGUNDY =
(the Handsome)
King of Castile
from 1506

JOANNA
(the Mad)
of Castile

CATHERINE =
of Aragon

HENRY VIII
Tudor
of England
1509-1547

HABSBURGS

CHARLES V
Habsburg
Holy Roman Emperor
King of Spain and Naples
1517-1556
(abdicated)

*MARY I TUDOR* ..... = ..... PHILIP II ......... = ..... *Anne*
(Bloody Mary)         King of Spain              *of Austria*
*Queen of England*    1556-1598
*1553-1558 d.s.p.*    [Armada 1588]

1554

PHILIP III
King of Spain 1598-1621

PHILIP IV
King of Spain 1621-1665
= *Mariana*

CHARLES II (the Bewitched)          *MARIA THERESA*
King of Spain 1665-1700 d.s.p.      = LOUIS XIV of France

WAR OF SPANISH SUCCESSION 1701-1714

( Son )                              BOURBONS

PHILIP V
King of Spain 1700-1724
Abdicated in favour of son LUIS,
but restored on son's death 1724-1746

FERDINAND VI                         CHARLES III
King of Spain 1746-1759             Half-brother of Ferdinand by Philip V's
d.s.p.                             2nd wife *Elizabeth Farnese Duchess of Parma*

WAR OF SPANISH INDEPENDENCE 1808-1814    CHARLES IV
                                         King of Sapin 1788-1807 (abdicated)
                                         = *María Luisa, g-dau. of Elizabeth Farnese*

Crown Assumed by Napoleon's
brother, JOSEPH BONAPARTE                FERDINAND VII
                                         Restored, King of Spain 1814-1833
                                         = *María Christina*

AMADEO OF SAVOY (the Gentleman King)     *ISABELLA II*
Son of Victor Emmanuel II (Italy)        *Queen of Spain 1833-1868 (deposed)*
Constitutional Monarch 1868-1872 (abdicated)

1st SPANISH REPUBLIC 1872-1874           ALFONSO XII
                                         Restored, King of Spain 1874-1885
                                         = *Maria Chrstina of Austria*

                                         ALFONSO XIII
                                         The Last King of Spain 1885-1931 (abdicated)
2nd SPANISH REPUBLIC 1931                = *Victoria Eugenia , dau. of Queen Victoria of Britain*

THE STEWART DYNASTY
*Noble Houses -- Supplement to Chart: The First High Stewards*

Matthew Stewart
4th EARL OF LENNOX
= *Margaret Douglas*
*dau. of Margaret Tudor ‡*
*by 2nd marriage to Earl Angus*

Sir James Stewart = *Margaret* = Richard Stewart Henry Stewart ... = ... < 2nd ... *MARY QUEEN OF SCOTS*
of Beath *Lindsay* 3rd LORD LORD DARNLEY 1554-1567
CONSTABLE OF *of the Byres* INNERMEATH M. 1567 (Executed by English)
DOUNE d. 1530
m. 1547

James Stewart John Stewart John Stewart *JAMES VI*
1st LORD DOUNE 4th LORD INNERMEATH 4th EARL OF ATHOLL 1567-1625
d. 1590 d. 1570 Chancellor k.1579 (James I of England)
= *Margaret Campbell* = *Elizabeth Betoun* = *Margaret Fleming* 1603-1625
*of Argyll* *of Creich* = *Anne of Denmark*

STUART KINGS
**Descend**

John Stewart
5th Lord Innermeath [See Charts]
Commissioner of Realm (d. 1586) HOUSE OF STUART
= *Helen Ogilvie of Airlie* & CONTEMPORARY
**MONARCHS II**
and
DESCENT TO CHARLES
**EDWARD STUART**

James Stewart 2 > < 2 1 >
2nd LORD DOUNE John Stewart = *Mary Ruthven* = John Stewart
2nd EARL MORAY 6th LORD INNERMEATH *of Gowrie* 5th EARL OF ATHOLL
( The Bonnie Moray ) 6th EARL OF ATHOLL d. 1595
k. 1592 d. 1603 (no male heir)
= *Elizabeth Stuart* = (1) *Margaret Lindsay*
*dau. of Regent James of Moray* *of Crawford*
*illegit. son of James V*

1 >
Henry Stewart = *Jean* Sir James Stewart = *Mary* *Dorothea*
LORD ST. COLME (Eoin Ciar) b. 1583 (senior heiress)
Constable of 7th LORD INNERMEATH = *William Murray*
Doune Castle 7th EARL OF ATHOLL *of Tullibardine*
d. 1612 Atholl Title confiscated
through dispute with senior
heiress and step-mother.
Innermeath Title terminated ATHOL Title
Earls of Moray Exiled to England 1618 by Privy Council Succeeds to Murray
**Descend** Recorded presumed d.s.p. 1625 (but d. 1659)
(Literature: Eoin Ciar Duine (Ensor Doone))
= (2) *Margaret Alasdair MacGregor*

## THE ROYAL STEWARTS & CONTEMPORARY HOUSES
*Scotland, England and France: 1371 – 1603*

| ENGLAND | SCOTLAND | FRANCE |
|---|---|---|
| PLANTAGENETS | STEWARTS | VALOIS |

**RICHARD II** (Bordeaux)  1377-1399
Son of the Black Prince,
and Grandson of Edward III
*d.s.p.*

**ROBERT II**  1371-1390
Son of Walter, 3rd High
Steward, and Marjorie Bruce
*= Elizabeth, dau. of Sir Adam
   Mure of Rowallan*

**CHARLES V**  1364-1380
(the Wise)
Son of John the Good
*= Joan of Bourbon*

**HENRY IV** (Bolingbroke)  1399-1413
[House of Lancaster]
Son of John O'Gaunt (Duke of
Lancaster), and Grandson
of Edward III
*= Mary de Bohun*

**ROBERT III**  1390-1406
[John, Earl of Carrick]
Son of Robert II
*= Anabella, daughter of
   John Drummond of Stobhall*

**CHARLES VI**  1380-1422
(the Mad)
Son of Charles V
*= Isabeau of Bavaria
   (Their daughter, Katherine,
   married Henry V of England)*

**HENRY V** (Monmouth)  1413-1422
[House of Lancaster]
Son of Henry IV
*= Katherine de Valois, daughter
   of Charles VI of France*

**JAMES I**  1406-1437
Son of Robert III
*= Joan Beaufort of Somerset
   g-dau. of John O'Gaunt*

**HENRY VI** (Windsor)  1422-1461
[House of Lancaster]
Son of Henry V
*= Margaret - daughter of Rayner,
   Duke of Anjou, Titular King of
   Jerusalem*
(Deposed by Edward Duke of York)

**JAMES II**  1437-1460
Son of James I
*= Mary, daughter of Arnold,
   Duc de Gueldres*

**CHARLES VII**  1422-1461
(the Well Served)
Son of Charles VI
*= Mary of Anjou*

**EDWARD IV**  1461-1483
[House of York]
Son of Sir Richard Plantagenet,
in descent from John O'Gaunt's
brother, Lionel, Duke of Clarence
*= Elizabeth - daughter of Richard
   Widville, Earl Rivers*

**JAMES III**  1460-1488
Son of James II
*= Margaret, daughter of
   Christian I of Denmark*

**LOUIS XI**  1461-1483
Son of Charles VII
*= Charlotte of Savoy*

**EDWARD V**  1483
[House of York]
Son of Edward IV
Murdered before coronation,
along with brother, Richard
*d.s.p.*

**CHARLES VIII**  1483-1498
Son of Louis XI
*= Anne of Brittany*

**RICHARD III**     1483-1485
*[House of York]*
Killed at Bosworth Field
Son of Sir Richard Plantagenet
and brother of Edward IV
= *Anne - daughter of Richard
   Melville, Earl of Warwick*

**JAMES IV**     1488-1513
Son of James III
= *Margaret Tudor, daughter
   of Henry VII of England*

**LOUIS XII**     1498-1515
*[Duke of Orleans]*
Grand-nephew of Charles VI
= 1. *Joan of Valois*
= 2. *Anne of Brittany*


### TUDORS

**HENRY VII**     1485-1509
Son of Edmund Tudor,
Earl of Richmond *[in descent
from Katherine de Valois, widow
of Henry V, and her 2nd husband,
Owen Tudor]* and Margaret Beaufort,
g-dau. of John O'Gaunt
= *Elizabeth of York, daughter
   of Edward IV*

**JAMES V**     1513-1542
Son of James IV
= (2) *Marie de Guise Lorraine,
   daughter of Claude, Duc
   d'Aumale*

**FRANCIS I**     1515-1547
Cousin of Louis XII
= 1. *Claude de France
   dau. of Louis XII*
= 2. *Eleanor of Austria*


**HENRY VIII**     1509-1547
Son of Henry VII
= (1) *Catherine, daughter of
   Ferdinand V of Aragon and Castille*
= (2) *Anne, daughter of Sir Thomas
   Boleyn, Earl of Ormonde*
= (3) *Jane, daughter of Sir John
   Seymour, and sister of Edward,
   Duke of Somerset*

**MARY QUEEN OF SCOTS**   1542-1587
*Daughter of James V and
Mary de Guise Lorraine*
= (2) *Henry Stewart, Lord
   Darnley, son of Matthew
   Earl of Lennox*

**HENRY II**     1547-1559
Son of Francis I
= *Catherine de Medici*


**EDWARD VI**     1547-1553
Son of Henry VIII and
Jane Seymour
*(Unmarried)*

**FRANCIS II**     1559-1560
Son of Henri II
(As Dauphin and King, Francis
was the first husband of *Mary
Stuart, Queen of Scots*)
d.s.p.


**JANE GREY**     1553-1554
*Daughter of Henry Grey,
Duke of Suffolk, and
g-dau. of Henry VII
[Inherited Crown by Will
of Edward VI]
(Executed)*


**MARY I**     1553-1558
*Daughter of Henry VIII
and Catherine of Aragon*
= Philip II of Spain
d.s.p.

**CHARLES IX**     1560-1574
Son of Henri II
and Brother of Francis II
d.s.p.


**ELIZABETH I**     1558-1603
*Daughter of Henry VIII
and Anne Boleyn
(Unmarried)*

**JAMES VI**     1567-1625
Son of Mary Queen of
Scots and Lord Darnley
JAMES I of England from 1603

**HENRI III**     1574-1589
Son of Henri II
and Brother of Francis II
d.s.p.

## DESCENT TO CHARLES EDWARD STUART
*Mary Queen of Scots' lineage*

JAMES V (STEWART) OF SCOTS
b. 1512    R. 1513-1542    d. 1542 Falkland
= 2nd (1538) Marie de Guise-Lorraine
(d. 1560) Dau. of Claude, Duc d'Aumale
|

*MARY (STUART) QUEEN OF SCOTS*
b. 1542    R. 1542-1567    (forced abdication)
Beheaded 1587 Fotheringhay Castle
= 2nd (1565) Henry Stewart, Lord Darnley
Master of Lennox. Murdered 1567
|

JAMES VI (STUART) OF SCOTS
b. 1566    R. 1567-1625    d. 1625 Herts
JAMES I OF ENGLAND 1603-1625
= (1589) Anne (d. 1619) Dau. of
King Frederick II of Denmark & Norway
|

CHARLES I (STUART) OF BRITAIN
b. 1600    R. 1625-1649    Beheaded 1649 London
= (1625) Henrietta Maria (d. 1669)
Dau. of King Henri IV of France
|

JAMES VII (STUART) OF SCOTS (II OF ENGLAND)
b. 1633    R. 1685-1688    (deposed by Whig Revolution - No abdication)
[Succeeded brother, Charles II Stuart]
d. Saint Germain-en-Laye 1701
= 2nd (1673) Mary Beatrix D'Este (d. 1718)
Dau. of Duke Alphonso IV of Modena (Italy)
|

JAMES FRANCIS EDWARD STUART - JAMES VIII OF SCOTS *de jure* (III OF ENGLAND)
(Chevalier Saint George) b. 1688    Proclaimed 1701    d. 1766
= (1719) Mary Clementina Sobieska (d. 1735) Dau. of Prince
James Lewis Sobieski (son of King Jan III of Poland)
|

CHARLES EDWARD LOUIS PHILIP CASIMIR STUART - *de jure* CHARLES III
b. 31 Dec 1720    Crowned (symb.) Sept 24th 1745    Succeeded 1766    d. 31 Jan 1788

## THE STUART KINGS & CONTEMPORARIES
*Britain and France: 1603 – 1688*

| ENGLAND | SCOTLAND | FRANCE |
|---|---|---|

**ENGLAND**

*ELIZABETH I TUDOR*  1558-1603
*Daughter of Henry VII
and Anne Boleyn
(Unmarried)*

**SCOTLAND**

JAMES VI STEWART  1567-1625
Son of Mary Queen of
Scots and Lord Darnley

James VI of Scots became James I
of England on Union of Crons
in 1603 [See ENGLAND column]

**FRANCE**

HENRI III                    1574-1589
Son of Henri II
and  Brother of Franicis II
*d.s.p.*

**STUARTS  KINGS OF BRITAIN**

[Union of Scots and English Crowns]  ← ← ⎤

**BOURBONS**

HENRY IV                    1589-1610
Son of Antoine de Bourbon
and Jeanne, Queen of Navarre
= 2. *Marie de Medici
(Their daughter, Henrietta,
married Charles I of Britain)*

JAMES I (VI of Scots)   1603-1625
Son of Mary Queen of Scots and
Henry Stewart, Lord Darnley
= *Anne , daughter of Frederick II
of Denmark and Norway*

CHARLES I                 1625-1649
Son of James I (VI)
= *Henrietta Maria  daughter
of Henry IV of France*
( Executed )

LOUIS XIII                 1610-1643
Son of Henri IV
[Policies under Cardinal
de Richelieu 1624-1642
= *Anne of Austria*

[Commonwealth Declared 1649]

Oliver Cromwell
Lord Protector          1653-1658

Richard Cromwell
Lord Protector          1658-1659

LOUIS XIV                 1643-1715
(The Sun King)
Son of Louis XIII
[Policies under Cardinal
Mazarin until 1661]
= *Maria Theresa , Infanta
of Philip IV of Spain*

[Stuart Restoration 1660]

CHARLES II                1660-1685
Son of Charles I
= *Katherine of Braganza, Infanta
of John IV of Portugal*
d. s. p. ( legit )

JAMES II (VII of Scots)   1685-1688
Brother of Charles II
= (1) *Anne, daughter of Edward
Hyde, Earl of Clarendon*
= (2) *Mary D'Este, daughter of
Alphonso IV of Modena*
( Deposed by Whig Revolution )

From the deposition of James VII,
the *de jure* Scottish succession
progressed (to the present day)
through his son, James Francis
Edward Stuart [ See Charts:
DESCENT TO CHARLES EDWARD STUART
and COUNTS OF ALBANY ]

## DESCENT TO MARGUERITE DE MASSILLAN
*House of d'Audibert de Lussan*

JACQUES D'AUDIBERT
Seigneur de Valros
Comte de Lussan 1645
= *Claudine*
*de Loudun*
|
PIERRE D'AUDIBERT
Comte de Lussan
= *Claudine*
*de Loudun*
|
GASPARD D'AUDIBERT
Comte de Lussan

| < --- > | --- > |
|---|---|
| (1) | (2) |
| = *Jeanne Bourdal* | = *Gabrielle* |
| *d'Aramon* | *de Pellegrin* |

GABRIEL D'AUDIBERT          SIMON D'AUDIBERT
Comte de Lussan            Lord of Massillan
= *Gabrielle de*
*Bourdos de Portes*

CHARLES D'AUDIBERT          GASPARD D'AUDIBERT
Comte de Lussan            Lord of Massillan
= *Marguerite d'Albert*

JACQUES D'AUDIBERT          LOUIS D'AUDIBERT
Comte de Lussan            Comte de Massillan
Baron de Beauvoir          = *Madeleine*
= *Jeanne de Beauvoir*     *du Pont*
*du Roure*

---

LAURENCE MIDDLETON
of that Ilk
= *Nicola Stratton*
*of Lauriston*
|
GILBERT MIDDLETON
Sheriff of Forfar
1516
= *Agnes Lauder*
|
JOHN MIDDLETON
of Middleton
= *Isabella Falconer*
*of Halkertoun*
|
ROBERT MIDDLETON
of Caldham
= *Katherine Strachen*
*of Therbstoun*
|
JOHN MIDDLETON
Earl of Middleton
= *Grizel Durham*
*of Easter Powrie*

---

NICHOLAS O'DEA
Baron of Ida
(Ireland)
= *Helena Bourke*
|
PATRICK O'DEA
Baron of Ida
b. 1567
|
THOMAS O'DEA
Baron of Ida
b. 1587
= *Cecily Archer*
|
JOHN O'DEA
Baron of Ida
c. 1610
(b. Naples)
= *Elizabeth Brown*

---

LOUIS DE ROHAN
MONTBAZON
= *Marie de Rohan-Gié*
|
RENE DE ROHAN-GIÉ
= *Jeanne d'Albret*
*Princess of Navarre*
|
RENE DE ROHAN-LÉON
= *Catherine*
*de Parthenay*
|
HENRI, DUC DE ROHAN
= *Marguerite*
*de Bethune Sully*

---

## HOUSE OF STUART

JAMES V OF SCOTS
1513-1542
= *Marie de Guise*
*Lorraine*
|
MARY QUEEN OF SCOTS
1542-1567    d. 1587
= *Henry Stewart*
*Lord Darnley*
|
JAMES VI (I) STUART
1567 (1603) - 1625
= *Anne of Denmark*
|
CHARLES I
1625-1649
= *Henrietta Maria*
*de France*

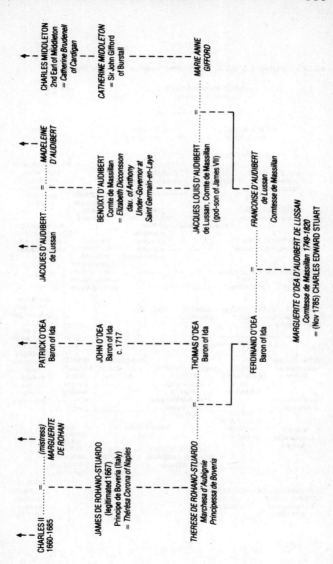

CHARLES II
1660–1685
= (mistress) MARGUERITE DE ROHAN

JAMES DE ROHANO-STUARDO
(legitimated 1667)
Principe de Boveria (Italy)
= Therèsa Corona of Naples

THERÈSE DE ROHANO-STUARDO
Marchesa d'Aubignie
Principessa de Boveria

PATRICK O'DEA
Baron of Ida

JOHN O'DEA
Baron of Ida
c. 1717

THOMAS O'DEA
Baron of Ida

FERDINAND O'DEA
Baron of Ida

JACQUES D'AUDIBERT
de Lussan

BENOIXT D'AUDIBERT
Comte de Massillan
= Elizabeth Dicconson
dau. of Anthony
Under-Governor at
Saint Germain-en-Laye

JACQUES LOUIS D'AUDIBERT
de Lussan, Comte de Massillan
(god-son of James VII)

FRANÇOISE D'AUDIBERT
de Lussan
Comtesse de Massillan

MARGUERITE O'DEA D'AUDIBERT DE LUSSAN
Comtesse de Massillan 1749–1820
= (Nov 1785) CHARLES EDWARD STUART

MADELEINE
D'AUDIBERT

CHARLES MIDDLETON
2nd Earl of Middleton
= Catherine Brudenell
of Cardigan

CATHERINE MIDDLETON
= Sir John Gifford
of Burstall

MARIE ANNE
GIFFORD

**HOUSES OF ROHAN & SOBIESKI** *Stuart related Houses of France and Poland*

PRINCE FERDINAND DE ROHAN
Archbishop de Cambrai
= (mistress)
*CHARLOTTE OF ALBANY*
dau. of Charles
Edward Stuart
by Clementina Walkinshaw
of Borrowfield

JULES HERCULE
Prince de Rohan
Duc de Montbazon
1726-1788

(married) <—

= *MARIE LOUISE
HENRIETTE
JEANNE DE LA
TOUR*, Duchesse
de Montbazon
1725-1781

—> (mistress)

= CHARLES EDWARD
STUART
Prince of Wales
1720-1788

CARDINAL HENRY
BENEDICT STUART
Duke of York
1725-1807 d.s.p.

PRINCE LOUIS
DE ROHAN
Cardinal-Archbishop
of Strasbourg
Grand Aumonier
of France

HENRI LOUIS DE ROHAN
Prince de Guéméné 1745-1809

CHARLES GODEFROID DE ROHAN-STUART
b. 1748  Mock death and burial in Jan 1749,
but died in England (Charles Stuart) 1820

**POPES FROM THE NORMAN CONQUEST**
*To the 1929 Lateran Treaty*

| POPE | TERM | POPE | TERM | POPE | TERM |
|---|---|---|---|---|---|
| Alexander II | 1061-1073 | Nicholas IV | 1288-1292 | Gregory XIII | 1572-1585 |
| Gregory VII | 1073-1085 | Celestine V | 1294 | Sixtus V | 1585-1590 |
| Victor III | 1086-1087 | Boniface VIII | 1294-1303 | Urban VII | 1590 |
| Urban II | 1088-1099 | Benedict XI | 1303-1304 | Gregory XIV | 1590-1591 |
| Paschal II | 1099-1118 | Clement V | 1305-1314 | Innocent IX | 1591 |
| Gelasius II | 1118-1119 | John XXII | 1316-1334 | Clement VIII | 1592-1605 |
| Callistus II | 1119-1124 | Benedict XII | 1334-1342 | Leo XI | 1605 |
| Honorius II | 1124-1130 | Clement VI | 1342-1352 | Paul V | 1605-1621 |
| Innocent II | 1130-1143 | Innocent VI | 1352-1362 | Gregory XV | 1621-1623 |
| Celestine II | 1143-1144 | Urban V | 1362-1370 | Urrban XII | 1623-1644 |
| Lucius II | 1144-1145 | Gregory XI | 1370-1378 | Innocent X | 1644-1655 |
| Eugene III | 1145-1153 | Urban VI | 1378-1389 | Alexander VII | 1655-1667 |
| Anastasius IV | 1153-1154 | Boniface IX | 1389-1404 | Clement IX | 1667-1669 |
| Adrian IV | 1154-1159 | Innocent VII | 1404-1406 | Clement X | 1670-1676 |
| Alexander III | 1159-1181 | Gregory XII | 1406-1415 | Innocent XI | 1676-1689 |
| Lucius III | 1181-1185 | Martin V | 1417-1431 | Alexander VIII | 1689-1691 |
| Urban III | 1185-1187 | Eugene IV | 1431-1447 | Innocent XII | 1691-1700 |
| Gregory VIII | 1187 | Nicholas V | 1447-1455 | Clement XI | 1700-1721 |
| Clement III | 1187-1191 | Callustus | 1455-1458 | Innocent XIII | 1721-1724 |
| Celestine III | 1191-1198 | Pius II | 1458-1464 | Benedict XIII | 1724-1730 |
| Innocent III | 1198-1216 | Paul II | 1464-1471 | Clement XII | 1730-1740 |
| Honorius III | 1216-1227 | Sixtus IV | 1471-1484 | Benedict XIV | 1740-1758 |
| Gregory IX | 1227-1241 | Innocent VIII | 1484-1492 | Clement XIII | 1758-1769 |
| Celestine IV | 1241 | Alexander VI | 1492-1503 | Clement XIV | 1769-1774 |
| Innocent V | 1243-1254 | Pius III | 1503 | Pius VI | 1775-1799 |
| Alexander IV | 1254-1261 | Julius II | 1503-1513 | Pius VII | 1800-1823 |
| Urban IV | 1261-1264 | Leo X | 1513-1521 | Leo XII | 1823-1829 |
| Clement IV | 1265-1268 | Adrian VI | 1522-1523 | Pius VIII | 1829-1830 |
| Gregory X | 1271-1276 | Clement VII | 1523-1534 | Gregory XVI | 1831-1846 |
| Innocent V | 1276 | Paul III | 1534-1549 | Pius IX | 1846-1878 |
| Adrian V | 1276 | Julius III | 1550-1555 | Leo XIII | 1878-1903 |
| John XXI | 1276-1277 | Marcellus II | 1555 | Pius X | 1903-1914 |
| Nicholas III | 1277-1280 | Paul IV | 1555-1559 | Benedict XV | 1914-1922 |
| Martin IV | 1281-1285 | Pius IV | 1559-1565 | Pius XI | 1922-1939 |
| Honorius IV | 1285-1287 | Pius V | 1566-1572 | | |

## REIGNING MONARCHS FROM THE WHIG REVOLUTION
*Britain and France – 1688 onwards*

### GREAT BRITAIN

#### ORANGE / STUART

**WILLIAM III**    1689-1702
Duke of Orange (Dutch)
Son of William of Nassau
and Mary Stuart, dau of
Charles I
And = *MARY II* (Stuart)    1689-1694
    Dau. of James VII (II)
    and 1st wife, Anne Hyde
    d.s.p.

*ANNE* (Stuart)    1702-1714
*Dau. of James VII (II)
and Anne Hyde of Clarendon
d.s.p.*

#### HANOVER

**GEORGE I**    1714-1727
[House of Guelph]
Duke of Brunswick-Luneburg
Son of Elector of Hanover (German)
= *Sophia Dorothy, dau. of George
    William, Duke of Zelle*

**GEORGE II**    1727-1760
Duke and Elector of Hanover
Son of George I
= *Whilhelmina Caroline
    dau. of John Frederick, the
    Margrave of Brandenburgh-Anspach*

**GEORGE III**    1760-1820
King of Hanover
Grandson of George II
Son of Frederick P.O.W.
= *Sophia Charlotte, dau. of
    Charles, Duke of Mecklenburg-
    Strelitz*

### FRANCE

#### BOURBON

Continuation of LOUIS XIV
until 1715 [See Chart:
STUART KINGS & CONTEMPORARIES ]

**LOUIS XV**    1715-1774
G.g-son of Louis XIV
Son of Louis, Duke of Burgundy
(d. 1712), son of Louis the
Dauphin (d.1711)
[Policies under Cardinal Fleury
to 1743]
= *Marie Leczinska of Poland*
Mistresses: (1) *Jeanne, Madame de
Pompadour* (2) *Marie, Madame du Barry*

FRENCH COLONIES (CANADA/INDIA) LOST
DURING SEVEN YEARS WAR 1756-1763

**LOUIS XVI**    1774-1793
Grandson of Louis XV
Son of Louis the Dauphin (d. 1765)
= *Marie Antoinette, daughter of
    Emperor Francis I and Maria Theresa*
Both Louis and *Marie Antoinette*
guillotined (1793) in Revolution

FRENCH REVOLUTION 1789-1799 ABOLISHED
ABSOLUTE MONARCHY IN FRANCE. SUPREME
COURT *PARLEMENT OF PARIS* ABOLISHED IN
1792 WHEN FIRST REPUBLIC PROCLAIMED

GEORGE IV      1820-1830
King of Hanover
Son of George III
= (2) *Caroline Amelia, dau.*
 *of Charles William Ferdinand,*
 *Duke of Brunswick-Wölfenbuttel*
Predeceased by daughter
No male heir

WILLIAM IV     1830-1837
King of Hanover
Brother of George IV
= *Amelia Adelaide, dau.*
 *of George Frederick, Duke*
 *of Saxe Meiningen*
Predeceased by daughters
No male heir

VICTORIA      1837-1901
*(Alexandrina Victoria)*
*Regina et Imperatrix*
*Niece of William IV*
*Dau. of his brother, Edward,*
*Duke of Kent, and Princess*
*Victoria Mary, dau. of*
*Francis Frederick, Duke of*
*Saxe-Saalfeld-Coburg*
= *Francis Albert, Prince of*
 *Saxe-Coburg-Gotha. Son of*
 *Ernest I of Saxe Coburg*
 *and Gotha*

SAXE COBURG-GOTHA

EDWARD VII     1901-1910
[Albert Edward]
Son of Queen Victoria
= *Princess Alexandra, dau.*
 *of Christian IX of Denmark*

LOUIS XVII     1793-1795
Nominal King of France
Son of Louis XVI
Died in prison

LOUIS XVIII    1795-1824
Count of Provence
Nominal King of France
Uncle of Louis XVII
Brother of Louis XVI
Lived in exile until 1814

COUP D'ETAT BY NAPOLEON BONAPARTE
BROUGHT REVOLUTION TO AN END IN NOV.
1799. HE WAS CONSUL FROM 1802, AND
EMPEROR NAPOLEON I OF THE FRENCH
1804-1815. INTRODUCED THE CIVIL *CODE
NAPOLEON*, WHICH STILL PROVIDES THE
BASIS OF FRENCH LAW. d. 1821

CHARLES X     1824-1830
Count of Artois
Brother of Louis XVI and XVIII
British exile in Revolution
Returned to France 1824
Abdicated 1830

LOUIS PHILIPPE   1830-1848
[The Citizen King]
Son of Duke of Orleans in
descent from Philip of Orleans,
brother of Louis XIV
Originally supported Revolution
against Bourbon monarchy. Styled
King of the French (not of France)
Abdicated d. (England) 1850

1848 REVOLUTION PROCLAIMED SECOND
REPUBLIC, WITH 44 SUCCESSIVE GOVERNMENTS
BETWEEN 1918 AND 1940

## WINDSOR

FAMILY NAME CHANGED TO WINDSOR
IN WORLD WAR I (1917) TO VEIL
GERMAN HERITAGE. WINDSOR WAS THE
SURNAME OF KING EDWARD III (d. 1377)

GEORGE V                          1910-1936
Son of Edward VII
= *Princess Mary of Teck*

EDWARD VIII                       1936
Duke of Windsor
1st son of George V
= *Mrs. Wallis Simpson*
  Abdicated

GEORGE VI                         1936-1952
[Prince Albert]
2nd son of George V
= *Elizabeth Bowes-Lyon, dau. of
  Claude, Earl of Strathmore*

ELIZABETH II                      1952-
*Daughter of George VI*
= (1947) Philip (Duke of Edinburgh)
  Son of Prince Andrew, son of King
  George I of Greece. Great-grandson
  of Christian IX of Denmark. Descended
  in female line via mother, *Princess
  Alice of Battenburg*, from the German
  House of Hesse, and from Queen Victoria.

  When Saxe Coburg-Gotha became Windsor
  in W.W.I, the BATTENBURG name was also
  changed to Mountbatten. Philip assumed
  the name of MOUNTBATTEN on gaining
  British citizenship in 1947.

EUROPEAN ECONOMIC COMMUNITY (COMMON
MARKET) – AN ORGANISATION OF WESTERN
STATES – WAS CREATED IN 1957 BY THE
TREATY OF ROME (NOW EUROPEAN UNION)

Subsequent to the 1830 abdication of King
CHARLES X, the House of Bourbon retained
its *de jure* heritage irrespective of the
politically elected Louis Philippe. Charles
X's nominated successor was his grandson, the
Duc de Chambord who was HENRY V 1830-1833.
He was succeeded by his nephew, Louis, Duc
d'Aquitaine, as LOUIS XIX 1833-1918. Louis
died with no son, but nominated the Spanish
Bourbon line to succeed. Thus, James, Duke
of Segovia, 2nd son of Alfonso III, became
JACQUES I OF FRANCE 1918-1975. His son, the
Duc d'Anjou and Cadiz, became ALFONSE I
1975-1989. The present successor is his son,
Louis Alfonso, Duc d'Anjou and Cadiz, who has
been *de jure* KING LOUIS XX from 1989

FRANCE FELL TO GERMANY IN WORLD WAR II

LIBERATED IN 1944. DE GAULLE ESTABLISHED
PROVISIONAL GOVERNMENT. FOURTH REPUBLIC
PROCLAIMED IN 1946

DE GAULLE RECALLED AS PRESIDENT OF THE
FIFTH REPUBLIC 1958. RESIGNED 1969

# BIBLIOGRAPHY

## Biblical and Scriptural

Aaron, R, *Jesus of Nazareth the Hidden Years*, (translated by F Frenhaye), Hamish Hamilton, London, 1962

Allegro, JM, *The Dead Sea Scrolls*, Penguin, Harmondsworth, 1964

Anderson, H, *Jesus and Christian Origins*, Oxford University Press, 1964

Baigent, M, Leigh, R and Lincoln, H, *The Dead Sea Scrolls Deception*, Jonathan Cape, London, 1991

Barclay, J, *The Mind of Jesus*, Harper & Row, New York, USA, 1960

Black, M, *The Scrolls and Christian Origins*, Thomas Nelson, London, 1961

Brandon, SGF, *The Fall of Jerusalem and the Christian Church*, SPCK, London, 1951

Brandon, SGF, *Jesus and the Zealots*, Charles Scribner's Sons, New York, USA, 1967

Brooke, G, *Temple Scroll Studies*, Sheffield Academic Press, 1989

Catchpole, DR, *The Trial of Jesus*, EJ Brill, Leiden, Netherlands, 1971

Chase, ME, *Life and Language in the Old Testament*, Collins, London, 1956

Cranfield, CEB, *The Gospel According to St. Mark*, Cambridge University Press, 1959

Danielou, J, *The Dead Sea Scrolls and Primitive Christianity*, (translated by S Attansio), New American Library, New York, USA, 1962

Dart, J, *The Laughing Saviour*, Harper & Row, New York, USA, 1976

Dodd, CH, *Historical Tradition in the Fourth Gospel*, Cambridge University Press, 1963

Doresse, J, *The Secret Books of the Egyptian Gnostics* (translated by P Mairet), Hollis & Carter, London, 1960

Dupont-Sommer, A, *The Essene Writings from Qumrân* (translated by G Vermes), Basil Blackwell, Oxford, 1961

Dupont-Sommer, A, *The Jewish Sect of Qumrân and the Essenes*, Vallentine Mitchell, London, 1954

Eisenman, RH, *Maccabees, Zadokites, Christians and Qumrân*, EJ Brill, Leiden, Netherlands, 1983

Eisenman, RH, *James the Just in the Habakkuk Pesher*, EJ Brill, Leiden, Netherlands, 1986

Faber-Kaiser, A, *Jesus Died in Kashmir*, Abacus/Sphere, London, 1978

Filliette, E, *Saint Mary Magdalene, Her Life and Times*, Society of St. Mary Magdalene, Newton Lower Falls, MA, USA, 1983

Finkel, A, *The Pharisees and the Teacher of Nazareth*, EJ Brill, Leiden, Netherlands, 1964

Fleetwood, The Revd J, *The Life of Our Lord and Saviour Jesus Christ*, William Mackenzie, Glasgow, c.1900

Finkel, A, *The Pharisees and the Teacher of Nazareth*, E.J. Brill, Leiden, Netherlands, 1964

Gaster, TH, *Samaritan Eschatology – Oral Law and Ancient Traditions*, Search, London, 1932

Grant, M, *The Jews in the Roman World*, Weidenfeld & Nicolson, London, 1973

Grant, M, *Herod The Great*, Weidenfeld & Nicolson, London, 1971

James, MR (editor), *The Apocryphal New Testament*, Clarendon Press, Oxford, 1924

Jeremias, J, *Jerusalem in the Time of Jesus*, SCM Press, London, 1969

Josephus, F, *The Jewish Wars* (translated by GA Williamson), Penguin, Harmondsworth, 1959

Josephus, F, *Antiquities of the Jews and Wars of the Jews* (translated by W Whitson), Thomas Nelson, London, 1862

Josephus, F, *The Works of Flavius Josephus*, Milner & Sowerby, London, 1870

Joyce, Donovan, *The Jesus Scroll*, Angus & Robertson, London, 1973

Kenyon, KM, *Jerusalem: Excavating 3000 Years of History*, Thames & Hudson, London, 1967

Kersten, H and Gruber, ER, *The Jesus Conspiracy*, Barnes & Noble, New York, USA, 1995

Knox, W, *Sources of the Synoptic Gospels*, Cambridge University Press, 1959

Lacordaire, Rev P, *Saint Mary Magdalene*, Thomas Richardson, Derby, 1880

Lewis, Rev LS, *St. Joseph of Arimathea at Glastonbury*, AR Mobray, London, 1927

Malvern, M, *Venus in Sackcloth*, Southern Illinois University Press, USA, 1975

Mead, GRS, *The Gnostic John the Baptiser*, John M Watkins, London, 1924

Milik, JT, *Ten Years of Discovery in the Wilderness of Judaea* (translated by J Strugnell), SCM Press, London, 1959

Osman, A, *The House of The Messiah*, Harper Collins, London, 1992

Osman, A, *Moses Pharaoh of Egypt*, Grafton/Collins, London, 1990

Pagels, E, *The Gnostic Gospels*, Weidenfeld & Nicolson, London, 1980

Patai, R, *The Hebrew Goddess*, Wayne State University Press, Detroit, USA, 1967

Perowne, S, *The Life and Times of Herod the Great*, Hodder & Stoughton, London, 1956

Perowne, S, *The Later Herods*, Hodder & Stoughton, London, 1958

Platt, RH (editor), *The Lost Books of the Bible*, World Publishing, New York, USA, 1963

Ringgren, H, *The Faith of Qumrân* (translated by ET Sander), Fondress Press, Philadelphia, USA, 1973

Robinson, JM (director), Coptic Gnostic Library: Institute for Antiquity and Christianity, *The Nag Hammadi Library*, EJ Brill, Leiden, Netherlands, 1977

Schonfield, HJ, *The Authentic New Testament*, Denis Dobson, London, 1956

Schonfield, HJ, *The Essene Odyssey*, Element Books, Shaftesbury, 1984

Schonfield, HJ, *The Passover Plot*, Element Books, Shaftesbury, 1985

Smallwood, EM, *The Jews Under Roman Rule*, EJ Brill, Leiden, Netherlands, 1976

Smith, M, *The Secret Gospel*, Victor Gollancz, London, 1974

Stone, M, *When God Was a Woman*, Dial Press, New York, USA, 1976

Thackery, HS, *Josephus the Man and Historian*, KTAV, Hoboken, NJ, USA, 1967

Thiering, B, *Jesus the Man*, Doubleday/Transworld, London, 1992

Times, The, *Atlas of the Bible*, Times Books, London, 1987

Vermes, G, *The Dead Sea Scrolls in English*, Pelican, Harmondsworth, 1987

Von Daniken, E, *Chariots of the Gods*, Souvenir Press, London, 1969

Walker, B, *Gnosticism*, Aquarian Press, Wellingborough, 1983

Williamson, GA, *The World of Josephus*, Secker & Warburg, London, 1964

Wilson, AN, *Jesus*, Sinclair Stevenson, London, 1992

Wilson, E, *The Dead Sea Scrolls*, Collins, London, 1971

Yadin, Y, *The Temple Scroll: Hidden Law*, Weidenfeld & Nicolson, London, 1985

Yadin, Y, *Masada: Herod's Last Fortress*, Weidenfeld & Nicolson, London, 1966

## Cults and Religion

Adamnan, St, *A Life of Saint Columba* (translated by Wentworth Huyshe), George Routledge, London, 1908

Aradi, Z, *Shrines of Our Lady*, Farrar, Strauss & Young, New York, USA, 1954

Baigent, M, Leigh, R and Lincoln, H, *The Messianic Legacy*, Jonathan Cape, London, 1986

Baldock, J, *Christian Symbolism*, Element Books, Shaftesbury, 1990

Bander, P, *The Prophecies of St. Malachy and St. Columbkille*, Colin Smythe, Gerrards Cross, 1979

Baring-Gould, S, *The Lives of the British Saints*, (with J Fisher), Cymmrodorion Society, London, 1907–1913

Bede (The Venerable of Jarrow), *The Ecclesiastical History of the English Nation* (translated by JA Giles), Dent/Everyman, London, 1970

Begg, ECM, *The Cult of the Black Virgin*, Arkana, London, 1985

Bernard de Clairvaux, *On the Song of Songs* (translated by K Walsh), Cistercian Publishers, Michigan, USA, 1976

Bowen, EG, *The Settlements of the Celtic Saints in Wales*, University of Wales Press, Cardiff, 1956

Bull, NJ, *The Rise of the Church*, Heinemann, London, 1967

Bultman, R, *Primitive Christianity in its Contemporary Setting* (translated by RH Fuller), Fontana/Collins, Glasgow, 1960

Butterworth, GW, (translator), *Clement of Alexandria*, Heinemann, London, 1968

Chadwick, H, *Priscillian of Avila*, Oxford University Press, 1976

Chadwick, H, *The Early Church*, Penguin, Harmondsworth, 1978

Chadwick, NK, *The Age of the Saints in the Early Celtic Church*, Oxford University Press, 1961

Clement (Saint) of Alexandria, *Clementine Homilies and Apostolical Constitutions* (translation), Ante-Nicene Library, T & T Clark, Edinburgh, 1870

Constantinus of Lyons (c.AD 480), *The Life of Saint Germanus of Auxerre* (in *The Western Fathers*), edited by W. Levinson, translated by FR Hoare, Sheed & Ward, London, 1954

Duncan, A, *Celtic Christianity*, Element Books, Shaftesbury, 1992

Eusebius, of Caesaria, *History of the Church from Christ to Constantine* (translated by GA Williamson), Penguin, Harmondsworth, 1981

Eusebius, of Caesaria, *Ecclesiastical History* (translated by CF Crusé), George Bell, London, 1874

Farmer, DH, *The Oxford Dictionary of Saints*, Clarendon Press, Oxford, 1978

Gilson, E, *The Mystical Theology of Saint Bernard* (translated by AHC Downes), Sheed & Ward, London, 1940

Gimbutas, M, *The Gods and Goddesses of Old Europe*, Thames & Hudson, London, 1974

Godwin, J, *Mystery Religions in the Ancient World*, Thames & Hudson, London, 1981

Gougaud, Dom L, *Christianity in Celtic Lands* (translated by M Joynt), Four Courts Press, Dublin, 1932

Graves, R and Podro, J, *The Nazarene Gospel Restored*, Cassell, London, 1953

Green, M, *The Gods of the Celts*, Alan Sutton, Gloucester, 1986

Halsberghe, GS, *The Cult of Sol Invictus*, EJ Brill, Leiden, Netherlands, 1972

Herford, RT, *Christianity in Talmud and Midrash*, Williams & Norgate, London, 1903

Hewins, Prof WAS, *The Royal Saints of Britain*, Chiswick Press, London, 1929

Jacobus de Voragine, *The Golden Legend* (translation by William Caxton, edited by G V O'Neill), Cambridge University Press, 1972

James, BS, *Saint Bernard of Clairvaux*, Harper, New York, USA, 1957

James, EO, *The Cult of the Mother Goddess*, Thames & Hudson, London, 1959

Jameson, A, *Legends of the Madonna*, Houghton Mifflin, Boston, USA, 1895

Johnston, Rev TJ, *A History of the Church of Ireland*, APCK, Dublin, 1953

Jonas, H, *The Gnostic Religion*, Routledge, London, 1992

Jowett, GF, *The Drama of the Lost Disciples*, Covenant Books, London, 1961

Knowles, D, *The Monastic Order in England*, Cambridge University Press, 1950

Kramer, S, *The Sacred Marriage Rite*, Indiana University Press, Bloomington, USA, 1969

Lewis, Rev LS, *Glastonbury, the Mother of Saints*, St Stephen's Press, Bristol, 1925

MacLean, GRD, *Praying With the Highland Christians*, Triangle/SPCK, London, 1988

Margoliouth, DS, *Mohammed and the Rise of Islam*, Putnam, London, 1931

Marsden, J, *The Illustrated Colmcille*, Macmillan, London, 1991

Martin, M, *The Decline and Fall of the Roman Church*, Secker & Warburg, London, 1982

Nash-Williams, VE, *The Early Christian Monuments of Wales*, University of Wales Press, Cardiff, 1950

Piggot, S, *The Druids*, Penguin, Harmondsworth, 1974

Pope, MH, *Song of Songs*, Garden City/Doubleday, New York, USA, 1977

Qualls-Corbett, N, *The Sacred Prostitute*, Inner City Books, Toronto, Canada, 1988

Rees, The Revd R, *An Essay on the Welsh Saints*, Longman, London, 1836

Rees, The Revd WJ, *Lives of the Cambro-British Saints*, Welsh MSS Society/Longman, London 1853

Ross, A, *Pagan Celtic Britain*, Cardinal/Sphere Books, London, 1974

Rutherford, W, *The Druids and Their Heritage*, Gordon & Cremonesi, London, 1978

Scott, J, *The Early History of Glastonbury*, Boydell Press, London, 1981

Taylor, G, *Our Neglected Heritage*, Covenant Books, London, 1969–74

Taylor, JW, *The Coming of the Saints*, Covenant Books, London, 1969

Wade-Evans, AW, *Welsh Christian Origins*, Alden Press, Oxford, 1934

Warren, FE, *The Liturgy of the Celtic Church*, Oxford University Press, 1881

## Ancient History and Prehistory

Daniel, G (editor), *Encyclopedia of Archaeology*, Macmillan, London, 1978

Guthrie, WKC, *The Greeks and Their Gods*, Methuen, London, 1950

Hawking, S, *A Brief History of Time*, Bantam Press, London, 1992

Kramer, S, *History Begins at Sumer*, Thames & Hudson, London, 1958

Michell, H, *Sparta*, Cambridge University Press, 1964

Rohl, D, *A Test of Time*, Century, London, 1995

Roux, G, *Ancient Iraq*, George Allen & Unwin, London, 1964

Woolley, CL, *Ur of the Chaldees*, Ernest Benn, London, 1930


## Mythology and Folklore

Ames, D (translator), *Greek Mythology* (from *Mythologie Générale Larousse*), Paul Hamlyn, London, 1963

Bromwich, R (translator), *The Welsh Triads*, University of Wales Press, Cardiff, 1961

Conran, A, *The Penguin Book of Welsh Verse*, Penguin, Harmondsworth, 1967

Crossley-Holland, K, *British Folk Tales*, Macmillan, London, 1971

Curtin, J, *Hero Tales of Ireland*, Macmillan, London, 1894

Davidson, HE, *Gods and Myths in Northern Europe*, Penguin, Harmondsworth, 1964

Delaney, F, *Legends of the Celts*, Hodder & Stoughton, London, 1989

Dillon, M, *The Cycles of the Kings*, Oxford University Press, 1946

Gantz, J (translator), *The Mabinogion*, Penguin, Harmondsworth, 1976

Graves, R, *The White Goddess*, Faber & Faber, London, 1961

Graves, R, *Mammon and the Black Goddess*, Cassell, London, 1965

Guest, Lady C (translator), *The Mabinogion*, John Jones, Cardiff, 1977

Hadas, M and Smith, M, *Heroes and Gods*, Freeport, New York, USA, 1965

Matthews, C, *Mabon and the Mysteries of Britain*, Arkana, London, 1987

O'Rahilly, T, *Early Irish History and Mythology*, Dublin Institute for Advanced Studies, 1946

Price, G (translator), *William, Count of Orange* (French trad), Dent, London, 1975

Rhys, J, *Celtic Folklore*, Clarendon Press, Oxford, 1901

Tatlock, JSP, *The Legendary History of Britain*, University of California, USA, 1950

Westwood, J, *A Guide to Legendary Britain*, Paladin, London, 1987

Williamson, J, *The Oak King, the Holly King and the Unicorn*, Harper & Row, New York, USA, 1986

## Celts, Romans and the Dark Ages

Chadwick, NK (editor), *Studies in Early British History*, Cambridge University Press, 1954

Chadwick, NK, *Celtic Britain*, Praeger, New York, USA, 1963

Chadwick, NK, *Celt and Saxon*, Cambridge University Press, 1964

Chadwick, NK, *The Celts*, Penguin, Harmondsworth, 1970

Cunliffe, B, *The Celtic World*, Bodley Head, London, 1979

Delaney, F, *The Celts*, Grafton/Collins, London, 1989

Dillon, M and Chadwick, N, *The Celtic Realms*, Weidenfield & Nicholson, London, 1967

Ellis, PB, *The Celtic Empire*, Constable, London, 1990

Gurney, R, *Celtic Heritage*, Chatto & Windus, London, 1969

Herm, G, *The Celts*, Weidenfeld & Nicolson, London, 1976

Hubert, H, *The Rise of the Celts*, Keegan Paul, London, 1934

Hubert, H, *The Greatness and Decline of the Celts*, Keegan Paul, London, 1934

Markale, J, *Women of the Celts* (translated by A Mygind, C Hauch and P Henry) Inner Traditions, Vermont, USA, 1986

Matthews, C, *The Celtic Tradition*, Element Books, Shaftesbury 1989

Nennius, *Historia Brittonium* (translated by J Morris), Phillimore, Chichester, 1980

Rees, A and B, *Celtic Heritage*, Thames & Hudson, London, 1961

Thomas, C, *Celtic Britain*, Thames & Hudson, London, 1986

Wood, M, *In Search of the Dark Ages*, BBC Books, London, 1981

## Scotland

Adam, F, *Clans, Septs and Regiments of the Scottish Highlands* (Revised by Sir T Innes of Learney), Johnston & Bacon, Edinburgh, 1965

Anderson, AO, *Early Sources of Scottish History* (Edited by M. Anderson), Paul Watkins, London, 1990

Anderson, J, *Scotland in Early Christian Times*, David Douglas, Edinburgh, 1881

Bain, J, *Calendar of Documents Relating to Scotland*, HM Stationery Office, Edinburgh, 1881–8

Bain, R, *The Clans and Tartans of Scotland*, Fontana/Collins, Glasgow, 1981

Barbour, J, *The Bruce*, William Mackenzie, Glasgow, 1909

Barrow, GWS, *Robert Bruce and the Community of the Realm of Scotland*, Eyre & Spottiswoode, London, 1965

Barrow, GWS, *The Kingdom of the Scots*, Edward Arnold, London, 1973

Chadwick, HM, *Early Scotland: The Picts, Scots and Welsh of Southern Scotland*, Cambridge University Press, 1949

Fairweather, B, *Highland Heritage*, Glencoe & N Lorne Folk Museum, Argyll, 1984

Harry, The Revd GO, *The Genealogy of the High and Mighty Monarch, James*, Simon Stafford, London, 1604

Hewison, JK, *The Isle of Bute in the Olden Time*, William Blackwood, Edinburgh, 1895

Kermack, WR, *Scottish Highlands, A Short History c.300–1746*, Johnston & Bacon, Edinburgh, 1957

Kermack, WR, *The Clan MacGregor*, Johnston & Bacon, Edinburgh, 1979

Maciain, RR, *The Clans of the Scottish Highlands*, Webb & Bower, Exeter, 1983

Mackenzie, Sir G, *A Defence of the Antiquity of the Royal Line of Scotland*, HM Printers, Andrew Anderson, Edinburgh, 1685

Mackie, JDA, *A History of Scotland*, Pelican, Harmondsworth 1964

Moncrieffe, Sir I, *The Highland Clans*, Barrie & Jenkins, London, 1982

Murray, J (Duke of Atholl), *Chronicles of Atholl and Tullibardine Families*, Ballantyne, London, 1908

Platts, B, *Scottish Hazard*, Proctor Press, London, 1985–90

Shaw, RC, *Post Roman Carlisle and the Kingdoms of the North-West*, Guardian Press, Preston, 1964

Skene, WF, *Chronicles of the Picts and Scots*, HM General Register, Edinburgh, 1867

Skene, WF, *Celtic Scotland*, David Douglas, Edinburgh, 1886–90

Starforth, M, *Clan MacDougall*, Bell & Bain Press, Glasgow 1960

Stewart, Maj J (of Ardvorlich), *The Stewarts*, Johnston & Bacon, Edinburgh, 1954

Watson, WJ, *The History of the Celtic Place Names of Scotland*, William Blackwood, Edinburgh, 1926

Ireland and Wales

Bartrum, PC, *Early Welsh Genealogical Tracts*, University of Wales Press, Cardiff, 1966

Charlsworth, MP, *The Lost Province*, University of Wales Press, Cardiff, 1949

Keating, G, *The History of Ireland – 1640* (translated by David Comyn and The Revd PS Dinneen), Irish Texts Society, London, 1902

Kenney, JF, *The Sources for the Early History of Ireland*, Four Courts Press, Dublin, 1966

Macneill, E, *Celtic Ireland*, Martin Lester, Dublin, 1921

Morris, J (translator), *Annales Cambriae* (The Annals of Wales), [Nennius, British History and the Welsh Annals], Phillimore, Chichester, 1980

Munch, PA and Goss, The Revd Dr, *The Chronicle of Man*, The Manx Society, Isle of Man, 1974

O'Rahilly, C, *Ireland and Wales*, Longmans Green, London, 1924

Rhys, J, and Brynmore-Jones, D, *The Welsh People*, T. Fisher Unwin, London, 1900

Skene, WF, *The Four Ancient Books of Wales*, David Douglas, Edinburgh, 1868

Simms, K, *From Kings to Warlords*, Boydell Press, London, 1987

Williams, AH, *An Introduction to the History of Wales*, University of Wales Press, Cardiff, 1962.

## England and Britain General

Blair, PH, *The Origins of Northumbria*, Northumberland Press, Gateshead, 1948

Copley, GK, *The Conquest of Wessex in the Sixth Century*, Pheonix House, London, 1954

Deacon, R, *A History of the British Secret Service*, Grafton/Collins, London, 1982

Deanesly, M, *A Medieval History of Europe 476–911*, Methuen, London, 1956

Feiling, K, *A History of England*, Book Club Associates, London, 1972

Garmonsway, GN (translator), *The Anglo-Saxon Chronicle*, Dent/Everyman, London, 1967

Geoffrey of Monmouth, *The History of the Kings of Britain* (edited by L Thorpe), Penguin, Harmondsworth, 1966

Gildas, *De Excidio et Conquestu Britanniae* (translated by M Winterbottom), Phillimore, Chichester, 1978

Green, VHH, *The Hanoverians 1714–1815*, Edward Arnold, London, 1948

Harvey, J, *The Plantagenets*, BT Batsford, London, 1959

Hodgkin, RH, *A History of the Anglo-Saxons*, Oxford University Press, 1952

Lloyd, LC, *The Origins of Some Anglo-Norman Families* (edited by C Clay and D Douglas), Harleian Society, Leeds, 1951

Oman, Sir C, *England Before the Norman Conquest*, Methuen, London, 1938

Paine, L, *Britain's Intelligence Service*, Robert Hale, London, 1979

Petrie, Sir C, *The Stuarts*, Eyre & Spottiswoode, London, 1937

Pryde, GS, *The Treaty of Union Between Scotland and England 1707*, Thomas Nelson, London, 1950

Seton, W, *Relations of Henry, Cardinal York, With the British Government*, The Royal Historical Society, London, 1919

Skeet, FJA, *The Life and Letters of HRH Charlotte, Duchess of Albany*, Eyre & Spottiswoode, London, 1922

Stenton, FM, *Anglo-Saxon England*, Oxford University Press, 1950

Thomas, C, *Britain and Ireland in Early Christian Times*, Thames & Hudson, London, 1971

Whitelock, D, *English Historical Documents (AD 500–1042)*, Eyre & Spottiswoode, London, 1955

William of Malmesbury, *Chronicles of the Kings of England*, Bell and Daldy, London, 1866

William of Malmesbury, *The Antiquities of Glastonbury* (translated by F Lomax), Talbot/JMF Books, Llanerch, 1980

## European History

Castries, Duc de (Académie Française), *The Lives of the Kings and Queens of France* (translated by A Dobell), Weidenfeld & Nicolson, London, 1979

Chadwick, NK, *Early Brittany*, University of Wales Press, Cardiff, 1969

Crankshaw, E, *The Fall of the House of Habsburg*, Longman, London, 1963

Davidson, MB, *The Concise History of France*, American Heritage, New York, USA, 1971

Davis, RHC, *A History of Medieval Europe*, Longmans Green, London, 1957

Deanesly, Margaret, *A History of Early Medieval Europe 476–911*, Methuen, London, 1956

Dill, Sir S, *Roman Society in Gaul in the Merovingian Age*, Macmillan, London, 1926

Giot, PR, *Brittany*, Thames and Hudson, London, 1960

Gregory of Tours, *A History of the Franks* (translated by L Thorpe), Penguin, Harmondsworth, 1964

Kendrick, TD, *A History of the Vikings*, Frank Cass, London, 1930

Lindsay, J, *The Normans and Their World*, Purnell, London, 1974

McKendrick, M, *A Concise History of Spain*, Cassell, London, 1972

Meade, M, *Eleanor of Aquitaine*, F Muller, London, 1978

Painter, S, *A History of the Middle Ages*, Macmillan, London, 1973

Roget, FF, *French History, Literature and Philology*, Williams & Norgate, London, 1904

Round, JH, *Calendar of Documents Preserved in France 918–1206*, Eyre & Spottiswoode, London, 1899

Round, JH, *Studies in Peerage and Family History*, Constable, London, 1901

Sackville-West, V, *Saint Joan of Arc*, Michael Joseph, London, 1936

Smith, GA, *The Historical Geography of the Holy Land*, Fontana/Collins, Glasgow 1966

Spence, K, *Brittany and the Bretons*, Victor Gollancz, London, 1978

Stanley, JE, *King René d'Anjou and his Seven Queens*, John Long, London, 1912

Tacitus, *The Annals of Imperial Rome*, Translated by M Grant, Cassell, London, 1963

Thompson, EA, *A History of Atilla and the Huns*, Clarendon Press, Oxford, 1948

Thompson, JM, *The French Revolution*, Basil Blackwell, Oxford, 1964

Thorpe, L (translator), *The Life of Charlemagne*, Penguin, Harmondsworth, 1979

Ullman, W, *A History of Political Thought in the Middle Ages*, Penguin, Harmondsworth, 1970

Wallace-Hadrill, JM, *The Long Haired Kings*, Methuen, London, 1962

Wells, HG, *The Outline of History*, Cassell, London, 1920

Zuckerman, AJ, *A Jewish Princedom in Feudal France*, Columbia University Press, New York, USA, 1972

## Knights Templars and Crusades

Andressohn, JC, *The Ancestry and Life of Godfrey of Bouillon*, University of Indiana Press, USA, 1947

Baigent, M and Leigh, R, *The Temple and the Lodge*, Jonathan Cape, London, 1989

Barber, M, *The Trial of the Templars*, Cambridge University Press, 1978

Birks, W and Gilbert, RA, *The Treasure of Montségur*, Crucible/Thorsons, London, 1987

Delaforge, G, *The Templar Tradition in the Age of Aquarius*, Threshold, Vermont, USA, 1897

Durman, E, *The Templars, Knights of God*, Aquarian Press, Wellingborough, 1988

Guilliame, de Tyre, *A History of Deeds Done Beyond the Sea* (translated by E A Babcock and AC Krey), Columbia University Press, New York, 1943

Howarth, S, *The Knights Templar*, Collins, London, 1982

Joinville, Sire J de, *Chronicles of the Crusades* (translated by M Shaw), Penguin, Harmondsworth, 1976

McMahon, N, *The Story of the Hospitallers of Saint John of God*, MH Gill, Dublin, 1958

Oldenbourg, Z, *Massacre at Montségur* (translated by P Green), Pantheon, New York, USA, 1961

Runciman, S, *A History of the Crusades*, Cambridge University Press, 1951

Seward, D, *The Monks of War*, Paladin/Granada, St Albans, 1974

Smith, JR, *The Knights of Saint John of Jerusalem and Cyprus*, Macmillan, London, 1987

## Freemasonry and the Rose Cross

Cartwright, EH, *Masonic Ritual*, Lewis Masonic, Shepperton, 1985

Fuller, JO, *Sir Francis Bacon*, East-West Publications, London, 1981

Gould, RF, *Gould's History of Freemasonry*, Caxton, London, 1933

Gray, T, *The Orange Order*, Bodley Head, London, 1972

Hamill, J, *The Craft, A History of English Freemasonry*, Crucible/Thorsons, London, 1986

Horne, A, *King Solomon's Temple in the Masonic Tradition*, Aquarian Press, Wellingborough, 1972

Jones, BE, *Freemasons' Guide and Compendium*, Harrap, London, 1956

Jones, BE, *Freemasons' Book of the Royal Arch*, Harrap, London, 1957

Knight, S, *The Brotherhood – The Secret World of the Freemasons*, Granada, St Albans, 1984

Lawrence, J, *Freemasonry, a Religion*, Kingsway, Eastbourne, 1987

Phillips, G, and Keatman, M, *The Shakespeare Conspiracy*, Century, London, 1994

Waite, AE, *The New Encyclopedia of Freemasonry*, Weathervane, New York, USA, 1970

Ward, JSM, *Who Was Hiram Abiff?*, Baskerville, London, 1925

Ward, JSM, *Freemasonry and the Ancient Gods*, Baskerville, London, 1926

Yates, FA, *The Rosicrucian Enlightenment*, Routledge & Kegan Paul, London, 1972

## Ancient and Esoteric Science

Adams, H, *Mont Saint Michel and Chartres*, Houghton Mifflin, Boston, USA, 1913

Arrien, A, *The Tarot Handbook*, Aquarian Press, Wellingborough, 1987

Bauval, R and Gilbert, A, *The Orion Mystery*, Heinemann, London, 1994

Bayley, H, *The Lost Language of Symbolism*, Williams & Norgate, London, 1912

Butler, EM, *The Myth of the Magus*, Cambridge University Press, 1948

Case, PF, *The Tarot*, Macoy, VA, USA, 1947

Cavendish, R, *The Tarot*, Michael Joseph, London, 1975

Charpentier, L, *The Mysteries of Chartres Cathedral*, Research Into Lost Knowledge Organization/Thorsons, Wellingborough, 1972

Dobbs, BJT, *The Foundations of Newton's Alchemy*, Cambridge University Press, 1975

Douglas, A, *The Tarot*, Victor Gollancz, London, 1972

Fell, C, *John Dee*, Constable, London, 1909

Harrison, M, *The Roots of Witchcraft*, Frederick Muller, London, 1973

Howard, M, *The Occult Conspiracy*, Rider/Century Hutchinson, London, 1989

Hulme, EF, *Symbolism in Christian Art*, Swann Sonnenschein, London, 1891

Lincoln, H, *The Holy Place*, Jonathan Cape, London, 1991

Lucie-Smith, E, *Symbolist Art*, Thames & Hudson, London, 1972

Mathers, SLM, *Astral Projection, Ritual Magic and Alchemy*, Aquarian Press, Wellingborough, 1987

Michell, J, *Ancient Metrology*, Pentacle Books, Bristol, 1981

Michell, J, *The Dimensions of Paradise*, Thames & Hudson, London, 1988

Pennick, N, *Sacred Geometry*, Turnstone, Wellingborough, 1980

Pincus-Witten, R, *Occult Symbolism in France*, Garland, London, 1976

Richards, S, *Levitation*, Thorsons, Wellingborough, 1980

Roberts, JM, *The Mythology of the Secret Societies*, Granada, St Albans, 1974

Rougemont, D de, *Love in the Western World* (translated by M. Belgion), Princeton University Press, New Jersey, USA, 1983

Silberer, H, *Hidden Symbolism of Alchemy and the Occult Arts*, Dover Publications, New York, USA, 1971

Steiner, R, *An Outline of Occult Science*, Anthroposophic Press, New York, USA, 1972

Von Franz, ML, *Alchemy*, Inner City Books, Toronto, Canada, 1980

## Heraldry and Chivalry

Aveling, ST, *Heraldry, Ancient and Modern*, Frederick Warne, London, 1873

Barber, R, *The Knight and Chivalry*, Longman, London, 1970

Brook-Little, JP, *Boutell's Heraldry*, Frederick Warne, London, 1969

Capellanus, A, *The Art of Courtly Love* (translated by JJ Parry), Columbia University Press, New York, USA, 1941

Foster, J, *The Dictionary of Heraldry*, Studio Editions, London, 1994

Fox-Davies, AC, *A Complete Guide to Heraldry*, TC & EC Jack, Edinburgh, 1929

Hooke, SH, *The Siege Perilous*, SCM Press, London, 1956

Kennedy, B, *Knighthood in the Mort d'Arthur*, DS Brewer, Cambridge, 1986

Platts, B, *Origins of Heraldry*, Proctor Press, London, 1980

## Arthurian History and Romance

Ashe, G, *Camelot and the Vision of Albion*, Heinemann, London, 1971

Ashe, G, *Avalonian Quest*, Methuen, London, 1982

Barber, R, *Arthur of Albion*, Boydell Press, London, 1971

Barber, R, *The Figure of Arthur*, Longman, London, 1972

Barber, R, *King Arthur in Legend and History*, Cardinal/Sphere, London, 1973

Barber, R, *The Arthurian Legends*, Barnes & Noble, New York, USA, 1993

Cavendish, R, *King Arthur and the Grail*, Weidenfeld & Nicolson, London, 1978

Chambers, AK, *Arthur of Britain*, Sidgwick & Jackson, London, 1966

Chrétien de Troyes, *Arthurian Romances*, Dent, London, 1987

Clarke, G (editor), *Life of Merlin*, University of Wales Press, Cardiff, 1973

Comfort, WW, *Arthurian Romances*, EP Dutton, New York, USA, 1914

Fife, G, *Arthur the King*, BBC Books, London, 1990

Geoffrey of Monmouth, *The Life of Merlin* (edited by J Parry), University of Illinois Press, USA, 1925

Goodrich, N, *Merlin*, Franklin Watts, New York, USA, 1989

Goodrich, N, *Arthur*, Franklin Watts, New York, USA, 1989

Jarman, AOH, *The Legend of Merlin*, University of Wales Press, Cardiff, 1960

Knight, G, *The Secret Tradition in Arthurian Legend*, Aquarian Press, Wellingborough, 1983

Layamon, *Arthurian Chronicles* (translated by E Mason), Dent, London, 1972

Loomis, RS, *Celtic Myth and the Arthurian Romance*, Columbia University Press, New York, USA, 1977

Loomis, RS, *Arthurian Literature in the Middle Ages*, Clarendon Press, Oxford, 1979

Malory, Sir T, *Le Mort D'Arthur*, New York University Books, USA, 1961

Malory, Sir T, *Tales of King Arthur* (edited by M Senior), Book Club Associates, London, 1980

Markale, J, *King Arthur, King of Kings* (translated by C Hauch), Gordon & Cremonesi, London, 1977

Matthews, C, *Arthur and the Sovereignty of Britain*, Arkana, London, 1989

Matthews, J, *The Arthurian Tradition*, Element Books, Shaftesbury, 1989

Morris, J, *The Age of Arthur*, Weidenfeld & Nicolson, London, 1973

Newstead, H, *Brân the Blessed in Arthurian Romance*, Columbia University Press, New York, USA, 1939

Phillips, G, and Keatman, M, *King Arthur, the True Story*, Century, London, 1992

Pollard, A, *The Romance of King Arthur*, Macmillan, London, 1979

Stewart, RJ, *The Mystic Life of Merlin*, Arkana, London, 1986

Tolstoy, Count N, *The Quest for Merlin*, Hamish Hamilton, London, 1985

Topsfield, LT, *A Study of the Arthurian Romances of Chrétien de Troyes*, Cambridge University Press, 1981

Wace, R, *Arthurian Chronicles* (translated by E Mason), Dent, London, 1972

## The Holy Grail

Anderson, F, *The Ancient Secret*, Research Into Lost Knowledge Organization/Thorsons, Wellingborough, 1953

Baigent, M, Leigh, R and Lincoln, H, *The Holy Blood and the Holy Grail*, Jonathan Cape, London, 1982

Bogdanow, F, *The Romance of the Grail*, Manchester University Press, 1966

Bryant, N (translator), *Perlesvaus*, DS Brewer, Cambridge, 1978

Burns, JE (editor) *The Vulgate Cycle*, Ohio State University Press, USA, 1985

Chrétien de Troyes, *Le Conte del Graal (The Story of the Grail)*, (translated by RH Cline), University of Georgia Press, USA, 1985

Chrétien de Troyes, *The Story of the Grail*, (translated by RW Linker), North Carolina Press, Chapel Hill, USA, 1952

Currer-Briggs, N, *The Shroud and the Grail*, Weidenfeld & Nicolson, London, 1987

Eisler, R, *The Chalice and the Blade*, Harper & Row, New York, USA, 1987

Evans, S, *In Quest of the Holy Grail*, Dent, London, 1898

Evans, S, *The High History of the Holy Grail* (translated by S Evans from *The Perlesvaus*), Dent/Everyman, London, 1912

Frappier, J, *Chrétien de Troyes and his Work* (translated by R Cormier), Ohio State University Press, USA, 1982

Furnival, FJ, (editor), *The History of the Holy Grail* (from *Roman l'Estoire dou Saint Graal* by Sires Robert de Boron). Translation by HL Skynner, Early English Text Society, N Turner, London, 1861

Jung, E, and Von Franz, ML, *The Grail Legends* (translated by A Dykes), Hodder & Stoughton, London, 1971

Loomis, RS, *The Grail – From Celtic Myth to Christian Symbolism*, University of Wales Press, Cardiff, 1963

Matarasso, PM, (translator), *The Quest of the Holy Grail* (from the *Queste del Saint Graal*), Penguin, Harmondsworth, 1976

Matthews, J, *The Grail – Quest for the Eternal*, Thames & Hudson, London, 1981

Matthews, J, *The Grail Tradition*, Element Books, Shaftesbury, 1990

Matthews, J, *Household of the Grail*, Aquarian Press, Wellingborough, 1990

Owen, DDR, *The Evolution of the Grail Legend*, Oliver & Boyd, London, 1968

Richey, MF, *Studies of Wolfram Von Eschenbach*, Oliver & Boyd, London, 1957

Sinclair, A, *The Sword and the Grail*, Crown, New York, USA, 1992

Skeels, D, *The Romance of Perceval*, University of Washington Press, USA, 1966

Starbird, M, *The Woman With the Alabaster Jar*, Bear, Santa Fe, New Mexico, 1993

Von Eschenbach, W, *Parzival* (edited by HD Sacker), Cambridge University Press, 1963

Waite, AE, *The Hidden Church of the Holy Grail*, Rebman, London, 1909

Webster, KGT (translator), *Lanzelet*, Columbia University Press, New York, USA, 1951

## Peerages and Formal Registers

Anderson, J, *Royal Genealogies*, 1732–1736
Burke's *Peerage and Baronetage*, 1840 etc.
    *Landed Gentry*, 1848 etc.
    *Extinct and Dormant Peerages*, 1952 etc.
Douglas, Sir Robert of Glenbervie,
    *The Peerage of Scotland*, 1764
    *The Baronage of Scotland*, 1798
Great Seal, Register of Scotland
Massue, Melville Henry (9th Marquis of
  Ruvigny & Raineval)
    *The Royal Blood of Britain*, 1903
    *The Jacobite Peerage, Baronage, Knightage
      and Grants of Honour*, 1904
    *The Titled Nobility of Europe*, 1914
Paul, Sir James Balfour (Lord Lyon)
    *Ordinary of Scottish Arms*, 1903
    *The Scots Peerage*, 1904–1914
Privy Seal, Register of Scotland

## Relevant Dead Sea Scrolls

Manual of Discipline–Community Rule, Damascus Document, Temple Scroll, Copper Scroll, Angelic Liturgy, Habakkuk Commentary, War Scroll, Psalms Commentary, Nahum Commentary, Messianic Rule of the Congregation.

## Nag Hammadi Codices and Gnostic Tractates

Prayer of the Apostle Paul, Apocryphon of James, Gospel of Truth, Treatise on Resurrection, Tripartite Tractate, Apocryphon of John, Gospel of Thomas, Gospel of Philip, Hypostasis of the Archons, On the Origin of the World, Exegesis on the Soul, Book of Thomas the Contender, Gospel of the Egyptians, Eugnostos the Blessed, Sophia of Jesus Christ, Dialogue of the Saviour, Apocalypse of Paul, Apocalypse of James, Apocalypse of Adam, Acts of Peter and the Twelve Apostles, Thunder – Perfect Mind, Authoritative Teaching, Concept of Our Great Power, Plato – Republic, Discourse on the Eighth and Ninth, Prayer of Thanksgiving, Asclepius, Paraphrase of Shem, Second Treatise of the Great Seth, Apocalypse of Peter, Teachings of Sylvanus, Three Steles of Seth, Zostrianos, Peter's Letter to Philip, Melchizedek, Thought of Norea, Testimony of Truth, Marsanes, Interpretation of Knowledge, Valentinian Exposition, On the Anointing, On Baptism, On the Eucharist, Allogenes, Hypsiphrone, Sentences of Sextus, Trimorphic Protennoia, Act of Peter, Gospel of Mary.

## Apocryphal Gospels, Acts and Epistles
### (Including Testimonies and Fragments)

Gospel According to the Hebrews, Gospel of the Ebionites, Gospel According to the Egyptians, Gospel of Matthias, Gospel of Peter, The Preaching of Peter, The Pistis Sophia, The Fayoum Gospel, Acts of Paul, Book of James, Book of Thomas, Gospel of Nicodemus, Gospel of Bartholomew, Book of John the Evangelist, Assumption of the Virgin, Acts of John, Acts of

Andrew, Acts of Thomas, Acts of Philip, Letters of Christ and Abgarus, Letter of Lentulus, Epistle to the Laodiceans, Correspondence of Paul and Seneca, Unknown Gospel.

## Forgotten Books and Discourses

Birth of Mary, Gospel of Eve, Lesser Questions of Mary, Prophecies of Parchor, Ascents of James, Book of Elxai, Memoria of the Apostles, Gelasian Degree, Stichometry of Nicephorus, Synopsis of Pseudo-Athanasius, Secrets of Enoch.

## Annals, Chronicles and Manuscripts

ANGLO-SAXON CHRONICLE
Compiled from 9th century (monastic various). Edited by B Thorpe 1861 [See also – GARMONSWAY, *England and Britain general*].

ANNALES CAMBRIAE
Compiled 10th century – MS to 924 Edited by Egerton Phillimore – *Y Cymmrodor 9* – Cymmrodorion Society 1888 [See also, J MORRIS, *Ireland and Wales*].

ANNALS OF CLONMACNOISE
Translated 1627 (from early MS) by Conell Mageoghagan.
Including *Synchronisms of Fland Mainistrech* – Compiled 11th century in Bute. Continuations: *The Book of Lecain* 1418. Edited by Denis Murphy – Royal Society of Antiquities of Ireland 1896.

ANNALS OF INNISFALLEN
Compiled 1215 Co Kerry – Bodleian MS. Dr C O'Connor edition – *Rerum Hibernicarum Scriptores* 1825.

ANNALS OF THE KINGDOM OF IRELAND OF THE FOUR
MASTERS
Compiled 1632–1636 – *Annals of Donegal* – Michael
O'Clery + 3 O'Clerys & Forfeasa O'Mulconry – Edited
by John O'Donovan – Dublin 1851.

ANNALS OF TIGERNACH
Compiled 1017–1088 – Tigernach Ua-Broein of Clonmacnoise. Edited by Whitley Stokes – *Revue Celtique*
1896.

ANNALS OF ULSTER
Compiled pre-1498 – Cathal MacManus, Fermanagh +
Continuation. Edited by WM Hennessey and R Mac-
Carthy – Dublin 1887–1901.

ARCHAELOGIA BRITANNICA
By Edward Lluyd – published 1707. Ref. *Hengwrt MSS*
catalogued by William Maurice 1658 (*Wynnstay MS 10*
– Nat. Lib. Wales) *Hengwrt MS 33* edit from *Wynnstay
MS 10* by Prof. AOH Jarman in *Ymddiddan Myrddin a
Thaliesin* [see *Arthurian History*]. *Hengwrt MS 33*
(Hanesyn Hen) copies in *Cardiff* and *Penairth MSS*. In-
cluding *Achu Brenhinoedd a Thywysogion, Bonedd yr Ar-
wyr, Hen Lwythau Gwynedd a'r Mars & Plant Brychan.*

BONEDD GWYR-Y-GOGLEDD
Lineage of the Men of the North – *Penairth* (Nat Lib.
Wales) *MS 45* (13th cty); *Penairth MS 75* (16th cty);
*Penairth MS 127* (c. 1510); *Penairth MS 128* (c.1560);
*Penairth MS 129* (early 16th cty); *Penairth MS 253* (16th
cty).

BONEDD-Y-SAINT
Lineage of the Saints – 12th cty. Various as given in
MSS: *Harleian* (Brit. Mus.); *Cae Cyriog MS 3* (Nat. Lib.

Wales); *Llangibby MSS* (Nat. Lib. Wales); *Llanstephan MS 28* (Nat. Lib. Wales); *Penairth MSS* (Nat. Lib. Wales); *Rawlinson B MSS* (Bodleian). *Achau'r Saint* tract – Pedigrees of the Saints in *MSS Cardiff* and *Penairth*.

BOOK OF BALLYMOTE
Compiled 15th century. Photo-fac. Anal. Robert Atkinson – Royal Irish Academy – Dublin 1887.

BOOK OF KELLS
Compiled (MS. copied) 12th century – Edited by J O'Donovan – Irish Archaeological Society 1846.

BOOK OF LEINSTER
Compiled 1160/1170 – *Book of Glendalough*. Including *Tract on the Picts – Leabhar Gabhala* – R Atkinson edition – Dublin 1880. Transcript by Joseph O'Longan – Facsimile, Royal Irish Academy, Dublin 1880.

BOOK OF LISMORE
Compiled 15th century – *Saints from B of L* edition – W Stokes 1890.

BOOK OF LLANDAFF
Compiled c.1132 – Edited by WJ Rees – Llandovery 1840.

BOOK OF UI MAINE
Orig. c.1394 – Irish Manuscripts Commission – Facsimile, Dublin 1942.

BREVIARY OF ABERDEEN
Compiled 1509/10 – Coll. Bishop William of Aberdeen – Editions: Spalding Club, Maitland Club, Bannantyne Club – all 1854.

CHRONICLE OF HOLYROOD
Compiled c.12th century Holyrood Abbey – Translated by Joseph Stevenson in *Church Historians of England* 1856.

CHRONICLE OF MAN
Compiled 13th century – Translated by Joseph Stevenson in *Church Historians of England* 1856.

CHRONICLE OF MELROSE
Compiled from 12th century – Translated by Joseph Stevenson in *Church Historians of England* 1856.

CHRONICLES OF THE KINGS
Including *Chronicle of the Picts; Chronicle of the Scots of Dalriata; Chronicle of Scotland* – Compiled from 14th century – Including *Chronicles of the Picts and Scots* – William Forbes Skene 1867 [See also – SKENE, *Scotland* book list].

COGNATIO BRYCHAN
*Cotton MS* (Brit. Mus.) *Domitian i* – Sir John Price of Brecon 1502–55. Egerton Phillimore text in *Y Cymmroder 9* – 1888. Wade-Evans text in *Y Cymmroder 19* – 1906 and *Vita Sanctorum Britanniae et Genealogiae* – Cardiff 1944.

DE SITU BRECHENIAUC
*Cotton MS* (Brit. Mus.) *Vespasian A xiv* – c.1200 Egerton Phillimore text in *Y Cymmroder 9* – 1888. Wade-Evans text in *Y Cymmroder 19* – 1906 and *Vita Sanctorum Britanniae et Genealogiae* – Cardiff 1944.

DE EXCIDIO ET CONQUESTU BRITANNIAE
Compiled 6th century – Gildas III – Translated by JA Giles 1841–48. Translated by Hugh Williams, Cymmro-

dorion Society 1899 [See also – GILDAS, *England and Britain General*].

## DOMESDAY BOOK
Compiled 1086 – Translations: *Victoria County Histories*.

## DUAN ALBANACH
Compiled 11th century. Irish MS. Dudley M'Firbis 1650. 19th century edit. by William Forbes Skene.

## HANES GRUFFUDD AP CYNAN
*Cotton MS* (Brit. Mus.) *Vitellius C ix* – c.1600; *Penairth MS 17* (Nat. Lib. Wales); *Penairth MS 267* by John Jones 1641. Text edits by Arthur Jones in *The History of Gruffydd ap Cynan* – Manchester 1910.

## HISTORY OF SCOTLAND
Compiled 14th century – John of Fordun, Chaplain of Church of Aberdeen. Edited by William Forbes Skene 1891/2. Recension: *Scotichronicon* by Walter Bower, Abbot of Inchcolm – Compiled 1441 – Including *Book of Paisley, Book of Scone, Book of Cupar, Chronicle of Icolmkill* – Edited by Thomas Hearne (Oxford) 1722, and Walter Goodall (Edinburgh) 1759.

## HISTORIA BRITONUM
Nennius edition 858 – *Harleian MS.* – *Vatican MS.* – *Paris MS.*
Saxon and Welsh additions – Irish and Pictish additions translated by JA Giles 1848. [See also – NENNIUS, *Celts, Romans*] *Chartres MS 98 Z* – c.900. *Vatican MS Reginae 1964 M* – 11th cty. *Harleian MS* (Brit. Mus.) *3859 H* – c.1100. Egerton Phillimore text in *Y Cymmrodor 7* – 1886. Wade-Evans edit. in *Y Cymmrodor 19* – 1906. *Cotton MS* (Brit. Mus.) *Vespasian D xxi* – 12th cty. *Cotton MS* (Brit. Mus.) *Caligula A viii* – 12th cty.

HISTORIA ECCLESIASTICA GENTIS ANGLORUM
Compiled 731 – Bede of Jarrow. Edited by C Plummer
– Oxford 1896 [See also – BEDE, *Cults and Religion*]. (2)
Edited by Bertram Colgrave and RAB Mynors – Oxford
1969.

HISTORIA REGUM BRITANNIE
Compiled c.1147 – Geoffrey of Monmouth – Translated
by JA Giles – Caxton Society 1844 [See also – GEOFFREY
OF MONMOUTH, *England and Britain General*].

HISTORY OF IRELAND
Compiled c.1640 – Geoffrey Keating. Translated by
David Comyn and The Revd Patrick S Dinneen – Irish
Texts Society 1902–1914 – 4 Volumes [See also – KEAT-
ING, *Ireland and Wales*].

JESUS COLLEGE MS
*J.C. Oxford MS 20* (Bodleian) – Pedigrees: *Ach Cunedda,
Ach Gryg, Ach Llewelyn ap Iorwerth, Ach Morgan ab
Owain, Ach Rhodri Mawr, Gwehelyth Brycheiniog, Gwehe-
lyth Buellt, Gwehelyth Ceredigion, Gwehelyth Dogfeiling,
Gwehelyth Dunoding, Gwehelyth Meirionydd, Gwehelyth
Rhos, Gwyr-y-Gogledd, Plant Brychan, Plant Ceredig, Plant
Cunedda.* 14th cty. *J.C. MS 20* – copies: *Penairth MS 120*
(Nat. Lib. Wales) – Edward Lluyd – c.1700; *Panton MS
15* (Nat. Lib. Wales) 18th cty. Evan Evans; *Harleian MS
4181* (Brit. Mus.) – Hugh Thomas c.1700.

MOSTYN MS
*Mostyn 117* (Nat. Lib. Wales) – 13th cty. Edits by JG
Evans in *Report on Manuscripts in the Welsh Language* –
Historical MSS Commission, London 1898–1910.

VITAI SANCTII

Lives of Saints: *Vita Beatissimi Cadoci – Cotton MS* (Brit. Mus.) *Vespasian A xiv* – c.1200 – Orig. Lifris of Llancarfan c.1100. AW Wade-Evans edits – *Vita Sanctorum Britanniae et Genealogiae* – Cardiff 1944. *Vita Sancti Carantoci – Cotton MS* (Brit. Mus.) *Vespasian A xiv* – Orig. 12th cty. AW Wade-Evans edit in *Vita Sanctorum Britanniae et Genealogiae. Vita Beati David – Cotton MS* (Brit. Mus.) *Vespasian A xiv* – Orig. Ricemarchus c.1090 AW Wade-Evans edit in *Vita Sanctorum Britanniae et Genealogiae. Vita Sancti Kentegerni – Cotton MS* (Brit. Mus.) *Titus A xix* – Orig. Anon. c.1150. *Vita Sancti Samsonis – Bibliothèque Municipale, Metz, MS 195* (11th cty); *Bibliothèque Mazarine, Paris, MS 1708* (c.1000); *Bibliothèque Nationale, Paris, MS 11758* (13th cty).

# INDEX

# INDEX

*Bloodline of the Holy Grail*

Published in conjuction with this book, and with the active help and support of the author, Peter Robson's Entropic art forms a series of prints which explore fascinating new dimensions of allegory and symbolism. These uniquely energized paintings probe the depths of arcane lore and sacred geometry to reveal ancient knowledge within and beyond the scope of *Bloodline of the Holy Grail*. For information concerning the print series and the chance to complete an intriguing quest and win valuable prizes, see Picture Credits 15 and 16; also Internet Address: http://www.entropic-art.com.

Also produced in association with this book is the haunting musical suite, *The Holy Spirit and the Holy Grail*. This has been composed by Adrian Wagner, great-great-grandson of Richard Wagner, composer of the famous 19th-century Grail-related operas *Parsival* and *Loehengrin*. Information concerning *The Holy Spirit and the Holy Grail* album (CD and cassette) may be obtained from Media Quest – Internet address: http://www.mediaquest.co.uk/awhshg.html